Cybercrime, Organized Crime, and Societal Responses

Emilio C. Viano
Editor

Cybercrime, Organized Crime, and Societal Responses

International Approaches

Springer

Editor
Emilio C. Viano
International Society of Criminology
Washington, DC, USA

ISBN 978-3-319-44499-4 ISBN 978-3-319-44501-4 (eBook)
DOI 10.1007/978-3-319-44501-4

Library of Congress Control Number: 2016948731

Printed on acid-free paper

This Springer imprint is published by Springer Nature
The registered company is Springer International Publishing AG
The registered company address is: Gewerbestrasse 11, 6330 Cham, Switzerland

To the memory of my parents, Giuseppe and Teresa Viano, who taught me, with their example, the value of commitment, work, and perseverance and who have encouraged and supported me in my studies and career with their generosity and sacrifices.

Introduction

Crime and criminality are at the same time centuries-old phenomena and ever changing realities powered by innovations in technology, communications, transportation, and other scientific advances.

According to the United Nations Office on Drugs and Crime (2013), at least 2.3 billion people, the equivalent of more than one third of the world's total population, have access to the Internet. Over 60 % of all Internet users are in developing countries, with 45 % of all Internet users below the age of 25 years. By the year 2017, it is estimated that mobile broadband subscriptions will approach 70 % of the world's total population. By the year 2020, the number of networked devices will outnumber people by six to one, transforming current conceptions of the Internet. In the hyperconnected world of tomorrow, it will become hard to imagine a "computer crime," and perhaps any crime, that does not involve some element of electronic evidence linked with Internet protocol (IP) connectivity.

The explosion of information and communications technologies in particular is totally transforming the way we live, work, interact, do research, find a mate, travel, transfer funds, do business, and share information. This transformation has truly taken place in the last 15 years and is still under way. The impact that it has on our daily lives, on society, on the government, and on crime is still unfolding and being assessed. The ever changing nature of the Internet of things and its dynamics makes prediction and planning difficult and uncertain. Since the law is famously always behind reality in society, there is no question that this is still a vastly unregulated field. The damaging consequences of this time delay are incalculable especially because criminality now can happen literally instantaneously via the Internet. The Deloitte's report (2015) on cybersecurity trends states that emerging technologies, coupled with a shifting threat profile, are challenging organizations to deal more and more with sophisticated "bad actors" that are motivated, skilled, and adaptable. The threat has shifted from the traditional hacker exploiting a target of opportunity to:

- Targets of choice and not chance. Attackers are increasingly targeting specific companies, products, services, and individuals.

- Involvement by organized crime. Low risks and high rewards are luring organized crime to cybercrime. The Internet facilitates its international operations, all types of trafficking and the movement of monies.
- State-sponsored cyber threats. Financial, political, and strategic objectives are motivating state-sponsored actors to compromise systems, steal intellectual property, or cause economic damage. Some countries are accused of already investing considerable resources in developing and engaging in cyber war and cyber attacks.
- Growing insider threats. Insider threats have risen due to economic conditions, layoffs, and increasing "privileged accesses" accorded to third-party vendors. The recent scandals originating in sensitive and secret electronic materials leaked to the press by Wikileaks, Julian Assange, Bradley Manning and Edward Snowden, to mention just the most famous whistleblowers, show how weak and disregarded privacy protections and guarantees are.
- Legislative initiatives and global implications. New cyber legislation and penalties for noncompliance are being developed, and global business models are being reconsidered since in their present form they may facilitate the commission and cover-up of international crimes.

Cyber warfare in particular is a growing concern among national security establishments and is one of the most serious national security challenges as it threatens critical economic and defense infrastructure (e.g., power grid, financial systems). Acts of cyber warfare are also feasible and reportedly have already taken place between different countries. One of the most well-known episodes was the attack and destruction of uranium processing centrifuges at the Natanz nuclear facility in Iran via the Stuxnet virus, a joint US-Israel project. The potential for similar destructive attacks also on the civilian critical infrastructure is obviously quite high and could be carried out by a governmental agency, foreign or domestic, or another private competitor or adversary. Most modern plants operate with a standardized industrial control system, so if someone gains control of one industrial control system, one can then infiltrate dozens or even hundreds more of the same type. Another frontier related to cyber communications and artificial intelligence is the rapid increase in the use of robots and drones for surveillance and also interventions that can violate people's privacy, residences, and be lethal. The use of a robot to find and kill a sniper who killed five police officers and wounded several others in Dallas, Texas, in the context of demonstrations and protests for the killings of civilians by police in Louisiana and Minnesota during early July 2016 is a troubling precedent and raises serious questions about the future use of new technologies by police. While many police forces have already used remote-controlled devices for detonating bombs or launching of nonlethal force like tear gas, employing one to kill a suspect is certainly unusual and quite possibly unprecedented (Graham, 2016). It opens a new frontier in the use of distance-controlled weaponry in civilian law enforcement, which will be controversial, especially when, some day, there may be substantial "collateral" damage.

That is why the **First Part** of the volume focuses on Cybercrime, the most timely and important subject of interest and concern in criminology today, given that it is the platform that supports the entire intricate web of human, financial, business, legal, and commerce interactions today and therefore most of what relates to crime as well. The term "cybercrime" refers to criminal conduct that impacts interests such as the proper functioning of computer systems and the Internet, the privacy and integrity of data stored or transferred in or through ICT, or the virtual identity of Internet users.

The first part of this book specifically addresses the issue of Cybercrime in some of its current manifestations. In the first chapter, **Emilio C. Viano** (USA) addresses the theme of cybercrime, providing an overall review of the basic definition, legal principles, and responses to this growing criminal justice reality. It systematically addresses the definition of cybercrime, the legal interests protected by the laws on Information and Communication Technology and Cybercrime. It addresses in depth the extent of criminalization, especially preparation and possession, and focuses on the issue of the challenges and limits of criminal legislation. It concludes with an analysis of the legal demands advanced by the internationalization of cybercrime, a typical characteristic of this type of crime, and ends examining projected trends for the future. The chapter is documented carefully and exhaustively.

Susan Edwards (UK) focuses on young women and school girls who have left their families to join ISIS. It explores the role of cyberspace in their recruitment, especially cyber grooming and gender in terrorism recruiting. Special attention is given to the law and the protection of the vulnerable. **Garima Jain** and **Sanjeev Sahni** (India) direct their attention to social pathologies that are beginning to appear in cyberspace, reporting on a pilot study in North India on the prevalence, attribution, and rationale behind Internet-based infidelity. **Malgorzata Skorewska Amberg** (Poland) tackles the difficult but necessary area of how to address a global threat through national legislation and how the legislative world can adapt to the new cyberspace society. This theme is continued by **Vanja Bajovic** (Croatia) writing on the challenges that the digital area presents to criminal procedure in cyberspace while **Steven Thaman** (USA) focuses on the use of information and communications technology in criminal procedure in the United States. He especially underlines how all of these practices involve invasions of privacy of the citizenry and thus must be examined within the framework of constitutionally protected privacy rights in the United States. **Part II** overall focuses on organized crime and trafficking, underlining at times how information and communications technology facilitates the reach and the operations of this global threat. There is no doubt that organized crime quickly embraced the information and communications technology to speed up, expand, facilitate, and strengthen their areas of influence and control. It has been said, for example, that initially the major factor supporting the rapid expansion of the Internet was access to pornography, the production of which has been notoriously controlled by organized crime, along with prostitution. Ironically, as the wealth in the world overall has increased and become more diffused, as a consequence, it allows more people worldwide access to goods and services previously unattainable that at times are illegal, prohibited, or obtainable only in manners damaging to the environment. Therefore they can be secured only through criminal commerce and trafficking. There is a vast market for illegally captured, killed, harvested, and exported fauna and flora that is driven and sustained by the increased wealth of countries where those items are considered very valuable as a sign of status and wealth or as traditional remedies to various infirmities and health problems. Thus various species of wild animals are now being decimated and in danger of disappearing like elephants for their ivory; rhinoceros for their horn that, reduced to powder and pills, supposedly restore sexual potency; sharks just for their fins that are used to make an expensive soup, a powerful status symbol at celebrations and weddings, in China; tigers for a "wine" made with their bones with various healing and curative powers, plus various roots, seeds, flowers, exotic birds, and other animals and plants. Antiquities and artwork are also smuggled worldwide to fulfill the demands of the newly wealthy. Humans are also included and trafficking in humans has skyrocketed in today's world. It is ironic that more than 150 years since the abolition of slavery in various parts of the world, slavery and indentured servitude are flourishing again in our very midst and by numbers much higher than in the seventeenth, eighteenth, and nineteenth centuries. A young woman being transported for a forced marriage or prostitution may be sitting next to us on an airplane or on a train or be held and forced to work in an establishment in a part of town that we cross every day. Chapters in Part II refer to some of these phenomena. **Francesca Calandra** and **Antonino Giorgi** (Italy) examine the destructive effects of the mafia as a global threat on the economic, environmental, and psychosocial spheres, especially focusing on the impact upon its victims. They stress the need to create intervention models to support the victims of the mafia to prevent further damage to the social fabric. **Ioana Neto** (Portugal) offers a methodological review of Social Network Analysis (SNA), addressing especially the usefulness of this type of analysis for criminal investigations, intelligence, and procedural and political matters. She intends to show how the SNA can be applied successfully in the study of organized criminal networks. **Hai Thanh Luong** (Vietnam) presents an extensive case study of drug trafficking trends and how to counteract them in the Mainland Southeast Asia and the Golden Triangle, one of Asia's two main opium-producing areas. In particular, he identifies main routes of transnational drug trafficking across Vietnam's borderland with its neighbors. He also presents and comments on the National Strategy of Vietnam to prevent, combat, and control drugs towards 2020. **Arun Kumar Acharya** (Mexico) focuses on another global theme, the trafficking of persons and the essential importance to reintegrate trafficked victims as an important human right. He analyses especially the response of the government of Mexico to this challenge. **Sanjeev P. Sahni**, **Garima Jain**, and **Indranath Gupta** (India) address a problem that is rampant in India—movie and software piracy—and focus especially on the countermeasures that have been considered by the movie and software industries. The authors stress that there is not enough evidence to connect piracy to those measures and those measures to the possible rates of piracy and therefore there is a need to ascertain the real dangers and the possible remedial measures to deter possible pirates. The next two chapters focus on juvenile delinquency, one of the major challenges of today especially in developing countries with their higher natality rates against a background of poor public education, limited or nonexistent health services, and no recreational facilities, career training, and employment opportunities. As the United Nations and the World Bank (2007:61) state, youth are disproportionately represented in statistics on crime and violence, both as victims and as perpetrators. In many developed countries, perpetrators of violent crimes are becoming younger and younger. Also there is increasing worry that, at least in some areas, young people are increasingly becoming responsible for violent crimes. Additionally, research has shown that delinquent behavior is mostly undertaken by youth in a group. Gang or group members, with varying degrees of organizational structure, are responsible for 66–75 % of all offenses carried out by young people together with the group or alone. Poverty and lack of employment are not, by themselves, the cause of violence. However, they play a major role when working in unison with other factors like racism, discrimination, inequality, exclusion, the availability of guns and drugs, and lack of access to capital, justice, and a decent education. On a more positive note, research as summarized by the United Nations and the World Bank (2007) shows that most first time offenders do not go on re-offending and that programs like diversion and community initiatives are much better responses to youth delinquency than arrest and incarceration. Unfortunately, regardless of research findings, placing young people in detention, including jail, is still the most frequent way to deal with youth offenders, even if they are still awaiting trial and are accused of minor infractions. As for most crime in general, crimes perpetrated by young people are mostly an urban phenomenon; likewise, being a victim of crime. **André Vilela Komatsu** and **Marina Rezende Bazon** (Brazil) report on an exploratory study in the city of Ribeirao Preto in the state of São Paulo, Brazil. Their premise is that engaging in antisocial activities among adolescents can vary, depending on the frequency and diversity of activities in which they participate and, even more importantly, the age of onset of participation. This may result in greater or lesser criminal engagement. Consequently, not all juveniles who might break the law are the same. It is crucial for the juvenile justice system to distinguish between different juvenile offenders arrested by police. The behavior of some of them will lead to greater criminal engagement that in turn is associated with persistent criminal lifetime trajectories. Using sophisticated statistical tests, the authors are able to distinguish five different groups or categories representing increasing levels of criminal engagement, with 5 being the highest level. This is an important insight to ensure the correct disposition of juvenile cases, stressing that youth in trouble should not all be considered at the same level of delinquency and treated the same. Treating them all the same may in turn lead to an increase in the criminality of those whose scores were actually low, that is, not indicative of a strong commitment to delinquency. **Ellen Van Damme** (Belgium) focuses on the reintegration of youth gang members in Honduras with the aim of broadening the knowledge of these processes as they unfold in Central America. Leaving a gang is difficult and risky and often entails being killed in the process. In the end, prevention at an early stage is the best remedy. **Part III** of the volume addresses society's responses to crime, not all of them necessarily positive or respectful of human rights. The first chapter in this section, authored by **Rick Sarre** (Australia), centers on the basic question of how we can best balance the rights of citizens to privacy, as envisioned in Article 12 of the U.N. Declaration of Human

Rights, with the legitimate interest of the State, media, employers, corporations, and even private citizens to obtain information on them and even observe, film, and monitor them. This chapter deals with the challenges to citizens' privacy when they face this expanded surveillance environment and examines the consequences of the choices that they themselves make. It is true, for example, that many of us provide a lot of information on ourselves on our own by posting information about all sorts of aspects of our lives on social media, for example. **Toshiko Sawaguchi** (Japan) dwells over criminology as a science that has to find its place among the various established ones. She recommends that criminology be considered a criminal regulatory science and envisions it as providing a general, unified theory spanning the fields of medicine, psychology, law, social science, and so on. In particular, she underlines how effective the field called "law and economics" would be within modern criminology. Continuing this examination of criminology, **Thomáš Strémy** and **Miroslava Vráblová** (Slovakia) compare criminal justice based on repressive approaches against new models founded on the principles of restorative justice. The latter is presented as one of the more modern and progressive current approaches to criminal law that deserves to be implemented into the Slovak criminal justice system. **Jennifer Stave** (USA) examines the role of the judiciary in keeping law and order in a community, especially in regard to violence reduction. She emphasizes that the key element here is trust in the institution. Drawing from 2438 municipalities and using a zero-inflated binomial model to test whether institutional trust is a necessary precondition to reform, she concludes that institutional trust is a key variable to be studied closely in future reform initiatives. **Smart Otu** (Nigeria) presents a case study of security or lack thereof in the public transportation system within the city and region of Abakaliki in Nigeria. This chapter is addressing how the system is not responding appropriately from many points of view to the high level of criminality, from petty property crimes to serious violent crimes, rape, and homicide, in and around the bus station and when the buses travel through certain dangerous neighborhoods or isolated rural areas. It is an especially interesting chapter from the perspective of environmental criminology and how modifying and retouching the design of a bus station, the area surrounding it, and the way in which people have access to the buses can impact the level of criminality, bringing in at this point the routine theory of criminality. Overall, this volume offers an international selection of scholarly contributions of high caliber from all continents of the world, underlining the growing internationalization of criminology, the universal concern about criminality, delinquency and victimization, and the overall theme of security in a world challenged by globalization, massive migration, the ubiquity of electronic communications, and the appearance and rapid growth of cybercrime, constantly morphing into new forms and expressions.

Washington, DC, USA Emilio C. Viano

References

Deloitte. (2015). *Cybersecurity Survey*. http://www2.deloitte.com/ca/en/pages/risk/articles/cyber-security-survey-2015.html

Graham, D. (2016). The era of lethal police robots has arrived. *Defense One*, July 11.

United Nations and World Bank. (2007). *Fact sheet on juvenile delinquency*. Retrieved from http://www.un.org/esa/socdev/unyin/documents/wyr11/FactSheetonYouthandJuvenileJustice.pdf

United Nations Office on Drugs and Crime. (2013). *Comprehensive Study on Cybercrime*. Retrieved February, from http://www.unodc.org/documents/organized-crime/UNODC_CCPCJ_EG.4_2013/CYBERCRIME_STUDY_210213.pdf

Contents

Contributors

Arun Kumar Acharya Universidad Autónoma de Nuevo León, Nuevo León, Mexico

Vanja Bajovic University of Belgrade, Faculty of Law, Belgrade, Serbia

Marina Rezende Bazon University of São Paulo, Ribeirao Preto, São Paulo, Brazil

Francesca Calandra University of Palermo, Palermo, Italy

Ellen Van Damme Catholic University of Leuven, Leuven Institute of Criminology, Leuven, Belgium

Susan S.M. Edwards Dean of Law, University of Buckingham, Buckingham, UK

Barrister, Door Tenant, 1 Gray's Inn Square, London, UK

Expert Witness, MEWI, Temple Chambers, London, UK

Antonino Giorgi Catholic University of the Sacred Heart, Brescia, Italy

Indranath Gupta O.P. Jindal Global University, Sonipat, Haryana, India

Garima Jain Jindal Institute of Behavioural Sciences, O.P. Jindal Global University, Haryana, India

André Vilela Komatsu University of São Paulo, Ribeirao Preto, São Paulo, Brazil

Hai Thanh Luong School of Global, Urban, and Social Science, RMIT University, Melbourne, Australia

Joana Neto University of Porto, Porto, Portugal

Smart Egwu Otu Federal University Ndufu Alike Ikwo, Ebonyi, Nigeria

Sanjeev P. Sahni O.P. Jindal Global University, Sonipat, Haryana, India

Rick Sarre School of Law, University of South Australia, Adelaide, Australia

Toshiko Sawaguchi Department of Legal Medicine, Showa University School of Medicine, National Institute of Public Health, Shinagawa, Japan

Małgorzata Skórzewska-Amberg Kozminski University School of Law, Warszawa, Poland

Jennifer Stave Justice Reform Initiative, Washington, DC, USA

Tomáš Strémy Comenius University, Trnava University, Bratislava, Trnava, The Slovak Republic

Stephen C. Thaman Saint Louis University School of Law, St. Louis, MO, USA

Emilio C. Viano International Society of Criminology, Washington, DC, USA

Miroslava Vráblová Comenius University, Trnava University, Bratislava, Trnava, The Slovak Republic

About the Editor

Emilio C. Viano has earned several academic law degrees [LLB (Honors) and three LL.Ms], an M.A. in Sociology & Anthropology, and a Ph.D. ("summa cum laude") in Sociology of Law at New York University.

Most recently, he has taught and done research mostly at American University, Washington DC, both in the School of Public Affairs and the Washington College of Law. He has also been a professor at the University of Paris (Sorbonne), Cordoba (Argentina), Panteion (Athens, Greece), Bologna (Italy), Shanghai International Studies University (SISU), and others.

His work in law, criminal justice issues, and governance has been recognized by his election as President of the International Society for Criminology (Paris), Member of the Board of Directors of the International Association of Penal Law and of the International Society of Social Defense, U.S. Voting Member of the International Penal & Penitentiary Foundation, Member of the Steering Committee of the Global Forum on Law, Justice and Development at the World Bank, and others. In 2012 he received the "Hans Von Hentig" Prize, the highest recognition of the World Society of Victimology, awarded only every 4 years. Among other awards and prizes, he also received two Fulbrights. He is a well-known and respected political analyst and commentator, often interviewed on CNN, UNIVISION, Voice of America, CCTV, and several radio stations and newspapers in South America, the United States and Europe.

Dr. Viano has vast experience with consulting assignments worldwide, especially in the developing world and particularly on security issues. He has worked extensively in Argentina, Brazil, Guatemala, Costa Rica, El Salvador, Malaysia, Thailand, Egypt, Algeria, South Africa, Mexico, and others. Most recently he served as senior consultant on Cybercrime Prevention at the World Bank and wrote the Cybercrime law under contract for a Central American country.

Part I
Cybercrime

Chapter 1
Cybercrime: Definition, Typology, and Criminalization

Emilio C. Viano

Defining Cybercrime

There is no universal accepted definition of cybercrime. Different definitions have been put forward by experts, the industry and scholars. Some have been used by various governments. They vary in their degree of specificity and breadth (Viano 2006:11).

Regardless of the definition, conceptualizing cybercrime raises several key questions, like where do the criminal acts take place in the real and digital worlds and with the help of which technologies; why are damaging activities undertaken; and who are the actors perpetrating the deviant acts?

The "Where" of Criminal Activities, Actors, and Victims.

When it comes to cybercrime, the location touches upon both the physical and digital domains. However, the fairly clear borderlines and places common in the physical world are not available in the virtual one. Interestingly, there are still some borders that distinguish the physical from the cyber world. The keyboard, the screen, the arrow, the password, all fulfill a mediating role between the physical and the virtual worlds. But once within cyberspace, the idea of a border is much more undefined. In the cyber world, there are obviously no clear cut geographic boundaries like in the physical world (Johnson and Post 1996: 1379).

Experts point out that some cybercrimes demand more technological know-how or a much bigger use of digital technologies in order to carry them out (Gordon and Ford 2006:15–19). For instance: phishing, theft of identity and distributed denial of service attacks presuppose a much deeper and better understanding of digital and electronic technologies. This as opposed to other cybercrime like, among others, downloading child pornography or engaging in cyber stalking, the so-called

E.C. Viano (✉)
International Society of Criminology, 2333 North Vernon Street,
22207-4036 Washington, DC, USA
e-mail: emilio.viano@gmail.com

E.C. Viano (ed.), *Cybercrime, Organized Crime, and Societal Responses*,
DOI 10.1007/978-3-319-44501-4_1

"point and click" crimes. Obviously, the deviant acts that need more technological know-how are also more deeply embedded in the virtual world than others.

Technology plays a major role in the definition of cybercrimes, depending on the role that it plays (Finklea and Thehoary 2015:3). In some cases, the electronic devices and the data that they contain are the intended target or victim of the crime. In other situations, the electronic or digital technologies are the actual tools used to perpetrate the crimes impacting individuals, organizations, or governmental entities. Finally, technology can store the fruits and the evidence of the crimes (Homeland Security 2011).

A Traditional View

One approach to cybercrimes is that they are just the digital edition of well-known, traditional offenses. It can be said that quite a few cybercrimes could actually be thought of as traditional or "real world" crimes, were it not for the virtual or cyberspace element. A common example is identity theft that can indeed happen in both the physical and electronic worlds. One can point out that it is only the "how" that is different. In both settings the criminal intent (obtain money, property or profit from it) and the result (private information identifying a person) are indeed the same. In the real world it is done by stealing someone's wallet, briefcase or mail. In the virtual world, the same information can be stolen by inducing a person to reveal such information to the thief who might pretend to be the bank or the credit card company verifying the customer's identity or by inserting "keystroke loggers" (that record the needed electronic information of the customer and transmit it electronically to the thieves for them to use). It is at the law enforcement level that one can see the difficulty and the struggle to make the transition from one level of reality to the other (Viano 2006:11–22).

Police are accustomed to physical evidence, to the "paper trail" and find it difficult to transpose all of this to the electronic world and investigate a crime on purely electronic grounds (Guinchard 2008: 1030). Thus, while organized crime has pioneered the use of electronic tools to carry out its criminal activities, the law can still be far behind. For example, in the United States, computer fraud (18 U.S.C. §1030) is not yet classified as a predicate offense for racketeering under the Racketeer Influenced Corrupt Practices Act (RICO) which is one of the most important tools to combat organized crime (Doyle 2016).

Major Definitions of Cybercrime

Susan Brenner (2007) distinguishes between:

1. Specifically defined cyber offenses
2. Migration of real world crime into cyberspace

D.S. Wall (2007) distinguishes between:

1. Computer integrity crimes :"Crimes against the machine"
2. Computer assisted crimes: "Crimes using the machine"
   This includes piracy.
3. Computer content crimes (violence, pornography): "Crimes in the machine"

In a previous typology of cybercrime, Wall distinguishes between:

Cyber-Trespass

Cyber-trespass encompasses the crossing of invisible, yet relevant boundaries of ownership online. Specifically, if an individual attempts to access a computer system, network, or data source, without the permission of the system owner, they are violating a recognized border of ownership. These activities are most closely associated with computer hackers.

Cyber-Deception/Theft

Cyber-deception (or theft) includes the use of ICT to steal information or illegally acquire items of value, whether from individuals or corporations. This category is innately tied to cyber-trespass since malicious hackers frequently attempt to capture sensitive information and data through trespassing. Hackers are increasingly targeting data repositories managed by financial, medical, and governmental institutions and online retailers to steal large amounts of data. Digital piracy may be the most frequently studied form of cybercrime at the moment, given some recent major hacking events. Cyber theft is then connected to online international markets where cybercriminals buy and sell stolen data and information acquired through various sources (Tosza 2013:115).

Cyber-Pornography and Obscenity

Cyber-pornography and obscenity encompasses the range of sexual expressions enabled by ICT-mediated communications and the distribution of sexually explicit materials online. Virtually all sexual fetishes and interests are represented in some way on the Internet. The anonymous nature of the Internet allows individuals to become part of virtual subcultures focused on activities that may not be accepted in the larger society and gain a sense of social support and validation. Cyber-porn and obscenity also includes pedophilia, where individuals seek out sexual or emotional relationships with children, and the production of child pornography (Viano 2013:347). Sex trade and sex tourism have also enormously expanded taking advantage of ICT. It has been said that these elements of cyber-pornography played a major role, at least initially, in the worldwide development of the Internet.

Cyber-Violence

Cyber violence includes the various ways that individuals can cause harm in real or virtual environments. Estimates of online harassment and bullying appear to have increased, especially across juvenile populations, due to greater access to technology and the social importance placed on virtual communications. It is important to note that this includes the use of technology in support of social unrest and prospective acts of terror. In fact, political and social movements are increasingly promoting their ideologies through the Internet and social media. This also includes recruiting new members to join, for example, ISIS. ICT has provided significant opportunities for terrorist groups and extremist organizations to further their objectives. The complex and intersecting nature of both crime and terror make it difficult to clearly separate these issues, particularly in virtual environments, due to the anonymous nature of electronic communications. There is some evidence of nation states and motivated individuals engaging in large-scale hacking attacks against political and military targets (Viano 2013:336). Similarly, politically driven groups have also employed hacking techniques to engage in serious strikes against governments and political organizations. ICT has greatly facilitated the interactions, collaborations, and even merger of organized crime, financial crimes, trafficking, and terrorism.

The Council of Europe(2001) distinguishes between:

1. Offenses against the confidentiality, integrity, and availability of computer data and systems
2. Computer-related offenses
3. Content-related offenses
4. Offenses related to infringements of copyright and related rights
5. Acts of a racist & xenophobic nature committed through computer systems (Council of Europe 2003).

Acknowledging that Information and Communications Technology (ICT) and cybercrime include quite diverse phenomena, we can distinguish three types of criminal conduct:

1. "Ordinary" criminal offenses, e.g., fraud or forgery, that are committed by means of information and communication technology, especially the World Wide Web;
2. Crimes directed against the proper functioning of ICT systems, e.g., hacking, manipulation of computer systems, or the destruction of stored data; and
3. Crimes against interests that are web-specific, e.g., the "theft" or manipulation of virtual personalities, Avatars, etc.

One can notice that the definition provided by Brenner is the simplest, more Spartan and technical one. At the opposite end is the typology developed by the Council of Europe that encompasses categories inspired by a broader moral and political agenda, driven for example by campaigns undertaken by the film and music industries to lobby lawmakers to write or amend laws so that their intangible assets are protected (Couldry 2008: 373). These efforts and others against racism, bullying, harassment and child pornography illustrate well that, in order to include them among cybercrimes, they have to be acknowledged and accepted as such by society first. Thus, they are good examples of a non-technical way to develop a typology of cybercrimes based on political and/or moral decisions to spur and support public awareness of this type of behaviors as reprehensible (Eskola 2012:122).

Legal Interests Protected by ICT and Cyber Criminal Law

General Aspects

Conventional Crimes "going digital"

ICT and the cyber space have enabled offenders to be more "efficient" than before when they wish to commit fraud, slander, copyright violations and other traditional crimes (Weigend 2013:51). They can use electronic equipment and/or the web in order to address, with one single mouse click, millions of potential victims or harm the reputation or the protected copyright of a single or multiple victims. But in these instances only the *modus operandi* differs from traditional forms of fraudulent or slanderous conduct; however, the affected interests remain the same.

Examples of "computerized or electronic" versions of traditional crimes contained in criminal codes are: fraud by using ICT systems, revelation of government secrets stored electronically, forgery of digitally stored data, defamation, stalking, or "cyber bullying" (Brenner and Rehber 2009). Copyright violation by illegally offering or downloading protected materials in the internet is another example of a "conventional" crime taking on a different quantitative (and perhaps qualitative) dimension.

Pornography (including child pornography) is today mainly transmitted and distributed electronically, hence some legal systems have introduced special criminal prohibitions against "cyber porn." Where perpetrators use social networks to initiate and establish contact with potential victims of sexual offenses—in particular with children—they cross the line between traditional crime (contacting children with the purpose of committing sexual acts on them) and the type of crime that depends on the existence of the internet. "Grooming" of children for potential sexual abuse through electronic communications has also been defined as a criminal offense in many jurisdictions (Weigend 2013:52).

New Offenses

Other forms of ICT and cybercrime focus on interests that were not in existence before computers and other electronics were invented and the advent of the World Wide Web. Most probably, the largest challenge of criminal law in this century is to properly ascertain and determine these newly surfacing legal interests; defend them from inappropriate obstacles and clashes; and simultaneously reduce the breadth of criminalization (Eskola 2012: 122). The last item is salient because the introduction and expansion of ICT and the origination of cyber space have unlocked several new possibilities and a new range of freedoms related to collecting information, using one's time, creativity when communicating, and seeking commercial interests (Weigend 2013:53). This should not be unnecessarily or disproportionately stifled in the name of security and combating criminality. Moreover, over the last quarter century, financial institutions, private industry and governments have increasingly relied on technology in order to access sensitive data and manage critical infrastructure, such as: electrical power grids, air traffic control, urban utilities including water and the functioning of hospitals, among others (Spidalieri 2015:3). As a consequence, the threat posed by cybercriminals has grown dramatically and afforded significant opportunities for terrorist groups and extremist organizations to strike and inflict considerable damage. Acts of cyber warfare are also feasible and reportedly have already taken place between different countries. One of the most well-known episodes was the attack and destruction of uranium processing centrifuges at the Natanz nuclear facility in Iran via the Stuxnet virus, a joint U.S.-Israel project. The potential for similar destructive attacks also on the civilian critical infrastructure is obviously quite high and could be carried out by a governmental agency, foreign or domestic, or another private competitor or adversary. Most modern plants operate with a standardized industrial control system, so if someone gains control of one industrial control system, one can then infiltrate dozens or even hundreds more of the same type. Another frontier related to cyber communications and artificial intelligence is the rapid increase in the use of robots and drones for surveillance and also interventions that can violate people's privacy, residency, and be lethal. The use of a robot to find and kill a sniper who killed five police officers and wounded several others in Dallas, Texas in the context of demonstrations and protests for the killings of civilians by police in Louisiana and Minnesota during early July 2016 is a troubling precedent and raises serious questions about the future use of new technologies by police. While many police forces have already used remote-controlled devices for detonating bombs or launching of nonlethal force like tear gas, employing one to kill a suspect is certainly unusual and quite possibly unprecedented (Graham, 2016). It opens a new frontier in the use of distance-controlled weaponry in civilian law enforcement, that will be controversial, especially when, some day, there may be substantial "collateral" damage.

Several legal systems stress the need to protect the functioning of ICT systems (computers, networks, etc.) through criminal laws (USGAO 2007:15). In a broader sense, the public trust in the "functioning" of ICT systems and of cyber space is seen as needing protection so that electronic communications and transactions can flourish and facilitate commerce, diffusion of information, and economic growth (Burns 2011:831). The main interests to be protected here are the confidentiality, integrity, and availability of information systems and electronic data (USGAO 2007:23).

Particular Interests

Interference with ICT systems

One fundamental interest is the "integrity" of private and public ICT systems, which is: the functioning of these systems according to their operating rules and the input furnished by the owners (Viano 2013:339). As any unauthorized interference can cause serious damage and undermine the trust in the proper functioning of the ICT system in question, many legal systems have adopted criminal sanctions to punish it (Chia 2012). Typical examples of this crime are the unauthorized transmission and changes of data, removal and destruction of data and software, as well as impeding access to an ICT system. Basically, this crime can be described as "computer sabotage" (Weigend 2013:54).

Hacking

To control, manipulate or sabotage an ICT system, one needs to gain access to it. However, since most ICT systems are usually shielded from unauthorized access, an intruder must penetrate and disable the security system used by the owners. Many legal systems consider this act of "hacking" someone else's ICT system as criminal, without taking into consideration the purpose of the offender (Koons 2015). Generally, the law categorizes the offense simply as entering a protected ICT system without authorization, even if the offender does not or does not intend or want to obtain information put in storage in the system (Weigend 2013:55). However, some countries, like the USA, distinguish between "white hat" and "black hat" hackers, depending on the intent of the hacker. Taking into account the public interest in the "integrity" of an ICT system, hacking can be categorized as an offense of "endangerment" (Hargrave 2012). It is important to note that, while "hacking" was originally conceived of as analogous to trespass, the trend in some jurisdictions has been toward punishing access to computer data per se (Clough 2011:145).

This issue also arises under the Council of Europe Convention on Cybercrime that criminalizes "offenses against the confidentiality, integrity and availability of computer data and systems" (Viano 2013:339). Since the criminal law traditionally provides protection only to limited forms of information, the increasing use of the criminal law to protect computer data therefore confers them a privileged status not enjoyed by information stored in other forms (Manes et al. 2007; ENISA 2009; Sen 2013).

The challenge for the law is to avoid over reaching and over breadth (Wall 2001, 2007/2010:183).

Illegal Monitoring

A related but different offense is the breach of the confidentiality of an ICT system by installing or using monitoring devices or software. Illegal (private) wiretapping is the precursor of this crime before the internet era. The perpetrator not only enters an ICT system without authorization but also attempts to obtain information that has been stored there or that will be transmitted from or to that system (Sembhi 2009).

Innovative Criminal Prohibitions

The cyber world not only offers several new possibilities for communication, commerce and the dissemination of information and opinion but also creates substantial new interests that can be harmed by others (Moitra 2004:105). Legal systems have created new categories and definitions of offenses specifically aimed at protecting individual interests in the cyber world (Steel 2010:503). For example, cyber harassment is defined as a criminal offense for any person to "use a network or electronic communications service or other electronic means to annoy or cause damage to his correspondent, or to install any device intended to commit the offense and the attempt to commit it" (Weigend 2013:56). Another risk associated with the internet is the fast dissemination of photos and images of persons without their consent or against their will (Viano 2013: 34. This does not affect only celebrities but ordinary persons as well, like in the case of pictures or videos depicting nudity or sex activities posted in revenge ("revenge porn") by people whose intimate relationship with someone else went sour, in order to embarrass or punish the other partner or to interfere with his or her existing or new relationships (Walls 2008:45).

The virtual world of cyber space is distinct from the real world, but there are connections between the two. For example, persons can be affected by the loss of "cyber goods" as much as by losing tangible property (Bilge et al. 2009; Westbrook 2006). This raises the question whether laws against theft and fraud, which primarily concern goods and property of the "real" world, can also be applied to the cyber world (Chein 2012:1069). In a 2012 Dutch case, the Dutch Supreme Court confirmed a conviction for theft of electronic goods (Kuchera 2008) (the RuneScape case: "these virtual goods are goods [under Dutch law], so this is theft"). Other legal systems and courts do not readily consider hacking as theft because hacking normally does not "permanently deprive" the victim of the goods (Rumbles 2011:354). The victim still has them on his or her system or hard drive. Hacking is a form of "involuntary" sharing and thus not theft. Stealing a person's virtual identity used for communication on the web affects a more "real" dimension. It is frequently related to attempts to defraud in concrete commercial transactions (Gercke 2007). For example, a perpetrator may illegally acquire the victim's access data and order goods from an Internet seller, receiving the goods but leaving the payment of the bill to the victim (Weigend 2013:57). In some legal systems (e.g., USA, Canada), illegally acquiring or using someone else's "means of identification" with the intent to commit an unlawful act is considered a crime and is sanctioned (U.S. Congress 1998). In other legal systems, courts have recognized and used the offense definitions (Viano 2013:346) of computer forgery, fraud by false representation, wrongful impersonation of another person, defamation, or dissemination of information that violates someone's personal privacy (Clough 2011:145). Given the considerable and valuable importance of the reputation and integrity of cyber personalities -particularly in social networks—the usurpation or falsification of a person's virtual identity has been criminalized, even when the perpetrator does not intend to cause material harm (Effross 1997:931). Sharing certain opinions, placing ads or divulging fake information under another person's cyber identity may do serious damage to that person's "good name" in the cyber world. This could have negative consequences for his or her career or standing in the community and even in his or her family, and may thus be regarded as being even more damaging than the financial loss generated through false orders placed with an online store (Moir and Weir 2008).

Extent of Criminalization: Preparation and Possession

Preparation

The somewhat elusive character of ICT and cybercrime, which can generate problems of proof of actual harm or endangering, has led to the widely adopted incrimination of acts in preparation of the harmful conduct itself (Brenner 2009). This generally also encompasses the mere possession of devices or software that can be used for attacking the integrity of ICT systems. This is remarkable because most legal systems do not normally regard the mere preparation of criminal conduct as qualifying for punishment, except when it relates to very serious crimes or to conspiracies. But in the area of ICT and cybercrime, many legal systems have complied with Article 6 of the Budapest Convention (or "Cybercrime Convention") that asks them to criminalize the production, sale, procurement for use, import, distribution or otherwise making available of devices, including computer programs, designed or adapted primarily for the purpose of committing any of the ICT offenses listed in the Convention (Schjolberg 2014:200). Similarly this applies to computer passwords, access codes, or similar data by which the whole or any part of a computer system is or can be accessed, with the intention to use it for perpetrating any of these offenses. Several legal systems have adopted almost literally this broad definition of preparatory acts from the Budapest Convention. Typical examples of preparatory acts along these lines are "phishing" of web addresses (Deleon 2008) or other personal data (e.g., bank account and credit card numbers, passwords) to be used in order to defraud persons or to do other harm to their interests on the net (Gercke 2011:14). The same applies to the production or sale of devices or software that can be used for hacking, for intercepting communications, for circumventing the protection of copyrighted material, and for child pornography (Viano 2013:340). A special form of preparatory conduct that has been criminalized in some legal systems is the "grooming" of children, that is, making contact with them through electronic communications, with the intent of subsequent sexual abuse or of producing pornographic material (Webster et al. 2012: Chaps. 3–5).

Possession

Criminalization extends in many legal systems- not only to those who produce or distribute devices or software that are suitable to be used for committing ICT or cybercrimes-but also to the mere possession of such tools, including those that are to be used for intercepting communication (Weigend 2013: 60). As to child pornography, the mere possession of certain materials, also in the form of data files, is frequently defined as a criminal offense. While there is a broad agreement that storing such materials in one's computer is a crime (as the sale and acquisition of child pornography perpetuates the illicit market of such materials and consequently promotes the abuse of children) opinions are divided as to whether "possession" extends (or should extend) to the mere viewing of pornographic material on the Internet (Exum 2010: 8; Weigend 2013: 61; Bacon 2011:1027; Howard 2004: 1227; McBath 2012:381). For some countries, the act of knowingly acquiring access to child-pornographic materials on the Internet is a crime, while others require some sort of permanent possession. Another debated issue is the question whether the prohibition only extends to "real" images of children in sexual poses or activities or also covers virtual images, e.g., computer-generated drawings or illustrations (Viano 2013:347–349; Silverstone 2006).

Responsibility of Providers

A number of criminal offenses can be committed by posting certain information, images, or statements on the internet (National White Collar Crime Center 2011). Libel and defamation, incitement to racial hatred, fraud, violations of copyright and pornography laws are the most common types of these crimes. For understandable technical reasons, committing these crimes is not feasible without using internet service providers (ISP) who are the intermediaries between those who wish to post information on the internet and those who receive it. The basic and hotly debated question is: to what extent may ISPs be made criminally responsible? (Viano 2013:342). Legal systems have provided different answers to this question, but the overall trend goes toward limiting the criminal liability to situations in which a provider has been made aware of criminal contents on a site under his control and does not take appropriate action. European legal systems have adapted their laws to the model established by the European Union E-Commerce Directive of 2000 (European Union 2000:OJ 178). In general, national transpositions have closely followed the form and content of the Directive. Member States, with the exception of the Netherlands, decided to transpose the Directive by a horizontal e-commerce law in order to create as clear and user-friendly a national framework as possible. Germany transposed the Directive by modifying its Teleservices Act.

The Directive provides that Member States shall not impose a general obligation on ISPs—including access providers, caching providers and hosts of websites—"to monitor the information which they transmit or store, nor actively to seek facts or circumstances indicating illegal activity"(European Union 2000: Art. 5, Internal Market Clause). The Directive attempts to prevent proactive censoring and the consequent chilling effects on the free flow of information (Center for Technology and Democracy 2012). However, this protection from criminal liability for providers has been limited in a number of ways:

First, providers lose this protection as soon as they go beyond serving as a mere conduit or providing a cache for cyber communications. This can happen, for example by initiating the transmission of data, selecting the receiver or modifying the information transmitted or stored.

Second, ISPs can be criminally liable when they have been alerted about the specific illegal content in their domain by an official agency or by users, but fail to promptly remove it. In France, ISPs are required to positively invite users to alert them to certain prohibited content, such as child pornography, incitement to violence and assaults on human dignity, and they must promptly remove from their sites contents that are "manifestly illegal" (COE 2007; Weigend 2013:63).

Specific Sanctions

In addition to imprisonment and fines, some legal systems envision sanctions that are specific to the offenses discussed here. For example, devices used in the commission of crimes can be confiscated (Viano 2013:341). Prosecutors may order an internet service provider to delete the domain name of a site that violates the law, e.g., by distributing child pornography. In France, the courts have the power to fine an offender up to EUR €1500 euros (US $1,923; GBP £1,292) and even to ban this person from using online communications for up to 1 year as a sanction for violating a copyright (Loi 2009) (In 2013 France ended the three strikes internet piracy ban deemed to be excessive, Ministry 2013). The general criminal law principle that sanctions should be proportionate to the seriousness of the crime should be underlined here. In some states, legislatures and courts tend to overreact to the threat of ICT and cybercrime by approving or imposing excessively high sentences for these new crimes (Ho et al. 2015).

Challenges to and Limits of Criminal Legislation

Keeping Updated with Technological Progress

In view of the fact that the pace of technological developments may quickly make the wording of a criminal statute obsolete, some legislatures try to keep up with the latest progress in various ways, from adopting what is deemed to be relative generic language not tied to the current technology available on the market or by adopting generalizations ("any electronic communication technology, regardless of its technological format or appearance") (U.S. Access Board 2000).

Respecting Constitutional Limits

Any criminalization of communications in cyber space is potentially in conflict with the freedom of expressing one's opinion, a constitutional right in most countries, and may also limit the freedom of the press and of artistic expression (Molina 2011:123; Ferzan 2013:685; Feinberg and George1990:1425) Infringements of these basic rights are permissible only if they are proportionate to what they seek to combat (U.S. Dept. of Commerce 2013). Some legal systems have also introduced in their constitutions the "harm principle" (Persak 2007). It limits the scope of the criminal law to conduct that is harmful or imminently dangerous to an interest worthy of protection (Gray and Smith 2003:90). This raises serious questions as to the criminalization of hacking that does not produce additional detrimental effects or as to the mere possession of the tools for hacking that could negatively impact the freedom to do research (J.S. Mill, 1859; Pontin 2013; Viano 2012:33). The actual application of criminal laws against ICT and cybercrime has the potential of violating the principle of culpability. This can happen, for example, when a court convicts a person of a crime only on the basis that their IP number was connected to a criminal activity but without proof that they intentionally committed, participated or supported the offense committed (Weigend 2013:67).

Alternatives to Criminalization

Honoring the *ultima ratio*-principle (Melander 2013; Wendt 2013; Dubber 2013), criminal law should be used only as a last resort for dealing with a social problem. The *ultima ratio* principle is a well known traditional principle of criminal law that emphasizes the repressive nature of the criminal justice system and classifies it as the last resort of the legislator. According to some, it is a principle honored mostly in its ubiquitous breach. Many consider criminal laws as the primary means of combating ICT and cybercrime, that is, the first line of defense. It must be stressed that, beside criminal law, there are both administrative and civil mechanisms to deal with cybercrime (Dubber 2010).

Administrative Measures

An important tool for administrative agencies is their power to order the removal of certain content or to "close down" offensive websites (Fuller 2001:2; Kibble 2008:497). In various states, this possibility is available for example, against websites providing child pornography. An administrative agency may order the access provider to block access to the website in question (Bernstein 2012:1457; BBC 2015; Cecil 2011; McCormack 2014:304). While these orders are issued to domestic access providers, they actually also cover access to websites operated abroad.

Civil Remedies

In many legal systems, individual victims can seek redress in the civil courts for damages incurred because of illicit activity on the net. However, this avenue is difficult, complicated and expensive to undertake for private victims. Therefore, it is seldom used, except in the case of a copyright violation (Cheh 1991:1325; Adler 2011; Marsh 2015:459; Salvador 2015:268).

Aspects of Internationalization

Cybercrime, almost by definition, transcends national borders (Viano 2013:338). This fact raises jurisdiction issues when there is the application of national laws to transnational conduct (Colangelo 2011:1019). It also makes international cooperation and harmonization in combating cybercrime a necessity.

Jurisdiction

Most states exercise their jurisdiction and apply their criminal laws to any offense that has been committed on their territory. This applies to cybercrime when the perpetrator acts illegally while being in the territory of the state in question (Brenner 2006). States also exercise their jurisdiction if the perpetrator acts abroad but the effect, as required by the definition of the particular offense, occurs on the state's territory. Another recognized basis for jurisdiction is the fact that the offense committed abroad has negatively affected, caused damages, or impacted the state that claims jurisdiction, or one of its citizens. In this latter case, there is normally a requirement of "double criminality," which means that, the act must be punishable both where it was committed and in the forum state. Another source of jurisdiction for a crime alleged to have occurred abroad is the use of an instrumentality located in the country intending to prosecute (for example, a bank or money services based in the country) in order to carry it out (President's Working Group 2000; Koops & Brenner 2006).

International Harmonization

Certain international legal instruments have been quite influential on the relevant legislation in many countries (Sweeney 2008:209). The greatest common denominator is the Council of Europe's Budapest Convention of 2001, which has had an impact on legislation even in those states that have not ratified it. In the European Union (EU) and even beyond, the EU Framework Decision 2005/222/JHA (European Union 2005) on attacks against information systems has a significant impact on national legislation. The EU Data Retention Directive 2006/24/CE

(European Union 2006) has similarly been implemented by most member states. However On 8 April 2014, the Court of Justice of the European Union declared the Directive invalid in response to a case brought by Digital Rights Ireland against the Irish authorities and others (CJEU 2014).

Additionally, certain EU instruments concerning the combat of individual crimes, such as the Framework Decision 2004/68/JHA (European Union 2003) on the sexual exploitation of children and child pornography, have been influential.

In general, there is remarkable convergence of various multilateral instruments on cybercrime in criminalizing acts against the confidentiality, integrity and availability of computer data and systems. Multilateral instruments connected with the African Union, the Council of Europe, the League of Arab States, the Economic Community of West African States, the Common Market for Eastern and Southern Africa, the Commonwealth and the International Telecommunications Union, all criminalize illegal access to: a computer system; illegal interception; illegal computer data and system interference; and the misuse of devices (Downing 2005:43; Kunze 2010:241; Miquelon-Weisman 2005:329; Goodman and Brenner 2002; Borisevich et al. 2012: 267). Others, like illegal access, acquisition and input of computer data and illegally remaining in a computer system to date, have received considerable less support. When it comes to computer-related acts, two categories—computer related forgery and fraud—are widely criminalized, with the exception of the Commonwealth of Independent States and the Commonwealth. Remarkably, identity theft has not yet been included in these multilateral instruments along with, by and large, extortion, spam, harassment, stalking, and bullying (Viano 2013:342). Computer solicitation or grooming of children has been included only in the Council of Europe Convention on Protection of Children against Sexual Exploitation and Sexual Abuse, also known as "the *Lanzarote Convention*"{COE 2007}, the first international treaty that addresses child sexual abuse that occurs within the home or family.

As to computer content-related acts, the most frequently criminalized are those involving child pornography and -to a lesser extent- dissemination of racist and xenophobic materials and related threats and insults (COE 2003). Genocide, terrorism, pornography (including facilitating access of a child to pornography), gambling, money laundering and illicit trafficking using electronic media technologies have been very rarely criminalized to date (INCB 2001; ITU 2009; Fafinski 2008:273).

Other areas that have received little attention to be classified as crimes in international treaties to date are (Viano 2013:347):

1. Violation of data protection measures for personal information;
2. Breach of confidentiality;
3. Use of forged or fraudulently obtained data;
4. Illicit use of electronic payment tools;
5. Acts against privacy;
6. Disclosure of details of an investigation; and
7. Failure to permit assistance.

It must be noted that we are discussing multilateral documents here. Individual countries may have already criminalized behaviors that have not yet been included in international treaties. The process of creating, offering for signature and ratifying international documents is much slower and difficult than domestic lawmaking. Also it is essential to keep in mind that what a multiparty treaty contains is not necessarily what the ratifying countries agree to adopt and/or to enforce. Frequently, ratification of treaties is predicated on "reservations," which means that the ratifying country does not fully or at all accepts one or more clauses of the document or that their implementation is subordinated to domestic law (Neumayer 2007:397). This happens especially in cases when the country's constitution and its interpretation (or the passage of domestic enabling legislation) place limits on the applicability and enforcement of the treaty. At times these "reservations" can effectively gut a treaty of its most important provisions, while the ratification rate of a treaty may give the mistaken impression of widespread acceptance and enforcement.

Shifting the Burden of Crime Prevention to the Consumer

There has been a movement towards shifting the burden of protection to users.

The reasoning is that, at least, some offenses in the Information and Communication Technology and cyber spheres could be easily prevented by exercising some caution on the part of those who become victims of these offenses. This can demonstrated by downloading antivirus software and by using strong passwords to protect one's account and operations via the internet. Some have argued that this effectively shifts the task of preventing cybercrime to the user who becomes responsible for her own protection instead of punishing the offender who takes advantage of an easy target. While many countries encourage users to use appropriate protection, only a few go to the extent of criminalizing "not using protection" (Smith et al. 2015:47). The reasoning for criminalization is that by not using antivirus software, the user not only makes him or herself vulnerable to victimization but he or she effectively allows or at least facilitates the use of his or her electronic devices to then further distribute malware and victimize others with considerable costs to society (Viano 2012:33).

Trends for the Future

Based on the analysis of the provisions of the multilateral instruments on cybercrime and the comparison checklist, one can perceive the following trends and needs, among others (Weigend 2013:73):

1. Addressing intent requirements, in view of lowering them, which would allow courts to dispose of problems of proof that are otherwise insurmountable;
2. Balancing the interests of copyright holders and those of users, allowing inexpensive access to music protected by copyright;
3. Criminalizing new types of harmful conduct like cyberbullying, cyberstalking, identity theft, spamming, and the illegal acquisition and distribution of data;

4. Protecting information and network systems from theft and other offenses;
5. Studying whether criminal liability of internet service providers (ISPs) should be increased;
6. Developing legislation on cybercrime systematically and uniformly
7. Begin to answer whether and how criminal law can cover a number of problematic behaviors that occur in Virtual Worlds (Viano 2012:33).

Conclusion

Cybercrime is the major threat to our society today from all perspectives: social life, privacy invasion, identify theft, financial crimes, fraud, harassment, bullying, slander, security of the community and of the country, cyberwarfare, industrial production, provision of electricity and water, communications, entertainment, and other essential or purely elective services. Cybercrime still does not command the attention, the concern, the prevention and the public education that other crimes, mostly violent crimes, elicit in our society. The unstoppable growth of information, communication, and entertainment technology, of artificial intelligence, and of robots urgently requires that the gap between reality and the law addressing it be closed as rapidly as possible and at the international level.

References

Adler, J. (2011). The public's burden in a digital age: Pressures on intermediaries & the privatization of internet censorship. *Journal of Law & Policy, 20*, 231.

Bacon, S. L. (2011). A distinction without a difference: "Receipt" and "Possession" of child pornography and the double jeopardy problem. *University of Miami Law Review, 65*(Spring), 1027.

BBC Monitoring Europe. (2015, March 23). *New bill gives Turkish government power to shut down Websites in four hours*, supplied by BBC Worldwide Monitoring.

Bernstein, A. (2012). Social networks and the law: Real remedies for virtual injuries. *90 N.C.L. Rev, 90*, 1457.

Bilge, L., Strufe, T., Balzaroti, D., & Kirda, E. (2009). *All your contacts belong to us: Automated identity theft attacks on social networks*. Retrieved from http://www.sba-research.org/wpcontent/uploads/publications/Bilge_AllYourContacts_2009.pdf.

Borisevich, G., Chernyadyeva, N., Frolovich, E., Pastukhov, P., Polyakova, S., Dobrovlyanina, O., et al. (2012). A comparative review of cybercrime law and digital forensics in Russia, the United States and under the convention on cybercrime of the Council of Europe. *Northern Kentucky Law Review, 39*(2), 267.

Brenner, S. (2006). Cybercrime jurisdiction. *Crime, Law and Social Change, 46*(4), 189–206.

Brenner, S. (2007). Cybercrime: Re-thinking crime control strategies. In Y. Jewkes (Ed.), *Crime online* (pp. 12–28). Cullompton, United Kingdom: Willan Publishing.

Brenner, S. (2009, May 6). "Thoughts, witches and crimes," CYB3RCRIM3: Observations on technology, law, and lawlessness. Retrieved from http://cyb3rcrim3.blogspot.com/2009/05/thoughts-witches-and-crimes.html.

Brenner, S. W., & Rehber, M. (2009–2010). "'Kiddie Crime?' The utility of criminal law in controlling cyber-bullying," *First Amendment Law Review 8*(1).
Burns, Brett. (2011-2012).Level 85 Rogue: When virtual theft merits criminal penalties. *UMKC Law Review*, *80*: 831, 845.
Cecil, N. (2011, November 6). MP demands law to force internet providers to remove gang videos. *The Evening Standard.*
Center for Technology & Democrac. (2012). Shielding the messengers: Protecting platforms for expression and innovation. Version 2, updated December; https://cdt.org/files/pdfs/CDT-Intermediary-Liability-2012.pdf.
Cheh, M. M. (1991). Constitutional limits on using civil remedies to achieve criminal law objectives: Understanding and transcending the criminal-civil law distinction. *Hastings L.J, 42*(July), 1325.
Chein, A. (2012). A practical look at virtual property. *St. John's Law Review, 80*, 3, Summer, 1059–1088.
Chia, T. (2012, August 20). Confidentiality, integrity and availability (CIA): The three components of the CIA triad. *IT Security Community Blog.*
CJEU. (2014). Court of Justice of the European Union. Case number C-293/12. *EUR-Lex, Official Journal of the European Union*. Retrieved April 8, 2014 from http://curia.europa.eu/juris/documents.jsf?num=C-293/12.
Clough, J. (2011). Data theft? Cybercrime and the increasing criminalization of access to data. *Criminal Law Forum, 22*, 145–170. doi:10.1007/s10609-011-9133-5. Springer 2011.
COE. (2003). See, for example, an additional protocol to the council of Europe convention on cybercrime: Council of Europe. http://conventions.coe.int/Treaty/Commun/ChercheSig.asp?NT=201&CM=&DF=&CL=ENG.
COE. Council of Europe. (2007, October 25). Additional protocol to the convention on cybercrime, concerning the criminalization of acts of a racist and xenophobic nature committed through computer systems. Retrieved July 1, 2010 from http://conventions.coe.int/Treaty/en/Treaties/Html/189.htm.
COE. (2007). Signed on 25 October 2007; effective on 1 July 2010; http://conventions.coe.int/Treaty/Commun/ChercheSig.asp?NT=201&CM=&DF=&CL=ENG.
Colangelo, A. J. (2011). A unified approach to extraterritoriality. *Virginia Law Review, 97*, 1019.
Couldry, N. (2008). Mediatization or mediation? Alternative understandings of the emergent space of digital storytelling. *New Media & Society, 10*(3), 373–391.
Council of Europe. (2001). Convention on cybercrime. Retrieved from http://conventions.coe.int/Treaty/EN/Treaties/html/185.htm.
Council of Europe. (2003). Additional protocol to the convention on cybercrime, concerning the criminalization of acts of a racist and xenophobic nature committed through computer systems. Retrieved from http://conventions.coe.int/Treaty/en/Treaties/Html/189.htm.
Deleon, N. (2008, March 26). Phishing scam targeting facebook users. Retrieved from http://techcrunch.com/2008/03/26/phishing-scam-targeting-facebook-users/.
Downing, R. (2005). Shoring up the weakest link: What lawmakers around the world need to consider in developing comprehensive laws to combat cybercrime. *Colum. J. Transnat'l L., 43*, 705.
Doyle, C. (2016). RICO: A brief sketch. Congressional research service, Report 96-850.
Dubber, M. D. (2010, December 1). The legality principle in American and German criminal law: An essay in comparative legal history. SSRN: http://ssrn.com/abstract=1735966 or http://dx.doi.org/10.2139/ssrn.1735966.
Dubber, Markus. (2013, July 3). *Ultima Ratio as Caveat Dominus: Legal principles, police maxims, and the critical analysis of law*, http://ssrn.com/abstract=2289479 orhttp://dx.doi.org/10.2139/ssrn.2289479.
Effross, W. A. (1997). High-tech heroes, virtual villains, and jacked-in justice: Visions of law and lawyers in cyberpunk science fiction. *Buffalo Law Review, 931*, 46.
Eskola, T. (2012). From risk society to network society: Preventing cybercrimes in the 21st century. *Journal of Applied Security Research, 7*(1), 122–150.

European Network and Information Security Agency (ENISA). (2009). Cloud computing: cloud computing: benefits, risks and recommendations for information security. Report No: 2009.
European Union. (2000). *Directive 2000/31/EC* of the European Parliament and of the Council of 8 June 2000 on certain legal aspects of information society services, in particular electronic commerce, in the Internal Market (Directive on electronic commerce), OJ L 178, 17.7.2000: 1.
European Union. (2003). Council framework decision 2004/68/JHA of 22 December 2003 on combating the sexual exploitation of children and child pornography.
European Union. (2005). *Council framework decision 2005/222/JHA of 24 February 2005 on attacks against information systems.* http://eur-lex.europa.eu/legal content/EN/ALL/?uri=CELEX%3A32005F0222.
European Union. (2006). Directive 2006/24/EC of the European Parliament and of the Council of 15 March 2006 on the retention of data generated or processed in connection with the provision of publicly available electronic communications services or of public communications networks and amending Directive 2002/58/EC.
Exum, J. J. (2010). Making the punishment fit the (Computer) crime: Rebooting notions of possession for the federal sentencing of child pornography offenses. *Richmond Journal of Law and Technology, 16*(Spring), 8.
Fafinski, Stefan Frederick. (2008). Computer use and misuse: The constellation of control. Ph.D. Dissertation, University of Leeds, School of Law 273–281.
Feinberg, J., & George, R. P. (1990). Crime and punishment: Moralistic liberalism and legal moralism: Harmless wrongdoing: The moral limits of the criminal law. *Mich.L.R, 88*, 1415.
Fernando, F. M. (2011). A comparison between continental European and Anglo-American approaches to overcriminalization and some remarks on how to deal with it. *New Crim. L.R., 14*, 123.
Ferzan, Kimberly Kessler. (2013). Prevention, wrongdoing, and the harm principle's breaking point. *Ohio St. J. Crim. L*, 685
Finklea, Kristin., Catherine A. Theohary. (2015). Cybercrime: Conceptual issues for congress and law enforcement," *CRS*, January 3.
Fuller, Kathleen. (2001). ICANN: The debate over governing the internet. *Duke L & Tech. Rev.* 2(February): 24.
Gercke, Marco. (2007). Internet-related identity theft. A discussion paper, http://www.coe.int/t/dghl/cooperation/economiccrime/cybercrime/documents/reportspresentations/567%20port%20id-d-identity%20theft%20paper%2022%20nov%2007.pdf.
Gercke, Marco. (2011). Legal approaches to criminalize identity theft. In: Handbook on Identity related Crime. pp. 146, New York: United Nations.
Goodman, M., & Brenner, S. (2002). The emerging consensus on criminal conduct in cyberspace. *UCLA Journal of Law and Technology, 3.*
Gordon, S., & Ford, R. (2006). On the definition and classification of cybercrime. *Journal of Computer Virology, 2*(July), 15–19.
Graham, David. (2016, July 11). The era of lethal police robots has arrived. Defense One.
Gray, John., G. W. Smith (eds.). (2003). *J.S. Mill on Liberty*. New York: Routledge, 2003: 90.
Guinchard, A. (2008). Cybercrime: The transformation of crime in the digital age. *Information, Communication and Society, 11*(7), 1030–1032.
Hargrave,Vick. (2012, June 17). Hacker, hacktivist or cybercriminal? *Trend micro simply security.*
Ho, Michael, Joyce Hung, & Michael Hasnick. (2015). *The carrot and the stick: Innovation versus anti-piracy enforcement*. The Copia Institute, October.
Homeland Security Newswire. (2011, April 19). An electronic trail for every crime, http://homelandsecuritynewswire.com/electronic-trail-every-crime.
Iain Moir., George R. S. Weir. (2008). Identity theft: A study in contact centres, Paper presented at the 4th International Conference on Global E-Security, University of East London, June. http://www.cis.strath.ac.uk/cis/research/publications/papers/strath_cis_publication_2243.pdf.
INCB. (2001). International narcotics control board, globalization and new technologies: challenges to drug law enforcement in the twenty-first century, 2001.
ITU (International Telecommunications Union). (2009). *Understanding cybercrime: A guide for developing countries*, pp. 30–40.

Johnson. David R., David Post, (1996). Law and Borders - The rise of law in cyberspace, Stanford law review, vol. 48 (May) 1379.
Kibble, M. B. (2008). Fear mongering, filters, the internet and the first amendment: Why congress should not pass legislation similar to the deleting online predators act. *Roger Williams U.L. Rev., 13*, 497.
Koons, Stephanie. (2015, January 22). Researchers examine role of "white hat" hackers in cyber warfare. *Phys Org, Technology, Security*.
Koops, B.-J., & Brenner, S. (Eds.). (2006). *Cybercrime and jurisdiction: A global survey*. Den Haag: T.M.C. Asser Press.
Kuchera, B. (2008). Dutch court imposes real-world punishment for virtual theft. *Ars Technica*.
Kunze, E. I. (2010). Sex trafficking via the internet: How international agreements address the problem and fail to go far enough. *J. High Tech. L., 10*, 241.
Loi. (2009). Loi favorisant la diffusion et la protection de la création sur Internet : Loi n° 2009-669 du 12 juin 2009 published in the JO n° 135 du 13 juin 2009. Décision du Conseil constitutionnel n° 2009-580 du 10 juin 2009.
Manes, Gavin W., Elizabeth Downing, Lance Watson, & Christopher Thrutchley. (2007). New federal rules and digital evidence, Conference on digital forensics, security and law.
Marsh, J. R. (2015). Predators, porn & the law: America's children in the internet era: A federal civil remedy for child pornography victims. *Syracuse L. Rev., 61*, 459.
McBath, J. E. (2012). Trashing our system of justice? overturning jury verdicts where evidence is found in the computer's cache. *American Journal of Criminal Law, 39*(Summer), 381.
McCormack, Wayne. (2014). U.S. judicial independence: Victim in the 'war on terror', *Wash & Lee L. Rev,* 71, 305.
Melander, Sakari. (2013). Ultima ratio in european criminal law. *Oñate Socio-Legal Series*, 3 (1).
Mill, John Stuart. (1859). *On Liberty*. The "harm" principle is fundamental to John Stuart Mill's approach to justifying or rejecting the intervention of the state through criminal law to prohibit, deter and punish certain behaviors. In On Liberty, Mill argues for 'one very simple principle, as entitled to govern absolutely the dealings of society with the individual in the way of compulsion and control'. That principle is that 'The only purpose for which power can be rightfully exercised over any member of a civilized community, against his will, is to prevent harm to others. His own good, either physical or moral, is not a sufficient warrant. In: John Gray., G.W. Smith (Eds.), *J.S. Mill on Liberty*, New York: Routledge, pp. 90, 2003.
Ministry. (2013). http://www.culturecommunication.gouv.fr/Presse/Communiques-de-presse/Publication-du-decret-supprimant-la-peine-complementaire-de-la-suspension-d-acces-a-Internet.
Miquelon-Weismann, Miriam F. (2005). The convention on cybercrime: A harmonized implementation of international penal law: What prospects for procedural due process. 3 *J. Marshall J. Computer & Info. L.* Winter 23: 329.
Moitra, S. D. (2004). Cybercrime: Towards an assessment of its nature and impact. *International Journal of Comparative and Applied Criminal Justice, 28*(2), 105–120.
National White Collar Crime Center. (2011). *Criminal use of social media*, http://www.iacpsocialmedia.org/Portals/1/documents/External/NW3CArticle.pdf.
Neumayer, Eric. (2007). Qualified ratification: Explaining reservations to international human rights treaties, *J. Legal Stud*, 397 June.
Pontin, J. (2013, February 20). Free speech in the era of its technological amplification. *Technology Review*.
Persak, Nina. (2007). *Criminalizing harmful conduct: The harm principle, its limits and continental counterparts*. Springer Science & Business Media.
President's Working Group. (2000, March). *The electronic frontier: The challenge of unlawful conduct involving the use of the internet.* A report of the President's Working Group on Unlawful Conduct on the Internet.
Salvador, J. (2015). Dismantling the internet mafia: RICO's applicability to cyber crime. *Rutgers Computer & Tech. L.J., 41*, 268.
Sarb Sembhi (2009). How to defend against data integrity attacks, computer weekly, 2009.

Schjolberg, Stein. (2014). *The History of Cybercrime: 1976-2014*, pp. 200, Books on demand (November 24, 2014). Stein proposes in article 5 of a new Convention for the creation of an International Tribunal on Cybercrime that these types of crime fall under the jurisdiction of the proposed Tribunal.
Sen, Jaydip. (2013). Security and privacy issues in cloud computing. http://arxiv.org/pdf/1303.4814.pdf.
Silverstone, R. (2006). *Media and morality: on the rise of the mediapolis*. New York: Wiley.
Smith, R. G., Raymond Chak-Chung Cheung, & Laurie Yiu-Chung Lau. (2015). *Cyber risks and perspectives: Eastern and western perspectives*. Palgrave Macmillan.
Spidalieri, Framcesca. (2015, November 3). *State of the states on cybersecurity*, Pell Center for International Relations.
Steel, A. (2010). The true identity of Australian identity theft offences: A measured response or an unjustified status offence? *University of New South Wales Law Journal, 33*, 503–531.
Sweeney, B. J. (2008). Global competition: Searching for a rational basis for global competition rules. *The Sydney Law Review, 30*(June), 209.
Tosza, S. (2013). Online social networks and violations committed using I.T. –identity fraud and theft of victual property. *Revue Internationale de Droit Penal, 84*, 115.
Ty, E. Howard. (2004). Don't cache out your case: Prosecuting child pornography possession laws based on images located in temporary internet files. *Berkeley Tech. L.J*, 19 (Fall):1227.
U.S. Access Board. (2000). Section 508, standards for electronic and information technology, Federal register, December 21.
U.S. Congress. (1998). Identity theft and assumption deterrence act of 1998. Title 18, U.S. Code, Sect.1028. Fraud and related activity in connection with identification documents, authentication features, and information.
U.S. Dept. of Commerce. (2013). Internet policy task force, copyright, creativity and innovation in the digital economy, July.
USGAO. (2007). *Public and private entities face challenges in addressing cyber threats*. U.S. Government Accountability Office, June.
Viano, E. C. (2012). Balancing liberty and security fighting cybercrime: Challenges for the networked society. In S. Manacorda (Ed.), *Cybercriminality: Finding a balance between freedom and security* (pp. 33–64). Milano, Italy: ISPAC.
Viano, Emilio C. (2013). Section II: Criminal law. Special part, information society and penal law, general report. *Revue Internationale de Droit Penal*, 84 (3–4), 336.
Viano, E. C. (2006). Cybercrime: A new frontier in criminology. *International Annals of Criminology, 44*(1/2), 11–22.
Wall, D. S. (2007). *Cybercrime*. Cambridge, U.K.: Polity Press.
Wall, D. S. (2001). Cybercrimes and the internet. In D. S. Wall (Ed.), *Crime and the Internet* (pp. 1–17). New York: Routledge.
Wall, D. S. (2015). Cybercrime as a conduit for criminal activity. In A. Pattavina (Ed.), *Information technology and the criminal justice system* (pp. 77–88). Beverly Hills CA: Sage Publications.
Walls, David S. (2008). Cybercrime, media and insecurity: The shaping of public perceptions of cybercrime, *International review of law, computers and technology*, 22 (1–2), 45-63. Special issue: Crime and Criminal Justice.
Webster, Stephen et al. (2012). *The European online grooming project final report*, March, especially chapters 3, 4 & 5. http://www.europeanonlinegroomingproject.com/media/2076/european-online-grooming-project-final-report.pdf.
Weigend, T. (2013). Information society and penal law: General report. *Revue Internationale de Droit Penal, 84*(1–2), 51.
Wendt, Rudolph. (2013). The principle of ultima ratio and/or the principle of proportionality. *Oñate Socio-Legal Series*, 3(1).
Westbrook, Theodore J. (2006). Owned: Finding a place for virtual world property rights, *Mich. St. L. Rev*, 779ff.

Chapter 2
Cyber-Grooming Young Women for Terrorist Activity: Dominant and Subjugated Explanatory Narratives

Susan S.M. Edwards

Young Women, Schoolgirls and IS/Daesh

Evidence submitted to the UK Home Affairs Select Committee on Countering Extremism (19th January 2016) estimated that between 700 and 800 people have travelled from Britain to Syria to join IS/Daesh. Of those, the British Home Secretary, in a statement on Counter Terrorism on January 5th, 2016, referring to Metropolitan Police statistics, said about half had returned. It is estimated that of those travelling to Syria, 50–60 are young women and teenage schoolgirls. It is widely accepted that these young women are "recruited" and "cyber-groomed" online via social media (Hoyle et al. 2015). Whilst the UK's much contested and debated "Prevent" agenda (see Coppock 2014; Edwards 2016) (the subject of objection by University lectures because of its challenge to freedom of speech and its essentialist vilification of Muslims and the subject of a unanimous vote against the strategy by the National Union of Teachers at its conference on March 28th, 2016) has focused on mosques, schools, universities and other public spaces as key venues of potential recruitment, it is evident that it is within the private spaces of the study and the bedroom, the park, the street or theatre etc., and in any internet geolocation, that cyber-grooming takes place. Yusra Hussein, (15 years of age) from Bristol, was reported to have travelled to Syria to marry and become a "Jihadi bride" was thought to have been recruited via the internet. Aqsa Mahmood, aged 20, from Glasgow, was reported to have encouraged terrorist acts via social media using the pseudonym "Umm Layth" and was also thought to have been recruited via

S.S.M. Edwards, B.A., M.A., Ph.D., L.L.M. (✉)
Dean of Law, University of Buckingham, Buckingham, UK

Barrister, Door Tenant, 1 Gray's Inn Square, London, UK

Expert Witness, MEWI, Temple Chambers, Temple Avenue, London EC4Y 0DA, UK
e-mail: susan.edwards@buckingham.ac.uk

E.C. Viano (ed.), *Cybercrime, Organized Crime, and Societal Responses*,
DOI 10.1007/978-3-319-44501-4_2

the internet. Salma and Zahra Halane, both 16 years of age, left their home in Manchester in 2014, and were said to have sent messages home to their families encouraging them to join IS. More recently, in 2015, Shamima Begum 15 years of age, Amira Abase and Kadiza Sultana (the "Bethnal Green Academy schoolgirls") left their London homes to join IS. Two of them are said to have entered into marriages arranged by IS. It has been reported that Amira Abase married an Australian "jihadi" who was killed fighting for IS and that Kadiza Sultana also got married and her husband has also died. It is believed that cyberspace was used to contact and recruit them. Contrary to the promulgated view that has so exercised the public imagination that such recruitment happens within Muslim communities and places where Muslims gather, a view which has authorised the over policing and over surveillance of these communities (see Fussey 2013), the communication and grooming is happening in secret online.

The use of young women by terrorist groups was the subject of investigation by the Home Affairs Select Committee on Counter Terrorism on January 28th, 2014, but at that time the involvement of young women was still viewed with some scepticism. Paul Flynn MP., a member of the Committee, put the following question to Gilles de Kerchove, EU Counterterrorism Coordinator, "On the 16th of this month, two women were arrested carrying a large sum of money to Syria. Is this, again, another trend that is obvious throughout Europe—of women being used as couriers for large sums of money? Gilles de Kerchove replied: "I had not heard many cases of that sort, but that is probably the first time we have seen that women are going to Syria" (Question 515). Arguably it is the gendered presumption of women's unlikely involvement in terrorist activity that no doubt contributed to the police failings to apprehend, intercept and return the "Bethnal Green Academy schoolgirls" notwithstanding that their families had reported the disappearance of these school girls who were legally "minors" immediately to the police. Significantly, two of the three girls were only 15 years of age, the oldest being only 16 years old (see Edwards 2015). The schoolgirls were observed at the border control and observed on CCTV standing in a bus station in Turkey for many hours before travelling on to Syria. These and other police failings were the subject of investigation by the Home Affairs Committee on 10th March 2015 (Home Affairs Committee, 10th March 2015 oral evidence.) Certainly by 2015, the evidence of young women leaving the UK to join IS was incontrovertible. However leaving the UK to travel to Syria was not criminalised until the Counter Terrorism and Security Act 2015 came into force in July 2015, this was after the young women mentioned above had left for Syria.

By 2015, a number of women were being prosecuted in the UK for using social media as a "tool for terrorism." For example in Runa Khan pleaded guilty in December 2014 to four offences under the Terrorism Act 2006 ss. 2, 3 which prohibits "dissemination" over the internet of material likely to be useful in terrorist activity. She had posted on Facebook an article entitled "Raising Mujahid Children", and used "WhatsApp", messaging her desire to travel to Syria. She was sentenced to 5 years imprisonment. On March 27th, 2015, Hana Khan was found guilty of funding terrorism (Terrorism Act 2000 s. 15). She had sent a man 1000 pounds, he had duped her into believing that he was her boyfriend. Tareena Shakil travelled to Syria with her 14 month old son to join IS and posted pictures of him on social media wearing an IS balaclava. In 2015, she returned to the UK. She was convicted of "encouraging acts of terrorism" (Terrorism Act 2006 s. 1) and being a member of IS, a "proscribed organization" (Terrorism Act 2000 s. 11). Her counsel, Tim Moloney QC, said she had developed friendships online after her marriage failed and that she was "groomed" by IS members. Evidence from her friends was adduced as to her character. They described her as an ordinary young woman, who was "fun loving" and who liked the Spice Girls". She was sentenced to a term of 6 years imprisonment on February 1st, 2016. In addition to young single women leaving to join IS, in 2015, three families left the UK for Syria to join IS. Muhammed Abdul Mannan and his extended family; Farzana Ameen and her husband Imran and five children, and a third family headed by three sisters, the Dawood sisters who left for Syria with their nine children. These families have not been intercepted and have not returned to the UK.

Official statistics on the prosecution of suspects for terrorist related offences under the Terrorism Act 2000 for the period 2014–2015, record 299 arrests, of which 118 persons were charged with an offence, of which 85 % were considered to be terrorist related offences. Fifty-two were proceeded against, and of these, 42 (81 %) were convicted, of whom 27 entered a guilty plea. The most common offence charged, is "preparation of terrorist acts" (Terrorism Act 2006 s. 5) This statutory section states, "(1) A person commits an offence if, with the intention of—(a) committing acts of terrorism, or (b) assisting another to commit such acts, he engages in any conduct in preparation for giving effect to his intention)". Significantly, the proportion of women arrested for terrorism related offences has increased since September 11th, 2001 and 12 % of offences (in 2014–2015) relate to 35 women (Official statistics on the prosecution of suspect terrorist activities and the operation of police powers under the Terrorism Act 2000 and subsequent legislation for year ending 31 March 2015).

Grooming in Cyber-Space for Terrorist Recruitment

Clive Walker and Maura Conway (2015, p. 156), examine the role played by mass communications technology in terrorist and extremist movements and identify the several legal measures introduced to deal with the use of the internet by extremist groups including the closing down of some online websites (p. 157), the criminalization of precursor activity as a preventative measure (p. 163), countering the ideology of terrorism through the creation of new crimes (p. 164) and the introduction of preventive measures in the "Prevent" policy. The "Prevent" policy places a duty on "responsible authorities" on a statutory footing with the Counter Terrorism and Security Act 2015 s. 26, which requires responsible authorities "To have regard to the need to prevent people from being drawn into terrorism". Fisher and Prucha (2014) in particular, point to the resilient and persistent jihadist presence on Twitter and especially to the dedicated "media mujahideen." Dilipraj (2015) also details the several ways in which "jihadist" groups have developed a network of Twitter accounts, chat rooms and forums etc. including the use of "You Tube" which continually gives them an ideological presence for jihadist propaganda. Certainly, cyber-space has played a significant role in facilitating and engaging support and recruitment to Syria including the grooming and recruitment of young women to become "jihadi brides" and to serve in other ways. The cyber-space platform is both determined and specific and part of what is recognised as an "electronic ribat" (Fisher and Prucha 2014).

By 2016, the UK government's concern with the potential of cyber-grooming for terrorist purposes and its limited understanding of how young people access cyber space resulted in directing its maladroit pre-emptive prevention strategy towards Muslim mothers who the government positioned as the key gatekeepers in preventing adult and teenage offspring being drawn into terrorism. The former UK Prime Minister David Cameron said on BBC Radio 4 on January 16th, 2016, "If you're not able to speak English, you're not able to integrate, you may find, therefore, that you have challenges understanding what your identity is and you could be more susceptible to the extremist message that comes from Daesh", and he went on to say that Muslim mothers unable to read English would be unable to "monitor" the behaviour of those in their families for whom they were responsible. This underscores a fundamental lack of understanding of how social media is accessed in that private space between the internet device and the user. The Home Affairs Select Committee on Countering Extremism on 19th January 2016, questioned David Anderson QC (Independent reviewer of terrorism legislation) on this very point. Chairman Mr Keith Vaz asked: "One of the points that the Prime Minister made yesterday is that he felt that it was a language problem and that, by giving Muslim mothers, in effect, £20 million to teach them how to speak English, this would somehow have an effect on stopping people going, because it is the Muslim mothers, in particular, who seem to be encouraging people. Do you agree with what the Prime Minister has said? Do you think that that is one way of making sure that people are more integrated?" (Question 930). David Anderson QC replied, "I think it is unfortunate that this whole question of language learning, which is a very important part of the integration and empowerment of women, should get mixed up with the business of ISIS".

In reality few parents, regardless of religion or ethnicity, are able to "police" or exercise this sort of control over their teenage sons or daughters. Michael Ellis, a member of the Home Affairs Select Committee (see Home Affairs Committee on Counter Terrorism 2015, 10th March 2015), put a question to the father of Amira Abase (one of the "Bethnal Green Academy schoolgirls") in which he raised his concern and also some degree of scepticism that the schoolgirls had access to their own passports. "The passports are in your possession and control at home and your daughter knew where they were… So you are assuming your daughter took the passport without your knowledge"? Mr. Abase replied, "Yes, of course, she is trustworthy. They are free." The reality is that parents have little understanding of social media and even less control over their adolescent offspring's activities in their use of cyber-space and many adolescent girls have access to their own passports without their being any suspicion of dereliction of parental duty.

How should the law should protect young people including young women from IS and the use by IS of the internet in recruiting them? The response of the UK government to IS/Daesh's use of cyber-space has been to strengthen existing criminal legislation by the Terrorism Act 2006 to include the internet. Section 3(1) (a) specifically prohibits the "encouragement" and dissemination of publications for terrorist purposes extending the offence to the internet. "(1) This section applies for the purposes of sections 1 and 2 in relation to cases where—(a) a statement is published or caused to be published in the course of, or in connection with, the provision or use of a service provided electronically; or (b) conduct falling within section 2(2) was in the course of, or in connection with, the provision or use of such a service." But there is even by 2016 still no specific provision which prohibits and criminalises terrorist grooming.

Grooming Young Women

As has already been pointed out the internet has been used to target young women and schoolgirls who are being groomed online to enlist them in a range of extremist and terrorist activities by encouraging them to leave the UK to join IS (see "Britain's Jihadi Brides" 2015). The role of young women is hugely important to IS as an army of domestic workers who provide all the domestic services required to support IS including the sexual services required by the men. Some women are marrying the so called jihadi fighters but it is unlikely even given the tenets of the interpretation of Islam that IS states it adheres to that women are providing sexual services within monogamy. Some women are clearly being used and abused merely to provide sexual services to many men. Thus the sexual abuse of women is operating at two levels first, within the context of forced marriage and second, outside marriage where women are providing a sexual service vicariously to several men. There is considerable agreement on this point. Jacoby (2015) argues that, "many women have accepted as their duty to contribute to violent Jihad by serving in domesticated roles as wives, mothers, caregivers, homemakers, community builders, and symbols of national unity" (p. 533). The gender based abduction and tactical use of young school girls by Boko Harem provides an insight into the use and abuse of women in this way (Zenn and Pearson 2014).

Willingness to succumb to a domestic role may well stand in sharp contradistinction to women's role in nationalist struggles and in revolutionary movements. Yet during the recruitment phase young women may well see themselves in this idealised role. It may also be the case that women are prepared to sacrifice any gains they might make for women's equality or for women as a group, to the common good of the so called jihad struggle. Research on "British Jihadists: Preventing Travel Abroad and Stopping Attacks at Home" conducted by the Henry Jackson Society, September 2014, reveals how ISIS offers advice on how to get to Syria, details of the idealised life that awaits young women, and their role and status as a wife in the jihad, all of which is very far removed from the reality that they experience on a daily basis. It is certainly not clear whether these women become involved volitionally, it is certainly more likely that they are coerced and compelled.

Not surprisingly the legal defence submissions and narratives in the Shakil, Khan, and Khan cases (above) present the defendant as a woman under duress, whose will has been overborne or else is a woman duped, tricked and misled. Such legal narrations however can only assist in mitigation of sentence. Some women are certainly woefully misled, and jihadists through social media are easily reaching schoolgirls and young women through cyber-space. Such women are the perfect target since they are single, unattached, without sexual experience and the ideal woman to indoctrinate, and groom to leave their homes to travel to Syria and to join these men with promises of status, role, significance and meaningful life in assisting in the creation of IS's perverted version of an Islamic state. The naivete of some of these women is telling, as Shakil (above) insisted: "For me, what it was about was living a Muslim life. I just wanted to live an Islamic life, not to kill anybody." The criminal law however does not capture these new offences of internet grooming for terrorism recruitment. The criminal law however does recognise "grooming" in the commission of sexual offences. The Sexual Offences Act 2003, s. 15, criminalises the meeting of a child following sexual grooming, etc., where the child is under 16: "Where A has met or communicated with another person (B) on at least one occasion (as amended by the Criminal justice and Courts Act 2015 s. 36), and intentionally meets B, or travels with the intention of meeting B in any part of the world or arranges to meet B in any part of the world." This offence was extended to online grooming Serious Crime Act 2015 s. 67 criminalising sexual communication with a child and is further extended under the Modern Slavery Act 2015 ss 2 and 3.

Trafficking Young Women

These young women who are going to Syria are not only "groomed", but they are being trafficked and certainly once outside the UK they are coerced and likely trafficked into sexual slavery. There is evidence that young women and men are trafficked to join IS and also trafficked within IS (cited in Jacoby, p. 537). "Even when girls join ISIS voluntarily, they may find themselves in situations of sexual slavery" (Jacoby p. 538). The recent introduction of the Modern Slavery Act 2015 provides for protection against slavery, servitude and forced labour. Section 2 (1) provides "A person commits an offence if the person arranges or facilitates the travel of another person ("V") with a view to V being exploited. (2) It is irrelevant whether V consents to the travel (whether V is an adult or a child). (3) A person may in particular arrange or facilitate V's travel by recruiting V, transporting or transferring V, harbouring or receiving V, or transferring or exchanging control over V. (4) A person arranges or facilitates V's travel with a view to V being exploited only if—(a) the person intends to exploit V (in any part of the world) during or after the travel." Once outside the UK these persons are extremely vulnerable as Jacoby points out (p. 538) "… those girls and women who already joined are now located in situations of armed conflict, outside the reach of international law, without diplomatic support and difficult, if not impossible, to rescue".

As for the young girls and young women recruited, groomed and trafficked by IS and those subsequently involved in terrorist related activities, should they be apprehended and intercepted or should they return to the UK are any defences available to them? The general defence of duress is available but the current criminal law defence is extremely restricted. The House of Lords judgment in *R v Hasan* [2005] reaffirmed the requirement of threat of death or serious injury. In addition it reinstated the earlier position that the threat was to be carried out immediately if the defence is to be operative. It is unlikely that any woman or young girl groomed or trafficked to join IS could rely on this defence since she may not be threatened with immediate death or serious bodily harm. The recent addition of the Modern Slavery Act 2015 s. 45, offers a defence akin to duress for those accused of trafficking offences where they are indeed themselves the victims of trafficking. So a person is not guilty of an offence if compelled and "(c) the compulsion is attributable to slavery or to relevant exploitation, and (d) a reasonable person in the same situation as the person and having the person's relevant characteristics would have no realistic alternative to doing that act". It would be for defence counsel to advance a defence on behalf of a trafficked victim of terrorism recruitment and trafficking. However, there would need to be a change of consciousness whereby those joining IS were perceived as compelled and as victims. It is only recently that international law recognised that trafficked persons were compelled to engage in criminal offences. In this regard the Council of Europe Convention on Trafficking in Human Beings (2005) Article 26 introduced a non punishment provision where there was evidence of coercion. However, the Convention did not consider trafficking or exploitation for a terrorist purpose. Significantly, the UK provision in the Modern Slavery Act s 45 which provides a defence of coercion where there is evidence of compulsion applies only to a very limited range of offences and expressly excludes terrorist offences under Schedule 4. Yet we are witnessing the victimisation, abduction, kidnapping and grooming of young girls through IS's use of cyber-space. After all like cyber-crime why meet face to face when you can recruit simply through social media and be thousands of miles away beyond the reach of the law. These young women are held in sexual slavery. This new slavery is presented to them as the professed "freedom" of IS. These women and schoolgirls believe that a life with IS/Daesh will offer them freedom, a choice of partners, ideologically supported by a belief that they are following their faith and fighting ideologically against a corrupt and colonialist Kufirist West.

Explaining Female Recruitment: Dominant and Subjugated Discourses

Repeatedly the seminal question asked, is whether there is anything distinct about the backgrounds, psychology, or religious commitment of these young women and schoolgirls that can be identified as contributing to their "vulnerability" or "susceptibility" for grooming and trafficking by terrorist groups. Invariably the answer is "No". However, a crisis of identity, a sense of grievance, and religious fanaticism have nevertheless been repeatedly identified by the UK government as significant factors in their recruitment, and are factors which have informed the UK governments "Prevent" strategy and Prevent duty guidance. (See https://www.gov.uk/government/

publications/prevent-duty-guidance). Vulnerability for terrorism is understood by the British government to mean something quite specific. "Most significantly, these 'vulnerabilities' are closely tied to issues of integration into, and social cohesion with, a normalised understanding of British society" (Martin 2014, p. 67). The Home Office took the view that communities who cannot or will not participate in all civic society "are more likely to be vulnerable to radicalization by all kinds of terrorist groups" (cited in Martin 2014, p. 67). Indeed, the former UK Prime Minister David Cameron echoed this sentiment when he said that those who are not integrated into the British way of life could be more susceptible to the extremist message that comes from Daesh. So in this new age there seems little space for recognition of different cultures with different identities (the Parekh ideal, Parekh 2005), and the multicultural ideal has indeed become a multicultural fallacy.

In looking to the narratives that are proposed to offer an explanation for those who have been recruited into terrorism some narratives have a privileged place whilst others are silenced. Michel Foucault in his lecture "Power and Knowledge"(1980) identifies what he calls subjugated knowledge as "… the historical contents that have been buried and disguised in a functionalist coherence or formal systemization. By 'subjugated knowledges' one should understand something else … namely a whole set of knowledges that have been disqualified as inadequate to the task or insufficiently elaborated; naive knowledges, located low down on the hierarchy, beneath the required level of cognition or scientificity" (1980, p. 81). But it is not simply that these knowledges have been buried by some accident of history, as Althusser (1970) in his analysis of what he calls ideological state apparatuses writes, "In other words, the school (but also other State institutions like the Church, or other apparatuses like the Army) teaches 'know-how', but in forms which ensure subjection to the ruling ideology or the mastery of its 'practice'". Knowledge that does not does not serve the state ideological apparatus or the dominant ruling, economic, intellectual or political force is knowledge or ideas that are consciously suppressed and "gulaged". Foucault, as did Althusser, also identifies the centrality of law in this process, "The system of right, the domain of the law, are permanent agents of these relations of domination, these polymorphous techniques of subjugation" (Foucault 1980, p. 96). This concept of "subjugated knowledge" is useful in examining the silencing and marginalisation of those explanations of terrorist activities which do not conform to the governmental agenda. There has been considerable discussion of the subjugation of alternate knowledges specifically within the field of terrorism studies (Jackson 2012) but little attempt to explore how this specifically operates in relation to understanding women's motivation for terrorist involvement.

The dominant official discourses explaining young women and schoolgirls leaving the UK to join IS have focused on the pressures of traditional Muslim family life and the role of religion. The gendering of these analyses demonstrates the incredulity and inability to understand how the apparently subjugated Muslim female can at the same time become a woman with agency. These explanations straddle the binaries of the trope of women being led and controlled on the one hand, or else inhabiting some demonic space out with femininity and womanhood on the other. The narratives and the understandings of the motives of these young women is very much presented from an orientalist perspective either they are vulnerable and victim, or else beyond redemption especially when they involve their own children, as in the cases of Shakil and Khan (above). The impact of oriental stereotyping imaginings on the shaping of official discourse and media representation is prominent in the work of Maryam Khalid (2011), Tami Jacoby (2015), and Kathy Lester and Edna Erez (2015). Khalid (2011, p. 18) examines the representation of men and women and argues that these sexual binaries are highly gendered where gendered orientalism marks "'Other' women as voiceless victims of a barbaric (male)" (p. 16). So that men are represented as "evil" and "barbaric" and women as the oppressed victim. Khalid significantly adopts the framework of analysis provided by Edward Said's *Orientalism* (1979) in her endeavour "to uncover the power relationships that underscore the representations of the 'Other' in the War on Terror" (p. 15). This has also led to the appropriation of the "saving women" of the East crusade rhetoric behind which to hide and veil the real motivation which is to conquer and dominate parts of the Middle East and justify military intervention. But are women who join IS always the voiceless victims or do they have agency? Laster and Erez (2015) certainly think that they have agency and they query how is it that in exceptional circumstances patriarchy lets women into what has been typically men's business. They suggest that the representation of women as passive, victims, helpless, maternal etc., actually provides women with an advantage (p. 88). This advantage lies in the element of surprise since the stereotypical expectation of such women is that they will be subservient and that this "reading" of women may determine the onlooker's response to her. Indeed, Fanon (1965), identified how the French military in Algeria "read" the veil as a symbol of subjugation and responded to women accordingly, yet women used the veil imbuing it with a new meaning and with a revolutionary potential as it enabled them to conduct bombing campaigns undetected. Jacoby (2015) however is not persuaded that such women have been able to free themselves from a subservient gendered life. She suggests that women "have accepted as their duty to contribute to violent jihad by serving domesticated roles as wives, mothers, caregivers, homemakers, community builders, and symbols of national unity" (p. 533). Jacoby identifies their role as part of "state building" and IS's manifesto for recruiting women who will give birth to the future Caliphate (p. 535). Mia Bloom (2011a) echoes this analysis of a state building agenda in that women are seen as little more than "baby factories" whose purpose is to populate the new "purist" Islamic state. Certainly some women have positioned themselves or been positioned by IS as "mothers" in this quest. Aqsa Mahmood otherwise reportedly known as "Umm Layth" (Mother of Layth), is reported to have written on a twitter account in her name, "We are created to be mothers and wives—as much as the western society has warped your views on this with a hidden feminist mentality." Zine (2006) is right when she argues that women are caught somewhere between orientalism and fundamentalism.

Dominant Discourses

Conservative Families-Subjugated Lives

The too conservative Muslim family has been suggested as one of the reasons that propel women into joining IS or else make them more vulnerable to its influence. Of those women who left for Syria did they come from families with proscribed and fixed gender roles? Were their life chances restricted by culture and custom? Were their educational, career and employment prospects, social and family opportunities limited? Is it the case that arranged marriage would have been the norm and expectation? Indeed, there is some academic support for this perception. Jacoby (2015, p. 538) suggest that "a Muslim girl may envision in ISIS an escape from unbearable social pressures to conform". Bloom has similarly argued that an oppressive culture may be a trigger making her vulnerable (Bloom 2011a, b). On the arranged marriage question within the Asian family, Sardar (2013) writes: "Arranged marriages work in this framework of extended family. They are the heartbeat of Asian tradition". The harsh reality of forced marriage cannot be ignored either. One thousand forced marriages have been recorded in the UK since the introduction of the Anti-Social Behaviour Crime and Policing Act 2014. The Forced Marriage Protection Unit reported that 40 % of victims were below 18 years of age. Domestic violence may also be another factor. Certainly, there is evidence that for some Asian and Muslim women the rates of unhappiness in families is high if suicide rates are indeed a measure of unhappiness. For example, Southall Black Sisters in their report "Sane and Safe" (see http://www.southallblacksisters.org.uk/reports/safe-and-sane-report/) stated that suicide rates among British women of Asian origin is twice the national average. Women under 35 were three times more likely to kill themselves than other ethnic groups citing domestic violence, abuse and arranged marriage as the main causes. Or is this commentary just Orientalism? On the other hand, if some Muslim women are under the control of their families how is it that they break free at all? The subjugation of women in their own communities, may certainly be a factor in vulnerabilising young women to the draw of a life with IS which is portrayed as freedom. But do families that exert control over their children produce children who become dissidents or terrorists any more than any other family forms? Or is this thinking just essentialism? However it is persuasive that whilst these women may be abandoning their immediate families at the same time they do not abandon what they regard as their culture, or what they reagrd as their religion and position themselves as contributing pro-actively to what they perceive as a "truly" Islamic movement which is also taking a stand against Western imperialism. IS propaganda presents IS to them as an altruistic and noble movement.

Pathological or "Nothing Exceptional"

Another enduring dominant explanatory narrative is the belief that the families from which these young women and schoolgirls are drawn must in some way be very different from other families. These suppositions formed the basis of questions the

Home Affairs Committee on Counter Terrorism (2015) 10th March 2015, put to Fahmida Aziz, first cousin to Khadija Sultana, and to Sahima Begum the sister of Shamima Begum and to Hussen Abase, father of Amira Abase (the families, of the "Bethnal Green Academy" schoolgirls). Yet, in all their answers the families confirmed that neither the schoolgirls nor their families were in any way distinct or different. In responding to the question from the Chairman of the Committee, "Had you any idea that they were being radicalised"? Hussen Abase, father of Amira Abase said, "Not at all". The older sister of Shamima Begum similarly responded, "My sister was into everything normal there was nothing to indicate … My sister was into any normal teenage things. She used to watch 'Keeping up with the Kardashians' and stuff like that." (Question 185). Nor said the witnesses did the school have any indicators.

Similarly, even where young girls have become involved in "promoting terrorism" there is still nothing in their family background to point to anything identifiably different about them or their families. Samina Malik, (*R v Malik* (*Samina Hussain*) [2008]), the so-called "lyrical terrorist", (the name she gave herself because she wanted to "be cool") was employed as a sales assistant in W. H. Smith's newspaper shop at Heathrow airport in London. She wrote so called "poems" on pieces of paper and on till receipts and then later posted them on social media. "The desire within me increases every day to go for martyrdom, the need to go increases second by second … Show the children videos and pictures of Mujahideen and tell them to become strong". At her trial the prosecution presented her as a "committed Islamic extremist who supports terrorism and terrorists". In her defence she said the poems were meaningless. She was convicted of the offence of "glorifying terrorism" (Terrorism Act 2000 s. 58) and sentenced to a term of 9 months imprisonment. On appeal against conviction (allowed) she said she wanted to "move on with her life" and "become a housewife." Such conservative gendered aspirations for her future life suggested that in fact she was indeed a very ordinary girl who wanted to "be cool" and no doubt felt frustrated and trapped in a dead end job as a sales assistant. Despite a wealth of evidence which confirms that there was nothing different about these young girls or indeed their families, government policies on counter-terrorism have been directed at the control and surveillance of the Muslim community en masse treating Muslims as a "suspect community" and stigmatising them.

Pathological Muslim Men

The dominant discourse and writings on Muslim men have stigmatised Muslim communities and focused on the danger they present and have represented Islam as fanaticism. The ideologies and tropes of Muslim men and Muslim male youth (see Lynch 2013) echo Edward Said's concerns (1997). The Muslim man is, as Khalid points out, especially at this time "a threat to be contained" (Khalid 2011, p. 23). In bolstering and grounding this representation, any male transgression is broadly publicised and used to caricature and stereotype all Muslim men in general terms. Susan Okin's "Is Multi culturalism bad for women?" (1999) for example, in exploring Islamic communities focuses on the worst instances of patriarchal culture within these communities including, honour killing indeed such practices are condemned by Muslim communities as unacceptable but nonetheless Okin proposes that "extinction" of the Islamic culture is the preferred solution. "In the case of a more patriarchal minority culture, no argument can be made on the basis of self-respect or freedom that the female members of the culture have a clear interest in its preservation. Indeed, they might be much better off if the culture into which they were born were either to become extinct (so that its members would become integrated into the less sexist surrounding culture) or, preferably, to be encouraged to alter itself so as to reinforce the equality of women …" (pp. 2, 3). Okin is not without her critics. Abu-Lughod (2015) makes the point that the iconic use of honour crime as an exemplar of cultural practices within Muslim communities stigmatises not only particular acts of violence but entire communities (Abu-Lughod, p. 114). For example, the recent representation in UK national public debate which focussed on a group of men in Bradford, England (who happened to be of Pakistani descent) and were responsible for the sex trafficking within the UK of young girls provides just one example of this essentializing. Jack Straw, MP. saw this sex trafficking of young girls by Pakistani men as a "suspect community" problem. Stigmatising the entire Pakistani community he said in 2011, "But there is a specific problem which involves Pakistani heritage men … who target vulnerable young white girls … We need to get the Pakistani community to think much more clearly about why this is going on and to be more open about the problems that are leading to a number of Pakistani heritage men thinking it is OK to target white girls in this way". Attempts to explain this problem have theorised this behaviour as an inevitable product of a community where sexual restrictions are placed on males and females limiting sexual encounters outside marriage suggesting that the cultural norms of Muslim communities forces them to prey on young non-Asian girls. What impact do these negative representations and the continual production and reproduction of these diatribes of hostility and racialized misrepresentation of whole communities have on the sense of identity and dignity of men and of women in these communities? To what extent does the pathologization and essentializing of all Muslim men in this way affect a collective sense of pride, identity, hurt and indignation?

Devoutness and Exposure to Radical Ideas

Devoutness is of course associated with peacefulness, grace, humility, righteousness, godliness, piousness and saintliness and always acting for the good and for the betterment of others. But when Islamic devoutness is considered it takes on a new meaning and has become warped by IS. The dominant discourse and understanding of devoutness when considered in the Islamic context is that it is a standard bearer of violent extremism. The notion that Islamic devoutness is in some way linked to radicalization, extremism and terrorism is also ingrained in the public mind. The Home Affairs Committee on Counter Terrorism 10th March 2015, explored the question of devoutness when questioning the families of the "Bethnal Green Academy schoolgirls". Michael Ellis, a member of the Committee asked, "Were here any indicators that the girls were becoming more devout in thinking. Had you noticed any difference"? The families of the schoolgirls resolutely said "No". Islam, the faith per se, is now positioned as the problem and believers in Islam as the enemy. No one questions the Christian Sunday worshippers or construes their manifestations of their faith as problematic or fanatical, nor continually presents images of them reciting the Lords prayer or the creed at Sunday services.

Subjugated Narratives

There are of course other reasons that can offer some understanding of why young women are drawn towards, drift into, are pulled, or coerced into joining IS, however these alternate understandings because they contest the dominant orthodoxy are subjugated. An analysis of the subjugated explanations include for example a consideration of inter alia, the impact and effect of the vilification of Muslim identity (see Kundnani 2014), a sense of outrage and frustration, a lack of opportunity and life chances, and a rejection of Western foreign policy in the Middle East. Arguably these may also be reasons for the alienation of young people which results in them travelling abroad to join IS (see Brown 2014).

A Justified Sense of Outrage

In this jurisdiction there is calcified and habituated Islamophobia within domestic policy on crime and policing, (see "Operation Champion" and over surveillance of Muslim communities mentioned above, Fussey 2013) and encroaching and enveloping "governmentality" (see the "Prevent" policy as an example of this). I use Foucaults concept of "governmentality" here since he identifies the power of the state through ideology, rhetoric and discourse to control and govern. Islamophobia is now so constituted in the ideological state apparatus in the Althusserian sense (Althusser 1970) and in the public mind that it has become a warped norm, habituated in media reportage, in public policy, in Counter Terrorism law, in the justification for suspension of the Human Rights Act 1998, in justifications for prohibiting the face veil or niqab, and in the recent refugee rhetoric and policy. It is true that the Oriental subject is essentialised, fetishised, demonised and racialised today more than Edward Said (1997) could possibly have envisioned when he wrote, "What is said about the Muslim mind, or character or religion or culture as a whole cannot now be said in mainstream discussion about Africans, Jews, other Orientals or Asians" (1997 p. xii). Said (1997) argued in his book *Covering Islam* that "what the media produce is neither spontaneous nor completely 'free': 'news' does not just happen" (p. 48), instead, there is a "qualitative and quantitative tendency to favor certain views and certain representations of reality over others" (Said 1997, p. 49). Young Muslim women and girls are inevitably affected by these negative representations of Islam and of Muslim men and of Muslim women and their families and their communities, racist attacks against their communities and against women within them who wear the niqab (MacKinnon 2010) and also against women who wear the hijab (see Edwards 2012, 2014a, b). These attacks are also characterised by a general ridicule of their faith which is accepted and permitted from the vehement defence of the Danish Cartoons to the defence of Charlie Hebdo as the principle of freedom of speech is perverted and those who wish to rain down hatred hide behind freedom of speech's noble claims. Are these subjugated narratives significant explanations for being drawn into terrorism related activities?

Western Foreign Policy and Domestic Policy

In a society where foreign policy interventions into Middle Eastern Muslim countries have included the killing of innocent civilians, and where Western governments bear responsibility for the shamefulness of Abu Ghraib (Eisenman 2007) and complicity in the torture of terror suspects in Guantanamo Bay (Luban 2007), there is indeed a justified outrage. A growing sense of despair arising from Western incursions into the Middle East may provide another reason for the alienation of many including Muslims who turn to IS. The role played by Western foreign policy in Afghanistan, Iraq, Libya and the Middle East in alienating and antagonising young people has not been mooted in UK government dialogue as possible causes of terrorist activity or of "radicalization". The Home Affairs Committee inquiry into "Countering Extremism" has not included in its questioning of witnesses in any real way any consideration of whether Western foreign policy might have contributed. However, Paul Flynn MP did perhaps exceptionally pose one such question when questioning Gilles de Kerchove (Question 545) at the Home Affairs Select Committee on Countering Extremism on 28th January 2014.

"Do your responsibilities and the responsibilities of the United Nations include the job of trying to build confidence and counteract this gulf of suspicion between the Western Christian world and the Eastern Muslim world, which is probably fuelled by the imbalance and the asymmetry of the weapons that they each have? Do you think that the use of drones—hugely sophisticated weapons that cannot be matched by the other side—is itself a cause of increasing terrorism, because terrorists, and those in that position, potential terrorists, feel themselves impotent to defend themselves and their communities against drones and other sophisticated equipment?"

Significantly, Eland (1998) was one of the early voices asking the so often unspeakable question that is whether foreign policy itself breeds terrorism.

Historically however those who question and contest Western foreign policy in the Middle East and suggest that the West shares some culpability for what happens there, have been silenced or else severely admonished. For example, Baroness Jenni Tonge, former Liberal Democrat MEP, when talking on the plight of the Palestinians in 2004, at a Palestine Solidarity Campaign meeting, said that if she was a Palestinian, she would consider becoming a suicide bomber herself. "If I had to live in that situation—and I say that advisedly—I might just consider becoming one myself." She was trying to understand despair and a desire to self-immolate, obliterate and die in this way. She was asked to apologise and eventually was forced to resign as a Liberal Democratic MP. Cherie Blair QC., the wife of Tony Blair a former UK Prime Minister said of the Palestinians in 2002: "As long as young people feel they have got no hope but to blow themselves up you are never going to make progress." The office of the Prime Minister apologised immediately. More recently, The Home Affairs Committee on Countering Terrorism January 19th, 2016 in its questioning of Shami Chakrabarti, the Director of Liberty who is well known for her opposition to British and Western foreign policy and for her staunch defence of human rights and liberty was subjected to a quite shameful, disgraceful and hostile questioning. Was this hostility and anger towards her an attempt to silence because she dared to provide a counter-narrative in critiquing the UK government's counter-terrorism policy? She continued to answer questions put to her with grace and measure "Look, I don't know but I think my instinct is—and this is just my life experience of having travelled up and down this land and been the daughter of migrants and met a lot of people, privileged people and vulnerable people—that there is a language problem with radicalisation, but it is the language of hate rather than the language of human rights". Western foreign policy and the silencing and minimalisation of torture atrocities (Foucault's "subjugated knowledge") that have been committed in Guantanamo Bay and in Abu Ghraib and the treatment of the Palestinian people (Viterbo 2014) all contribute to a justifiable sense of resentment. David Anderson QC, the Independent reviewer of anti-terrorist legislation more recently acceded that one of the reasons why young people are turning to terrorism, "it could be, one often hears, the foreign policy grievance" (Home Affairs Select Committee 19th January 2016, Question 926).

When Hate Speech Hides Behind Satire

The quite appalling Charlie Hebdo killings in Paris in 2015 seemed in the understandable outrage and tragic aftermath to unleash a justification of hate speech, albeit unintended, by describing any verbal attack on Muslims however denigrating as just a matter of satire. Michael Ondaatje and Peter Carey were just two of many who were of the opinion that the Charlie Hebdo killings were used to legitimate a freedom of speech that permitted Muslim hatred. Carey said, "A hideous crime was committed, but was it a freedom-of-speech for PEN America to be self-righteous about ... All this is complicated by PEN'S seeming blindness to the cultural arrogance of the French nation, which does not recognize its moral obligation to a large and disempowered segment of their population." The rising Islamophobia hiding behind satire in the USA for example is demonstrated in the organising of the "Draw the Prophet Mohammed" cartoon contest in Texas, organised by the American

Freedom Defense Initiative (AFDI) at which Geert Wilders who leads the Dutch right wing "party for Freedom" gave a keynote speech.

Muslim women share a sense of outrage with regard to the vilification of their communities and religion which is now perpetrated against them as part of "popular culture." They have also to contend with the misrepresentations of Islamic clothing allegedly satirised by haute couture fashion houses and some so called feminist groups who either ridicule their attire or else define for Muslim women what liberation should look like. FEMEN provides just one example of the way in which so called feminism and satire can be used in vilification when in 2012 they held what they called a "Topless Jihad" and called for "Bare breasts against Islamism!" Yet they did this baring their breasts whilst covering their head in a hijab. This acclaimed and self-professed expression of feminism denigrated the hijab in graphically alluding to the sexual freedom of women through nakedness and the oppression of Islamic women through coveredness. Implicit in this demonstration was the message that removal of "her" Islamic clothing would free her from her oppression and save her (Khalid 2011, p. 22).

This anti-Muslim epidemic has turned into a crusade and has contributed to an increase in physical assaults on Muslims. Criminal Statistics England and Wales for 2011/12 and 2012/13 and 2014/15 estimate an average of 70,000 incidents of religiously motivated hate crime annually with Muslim adults the most likely to be a victim of religiously motivated hate crime. In 2012/13, the police recorded 1573 religious hate crimes, around one-quarter (24 %) of religious hate crimes were violence against the person. Figures for 2015 indicate that the number of race hate crimes has increased by 15 %, up 5464, to 42,930 offences over the previous year (see also Awan and Zempi 2015). Since Brexit (UK's exit from the EU) hate crimes against Muslims and other immigrants has dramatically increased.

Legal Responses in Criminal and Family Law

The introduction of criminal law measures and the imaginative application of existing family law and inherent jurisdiction measures in the UK is a direct response to these images and tropes of those who leave for Syria, such that women are perceived either as offenders with agency or as victims who are vulnerable and in need of protection. The criminal law measures reflect the tendency to position those who leave for Syria including men and women as persons with agency, who are deliberate in their planned, intentious acts and who act with volition, such that punishments are harsh with little consideration of rehabilitation. In this regard the government attributes the causes of terrorism to radicalization, nihilism and religious extremism which becomes the dominant force in driving the legal agenda (Jackson 2015, p. 14). The family courts in their dealings with young schoolgirls at least, position them quite differently, as without agency, coerced and controlled.

Criminal Law and Prevention and Punishment

As part of the counter-terrorist strategy, the criminal law provisions especially the Counter Terrorism and Security Act 2015 has introduced for the first time pre emptive provisions to prevent persons suspected of going to join IS from doing so. Section 1 and Schedule 1 provides for the seizure of passport and travel documents "where a person is suspected of intending to leave Great Britain or the United Kingdom in connection with terrorism-related activity." Here, "terrorism" and "terrorist" have the same meaning as in the Terrorism Act 2000 (ss. 1 (1) to (4), 40). "(1) In this Act 'terrorism' means the use or threat of action where—(a) the action falls within subsection (2), (b) the use or threat is designed to influence the government or an international governmental organisation or to intimidate the public or a section of the public, and (c) the use or threat is made for the purpose of advancing a political, religious [racial] or ideological cause." Section 17 provides for travel bans. For those who having left wish to return (Shakil above) "temporary exclusion orders" (ss. 2–4), may be put in place. However return is permitted only by the Secretary of State (ss. 5–8) and upon return the returnee is subject to a Terrorism Prevention and Investigation Measures notice (TPIM) under the Terrorism Prevention and Investigation Measures Act 2011 s. 9. These exclusion measures are further bolstered by a provision under the Immigration Act 2014 s. 66, which provides for the deprivation of citizenship.

In response to the terror threat the reach of the law has also extended into arenas of social and private life through the monitoring, policing and surveillance of "suspect communities". In analysing this tendency Martin (2014, p. 64) develops Foucault's construct of "governmentality." In the UK, the "Prevent" strategy (referred to earlier) is an expression of this "governmentality" setting down in law, and mandated by the Counter Terrorism and Security Act 2015, s. 26, the requirement that all "responsible authorities" develop anti radicalization strategies. Section 26 of the Act says specified authorities in the exercise of their functions, are to have "due regard to the need to prevent people from being drawn into terrorism". This strategy is being developed in the absence of a definition of radicalization or extremism. The latest prevention efforts for "de radicalization" for those considered at risk of terrorist recruitment have been met with criticism and incredulity. The National Police Chiefs' Council (NPCC) has recorded that 1800 children have been referred to the "de radicalization"—Channel programme. The "moral panic" over terrorism, the racist assumptions about and grotesque demonization of the Muslim community, the reflexive willingness and crass thoughtlessness of compliance officers in schools and Universities tasked with the section 26 duty, points to its overwhelming failure. For example, in one case a child who could not spell and in a school essay wrote that he lived in a "terrorist" house when in fact he meant "terraced", found himself under investigation. Another referral to the de radicalization programme involved a teenage boy who was the subject of investigation because he was raising money for Palestinian children and wore a badge at his school which said "Free Palestine." As Gearson and Rosemont (2015) suggest the "Prevent" and de-radicalization programme is in urgent need of reassessment. Other UK anti-terror laws, include the Terrorism Act 2000, which makes criminal possessing "information of a kind likely to be useful to a person committing or preparing an act of terrorism", being a member of a proscribed organisation, and fundraising for a terrorist purpose. Section 44 of the 2000 Act also extend police powers permitting stop and search without suspicion which allows over surveillance of Muslim communities. It is now amended to include "without suspicion in a specified area where she or he reasonably suspects an act of terrorism is about to occur the act states in exceptional circumstances".

Additionally, the law post 9/11, permitted a different treatment of "the other"—the foreigner, and the Anti-terrorism, Crime and Security Act 2001, exempted foreign nationals from the legal and human rights protections available to everyone else. This exemption of foreign nationals from laws protection in the UK, is also reflected in US and Canadian law and demonstrates what Saito (2009, p. 75) calls the "exceptionalism" tendency. This leads to the lawlessness of nation states as Mégret (2006), Bahdi (2011), Sands (2006, p. 205), Kennedy (2006) and others observe. Under the 2001 Act, the Secretary of State could certify foreign nationals as "detainees" and detain them without charge or trial on the basis that they might pose a security risk. The detention of fourteen foreign nationals followed until, the House of Lords in *A (FC) and others (FC) (Appellants) v Secretary of State for the Home Department (Respondent)* (2004) ruled that indefinite detention of non UK nationals, without charge or trial was incompatible with Article 5 of the ECHR (Edwards 2008, p. 221). Baroness Hale in her judgment said, "235. Are foreigners and nationals alike for this purpose? The Attorney General argued that they are not. The foreigners have no right to be here and we would expel them if we could. We only have to allow them to stay to protect them from an even worse invasion of their human rights. Hence, he argued, the true comparison is not with suspected international terrorists who are British nationals but with foreign suspected international terrorists who can be deported. This cannot be right. The foreigners who can be deported are not like the foreigners who cannot. These foreigners are only being detained because they cannot be deported. They are just like a British national who cannot be deported. The relevant circumstances making the two cases alike for this purpose are the same three which constitute the problem: a suspected international terrorist, who for a variety of reasons cannot be successfully prosecuted, and who for a variety of reasons cannot be deported or expelled. [She continued] 238. No one has the right to be an international terrorist. But substitute 'black', 'disabled', 'female', 'gay', or any other similar adjective for 'foreign' before 'suspected international terrorist' and ask whether it would be justifiable to take power to lock up that group but not the 'white', 'able-bodied', 'male' or 'straight' suspected international terrorists. The answer is clear". The government then replied with the Prevention of Terrorism Act 2005 introducing measures including "control orders" where the Secretary of State could order persons to be detained in their homes for initially up to 18 h if they were considered to pose a security risk. Control orders were later the subject of legal challenge and replaced by TPIMS. Discussed by Mythen (2011, p. 177) this legal measure he argues demonstrates the way in which the law is used to pre-emptively manage what it perceives to be a risk.

Family Law, Protection and Rehabilitation

Turning to the family courts their recent dealings with young people and especially young girls joining IS reflects a very different approach altogether. The approach is one of protection and this is not merely because those involved are minors but because of a different perception of how people, and in this case young people, become involved, informed by a view that young people are groomed, beguiled and inveigled. The family courts have responded differently in invoking protective measures, including placing adolescent minors in the care of the local authority (Children Act 1989 s. 31) because of the risk of "significant harm", or else placing them into the care of the court under the inherent jurisdiction of wardship. In March 2015, in *London Borough of Tower Hamlets v M and Others/In the matter of M (Children)* [2015] the presiding judge, Mr. Justice Hayden, imposed a travel ban preventing five teenage girls from travelling abroad to Syria to join IS. He also imposed a travel ban in connection with a 16-year-old boy from a family where two older brothers had died fighting in Syria. He said of these two cases.

"[1] Last week, I heard two cases, both of which were brought by local authorities who were concerned that a number of young people, all minors in their areas, were at risk of leaving the country to travel to ISIS countries, particularly Syria … [3] The cases involved both girls and boys, each of whom was at risk, to my mind self-evidently, of significant harm in the sense contemplated by section 31 (ii) of the Children Act 1989. [4] The risk plainly differs according to gender but is nonetheless grave in both instances and does not need to be spelt out … [10] Thus, pursuant to this jurisdiction [wardship], I made orders relating to the retrieval of the passport of each of the young people concerned in order to use the full powers at the court's disposal to endeavour to prevent the wards leaving the United Kingdom".

Wardship has also been used to retrieve children who have already left the jurisdiction. For example, wardship was invoked in the case of the disappearance of the 3 year old Madeline McCann in April 2008 through what are called 'seek and find' orders (Welstead and Edwards 2013, p. 421). In *Re M (children)* [2015] a family who had left the country with their four children ages ranging from 20 months to 7 years of age were intercepted and returned to the UK. Sir James Munby, President of the Family Division said:

"There is always, every minute of every day and night throughout the year, a judge of the Family Division on duty, 'out of hours', to deal with cases so urgent that they cannot wait. This case, I believe, shows the system working well. The court became involved in the early morning of Tuesday 5 May. The children had returned to this country by the middle of the afternoon of Thursday 7 May." Later that year in *In the matter of M (Children) (No 2)* [2015] wardship was withdrawn due to the co-operation of the parents.

Care proceedings have also been pursued successfully where the protection of adolescents has been paramount. In *London Borough of Tower Hamlets v B* [2015] Mr Justice Hayden, in providing the background to this case said, "This case comes before me consecutively with a number of other cases within the Borough of Tower

Hamlets, each of which involves intelligent young girls, highly motivated academically, each of whom has, to some and greatly varying degrees, been either radicalised or exposed to extreme ideology promulgated by those subscribing to the values of the self-styled Islamic State."

In this case he local authority sought the removal of all the children of the family, including the male children on the basis that: "So corrosive and insidious are the beliefs in this household, it is argued, so pervasive is the nature of the emotional abuse, so complete is the resistance to intervention, and so total the lack of co-operation, that the emotional safety of the boys, the Local Authority says, cannot be assured." Care orders were granted in respect of the female and male adolescents of the household.

In *Z (A Child)*, in April 2015 a young female adolescent was detained at an airport under the Terrorism Act 2000, Sch.7 after attempting to board a flight to Turkey with a single ticket. The terrorism unit was alerted and she was returned to her family and her passport seized. These and other cases resulted in Sir James Munby, President of the Family Division, on 8th October 2015 issuing guidance on 'Radicalisation cases in the family courts' in which he set out the procedures to be adopted in such cases to ensure not punishment but protection either through wardship or local authority care proceedings. The remarks of Mr Justice Hayden in the *Tower Hamlets* case (*In the matter of M (Children)* [2015]) above perhaps captures the objectives of the family courts which are distinctly different from the government's agenda. "All involved must recognise that in this particular process it is the interest of the individual child that is paramount. This cannot be eclipsed by wider considerations of counter terrorism policy or operations, but it must be recognised that the decision the court is being asked to take can only be arrived at against an informed understanding of that wider canvas."

Conclusion

It is true as Orford (2007, p. 398) writes "the upheaval of 9/11 has altered international law". It has also altered domestic law, Muslims find themselves over-surveilled, over-policed and outlawed. In the presence of all this vilification do these young women who leave the UK to join ISIS see themselves as part of a global resistance movement? And when attacked body and soul from all angles is it easier for the terrorist recruiter and groomer to inculcate young women's minds through using the platform of cyber space with an ideology that justifies their involvement. If the use of cyber space as a vehicle for terrorist recruitment is to be challenged, then strategies which go beyond shutting down of chatrooms or intercepting communications need to be developed; these strategies should lie within understanding the subjugated narratives responding to the sense of adolescent and young women's alienation. These strategies and policies and law must challenge, contest and prohibit the demonization of Muslim communities. These strategies must also provide some protection and defence for young women and adolescent girls who are recruited into terrorist activity.

References

Abu-Lughod, L. (2015). *Do muslim women really need saving?* Harvard: Harvard University Press.

Althusser, L. (1970). Ideology and ideological state apparatuses. In L. Althusser (Ed.), *Lenin and philosophy and other essays*. New York: Monthly Review Press.

Bahdi, R. (2011). Before the law: Creeping lawlessness in Canadian National Security. In V. Bajc & W. de Lint (Eds.), *Security and everyday life* (pp. 143–156). London: Routledge.

Bloom, M. (2011a). *Bombshells: The many faces of women terrorist*. Toronto, ON: Penguin Press.

Bloom, M. (2011b). Bombshells: Women and terror. *Gender Issues, 28*(1–2), 1–21.

Brown, K. (2014, October 6). Analysis: Why are Western women joining Islamic State? *BBC News*.

Coppock, V. (2014). Can you spot a terrorist in your classroom? Problematizing the recruitment of schools to the 'War on Terror' in the United Kingdom. *Global Studies of Childhood, 4*(2), 115–126.

Edwards, S. (2008) Human Sacrifices at the Altar of Terrorist Control - (Secretary of State for the Home Department v MB; Secretary of State for the Home Department v AF [2007] UKHL 46). *Denning Law Journal, 20*(1), 221–238.

Edwards, S. S. M. (2012). For her own good! Criming the niqab. *International Family Law, 2*, 203–208.

Edwards, S. S. M. (2014a). Proscribing unveiling–law: A chimera and an instrument in the political agenda. In E. Brems (Ed.), *The experiences of face veil wearers in Europe and the law* (pp. 278–296). Cambridge: Cambridge University Press.

Edwards, S. S. M. (2014b). SAS v France (application no 43835/11) unreported, July 1, 2014 (ECtHR). *Denning Law Journal, 26*, 246–260.

Edwards, S. (2015). Protecting schoolgirls from terrorism grooming. *International Journal of Family Law, 3*, 236–248.

Edwards, E. (2016). Closure through resilience: The case of prevent. *Studies in Conflict and Terrorism, 39*(4), 292–307.

Eisenman, S. (2007). *The Abu Ghraib effect*. London: Reaktion Books.

Eland, I. (1998, December). Does U.S. intervention overseas breed terrorism? The historical record. *CATO Institute Foreign Policy Briefing, 50*, 1–24. Retrieved from http://www.cato.org/pubs/fpbriefs/fpb-050es.html.

Fanon, F. (1965). *Studies in a dying colonialism*. New York: Monthly Review Press.

Foucault, M. (1980). *Power/knowledge selected interviews and other writings 1972–1977*. In C. Gordon (Ed.), New York: Pantheon Books.

Fussey, P. (2013). Contested topologies of UK counterterrorist surveillance: The rise and fall of Project Champion. *Critical Studies on Terrorism, 6*(3), 351–370.

Gearson, J., & Rosemont, H. (2015). CONTEST as strategy: Reassessing Britain's counter terrorism approach. *Studies in Conflict and Terrorism, 38*, 1038–1064.

Jackson, R. (2012). Unknown knowns: The subjugated knowledge of terrorism studies. *Critical Studies on Terrorism, 5*(1), 11–29.

Jackson, R. (2015) The Epistemological crisis of counter-terrorism. *Critical Studies on Terrorism, 8*(1), 33–54.

Jacoby, T. (2015). Jihadi brides at the intersections of contemporary feminism. *New Political Science, 37*(4), 526–542.

Kennedy, D. (2006). *Of war and law*. Princeton: Princeton University Press.

Khalid, M. (2011). Gender, orientalism and representations of the 'Other' in the War on Terror. *Global Change, Peace & Security, 23*(1), 15–29.

Kundnani, A. (2014). *The Muslims are coming*. London: Verso.

Laster, K., & Erez, E. (2015). Sisters in terrorism? Exploding stereotypes. *Women and Criminal Justice, 25*(1–2), 83–99.

Luban, D. (2007). The torture lawyers of Washington. In D. Luban (Ed.), *Legal ethics and human dignity* (pp. 162–206). Cambridge: Cambridge University Press.

Lynch, O. (2013). British Muslim youth: Radicalisation, terrorism and the construction of the 'other'. *Critical Studies on Terrorism, 6*(2), 241–261.
MacKinnon, V. (2010). Lifting the veil on terrorism: An analysis of the relationship between women's oppression and terrorism. *Homeland Security Review, 4*(2), 93–118.
Martin, T. (2014). Governing an unknowable future: The politics of Britain's prevent policy. *Critical Studies on Terrorism, 7*(1), 62–78.
Mégret, F. (2006). From 'savages' to 'unlawful combatants': A postcolonial look at international law's 'other'. In A. Orford (Ed.), *International law and its others* (pp. 265–317). Cambridge: Cambridge University Press.
Mythen, G. (2011). The pre-emptive mode of regulation: Terrorism, law and security. In V. Bajc & W. de Lint (Eds.), *Security and everyday life* (pp. 168–184). London: Routledge.
Okin. S. M. (1999). *Is multiculturalism bad for women? Part 1: Is multi culturalism bad for women*. In J. Cohen, M. Howard, & M. Nussbaum (Eds). Princeton University Press.
Parekh, B. (2005). *Rethinking multiculturalism: Cultural diversity and political theory*. London: Palgrave Macmillan.
Said, E. W. (1979). *Orientalism*. London: Vintage.
Said, E. W. (1997). *Covering Islam: How the media and the experts determine how we see the rest of the world*. London: Vintage.
Saito, N. T. (2009). Colonial presumptions: He war on terror and the roots of American exceptionalism. *Georgetown Journal of Law and Modern Critical Race Perspectives, 1*(1), 67–110.
Sands, P. (2006). *Lawless world making and breaking global rules*. London: Penguin.
Viterbo, H. (2014). Seeing torture anew: A transnational reconceptualization of state torture and visual evidence. *Stanford Journal of International Law, 50*(2), 281–317.
Walker, C., & Conway, M. (2015). Online terrorism and online laws. *Dynamics of Asymmetric Conflict, 8*(2), 156–175.
Welstead, M., & Edwards, S. (2013). *Family law*. Oxford: Oxford University Press.
Zenn, J., & Pearson, E. (2014). Women, gender and the evolving tactics of Boko Haram. *Journal of Terrorism Research, 5*(1). doi:10.15664/jtr.828
Zine, J. (2006). Between orientalism and fundamentalism: Muslim women and feminist engagement. In K. Hunt & K. Rygiel (Eds.), *(En)Gendering the war on terror: War stories and camouflaged politics* (pp. 27–50). Hampshire: Ashgate Publishing Limited.

Web References

Ameen (Farzana). Retrieved from http://www.telegraph.co.uk/news/uknews/law-and-order/11931632/Mother-feared-to-have-taken-children-to-Syria-said-she-was-doing-what-was-best-for-them.html.
Awan, I., & Zempi, I. (2015, October). *We fear for our lives: Offline and online experiences of anti-Muslimhostility*.Retrievedfromhttp://discoversociety.org/2015/10/06/we-fear-for-our-lives-offline-and-online-experiences-of-anti-muslim-hostility/.
Bethnal Green Academy schoolgirls. Retrieved from http://www.huffingtonpost.co.uk/2016/01/19/london-schoolgirls-who-fled-to-isis-are-being-held-hostage-reveals-lawyer_n_9016900.html, http://www.telegraph.co.uk/news/uknews/11461693/Sisters-of-the-missing-jihadi-brides-to-face-radicalisation-tests.html.
Blair (Cheri). *Anger at Cherie 'sympathy' for suicide bombers 19th June 2002*. Retrieved from http://www.telegraph.co.uk/news/worldnews/middleeast/jordan/1397696/Anger-at-Cherie-sympathy-for-suicide-bombers.html.
Britain Jihadi Brides. *BBC two documentary transmitted 8th April 2015 Director Fatima Salaria*. Retrieved from http://www.bbc.co.uk/programmes/b05qq4c0.

Henry Jackson Society. (2014, September). *British Jihadists: Preventing travel abroad and stopping attacks at home*. Retrieved from http://henryjacksonsociety.org/2014/09/12/british-jihadists-preventing-travel-abroad-and-stopping-attacks-at-home/.

Home Office, Office for National Statistics and Ministry of Justice. (2013, December). *Criminal Statistics England and Wales for 2011/12 and 2012/13. An overview of hate crime in England and Wales*. Retrieved from https://www.gov.uk/government/uploads/system/uploads/attachment_data/file/266358/hate-crime-2013.pdf.

Dawood sisters. Retrieved from http://www.theguardian.com/uk-news/2015/jun/21/police-complicit-radicalisation-missing-sisters-claim-family-lawyers.

Dilipraj, E. (2015). Challenges of terrorism in cyber space. *Defence and Diplomacy, 4*(3). http://www.academia.edu/14294516/CHALLENGES_OF_TERRORISM_IN_CYBER_SPACE.

FEMEN Femen's Topless Jihad. Retrieved from http://www.thenation.com/article/femens-topless-jihad/.

Fisher, A., & Prucha N. (2014). *The call-up: The roots of a resilient and persistent jihadist presence on twitter*. Retrieved from https://globalecco.org/en_GB/the-call-up-the-roots-of-a-resilient-and-persistent-jihadist-presence-on-twitterctx.

Forced Marriage Unit statistics. (2013, January to December). Retrieved from https://www.gov.uk/government/uploads/system/uploads/attachment_data/file/291855/FMU_2013_statistics.pdf.

Free Palestine badge referral. Retrieved from http://www.independent.co.uk/news/uk/anti-terror-police-question-schoolboy-for-wearing-pro-palestine-badge-a6873656.html.

Halane (Salma and Zahra). Retrieved from http://www.telegraph.co.uk/news/worldnews/middleeast/syria/11387424/Target-practice-Teenage-British-twins-train-in-Syria.html.

Home Affairs Committee. (2015, January 28). *Counter-terrorism, seventeenth report of session 2013–14 report, together with formal minutes and oral evidence*. Retrieved from http://www.publications.parliament.uk/pa/cm201314/cmselect/cmhaff/231/140128.html.

Home Affairs Committee. *Countering extremism 10th March 2015 oral evidence*. Retrieved from http://www.parliament.uk/business/committees/committees-a-z/commons-select/home-affairs-committee/news/150306-ct-ev.

Home Affairs Committee. *Oral evidence: Countering extremism, HC 428 Tuesday 19th January 2016*. Retrieved from http://www.parliament.uk/business/committees/committees-a-z/commons-select/home-affairs-committee/news-parliament-2015/160115-countering-extremism-evidence/.

Operation of police powers under the Terrorism Act 2000 and subsequent legislation: arrests, outcomes and stops and searches, Great Britain, financial year ending 31st March 2015. Retrieved from https://www.gov.uk/government/publications/operation-of-police-powers-under-the-terrorism-act-2000-financial-year-ending-march-2015/operation-of-police-powers-under-the-terrorism-act-2000-and-subsequent-legislation-arrests-outcomes-and-stops-and-searches-great-britain-financial.

Hoyle, C., Bradford, A., & Frenett, R. (2015). *Becoming Mulan? Female western migrants to ISIS. Report of the Institute for Strategic Dialogue*. Retrieved from http://www.strategicdialogue.org/.

Hussein (Yusra). Retrieved from http://www.theguardian.com/uk-news/2014/oct/03/yusra-hussein-teenager-uk-missing-bristol-syria.

Khan (Hana). Retrieved from http://www.dailymail.co.uk/news/article-2965588/Girlfriend-jihadi-fighter-faces-jail-sending-1-000-fund-terrorist-activities-Syria.html.

Khan (Runa). Retrieved from http://www.bbc.co.uk/news/uk-england-30439913.

Mahmood (Aqsa). (2015, 22 February). Retrieved from http://www.independent.co.uk/news/uk/home-news/aqsa-mahmood-branded-a-disgrace-by-her-parents-after-claims-she-recruited-three-uk-girls-flying-to-10062151.html; http://www.independent.co.uk/news/uk/crime/the-glasgow-teenager-who-dropped-out-of-university-to-marry-an-isis-fighter-in-syria-9706610.html.

Mannan (Muhammed Abdul). Retrieved from http://www.independent.co.uk/news/uk/home-news/muhammed-abdul-mannan-grandfather-who-left-britain-to-join-isis-was-tricked-says-son-10379112.html.

Metropolitan Police statistics. Retrieved from http://content.met.police.uk/Article/Counter-Terrorism Command/1400006569170/1400006569170.
Prevent strategy and prevent duty guidance. Retrieved from https://www.gov.uk/government/publications/prevent-duty-guidance.
Sardar, Z. (2013, September 13). *Life and style first person–Family The Guardian*. Retrieved from http://www.theguardian.com/lifeandstyle/2008/sep/13/family1.
Shakil (Tareena). (2016, February 1). *BBC News*. Retrieved from http://www.bbc.co.uk/news/uk-england-35460697.
Southall Black Sisters report. "*Sane and Safe*." Retrieved from http://www.southallblacksisters.org.uk/reports/safe-and-sane-report/.
Straw(Jack).Retrievedfromhttp://www.theguardian.com/world/2011/jan/08/jack-straw-white-girls-easy-meat.
Terraced house referral. Retrieved from http://www.dailymail.co.uk/wires/pa/article-3410178/1-800-children-referred-Channel-radicalisation-programme-four-years.html.

Cases

London Borough of Tower Hamlets v B [2015] EWHC 2491.
London Borough of Tower Hamlets v M and Others [2015]/*In the matter of M (Children)* [2015]. EWHC 1433 (Fam)EWHC 869 (Fam).
R v Hasan [2005] 4 All ER 685.
R v Malik (Samina Hussain) [2008] EWCA Crim 1450.
Re M (children) [2015] EWHC 1433 (Fam). [2015] 2 FLR, Fam. Law 893.
Re M (children) No 2 [2015] EWHC 2933 (Fam).
Re Z [2015] EWHC 2350.

Chapter 3
Understanding Attribution Bias and Reasons Behind Internet Infidelity in India

Garima Jain and Sanjeev P. Sahni

Background

Internet Infidelity—a new and escalating twist to the age-old problem of adultery. Defining infidelity has become relatively harder with the advent of technology. There is no universally accepted definition. Internet Infidelity constitutes intimate chat sessions, sexually stimulating conversations, cybersex, exchanging sexual self-images, online dating, online flirting, and using online pornography (Hertlein and Piercy 2006). Globally researchers, legislators, and academicians acknowledge that there is limited research characterizing Internet Infidelity (e.g., Moller and Vossler 2015; Varnado 2013). Limited research in this area suggests that online romantic relationship outside of marriage can lead to marital discord, separation, and divorce (Maheu and Gordon 2000).

Victimologists and psychologists mentioned that victims of online infidelity experienced a range of emotions (such as mistrust, suspicion, fear, lack of intimacy, hurt, betrayal, rejection, abandonment, devastation, depression, loneliness, shame, isolation, humiliation, jealousy, anger, rage, and loss of self-esteem) leading to the psychological abuse of the uninvolved partner (Young 2004). With the Internet, we are moving away from physical ideas about infidelity and acknowledging emotional infidelity and psychological abuse. According to WHO report (2012) intimate partner violence is the most common type of violence against women, affecting 30 % of women worldwide. Therefore, it is imperative to address the issue of Internet Infidelity at the nascent stages. This has the potential to aggravate intimate partner violence, emotional and psychological abuse of the partner and children.

There is much popular debate whether having sexual or romantic conversation online should be classified as "infidelity." According to Uberoi (2001), marriage in

G. Jain (✉) • S.P. Sahni
Jindal Institute of Behavioural Sciences, O.P. Jindal Global University, Haryana 131001, India
e-mail: gjain@jgu.edu.in; drspsahni@jgu.edu.in

E.C. Viano (ed.), *Cybercrime, Organized Crime, and Societal Responses*,
DOI 10.1007/978-3-319-44501-4_3

Indian context is governed by sexual as well as emotional exclusivity. Russell (2003) further argued that flirtatious behavior or sexual involvement with anyone else than your partner is considered unacceptable within moral, ethical, political, cultural, and religious ambit. As per the Section 497 of Indian Penal Code (IPC), adultery is considered a punishable offense in India (Mahapatra 2011). It is estimated lately that divorce rates in India are increasing gradually. Family court officials reported that number of divorce applications have increased 2–3 times in cities such as Mumbai, Delhi, Bengaluru, Kolkata, and Lucknow over the past 5 years. In 2005, the divorce rates was determined as 1 per 1000 as compared to 13 per 1000 in 2015. There is a gradual increase in divorce rates of India over the past 10 years (Dutt 2015). While on the other hand, existing divorce rates in India is much lower than other parts of the world. For example divorce rate in the USA is 53 % and in Europe is 60 % (Engel 2014).[1] But, since India does not maintain any central or state-wise registry for divorce data, there is high probability that cited figure is underestimated (Dutt 2015). According to a report in The Times of India (2012) and New Indian Express (2014) there is a staggering demand of family courts, high pending cases of divorce and marital disputes in India which further supports the above argument (Umbrajkar 2012; Durgam 2014). Out of the total 4000 divorce cases filed in Bangalore jurisdiction, 40 % of the cases were being sought on the ground of adultery and extramarital affair (Mukherjee 2014). It has been seen that most of the clients came up with recorded messages of their spouse on Whatsapp, Facebook, Twitter, etc. as a proof of their infidelity (Mukherjee 2014). Lee (2010) studied relationship between divorce and technology and cited that according to British statistics, one in five divorce petitions cite Facebook as a cause. 14 % of the respondents admit that common reason of checking their partner's social media accounts is to identify evidence of infidelity. It can be concluded that number of couples filing divorce in metropolitan cities are going up by leaps and bounds. Due to changing lifestyle patterns and high exposure to technology in metropolitan cities, Internet is becoming a safe resort for partners to maintain a secretive virtual relationship.

Due to asynchronous, accessible, and ambiguous nature of Internet, the virtual affair remains hidden in the overwhelming majority of cases. Hence, Mileham (2007) argued that not only online relationships carry "forbidden" quality, but they also require lying to the partner and omitting the truth. The present study is first of its kind where reasons, attribution, and motivation of general public in India about Internet Infidelity are discussed. The first part of the present study unveils various defense mechanisms employed by Indian respondents while indulging in Internet Infidelity. The second part brings a comparative perspective about the reasons behind their involvement in online infidelity between respondents who were "married" and "in a relationship."

[1] http://www.businessinsider.in/MAP-Divorce-Rates-Around-The-World/articleshow/35606389.cms.

Introduction

A study on 97 societies from Demographic Yearbook of United Nations between 1947 and 1992 indicated that closer to 93.1 % of women and 91.8 % of men marry by the age 49 (Fisher 1989). This clearly indicates Pair Bonding is a hallmark of Humanity (Rosenberg and Feder 2014). Our need to connect with other individuals is more fundamental than other basic needs as described by Abraham Maslow as basic physiological needs (food, shelter, water). Lieberman (2013) demonstrated using fMRI (frontal Magnetic Resonance) that our brain responds to social pain and pleasure as effectively as the physical pain and pleasure. He found that deepest contentment lies in an individual's ability to stay faithful and committed to the most important people in our lives. This further restrains our selfish impulses to protect our primary relationship. From this perspective fidelity is viewed as more satisfying and gratifying rather than infidelity.

Despite professed commitment with monogamy, infidelity is widespread (Mileham 2007). The frequency and expression of infidelity is defined by myriad psychological, cultural, sociological and economic variables (Tsapelas et al. 2011).

The ways in which individuals become involved in interpersonal relationships has changed at a dramatic rate during the last 20 years. Greenfield (1999) that 42 % of compulsive Internet users are engaged in an affair while online. Internet is regarded as a Social Technology; bringing a revolution in interpersonal relationships (Tyler 2002). The combination of available stimulating visual content, lack of visual cues between communicators, easy accessibility, autonomous, anonymous identity, and asynchronous nature of communication has contributed to highly psychoactive experiences while online (McKenna and Bargh 2000). Therefore, Internet Infidelity presents a challenge not only for researchers but also for couple counselors working therapeutically with infidelity cases.

This chapter attempts to understand the distinct reasons, motivation, justification and rationalization process that occurs on the part of the individual involved in online infidelity. It is the first empirical research which investigates: (a) distinct rationalization, justification, attribution bias employed by perpetrators of Internet Infidelity. (b) investigates the reasons behind involvement in Internet Infidelity. By examining relatively large sample, we are able to provide coherent and organized view on the reasons and defenses behind the act of cheating on primary relationship that will inform both clinicians and researchers in the field.

Literature Review

From a moral and ethical point of view, infidelity is a direct attack on emotional investment the other person has made in a relationship (Treas and Giesen 2000). Online infidelity is significantly contributing towards disruption of primary relationship, consequently leading to separation/divorce (Barak and Fisher 2003; Schneider 2000).

It has been established that there exist a gender difference pertaining to infidelity in general. Commitment and Monogamy are considered less attractive by males than females (Sheppard et al. 1995; Whitty 2005). It is further corroborated by the fact that women are more likely to get upset by emotional infidelity than by sexual infidelity. There are numerous studies and scholarly articles on understanding reasons behind cheating or betrayal as a function of gender differences (Barak and Fisher 2003; Treas and Giesen 2000). Yeniceri and Kökdemir (2006) hypothesized a questionnaire to study reasons behind infidelity to lay theories about infidelity and found a significant difference between men and women with respect to reasons behind act of cheating or betrayal. Mileham (2007) elaborated that the reason behind indulgence of women in the act of infidelity is to mate-switch, i.e., finding more desirable partner without giving up security and protection from the primary relationship or current partner. In another study by Shackelford et al. (2002) participants were asked to imagine a scenario of infidelity by their partner and studied the consequent reactions following the imagined situation. It was concluded that men are more likely to terminate the relationship following sexual infidelity as compared to women.

Mileham (2007) identified **Behavioral Rationalization**, where 80 % of the participants justified that due to absence of physical contact, online liaisons do not qualify for infidelity.

How can this be cheating if I'm not touching anyone?

Virtual sexual or romantic exchanges are perceived as fantasy entertainment and do not count as unfaithfulness.

Brand et al. (2007) postulate that the objective behind rationalizing unfaithfulness by men and women involved in online extradyadic relationship is to avoid the crushing guilt and to serve their self, thereby facilitating self-protection. Similarly, Whitty (2003) explored Internet Infidelity by studying 234 junior-level students in an introductory psychology class. Author administered two versions of projective test and discovered that the involved partner in Internet Infidelity experienced guilt and shame about the affair. It was further found loss of self-esteem for the involved partner.

Paul David illustrated that infidelity can be explained by Game theory model, Prisoner's Dilemma, which provides a useful framework for understanding how individual's decision making in committed relationship can adhere to predictable patterns of self-interest. Higher the self-interest is rewarded in short-run, the more likely individual will cheat. While on the other hand, more individuals understand the importance of long-term perspective of maintaining and sustaining our committed relationship, the more people will be faithful to each other (Gottman and Silver 2012).

Online romantic relationships adversely affect marriage and de facto relationship, leading to divorce (Merkle and Richardson 2000; Young et al. 2000) or wife battering and wife killing (Wilson and Daly 1995). Infidelity or "Cheating" result in anguish, depression, fury, and humiliation on uninvolved partner (Cano and O'Leary 2000; Buunk and Van Driel 1989). Facing direct consequences of infidelity can enfeeble the cheater. Foster and Misra (2013) propose that perpetrators of infidelity debilitate about their indiscretions and experience symptoms of dissonance (e.g., discrepancy in self-concept, emotional and psychological discomfort). Cognitive dissonance theory predicts that discrepancy between thoughts and behavior leads to discomfort (Petty and Brinol 2010). Hence, individuals generate rationalization to preserve the impression that their behavior and attitude are consistent (Foster 2005).

In the present study we attempt to identify individuals who have had been involved in online romantic/sexual conversation with anyone else other than their partner and the reasons behind their involvement is understood. Further, the present research also focused on understanding the attribution bias, justification, and rationale behind involvement of individuals in online infidelity.

Aims/Objective

We seek to study the following objectives in this chapter:

(a) **Study 1: investigates distinct rationalization, justification and attribution bias employed by perpetrators of Internet Infidelity.** We divided the sample respondents of the study in two Groups; **Group A** constitutes men and women who admitted their involvement in online infidelity and **Group B** constitutes the individuals who do not have an engagement in Internet Infidelity.

(b) **Study 2 investigates the reasons behind involvement in Internet Infidelity**. Researchers of the present study further divided respondents of Group A in two strata: **Married** and **In a Relationship**.

The authors demonstrated significantly different reasons behind involvement in extradyadic online relationship between respondents who were Married and Those In a Relationship.

Methodology

The data for this exploratory study is collected through convenience sample, using a combination of online and offline methods and disseminated to the social contacts of the authors. The sample was collected from urban part of Delhi and neighboring states in northern India. An anonymous self-administrative survey was formulated comprising of 14 items. The survey was limited to individuals who were either married or in a de facto relationship.

Participants' Profile

Four hundred and eighty-nine respondents were included in the final sample, of which 58.3 % were men and 41.7 % were women. One hundred and sixty-six respondents (34 %) of the sample admitted their involvement in Internet Infidelity, i.e., **Group A**, while on the other hand, 220 respondents (66 %) said that they have never committed online infidelity: **Group B**. Of the total sample, 83.4 % were in a relationship and 16.6 % were married.

The participants predominantly defined themselves as heterosexual, with 7.2 % considering themselves as homosexual and 4.1 % as bisexual. Data with or without non-heterosexual participants did not change any of the findings. Therefore, authors decided to retain responses from non-heterosexual participants.

Over 56.6 % were 19–24 years old. Meanwhile, a majority of the participants (68.9 %) were students. The sample largely consisted of upper middle class family with monthly income of over INR 50,000 (66.7 %).

GROUP A (Individuals who admitted their involvement in Internet Infidelity): Majority of sample in Group A (57.8 %) falls in the age group of 19–24 years and 24 % were 25 years and above. It was found that men were more likely to be engaged in online romantic relationship than women. In the present study, 72.9 % were males and 27.1 % were females. Since study was limited to individuals, who were either married or in a relationship, it was found that while 84.9 % were in a relationship, 15.1 % were married. Further, majority of the respondents consists of individuals from upper middle class family with monthly income over INR 50,000.

GROUP B (Individuals who do not have any involvement in Internet Infidelity): 56.2 % falls in the age group of 19–24 years and 22.4 % belongs to 25 years and above. Ratio of men to women in Group B is almost same. While 50.6 % were men, 49.4 % were women. 82.6 % were in a relationship, and 17.4 % were married.

Study 1

Distinct rationalization, justification and attribution bias employed by perpetrators of Internet Infidelity

All participants were asked the possible reasons behind **disengagement of people in general** to have a romantic/sexual online conversation with someone other than their partner. Respondents of both Group A and Group B were allowed to select as many options as applied. Possible answers were: **(a) Strong Moral Values; (b) Religious Principles; (c) Not Wanting to Cheat on One's Partner; (d) Fear of Being Caught; (e) Lack of Knowledge; (f) Internet Inaccessibility.** We also provided an "other" response (there was no reliable patterns in those "other" response).

Result and Discussion

- Of 166 respondents in Group A (refer Fig. 3.1), more than half of the respondents (51.8, 54.8, and 50 %) attributed **"Lack of Knowledge," "Fear of Being Caught," and "Internet Inaccessibility"** as leading causes behind disengagement of individuals in Internet Infidelity. On the other hand, only 26.5, 13.3, and 21.7 % of the participants in Group A attributes **"Strong Moral**

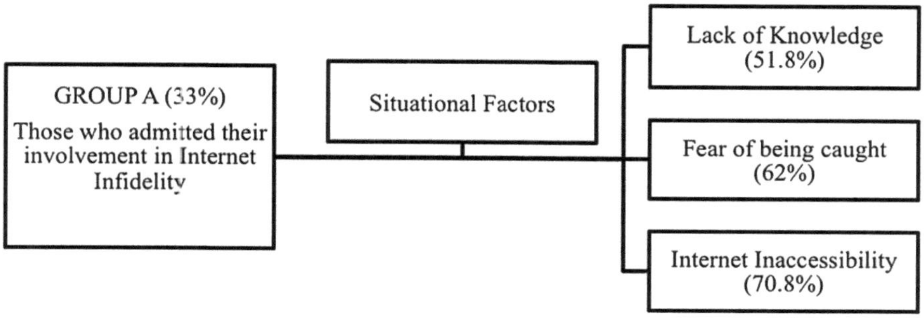

Fig. 3.1 Why do you think people do not indulge in Internet Infidelity?

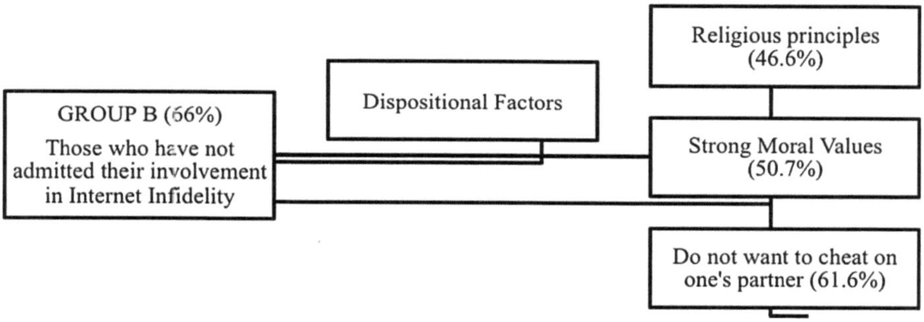

Fig. 3.2 Why do you think, people do not indulge in online infidelity?

Values," "Religious Principles," and "Not Wanting to Cheat on One's Partner" behind disengagement of general population in online infidelity respectively.

- 50, 46, and 50.6 % of the total respondents in Group B ($n=322$) perceive and attribute **"Strong Moral values," "Religious Principles,"** and **"Do Not Want to Cheat on One's Partner"** behind disengagement of people in Internet Infidelity (refer Fig. 3.2). On the other hand, 13, 32, and 10.9 % in Group B attributes **"Lack of Knowledge," "Fear of Being Caught,"** and **"Inaccessibility to Internet"** behind disengagement of people in general such acts.
- Authors were able to categorize the factors in two major clusters, depending on the distinguished responses by Group A and Group B participants: **Dispositional/ Personality Factors** ("Strong Moral Values," "Religious Principles," and "Not Wanting to Cheat on One's Partner") and **Situational/ External factors** ("Lack of Knowledge," "Fear of Being Caught," and "Inaccessibility to Internet").
- Consistent with our findings, The Meta-Analysis of GROUP A suggested that there is an overall significant relationship ($p<0.005$) between Inaccessibility to Internet and Lack of Knowledge ($r=0.675$); significant relationship ($p<0.005$) between Lack of Knowledge and Fear of Being Caught ($r=0.565$); significant relationship ($p<0.005$) between Inaccessibility to Internet and Fear of Being Caught ($r=0.604$) (refer Table 3.1).

Table 3.1 Reasons behind involvement in Internet Infidelity

Group A		Lack of knowledge	Scared to be caught	Strong moral values	Religious principles	Inaccessibility to Internet	Do not want to cheat
Lack of knowledge	Pearson correlation	1	0.565[a]	–0.404[a]	–0.227[a]	*0.675*[a]	–0.048
	Sig. (2-tailed)		0.000	0.000	0.003	*0.000*	0.537
	N	166	166	166	166	166	166
Scared to be caught	Pearson correlation	*0.565*[a]	1	–0.340[a]	–0.186[b]	*0.604*[a]	–0.005
	Sig. (2-tailed)	*0.000*		0.000	0.016	*0.000*	0.951
	N	166	166	166	166	166	166
Inaccessibility to Internet	Pearson correlation	*0.675*[a]	*0.604*[a]	–0.409[a]	–0.178[b]	1	–0.088
	Sig. (2-tailed)	*0.000*	*0.000*	0.000	0.022		0.261
	N	166	166	166	166	166	166

[a]Correlation is significant at the 0.01 level (2-tailed)
[b]Correlation is significant at the 0.05 level (2-tailed)

Table 3.2 Reasons behind involvement in Internet Infidelity

Group B							
		Lack of knowledge	Scared to be caught	Strong moral values	Religious principles	Inaccessibility to Internet	Do not want to cheat
Strong Moral values	Pearson correlation	−0.240[a]	−0.441[a]	1	*0.636*[a]	−0.210[a]	*0.603*[a]
	Sig. (2-tailed)	0.000	0.000		0.000	0.000	0.000
	N	322	322	322	322	322	322
Religious principles	Pearson correlation	−0.209[a]	−0.373[a]	*0.636*[a]	1	−0.262[a]	*0.574*[a]
	Sig. (2-tailed)	0.000	0.000	0.000		0.000	0.000
	N	322	322	322	322	322	322
Do not want to cheat	Pearson correlation	−0.134[b]	−0.346[a]	*0.603*[a]	0.574[a]	−0.214[a]	1
	Sig. (2-tailed)	0.016	0.000	0.000	0.000	0.000	
	N	322	322	322	322	322	322

[a]Correlation is significant at the 0.01 level (2-tailed)
[b]Correlation is significant at the 0.05 level (2-tailed)

- Meta-analysis of Group B revealed significant relationship between "Strong Moral Values, Religious Principles, and Do not Want to Cheat on One's Partner." Pearson's Correlation (2 tailed) suggested that there is an overall significant relationship ($p<0.005$) between Strong Moral Values and Religious Principles ($r=0.636$), Strong Moral Values and Do not Want to Cheat on One's Partner ($r=0.603$) ($p<0.005$), between Do not Want to Cheat on One's Partner and Religious Principles ($r=0.574$) ($p<0.005$) (refer Table 3.2).

The findings clearly indicate that participants in Group A (those who are involved in Internet Infidelity) attribute **Situational or External factors** behind disengagement of people in general in the act of infidelity. And participants in Group B (those who are not involved in Internet Infidelity) attribute **Dispositional or Personality factors** behind disengagement of individuals in general behind their involvement in Internet Infidelity.

Discussion

The aim of the research is to understand the distinct attribution process, cognitive distortion, rationalization, and excuses employed by perpetrators of Internet Infidelity. Most of the burgeoning literature on attribution process can be established by the work of Heider (1944, 2013). According to Heider, causal explanation of human behavior is the distinction between internal or dispositional and external or environmental factors (Jones and Davis 1965a, b). Maruna and Mann (2006) have established that excuses are those justification that involve element of externality (outside the personality trait of the person, cause by external force), uncontrollability (cause beyond person's control), and unintentionality (the behavior was enacted involuntary and by chance) leading to cognitive distortions.

Plethora of research studies, ranging from field based ethnographies to laboratory based experiments disclose that individuals tend to formulate justifications and post hoc excuses when they indulge in activities that is perceived to be unacceptable or exasperating (Snyder and Higgins 1988; McCrea 2008).

Our findings suggested that respondents who admitted their involvement in Internet Infidelity (Group A) attributed external or situational factors (Internet Inaccessibility, Lack of Knowledge, Fear of Being Caught) behind disengagement of people in Internet Infidelity and the participants who do not have any involvement in Online Infidelity (Group B) attributed internal or dispositional factors (Strong Moral Values, Religious Principles, and Not Wanting to Cheat on One's Partner) behind disengagement of people in Internet Infidelity. Researchers postulate that people consider infidelity as morally unacceptable (Daines 2006). As illustrated in the present study, perpetrators of Internet Infidelity (Group A) accredit situational or external factors behind non indulgence of people in Internet Infidelity, thereby projecting their behavior as a responsible element of environmental factor. While, on the other hand, individual respondents with no history of Internet Infidelity (Group B) ascribed Dispositional or personal factors behind disengagement of individuals in such acts, thereby attributing their personal factors behind their non-indulgence in extradyadic online relationship. Jones and David (1965a, b) suggest that Individuals reasonably tend to account for their negative actions as caused by agents outside their control, i.e., situational. The overall tendency of an individual to overestimate personal or dispositional factors relative to environmental factors while perceiving behavior of others is called "Fundamental Attribution Error."

This process of attribution, excuse making, and justification can be traced back from psychoanalytical school of thought on ego defense mechanism to neutralization theory of criminology. Denial of Responsibility, condemnation of condemners are some of the neutralization techniques identified by Sykes and Matza (1957). Similarly, social cognitive theory of Morality by Bandura (1990) ascertain following techniques to avoid self-condemnation: Diffusion or Displacement of responsibility, distorting the consequences of an action, assuming the role of victim for oneself.

The attribution process established by the respondents in the present study can be explained by Self Presentation theory of Fundamental attribution error. Attributing external factors such as Lack of Knowledge, Internet Inaccessibility, and Fear of Being Caught by One's Partner is mediated by a desire to preserve a positive public image rather than private self-image (Topalli 2005).

Due to greater degrees of uninhibited behavior, secrecy of online activities, dysfunctional sexual relationship with partners extra dyadic online relations can disrupt primary relationship and consequently may result in divorce and separation (Cooper et al. 2000). It has been alleged that Internet Infidelity presents a challenge for counselors or therapists which was exemplified as online infidelity surpass the traditional definition of infidelity both in terms of sexual intercourse and broader categories of sexual behavior. Johnson (2005) stated that the distinction between emotional and sexual infidelity is hard to make in practice.

Hertlein and Stevenson (2010) identified seven factors related to Internet related intimacy problems (IRIPs) known as Seven A's. It has been stated by King (1999) that Internet is *acceptable* as a mode of communication. Internet is *accessible*, *affordable* and sustains *anonymity* of the user. Further, approximation to real life interactions is facilitated (Hertlein and Sendak 2007a, b), allows *ambiguity* for non-acceptable actions or behavior (Hertlein 2009) and provides *accommodation/adjustment* in terms of the real self and ideal self (Tittle and Botchkovar 2005). As aforementioned, individuals feel restricted in their day to day life driven by societal norms, values and rules, which confines and constrain their day to day actions and behavior. This sometimes leads to exhibition of opposite behavior. Due to anonymity and ambiguity ensured, Internet provides an opportunity to individuals to deviate from their real personality (Johnson 2005). This further escalate tension between "real" and "ought" self, leading to distorted self concept. Individuals employ various defense mechanisms, justification, excuses, cognitive and attribution bias to accommodate the gap in their Self-Concept.

Moller and Vossler (2014) argued that perpetrators of online infidelity decline the act cheating behind their involvement by claiming that there was no sexual act involved. This further contributes towards greater tendency of men and women involved in online infidelity to commit attribution bias. As a result, they do not consider themselves responsible and accountable behind their action. This proposes even a greater challenge and dilemma for counselors, psychologists and therapist in treatment. It becomes difficult for the therapist to make the involved partner realize his responsibility and accountability towards his actions and its consequent impact in his/her primary relationship.

Study 2

Reasons and Causes Behind Involvement of People in Internet Infidelity

For the purpose of understanding reasons behind involvement in Internet Infidelity, we compared the respondent of Group A with two categories: Married and In a Relationship.

Of the total respondents in Group A, who admitted their involvement in having romantic/sexual conversation with someone else than their partner, 25 (15.2 %) are married and 141 (84.8 %) are in a relationship.

Group A (Married): Eighty percent of the married respondents were 25 years and above. Sixty-eight percent male and 32 % female. Sexual Orientation was reported with majority (62 %) being heterosexual; however, three male respondents (12 %) reported orientation towards same sex. Except 12 % who were students, 88 % were employed either in government/private jobs or had their own business units/ventures. Fifty-six percent belong to nuclear family; 24 % joint family; 12 % broken family. While 36 % never used web camera while engaging in Internet Infidelity, 56 % have reported to employ web camera while indulging in secondary online relationship.

Group B (in a relationship): Researchers of present study further revealed that majority respondents who admitted their involvement in Internet Infidelity belonged to young Net Generation. Maximum respondents (80 %) were less than 24 years, with 85 % undergoing under graduation. Sixty percent belong to nuclear family, forty six to joint family, 6 % broken family. While 35 % denied using web camera, 56.4 % reported to have used web camera while engaging in online sexual/textual conversation.

The purpose of the research is to study the **reasons** behind involvement of men and women in online sexual communication. It was revealed that 166 (34 %) of the total respondents admitted their involvement in online sexual/romantic conversation with person other than their partner (primary relationship) whereas 322 (66 %) responded negatively to indulging in online infidelity. More than half of the men and women who admitted their involvement in Internet Infidelity lie in the age group of 19–24 years and 24.1 % are 25 years or above.

In the present study, more males (72.3 %) as compared to females (27.1 %) admitted their involvement in Internet Infidelity.

Result and Findings

Respondents were asked about the frequency of their involvement in online sexual conversation. Using a 5 point Likert scale of 1–5, where 1 refers to Never and 5 Very frequently, 2/5th of total respondents were found to have involved in online romantic/sexual conversation once or twice and 3/5th were involved either very often or very frequently. While 35 % of the respondents in Group A have never used web camera, 56 % reported to have used web camera while engaging in cyberspace infidelity.

The authors analyzed that relative to individuals who were in a relationship, married respondents are more likely to endorse reasons for cheating that indicated need for Emotional Support, Loneliness, Boredom, and Frustration, whereas majority of those who were in a relationship recognize Desire to explore and Peer Pressure as reasons behind their involvement.

The authors analyzed that relative to 10 % individuals who were in a relationship, 60 % married respondents attributed Need for Emotional Support behind cyberspace secondary relationship. Pearson Chi Square = 36.6, $p = 0.00$.

Married respondents are more likely to attribute Loneliness (72 %) than the one in a relationship (23.6 %). Pearson Chi Square = 11.67, $p = 0.01$. Further, 56 % married attributes boredom in primary relationship behind their involvement in Internet Infidelity. Pearson Chi Square = 15.311; $p = 0.00$. In addition, 52 % married respondents recognize frustration relative to 14 % respondents who were in a relationship. Pearson Chi Square = 27.341; $p = 0.00$.

On the other hand, we found that respondents who were in a relationship were marginally more likely to attribute "Desire to Explore" behind their indulgence in online infidelity (50.7 % of respondents who were in a relationship as compared to 26 % married.). Fifty-nine percent in a relationship also perceives "Peer Pressure" as compared to only 4 % of those who were married. Pearson's Chi Square = 13.336; $p = 0.01$.

We further examined the reasons behind involvement in Internet Infidelity of Group A respondents using independent sample t-test. According to the married perpetrators of infidelity report, married respondents ($M = 0.56$, $\sigma = 0.507$) are more likely to ascribe emotional support behind their involvement in InternetInfidelity as compared to those who were in a relationship ($M = 0.10$, $\sigma = 0.301$), $t = 8.684$; $p = 0.00$. Married respondents ($M = 0.60$, $\sigma = 0.500$) are more likely to attribute loneliness as a factor as compared to those who were in a relationship ($M = 0.24$, $\sigma = 0.426$), $t = 12.873$; $p = 0.00$. Married participants ($M = 0.56$, $\sigma = 0.507$) were more likely to attribute Boredom as an attribution as compared to those who were in a relationship ($M = 0.19$, $\sigma = 0.396$), $t = 8.165$; $p = 0.00$. Married respondents ($M = 0.52$, $\sigma = 0.510$) were more likely to attribute Frustration as a factor as compared to those who were in a relationship ($M = 0.10$, $\sigma = 0.310$), $t = 9.936$; $p = 0.00$.

On the other hand, assessing the report of respondents who were in a relationship ($M = 0.51$, $\sigma = 0.502$), it was found that Desire to explore behind their indulgence as compared to married people ($M = 0.306$, $\sigma = 0.490$), $t = 13.481$; $p = 0.00$. And, In a relationship respondents ($M = 0.42$, $\sigma = 0.496$) were more likely to attribute Peer Pressure as factor behind their involvement in Internet Infidelity as compared to those who were married ($M = 0.04$, $\sigma = 0.200$); $t = 6.486$, $p = 0.00$.

The finding was further supported by administering One-Way ANOVA analysis. There is a statistically significant difference ($p = 0.00$) in the mean attributions (Emotional Support, Loneliness, Peer Pressure, Bored in Primary Relationship, and Frustration) between the two groups of respondents.

Discussion

In the present study, we tried to establish online infidelity through the lens of individuals who are married and in a relationship and bringing a comparative perspective between the two sets of respondents in Indian context. Married respondents attributed **Emotional support, Loneliness, Boredom,** and **Frustration** behind their involvement in Internet Infidelity, while those who are "in a relationship" attribute **Peer Pressure** and **Desire to Explore.**

Recent study observes how married people report high probability (five times) of searching sexual or Emotional online relations than singles (Albright 2008).

Pittman and Pittaman-Wagers (1985) found that more than 90 % of divorces were related to marital infidelity. Social exchange theory states that people will stay in a relationship in part when attractive outsiders are not readily available (Rusbult 1993; Rusbult et al. 1986). The Internet provides ready access to a huge pool of potentially attractive others: Perhaps people already married or in committed relationships are unhappy and are "testing the waters" to see if an attractive other would respond to them online, allowing them to transition out of the marriage.

Dew et al. (2006) studies 508 heterosexual men and concluded that common use of cybersex was for isolated sexual purposes, social sexual purposes, or for a search for offline relationships. In addition to being affordable, the accessibility and anonymity of online sexual activities (OSA) are particularly relevant (Cooper 1998; Daneback et al. 2005; Ross et al. 2005). It is easier to access sexually explicit websites and chat rooms from home, work places, telephones and other electronic devices. These locations allow for both clandestine and convenient forms of communication. Married men and women can meet potential sexual partners while keeping their identity and marital status anonymous. Married men get involved in online infidelity as a convenient escape from life's pressures (Young et al. 2000). Chaney and Dew (2003) discovered that both married and non-married adult males engaged in a form of disassociation from negative emotional states (e.g., depression, anxiety) when compulsively engaging in OSA. Finally, married men may choose to engage in online sexual behaviors because they perceive less stigma attached to meeting individuals online compared to meeting potential sexual partners in person.

A University of Florida researcher, Beatriz Mileham, studied Internet Infidelity as part of her doctoral dissertation, interviewing 76 men and 10 women who used popular chat rooms for the "Married But Looking" crowd. Most of the participants insisted they loved their spouses, but were still compelled to seek a romantic encounter via the Internet due to boredom or their partner's perceived lack of interest in sex.

The courts, however, have argued that the role of online compulsivity as a mental disorder in the defense of online sexual deviancy cases. For example, one landmark case, the United States versus McBroom, successfully demonstrated that the client's downloading, viewing, and transferring of Internet pornography was less about erotic gratification and more about an emotional escape mechanism to relieve mental tension (Cooper 2003).

It is argued that principle of hierarchy in Indian families along with patrilocal ideology in Indian structure family is prevalent in many families of India. It is viewed that in such a set up, expressing romantic and intimate relationship is regarded as disruptive and senior member of the family adopt the role of controlling romantic complex. Lack of expressed intimacy between husband and wife leads to lack of emotional support; commitment, frustration, and monotonous nature of relationship. In a cross-cultural study of American, Asian Indian, and Turkish Young Adult on perceived attitude towards romanticism, it was found that Indians have the lowest romanticism score followed by Turkish and American (Medora et al. 2002). It is further exuberated by the study done by Caldwell et al. (1983) in New Delhi on men of Aggarwal Community. An overwhelming 56 % men felt closer to their mothers than their wives. India had witness a transformation from joint family to nuclear family set up in metropolitan and urban parts of India. Due to collectivistic nature of Indian society, intimate and romantic expression of love is still not encouraged, leading to conflicts and infidelity between couples (Medora et al. 2002).

Limitations of Study

There are several limitations of the study. The most important limitation is that this sample represents a convenience sample of individuals recruited online keeping their identity anonymous. Because of the small sample size and low response rate to the survey, caution must be taken in generalizing the result of the present study. It is important to point out that majority of the studies on Internet Infidelity were published by western countries; there is no published study on identifying reasons and attributions while involving in Internet Infidelity in India. We, therefore, had to draw from inferences from studies published on general topics of marriages, adultery, and family relations.

Conclusion

India is a collectivistic society where moving out of marriage was considered unacceptable due to social norms (Medora et al. 2002). With technological advancement, changing lifestyles, more and more women entering workforce, Indian society is witnessing a transformation towards nuclear families and individualism (Raina 2012; Dummett 2011). India's old taboos are being challenged. There has been 100 % increase in divorce rates in India in the last 5 years alone (Dummett 2011). Owing to recent hacking of ashleymadison.com (Tagline: "Life is short, Have an affair"), a website for married people, or those who are in committed relationship, looking to cheat their spouses or partners, Indians were found as one of the top users in the infidelity website with over 2.7 Indian lakh users registered. Based on the leaked data, majority of Indian users were from New Delhi, Mumbai, Chennai, and Kolkata (Dhapola 2015). While majority of worldwide users were men, surprisingly, for India, substantial number were women were registered as compared to men-reflecting the changing attitude towards relationship in India (Sonwalker 2015). The present study has given an insight on motivation, rationalization, excuses, justification, and various reasons employed by those respondents who admitted their involvement in Internet Infidelity. Lack of emotional support, boredom, frustration, and loneliness were identified as reasons by urban married Indians to get involved in Internet Infidelity. The chapter also gives an insight on excuses and justification employed by perpetrators of Internet Infidelity. It has not only reflected changing dynamics of relationships but also modern challenges faced by couples in marriages in India.

References

Albright, J. M. (2008). Sex in America online: An exploration of sex, marital status, and sexual identity in Internet sex seeking and its impacts. *Journal of Sex Research, 45*(2), 175–186.
Bandura, A. (1990). Perceived self-efficacy in the exercise of personal agency. *Journal of Applied Sport Psychology, 2*(2), 128–163.
Barak, A., & Fisher, W. A. (2003). Experience with an Internet-based, theoretically grounded educational resource for the promotion of sexual and reproductive health. *Sexual and Relationship Therapy, 18*(3), 293–308.
Brand, R. J., Markey, C. M., Mills, A., & Hodges, S. D. (2007). Sex differences in self-reported infidelity and its correlates. *Sex Roles, 57*(1–2), 101–109.
Buunk, B. P., & Van Driel, B. (1989). *Variant lifestyles and relationships*. USA: Sage Publications, Inc.
Cano, A., & O'Leary, K. D. (2000). Infidelity and separations precipitate major depressive episodes and symptoms of nonspecific depression and anxiety. *Journal of Consulting and Clinical Psychology, 68*(5), 774.
Chaney, M. P., & Dew, B. J. (2003). Online experiences of sexually compulsive men who have sex with men. Sexual Addiction & Compulsivity,10(4), 259–274.
Caldwell, J. C., Reddy, P. H., & Caldwell, P. (1983). The causes of marriage change in South India. Population Studies, 37(3), 343–361.
Cooper, A. (1998). Sexuality and the Internet: Surfing into the new millennium. CyberPsychology & Behavior, 1(2), 187–193.
Cooper, A., Delmonico, D. L., & Burg, R. (2000). Cybersex users, abusers, and compulsives: New findings and implications. *Sexual Addiction & Compulsivity: The Journal of Treatment and Prevention, 7*(1–2), 5–29.
Cooper, A. (Ed.). (2013). Cybersex: The dark side of the force: A special issue of the Journal Sexual Addiction and Compulsion. Routledge.
Daines, B. (2006). Violations of agreed and implicit sexual and emotional boundaries in couple relationships–some thoughts arising from Levine's 'A clinical perspective on couple infidelity'. *Sexual and Relationship Therapy, 21*(1), 45–53.
Daneback, K., Cooper, A., & Månsson, S. A. (2005). An Internet study of cybersex participants. Archives of Sexual Behavior, 34(3), 321-328..
David, P. Infidelity: The Prisoner's Dilemma.
Dew, B., Brubaker, M., & Hays, D. (2006). From the altar to the Internet: Married men and their online sexual behavior. Sexual Addiction & Compulsivity, 13(2-3), 195-207.
Dhapola, S. (2015, August 26). Cheating website Ashley Madison hacked: Everything you need to know. *The Indian Express*. Retrieved from http://indianexpress.com/article/explained/what-ashley-madison-data-breach-means-who-it-impacts/.
Dummett, M. (2011). Not so happily ever after as Indian divorce rates doubles. *BBC News*. Retrieved from http://www.bbc.com/news/world-south-asia-12094360.
Durgam, J. K. (2014, October 7). 1000 divorce cases filed every month. *The New Indian Express*. Retrieved from http://www.newindianexpress.com/cities/hyderabad/1000-Divorce-Cases-Filed-Every-Month/2014/10/07/article2465777.ece.
Dutt, A. (2015, January 4). How and why number of young Indian couples getting divorced has risen sharply. *The Hindustan Times*. Retrieved from http://www.hindustantimes.com/sex-and-relationships/how-and-why-number-of-young-indian-couples-getting-divorced-has-risen-sharply/story-mEuaEoviW40d6slLZbGu6J.html.
Fisher, H. E. (1989). Evolution of human serial pairbonding. *American Journal of Physical Anthropology, 78*(3), 331–354.
Foster, J. D. (2005). *Using cognitive dissonance theory to investigate the thoughts and behaviors of individuals who commit romantic infidelity*. Doctoral dissertation. Retrieved from https://getd.libs.uga.edu/pdfs/foster_josh_d_200508_phd.pdf.
Foster, J. D., & Misra, T. A. (2013). It did not mean anything (about me) Cognitive dissonance theory and the cognitive and affective consequences of romantic infidelity. *Journal of Social and Personal Relationships, 30*(7), 835–857.

Gottman, J., & Silver, N. (2012). *What makes love last?: How to build trust and avoid betrayal*. New York: Simon and Schuster.
Greenfield, D. N. (1999). *Virtual addiction: Sometimes new technology can create new problems*. The Center for Internet Studies@ Psychological Health Associates.
Heider, F. (1944). Social perception and phenomenal causality. *Psychological Review, 51*(6), 358.
Heider, F. (2013). *The psychology of interpersonal relations*. USA: Psychology Press.
Hertlein, K. M. (2009, September). *Distinguishing Internet infidelity from Internet addiction*. Workshop presented at the Annual Nevada State Recovery Conference, Las Vegas, NV.
Hertlein, K. M., & Piercy, F. P. (2006). Internet infidelity: A critical review of the literature. *The Family Journal, 14*(4), 366–371.
Hertlein, K. M., & Sendak, S. K. (2007). *Love "bytes": Internet infidelity and the meaning of intimacy in computer-mediated relationships*. In Annual Conference of Persons, Intimacy, and Love, Salzburg, Austria.
Hertlein, K. M., & Stevenson, A. (2010). The seven "As" contributing to Internet-related intimacy problems: A literature review. *Cyberpsychology: Journal of Psychosocial Research on Cyberspace, 4*(1), 1.
Johnson, S. (2005). Your Cheatin'Heart: Myths and absurdities about extradyadic relationships. *Journal of Couple & Relationship Therapy, 4*(2–3), 161–172.
Jones, E. E., & Davis, K. E. (1965a). From acts to dispositions the attribution process in person perception. *Advances in Experimental Social Psychology, 2*, 219–266.
Jones, E. E., & Davis, K. E. (1965b). From acts to dispositions the attribution process in person perception. In L. Berkowitz (Ed.), *Advances in experimental social psychology* (pp. 219–266). New York: Academic Press.
Kenneth Paul Rosenberg, M. D., & Laura Curtiss Feder, P. (Eds.). (2014). *Behavioral addictions: Criteria, evidence, and treatment*. Elsevier, UK: Academic Press.
King, S. A. (1999). Internet gambling and pornography: Illustrative examples of the psychological consequences of communication anarchy. *CyberPsychology & Behavior, 2*(3), 175–193.
Lee, A. (2010). Technology and divorce: A correlation? *The Huffington Post in association with The Times of India group*. Retrieved from http://www.huffingtonpost.com/entry/technology-and-divorce-a-_n_794643.html?section=india.
Lieberman, M. D. (2013). *Social: Why our brains are wired to connect*. UK: Oxford University Press.
Mahapatra, D. (2011, December 3). Adultery law biased against men, says Supreme Court. *The Times of India*. Retrieved from http://timesofindia.indiatimes.com/india/Adultery-law-biased-against-men-says-Supreme-Court/articleshow/10964790.cms.
Maheu, M. M., & Gordon, B. L. (2000). Counseling and therapy on the Internet. *Professional Psychology: Research and Practice, 31*(5), 484.
Maruna, S., & Mann, R. E. (2006). A fundamental attribution error? Rethinking cognitive distortions†. *Legal and Criminological Psychology, 11*(2), 155–177.
McCrea, S. M. (2008). Self-handicapping, excuse making, and counterfactual thinking: Consequences for self-esteem and future motivation. *Journal of Personality and Social Psychology, 95*(2), 274.
McKenna, K. Y., & Bargh, J. A. (2000). Plan 9 from cyberspace: The implications of the Internet for personality and social psychology. *Personality and Social Psychology Review, 4*(1), 57–75.
Medora, N. P., Larson, J. H., Hortacsu, N., Hortagsu, N., & DAVE, P. (2002). Perceived attitudes towards romanticism; a cross-cultural study of American, Asian-Indian, and Turkish young adults. *Journal of Comparative Family Studies, 33*(2) 155–178.
Merkle, E. R., & Richardson, R. A. (2000). Digital dating and virtual relating: Conceptualizing computer mediated romantic relationships. *Family Relations, 49*(2), 187–192.
Mileham, B. L. A. (2007). Online infidelity in Internet chat rooms: An ethnographic exploration. *Computers in Human Behavior, 23*(1), 11–31.
Moller, N. P., & Vossler, A. (2015). Defining infidelity in research and couple counseling: A qualitative study. *Journal of Sex & Marital Therapy, 41*(5), 487–497.
Mukherjee, S. (2014, June 25). Adultery cases on rise: Chat trails give divorce lawyers new-age ammunition. *The Times of India*. Retrieved from http://timesofindia.indiatimes.com/city/ben-

galuru/Adultery-cases-on-the-rise-Chat-trails-give-divorce-lawyers-new-age-ammunition/articleshow/37141369.cms.

Petty, R. E., & Brinol, P. (2010). Attitude change. In R. F. Baumiester & E. J. Finkel (Eds.), *Advanced social psychology: The state of the science* (pp. 217–259). New York: Oxford.

Pittman III, F. S., & Wagers, T. P. (1995). Crises of infidelity. Guilford Press.

Raina, P. (2012). For Indian women, divorce is a raw deal. *The New York Times*. Retrieved from http://india.blogs.nytimes.com/2012/03/22/for-indian-women-divorce-a-raw-deal/?src = rechp&_r=0.

Ross, M. W., Månsson, S. A., Daneback, K., Cooper, A., & Tikkanen, R. (2005). Biases in internet sexual health samples: Comparison of an internet sexuality survey and a national sexual health survey in Sweden. Social Science & Medicine, 61(1), 245–252.

Russell, M. (2003). Infidelity online. *The Post-Bulletin, 78*, E4.

Rusbult, C. E. (1993). Understanding responses to dissatisfaction in close relationships: The exit-voiceloyalty-neglect model.

Rusbult, C. E., Johnson, D. J., & Morrow, G. D. (1986). Determinants and consequences of exit, voice, loyalty, and neglect: Responses to dissatisfaction in adult romantic involvements. Human relations, 39(1), 45-63.

Schneider, J. P. (2000). Effects of cybersex addiction on the family: Results of a survey. *Sexual Addiction & Compulsivity: The Journal of Treatment and Prevention, 7*(1–2), 31–58.

Shackelford, T. K., Buss, D. M., & Bennett, K. (2002). Forgiveness or breakup: Sex differences in responses to a partner's infidelity. *Cognition & Emotion, 16*(2), 299–307.

Sheppard, V. J., Nelso, E. S., & Andreoli-Mathie, V. (1995). Dating relationships and infidelity: Attitudes and behaviors. *Journal of Sex & Marital Therapy, 21*(3), 202–212.

Snyder, C. R., & Higgins, R. L. (1988). Excuses: Their effective role in the negotiation of reality. *Psychological Bulletin, 104*(1), 23.

Sonwalker, P. (2015, October 9). Indians among top users of infidelity website Ashley Madison. *The Hindustan Times*. Retrieved from http://www.hindustantimes.com/tech/indians-among-top-users-of-infidelity-website-ashley-madison/story-Q1e6aVwUObBHRzsuoEcKKJ.html.

Sykes, G. M., & Matza, D. (1957). Techniques of neutralization: A theory of delinquency. *American Sociological Review, 22*(6), 664–670.

Tittle, C. R., & Botchkovar, E. V. (2005). Self-control, criminal motivation and deterrence: An investigation using Russian respondents. *Criminology, 43*(2), 307–354.

Topalli, V. (2005). When being good is bad: An expansion of neutralization theory*. *Criminology, 43*(3), 797–836.

Treas, J., & Giesen, D. (2000). Sexual infidelity among married and cohabiting Americans. *Journal of Marriage and Family, 62*(1), 48–60.

Tsapelas, I., Fisher, H. E., & Aron, A. (2011). Infidelity: When, where, why. In W. R. Cupach & B. H. Spitzberg (Eds.), *The dark side of close relationships II* (pp. 175–195). New York: Routledge.

Tyler, T. R. (2002). Is the Internet changing social life? It seems the more things change, the more they stay the same. *Journal of Social Issues, 58*(1), 195–205.

Uberoi, P. (2001). A suitable romance? Trajectories of courtship in Indian popular fiction. In M. Shoma (Eds.), *Images of the 'modern woman in Asia: Global media, local meanings'* (pp. 169–187). Taylor and Francis: London and New York.

Umbrajkar, M. (2012, July 22). Increase the number of family courts in Pune. *The Times of India*. Retrieved from http://timesofindia.indiatimes.com/city/pune/Increase-the-number-of-family--courts-in-Pune/articleshow/15092692.cms.

Varnado, S. (2013). Avatars, Scarlet'A's, and Adultery in the technological age. *Arizona Law Review, 55*(2), 371–416.

Vossler, A., & Moller, N. P. (2014). "The relationship past can't be the future": couple counsellors' experiences of working with infidelity. Sexual and Relationship Therapy, 29(4), 424–435.

Whitty, M. T. (2003). Pushing the wrong buttons: Men's and women's attitudes toward online and offline infidelity. *CyberPsychology & Behavior, 6*(6), 569–579.

Whitty, M. T. (2005). The realness of cybercheating men's and women's representations of unfaithful Internet relationships. *Social Science Computer Review, 23*(1), 57–67.
Wilson, M., & Daly, M. (1995). The man who mistook his wife for a chattel. In J. H. Barkow, L. Cosmides, & J. Tooby (Eds.), *The adapted mind* (pp. 289–322). New York: Oxford.
World Health Organization. (2012). *Understanding and addressing violence against women*. Retrieved from http://apps.who.int/iris/bitstream/10665/77432/1/WHO_RHR_12.36_eng.pdf.
Yeniceri, Z., & Kökdemir, D. (2006). University students' perceptions of, and explanations for, infidelity: The development of the Infidelity Questionnaire (INFQ). *Social Behavior and Personality: An International Journal, 34*(6), 639–650.
Young, K. S. (2004). Internet addiction a new clinical phenomenon and its consequences. *American Behavioral Scientist, 48*(4), 402–415.
Young, K. S., Griffin-Shelley, E., Cooper, A., O'mara, J., & Buchanan, J. (2000). Online infidelity: A new dimension in couple relationships with implications for evaluation and treatment. *Sexual Addiction & Compulsivity: The Journal of Treatment and Prevention, 7*(1–2), 59–74.

Chapter 4
Global Threats But National Legislations—How to Adapt to the New Cyberspace Society

Małgorzata Skórzewska-Amberg

Introduction

The Internet, in its initial phase of development, was primarily a channel for communication and data exchange within the scientific community. For many years only scholars, universities and research institutions had access to the network (Garfinkiel and Spafford 1997, p. 435; Gilster 1995, p. 29; Gołaczyński 2007). Even in 1994, after the opening of the Internet to the world, it was stated that the unusual freedom of expression and the availability of information in the Internet suggest that it may launch a new era for the exchange of information between human beings (Cerf 1995, p. 23). Today, a little more than 20 years later, the world faces the problem of whether and how the exchange of information should be controlled.

The World Wide Web is essentially an inexhaustible source of information and a convenient channel to search and distribute information basically in real time. Through the ICT an information society has evolved—a new type of highly developed and truly global society in which full access to services and information is ensured through ICT technology (Bangemann 1994), enabling the acquisition, processing, storage and dissemination of audio, visual, textual and numeric information through computer networks.[1]

[1] Cf Directive 98/34/EC of the European Parliament and of the Council of 22 June 1998 laying down a procedure for the provision of information in the field of technical standards and regulations, OJ L 204, 21/07/1998 p. 37; amended by Directive 98/48/EC of the European Parliament and of the Council of 20 July 1998 amending Directive 98/34/EC laying down a procedure for the provision of information in the field of technical standards and regulations, OJ L 217, 05/08/1998 p. 18.

M. Skórzewska-Amberg (✉)
Kozminski University School of Law, Warszawa, Poland
e-mail: msa@domus-amberg.com

E.C. Viano (ed.), *Cybercrime, Organized Crime, and Societal Responses*,
DOI 10.1007/978-3-319-44501-4_4

The information society is heavily dependent on IT systems. On the one hand life becomes easier—a lot of things can be done online and in real time, virtually unlimited access to information accessible at any time has been achieved, electronic signature allows, among others, to conclude contracts at distance, settle taxes etc. On the other hand, however, cyberspace has not become exactly a safe place and, unfortunately, is increasingly being used to not only commit crime but also violate social norms.

Transmission of data, including sensitive data, is done electronically, which raises the need for its effective protection. At the same time, widespread availability of the Internet[2] increases the risk of unauthorised access to such data.

The technological revolution has given the man a powerful tool, but has made at the same time vulnerable to an extent not previously encountered. Every rapid development in any field has always been and will be a challenge. More closely—not so much the technological development in itself, but the adaptation of social standards, including in particular the regulatory framework.

Threats in ICT networks are more and more common and increasingly diverse. Their character and structure changes with the development of technology and ever wider participation of the global society in ICT networks. The first type of attacks to be noticed was those which can be considered as vandalism, the second type—attacks aimed at theft of identity or financial information. Targeted attacks (Advanced Persistent Threat, APT), specialised, comprehensive and staged, directed at specific targets can be recognised as the third type of attacks (Attack and Defence 2013, p. 12). Criminals conducting attacks are more and more able to mask their malicious applications and carry them out in an increasingly sophisticated way, making the effective operation of standard security systems difficult or even impossible. Crime (including organised crime) quickly adapts to the environment of advanced technology using ICT systems to commit crimes, more and more often on a global scale. Automated networks are used today for example in economic espionage, extortions, frauds related to financial transactions.

The danger of uncontrolled use of computer and computer networks has been increasingly noticed in the last few years. However, the task of translating the language used by modern technology into proper and effective legal language, reflecting behaviour ostensibly unimportant or of seemingly minor consequence—but in reality causing major damage—turned out to be a most difficult one. At the same time, technology development continues to take a much faster pace than the evolvement of legislation.

Newly adopted law should include the widest possible range of behaviour in cyberspace. This objective is not only of utmost importance and urgency, but also a considerable challenge, especially from the point of view of criminal law. Criminal law is by its very nature repressive and requires precise definition of both the act and the punishment. In the case of constantly evolving cyberspace description of the offenders, behaviour must leave a certain margin, enabling it to adapt the standard to a changing criminal behaviour in the cyberspace.

---

[2]In the middle of 2014 more than 42 % of the world population were Internet users (http://www.internet-worldstats.com/stats.htm, accessed 31 March 2015).

Violence in Cyberspace

Violence in the cyberspace ("cyberbullying") is defined as intentional and repetitive action against individuals or organisations, performed using the ICT (especially the Internet).

Cyberbullying can take a variety of forms, including impersonation (in particular identity theft), disclosure of another person's private information, posting insulting or defamatory information about another person, posting crafted materials relating to another person (including primarily images), blackmail, and threat.

Global computer networks, especially the Internet, are to be considered as means of mass communication (like newspapers, radio, television). The harm caused by such means (e.g. dissemination of false information or photos) is generally very difficult to fix (Szkotnicki 1995, p. 28). The effect of humiliation or loss of public trust can in many cases be irreversible.

To the content appearing in a public network forum the provisions of the Polish Penal Code concerning offences against public order[3] can usually be applied, as well as the provisions in connection to crimes against freedom of conscience and religion[4] and crimes against honour and physical integrity—criminalising defamation[5] (Article 212 of the Penal Code) and insulting another person made by means of mass communication (Article 216 § 2 of the Penal Code).

A different kind of act, which can be committed with the use of computer networks, is acts aiming at threats against other persons. An example of such act is the sending of threatening letters by electronic mail or publishing material of threatening character on network sites. The provisions of the Penal Code apply to unlawful threat defined in Article 115 § 12 of the Penal Code either as a punishable threat, i.e. threatening another person to commit an offence to its detriment or harm people close to that person, or as the threat of causing a criminal proceeding or publish messages offensive to the threatened or to people close to the threatened.[6] To commit an offence under Article 190 § 1 of the Penal Code it is necessary that the threat causes in the threatened person a justified fear that the threat will be fulfilled. The prosecution is carried out on the request of the victim (Article 190 § 2 of the Penal Code).

Illegal threats based on national or ethnic identity, race or with reference to religious denomination (or lack of it), as well as public instigation of violence or illegal threats with reference on such basis, applies to penalty according to Article 119 of the Penal Code.

---

[3] Public promotion of fascism or any other form of totalitarian systems or public incitement to discord on the national, ethnic, racial or religious background (Article 256 of the Penal Code), as well as defamation based on national identity, ethnicity, racism, religious affiliation or lack of denomination (Article 257 of the Penal Code).

[4] Insult religious feelings of other persons committed by public offence towards religious cult objects (Article 196 of the Penal Code).

[5] Libel natural and legal persons or organisations without legal personality with regard to such acts or features, which could bring discredit in the face of public opinion or result in loss of confidence, necessary for a given position, occupation or kind of activity.

[6] According to the Article 115 § 12 of the Penal Code announcement to cause criminal proceedings does not constitute a threat, if it is only to protect the law violated by offence.

Blackmail, i.e. the use of violence or unlawful threat to compel another person to carry out certain acts, omissions or abolition is punished under Article 191 of the Penal Code.

With the exceptions provided for by law, provisions of the criminal law provide for the punishment of application ia: unlawful threat in order to influence the official acts of government authority, other state or local government authority (Article 224 § 1 of the Penal Code), a public official or a person foster to aid (Article 224 § 2 of the Penal Code), the court (Article 232 of the Penal Code), as well as in order to influence a witness, expert, translator, prosecutor or the accused (Article 234 of the Penal Code).

Penalised is also public provocation to commit a misdemeanour or treasury offence (Article 255 § 1 of the Penal Code), crime (Article 255 § 2 of the Penal Code) and public preaching of the offence (Article 255 § 3 of the Penal Code). Qualified type of the public provocation to commit a misdemeanour is, described in Article 119 § 2 of the Penal Code, public incitement to commit a crime of violence or threats against a person or group of persons because of their national, ethnic, racial, political or religious affiliation or lack of denomination.

A threat to commit a criminal act of terrorist character is also considered an illegal threat.

From the point of view of cyberspace behaviour, an interesting question is the possibility to ensure the protection of the individual whose rights are being violated (e.g. defamation or blackmail), in a situation where the infringer can not be unambiguously determined due to the anonymity of access to the network.

Harassment (cyberstalking) is a distinct form of violence in the cyberspace. In the case of violence as well as harassment, the forms of action are similar, but in the case of harassment, action against the perpetrator is targeting specific person with whom the pursuer have a bond. In cases of harassment there is a desire to control the harassed people, even through attacking members of the harassed person's family or other close persons (Kosińska 2008, p. 34).

The criminal law does not define the concept of harassment. Therefore it seems reasonable to use a language definition which describes harassment as continuing tormenting, bothering, harassing and teasing someone, not giving a moment's peace (Szymczak 1979, p. 317).

Such actions can not be single ones (a dictionary describes harassment as a constant, and the legislator has added persistent, i.e. long-drawn, difficult to eradicate, burdensome). Actions which can be regarded as cyberstalking are for example unauthorised creation of social media profiles of harassed person, forcing a meeting with the tormented person (Kosińska 2008, pp. 33–34; Bocji 2004, pp. 9–13), publishing pictures of harassed person in the network.

Prohibition of harassment (including harassment in cyberspace) is included in Article 190a § 1 of the Penal Code, which penalise actions of a perpetrator who through persistent harassment of another person or persons close to him/her,[7] rises a legitimate sense of danger or indeed violates his/her privacy.

[7] According to Article 115 § 11 of the Penal Code person close to someone means spouse, ascendant, descendant, sibling, relative in the same line or degree, the adopted person and his or her spouse, as well as a person staying in cohabitation.

With the development of computer networks, including mobile network, sexting, i.e. sending sexually explicit messages (i.e. naked or half-naked pictures)—primarily between mobiles, becomes a growing problem. The phenomenon began with the sending of photos between emotionally involved adolescents, increasingly turned into violence—attack on an individual in cyberspace. Sexting is criminalised in Article 191a of the Penal Code, which protects the privacy and intimacy of individual prohibiting fraudulent, or made with the use of violence or illegal threat, recording of a naked person or person in the course of sexual activity, as well as dissemination of the image of a naked person or person in a sexual act carried out without the consent of the person whose image was recorded.

Fraud and Identity Theft

Fraud can be defined, in the simplest possible way, as consciously misleading of someone—for the fraudster's benefit. There is no doubt that for example the sale of a non-existing item can be classified as a fraud. But what happens when for example a non-existing person takes a loan in the name of a real person, e.g. by stealing his or her data such as tax identification number or social security number?

In the era of rapid development of information and communication technologies, issues of impersonation, i.e. adopting a different identity, becomes increasingly important. Of course, hiding one's own identity does not always means a violation of the law, but we deal more and more often with identity thefts in order to for example defraud credit or to create entirely fictitious identity, e.g. in social networking services—in order to harm another person.

Fraud

Spoofing, i.e. tampering with network services and protocols in order to hide the identity of the perpetrator, is an example of cyberspace fraud. With the use of various spoofing methods,[8] it is possible to i.a. gain unauthorised network access to such confidential information as login, passwords, credit card numbers and personal data.

Fraud, defined in Article 286 § 1 of the Penal Code, is bringing another person to unfavourable disposition of one's own or someone else's property by misleading this person or making use of any mistake, as well as taking advantage of this person's inability to assess properly the actions taken—in order to gain financial benefit.

[8] Spoofing is very general form and a whole series of its variations can be distinguished. For example *IP spoofing* consisting of sending messages (IP datagrams) with changed IP of the sender in order to make it difficult or impossible to disclose the real source of information; *data spoofing* modifies data between hosts in a communication session; *e-mail spoofing* is when unauthorised electronic mail is sent in the name of other persons.

Misleading is described as behaviour intended to cause a false perception of reality (e.g. concealing defects in purchased goods), while the use of mistake—lack of correction, clarification or specification of the actual state of affairs (Skorupka 2000, p. 45). Taking advantage of a person's inability to assess properly the actions taken, means persuading this person to dispose of the property, at the moment he or she is not in a position to properly assess the significance and consequences of their actions (Skorupka 2000, p. 45). Such inability may be permanent or temporary, or even momentary.[9]

Unfavourable disposition includes any property decisions (Górniok 2002, pp. 11–12), while identity between the person making the disposition of the confiscated property and the wronged person is not necessary. What matters only is the identity of the "deceived" person (Korczyński and Koszut 2002, p. 17).

The criminal condition of the actions described in article 286 of the Penal Code is directed towards the person—body, who can commit a mistake, or be in a condition excluding the correct understanding of the actions taken. The problem arises when financial benefit obtained by the offender, or the wrong caused by the offender's deed, result from data processing system. In such case a machine cannot be blamed, for the mode of its action is determined by a human who controls it. From the point of view of the discussed issues, two cases are of particular interest: firstly, error of the person compiling software; secondly, human activity with the intention to cause damage or to profit. Such activity can consist of altering the software, introduce incorrect data or manipulate the result of processing.[10]

A malfunctioning software causing, e.g. adding sum fractions to bank accounts in connection with financial transactions does not have to be aimed to violate the law. Such software should not be introduced before the end of its testing period, making sure that such mistakes and irregularities will not take place. If the operation of such software nonetheless results in unintentional change of property of a wronged person, then liability shall be applied—but not for fraud since the action was not taken in order to obtain financial benefit by misleading or making use of any mistake. However, activity intended to obtain financial benefit or to cause damage to another person by affecting data processing or violation of digital information is an activity which shall be liable under criminal law as a fraud.

The condition of liability according to Article 287 of the Penal Code is an activity intended to obtain financial benefit or cause damage to another person.

---

[9] The Supreme Court, in the judgment of 30 August 2000 (V KKN 267/00, OSNKW 2000, no. 9-10, item 85), indicates that the constituent elements of the offence, described in Article 286 § 1 of the Penal Code, will be filled if the perpetrator, "acting in the manner described in this article, leads the other person to dispose of the property in a way that is detrimental to the interests of this person or other wronged person", while stressing that "the injury to the property is not a necessary condition to accept that there has been so understood unfavourable disposition".

[10] Computer fraud, from a technical point of view, takes most often the form of input, software or output manipulation. Input manipulation means unauthorised entering, concealing or modifying data in a computer system (adding, for example, fictitious overtime figures into the system). Software manipulation is the change of software operation to enable fraud (for example altering a software serving finance transactions in such a way that fractions emerging from normal rounding off sums are transferred to an account of the perpetrator). Output manipulation most often facilitates concealing other committed offences.

Computer Fraud

Criminal liability for computer fraud is described in Article 287 of the Penal Code as fraud committed with the use of devices for automatic processing, storing or transferring of data. Computer fraud comprises no element of misleading another person by the offender or making use of his or her mistake. To exhaust the constituent elements of the offence, the fact of technological influence on data processing is essential. Also the activity of the offender who acts in order to obtain financial benefit or to cause damage to another person is not aimed directly at the wronged person (Michalski 2010, p. 1174). Not only the activity consisting of changing (or erasing) data stored in the computer system, modifying or interfering in data processing software operation or changing the information as a result of processing but also mechanical interference in the data processing devices or connecting to the system of data transmission, meet the criteria of the offence described in Article 287 of the Penal Code. Change, deletion or entry of data, i.e. modification of information on data storage device, meet the criteria of the offence described in Article 287 of the Penal Code. Such modifications can be made both on the actual data storage device and in the ICT networks. The offence may involve for example redirection of bank transfers or such modification of the financial application which results in adding bank interests to the account of the unauthorised person. Another example of computer fraud is *carding*, i.e. activity involving the use of legal tenders from a credit card whose number has been stolen, e.g. while carrying out financial transaction on the Internet.

An essential question refers to specifying the subject of protection described in Article 287 of the Penal Code, especially with respect to new types of fraud, distinguished by ICT, in particular phishing[11] or pharming.[12] Placing computer fraud in the chapter referring to offence against property indicates that the aim of Article 287 of the Penal Code is the protection of property. According to Article 44 of the Civil Code, property is the ownership or other proprietary rights (both real rights other than property and proprietary rights resulting from the relations between property and persons). Article 287 of the Penal Code protects the property, i.e. all the proprietary rights confirmation of which is the record in the system storing, processing or automatically transmitting the data or the record on the computer data storage device, or property which refers to such record (Michalski 1999, p. 220).

The condition of liability according to Article 287 of the Penal Code is the activity intended to obtain financial benefit or cause damage to another person.

[11] Phishing is a form of e-mail spoofing and consists primarily of sending messages in the name of a trusted sender (e.g. auction sites, social web portals, financial institutions) while providing links to concocted Internet sites—in order to extort information (including information which can be used for identity theft) or to cause damage.

[12] Pharming consist of redirecting the user to a concocted www site (often difficult to distinguish from the authentic one), while making it possible to extract confidential information (including information which can be used for identity theft) or to cause damage.

Identity Theft

Identity theft is a form of usurpation of another person's identity, impersonation of another person by assuming that person's identity—usually to cause harm or to gain unfair advantage. Identity theft occurs when someone uses information identifying another person (e.g. name and surname of another person), without this person's authorisation and in order to cause harm.

There are several basic categories of identity theft[13]:

- Criminal identity theft (impersonating another person to commit an offence).
- Financial identity theft[14] (impersonating another person in order to obtain credit, goods or services).
- Identity cloning (impersonating another person in order to use its identity in everyday life).
- Medical identity theft (impersonating another person in order to receive medical care and medicines).
- Identity theft of children (children data used to gain unfair advantage).

Identity theft, more specifically impersonating another person, is criminalised in Article 190a § 2 of the Penal Code, which penalises the behaviour of the offender who while pretending to be another person, uses an image or other personal information of this person—in order to cause personal or financial harm.

Article 6 § 1 of the Data Protection Act of 29 August 1997 (consolidated text: Journal of Laws of 2014 item 1182) defines personal data as any information relating to an identified or identifiable natural person. On the one hand, therefore, "personal data are any information relating to an identified or foreseeable to identify person, and not only such information, which are used to identify" (Barta et al. 2011, p. 344), on the other hand—it is not clear if for example information about digital profiles (such as username or login, password) always can be considered as personal data. Identity theft is a directional crime carried out in order to cause personal or financial harm. However, the law does not regulate the issue of unauthorised collecting of data that could be used for identity theft or impersonation another person (particularly in the ICT era). The content of Article 190a § 2 of the Pena Code clearly indicates that the aim of the perpetrator is to cause harm to the impersonated person. It remains an open question when it comes to impersonating another person without any intention of causing harm, as well as in cases when the perpetrator accept that the impersonated person suffers harm, but when the real aim of the perpetrator's

[13] According to the Identity Theft Resource Center, a non-profit organisation dedicated to identity theft monitoring and providing assistance to identity theft victims (8 March 2014 at http://www.idtheftcenter.org).

[14] This category can also include the so-called. administrative identity theft (governmental identity theft), including i.a. theft of personal data in order to obtain documents (e.g. driving licence), unemployment benefits or other state benefits etc.

action is to cause harm to someone else entirely. It seems that regardless of any questions asked in connection to this provision, it could be worth to consider to eliminate the determination of the person to whom the offender causes harm and to leave the provision as follows "the same punishment shall be subject to whoever pretends to be another person, uses his or her image or other personal information in order to cause personal or financial harm shall be subject to the punishment of ...".

There is no doubt that article 190a § 2 of the Penal Code penalises only such behaviour of the offender, which concerns a really existing person. The data of fictitious person are not personal data within the meaning of the Data Protection Act.

However, it seems worth to consider a discussion on the criminalisation of impersonation someone else for the sole purpose of hiding one's identity (without the element of harming a person whose identity is being used), in order to harm another person. The problem of creating a fictitious identity (in particular digital profiles) in order to harm another person may increase in the future, e.g. in order to use such profiles as a tool of blackmail or threats.

The *ratio legis* of the article 190a § 2 of the Penal Code is "first of all to ensure the protection of the freedom of decision how information about your personal life can be used", so it seems that the subject of the protection is freedom of decision, i.a. on the use of someone's personal information. Identity theft in the intention of the Polish legislator is a form of stalking—it is, moreover, indicated by gathering these two crimes in one provision. In the doctrine, it is pointed out that given the nature of the offence, a better place for its implementation would be a chapter on offences against honour and physical integrity (Lach 2012), but it seems that the assignment of identity theft crimes against freedom is correct, since the freedom of the individual, including primarily the freedom of decision, is being violated when the perpetrator impersonating another person acts as if being made on his or her behalf, although without authorisation and with the intention to cause him or her harm.

Is It Always a Fraud and Just a Fraud?

Comparing the definitions of fraud and identity theft, elements of joint-action can be seen—deliberate and unauthorised actions with the intention to cause harm to a person against whom the action is directed.

The premise of criminality of the action described in the article 286 of the Penal Code is an action directed at the person in question, an object who can make a mistake or be in a position where he or she is not able to properly assess the significance and consequences of their action. The purpose of article 286 of the Penal Code is undoubtedly property protection.

Article 287 of the Penal Code protects all proprietary rights confirmed by the corresponding record in the system storing, processing or automatically transmitting the data or the record on the computer data storage device, or property which refers to such record (Michalski 1999, p. 220). Thus if computer data[15] are not connected with proprietary rights, violation of their integrity is not subject to the provisions of property protection but is subject to the provisions described in the chapter referring to the offence against information protection. Therefore, the type of computer data, and more specifically—relation between such data and property rights, or the lack of it—determines the classification of the offence—it could be a fraud, but in many cases it is to be considered a violation of the integrity of the information, or action against protection of information—and not a fraud.

The condition of being liable according to Article 287 of the Penal Code is the activity intended to obtain financial benefit or cause damage to another person. An activity intended to do this is not necessary when it comes to offence against information protection (Michalski 2010, p. 1174).

Therefore, in many cases, fraud in a common meaning will be treated by criminal law as a number of very different behaviours. What connects these behaviours is the purpose to cause harm to another person. Economic loss whenever the law defines as fraud, and personal harm whenever it is a case of identity theft. It should be noted as well that in some cases, an activity that seems to fill the description of identity theft—ultimately can be also be punishable as fraud—for instance, if the perpetrator wants to harm another person and to do this impersonates that person using his or her identification data. As a result of the perpetrator's activities, the impersonated person is considered to be a fraudster. If the offender misleads a third person and brings that person to unfavourable disposition of his or her property, then the offender is guilty of fraud. If the confidence of the cheated person to the person whose data was used is undermined—the perpetrator may also be responsible for identity theft.

Theft of Virtual Goods

Activities undertaken in virtual reality exist only in that framework (i.e. in a reality artificially created) and should not exert direct effects in the real world. At the same time, the technological revolution, making societies heavily dependent on ICT, had moved a large part of human activity to the cyberspace, while allowing such activity to cause consequences in the real world. From the legal point of view the distinction between virtual reality and virtual space (cyberspace) is extremely important. The cyberspace is part of a virtual reality, its subset covering a platform of storing, processing and transmitting information. Actions taken in the cyberspace will be of interest to the law, as long as they—at least in theory—have implications in the real world.

An example of such penetration of the virtual and real world are computer games. Player profile, in particular one that has won all sorts of game-related bonuses and

[15] Computer data, mentioned in Article 287 par. 1 of the Penal Code, is all data, manipulation of which may lead to obtain financial benefit or cause damage to another person.

perks as extra weapons, can often be worth a lot, e.g. when the player passes his profile to another person. Only in the USA it is a market worth billions of dollars (Herzfeld 2012). These profiles can have a tangible material value, measured in total amount obtained, e.g. from the sale of such profile.

These types of goods are increasingly subject to theft—in the usual meaning of the word. Virtual property can be acquired as a result of unauthorised access to a computer system, phishing or pharming attacks etc. (Newman 2007; Cluley 2010). It happens, however, that access to such virtual goods is obtained through for example extortion or robbery. The first case should be considered on the basis of legal provisions protecting data integrity (where the information as such is the subject of an offence, i.e. unauthorised access to a computer system, destruction, alteration or concealment of information etc.) or penalising fraud. In the second case the situation is more complicated.

The subject matter of the theft provided under Article 278 of the Penal Code is someone else's movable property. The Civil Law defines property as a tangible item. However, from a civil point of view property could also consist of documents providing the existence of a right and of securities. *Sui generis*, money is property as well. Also the Penal Law (Article 115 § 9 of the Penal Code) defines money or other means of payment as well as documents entitling to a sum of money as property. For example, a payment card is such a document.

The Penal Code uses the term "movable property", which in some circumstances can cause unnecessary narrowing of the responsibility on the part of the offender. It would be worth considering to restore the term "property" rather than use the rather civilistic expression "movable property" to describe the executive subject of the crimes against property. In certain circumstances not only a computer hardware, but also digitally stored data, could be treated as an object to which the provision relates. If the concept of property is to be treated in the same way as in the previous Penal Codes (1932 and 1969), then also a document of material value should be considered as a property. That would, in certain cases, allow to prosecute also as theft, digital data breaches, e.g. if the infringement applies to the publication of an ordered text intended to be published. It would be also interesting to stretch the concept of property on virtual goods that may have material value, e.g. through sale of such goods.

Anonymity in the Network—A Value or Problem?

One of the biggest challenges that the law sooner or later will have to confront, primarily in the context of the protection of the rights of the individual, is the problem of the anonymous user of network services. It becomes necessary to start the analysis and discussion of whether the right to anonymity of networks users is a fundamental one and to which degree it is a value—and therefore should not be subject to restrictions, or if it also can be a threat—which raises the need to develop rules limiting the anonymity of the user in a way that not violates the personal rights of the user. The problem of anonymity, or more precisely—difficulties in identifying the user (and not only the IP address of the host)—and hence the perpetrator—is essential. Solutions that enable the protection of the rights of the individual, regardless of the setting of the perpetrator, should therefore be developed and adopted.

The discussion on methods of securing the rights of the individual in a situation of their violation in the cyberspace should not be omitted. It is important to consider, first of all, cases where the direct infringer can not be determined (for example, when the IP address of the host is known, but it could not be conclusively determined who benefited from the terminal), or when the perpetrator can be determined, but when the content that is of interest of the law, available in its national jurisdiction, physically is outside the country.

It should be remembered that most of the currently used devices with Internet access are equipped with a webcam (i.e. laptops, tablets, netbooks, smartphones). It is not difficult to imagine a situation in which such a device can be used as a remote-controlled tapping device, acting without the knowledge of its user. This is just one of the many cases in which anonymity of the network user, who remotely runs processes in other devices connected to the network, can prevent legal protection of the individual.

The anonymity of Internet users,[16] threats to privacy and lack of control over illegal content posted on the Internet are a growing problem and can often constitute a violation of freedom and security of an individual.

Observing the discussion on the issue of limitation of anonymity in the Internet or blocking certain content, or in general—limitations of unfettered freedom of access to the network—it seems that someone may wonder if Thomas Hobbes was entirely wrong, denying Aristotle's thesis about the social nature of man. Hobbes, in his *philosophia civilis,* recognised the human being for an egoist, whose sole purpose is the own good and the good is everything that serves his purposes—even if it is bad for another individual, being contrary to the interests of that individual. It is for reason and fear of harm Hobbes derived the creation of the state (Tatarkiewicz 2001, p. 68). The state created a law, and the law defined the limitations of freedom. The legal limitation of freedom of individual is defined by the measure of freedom of another man.

The law should be integrally linked with freedom. John Stuart Mill pointed out that the law is intended to guarantee that the freedom of the individual is not violated as a result of the activities of another individual. "The only purpose for which power can be rightfully exercised over any member of a civilised community, against his will, is to prevent harm to others" (Mill 1998, p. 68).

[16] University, research or corporate networks are mostly intended for users whose identity is known to the network administrator and the authors of any information provided within the network are relatively easy trackable (although users with the guest access may be a problem). Also, the Internet Service Provider (ISP) in most cases it is able to provide information about the IP address (host address on the network; IP address prefix indicates a network, while the address suffix—particular computer on the network indicated by the prefix)—although it not always mean that is possible to determine the identity of a particular person.

It seems inevitable that solutions that reduce to some extent the anonymity of network users have to be introduced. It should be emphasised that this is not about a disclosure of identity to other users, but to provide for the possibility to determine a specific person in case of violation of the law. For instance, an electronic signature can be used to ensure the possibility of establishing a network user's identity. If it is possible to associate the user with a particular person[17]—then only such user are liable for the actions in the network. Otherwise, i.e. if the service provider does not require proof of identity of the service recipient, then imposing on a service provider an obligation to assist law enforcement in his/her services could be considered.[18] Such an obligation could for example include the need for constant supervision of the content available through his/her services, and erase what violates the law.

There is a consensus as for the fact that unlawful content should be eliminated from the Internet. However, this consent relates to the removal of prohibited content, not blocking access to it. The problem of information prohibited by law lies in the fact that they are not always to be found in places which are under the jurisdiction of a state, whose law criminalises such information. It is also impossible to remove illegal content without the permission and cooperation of the State, where the servers that provide such information are located. The solution to be considered in such situations is the blocking of websites providing illegal content. Discussion on blocking and removal of websites containing content prosecuted by the law is very lively, albeit not a new one. Objections raised concerning the lack of effectiveness of such actions are of course legitimate, however it does not change the fact that blocking websites containing illegal content works in some European countries (in some stipulated by law, in others as the result of an agreement between ISP) and in a situation where most of the pages containing banned content are located on servers outside the jurisdiction of the EU Member States—is currently the simplest solution of the problem.[19]

Over the centuries jurisprudence continually emphasises that power should serve justice and the general good, otherwise it results in the formation of law devoid of legitimacy. Herbert Hart emphasising the primacy of the law in relation to policy, states that ensuring the autonomy of law protects it from instrumental use, and determining the functioning of the state makes the operation of power predictable and objectified (Oniszczuk 2008, p. 485).

---

[17] During registration a user should credibly prove his/her identity and links with the name, which is used in the network.

[18] Within the framework of the European Union, the liability of service providers (or more precise—when the service provider is not liable for the service content) is defined in Directive 2000/31/EC of the European Parliament and of the Council of 8 June 2000 on certain legal aspects of information society services, in particular electronic commerce, in the Internal Market (Directive on electronic commerce, OJ L 178, 17.7.2000, p. 1).

[19] For example Article 25 of the Directive 2011/92/EU of the European Parliament and of the Council of 13 December 2011 on combating the sexual abuse and sexual exploitation of children and child pornography, and replacing Council Framework Decision 2004/68/JHA (OJ L 335, 17.12.2011, p 1), requiring fast removal of websites containing illegal materials (in this case related to child pornography)—provides for the possibility to block access to Internet pages containing or disseminating child pornography, if these sites can not be deleted.

The proposed solutions have therefore *raison d'être* only in a democratic state with rule of law. In any other case it may constitute a threat to the individual. Here John Locke may be recalled. According to him the rule of law in a country serving the public good can not be random, unjustified and arbitrary, but should be based on established and announced rights. Established standards and constituted according to them, the law can not violate the rights of individuals (Locke 2002, pp. 60–66).

Freedom and its limitation in the name of freedom of another, in the name of human being or state security—remains an extremely difficult problem, the solution of which certainly requires a balance between security requirements and guarantees of freedom and civil rights. It can be considered that action in accordance with Immanuel Kant's categorical imperative "Act in accordance with that maxim which can at the same time make itself into a universal law" (Kant 2002, p. 55), could postpone the need for resolving the problem of freedom and security in cyberspace by a way of legislation. Those who argue that the Internet should remain free, unfettered, anonymous and uncontrolled, should, however, bear in mind the words of Aristotle: in "a democracy under the law there are no demagogues (…). Demagogues arise (…) where the laws are not sovereign" (Aristotle 1995, p. 275).

Crimes of Terrorist Nature

In the future it can be expected that attacks on computer systems will be even more common, primarily aimed at structures on which modern societies are built. The target of a terrorist attack could constitute a computer network or more preferably public, social or economic structures (for example banks, research institutions, nuclear plants etc.), all functioning on the basis of such networks.

A terrorist attack is most often associated with bombing, but it should be assumed that cyberspace will soon be the primary arena for terrorist attacks, and in the coming years it is expected that attacks on computer systems will be increasingly more common. It is expected that the target of such attacks will mainly be the banking infrastructure and other so called critical infrastructure. Successful attacks of this kind have already taken place i.a. in Estonia, Lithuania and Georgia.

Such spectacular attacks can, of course, both be detected, as well as prevented. However, this can not be achieved without close international cooperation, both in the field of lawmaking, as well as law enforcement.[20]

Responsibility for participation in an organised group or association aimed at committing a crime, in particular a group or a compound of an armed nature, or intended

---

[20] In Europe, such cooperation is carried out within the European Network and Information Security Agency (ENISA), whose task is to ensure an effective level of security in networks and information systems in the EU. In 2008 NATO Cooperative Cyber Defence Centre of Excellence was established in Tallin. From 2013, within Europol, also operates the European Cybercrime Centre (EC3).

to commit terrorist crimes, is governed by the provisions of the criminal law of most States. European Union members are obliged by Council Framework Decision of 13 June 2002 on combating terrorism (OJ L 164, 22.6.2002, p 3) to take the necessary measures to ensure the adoption of a specific definition of terrorist offences, including offences relating to a terrorist group, offences linked to terrorist activities and to establish more severe penalties, if the offence is related to terrorism.

Polish solutions in that field are that the crime of terrorist nature is an offence, punishable by imprisonment with a maximum of at least 5 years, intended to seriously intimidate or coerce public authorities of the Republic of Poland or of another State or an international organisation authority to perform or abstain from certain activities, or causing a serious disturbance in constitutional system or the economy of the Republic of Poland, another state or an international organisation (Article 115 § 20 of the Penal Code). Such threats are considered in itself a terrorist crime (Wąsek 2005, p. 874).

These behaviours can fill the constituent elements of the offence, i.a. intentional disclosure or use of state secrets, where the direct object of protection are fundamental interests of the State (Article 265 § 1 and 2 of the Penal Code); the so-called computer sabotage, by calling potential danger to public by the criminal impact on automatic processing, gathering or transmission of computer data (Article 165 § 1 point 4 of the Penal Code) or sabotage in relation to computer data of particular importance for national defence, public security, functioning of government administration, other state authority or institution or local government (Article 269 of the Penal Code); significant disruption of a computer system or data communications network (Article 269a of the Penal Code), as well as money laundering, i.e. taking actions that may frustrate or significantly hinder the criminal origin of means of payment, securities and other items described in Article 299 § 1, 2, 5 and 6 of the Penal Code, which is closely linked with the provisions of the Act of 16 November 2000 on Combating Money Laundering and Financing of the Terrorism (consolidated text Journal of Laws of 2014 item 455).

The criminalisation of participation in an organised terrorist group is to be found in Article 258 of the Penal Code.

Polish Penal Code shall also be applied to a foreigner who committed a terrorist offence abroad (Article 110 § 1 of the Penal Code). Also Article 16 paragraph 1 point 12 of the Act of 28 October 2002 on liability of collective entities for acts prohibited under penalty (consolidated text: Journal of Laws of 2014 item 1417, as amended) provides liability of a collective entity, if the person acting on its behalf or cooperating with it, committed a terrorist offence. These regulations are the result of the obligation imposed by Article 9 and Article 7 of the Council Framework Decision of 13 June 2002 on combating terrorism (OJ L 164, 22.6.2002, p 3).

Terrorist groups and associations, as well as organised crime, their financing and organisation, as well as the availability of equipment has an international dimension. Hence the need for international cooperation in control of the trade in arms, explosives, equipment and components for the production of weapons and manufacturing bombs and transportation of used components.

Convergence of the Law—A Necessity in Information Society

The Internet evolved on the basis of lack of fixed, strict rules of conduct, but this has not meant an absence of rules in general. The scientific community was able to effectively enforce respect for freedom of all its network users, where the excessive freedom of action of some menaced the freedom of others. The development of a global network and its free and open public access has forced a legal intervention. This is to cover the Internet as a public medium used by individuals whose freedom must be protected but whose unlawful action must be punished.

The nature of the global network is its sheer size and the fact that it is global, and thus with different territorial affiliation of the network nodes. A global network linked to different legal systems is a primary concern and one that is difficult to solve. In the second half of the twentieth century, two opposing ideas of the legal system in cyberspace have emerged. According to one of them autonomous and sovereign legal order in cyberspace should be created (Hardy 1994; Johnson and Post 1996), according to the other—legal actions carried out in the cyberspace relate to physical entities and should therefore remain subject to the legal authority of its jurisdiction (Goldsmith 1998; Reed 2004).

It should be emphasised that these two concepts are primarily related to issues concerning commercial transactions in the network. Today, one of the most pressing problems of global networks are violations which fall within the area of criminal law—and criminal law should not be beyond the control of the state.

A convergence of different legal systems could be an effective solution to the problems of criminal violations in global networks, and more specifically harmonisation of the law in close international cooperation. A case in point would be the EU legislation, which produces a legal framework for the domestic law of the Member States. The problem, however, will always appear on the edge between different legal cultures, especially with regard to the prohibition of certain conducts, and theirs criminalisation. Infringements in cyberspace are classic examples highlighting such ambiguity. Situations which today can not be anticipated, or which recently have been seen as belonging to the realm of fantasy, and which suddenly becomes a reality will happen more and more often. Technology is obviously developing much faster than the legislative process. It is also vital that the language, used by modern technology must be translated into the language of the law. Adopted law should include the widest possible range of behaviours in cyberspace.

The creation of a fully autonomous legal system applicable in cyberspace does not seem neither realistic nor practical. The ongoing technical and social development on a global scale and the increasingly close integration of the cyberspace with the real space—whereas these two intertwined faces of the future global society will be difficult to separate—indicates that autonomous legal solutions for the cyberspace are not a feasible path to follow. It should also be noted that the imposition of any restrictions on the Internet freedom is met with fierce opposition and raises widely heated debate. It seems obvious that the international community has to strive for a legal system which is both common, rather than national, when it comes to the fundamental elements with global implications, as well as applicable to whatever aspect of the society it has to deal with—within the cyberspace or in the real space.

Conclusions

The rate of growth of the Internet allows to assume that undesirable behaviours will appear faster and at the increasingly common scale. It is difficult to predict what new—or indeed known but improved—methods of breaches of the security of the network and information transmitted with its use and safety of users benefiting from it may soon arise.

Reliable protection of interests of the users of computer networks may be the use of cryptography, but it also has negative consequences. Communicating by means of transmitting encrypted information to a large degree protects privacy and a subsequent confidentiality of correspondence, but at the same time substantially hinders the ability to read the information in those cases that due to other protected goods require a violation of such secrecy,[21] e.g. when the authorised bodies intercepts encrypted content. Modern cryptographic techniques enable very effective encryption, where the only way to uncover the content is through uneconomical, brute attack. Therefore legislators seek to protect the interests of the state, where there is authorised interception of data transmission. Provisions concerning authorised data interception often impose on entities that provide cryptographic support an obligation to decrypt intercepted content (§ 7 and § 8 of the regulation of Minister of Justice dated 24 June 2003 on technical preparation of the network used for transmission of information (...) to control transfers of information and manner of making, registration, storage, playback, and destruction of records with controlled transfers, Journal of Laws of 2003 No 110 item 1052). However, there is no legal possibility[22] to order the decryption of communication to the person which, for example has itself prepared a code of an encryption algorithm (e.g. using the available algorithms).

Attacks on the financial sector are increasingly common, primarily with banks and other financial institutions as targets. One of the simplest examples of spoofing

[21] Authorization to acquaint with the content of transmitted information is included in the rules of procedure and made subject to a number of conditions, of which the most important are: suppression of the possibility of data transmission interception in a situation in which there is a reasonable suspicion of committing the offence; the need to obtain the consent of the court to intercept the information content and the supervision of the competent authorities on the process of information interception (Article 218, 218a, 230a, 236-242 of the Code of Criminal Procedure, Article 159, 160, 161, § 2, 179, 180 of the Telecommunications Law of 16 July 2004 (consolidated text: Journal of Laws of 2014 item 243, as amended) and the provisions concerning the surveillance other than trial one contained in specific laws).

[22] In accordance with the generally applicable legal principle that no one may be forced to disclose an evidence incriminating him or herself.

(e-mail spoofing, and more specific phishing) is sending letters allegedly coming from reputable senders (very often PayPal or Apple). Such letter, frequently referring to alleged attempts of unauthorised access, contains a request to change personal data, offering a link to a page (which of course is controlled by an offender) where such change should be made. The innovative tools and new methods of extortion and theft of funds from bank accounts are more and more common, also in Poland. That includes new malware (such as PowerZeus, vmZeuS, Citadela, VBKlip), infections of mobile devices (E-Security, Antivirus), attacks on routers and DNS servers—in order to force payment,[23] ransomware[24] attacks.

Criminals usually try to get as much information as they can, normally more than they are entitled to. They often focus on information vulnerable from a security perspective, e.g. access codes, or try to change the content of electronic transmissions. Malware and botnets[25] are the most commonly used for this type of action.

The basic principle of protection against any attack remains the same, the data is safe in the extent to which the weakest point in the security chain is protected. An important aspect, if not the most important, is to educate and train of users of ICT—in combination with the use of different protection schemes.

Certain behaviours becoming an increasing threat in the ICT era are not criminalised per se (e.g. the creation of fictitious identities, stealing virtual goods), while others are only criminalised in some countries (e.g. identity theft). Many of the existing legislative solutions do not cover certain activities in the cyberspace. Identity theft is just one example. Existing solutions, if dealt with in the context of cyberspace, raise two doubts concerning the scope and limit of criminalisation. Firstly, is possession of digital data, which can potentially be used to impersonate a real person, in itself an act to cause damage? Secondly, should the sole act to create fictitious identity in order to cause damage to another person be criminalised?

Cloud computing, which is developing very dynamically, also makes it necessary to rethink the existing legal solutions—including those concerning privacy aspects. Legal issues related to cross-border flow of personal data can be indicated here—existing solutions do not envisage a situation in which data managed in a particular country may be processed in the cloud—i.e. in a place which may be both uncertain and variable. Given that cloud computing provides a lot more of computer power and software tools are cheaper than existing "stationary" solutions, it is

[23] Attacks are designed to impede or prevent the operation of the service. Frequently visited sites, like common auction sites and banks are the most frequent targets. The requirement to stop the attack is to pay the criminals a certain amount of money.

[24] Ransomware attacks are so far mostly infecting a computer with malware (worms, exploit kits, etc.), causing the computer to lock. A message is displayed on the computer screen informing that suspicious activity of the computer was detected by the police and that there is a need to pay a fine to have the lock removed.

[25] A group of computers infected with malware, hidden from the computer user. The bootmaster (the bootnet owner) remotely controls the computers included in the botnet with the use of managing servers, enabling for example remote distribute malware or to perform other attacks with the use of botnet.

expected in the not too distant future that programming and processing outside the cloud may become less and less common and in the end uneconomic. The law should be prepared for this.

In view of constantly evolving technologies, it is difficult to talk about any specific anticipation of problems that can be encountered in the distant future—especially considering that the future that even a decade ago appeared to be distant, is examined in terms of the past, due to the ongoing technological revolution. It should be noted, however, that the infringing actions in cyberspace are no longer exclusively the domain of "classic" crime and become increasingly part of an information warfare. Violation of the integrity of information, cyberbullying (in particular threat and blackmail), actions destabilising the financial system, attacks on critical infrastructure are increasingly part of organised intelligence activities.

Presented here is only a fraction of the problems associated with the lawmaking and law enforcement in the information society. The huge challenges of copyright protection and combating piracy on the net, uneven development of computerisation in public life in various countries and the difficulties posed by this also in dealings with the administration for people who are permanently resident outside the place of "administrative affiliation" etc. should not be forgotten. A lot has already been done, there is a wealth of well-used legislative experience of other countries, the endeavours made by the United Nations, the Council of Europe and the OECD, and above all the indication of the European Union law. The challenge is still huge.

Once again, as many times in the past, the forms of threat are continuously changing, while their content remains fairly constant. And how many times in the future—the law, without changing its substance, must adapt itself to a changing reality?

References

Aristotle. (1995). *The politics. Oxford World's classics ebook*. Oxford: Oxford University Press.

Bangemann, M. (1994). *Report: Europe and the global information society*. Retrieved May 4, 2015, from http://cordis.europa.eu/news/rcn/2730_en.html.

Barta, J., Fajgielski, P., & Markiewicz, R. (2011). *Ochrona danych osobowych. Komentarz*. Warszawa: Wolters Kluwer Polska.

Bocji, P. (2004). *Cyberstalking: Harassment in the Internet age and how to protect your family*. Westport, CT: Praeger Publishers.

Cerf, V. G. (1995). Przedmowa. In P. Gilster (Ed.), *Internet. Przewodnik użytkownika* (pp. 23–25). Warsaw: Wydawnictwa Naukowo-Techniczne.

Cluley, G. (2010). *Police search for stolen virtual furniture from Habbo Hotel*. Retrieved May 7, 2015, from https://nakedsecurity.sophos.com/2010/06/01/police-search-stolen-virtual-furniture-habbo-hotel.

Attack and Defence 2013. (2014). *Report: Attacks and methods of defence on the Internet in Poland*. Retrieved May 4, 2015, from https://www.cybsecurity.org/wp-content/uploads/2014/01/Raport_AiO2013.pdf.

Garfinkiel, S., & Spafford, G. (1997). *Bezpieczeństwo w Unixie i Internecie*. Warszawa: Wydawnictwo RM.

Gilster, P. (1995). *Internet. Przewodnik użytkownika*. Warszawa: Wydawnictwa Naukowo-Techniczne.

Gołaczyński, J. (2007). *Umowy elektroniczne w prawie prywatnym międzynarodowym*. Warszawa: Wolters Kluwer Polska.
Goldsmith, J. L. (1998). Against cyberanarchy. *The University of Chicago Law Review, 65*, 1199–1250.
Górniok, O. (2002). "Niekorzystne rozporządzenie" i "cudze mienie" jako znamiona przestępstwa oszustwa (na tle niektórych sposobów wyłudzeń nieruchomości). *Prokuratura i Prawo, 9*, 7–13.
Hardy, I. T. (1994). The proper legal regime for cyberspace. *University of Pittsburgh Law Review, 55*, 993–1055.
Herzfeld, O. (2012). *What is the legal status of virtual goods?* Retrieved July 6, 2015, from http://www.forbes.com/sites/oliverherzfeld/2012/12/04/what-is-the-legal-status-of-virtual-goods.
Johnson, D. R., & Post, D. (1996). Law and borders—The rise of law in cyberspace. *Stanford Law Review, 48*, 1367–1402.
Kant, I. (2002). *Groundwork for the metaphysics of morals*. (A. W. Wood, Ed., Trans.). London: Yale University Press.
Korczyński, R., & Koszut, R. (2002). Oszustwo komputerowe. *Prokuratura i Prawo, 2*, 17–38.
Kosińska, J. (2008). Prawnokarna problematyka stalkingu. *Prokuratura i Prawo, 10*, 33–47.
Lach, A. (2012). Kradzież Tożsamości. *Prokuratura i Prawo, 3*, 29–39.
Locke, J. (2002). *The second treatise of government and a letter concerning toleration*. Mineola, NY: Dover Publications.
Michalski, B. (1999). *Przestępstwa przeciwko mieniu*. Warsaw: C.H.Beck.
Michalski, B. (2010). Rozdział XXXV. Przestępstwa przeciwko mieniu. In A. Wąsek & R. Zawłocki (Eds.), *Kodeks karny. Część szczególna. Tom II* (pp. 866–1293). Warszawa: C.H.Beck.
Mill, J. S. (1998). *On liberty*. London: Penguin Books.
Newman, L. (2007). *Six teens arrested for virtual crime in Habbo Hotel*. Retrieved May 7, 2015, from http://www.technologytell.com/gaming/18923/six-teens-arrested-for-virtual-crime-in-habbo-hotel.
Oniszczuk, J. (2008). *Teoria i filozofia prawa*. Warsaw: C.H.Beck.
Reed, C. (2004). *Internet law: Text and materials*. New York: Cambridge University Press.
Skorupka, J. (2000). Wady oświadczenia woli w wybranych przestępstwach gospodarczych. *Przegląd Sądowy, 4*, 38–54.
Szkotnicki, W. (1995). Przestępstwo zniesławienia i próby nowej jego prawnej regulacji. *Przegląd Sądowy, 5*, 21–63.
Szymczak, M. (Ed.). (1979). *Słownik języka polskiego* (Vol. 2). Warsaw: Wydawnictwa Naukowe PWN.
Tatarkiewicz, W. (2001). *Historia filozofii*. Warsaw: Wydawnictwa Naukowe PWN.
Wąsek A. (2005). *Kodeks karny. Komentarz*. In O. Górniok, S. Hoc, M. Kalitowski, S.M. Przyjemski, Z. Sienkiewicz, J. Szumski, L. Tyszkiewicz, & A. Wąsek (Eds.) (pp. 856–1493). Gdańsk: Wydawnictwo ARCHE.

Chapter 5
Criminal Proceedings in Cyberspace: The Challenge of Digital Era

Vanja Bajovic

Introduction

The emergence of modern European states in the late eighteenth and the early nineteenth century went hand in hand with the introduction of comprehensive legal codifications as one of the basic reflections of the State, i.e. the nation. In spite of later modifications of legal solutions, the basic principles have remained the same—the right of the State to incriminate and sanction punishable behaviours in its territory is considered to be a part of national sovereignty many states are unwilling to waive, even today. Development of modern technologies and transfer of daily activities from physical to non-physical—cyber world, call into question some of the basic principles these codes are founded on. The principle of territoriality is hardly applicable in non-territorial space; the principle of guilt is challenged in the light of young ages of cybercrime offenders; the principle of legality (*nulla poena sine lege*) is tested by the new forms of computer crimes. However, it seems that digital revolution did not bring many changes in the area of criminal law and procedure, except some new incriminations and few international instruments prevalently symbolic in character. The first part of the paper aims to explain why this approach is unsustainable, explaining non-applicability of these principles to digital environment. In addition to substantive law, the use of computers in criminal activity poses significant challenges for traditional rules of criminal procedure. The problems are related to non-reporting of cybercrimes, difficulties in their detection, investigation and prosecution, collection of digital and electronic evidence, jurisdictional dilemmas and other procedural issues explained in the second part.

Anonymity of network users is recognized as the biggest advantage but, at the same time, also as one of the biggest drawback of the Internet. It certainly contributes

V. Bajovic (✉)
University of Belgrade, Faculty of Law, Belgrade, Serbia
e-mail: bajovic@ius.bg.ac.rs

E.C. Viano (ed.), *Cybercrime, Organized Crime, and Societal Responses*,
DOI 10.1007/978-3-319-44501-4_5

to the freedom of expression but, at the same time, it encourages the flourishing of criminal activities and hinders the identification of cybercrime offenders. Relaying on biometrics, as the most accurate identification mechanism, could significantly contribute to the cyber security but, on the other hand, there is a fear that such mechanisms will undermine cyber freedom and privacy. Finally, some practical suggestions are given, more with the purpose to start thinking about new solutions than to lay out detailed proposals.

Traditional Criminal Law in Cyber Environment

Principle of Territoriality

Criminal law is based on the territorial principle that guaranties exclusive authority to the State to deal with criminal offences arising within its territory. The right of the State to incriminate and punish criminal behaviour within its borders is based on ideological and political reasons and considered as a part of the state's national sovereignty. Eighteenth-century philosophers like Montesquieu, Russo and Voltaire pointed out the importance of territoriality principle that was particularly affirmed during the Renaissance, in the time of emergence and development of modern national states. Before that the rule was that every individual is guided by his national law, and is punished according to it, regardless the territory where the crime was committed (Cassese 2005, pp. 326–329). According to territoriality principle, the basic criterion for determination of jurisdiction is the place where the crime was committed. Traditional, physical-world crimes imply territorial connection between criminal act and its consequence—they are usually in the same place or, at least, within the borders of the same country. Other jurisdictional principles are the principle of nationality (personal jurisdiction) that implies jurisdiction of the state whose citizen is an offender, the protective principle that allows a state to assert jurisdiction over a person whose conduct threatens security of that state, and the universal principle that allows the state to claim jurisdiction over an accused, regardless of the place of commission and offender's nationality. The personal, protective and universal principles are applied subsidiarily and under certain conditions, in accordance with the internal state law (Cryer et al. 2008, pp. 40–53).

All these principles are challenged by the development of modern technologies. The territorial principle logically implies "territory" or physical borders between the states established by international law, but technological changes alter the understanding of territorial sovereignty. Cyberspace is not a territorial space, it does not recognize physical or territorial borders, and neither is it familiar with the concept of nationality. It is not a fixed, determined space, but rather a constructed area that functions according to principles that cannot be controlled or changed by individuals. As such, cyberspace is changeable, fluid and unsuitable for regulation according to traditional jurisdictional rules (Goldstone and Shave 1998; Marion

2010) and there is still lack of any definitive jurisdiction or consistent global legislation (Brenner and Koops 2004; Yar 2006; Bryant et al. 2008; Schmalleger and Pittaro 2009).

Unlike traditional criminal offences, cybercrimes usually imply territorial "disconnection" between the act and the consequence, they are in different places and, quite often, on different continents. According to UNDOC report (2013, p. 55) between 50 and 100 % of cybercrimes involve a transnational element. Cybercrimes do not require territorial proximity between the offender and the victim and a cybercriminal can commit multiple crimes all over the world in the blink of an eye. The number of victims is much higher compared to traditional offences. The "Love Bug" virus, that appeared in 2000 and spread around the world in 2 h, is a good illustration of the problem.

> The virus was spread in an email with the subject line "I love you". The message contained an attachment whose opening would destroy files, steal passwords, and delete graphic or musical files from the computer. It affected over fifty million of computers, and, among others, the systems of the NASA and the CIA. Because of that virus, many large corporations decided to completely shut down their email systems, which resulted in enormous economic damage, estimated at between 2 and 10 billion dollars (Brenner and Koops 2004, pp. 6–7).

Application of the territorial principle would imply jurisdiction of the state where the offender committed the criminal act (the state where the computer was physically located) or where the consequence appeared, but in cyberspace, the following problems arose. First, it is not always easy to locate the computer from which the crime was committed—cybercriminals can easily hide their identity, without leaving physical evidence at the scene. Digital evidence, on the other hand, is easily lost, destroyed or altered. Even if the crime was located, it could happen that the offender was found there "by chance" without anything that would link him to the territory of that state. Goldstone and Shave (1998, p. 1939) argued jurisdiction of the victim's state pointing out that 'victim countries have legitimate interests to prosecute crimes against the State, crimes that take place within their borders, and crimes upon their citizens'. However, the consequence criteria are also hardly applicable, having in mind that countries are usually unwilling or unable to extradite their nationals. Even if a country is willing to extradite the perpetrator, it is possible to extradite him only to one country at a time, but since cybercrimes usually imply many victims located all over the world, this immediately gives rise to the conflict of jurisdictions. Brenner and Koops (2004, p. 3) rightly state that jurisdiction in cyberspace is a tricky issue.

If, for instance, the perpetrator committed a computer fraud from his computer located in one country, against the citizen of another country, both these countries could claim jurisdiction. Possible extradition requires the existence of double criminality, i.e. that both countries incriminate computer fraud. In addition, for extradition to be allowed, the requirement is that the crime was not committed in the territory of the requested country, against the requested country or against its citizens. In the above case, however, the fraud was actually committed in the territory of the requested country (where the computer was located) which automatically excludes extradition. With computer-related criminality, these two principles inevitably come into conflict. If a state does not incriminate a certain act committed through computers as a criminal offence, extradition is impossible because the double criminality requirement is not satisfied. On the other hand, if it does incriminate such an act, extradition is still impossible since the act was committed in the territory of that country.

Principle of Legality

According to this principle, the person cannot be punished for an act that was not criminalized by the criminal code at the time the alleged offence occurred. It is expressed by the Latin maxim *Nullum crimen, nulla poena sine lege*, and represents the basic principle of criminal law in continental Europe. Technology is faster than the law and for the legislator it is hardly possible to quickly and immediately criminalize all cybercriminals' "inventions". For example, the creator of the above-mentioned Love Bug virus has never been punished, since at that time, spreading computer viruses was not regulated by the Criminal Code of the Philippines. Even today some countries still lack cybercrime regulations and as such could represent a safe haven for cybercriminals. Besides, cybercriminals are able to exploit the gaps in existing criminal law originating from constant technological innovations or variations and conflicts of substantive laws of different countries.

It is still illusionary to talk about universal criminal law, having in mind moral, political and legal differences between the states. Therefore, certain behaviour may be considered a criminal offence in one country but not in another. Moreover, what is considered a criminal activity in one state may be specially protected in the other (Swire 2005). For example, while the so-called hate speech is banned in many countries, particularly in Europe, in the United States it is protected by the First Amendment to the U.S. Constitution, and considered as freedom of expression. Illustrative in that regard is the case *Licra v. Yahoo* discussed by Greenberg (2003) and Brenner and Koops (2004).

> Criminal proceedings were brought in the French courts against Yahoo Inc. because of the sale of memorabilia from the Nazi period by Internet auction, contrary to Article R645-1 of the French Criminal Code that prohibits "wear or exhibit" in public uniforms, insignias and emblems which "recall those used" by the Nazi regime. Yahoo Inc. contested jurisdiction of the French court, claiming that servers were located in the territory of the USA and that the First Amendment to the U.S. Constitution guarantees freedom of speech and expression. Yahoo has decided to remove contradictory auction, but explicitly pointed out that such decision 'should not be considered as the execution of the French judgment, but the as a moral obligations toward Jews in America.'

Although the territorial principle empowers the state to punish illegal activities within its territory, it is hardly applicable in such cases, because of the lack of territorial borders within the cyberspace and the lack of universal criminal law that would be equally implemented everywhere.

Principle of Guilt

According to the principle of guilt or individual subjective responsibility, the person can be criminally liable only if he is guilty, i.e. if he possesses a mental attitude towards his act. In cyberspace, the principle is challenged from the perspective of offenders' ages and criminal intentions. Statistics shows that cybercriminals are much younger compared to "real-world" offenders. Some researches (Li 2008) indicate that 37 % of perpetuators are between the age of 17 and 25, while 61 % of hackers starting between the ages of 10 and 15 years! (UNODC 2013, p. 42).

Various jurisdictions differ in regard to the minimum age of criminal responsibility but, having in mind the 'availability' of computers and computer literacy of today's children, the perpetrator of a serious cybercrime could be a child whose age is the obstacle for criminal prosecution and punishment.

Criminal offence implies existence of criminal intent or negligence in the cases when the law explicitly provides liability for negligence. According to Serbian Criminal Code, all criminal offences against the security of computer data could be committed only with an intent, while some offences require the existence of special intent or purpose. Computer sabotage, for example, can be committed only with intent to prevent or considerably disrupt the procedure of electronic processing and transfer of data, crime of creating and introducing of computer viruses exists only if the virus was created with intent of its introduction into another's computer or computer network, while for computer fraud and unauthorized use of computer or computer network is required an intent of acquiring unlawful material gain.

Criminal intent or premeditation means that the perpetrator acted knowingly (he was aware of his action) and willingly (he wanted to commit an offence, or was aware that he could commit it and consented to its commission), but the problem arises when an offender hacked the network out of fun or for some other reason, without criminal intent. For example, a few months ago, Serbian hackers entered into the Serbian state network and stole the entire national database, including ID numbers, phone numbers, addresses and other personal data of Serbian citizens, but for "altruistic" purpose—they wanted to prove that the state security system is weak, that privacy of Serbian nationals is threatened and that state authorities need to improve security of their computers. It is also questionable whether the creator of the above-mentioned Love Bug virus could be punished (even if the act was criminalized in the Philippines), bearing in mind that the virus was created out of fun by a curious student who had no intention of further spreading it! Goodman and Brenner (2002, p. 156) survey showed that in more than 70 % of cyber attacks, motivation was curiosity of perpetuators! From a purely procedural aspect, the question of criminal intent remains open in such cases, and it is for the prosecutor to prove it "beyond any reasonable doubt". However, cybercrime cases explained before raise a doubt whether the intent of their perpetrators could be undeniably considered as "criminal intent".

Procedural Issues

Apart from substantive law, cyberspace seriously challenges criminal procedure as well. Procedural problems are reflected in underreporting of cybercrimes, difficulties in detection of offenders and collection of evidence, lack of technical knowledge on the part of procedural actors and so on.

Underreporting of cybercrimes is recognized as one of the biggest obstacle for their efficient suppression (EUROPOL 2007; Wall 2007/10) and the reason for the lack of concrete statistical data on these offences. In this regard, cybercrimes show one paradox—the level of cybercrime victimization is much higher while the level of their reporting is much lower compared to traditional criminality. According to UNODC report (2013, p. 118) only one percent of cyber offences are reported to the police. Wall (2007/10, p. 194) also found that only about 120–150 Internet-related offences per 1 million had been reported to the police during 1 year, and most of these were minor frauds over which no further action was taken. This is explained by the lack of awareness of victimization (Wall 2007/10, p. 194), lack of confidence in the capacity of state authorities to address cybercrime, victims' shame and embarrassment or fear for corporate credibility. In some cases, users are not even aware of the fact that they were a victim of the cybercrime, in others the nature of the crime prevents its reporting. In Charney & Kent study (1996), as cited by Katyal (2001, p. 1020), 38,000 government computers were deliberately attacked and 65 % of them were successfully hacked. Systems administrators detected only 4 % of those penetrations, and of the 4 %, only 27 % of them were reported. In other words, there were only 267 reports by administrators arising from the successful penetration of the 24,700 machines—about 1 report per 100 violations.

Mass victimization is one more typical feature of cybercrimes. Rather than stealing millions from one bank account or stealing one credit card and overcharging it, a cybercriminals would prefer to steal a few Euros from millions of accounts, or to steal thousands of credit cards and charge them with small amounts. In that way, the account owner is not aware that he was robbed, and even if he notices the transaction, he will turn a blind eye to it, rather than to go through a complicated legal procedure for a few Euros. It is also questionable whether police would react at all without many such reports, given the amount of damage caused to one person. A bank could notice such transactions, but banks, companies and corporations quite often do not report cybercrime in fear of losing their reputation among customers and clients.

Even when the crime is reported, the chances that the perpetrator will be detected and punished are smaller compared to traditional crimes. Collection of digital evidence and solving the case with computer-related criminal offences is quite different from any classic gathering of substantive evidence and so is the way the crimes are committed. To illustrate this, let us assume that an unauthorized intrusion into a certain bank's IT system was committed for the purpose of acquiring unlawful material gain. The first step in commission of the act was to log into the network using the services of an Internet provider. In practice, the perpetrator hardly ever commits the crime directly from his own computer; instead, he would hack into several poorly protected computers (the so-called intermediaries) in order to cover up his electronic traces. Thus, from one or more intermediary computers, the perpetrator hacks the password and brings down the electronic protection system which enables him to transfer a certain amount of money from the bank accounts to his temporarily opened account. However, any and all pieces of information exchanged through the network are recorded on the servers and accessible to network administrators who can inspect the memorized files.

Hence, the first step in the investigation is to collect all data found in the bank's computer but, more of than not, such data are of no big help. The investigator can learn that an unknown person from an unknown location accessed the system without authorization and, possibly, the IP address from which the access was made. Since the access was made from intermediary computers, it is necessary to check all unauthorized accesses to those computers as well, also via their respective IP addresses, in order to get to the perpetrator's account. Finally, the investigation finds its way to the computer from which the crime was committed and collects from it digital evidence indicating a series of log-ins and intrusions into different unprotected computer systems. Operating systems, namely, record all activities performed on the computer and even deleted files can be recovered/reconstructed. The problem, however, arises when a chain of intermediary computers used to access the bank's system is broken. In this case, it is necessary to resort to the network supervision system the coverage of which depends on the location and configuration of the monitoring device. This action is driven by a "gut feeling" that the criminal activity may be repeated or is still underway, enabling the police to reconnect the chain by pinpointing the missing link (Clark and Diliberto 1996; Kerr 2005).

Cybercriminals are hidden behind usernames and their identification is hardly possible without Internet Service Providers. Without their cooperation, it is difficult to figure out the identity of a perpetrator and to determine his location in real space. However, ISPs are obliged neither to possess personal information of subscribers, nor to preserve digital evidence forever. Having in mind ISPs ability to monitor web traffic, scan websites and e-mails for pirated software and viruses and other threats in this area, ISP liability for criminal offences committed in cyberspace was suggested. There is a belief that such liability may increase net control, since ISPs will care more about behaviour of the network users, requiring for example, ID or other personal data for opening an e-mail account or searching the web (Katyal 2001; Brenner 2004). But liability of internet providers for the actions of their users would mean objective and collective liability for the others, which is contrary to the above-mentioned principle of guilt.

Even when the perpetrator is identified, his guilt must be proved beyond any reasonable doubt, which requires collection and presentation of evidence. Investigation of physical, "real" crimes includes the collection of physical evidence and eyewitness testimony. Investigation of cybercrimes includes the collection of digital or electronic evidence that can exist in the form of computer files, transmissions, logs and network data. Internet users store their private information on remote servers and that information is available to the systems administrator who can look through the stored files. Therefore, the initial step of most computer crime investigation is the collection of stored evidence from service providers.

Non-territoriality of the cyberspace generates additional problems in this regard. Having in mind the trans-border element of cybercrimes, it is quite often the case that the computer from which the offence was committed is located in a foreign state and therefore, the digital evidence is also located on a foreign server. In the "traditional" criminal proceedings, collection of the evidence located in a foreign country is done through international legal assistance, with the consent and assistance of the requested State. However, this procedure could take a few months, even years (Seitz 2004, p. 4), while digital evidence must be obtained very fast, before it is modified, destroyed or altered.

Therefore, the question is, whether the competent authorities of one country are authorized to collect digital evidence and data from the servers and computers located in another country, without the knowledge and consent of that country, or such a behaviour would be considered as violation of the national sovereignty and territorial principle? Gorshkov-Ivanov case before the US Supreme Court is a good illustration of the problem (Seitz 2004; Brenner and Schwerha 2002; Brenner and Koops 2004).

Late in 1999, two Russian citizens hacked into the networks of several US banks, credit card institutions, and Internet service providers, gained access to credit card numbers and used these to commit fraud. Later on, they blackmailed affected companies to hire them as security consultants since they have unrestricted access to the firms' networks and threatened to delete all important data. The Federal Bureau of Investigation ("FBI"), which had been called upon to investigate, established a pseudo-firm allegedly specialized in security consultation and offered jobs to the suspects. In order to demonstrate their skills, the suspects flew to Seattle, where FBI agents provided them a computer with a special "sniffer" program installed in its keyboard. In order to retrieve software they needed for the demonstration, the suspects accessed their server in Russia over the Internet, but the sniffer program recorded their passwords. This enabled the FBI to obtain incriminating evidence against them. But the problem was that in fact, all electronic evidence was located on the server that was physically located in Russia. Therefore, the question was whether the FBI agents were allowed to obtain such evidence without the knowledge and consent of the foreign state.

During the trial, the defendants argued that FBI agents violated the Fourth Amendment to the U.S. Constitution that protects from unreasonable search and seizures, and asked for the exclusion of all digital evidence. The Court rejected the request under the explanation that the Fourth Amendment is not applicable, since the computer was not the property of an American citizen nor it was located in the US, and the agents had probable cause to act without a search warrant, because otherwise all evidence would have been destroyed (Smith 2007, p. 173). The position of the court was later confirmed by the executive government, and the US Department of Justice pointed out that the consent of the country where digital evidence is located is required, but in extraordinary situations, such as, for example, the risk of a terrorist attack, it is possible to obtain information from a foreign server without or before the consent of the foreign state (United States Department of Justice 2002, pp. 25–27).

German theory has quite the opposite view, claiming that trans-border search is impermissible without explicit consent of the affected state, because of the violation of the principle of territoriality. The principle of territoriality, including the sole right of each country to decide whether or not criminal investigations may be undertaken in its territory, must not be annulled by novel communication media such as the Internet. Without an explicit consent of the state where the server is located, such evidence is unlawful and must be excluded (Seitz 2004).

According to the Council of Europe's Convention on Cybercrime, a Party may, without the authorization of another Party access publicly available (open source) stored computer data, regardless of where the data is located geographically or access or receive, through a computer system in its territory, stored computer data located in another Party, if the Party obtains the lawful and voluntary consent of the person who has the lawful authority to disclose the data to the Party through that computer system (Art. 32). Following that trans-border access to stored computer data located in another country is allowed and unconditioned in the case of publicly available data, but "public" data are not quite common in the case of criminal offences. Faced simultaneously with the necessity of immediate reaction in regard to collection of digital evidence, and with the obligation to protect the national sovereignty and territorial principle, creators of Convention found solution in the establishment of special points of contacts (the so-called 24/7 network) that are available 24 h, seven days a week, in order to provide immediate assistance in investigation and for the collection of evidence in electronic form (Article 35 of the Convention). However, this provision does not resolve the problem of extra-territorial collection of digital evidence, having in mind limited number of the countries which ratified the Convention.

Even when electronic and digital evidence is collected, its production is still a challenge in court. Digital evidence must be connected to a specific person, in other words, the prosecutor has the burden to prove that the particular person controls the particular account. Anonymity of cyberspace users impedes this task. Additional problem in cybercrimes prosecution is the lack of technical expertise of police, prosecutors and judges what is, according to some authors (Shinder and Cross 2002) a major obstacle in writing, enforcing, prosecuting and interpreting cybercrime laws.

Biometric Passwords and Two Tracks Criminal Proceedings

All regulatory aspects of cyberspace entail the problem of controlling it. One of the basic characteristic of Internet, quite often listed also as its major advantage, is anonymity of its users. "One of the Internet's greatest strengths—its open anonymous nature—is also its greatest weakness, making it ripe for abuse and attracting attention from an array of unsavory individuals and advocacy groups including terrorists, neo-Nazis, pornographers and pedophiles" (Parker 1998, p. 114). Presumably, the freedom of the Internet relies precisely on the anonymity and unrecognizability on the network, providing an opportunity to express oneself without being censored and to visit various websites without fear of being recognized.

Such anonymity certainly contributes to improvement in terms of freedom of expression and therefore any form of Internet control, as a rule, provokes fierce resistance and is labelled unacceptable. This virtual or cyberspace is seen as the only place where a person can be all he wants to be, search whatever he feels like searching, view the contents which might be otherwise considered incompatible with his reputation, position and image, so it is no wonder why any attempt to control the Internet is interpreted as an attack on personal freedom. Quite like hiding behind the mask, covering one's identity by wearing a wig, cap or sunglasses in real world, using a username instead of one's own increases personal sense of security which, in turn, encourages people to leave more provocative comments or browse most different contents. On the other hand, this same anonymity in cyberspace greatly encourages computer-related criminality. According to space transition theory, people behave differently when they move from one space to another and in the cyberspace identity flexibility, anonymity of users and lack of deterrence factor are recognized as the biggest incentives for criminal behaviour (Jaishankar 2008, p. 292). Rules are not respected only out of fear of criminal sanction but also out of fear of moral judgment, and the "online anonymity" is widely believed to prevent the development of moral norms in the virtual environment and encourage an individual to behave in a way he would not dare to in the real world, given his position and reputation (Lessing 2006). Online anonymity may weaken a person's "ability to regulate behaviour, … and he/she will be less likely to care what others think of his or her behaviour" (McKenna and Bargh 2000, p. 61). After all, child pornography would certainly not be so widespread on the Internet if it had no audience.

Besides easing commission of criminal acts in terms of morality, online anonymity greatly hinders identification and location of perpetrators. Thus, the question is whether the present situation is sustainable given the growing trends of transferring everyday's activities into the world of virtual reality. As Viano (2012, p. 33) aptly states "the very way in which we communicate, learn, get the news, see reality, relate to one another, find friendship, love, companionship, obtain advice and information has changed dramatically from that one of the previous generation and is constantly changing with new technological innovations…" It is reasonably to believe, therefore, that in the years to come, classic criminality will be, for the most part, replaced by cyber one. Still, despite all the specificities of cyberspace, the states continue to vehemently hold on to their national sovereignty, trying to harness even the Internet within their own national boundaries by regulating it in a traditional way—through domestic regulations and international conventions which are mostly of merely symbolic nature. With cyber criminality on the rise and given the devastating statistics pertaining to reporting, solving and proving these crimes, such an approach proves to be unsustainable. Cyberspace must be given extraterritorial status and it has to be observed as a space "in its own right" governed by specially designed principles.

Just like the states which regulate the entry and movement of foreign nationals in their respective territories through visas and passports, a more robust control of movement through the cyberspace is necessary in response to the growing criminal activities in cyber area. An adequate solution could be found in development, promotion and mandatory introduction of biometric security systems which would allow access to the Internet base on fingerprints and other biometric features. Vacca (2007, p. 589) defines biometrics as "the science of automatic identification or identity verification of individuals using physiological or behavioural characteristics". Since it provides identity assurance on the highest level, biometric data can be used reliably to recognize individuals quickly, anywhere and at any time throughout their entire life. Consequences of this technology are analysed by numerous scholars (Feldman 2003; Jain et al. 2011, Donohue 2012), and advantages of biometric identifications are many. Having in mind that biometric data is a "unique signifier, it is perceived to be the most reliable and fraud-resistant form of identification data" (Hu 2013, pp. 1477–1478). Every person has a unique fingerprint composed of grooves and ridges that cannot be forgotten, stolen or falsified. Accordingly, 'logging on' in this way would eliminate the need to memorize passwords and usernames at the same time denying access to unauthorized persons. Moreover, the reliability of biometric identification would facilitate both detection of cybercrime perpetrators and proving their crimes by providing undisputable evidence that a certain account was used precisely by the perpetrator.

However, biometric identification, per se, does not solve the problem of criminal prosecution and punishment of the perpetrator. The accused must be given all the guarantees associated with the fair trial proclaimed in the Universal Declaration of Human Rights, the European Convention for the Protection of Human Rights and many other domestic and international instruments. To that end, classic procedural mechanism must be reorganized and adjusted to fit the cyber environment.

As it was explained earlier, only a negligible percentage of cybercrimes is reported to the police. Reporting the crime implies going to the police station, filling out certain forms, giving the statement and so on, and passing through all this procedure is usually seen as "not worthy" in the cyber domain. If a computer is "infected" by viruses, it is far simpler to call an IT specialist to solve the problem than to demand from the police to find the perpetrator who might be thousands of miles away. Also, for instance, if Facebook profile has been stolen, hacked or misused in any other way, the easiest way to proceed would be to contact the Facebook systems administrators and ask them to solve the issue, rather than to report the attack against the privacy, identity theft or other criminal acts committed, to the relevant authorities. Wall's (2005) research showed that relatively few internet offences were reported directly to the police. Most users seem to have adopted the idea that 'what happens in the cyberspace stays in the cyberspace', and this is precisely what should be the underlying concept of the procedural regulation of cyber criminality.

Accordingly, it would be desirable to establish and promote online reporting centres as the place to report all criminal acts committed in the cyberspace. It is believed that establishment of new reporting sites for different types of harmful behaviour will increase the relative power of the internet users and users groups (Wall 2007/10, p. 188). In addition to that, creation of universal cyber police should be considered, with the exclusive competence to "cruise" the cyberspace posing as a deterrent to potential cybercriminals, find suspects and collect digital evidence regardless of physical location of the server or nationality of the Internet provider. Biometric codes for gaining access to cyberspace would make the monitoring of persons "visiting" cyberspace and finding criminal offenders much easier, given the fact that they constitute a clear and undisputable proof of all the activities a certain person committed using a computer. Numerous classic defences such as alibi, mental incompetence, etc. are excluded given the infallibility of biometric identification. For instance, the accused cannot claim that he did not use the given device, since the biometrics is infallible. At the same time such a solution would, encourage users' "self-protection" by way of not forgetting to use their unique password, that is their fingerprint, to log in and log out. Physical violence, like cutting fingers in order to gain access to the system, could be automatically prevented by developing the technology which would react to fingerprints under certain body temperature only. Therefore, the only plausible defence would be duress, but this would transfer us from the online to the offline world, which means that duress, just like any other criminal act, should be reported to the competent authorities and prosecuted in regular criminal process. In that case, the perpetrator of duress would at the same time be considered to be indirect perpetrator of the criminal offence in the cyberspace.

Cybercriminals are "real" people, nationals of certain countries, and their "online" identification must be followed by their criminal prosecution and punishment. Cyber police are not the court of law and therefore it cannot provide all fair trial guarantees nor can it impose a criminal sanction. Besides, cyber authorities are not able to put the offender in prison or to provide restitution for the victim. Fair and impartial trial, right to defence, cross-examination of witnesses and presentation of other evidence as well as other procedural guarantees could be ensured only in the procedure before the existing, independent and impartial courts.

Accordingly, once the cyber authorities have completed their job, i.e. found the perpetrator and collected digital evidence, the case is forwarded to the competent state authorities for the purpose of criminal prosecution and punishment of the perpetrator. Still, the problems we already mentioned are not going away. The competent state might not have the adequate cyber regulations and adequately trained procedural actors to prosecute the case and present digital evidence. Besides, lengthy trials do not provide effective protection of cyberspace from cybercriminals. To ensure such protection, the cyber police must be given authority to impose a special measure—temporary prohibition of access to the Internet. Analogously to deportation from the sovereign territory of a state, this measure too, would imply a temporary deportation of perpetrators of criminal offences from the cyberspace for the purpose of protecting law-abiding users. Since the measure does not constitute a criminal sanction, the question of fair trial guarantees is excluded. Such guarantees are ensured in the "second track" proceedings before the national court, while this measure could be compared to the measure of detention in a regular criminal process, imposed for the purpose to prevent re-offending.

The imposition of this measure would certainly have a deterring effect against potential cybercriminals, some of whom would find the prohibition to access the Net to be harsher than a prison or a fine penalty. In addition, the temporary "deportation" from cyberspace would motivate the offenders not to avoid trials and countries lacking cyberspace-related legislation would become less attractive to cybercriminals. To exploit the preventive effect to the fullest, the measure of prohibition of access to the Internet should be added to the existing range of criminal sanctions at national levels.

Conclusion

The development of cyberspace and use of computers in criminal activity pose significant challenges for criminal law. Devastating statistics pertaining to reporting and prosecuting of this type of crimes shows that traditional criminal justice instruments are not adequate tools for efficient suppression of cyber criminality. Unlike traditional 'physical world' criminal offences, cybercrimes are characterized by mass victimization, global reach, territorial disconnection between act and consequence, younger ages of criminal offenders, gaps in the criminal legislations due to the constant technological development. Procedural problems are reflected in underreporting of cybercrimes, difficulties in detection of offenders and collection of digital evidence, jurisdictional dilemmas and lack of technical knowledge on the part of procedural actors. Therefore, all efforts to fight cyber criminality cannot bring satisfactory results as long as we use old tools in the new cyber environment.

Cyberspace is a borderless space and it cannot be regulated partially, on the national or regional level. As a particular, separated area, it must have special, supranational authorities empowered with exclusive jurisdiction to receive online complaints, collect electronic evidence regardless of the physical location of servers and detect cyber perpetrators. Not unlike the national states that protect the order within their boundaries, cyber authorities must be authorized to 'deport' the person who breaks the law and prohibit him from entering this 'non-physical' territory. In this regard, introduction of the particular measure—prohibition of access to cyberspace, will have deterrent effect on potential cyber offenders and protective effect on law-abiding users. The presumption of innocence is preserved having in mind preventive, temporary and non-punitive nature of this measure. This presumption, as well as other procedural guarantees, is still provided in a regular 'offline' trial before the national court. That is exactly the point of two track criminal procedure—one before the cyber authorities, another before the regular courts.

Since implementation of these ideas requires stronger identification of Internet users, development and promotion of biometric security systems is strongly supported. Instead of traditional usernames and passwords, fingerprints could be a new "passport" for the entrance into the cyberspace that provides easy, reliable and accurate identification of the offender. Development of biometric authentication devices is not obstructed with technological obstacles, but with the privacy concern. There is immediate fear that such technology would jeopardize cyber anonymity and freedom, but the question to be asked first is whether the Internet is as free as we want to believe it is? Haggerty and Ericson (2000, p. 605) stated that one of the great public misperceptions about the Internet is the myth of anonymity—in fact networked technology leans in the opposite direction, to the point that we are now in danger of experiencing what has been described as 'the disappearance of disappearance'. Choi (2013, p. 503) rightly points out that the activities of groups like Anonymous, LulzSec and WikiLeaks, as well as the uses of Internet-based organizing during the Arab Spring revolution, have enhanced the romanticism and notoriety of anonymity. Interception of communications and electronic surveillance are regular tools in cybercrime investigations and without the ability of state authorities and internet providers to monitor network traffic, the fight against cybercrime would be lost beforehand. Therefore, the use of biometrics will not change anything in regard to existing possibilities of Internet control, but it can significantly contribute to the identification of criminal offenders, providing powerful connection between the defendant and the crime.

References

Brenner, S., & Schwerha, J. (2002). Transnational evidence gathering and local prosecution of international cybercrime. *Journal of Computer & Informaton Law, 20*, 347–395.

Brenner, S. (2004). Toward a criminal law for cyberspace: Product liability and other issues. *Boston University Journal of Science & Technology Law, 10*(2), 1–113.

Brenner, S., & Koops, B. J. (2004). Approaches to cybercrime jurisdiction. *Journal of High Technology Law, 4*, 1–46.

Bryant, R., et al. (2008). *Investigating digital crime*. New York: Wiley.

Cassese, A. (2005). *International law*. Oxford: Oxford University Press.

Choi, B. H. (2013). The anonymous Internet. *Maryland Law Review, 72*, 501–570.

Clark, F. & Diliberto, K. (1996). *Investigating computer crime*. Boca Raton, Fla.: CRC Press.

Cryer, R., Friman, H., Robinson, D., & Wilmshurst, E. (2008). *An introduction to international criminal law and procedure*. New York: Cambridge University Press.

Donohue, L. (2012). Technological leap, statutory gap and constitutional abyss: Remote biometric identification comes of age. *Minnesota Law Review, 97*, 407–559.

EUROPOL. (2007). *High tech crimes within the EU: Old crimes new tools, new crimes old tools*. Retrieved June 10, 2015, from https://www.enisa.europa.eu/activities/cert/events/files/ENISA_Europol_threat_assessment_2007_Dileone.pdf.

Feldman, R. (2003). Considerations on the emerging implementation of biometric technology. *Hastings Communications and Entertainment Law Journal, 25*, 653–682.

Goldstone, D., & Shave, B. (1998). International dimension of crimes in cyberspace. *Fordham International Law Journal, 22*, 1925–1971.

Goodman, M. D., & Brenner, S. (2002). The emerging consensus on criminal conduct in cyberspace. *International Journal of Law and Information Technology, 10*. Retrieved February 2, 2016, from http://www.lawtechjournal.com/articles/2002/03_020625_goodmanbrenner.php.

Greenberg, M. (2003). A return to Lilliput: The LICRA v. Yahoo! Case and the regulation of online content in the world market. *Berkeley Technology Law Journal, 18*, 1191–1258.

Haggerty, K., & Ericson, R. (2000). The surveillant assemblage. *British Journal of Sociology, 51*(4), 605–622.

Hu, M. (2013). Biometric ID cybersurveillance. *Indiana Law Journal, 88*, 1475–1558.
Jain, A., Ross, A., & Nandakumar, K. (2011). *Introduction to biometrics*. New York: Springer.
Jaishankar, K. (2008). Space transition theory of cybercrimes. In F. Schmalleger & M. Pittaro (Eds.), *Crimes of the Internet* (pp. 283–301). Upper Saddle River, NJ: Prentice Hall.
Katyal, N. K. (2001). Criminal law in cyberspace. *University of Pennsylvania Law Review, 149*, 1003–1114.
Kerr, O. (2005). Digital evidence and the new criminal procedure. *Columbia Law Review, 105*, 279–318.
Lessing, L. (2006). *Code and other laws of cyberspace*. New York: Basic Books.
Li, X. (2008). The criminal phenomenon on the Internet: Hallmarks of criminals and victims revisited through typical cases prosecuted. *University of Ottawa Law & Technology Journal, 5*, 125.
Marion, N. E. (2010). The council of Europe's cyber crime treaty: An exercise in symbolic legislation. *International Journal of Cyber Criminology, 4*, 699–712.
McKenna, K., & Bargh, J. (2000). Plan 9 from cyberspace: The implications of the Internet for personality and social psychology. *Personality and Social Psychology Review, 4*, 57–75.
Parker, D. (1998). *Fighting computer crime: For protecting information*. New York: Wiley.
Schmalleger, F., & Pittaro, M. (2009). *Crimes of the Internet*. Upper Saddle River, NJ: Prentice Hall.
Seitz, N. (2004). Transborder search: A new perspective in law enforcement? *Yale Journal of Law and Technology, 7*(1), 23. Retrieved February 2, 2016, from http://digitalcommons.law.yale.edu/yjolt/vol7/iss1/2.
Shinder, D., & Cross, M. (2002). *Scene of the cybercrime*. New York: Syngress.
Smith, R. G. (2007). Crime control in the digital age: An exploration of human rights implications. *International Journal of Cyber Criminology, 1*(2), 167–179.
Swire, P. P. (2005). Developments in the law: The law of cyberspace. *Harvard Law Review, 112*, 1574–1704.
UNODC. (2013). *Comprehensive study on cybercrime*. Retrieved from https://www.unodc.org/documents/organized-crime/UNODC_CCPCJ_EG.4_2013/CYBERCRIME_STUDY_210213.pdf.
United States Department of Justice. (2002). *Searching and seizing computers and obtaining electronic evidence in criminal investigations*. Retrieved May 12, 2015, from http://www.usdoj.gov/criminal/cybercrime/s&smanual2002.pdf.
Vacca, J. (2007). *Biometric technologies and verification systems*. Amsterdam: Butterworth-Heinemann.
Viano, E. (2012). Balancing liberty and security fighting cybercrime: Challenges for the networked society. In Manacorda S. (Ed.), *Cybercriminality: Finding a balance between freedom and security* (pp. 33–63). Milano: ISPAC. Retrieved February 2, 2016, from http://ispac.cnpds.org/publications-27-cybercriminality-finding-a-balance-between-freedom-and-security-27.html.
Wall, D. S. (2005). The Internet as a conduit for criminals. In A. Pattavina (Ed.), *Information technology and the criminal justice system* (pp. 77–98). Thousand Oaks, CA: Sage.
Wall, D. S. (2007/10). Policing cybercrimes: Situating the public police in networks of security within cyberspace (revised May 2010). *Police, Practice & Research: An International Journal, 8*(2), 183–205.
Yar, M. (2006). *Cybercrime and society*. London: Sage Publishing Ltd.

Chapter 6
The Use of Information and Communications Technology in Criminal Procedure in the USA

Stephen C. Thaman

Introduction

Law enforcement organs in the USA use information and communications technology (ICT) in conducting three types of surveillance useful for solving crimes and bringing criminals to justice: (1) the physical surveillance of people in public spaces; (2) the surveillance of private communications; and (3) the surveillance of transactions in which people engage (Slobogin 2005).

ICT is also used, however, in data mining, that is, in synthesizing and comparing data contained in large databases containing the fruits of the aforementioned three types of surveillance, in order to help solve criminal cases. Data mining can be "target-driven" and involve obtaining information about an identified suspect. It can be "match-driven" to see whether a particular person is a "person of interest." Finally, it can be "event-driven" and designed to discover the as of yet unknown perpetrator of a past event, and involves what is called "pattern-based surveillance" (Slobogin 2008).

All of these practices involve invasions of privacy of the citizenry, and thus must be discussed in light of the case law of the US Supreme Court (USSC) interpreting the extent of privacy rights in the USA. After a discussion of this foundational case law, we first look at US laws and jurisprudence in relation to the interception of the content of confidential communications, for these laws are the "gold standard" for privacy in the USA. We then discuss physical surveillance and finally transactional surveillance both to solve particular crimes and also to create massive data banks for the purpose of solving future crimes through data mining. In each of these areas, we compare the rules for normal criminal cases, with the special regimes applying to

S.C. Thaman (✉)
Saint Louis University School of Law, 100 N. Tucker Avenue,
St. Louis, MO 63101-1930, USA
e-mail: thamansc@slu.edu

E.C. Viano (ed.), *Cybercrime, Organized Crime, and Societal Responses*,
DOI 10.1007/978-3-319-44501-4_6

investigations relating to national security and antiterrorism. We will also discuss the data bases which are key to government criminal investigations, and the private enterprises that cooperate, voluntarily or under threat of law, with the data mining and surveillance efforts.

Collecting Information as to Movements and Activities in Public Spaces

Use of Surveillance Cameras and Facial Recognition Technology

Activity in public places or "open fields" is not generally protected by the 4.Amend. It is thus not a "search" within the meaning of the 4.Amend. for police to mount a video camera to secretly record comings and goings in the front yard of a suspect's home (*State v. Holden* 1998), or in front of public establishments such as bars (*State v Augafa* 1999). Use of motion-activated video cameras in "open fields" is also permissible without judicial authorization (*United States v Vankesteren* 2009). Recording street-corner drug deals, either from a distance by using "bionic ears" and binoculars (*Stevenson v State* 1996), or by outfitting an informer's automobile with a video camera have not violated State privacy protections (*State v Clark* 1996). Using cameras in semipublic places like hospitals (*United States v Gonzalez* 2003), or open businesses (*Cowles v State* 2001) also arouses no 4.Amend. concerns. Once information has been revealed in public, the police then may subject that information to technologically assisted interpretation and evaluation without further implicating the 4.Amend.

There is thus no constitutional impediment to using facial recognition technology in relation to photographs or videotapes of persons in public.

It was also recently revealed, that the NSA has been gathering "millions" of images per day of people from communications it secretly intercepts, of which around 55,000 per day are of sufficient quality to apply increasingly sophisticated facial recognition technology (Risen and Poitras 2014).

Automatic License Plate Recognition (ALPR) and Warrant Checks

ALPR cameras are used in many jurisdictions. All Oklahoma license plates are now ALPR-compatible. New York State uses the system to catch car thieves and to scan parking lots for visitors who have outstanding warrants. The system is used to stockpile, from each license plate capture, images, dates, times and GPS coordinates which can help place a suspect at a scene, aid in witness identification, pattern recognition or the tracking of individuals. Such data can be used to create specialized databases that can be shared among police departments (Automatic Number Plate Recognition 2015). Oakland, California received $12 million in federal grants to use on antiterrorist surveillance at its large port, but it has instead used the money for massive surveillance related to ordinary law enforcement, "from gunshot-detection sensors in the barrios of East Oakland to license plate readers mounted on police cars patrolling the city's upscale hills" (Sengupta 2013b).

Police officers may also routinely access a computer to determine whether a particular license plate is associated with prior criminal violations, or whether an arrest warrant has been issued for its owner or regular user. They may do this without stopping the vehicle, or after a valid vehicle stop, where they may directly check the records for the driver or the passenger.

If the stop of the vehicle was unlawful, then some courts prevent use of the information gained from the warrant check. If a lawful stop, however, is excessively prolonged in order to perform a warrant check, some courts forbid use of the warrant information (*United States v Boyce* 2003; *United States v Fernandez* 2010; *People v Harris* 2008). Other courts, however, allow prolongation for a reasonable time to consummate the warrant check (*State v Williams* 2003).

No individualized suspicion is needed to run the name of either a driver or a passenger through the national computer system (*State v Sloane* 2008).

Use of Tracking Devices

1. The "Beeper" Cases

No 4.Amend. implications arose, traditionally, from police following suspects in public. In a couple of cases, police attached an electronic tracking device, or "beeper," to containers of precursor chemicals used in manufacturing illegal narcotics, and then trailed the purchaser of the containers by activating the "beeper." The USSC found no illegal search or seizure in the act of attaching the "beeper" to the container, because it did not yet belong to the suspect and he therefore had no reasonable expectation of private in its interior. And the Court also deemed that trailing suspects in public did not violate the 4.Amend., because police could have used more traditional methods to do the same surveillance (*United States v Knotts* 1983).

If police, however, use the devices to track location inside of the home, judicial authorization would be needed, because it would be a "search" in violation of a reasonable expectation of privacy (*United States v Karo* 1984). Recently, the New York Police's strategy of putting tracking devices in decoy pill bottles to deter pharmacy robberies, was upheld by the courts for the same reason (Goldstein 2015).

2. The Use of Global Positioning Systems (GPS) Technology for Tracking

Although lower courts had applied the rationale of the "beeper" cases to the use of GPS technology, a recent decision by the USSC has cast doubt on the continued validity of their earlier approach. In *United States v Jones* (2012a, b) the USSC held, however, that the 4.Amend. was violated when police attached a GPS device to a suspect's automobile and engaged in a 4-week surveillance of the suspect's movements. The majority did not, however, find that judicial authorization was needed for the long-term surveillance, but only that the act of attaching the device to the suspect's property was an unlawful "seizure" and violated the 4.Amend., as the automobile belonged to the suspect at the time the device was attached. Five Justices, however, writing in different opinions, did seem to hint that long-term surveillance might violate the 4.Amend. (McAllister 2012, p. 493).

Justice Sotomayor opined:

> GPS monitoring generates a precise, comprehensive record of a person's public movements that reflects a wealth of detail about her familial, political, professional, religious, and sexual associations...[such as] trips the indisputably private nature of which takes little imagination to conjure: trips to the psychiatrist, the plastic surgeon, the abortion clinic, the AIDS treatment center, the strip club, the criminal defense attorney, the by-the-hour motel, the union meeting, the mosque, synagogue or church, the gay bar and on and on. The Government can store such records and efficiently mine them for information years into the future... And because GPS monitoring is cheap in comparison to conventional surveillance techniques and, by design, proceeds surreptitiously, it evades the ordinary checks that constrain abusive law enforcement practices: such as limited police resources and community hostility...Awareness that the Government may be watching chills associational and expressive freedoms. And the Governments unrestrained power to assemble data that reveal private aspects of identity is susceptible to abuse. The net result is that GPS monitoring—by making available at a relatively low cost such a substantial quantum of intimate information about any person whom the Government, in its unfettered discretion, chooses to track—may alter the relationship between citizen and government in a way that is inimical to democratic society. I would take these attributes of GPS monitoring into account when considering the existence of a reasonable societal expectation of privacy in the sum of one's public movements. I would ask whether people reasonably expect that their movements will be recorded and aggregated in a manner that enables the Government to ascertain, more or less at will, their political and religious beliefs, sexual habits, and so on (*United States v Jones* 2012a, b).

Justice Alito, in another concurring opinion, also questioned whether the old USSC approach to public tracking could still stand in the modern technological era:

> Recent years have seen the emergence of many new devices that permit the monitoring of a person's movements. In some locales, closed-circuit television video monitoring is becoming ubiquitous. On toll roads, automatic toll collection systems create a precise record of the movements of motorists who choose to make use of that convenience. Many motorists purchase cars that are equipped with devices that permit a central station to ascertain the car's location at any time so that roadside assistance may be provided if needed and the car may be found if it is stolen.
>
> Perhaps most significant, cell phones and other wireless devices now permit wireless carriers to track and record the location of users—and as of June 2011, it has been reported, there were more than 322 million wireless devices in use in the United States. For older phones, the accuracy of the location information depends on the density of the tower network, but new "smart phones," which are equipped with a GPS device, permit more precise tracking. For example, when a user activates the GPS on such a phone, a provider is able to monitor the phone's location and speed of movement and can then report back real-time traffic conditions after combining ("crowdsourcing") the speed of all such phones on any

> particular road. Similarly, phone-location-tracking services are offered as "social" tools, allowing consumers to find (or to avoid) others who enroll in these services. The availability and use of these and other new devices will continue to shape the average person's expectations about the privacy of his or her daily movements.
>
> Under this approach, relatively short-term monitoring of a person's movements on public streets accords with expectations of privacy that our society has recognized as reasonable. But the use of longer term GPS monitoring in investigations of most offenses impinges on expectations of privacy (*United States v Jones* 2012a, b).

Some US courts had already adopted the position of Justices Sotomayor and Alito that long-term tracking is not "reasonable" under the 4.Amend. before the *Jones* decision (*United States v Garcia* 2007; *State v Jackson* 2003; *People v Weaver* 2009; *United States v Maynard* 2010; *United States v Jones* 2012a, b), but others have followed their approach after the decision (*State v Zahn* 2012; *State v Brereton* 2013; *Commonwealth v Rousseau* 2013). Several states require a warrant before GPS devices may be used (see McAllister 2012, p. 506).

3. Cellphone Site Location Tracking

As was noted by Justice Alito, as a cell phone moves, its signals are picked up by different cell phone towers located within close geographic proximity. Precise locations can be determined by analyzing signals from such towers, their strength and the angle of signal reception (Casey 2008, p. 1009). Courts have generally applied the same rationale in *Knotts* to allow police to secure from a cell phone service the location of a subscriber's phone without requiring a warrant for the purpose of tracking the person's movements (*United States v Forest* 2004; *Devega v State* 2010; *In re Application of United States of America for Order Directing Provider of Electronic Communication Service to Disclose Records to Government* 2010; *State v Subdiaz-Osorio* 2014).

Service providers maintain records of cellphone site location information (CSLI). Historic CSLI refers to the records maintained by providers that list the cell sites with which a subscriber's cell phone communicated at previous points in time, whereas prospective CSLI refers to the cell sites that a subscriber's cell phone will communicate with at a future point in time. Under the Stored Communications Act (SCA) law enforcement agencies may compel service providers to disclose prospective or historic CSLI for a particular cell phone in the course of a criminal investigation (18 USC §§ 2701–12; see Fox 2012, p. 771).

The government began to use simple pen register orders, which do not require probable cause, not only to gain access to numbers called, but also to track the location of the cellphone user. In 2005, however, a federal judge rejected the government's application to track the cellphone location of a suspect, claiming that the authorities needed a normal search warrant based on probable cause due to the increased interference with privacy (*In re Application of the United States for an Order Authorizing the Use of a Pen Register & a Trap & Trace Device* & (2) *Authorizing Release of Subscriber Info. & Cell Site Info* 2005). This decision was followed by 15 "pen register" decisions in other lower federal courts. In 11 of these cases, the courts have refused to issue the order and in four, they have allowed gathering the cell-site information. The government appealed none of these decisions. One New York State court has itself issued contradictory decisions. One panel required "probable cause" for disclosure of historic CSLI (Fox 2012, p. 783), whereas the other required only "reasonable grounds" for the discovery of prospective CSLI, which involved monitoring future movements of the suspect (*In re Application of the United States for an Order Authorizing the Use of a Pen Register & a Trap & Trace Device* & (2) *Authorizing Release of Subscriber Info. & Cell Site Info*2005, citing *In re Application of the U.S. for an Order Authorizing the Use of Two Pen Register and Trap and Trace Devices* 2008). On the other hand, the federal district court in Maryland has indicated that historic CSLI is not protected by the 4.Amend. because the defendants in that case "voluntarily transmitted signals to cellular towers in order for their calls to be connected," and the service provider "then created internal records of that data for its own business purposes" (McAllister 2012, pp. 518–520). A federal appeals court recently adopted this argument and held that historical CSLI held by service providers are "business records" and not protected by the 4.Amend. (*In re Application of United States for Historical Cell Site Data* 2013).

The trend appears to be in the direction of requiring a probable cause warrant to disclose cellsite location (Casey 2008, p. 1016; For cases requiring a warrant and probable cause, see *In re Application of the United States* 2011; *In re Application of the United States*, S D Tex 2010; *In re Application of the United States* E D N Y 2010, cited in (McAllister 2012, 520).

Bills have been proposed in the US Congress and in Delaware, Maryland, and Oklahoma that would require police to obtain judicial authorization before demanding location records from cellphone carriers and California passed such a law, but it was vetoed by the Governor (Sengupta 2012).

Sophisticated new technology has now given the NSA the ability to track the activities and movements of people almost anywhere in the world without actually watching them or listening to their conversations. When separate streams of data are integrated into large databases—matching, for example, time and location data from cellphones with credit card purchases or E-ZPass use—intelligence analysts are given a mosaic of a person's life that would never be available from simply listening to their conversations. Just four data points about the location and time of a mobile phone call make it possible to identify the caller 95 % of the time. Intelligence and law enforcement agencies also use a new technology, known as trilaterization, that allows tracking of an individual's location, moment to moment. The data, obtained from cellphone towers, can track the altitude of a person, down to the specific floor in a building (Risen and Lichtblau 2013).

In addition, NSA, working with its British counterpart, have expanded their surveillance in a program called "mobile surge," to include the many "leaky apps" used by smartphone and android phone users which spew out information, accessible by NSA, not only about the user's location, sex, and age, but which also make accessible address books, buddy lists, telephone logs and the geographic data embedded in photographs when someone sends a post to the mobile versions of Facebook, Flickr, LinkedIn, Twitter and other Internet services. A special target of the program is also "Google maps" which reveals a large amount of information about the movements of those spied upon (Glanz et al. 2014). The NSA and the British have also been infiltrating the world of video games, because they think that potential terrorists use these games to communicate. The spy agencies have themselves created make-believe characters in the games, which they hope will be attractive to terrorists (Mazzetti and Elliot 2013).

The Use of Drones

1. Civilian Use of Drones

Drones can record video images and produce heat maps. They can track fleeing criminals, or political protesters. The Department of Homeland Security (DHS) has offered grants to help local law enforcement buy Drones. Drone manufacturers began to market small, lightweight devices specifically for policing. They are already used to monitor movement on the US borders and by a handful of police departments. Drones for civilian-use are not armed and run on relatively small batteries and fly short distances. In principle, various sensors, including cameras, can be attached to them.

Citizens and civil rights organizations, however, are wary of them and Charlottesville, Virginia, became the first city to restrict their use in February of 2013, and enacted a rule excluding any evidence obtained from a drone. Public protests led the Seattle Police Department to return its two unused Drones. The federal Congress also introduced a bill in February of 2013 prohibiting the use of Drones for targeted surveillance of individuals or property without judicial authorization. In early February of 2013, Virginia passed a 2-year moratorium on the use of drones in criminal investigations. In several states, including Arizona and Montana, proposals would require the police to obtain a search warrant before collecting evidence with a drone (Sengupta 2013a).

2. Use of Drones for Targeted Killings

Un-manned surveillance aircraft or "Drones" have been used by the CIA and the US Army to assassinate upwards of 3000 alleged terrorists in Afghanistan, Pakistan, Yemen, and Somalia, and in doing so, have caused considerable collateral casualties (Shane 2013a). The Drone strikes have also killed four Americans, including Anwar al-Awlaki (Savage and Baker 2013).

The decision as to who is put on the "kill lists" is made secretly within the executive branch of government. In relation to the CIA killings, CIA Director John Brennan is the principal coordinator of the "kill list" and President Obama allegedly signs off on each person designated for assassination. While the program has eliminated some high Al Qaeda leaders, it now appears to be focusing on lower level cadre, many of whom could have probably been arrested and subjected to a civilian or military trial (Worth et al. 2013). The revelations of Edward Snowden have also shown that the NSA is also deeply involved in gathering information for use in target killings (Miller et al. 2013).

Uproar over this highly suspect use of Drones has led Congress to discuss whether a new secret court, like the Foreign Intelligence Surveillance Court (FISC), should be established to decide on which persons should be targeted for execution (Shane 2013b). A judge hearing a civil suit brought by relatives of the slain Americans strongly intimated that courts should have a role in the decisions leading to the strikes (Shane 2013c).

Collecting Information as to Activities in Homes and Other Private Spaces

Use of Thermal Imagery and Its Extension to Other Technologies

Thermal imaging technology is based on the electronic capture and imaging of a target's radiated or reflected energy in the thermal portion of the electromagnetic spectrum. It collects and visualizes the thermal energy emitted from all objects by collecting infrared light and focusing it with a lens onto a series of mirrors that direct it onto a detector. The detector then translates the light into an electronic signal that can be displayed on a screen, or amplified, processed, and stored on videotape to be used later as evidence. This technology, the wartime use of which was to detect, for instance, the presence of North Vietnamese or Viet Cong soldiers in the jungles of South Vietnam, is now mainly used to detect excessive use of electricity in homes, symptomatic of the indoor production of marijuana using high power lamps.

Most courts found that training this technology on a house was not a "search" within the 4.Amend., because there was no penetration of the house, and because the energy radiated was seen to be similar to waste or "garbage," without constitutional protection, or because the detection of energy use was like a *sui generis* search that did not otherwise disturb the privacy of the occupants of houses. This approach changed, however, when the USSC held in 2001, that the use of any technology that reveals anything inside the house, even as mundane as the amount of energy used, is protected by the 4.Amend., because "all details are intimate details, because the entire area is held safe from prying government eyes" (*Kyllo v United States* 2001).

The *Kyllo* decision would seem to indicate, that a search warrant under the 4. Amend. based on "probable cause" would be required to train a thermal imager on a house. Some courts, however, have engaged in "reasonableness clause balancing" and held that only "reasonable suspicion" was necessary due to the minimal extent of the intrusion (*United States v Kattaria* 2007).

In March of 2013, the USSC avoided, however, deciding whether a "canine sniff" of a dwelling was a "search" by claiming that the officer and dog illegally trespassed on the front doorstep of the house, thereby making the sniff the fruit of the illegal trespass (*Florida v Jardines* 2013). Even before *Jardines*, some courts had held that a canine sniff of a dwelling did constitute a search, and had to be based on probable cause and a warrant (*United States v Thomas* 1985; *State v. Young* 1994). Others had engaged in reasonableness clause balancing and held that reasonable suspicion was sufficient to conduct such an investigative measure because the main reason for such searches was to gather evidence, which would eventually constitute "probable cause" for the issuance of a search warrant (*State v Ortiz* 1999; *State v Davis* 2007; Some courts even require reasonable suspicion for the canine sniff of an automobile, *State v Wiegand* 2005; *State v Tackitt* 2003; *People v Devone* 2010).

Hacking into Computers Located in the Home with Viruses or Other Technology

Commentators speculated that a "perfect computer search" might be possible, if a program could be created that would only find digital contraband, say, in the form of a clearly illegal photograph constituting child pornography. Under the *sui generis* doctrine, no probable cause or even a warrant would be necessary, hypothetically, to conduct such a programmed search (Adler 1996, p. 1098). After the decision in *Kyllo* this would no longer hold if the computer containing the contraband was located in a home.

Already in 2001 it was reported that the FBI was developing software capable of inserting a computer virus onto a suspect's computer and obtaining encryption keys. The software, known as "Magic Lantern," enables agents to read data that had been scrambled, a tactic often employed by criminals to hide information and evade law enforcement. The use of "Carnivore," had proved useless against suspects clever enough to encrypt their files.

Magic lantern installs the so-called "keylogging" software on a suspect's machine that is capable of capturing keystrokes typed on a computer. By tracking exactly what a suspect types, critical encryption key information can be gathered, and then transmitted back to the FBI. The virus can be sent to the suspect via e-mail, perhaps through a trusting friend or relative. The virus then watches for a suspect to start a popular encryption program. It then logs the passphrase used to start the program, essentially giving agents access to keys needed to decrypt files (Sullivan 2001).

Before *Kyllo* a court held that federal agents did not violate either the 4.Amend. or the wiretap statute by obtaining a search warrant which authorized the installation of a "magic lantern" key logger device on a defendant's personal computer and using the device to discover the passphrase to an encrypted file (*United States v Scarfo* 2001).

There are three main approaches to remote searches of computers through the use of "Trojan Horse" or "Magic Lantern"-type technologies. Twenty-two States and federal law require a search warrant based on normal 4.Amend. principles, including exceptions such as that for "exigent circumstances." Twelve States require a search warrant, but have standards which offer more privacy protection than does the 4.Amend. Finally, 16 States prohibit all remote computer searches (Brenner 2012, p. 54).

Secretly Entering a Home or Office to Access Computers

Even before 9–11, federal courts authorized so-called "sneak and peek" warrants, that is, warrants that authorized law enforcement authorities to secretly enter dwellings and other private spaces to gather information relating to future or ongoing criminal activity, often by accessing computers (*United States v Villegas* 1990; *United States v Villegas* 1999).

"Sneak and peek" warrants were codified with the passage of the US PATRIOT Act in October 2001, which amended the law (§ 213 US PATRIOT Act; 18 USC § 3103(a)), to allow a delay in notifying the party whose premises were searched for a "reasonable time" where immediate notice would have an "adverse result." An "adverse result" can include: (1) endangering the life or physical safety of an individual, (2) flight from prosecution, (3) destruction of or tampering with evidence, (4) intimidation of potential witnesses, or (5) otherwise seriously jeopardizing an investigation or unduly delaying a trial (18 USC § 2705(a)(2)). Such "sneak and peek" searches are also allowed, upon warrant issued by the FISC, subject to similar conditions as required for FISA wiretaps (50 USC §§ 1822–24). US persons who have been the subject of a search under the FISA provisions will only be notified of the search when "the Attorney General determines there is no national security interest in continuing to maintain the secrecy of the search" (50 USC § 1825(b)).

From April 2003 to January 2005, the federal government used "sneak and peek" warrants 108 times, an average of five warrants per month, which was a sharp increase from 47 warrants between October 2001 to April 2003, i.e., fewer than three a month. The DOJ claimed they were used in less than .2% of searches (Lichtblau 2005).

Warrants to Seize and Search Computers in the Home

One clearly needs a search warrant, based on probable cause, to enter a house and to seize a computer. A second issue is whether one needs a second search warrant, also based on probable cause, designating what on the computer's hard drive may be searched for and copied (*State v Ruck* 2013, computer legally seized in probation search, but warrant required to search hard drive). Courts routinely hold that a warrant to search for information located on a computer allows executors thereof to seize the computer and conduct a thorough search of all files on the computer so as to separate relevant files from unrelated files (*Guest v Leis* 2001).

1. Probable Cause that Illegal Files Will Be Found on a Computer

Law enforcement investigators will often note a specific internet account or internet protocol showing that a person accessed a child pornography website and subpoena the service provider to determine the address associated with the account, and then seek a search warrant for the home computer at that address. Visiting or becoming a member of such a website is usually enough to constitute probable cause to issue a search warrant for a home computer (*United States v Kennedy* 2000; *United States v Hambrick* 1999; *United States v Forrester* 2008, cited in Kerr 2010, pp. 1026–1027; *United States v Martin* 2005; *United States v Gourde* 2006; *United States v Wagers* 2006; *United States v Shields* 2006; *United States v Frechette* 2009). Other courts, however, require more evidence (Another panel of the Second Circuit strongly disagreed with the *Martin* decision but felt it had to upheld a similar case due to *stare decisis* (*United States v Coreas* 2005). Some courts have also held that the physical possession of images of child pornography provide probable cause that the person's home computer will also contain such images (*United States v McArthur* 2009).

2. Specificity of a Warrant for Computer Files

Courts generally require a search warrant to search files on a seized computer, unless some exception to the warrant requirement (like search incident to arrest or consent) exists (*State v Rupnick* 2005). As with the search of a lawyer's office, the search warrant must particularize which of the numerous files on a computer may be copied from the computer hard drive.

Thus, a search warrant that authorized police officers to seize "any and all computer software and hardware, computer disks, disk drives and any and all visual depictions, in any format or media, of minors engaging in sexually explicit conduct" was sufficient not only to seize the computer, but also to conduct an off-site search of files the defendant had previously deleted (*United States v Upham* 1999).

Sometimes, courts will save an overbroad warrant on the argument that the business searched was "permeated with fraud." This argument was used to justify a brief, warrantless seizure of computers in one case (*United States v Bradley* 2011). But in a case alleging a business "permeated by fraud" the warrant, which authorized a search for "evidence of crimes that includes but is not limited to, records and documents, contracts, or correspondence, computer hardware, software, passwords, telephone toll records, all fax machines, all telephone answering machine, cassettes, typewriter ribbons, phone numbers contained in the memory of an automatic telephone dialer, and caller ID box," was held to violate the 4.Amend. specificity requirement because it could have been more precise (*United States v Bridges* 2003).

If probable cause does exist, but the warrant itself does not particularly describe the place to be searched or the things to be seized, or there is a mistake on the warrant, courts may choose not to exclude the evidence based on the "good faith" rule (*Massachusetts v Sheppard* 1984). The "good faith" exception has also been applied to search warrants that are "overbroad" in not sufficiently limiting the officers' discretion as to which documents or files they may open and read.

Thus, a warrant that allowed seizure of "all business records, files, papers, computer hard drives and discs, correspondence and other material constituting evidence of immigration fraud" was held to be overbroad in terms of the 4.Amend., but sufficiently particular for federal agents to have relied in "good faith" on its validity, thus allowing the evidence to be used at trial (*United States v Kouzmine* 1996).

One federal appeals court held that a search warrant authorizing the wholesale seizure of computer storage media for later off-site examination by law enforcement officers was overly broad absent a supporting affidavit giving a reasonable explanation as to why such a blanket seizure is necessary. Nevertheless, the court applied the "good faith" exception (*United States v Hill* 2006). The Nebraska Supreme Court also found a search warrant for a mobile phone to be overbroad for not specifying what conversations or data was to be seized (*State v Henderson* 2014). The Kentucky Supreme Court, however, recently held that a search warrant need not specify the component of the cell phone which was to be searched (*Hedgepath v Commonwealth* 2014).

3. Overbroad Execution of a Computer Search

It is first fairly typical, that police will make a complete "read-only" copy of a seized hard drive of the suspect computer. Government agents will then search this copy for the files indicated in the search warrant (Kimel 2013, p. 962).

The USSC has approved of searchers briefly examining each file in the office of a lawyer suspected of real estate fraud, to see if it belongs to the category of files subject to seizure according to the warrant (*Andreson v. Maryland* 1976). Some courts apply this broad approach to a search of a computer (*United States v Richards* 2011; *US v Giberson* 2008; *United States v Christie* 2013). One court noted: "Computer records are extremely susceptible to tampering, hiding, or destruction, whether deliberate or inadvertent. Images can be hidden in all manner of files, even word processing documents and spreadsheets. Criminals will do all they can to conceal contraband, including the simple expedient of changing the names and extensions of files to disguise their content from the casual observer" (*United States v Hill* 2006; *United States v Adjani* 2006).

A minority of courts, however, require special search protocols to limit the exploratory nature of searches of computerized material. In a similar vein, one federal judge has recently criticized DOJ officials for submitting patently overbroad warrants for searching suspects' e-mail accounts, whereas other courts will allow officers to look at each e-mail first to see if it fits within the scope of the warrant (Apuzzo 2014).

Sometimes an authorized computer search for business records will come upon, for instance, files with jpg. suffixes, usually indicating photographs. A narrow approach to computer searches might say the opening of such a "photo" file would be beyond the scope of the warrant (see *United States v Carey* 1999). If the photo file has a tag that seems to indicate possible child pornography, then the "plain view" doctrine might apply (*Frasier v State* 2003). Some courts have approved broad applications of the 4.Amend.'s plain-view doctrine to uphold sweeping searches of suspects' personal computers (*United States v Mann* 2010; *United States v Williams* 2010).

On the other hand, one federal court of appeal has issued a directive that the government may no longer simply rely on the plain view doctrine in cases in which the investigators rely on the intermingling of computerized records to justify a broad seizure and examination of electronically stored records (*United States v Comprehensive Drug Testing, Inc* 2010).

Where a search warrant authorizes the seizure of certain "documents" or "written material" some courts will allow law enforcement to seize computers as "containers of written documents" (*People v Gall* 2011). Other courts will find the seizure of a computer to be beyond the scope of the search unless the affidavit for the warrant specifically mentions computers, because of the particularly intrusive nature of computer searches (*United States v Paxton* 2009).

4. Third Party Consent as Applied to Computers

No search warrant is needed, of course, if the owner of the computer consents to have the computer seized and searched. Unqualified consent to search premises has been held to extend also to computers found therein (*United States v Al-Marri* 2002; *United States v Lucas* 2011, consented to search of house or narcotics and "records" related to narcotics sale). Criminal investigators may also rely on the consent of co-owners, or even co-users of a computer to conduct a search without the need to secure judicial authorization. Police thus legally searched the hard drive of a company executive's office computer pursuant to the consent provided by his company's chief financial officer (*United States v Ziegler* 2007).

The doctrine of "apparent consent" may also be relied on. Thus in one case, police relied on the apparent authority of the suspect's father to consent to the search of the son's computer, and even did not require police to inquire into whether the computer files were password-protected (*United States v Andrus* 2007). In another case, police relied on the apparent consent of defendant's girlfriend who had spent the night at defendant's abode and was allowed to use his computer and discovered child pornography (*State v Sobczak* 2013). A Texas court actually found that a man who gave a babysitter a tour of the master bedroom in which a computer was located, "consented" to the babysitter's use of the computer (*Baird v State* 2013).

But, as with other spaces searched pursuant to consent, the police may not exceed the scope of the consent obtained. Thus, if police only obtained consent to search a computer for viruses and other evidence of bank fraud, they could not look for child pornography in image files (*People v Prinzing* 2009). Consent to search a premises for a person, for instances, could not be extended to searching a computer in the house (*United States v Turner* 1999). But unrestricted consent to search a car has been held to extend to the seizing of pagers and the calling up of messages stored thereon (*United States v Reyes* 1996).

At least one court has refused to apply the rule of *Georgia v. Randolph* (2006), to a situation where one computer user refuses to let police search the computer in the presence of another user (*United States v King* 2010).

5. Encryption and Compelled Divulgation of Encryption Technology

When law enforcement authorities seek to compel a suspect to turn over encryption technology so as to be able to decipher encrypted files, concerns protected by the Fifth Amendment (5.Amend.) of the US Constitution, which prohibits the state from compelling anyone in a criminal case to be a witness against himself, arise.

Analysis of this issue is often based on a USSC case which dealt with state compulsion of a suspect to sign forms directing any foreign banks in which he had accounts to turn records over to a grand jury investigating fraud. The "consent order," which was phrased so as to not constitute an admission that any accounts existed, or to name the banks, was held to not violate the 5.Amend. The court said that the compulsion in this case was more like "being forced to surrender a key to a strong box containing incriminating documents" than to "being compelled to reveal the combination to petitioner's wall safe," the latter of which would be "testimonial" and require the suspect to "disclose the contents of his own mind," which would implicate the protection against self-incrimination according to the case law of the USSC (*Doe v United States* 1988).

Normally, if the government subpoenas business records with self-incriminating contents, the defendant may not claim the 5.Amend. privilege against self-incrimination in relation to the contents of those papers, because the government did not compel him/her to create their self-incriminating contents. But the defendant may claim the 5.Amend. to resist turning over the papers, if the act of turning them over would be "testimonial," i.e., would aid the government in proving either that the documents exist, that they are authentic, or that they are in the possession of the defendant (*Fisher v United States* 1976; *United States v Doe* 1984). In addition, when the subpoena requires the defendant to search through numerous documents and match them to the one's allegedly in his possession according to the subpoena, the USSC has indicated that this identification process would require the defendant to "use the contents of his mind" in identifying the documents, which would be tantamount to answering a series of interrogatories in a deposition (*United States v Hubbell* 2000).

A person may not, however, resist a document or records subpoena, on the above-mentioned grounds, if his or her possession of the document or records is a "foregone conclusion" in the sense that response to the subpoena would not provide the government any information that it did not already have. The "foregone conclusion" doctrine would apply to most corporate records which corporations are required by law keep (*Fisher v United States* 1976; *United States v Doe* 1984).

In one case, a grand jury subpoenaed a defendant in a child pornography case and sought to compel him under oath to reveal the passwords to all of his computers. The court cited the *Doe* case and held that this would violate the 5.Amend., as the grand jury was not seeking documents or objects, but testimony in the form of the passwords, thus equating the passwords more to "combinations" than the "key" to a safe (*United States v Kirschner* 2010; discussed in Bales 2012, p. 1302). Similar decisions have been reached in child pornography cases where the grand jury had sought to compel the defendant to produce and decrypt his computer hard drives (*In re Grand Jury Subpoena Duces Tecum* 2012; cited in Bales 2012, pp. 1302–1303).

Several lower federal courts have required a suspect to produce and to decrypt computer files, and have used the "foregone conclusion" exception as a basis for its decision (Engel 2012, pp. 568–569). In one case, the FBI, as part of a mortgage fraud investigation, executed a search warrant at defendant's home and seized, among a number of computers, an encrypted laptop found in the defendant's bedroom along with indications that she used it. A court order to compel her to "to produce the unencrypted contents of the computer" and the encryption keys was held not to violate her 5.Amend. privilege against self-incrimination, because of the "foregone conclusion" that she was the primary user of the computer (*United States v Fricosu* 2012; discussed in Engel 2012, pp. 563–566). The Massachusetts Supreme Judicial Court also, while recognizing that being compelled to provide encryption tools is "testimonial," held that the defendant's possession of the tools and ability to decrypt had already been revealed through his own boasting (*Commonwealth v Gelfgatt* 2014).

It becomes immeasurably more difficult for government to compel a suspect to give up the password or the encryption tools for suspect files, if the encrypted files are not on the suspect's own computer hard-drives, but are stored in the files of an ICT provider somewhere far away from the defendant's computer, or as some call it, in the "cloud." An encrypted file stored in the cloud will often be very difficult to trace back to an individual, whether because of technical issues or because the file locations are shared among many individuals. This means that the act of producing a password or encryption key, whether it is solely in the suspect's mind or on a written document, will implicitly communicate that the person with the password or key has access to or possession of the electronic files (Engel 2012, pp. 568–569).

In reality, however, it appears that the government is seldom impeded in its investigations by encryption software, as very few criminal suspects, at least as of 2006, made use of it (Schwartz 2008, p. 293). In addition, NSA has used "supercomputers, technical trickery, court orders and behind-the-scenes persuasion to undermine the major tools protecting the privacy of everyday communications in the Internet age," according to documents disclosed by Edward Snowden. The NSA hacked into computers to record messages before they were encrypted, and coerced some companies to turn over their master encryption keys. It also secretly introduced weaknesses into the encryption standards used around the world. The NSA spends more than $250 million a year in its Sigint Enabling Project which is designed to undermine commercial encrypting programs. This massive assault on encryption devices, code-named "Bull Run," has achieved what the Clinton Administration failed to do with its attempt to compel installation of a "clipper chip" in the 1990s (Perlroth et al. 2013).

Use of Informants to Electronically Surveil Activities in the Home

Since the string of decisions ending with *United States v. White* (1971), conversations in homes may be surveilled by police without a warrant, if the police can manage to get their wired informant accepted as a guest in the suspect's home or private space. The theory is that the suspect has "assumed the risk" of communicating with him or in his presence (see *Almada v State* 1999). Using a wired informer has even been allowed when the informer did not speak the language, nor understand the contents of the recorded conversation (*United States v Longoria* 1999).

The *White* case inspired, however, a strong dissent by Justice Harlan, who questioned whether "we should impose on our citizens the risks of the electronic listener or observer without at least the protection of a warrant requirement." Justice Douglas, also dissenting in *White*, called electronic surveillance "the greatest leveler of human privacy ever known" which penetrates "all the walls and doors which men need to shield them from the pressures of a turbulent life around them and give them the health and strength to carry on." He said that "[m]onitoring, if prevalent, kills free discourse and spontaneous utterances. Free discourse—a First Amendment value—may be frivolous or serious, humble or defiant, reactionary or revolutionary, profane or in good taste; but it is not free if there is surveillance. Free discourse liberates the spirit, though it may produce only froth. The individual must keep some facts concerning his thoughts within a small zone of people. At the same time he must be free to pour out his woes or inspirations or dreams to others. He remains the sole judge as to what must be said and what must remain unspoken. This is the essence of the idea of privacy implicit in the First and Fifth Amendments, as well as in the Fourth" (*United States v. White* 1971).

Several States have followed the dissents in *White* and required police to secure a judicial warrant before sending a wired informant into a dwelling (*People v Beavers* 1975; *State v Glass* 1978; *Commonwealth v Brion* 1995; *State v Bridges* 1997; *State v Geraw* 2002; *State v Mullens* 2007), or at least the approval of a high-level prosecutor (*State v Worthy* 1995, based on reasonable suspicion).

Some federal courts allow the secret installation of audio or video monitoring devices in a suspect's private dwelling without a warrant if the police have an informant present in the house during the surveilled conversation or activities (*United States v Yonn* 1983; *United States v Myers* 1982; *United States v Lee* 2004). Other federal courts would, however, require judicial authorization under Title III (the wiretap statute) in such a situation (*United States v Padilla* 1975).

The prevailing view, however, is that warrantless, surreptitious videotaping inside a home by a person who has been invited into the residence does not violate the 4.Amend. (*United States v Davis* 2003; *United States v Wahchumwah* 2012). If government authorities cannot gain consensual entrance into a home to use secret recording devices or video cameras, then they must obtain judicial authorization which follows the guidelines set out in Title III, the wiretap statute.

Video Surveillance in the Home

Although secret videotaping in a home or other private space is not covered in Title III, the US wiretap statute, nor considered to be an "interception" under that statute (*United States v Torres* 1984), federal courts in their case law have created requirement of a "super warrant" which closely tracks the requirements of Title III, including the 30 day-limit (*United States v Koyomejian* 1992; see also *United States v Falls* 1994; *United States v Mesa-Rincon* 1990; *United States v Cuevas-Sanchez* 1987; *United States v Biasucci* 1986; *States v Page* 1996). Video surveillance in the home is also, according to one court, only permissible for a crime that could be the subject of a wiretap under Title III (*United States v Williams* 1997).

Access to Electronically Stored Information in Private Possession in General

Accessing Portable I-Phones, Pagers, and Other Portable Electronic Storage Devices

In 2014, the USSC tightened its rule on searches incident to arrest in holding that police could no longer treat a computer or smart phone as a mere "container" searchable without probable cause or a warrant after the arrest of its possessor. Barring exigent circumstances police must now get a search warrant to access the stored information on such a device (Riley v. California, 2014).

Some courts have required a search warrant to search a confiscated cellphone or iPhone, even if the information could have been obtained by court order from the service provider (*State v Boyd* 2010). One federal court, however, determined that police may record numbers called on a pager when it is seized in the "on" position, because the suspect, in making the call to the pager, assumed the risk that his message would be received by whomever happened to be in possession of the pager at the time (*United States v Meriwether* 1990).

Transactional Surveillance and General Access to Records in the Hands of Third Parties

Traditional USSC case law stripped citizens of privacy when, due to a service agreement with a bank, telephone company, internet provider, or other business, they turned over otherwise private information to this provider as a condition for receiving the service. Because no 4.Amend. protection is given, a judicial warrant based on probable cause is not required to access this information. Various coercive measures may be used by the government, some involving court participation, such as court orders and subpoenas, others not, such as National Security Letters (NSLs) and informal government "requests" to obtain such information. Information from such surveillance and access may be used in an ongoing investigation, or may just be stored in one of the government's many databases and subjected to data mining in the future.

Banking and Financial Transactions

1. Requirement of Subpoena or Search Warrant

Congress has passed legislation prohibiting the government from obtaining records from a financial institution except by subpoena or search warrant (12 USC § 3410–22). The USSC upheld the use of a subpoena to obtain banking records, because it held that the bank customer has no reasonable expectation in the bank's microfilms of checks, deposit slips, and other financial records compiled by the bank (*Miller* 1976). These subpoenas are not based on "probable cause," but may be issued if "there is reason to believe that the records sought are relevant to a legitimate law enforcement inquiry."

While subpoenas are also sufficient in New Jersey, that State's more protective Constitution requires that the subpoena be issued by a grand jury and allows the customer a period of time to object to the release of the records (*State v McAllister* 2004). Other States also give enhanced protection (*People v Nesbitt* 2010; *People v Mason* 1999, requiring "probable cause" for the issuance of a subpoena).

It recently became known that the CIA has secretly been gathering massive amounts of information about international money transfers without resorting to subpoenas or court orders. This practice has been supposedly authorized by the FISC, but the government has refused to make the decisions which allegedly did so public. The CIA claims the practice is authorized by the Patriot Act (Savage and Mazzetti 2013).

2. Cooperation Required by Financial Institutions

Banks are required by the Bank Secrecy Act of 1970 (BSA) (Pub L 91-508), to maintain records of their client's identities, to microfilm certain checks and to keep records of other items. The BSA also authorizes the Secretary of the Treasury to require financial institutions to file reports of certain payments, receipts, or transfers of currency or other monetary instruments, including those in excess of $10,000. These "currency transaction reports" are sent to the Financial Crimes Enforcement Network (FINCEN) which keeps them in computerized storage and makes them accessible to law enforcement (Thaman 2001). These provisions have been upheld by the USSC (*California Banker's Ass'n* 1974).

Government Access to Information from Other Service Providers

Since the USSC does not grant 4.Amend. protection to information given to service providers, the government can access this information without a showing of probable cause. As with bank records or communications metadata, even if the law requires a subpoena, the violation of this law will not usually lead to suppression of evidence gathered in the federal system. Courts have thus found no reasonable expectation of privacy in records of electricity use (*People v Stanley* 1999), in pharmacy prescription records (*State v Russo* 2002), or in medical records from a public health clinic (*State v Mubita* 2008; *Commonwealth v Efaw* 2001).

Some States accord a greater respect for privacy in such records. Thus, the Washington Supreme Court found a violation of its constitutional right to privacy when a public utility turned over records of a suspect's use of electricity without having gotten a court order and held that the evidence could not be used (*In re Maxfield* 1997). Washington also recognizes an expectation of privacy in one's name in a hotel registry, but would allow access to the information with reasonable suspicion (*State v Jordan* 2007; *In re Pers Restraint of Nichols* 2001). Some courts also require a search warrant for prescription drug records (*Douglas v Dobbs* 2005; State v. Skinner).

Mail Covers

"Envelope information" is the metaphor used for communications metadata, and, of course, the address and return address one affixes to a letter or package is much more public than an e-mail address or a website one visits. In its voracious appetite for data, the US government has instituted the Mail Isolation Control and Tracking program, in which computers of the US Postal Service photograph the exterior of every piece of paper mail that is processed in the USA, about 160 billion pieces, for instance, in 2012. It is not known how long the government saves the images.

Traditionally, criminal investigators would only request "mail covers" on a case by case basis, when one had localized a suspected criminal. The same was true, of course, for wiretaps and pen registers. No judicial control is necessary: all the investigator has to do is to fill out a form to get the information. Mail cover surveillance requests, which are almost always granted by the US Postal Service, are granted for about 30 days, and can be extended for up to 120 days. Requests can be related to criminal activity or national security. Criminal activity requests average 15,000–20,000 per year. Officials need probable cause, and a warrant, of course to open a letter (Nixon 2013, 2014).

The Problem of Secret Interception of Data with No Notification Provisions and Its Shared Use by National Security and Criminal Enforcement Organs

The Right to Discover Whether One Was a Target of Secret Surveillance

The government need not inform a person that he or she has been the subject of surveillance under the Foreign Intelligence Surveillance Act (FISA), nor whether the government has installed pen/trap devices, or gathered stored communications metadata or electronic communications by subpoena or NSL directed to service providers. As a matter of fact, no lawyer has ever gotten discovery of the records which gave rise to a FISA search since the promulgation of FISA in 1978 (Savage 2014).

In the wake of the revelation of the secret NSA interceptions during the administration of George W. Bush, several lawsuits were filed by NGOs on behalf of persons attempting to ascertain whether they had their confidential communications intercepted during that long-term operation. An Islamic charity sued President Bush and other executive branch entities, alleging that it was subjected to warrantless electronic surveillance under the NSA program, but the government claimed that the "state secrets" privilege prevented it from revealing the information for the purposes of the lawsuit (*Al-Haramain Islamic Foundation Inc v Bush* 2007).

The American Civil Liberties Union (ACLU) sued the government on behalf of a group of lawyers and journalists alleging that the program violated FISA and that they had likely had their conversations intercepted thereunder, and another group of citizens sued AT&T on account of its collaboration with the allegedly illegal NSA program. In both cases, the government moved to dismiss the suits, either on the ground that the plaintiffs lacked standing, i.e., could not prove their conversations were intercepted, or because "state secrets" would have to be revealed in defending the suit. In both cases, the plaintiffs were ultimately denied relief based in the allegation of "state secrets" (*ACLU v NSA* 2007; *Hepting v AT&T* 2006; see Casey 2008, pp. 1020–1025).

The US chapter of Amnesty International challenged the NSA wiretap program on behalf of certain lawyers, human rights, labor, legal, and media organizations whose work requires them to engage in sensitive and sometimes privileged telephone and e-mail communications with colleagues, clients, sources, and other individuals located abroad. The complaint alleged that some of the persons with whom the plaintiffs communicated could be people that the government believes are associated with terrorist organizations and that the provision of the 2008 amendments of FISA, 50 U.S.C. §1881a, which allow such surveillance, would prevent them from engaging in their livelihood through the use of international correspondence by telephone or e-mail. The USSC denied the plaintiffs standing, claiming they could present no clear evidence that their conversations had been intercepted, or that future threatened injury was "certainly impending" and thus no "case or controversy" existed, which the court could entertain (*Clapper v Amnesty Intern USA* 2013).

The government's lawyer in *Clapper*, in his arguments, alleged that the only way a person could have "standing" to challenge secret NSA wiretaps, and to find out if her communications were intercepted in the first place, would be if she were charged in court and the government filed a notice of intent to use the intercepted communications in its case.

Nevertheless, in subsequent prosecutions, federal prosecutors have refused to make the promised disclosures, even after charges have been filed, thus undercutting the assurances the government lawyer had made to the USSC in *Clapper* (Savage 2013). This situation is now changing and the government has notified some defendants in pending and final cases that they were subjected to the secret wiretapping (Savage 2013).

"Hand-Off" Procedures to Avoid Notification Requirements of Title III or Other Laws

The wiretap "hand-off" procedure was used by investigators in Los Angeles beginning in the 1980s. It involves an initial issuance of a wiretap order by a judge. Once the wiretap yields evidence of criminal conduct, the investigating agents would then transmit the information to another unit without expressly stating that the information was discovered through a wiretap. The receiving unit then conducts further investigation. Evidence gathered during that second investigation would yield independent probable cause to arrest the targets. The defendant would be prosecuted without ever knowing that he was subjected to the wiretap surveillance (*Whitaker v Garcetti* 2003).

"Hand off" procedures were also apparently the main tool used to develop the material gathered in the secret NSA surveillance programs. This arguably illegally gathered information was secretly fed back into the established legal system of telecommunications surveillance. It has been estimated that from 10 % to 20 % of FISA warrants annually are based on information gathered in the secret NSA domestic surveillance program (Schwartz 2008, p. 307).

The secret NSA program has led, in the words of one commentator, to a "secret parallel system of telecommunications surveillance," where information collected in it is fed back into the official system in a fashion that leaves no traces. The system is "built on secret presidential authorizations, secret DOJ legal opinions; nonbinding presidential promises; an executive that refuses to provide Congress and the public with necessary information; and, most recently, acquiescent congressional legislation enacted in ignorance of the true dimensions of NSA activities" (Schwartz 2008, p. 309).

The Problem of Removing the "Wall" Between Traditional Law Enforcement and National Security Information Gathering

Since involvement of the Army and CIA in domestic surveillance of anti-Vietnam War and Black Power activists in the 1960s and 1970s, there was a concerted effort to separate traditional law enforcement from intelligence gathering. This so-called "wall" between the two arms of government meant that only FISA would be used for intelligence wiretaps and Title III for conventional organized crime investigations. Although the President had authority prior to the enactment of FISA to conduct national security wiretaps, federal courts would exclude evidence gained from such wiretaps when it turned out that the investigation had become, primarily, a conventional criminal enforcement operation (*United States v Truong Dinh Hung* 1980).

Even before 9–11, however, evidence legally gathered through a FISA wiretap could be used in a criminal prosecution against a US person (*United States v Duggan* 1984; *United States v Nicholson* 1997; *United States v Pelton* 1987; *United States v Sarkissian* 1988). After 9–11, however, the standard for a FISA wiretap was lowered to require only that a "significant purpose" of the wiretap was aimed at foreign intelligence, instead of the "primary purpose" language that existed in the original version of FISA. The Patriot Act intentionally aimed at removing the so-called "wall." This made it easier for FISA wiretaps to be simultaneously used for foreign intelligence as well as for conventional criminal investigation. And, with the lower threshold, as long as the wiretap can be justified under FISA, the evidence may be used in a conventional criminal prosecution as well (*United States v Ning Wen* 2006). The FISA Appeals Court has also ruled conclusively that there is no harm in "sharing" of material between law enforcement and intelligence operatives and that no such "wall" ever really existed (*In re: Sealed Case* 2002).

Because of the more flexible rules for FISA wiretaps, metadata orders and NSLs, the bulk of which are acquired by NSA and FBI, lesser law enforcement entities, such as the Drug Enforcement Administration (DEA) seek to tailor their requests for wiretaps to fall within the categories of terrorism or national security, but the NSA is often reluctant to allow more conventional law enforcement agencies access to its huge archives of electronic metadata (Lichtblau and Schmidt 2013).

The Search for a New Paradigm

It is becoming clear to more scholars, judges, and the public in the USA, that the traditional 4.Amend. approach to privacy protection is obsolete in the digital age. Even before the revelations of Edward Snowden in June, 2013, Justice Sotomayor, in *United States v. Jones* indicates that it is time for a change. She wrote:

> [I]t may be necessary to reconsider the premise that an individual has no reasonable expectation of privacy in information voluntarily disclosed to third parties. This approach is ill suited to the digital age, in which people reveal a great deal of information about themselves to third parties in the course of carrying out mundane tasks. People disclose the phone numbers that they dial or text to their cellular providers; the URLs that they visit and the e-mail addresses with which they correspond to their Internet service providers; and the books, groceries, and medications they purchase to online retailers (…). I for one doubt that people would accept without complaint the warrantless disclosure to the Government of a list of every Web site they had visited in the last week, or month, or year. But whatever the societal expectations, they can attain constitutionally protected status only if our Fourth Amendment jurisprudence ceases to treat secrecy as a prerequisite for privacy. I would not assume that all information voluntarily disclosed to some member of the public for a limited purpose is, for that reason alone, disentitled to Fourth Amendment protection. Privacy is not a discrete commodity, possessed absolutely or not at all. Those who disclose certain

> facts to a bank or phone company for a limited business purpose need not assume that this information will be released to other persons for other purposes (*United States v Jones* 2012a, b).

For the new generation of users of social media, such as Facebook, Twitter, Linked-In, etc., electronic communications of feelings and ideas can be seen as a surrogate for conversations which might earlier have taken place in a protected place like a home or a telephone conversation. The fact that one must enlist a service provider to facilitate these exchanges, according to this opinion, is not a sufficient reason for denying the protection that the 4.Amend. gives to homes, and telephone conversations (Ghoshray 2012, pp. 82–85; McAllister 2012, pp. 499–500).

The USSC has gradually extended the realm of privacy, first in the home, with decisions preventing use of a thermal imager (*Kyllo*) or a canine sniff (*Florida v. Jardines*), and even in automobiles, with the limitation of searches incident to arrest under *Gant*. But the decision in *Jones* and the strong concurring opinions of Justices Sotomayor and Alito, along with State court and lower federal court decisions limiting long-term surveillance in public places by GPS or cellphone location, seem to indicate a trend in the courts of recognizing the new necessities of protection in this era of massive use of ICT and the switch in the understanding of the population on what should be kept from government eyes.

This new approach to the 4.Amend., reflected in the concurring opinions in *Jones*, focusing on the totality of the actions of law enforcement in its surveillance of a suspect, and not on whether each sequential step taken by law enforcement comports or not with USSC interpretations of the 4.Amend., i.e., was, or was not a "search" according to the high court's jurisprudence, has been labeled a "mosaic theory" of the 4.Amend. (see generally, Kerr 2012). This approach appears to denigrate the traditional "inside-outside" demarcations which characterized the court's jurisprudence: i.e., all in the house, in private is protected, all in public, revealed to a third person, "envelope" information, is not (supporting the "inside-outside" approach and rejecting the "Mosaic" approach see Kerr 2012, pp. 346–353).

The outrage at the new revelations, by Edward Snowden, of the massive NSA data mining and surveillance aimed at US citizens and foreign citizens and governments, is also indicative of the fact that the USSC's interpretation of the 4.Amend. is falling behind the times. Sociological studies have shown, indeed, that the majority doctrines applied by the USSC in relation to using pen registers, GPS tracking devices, or cellphone site location do not correspond to the expectations of privacy held by a significant majority of society (McAllister 2012, pp. 512–529; Slobogin 2008, pp. 333–336).

Some critics suggest a rejection of the "reasonable expectation of privacy" test in favor of a test based on expectations of "security" from government intrusion, thus returning to the language of the 4.Amend. which says that the people should be "secure in their persons, houses, papers and effects" (Casey 2008, pp. 1030–1031).

In the area of data mining, Christopher Slobogin suggests that we should reject the one-size-fits-all approach of USSC case law that treats all information given to a third party as lacking 4.Amend. protection. He feels simple subpoenas should suffice for obtaining corporate and most public records, but probable cause and a warrant should be required to obtain records containing the most personal information, such as bank records, telephone records and ISP logs. A court order, based on reasonable suspicion, on the other hand, would suffice when the government sought to obtain records that are quasi-private, such as power consumption, or school records (Slobogin 2008, p. 337).

Slobogin differentiates between target-driven searches, and "event driven" cases where public or quasi-public information is matched in response to an investigation of a crime, in order to identify possible suspects. Since these types of searches only involve matching one or two bits of information (whether a person lived in a certain city during a certain period or bought a particular type of shoe). Here one's record is merely one of hundreds or thousands, and will be discarded or at least ignored if it does not prove of interest to investigators. For this type of data mining, no judicial order would be needed (Slobogin 2008, p. 338).

The uproar about the Snowden revelations nearly led to the US House of Representative imposing restrictions on the powers of the NSA to intercept *en masse* communications metadata (Weisman 2013), and there is evidence that the public is losing confidence in the spy agencies, CIA and NSA, and the government in general due to the phone and internet surveillance, the use of Drones, and the earlier scandals around the use of torture (Shane 2013d). Hopefully this means that changes may be on the way.

References

Adler, M. (1996). Cyberspace, general searches, and digital contraband: The fourth amendment and the net-wide search. *Yale Law Journal, 105*, 1093.

Apuzzo, M. (2014, March 19). Judge Rebukes Justice Dept. for Requesting Overly Broad E-Mail Searches. *New York Times*. Retrieved July 9, 2015, from http://www.nytimes.com/2014/03/20/us/judge-rebukes-officials-over-requests-for-broad-email-searches.html?ref=us.

Automatic Number Plate Recognition. (2015). *Wikipedia*. Retrieved March 22, 2015, from http://en.wikipedia.org/wiki/Automatic_number_plate_recognition#United_States.

Bales, C. (2012). Unbreakable: The fifth amendment and computer passwords. *Arizona State Law Journal, 44*, 1293.

Brenner, S. (2012). Encryption, smart phones, and the fifth amendment. *Whittier Law Review, 33*, 525; 533–534.

Casey, T. (2008). Electronic surveillance and the right to be secure. *University of California Davis Law Review, 41*, 977.

Engel, J. (2012). Rethinking the application of the fifth amendment to passwords and encryption in the age of cloud computing. *Whittier Law Review, 33*, 543.

Fox, C. (2012). Checking in: Historic cell site location information and the stored communications act. *Seton Hall Law Review, 42*, 769.

Ghoshray, S. (2012). Looking through the prism of privacy and trespass: Smartphones and the fourth amendment. *University of the District of Columbia David A. Clarke School of Law Review, 16*, 73.

Glanz, J., Larson, J., & Lehren, A. W. (2014, January 27). Spy agencies tap data streaming from phone apps. *New York Times*. Retrieved July 9, 2015, from http://www.nytimes.com/2014/01/28/world/spy-agencies-scour-phone-apps-for-personal-data.html?ref=world&_r=0.

Goldstein, J. (2013, January 15). Police to use fake pill bottles to track drugstore thieves. *New York Times*. Retrieved July 9, 2015, from http://www.nytimes.com/2013/01/16/nyregion/ny-police-to-track-drugstore-robbers-via-decoy-bottles.html.

Kerr, O. (2010). Applying the fourth amendment to the Internet: A general approach. *Stanford Law Review, 62*, 1005.

Kerr, O. (2012). The mosaic theory of the fourth amendment. *Michigan Law Review, 111*, 311.

Kimel, C. (2013). DNA profiles, computer searches, and the fourth amendment. *Duke Law Journal, 62*, 933.

Lichtblau, E., & Schmidt M. S. (2013, August 3). Other agencies clamor for data N.S.A. compiles. *New York Times*. Retrieved July 9, 2015, from http://www.nytimes.com/2013/08/04/us/other-agencies-clamor-for-data-nsa-compiles.html?ref=us.

Lichtblau, E. (2005, April 5). Justice Dept. Defends Patriot Act Before Senate Hearings. *New York Times* (p. A21).

Mazzetti, M., & Elliot, J. (2013, December 9). Spies infiltrate a fantasy realm of online games. *New York Times*. Retrieved July 9, 2015, from http://www.nytimes.com/2013/12/10/world/spies-dragnet-reaches-a-playing-field-of-elves-and-trolls.html?ref=world.

McAllister, M. (2012). The fourth amendment and new technologies: The misapplication of analogical reasoning. *Southern Illinois University Law Journal, 36*, 475.

Miller, G., Tate, J., & Gellman, B. (2013, October 16). Documents reveal N.S.A.'s extensive involvement in targeted killing program. *Washington Post*. Retrieved July 9, 2015, from http://www.washingtonpost.com/world/national-security/documents-reveal-nsas-extensive-involvement-in-targeted-killing-program/2013/10/16/29775278-3674-11e3-8a0e-4e2cf80831fc_story.html.

Nixon, R. (2013, July 3). U.S. postal service logging all mail for law enforcement. *New York Times*. Retrieved July 9, 2015, from http://www.nytimes.com/2013/07/04/us/monitoring-of-snail-mail.html?ref=us.

Nixon, R. (2014, October 27). Report reveals wider tracking of mail in U.S. *New York Times*. Retrieved July 9, 2015, from http://www.nytimes.com/2014/10/28/us/us-secretly-monitoring-mail-of-thousands.html?ref=us.

Perlroth, N., Larson, J., & Shane, S. (2013, September 5). N.S.A. able to foil basic safeguards of privacy on web. *New York Times*. Retrieved July 9, 2015, from http://www.nytimes.com/2013/09/06/us/nsa-foils-much-internet-encryption.html?ref=world.

Risen, J., & Lichtblau, E. (2013, June 8). How the U.S. uses technology to mine more data more quickly. *New York Times*. Retrieved July 9, 2015, from http://www.nytimes.com/2013/06/09/us/revelations-give-look-at-spy-agencys-wider-reach.html?ref=world&_r=0.

Risen, J., & Poitras, L. (2014, May 31). N.S.A. collecting millions of faces from web images. *New York Times*. Retrieved July 9, 2015, from http://www.nytimes.com/2014/06/01/us/nsa-collecting-millions-of-faces-from-web-images.html?ref=us.

Savage, C., & Baker, P. (2013, May 22). Obama, in a shift, to limit targets of drone strikes. *New York Times*. Retrieved July 9, 2015, from http://www.nytimes.com/2013/05/23/us/us-acknowledges-killing-4-americans-in-drone-strikes.html?ref=us.

Savage, C., & Mazzetti, M. (2013, November 14). C.I.A. collects global data on transfers of money. *New York Times*. Retrieved July 9, 2015, from http://www.nytimes.com/2013/11/15/us/cia-collecting-data-on-international-money-transfers-officials-say.html.

Savage, C. (2013, July 25). Roberts's picks reshaping secret surveillance court. *New York Times*. Retrieved July 9, 2015, from http://www.nytimes.com/2013/07/26/us/politics/robertss-picks-reshaping-secret-surveillance-court.html?ref=us.

Savage, C. (2014, June 17). Lawyer not entitled to see classified surveillance material court rules. *New York Times*. Retrieved July 9, 2015, from http://www.nytimes.com/2014/06/18/us/lawyer-not-entitled-to-see-classified-surveillance-material-court-rules.html?ref=us.

Schwartz, P. (2008). Reviving telecommunications surveillance law. *University of Chicago Law Review, 75*, 287.

Sengupta, S. (2013a, February 15). Rise of drones in U.S. drives efforts to limit police use. *New York Times*. Retrieved July 9, 2015, from http://www.nytimes.com/2013/02/16/technology/rise-of-drones-in-us-spurs-efforts-to-limit-uses.html?ref=us&_r=0.

Sengupta, S. (2013b, October 13). Privacy fears grow as cities increase surveillance. *New York Times*. Retrieved July 9, 2015, from http://www.nytimes.com/2013/10/14/technology/privacy-fears-as-surveillance-grows-in-cities.html?ref=us.
Shane, S. (2013a, April 7). Targeted killing comes to define war on terror. *New York Times*. Retrieved July 9, 2015, from http://www.nytimes.com/2013/04/08/world/targeted-killing-comes-to-define-war-on-terror.html?ref=world&_r=0.
Shane, S. (2013b, February 8). Debating a court to vet drone strikes. *New York Times*. Retrieved July 9, 2015, from http://www.nytimes.com/2013/02/09/world/a-court-to-vet-kill-lists.html?ref=us&_r=0.
Shane, S. (2013c, July 19). Surveillance court renews order for phone call data. *New York Times*. Retrieved July 9, 2015, from http://www.nytimes.com/2013/07/20/us/surveillance-court-renews-order-for-phone-call-data.html?ref=us.
Shane, S. (2013d, July 25). Spy agencies under heaviest scrutiny since abuse scandal of the 70's. *New York Times*. Retrieved July 9, 2015, from http://www.nytimes.com/2013/07/26/us/politics/challenges-to-us-intelligence-agencies-recall-senate-inquiry-of-70s.html?ref=us.
Slobogin, C. (2005). Transaction surveillance by the government. *Mississippi Law Journal, 75*, 139.
Slobogin, C. (2008). Government data mining and the fourth amendment. *University of Chicago Law Review, 75*, 317.
Sullivan, B. (2001, November 20). FBI software cracks encryption wall. *MSNBC*. Retrieved July 9, 2015, from http://www.nbcnews.com/id/3341694/#.UZCVKcrLsoE.
Thaman, S. C. (2001). Landesbericht U.S.A. In W. Gropp & B. Huber (Eds.), *Rechtliche Initiativen gegen organisierte Kriminalität*. Freiburg im Breisgau: Max-Planck-Institute for Foreign and International Comparative Law.
Weisman, J. (2013, July 24). House defeats effort to rein in N.S.A. data gathering. *New York Times*. Retrieved July 9, 2015, from http://www.nytimes.com/2013/07/25/us/politics/house-defeats-effort-to-rein-in-nsa-data-gathering.html?ref=us.
Worth, R. F., Mazzetti, M., & Shane, S. (2013, February 6). Hazards of drone strikes face rare public scrutiny. *New York Times* (p. A1, A10).

United States Court Cases

ACLU v. NSA, 493 F 3d 644, 655-57 (6th Cir 2007).
Al-Haramain Islamic Foundation Inc v Bush, 507 F 3d 1190, 1193 (9th Cir 2007).
Almada v State, 994 P 2d 299, 307-08 (Wyo 1999).
Andresen v Maryland, 427 US 463, 473 (1976).
Baird v State, 398 S W 3d 220, 230 (Tex Crim App 2013).
California Banker's Ass'n, 416 US 21, 53-54 (1974).
Clapper v. Amnesty Intern USA,133 S Ct 1138, 1148-49 (2013).
Commonwealth v Augustine, 4 N E 3d 846, 867 (Mass 2014).
Commonwealth v Bender, 811 A 2d 1016 (Pa Super 2002).
Commonwealth v Brion, 652 A 2d 287, 289 (Pa 1995).
Commonwealth v Efaw, 774 A 2d 735 (Pa 2001).
Commonwealth v Gelfgatt, 11 N E 3d 605, 615-16 (Mass 2014).
Commonwealth v Rousseau, 990 N E 2d 543, 551–53 (Mass 2013).
Cowles v State, 23 P 3d 1168, 1172 (Alaska 2001).
Devega v State, 689 S E 2d 293, 299–300 (Ga 2010).
Doe v United States, 487 US 201, 214–19 (1988).
Douglas v Dobbs, 419 F 3d 1097, 1102 (10th Cir 2005).
Fisher v United States, 425 US 391, 408 (1976).
Florida v Jardines, 133 S Ct 1409, 1416 (2013).

Frasier v State, 794 N E 2d 449, 465 (Ind App 2003).
Georgia v Randolph, 547 US 103, 109–23 (2006).
Guest v Leis, 255 F 3d 325, 335, 342 (6th Cir 2001).
Hedgepath v Commonwealth, 441 S W 3d 119, 130–31 (Ky 2014).
Hepting v AT&T, 439 F Supp 2d 974 (N D Cal 2006).
In re Application of the U.S. for an Order Authorizing the Use of Two Pen Register and Trap and Trace Devices, 632 F Supp 2d 202, 211 (E D N Y 2008).
In re Application of the United States for an Order Authorizing the Use of a Pen Register & a Trap & Trace Device & (2) Authorizing Release of Subscriber Info. & Cell Site Info., 384 F Supp 2d 562, 564 (E D N Y 2005).
In re Application of the United States, 736 F Supp 2d 578, 579 (E D N Y 2010).
In re Application of the United States, 747 F Supp 2d 827, 846 (S D Tex 2010).
In re Application of the United States, 809 F Supp 2d 113, 116, 127 (E D N Y 2011).
In re Application of United States for Historical Cell Site Data, 724 F 3d 600, 610–12 (5th Cir 2013).
In re Application of United States of America for Order Directing Provider of Electronic Communication Service to Disclose Records to Government, 620 F 3d 304, 312–13 (3d Cir 2010).
In re Grand Jury Subpoena Duces Tecum Dated March 25, 2011, 670 F 3d 1335, 1346, 1352–53 (11th Cir 2012).
In re Maxfield, 945 P 2d 196, 200–01 (Wash 1997).
In re Pers Restraint of Nichols, 256 P 3d 1131, 1135 (Wash 2001).
In re: Sealed Case No's 02-001, 02-002, 310 F 3d 717, 721 (USFIS App 2002).
Kyllo v United States, 533 US 27, 37 (2001).
Massachusetts v Sheppard, 468 US 981, 987–88 (1984).
People v Beavers, 227 N W 2d 511, 514 (Mich 1975).
People v Devone, 931 N E 2d 70, 74 (N Y 2010).
People v Gall, 30 P 3d 145, 153 (Colo 2011).
People v Harris, 886 N E 2d 947 (Ill 2008).
People v Mason, 989 P 2d 757, 760 (Colo 1999).
People v Nesbitt, 938 N E 2d 600, 605–06 (Ill App 2010).
People v Prinzing, 907 N.E.2d 87, 99–100 (Ill App 2009).
People v Stanley, 86 Cal Rptr 2d 89, 93 (Cal App 1999).
People v Weaver, 909 N E 2d 1195, 1199–1202 (N Y 2009).
Riley v. California, 134 S.Ct. 2473 (2014).
State v Augafa, 992 P 2d 723, 734 (Haw App 1999).
State v Boyd, 992 A 2d 1071, 1082–83 (Conn 2010).
State v Brereton, 826 N W 2d 369, 379 (Wis 2013).
State v Bridges, 925 P 2d 357 (Haw 1997).
State v Clark, 916 P 2d 384, 390 (Wash 1996).
State v Davis, 732 N W 2d 173, 182 (Minn 2007).
State v Domicz, 907 A 2d 395, 402–04 (N J 2006).
State v Earls, 70 A 3d 630, 645 (N J 2013).
State v Geraw, 795 A 2d 1219, 1225–26 (Vt 2002).
State v Glass, 583 P 2d 872, 875 (Alaska 1978).
State v Henderson, 854 N W 2d 616, 632–33 (Neb 2014).
State v Holden, 964 P 2d 318, 322 (Utah App 1998).
State v Jackson, 76 P 3d 217, 224 (Wash 2003).
State v Jordan, 156 P 3d 893, 898 (Wash 2007).
State v McAllister, 840 A 2d 967, 969 (N J App 2004).
State v Mubita, 188 P 3d 867, 875 (Idaho 2008).
State v Mullens, 650 S E 2d 169, 190 (W Va 2007).
State v Ortiz, 600 N W 2d 805, 817 (Neb 1999).

State v Page, 911 P 2d 513 (Alaska 1996).
State v Ruck, 155 Idaho 475, 484 (2013).
State v Rupnick, 125 P 3d 541, 547–48 (Kan 2005).
State v Russo, 790 A 2d 1132, 1140–41 (Conn 2002).
State v Skinner, 10 So 3d 1212, 1217–18 (La 2009).
State v Sloane, 939 A 2d 796, 803–04 (N J 2008).
State v Sobczak, 833 N W 2d 59, 71–73 (Wis 2013).
State v Subdiaz-Osorio, 849 N W 2d 748 (Wis 2014).
State v Tackitt, 67 P 3d 295, 302–03 (Mont 2003).
State v Wiegand, 645 N W 2d 125, 137 (Minn 2005).
State v Williams, 590 S E 2d 151, 154–55 (Ga App 2003).
State v Worthy, 661 A 2d 1244 (N J 1995).
State v Young, 867 P 2d 593 (Wash 1994).
State v Zahn, 812 N W 2d 490, 498 (S D 2012).
Stevenson v State, 667 So 2d 410, 411–12 (Fla App 1996).
Tracey v State, 152 So 3d 504, 524–26 (Fla 2014).
United States v Adjani, 452 F 3d 1140, 1150 (9th Cir 2006).
United States v Al-Marri, 230 F Supp 2d 535, 539–40 (S D N Y 2002).
United States v Andrus, 483 F 3d 711, 719–22 (10th Cir 2007).
United States v Biasucci, 786 F 2d 504, 510–11 (2d Cir 1986).
United States v Boyce, 351 F 3d 1102, 1107, 1111 (11th Cir 2003).
United States v Bradley, 644 F 3d 1213, 1259–61 (11th Cir 2011).
United States v Bridges, 344 F 3d 1010, 1016 (9th Cir 2003).
United States v Carey, 172 F 3d 1268, 1273 (10th Cir 1999).
United States v Christie, 717 F 3d 1156, 1164–66 (10th Cir 2013).
United States v Comprehensive Drug Testing, Inc, 621 F 3d 1162, 1171–72 (9th Cir 2010).
United States v Coreas, 419 F 3d 151, 157–59 (2d Cir 2005).
United States v Cuevas-Sanchez, 821 F 2d 248, 252 (5th Cir 1987).
United States v Davis, 326 F 3d 361, 365–66 (2d Cir 2003).
United States v Davis, 754 F 3d 1205, 1217 (2014).
United States v Doe, 465 US 605, 612–14 (1984).
United States v Duggan, 743 F 2d 59, 78 (2d Cir 1984).
United States v Falls, 34 F 3d 674, 680 (8th Cir 1994).
United States v Fernandez, 600 F3d 56 (1st Cir 2010).
United States v Forest, 355 F 3d 942, 950–51 (6th Cir 2004).
United States v Forrester, 512 F 3d 500, 509–11 (9th Cir 2008).
United States v Frechette, 583 F 3d 374, 379 (6th Cir 2009).
United States v Fricosu, 841 F Supp 2d 1232, 1237 (D Colo 2012).
United States v Garcia, 474 F 3d 994 (7th Cir 2007).
United States v Gonzalez, 328 F 3d 543, 548 (9th Cir 2003).
United States v Gourde, 440 F 3d 1065, 1071 (9th Cir 2006).
United States v Hambrick, 55 F Supp 2d 504, 508 (W D Va 1999).
United States v Heatley, 41 F Supp 2d 284 (S D N Y 1999).
United States v Hill, 459 F 3d 966, 975–77 (9th Cir 2006).
United States v Hill, 459 F 3d 966, 978 (9th Cir 2006).
United States v Hubbell, 530 US 27, 43 (2000).
United States v Jones, 132 S Ct 945, 946 (2012).
United States v Jones, 132 S Ct 945, 957 (2012).
United States v Karo, 468 US 705, 714–18 (1984).
United States v Kattaria, 503 F 3d 703, 707 (8th Cir 2007).
United States v Kennedy, 81 F Supp 2d 1103, 1110 (D Kan 2000).
United States v King, 604 F 3d 125, 134–37 (3d Cir 2010).
United States v Kirschner, 823 F Supp 2d 665, 668–69 (E D Mich 2010).
United States v Knotts, 460 US 276, 282 (1983).
United States v Kouzmine, 921 F Supp 1131, 1135 (S D N Y 1996).

United States v Koyomejian, 970 F 2d 536, 542 (9th Cir 1992).
United States v Lee, 359 F 3d 194, 199–203 (3d Cir 2004).
United States v Longoria, 177 F 3d 1179, 1183–84 (10th Cir 1999).
United States v Lucas, 640 F 3d 168, 177–78 (6th Cir 2011).
United States v Mann, 592 F 3d 779, 785 (7th Cir 2010).
United States v Martin, 426 F 3d 68, 74–75 (2d Cir 2005).
United States v Maynard, 615 F 3d 544, 560–63 (D C Cir 2010).
United States v McArthur, 573 F 3d 608, 613 (8th Cir 2009).
United States v Meriwether, 917 F 2d 955, 959 (6th Cir 1990).
United States v Mesa-Rincon, 911 F 2d 1433, 1437 (10th Cir 1990).
United States v Miller, 425 US 435, 442 (1976).
United States v Myers, 692 F 2d 823, 859 (2d Cir 1982).
United States v Nicholson, 955 F Supp 588, 590–93 (E D Va 1997).
United States v Ning Wen, 471 F 3d 777 (7th Cir 2006).
United States v Padilla, 520 F 2d 526, 528 (1st Cir 1975).
United States v Paxton, 573 F 3d 859, 861–62 (9th Cir 2009).
United States v Pelton, 835 F 2d 1067, 1075–76 (4th Cir 1987).
United States v Purcell, 236 F 3d 1274, 1279 (11th Cir 2001).
United States v Reyes, 922 F Supp 818, 833–34 (S D N Y 1996).
United States v Richards, 659 F 3d 527, 539–40 (6th Cir 2011).
United States v Sarkissian, 841 F 2d 959, 965 (9th Cir 1988).
United States v Scarfo, 180 F Supp 2d 572, 578 (D N J 2001).
United States v Shields, 458 F 3d 269, 278 (3d Cir 2006).
United States v Thomas, 757 F2d 1359, 1367 (2d Cir 1985).
United States v Torres, 751 F 2d 875, 880–82 (7th Cir 1984).
United States v Truong Dinh Hung, 629 F 2d 908 (4th Cir 1980).
United States v Turner, 169 F 3d 84, 88–89 (1st Cir 1999).
United States v Upham, 168 F 3d 532, 535 (1st Cir 1999).
United States v Vankesteren, 553 F 3d 286, 290–91 (4th Cir 2009).
United States v Villegas, 899 F 2d 1324, 1335–36 (2d Cir 1990).
United States v Wagers, 452 F 3d 534, 542–43 (6th Cir 2006).
United States v Wahchumwah, 704 F 3d 606 (9th Cir 2012).
United States v White, 401 US 745, 749–51, 762–63, Douglas dissent at 756, Harlan dissent at 786 (1971).
United States v Williams, 124 F 3d 411, 417 (3d Cir 1997).
United States v Williams, 592 F 3d 511, 521–24 (4th Cir 2010).
United States v Yonn, 702 F 2d 1341, 1347 (11th Cir 1983).
United States v Ziegler, 474 F 3d 1184, 1191–92 (9th Cir 2007).
US v Giberson, 527 F 3d 882, 889–90 (9th Cir 2008).
Whitaker v Garcetti, 291 F Supp 2d 1132, 1138 (C D Cal 2003).

United States Statutes

§ 213 US PATRIOT Act
12 USC § 3410–22.
18 USC § 2705(a)(2).
18 USC § 3103(a).
18 USC §§ 2701–12.
50 USC § 1825(b).
50 USC §§ 1822–24.
Pub L 91-508, 84 Stat 1114 (1970).

Part II
Organized Crime, Trafficking and Delinquency

Chapter 7
The Mafia Psychology: The Study of the 'Ndrangheta and the Cosa Nostra

Francesca Calandra and Antonino Giorgi

Introducing the "Subjectual Group Analysis" and Exploring the "Mafia Psychism"

In this chapter the brief explanation of the Subjectual Group Analysis' theoretical framework covers a key role in the deepening of the Mafia Psychism.

The Subjectual Group Analysis consists of the specific Italian development of Foulkesian group analysis (Lo Verso and Di Blasi 2011). This theoretical and methodological approach is a fundamental part of the clinical work and in order to explain the dynamics existing between the psychological internal and external field of family emotion and relationships, is interlaced with the Epistemology of complexity (Lo Verso 1998), the theories on the plasticity of the brain (Gabbard 2007; Elliot et al. 2010), the hermeneutics (Gadamer 1960), and the cultural anthropology.

Specifically, the term "subjectual" is used with the aim to refer to the unconscious and internal world as a "place" populated by relationships (historically and as a group) which exist individually. Hence, the "relational field" in which the individuals are included since its birth is related to the familiar context lived. For this reason the "family" could be considered the necessary passage in linking interpersonal and internal world of people. According to this theory, each individual is the resultant of the mixture of some overpersonal psychic factors (i.e., biological, ethnic-anthropological, transgenerational, institutional, and socio-communicative). Seeing as "the group is indeed the matrix of psychological life" (Foulkes 1975), also the understanding of Mafia Psychism does not exclude the intimate linking

F. Calandra (✉)
University of Palermo, Palermo, Italy
e-mail: francescamaria.calandra@gmail.com

A. Giorgi
Catholic University of the Sacred Heart, Brescia, Italy
e-mail: Antonino.Giorgi@unicatt.it

E.C. Viano (ed.), *Cybercrime, Organized Crime, and Societal Responses*,
DOI 10.1007/978-3-319-44501-4_7

between culture, family, individual and criminal organization. Therefore, the central concept of the psychic family field, anthropologically influenced, is essential not only for the understanding of the transpersonal and foundational aspects of the personality (Lo Verso 1998; Lo Verso et al. 2003; Lo Verso 2005, 2013), but also for the investigation of the working principles that distinguish the mafia psyche. Although the *group* has already described by Foulkes *as the place of birth of psychic life*, at the same time the psychic family field might produce mental illness and psychopathological diseases. The latter hypothesis could be true if individual was assimilated in familiar pattern characterized by the impossibility to modify the intergenerational code received. In this condition of *saturation* of the familiar matrix, the interpersonal ties and boundaries are rigid, monolithic; the cultural and symbolic heritage it cannot be changed, but only repeated again and again as in a form of *fundamentalism*. Hence, belonging to such psychic family field means being a robot, a replicant, a clone.

Several studies pointed out the continuity between data collected on mafia field and this theoretical model.[1] Therefore, according to the data collection, the mafia psychism could be considered as an *organizational identity, anthropologically* and *psychically* founded (Lo Verso, 1998; Lo Verso, 2005; Lo Verso and Di Blasi 2011; Giorgi 2007; Gozzoli et al. 2014).

Specifically, mainly the oldest mafia organizations, as Cosa Nostra and 'Ndrangheta, answer to the need for identity of their affiliates in order to establish the total control of them. In fact, providing an overindividual identitary configuration to each own members, the organizations could affirm their supremacy on people and territories. Nothing can be more superior than the mafia organizations. Therefore, the strength of mafia identity is primarily based on the denial of the subjectivity of its affiliates; there is no space neither for diversity, nor personal identity. The hypertrophic dimension of the organizational identity allows the mafias to survive and replicate their selves, their structure and their functioning all over the

[1] The Department of Psychology of Palermo University has started to investigate this phenomenon since the 1990s until today. After Cosa Nostra fatal attack on anti-mafia judges Giovanni Falcone, and Paolo Borsellino, and after the increasing of mafia affiliates who started to collaborate with justice, there was a fast growth of people belonging to mafia families who were in need of help and who started to turn to the public health service. The most common psychopathology among the sons and the daughters of who were involved in Mafia affairs, consisted in troubles related to identity (i.e., depression, drug addiction, personality disorders). Moreover in 1990s was also possible to collect data from lawyers and prosecutors. In this first phase, qualitative analysis was favorite. During the second period started between 1999 and 2000, the research studies were performed through the aid of qualitative and quantitative approaches that focus on action-research aspects related mainly on local public administration, politicians and racket victims. In this period was also possible considering the direct testimonial account of collaborators of justice. The last period is placed from 2006 until today and involved not only local public administration, but also citizens, students, voluntary association, professionals and anyone who suffered directly and indirectly the mafia exposure. The research approach chosen is related to observational studies carried out through clinical and social groups of elaboration and analysis of trial documents to deepen the understanding of the most powerful and diffused criminal organization all over the world (i.e., 'Ndrangheta and Cosa Nostra).

world. The belonging is so strong that if an affiliate was to escape to the mafia organization, he could be murdered. For the affiliates separation means "not to be," becoming "nobody." Usually people who have decided to collaborate with justice in their testimonial accounts refer about a state of mind in which subjectivity is absent.[2] The affiliates follow the dispositions imposed by the organization as a soldier would. Hence, the mafia members seemed as killing machines without fears and desires.

The consistency of this identity aspect is mainly diffused in criminal organization in which the belonging of the affiliate is perfectly coincident with his blood family. In this case, the mafia is not only an organization but first of all is an "identity," an ultra-fundamentalist religion, in which people don't have an individual mind, but only a belonging to a group. Undoubtedly, the "punciuta" known also as "baptism" rite,[3] represents the moment in which the affiliate devotes his self to the criminal organization. From this moment, the condition of psychic fundamentalism lived makes the affiliate almighty, powerful and as a God capable of deciding whether a person should live or die (Lo Verso and Lo Coco, 2003). Who allows the diffusion of this fundamentalist identity across the mafia organization are the women. The female contributes to guarantee the affective equilibrium of the entire family, including men. The women of mafia *are the honor* as they provide to preserve the "pedagogy of revenge" on which the mafias are built. Therefore, even if for several years it was thought in the total absence of women in attending criminal activities, as Alessandra Dino phrases "women have always been present in Mafia Context, whether carrying out explicitly criminal roles or providing indispensable daily support (Dino 2012: 323). Hence, the "submerged centrality" (Principato and Dino 1997) attributed to the women in order to protect the organization and its stability, now reveals that the female in criminal organizations is being fully involved in the clan's activities. Everything in the world of mafia has always served the power purpose, including its internal ethic-behavioral codes, the psychic structure of its members, the organizational dynamics. Therefore, this is the reason why there is a fundamental incompatibility between the mafias and the civil societies.

In the era of the liquid Post Modernity, also mafias expand their hegemony by becoming more rich and flourishing, with destructive effects on the economic, environmental and psycho-social spheres (Viano et al. 2003). In particular, "homo mafiosus" is the symbol of the denial of individual's existence (Giorgi and Lo Verso 2011).

This chapter addresses the thematic issues related to the Mafia Psychism and Mafias' organizational culture, as well as the devastating psychological and social impacts on its victims (Giannini and Cirillo 2012). The deepening of these themes is based primarily on the phenomenological and interpretative analysis (Smith et al. 2009) of two single case studies. Specifically, in the first single case, data are taken from the experience of Sicilian entrepreneurs extorted by Cosa Nostra, while in the

---

[2] One of the common reaction of people who collaborate with justice is justify themselves for criminal offenses committed, by attributing all the responsibilities to the their mafia roots (i.e., it is not my fault, because I came from that root and so I cannot be anything other than that type of tree.

[3] During this rite, the finger of the new member of the organization is pricked and the blood drops would be let to fall on a sacred image. The affiliate has to declare, while burning the sacred image in his hand: "may I burn like this image if I ever betray the organization."

second, 'Ndrangheta is narrated through words, thoughts, reasoning and reflections of who was affiliated. Besides to the examination of the theoretical basis on which the mafia psychism is founded, the introductory section of this contribution also aims to provide a brief exploration of the main characteristics that equate and discriminate the Sicilian Mafia by the Calabrian 'Ndrangheta. Another section of the chapter describes the qualitative approach to the research and the methodology employed, while the last section of the chapter remind us of the need to create multidisciplinary initiatives to prevent the risk of psychopathological drifts for mafias' victims (see Coppola et al. 2010, 2011; Giannone and Ferraro 2014; Coppola and Formica 2014; Gozzoli et al. 2014; Giorgi et al. 2014; Calandra and Giorgi 2015).

The Difference Between Cosa Nostra and 'Ndrangheta

Even if, the Italian Mafia-type organization are four, in order to introduce the subsequent single case studies, is more relevant deal with the Sicilian Cosa Nostra and the Calabrian 'Ndrangheta. These organizations show common traits but also specific characteristics. One of the common traits is related to the capacity of this two types of Mafias to impose their control on the territory and on the community by using the contextualized concepts of family, power, and respect. Thanks to their fascinating image these criminal organization are able to manipulate election and to install their men in administrative positions even far away from the territories they control.

The Sicilian Mafia

The possibility to know for the first time the overall structure of Cosa Nostra was provided by the first mafia member who decides to collaborate with the Italian law-enforcement in the 1980s, revealing the *organizational theorem*. For the first time the fascination image depicted by a lot of cinematographic masterpieces and popular beliefs was totally destroyed. The name of world's most famous criminal organization, finally it was pronounced by Tommaso Buscetta *in the specially Ucciardone bunker courtroom* built during the "Maxi Trial" started on 10 February 1986.[4] At this point, the Buscetta's testimonial account unveiled the real essence of the Sicilian Mafia, its internal structure and the rigid hierarchy governing it. In 1984, Tommaso Buscetta explained to the prosecutors the command structure of a typical clan.

[4] The definition of "Cosa Nostra" had first emerged in the testimonies of Leonardo Vitale in the early 1960s, but since his revelations were considered unreliable, only 20 years after thanks to Tommaso Buscetta was possible to confirm that Cosa Nostra was the name of the whole organization, on both sides of the Atlantic. What happened to Leonardo Vitale has proved the ability of the organization to manipulate the communication. In this case the discrediting of the witness was accomplished by the Cosa Nostra through the misleading use of the insanity of the member who has decided to leave the organization.

According to this testimonial account, Cosa Nostra was described as a hierarchical and centralized organization consisting of about 100 groups. Each clan, also known as "family" or "borgata" is led by a "boss" (capofamiglia), who is aided by an underboss (capo bastone or sotto capo) and supervised by one or more advisers (consigliere). Under his command are groups of about ten "soldiers" (decina). Each decina is led by a capodecina. In the Cosa Nostra Sicilian Mafia, the membership to the organization is ruled by a simple principle. People who become affiliates cannot have any close links with a lawman, such as a policeman or a judge. There is no strict age limit: boys as young as 16 have been initiated (Gambetta 2009: 67). Moreover, the members of a "family" do not need necessarily to be related by blood. An interesting point is related to the functioning and the main role covered by the multiple commissions existing. Each province of the Sicily has its own Commission. Clans are organized into districts (mandamenti) of three or four geographically adjacent clans. Each district elects a representative (capo mandamento) to sit on its Provincial Commission (Paoli 2003: 53). The power of commissions is limited and clans are independent. The commission has a consultation role and acts in order to regulate the use of the violence between the organization as well as the succession issues (Paoli 2003; Gambetta 2009). In fact in the cases in which a boss dies or retires, commission could be replaced him with a temporary regent. Therefore, in spite of for a long time the existence and the importance of mafia was denied by common people, the church, and the government in a sort of social removal; finally with the "pizza connection" operation was possible to discover the vast drug smuggling ring in which Cosa Nostra families in New York and Sicily are involved as well as the main money laundering schemes employed by the criminal organization. In addition to the heroin and cocaine trafficking, the illicit activities of the criminal organization Cosa Nostra are related to racketeering, extortions, protection money, usury, and total control of all territories occupied. Today the organization has moved his criminal affairs in South Africa, Canada, the USA, Venezuela, and Spain, but nevertheless its capacity to adapt to local restrictions and opportunities, modifying its modus operandi, and attending to money laundering and participation in illegal markets, the core business of the group remained in the region of origin. Moreover, usually Cosa Nostra do not try to replicate its basic structures away from Sicily, but organization tends to send emissaries. This is only one of the aspects that characterized specifically the main difference between Sicilian Mafia and Calabrian 'Ndrangheta.

The Calabrian 'Ndrangheta and the Law-Enforcement Operation "Crimine-infinito"

Even if until recent years, the Calabrian 'Ndrangheta has received less attention than Cosa Nostra, nowadays this criminal organization could be considered the most powerful organized crime groups in the world. The media started to talk about 'Ndrangheta only on 15 August 2007.

How it happened in Germany during the 'Duisburg massacre' showed us the murderous nature of the organization. An old blood feud between two powerful clans from San Luca, the Pelle-Vottari and the Nirta-Strangio provoked the killing of six Calabrians in front of a pizzeria in the town. The tight relation between the massacre and the 'Ndrangheta was evidenced through the finding of burned holy image in the pocket of one of the victims. The dramatic escalation of the 'Ndrangheta, known also as *onorata società*, was sufficient to establish that it was not a rural or backward organization with limited scope, but as the President of the United State (2011) phrases "'Ndrangheta has to recognized as a major threat not only in Italy but also in many other countries where it operates," including Germany, Spain, the Netherlands, France, Belgium, Switzerland, Canada, the USA, Colombia, and Australia (OFAC 2012). Specifically, the dominant position of the organization on the European cocaine market is due to the excellent relationship with the producers.[5]

A number of factors contributed to mark the distinction between the 'Ndrangheta and the Sicilian mafia. Undoubtedly the law enforcement operation in the 1980s and 1990s contributed to weaken Cosa Nostra and its structure, by ignoring the other criminal phenomena. At the same time the great wave of pentiti (literally, repentants), who started to collaborate with justice as well as the rapid changes in the market of drug trafficking that obliged Cosa Nostra to downscale their presence in some market and the simultaneous capacity of the 'Ndrangheta to filled those gaps.

Besides to these interesting points, the other key aspects that contributed to differentiate Sicilian and Calabrian criminal organizations could be traced in the perfect overlapping of the blood ties and of the peculiar structural and functional organogram of the 'Ndrangheta, as well as the aptitude of this organization to colonize new territories and the attempts to exert its influence over Calabrese migrant communities (compatriot ties).

These assumptions were highlighted by the two exceptional law enforcement operations mounted on 15 July 2010. The first investigation (operation Il Crimine) led to the arrest of people who belong to organization in Calabria and for the first time recorded the secret annual 'Ndrangheta meeting at the Sanctuary of Our Lady of Polsi. The second one focused on the stable presence of the 'Ndrangheta in Milan. Therefore, after the capture of more than 300 people it was possible to collect some important evidences. Specifically, it emerged the habit of the 'Ndrangheta to reproduce abroad perfect copies of its operational structures, the 'Ndrine (or Clans) and the Locali, which still fall under the supreme authority of the Calabrian Crimine. Each constitutional power units showed a Pyramidal Structure, the "Crimine" or "Provincia," but at the same time the inquiries confirmed the presence of exchange relationship between the different "locali." The latter are built by following the "geographic homogeneity principle." According to this principle, Lombardy areas partitions are equal than Calabria's territorial divisions. Moreover territories are ruled by the same family organogram that prevailing in Calabria. As Gratteri and

[5] Besides to the cocaine market, many several investigations have demonstrated the involvement of the 'Ndrangheta in environmental crime (illegal waste dumping) and in human trafficking.

Nicaso (2009) suggested, the 'Ndrangheta is the only criminal organization, that reproduces the same organizational form of the original places all over the world.

"Colonization" it is a brilliant definition (Dalla Chiesa and Panzarasa 2012) used to illustrate the expansion of the 'Ndrangheta outside its native region of Calabria. Thanks to the combination of gemmation[6] and co-optation[7] strategies the 'Ndrangheta is able to pursue not only the possibility to implant perfect copies of its essential structures in territories occupied, but also the progressive infiltration in new economic and social environments.

The immense corruptive power of the Calabrian 'Ndrangheta as well as its immense liquidity make the criminal organization able to achieve a position of quasi-monopoly in selected sectors (i.e., construction, real estate and transport). Hence, the successful growth of the 'Ndrangheta in new territories is also due to the solidity, versatility and adaptability of its structure. The Ranks (doti) and the offices (cariche) are the main structural elements of the internal hierarchy of the criminal organization that provide the strengthening trust among the members, even at a great distance from the motherland (Paoli 2003; KLPD 2011). The partition of the ranks and of the offices usually indicates each affiliate's status within the 'Ndrangheta. Usually a "'ndrina" gathers 'Ndrangheta families through social ties based on marriage or godfatherhood in order to control a specific territory (Paoli 2007). The 'Ndrine that belongs to the same area may form a "Locale." Therefore the coincidence of the partition of the ranks and the division of the territories is aimed at the reinforcement the cohesion of the criminal group and to the reduce the risk of betrayal (FAJ 1973). The complex functioning of the internal hierarchy of the "Ndrangheta is characterized not only by the horizontal plan but also by two main tiers that allow to arrange the criminal organization vertically. It is about the higher society (società maggiore) and the lower society (società minore), especially each of these is made up by multiple ranks (Paoli 2003). In Calabrian 'Ndrangheta the membership is ruled primarily by the blood ties. It means that if you born in a 'Ndrangheta family you are already an affiliate. Specifically a woman who belongs to the organization since her birth has affiliated as "sorella d'omertà," while a man in the same condition has affiliated as "giovane d'onore." People without blood ties could be affiliated as "contrasto onorato." Usually thanks to the affiliation ceremonies and the mythological rituals, as the "baptism" (battesimo) is possible to become a member of the criminal organization. Who is affiliated can enter in the lower society, by covering the lower ranks (picciotto, camorrista, sgarrista). La Santa, known also as "higher society" comprises, instead, members who have reached higher ranks (santista, vangelo, trequartino, quartino, quintino, crociata, stella, bartolo, mammasantissima, infinito e conte Ugolino. Specifically, the latter ranks have been discovered during the last law enforcement operation called Crimine-Infinito).

[6] The capacity of the 'Ndrangheta to serve of the weakening of the social ties, allows to the organization to subjugate and to exploit relationships in order to monopolize the economic sources and to obtain social legitimation (Arlacchi, 1983).

[7] The co-optation does not consider the use of violence. The territory is defeated by influencing indirectly the economics and the politics.

The mediator between these two different societies is the "capo giovane." Each locale is made up by 49 affiliates with specific function. Specifically, this structural component of the organization includes the "copiata," a triumvirate that consisting of a "capo locale," a "capo Crimine," and a "contabile." The Copiata is directed by a "maestro di Giornata," who controls the internal directives and who settles the emerging disputes (Gozzoli et al. 2014).

Usually, offices are assigned to higher-ranked affiliates. The boss of the locale is the capobastone or capolocale. The complex system of the organizational structure of the 'Ndrangheta was detected also in Milan, where 16 locali are discovered, but as stated in the order judicial of Crimine-infinito (Direzione Nazionale Antimafia, 2010; Ciconte 2010: 64) is probably that this number may be underestimated. According to the data emerged from this operation, the hierarchical structure of the 'Ndrangheta allows to the criminal organization to infiltrate in the political and economic environments, to do business with white-collars, by showing its remarkable capacity for corruption.

Through the blood and communities ties, the affiliation ceremonies and the ranks multiplication, the 'Ndrangheta reinforces the cohesion of the criminal group. Specifically, through the belonging to the organization, each affiliate can obtain a status of power or social acknowledgement who has never experienced in his daily life and in the society in which he lives (Ciconte 1992, 2010).

Qualitative Position in Data Collection. A Methodological Overview

Qualitative research is the resultant of a complex historical field. In fact, since the beginning it has had to face many challenges and resistances. Among them, especially in North America, it could be possible to identify some moments which have marked and crosscutting the subsequent developments of this research methodology until today. In particular, traditional period (1900–1950) is associated with the positivist, while the modernist age (1950–1970) and blurred genres moments (1970–1986) are connected to the appearance of post positivist arguments. The diffusion of non-positivist perspectives (hermeneutics, structuralism semiotics, phenomenology, cultural studies, and feminism[8]) represented undoubtedly an important

[8] According to structuralism any system is made up of a set of oppositional categories embedded in language. If semeiotics could be considered the science of signs, post-structuralism considered language as an unstable system of referents, making it impossible to ever completely capture the meaning or an action, text, or intention. It was only thanks to post modernism, developing since World War II, if is possible privileges no single authority, method, or paradigm. In this context, hermeneutics talks about the importance of the interpretative process in collective meaning construction. The latter aspects were the central core of phenomenology and of its diffusion, thanks to the works of Edmund Husserl, Martin Heidegger, Jean-Paul Sartre, Maurice Merleau-Ponty, and Alfred Schutz. In the same period, we have attended to the diffusion of the most important waves (critical theory, feminism, post-structuralism) connected to cultural studies.

turning point in the development of qualitative methodology and its employment. At the same time, the crisis of representation (1986–1990) and the new ethnographies (1990–1995), concurrently to post-experimental inquiry (1995–2000) have played a key role in the methodological frame that drives present (2000–2010) and future epistemological and methodological viewpoints in qualitative research. In the last three decades, "the overlapping of these moments has produced also a relevant mutation of researcher's role and of the ways in which results should be presented and used" (Devers 1999: 1154). Even if qualitative research means different things in each of these moments, already in 1992, Nelson and his colleagues tried to give an exhaustive definition. According to them "qualitative research is an interdisciplinary, transdisciplinary, and sometimes counterdisciplinary field". It crosses the humanities and the social and physical sciences. Qualitative research is many things at the same time. It is multiparadigmatic in focus. Its practitioners are sensitive to the value of the multimethod approach. They are committed to the naturalistic perspective, and to the interpretative understanding of human experience. At the same time, "the field is inherently political and shaped by multiple ethical and political positions" (*ivi*: 6). The diffusion of the most famous definition of qualitative research is due undoubtedly to Denzin and Lincoln's (2008a, b) third edition of Collecting and Interpreting Qualitative Materials. In the introductory chapter entitled, "The Discipline and Practice of Qualitative Research," authors argue this research methodological field as "a situated activity that locates the observer in the world" (*ivi:* 3). So according to this perspective "qualitative research consists of a set of interpretive, material practices that make the world visible. These practices transform the world. They turn the world into a series of representations, including field notes, interviews, conversations, photographs, recordings, and memos to the self" (*ibid.*). At this level, "qualitative research involves an interpretive, naturalistic approach to the world" (*ivi*: 5). This means that qualitative researchers study things in their natural settings, attempting to make sense of or interpret phenomena in terms of them (Keller and Keller 1996; Vygotsky 1978).[9] This methodological domain "involves the studied use and collection of a variety of empirical materials—case study, personal experience, introspection, life story, interview, artifacts, and cultural texts and productions, along with observational, historical, interactional, and visual texts—that describe routine and problematic moments and meanings in individuals' lives" (see also Becker 1986; Gupta and Ferguson 1997). Accordingly, "qualitative researchers deploy a wide range of interconnected interpretive practices, hoping always to get a better understanding of the subject matter at hand. It is understood, however, that each practice makes the world visible in a different way. Hence, there

[9] According to several authors "all settings are natural, that is, places where everyday experience takes place." Qualitative researchers study people doing things together in the places where these things are done. There is no field site or natural place where one goes to do this kind of work. The site is constituted through our interpretive practices. Historically, analysts have distinguished between experimental (laboratory) and field (natural) research settings; hence the argument that qualitative research is naturalistic. Activity theory erases this distinction.

is frequently a commitment to using more than one interpretive practice in any study" (Nelson 1992: 8).

Certainly as Miles and Huberman (1994: 11) remember "qualitative data appear to us in term of words rather than number." For this reason each attempt to leave out "noise" from research inquiry, often overlaps with the loss of the core people experience (Langridge 2004: 260). In this perspective qualitative research is focused on ordinary events in natural settings in order to know how happens in the real life (Miles and Huberman 1994: 27). It deal with "to understand" and "to represent" people reactions and experience through situation "lived and faced" (Elliot, et al. 1999: 216). Therefore qualitative research is intensive (examine in depth) and case oriented (not variables control influenced), not extensive (results are extended to the population by employing inference, sample is representative for a particular phenomenon, the survey of variables frequency in the population examined is primary).[10] This approach answers the question "which things do exist?" rather than "how much things do exist?"; this idea allows to explore the reason, the thing and the mean (Walker 1985: 3). Researcher has to centered his attention on "participant meaning" (Willig 2001: 9). Hence, Marecek (2003) has preferred to use the term "qualitative positions" in order to refer to qualitative method and to underline the importance of the subjectivity in the whole understanding of data examined. The distinctive core of qualitative research is oriented towards the employment of open-ended data collection, the use of words and visual imagines in place of statistical data to describe events of psychological experience and flexibility, together with the

[10] Qualitative research differs from quantitative research in five significant ways. The first point of difference is centered on the divergent way to deal with reality inquiry. Specially, the quantitative approach has been used for of isolating causes and effects, operationalizing theoretical relations, and measuring and quantifying phenomena, allowing the generalization of findings. Conversely the aim of qualitative analysis is a complete, detailed description. The second distinction within quantitative and qualitative methodology is connected to acceptance of postmodern sensibilities issue. Quantitative research use positivist method, refusing free of individual bias and subjectivity; on the other side, qualitative approach reject this radical trend to seek alternative methods for evaluating their work, including verisimilitude, emotionality, personal responsibility, an ethic of caring, political praxis, multivoiced texts, dialogues with subjects, and so on. Another aspect connected to the discrepancy within qualitative and quantitative research approach refers the possibility to capture the Individual's Point of View. Inferential Empirical methods employed by many quantitative researcher does not allow to get closer to the actor's perspective; conversely, this is it could be considered a foundational aspect of qualitative framework method. The second last issue that produce a gap between this two methodological field in scientific research it could be connected to the different way to contextualize everyday life constraints. Specifically, qualitative researchers try come against the constraints of the everyday social world and its embeddedness in human behavior, promoting an ideographic, case-based framework in order to direct their attention to the specifics of particular cases. Contrarily quantitative researchers seek a nomothetic or etic science based on probabilities derived from the study of large numbers of randomly selected cases. The last one point of heterogeneity between qualitative and quantitative dealing with the securing rich descriptions matter. While qualitative researchers believe that rich descriptions of the social world are valuable, quantitative researchers, with their etic, nomothetic commitments, are less concerned with such detail. According to their idea details interrupt the process of developing generalization, for this reason they are deliberately unconcerned with such descriptions.

importance given to perceptions, assumptions, prejudices of the subjects involved (Van Maanen 1988: 209). Using a qualitative approach means to start from "research questions" (Willig 2001: 19) driven by a flexible analysis process, based on ethical and political context relevance, and to leave the deterministic certainty of defined hypothesis, as in the case of quantitative research approach. Thus, doing qualitative research means to transform the researcher in a "bricoleur.[11]" The origins of bricolage research can be attributed to Anthropologist Claude Levi-Strauss's works (1966). Even if the use of this metaphor was originally employed to refer to structuralist project (Lincoln 2001), later scholars as Denzin and Lincoln (1999, 2003), Kincheloe (2001, 2004a, b, c, d, 2005) and Berry (2004a, b, 2006, 2011) have adopted this concept in relation to research within a post-structuralist frame,[12] to conceptualize this idea as an eclectic approach to social inquiry (Rogers 2012). Thus when the metaphor is used within the domain of qualitative research, for authors, who have been mentioned, *bricolage* overlaps with methodological practices explicitly based on notions of critical, multi-perspectival, multi-theoretical, and multi-methodological approach. Thus, phenomena have explored through multiple, and sometimes competing, theoretical and methodological perspectives by denoting an eclectic, a flexible and a plural frame to operate on data. In this way, methodological approaches based on multiplicity enable researchers to introduce a lot of possibilities for knowledge construction and epistemological and political dimensions through their inquiry (Kellner 1999; Berry 2004a). In this context, adopting a bricolage approach helped researchers respect the complexity of meaning-making processes and the contradictions of the lived world (Denzin and Lincoln 1999). As they suggest there are five types of bricoleurs who embrace this

---

[11] To clarify the meaning "bricoleur" it would be necessary to argue the etymological foundation of "bricolage." The latter term comes from a traditional French expression which denotes craftspeople who creatively use materials left over from other projects to construct new artifacts. In reverse of the work of engineers, who follow set procedure and have a list of specific tools to carry out their work, bricoleurs use only the tools and material "at-hand."

[12] Structuralism originated in linguistics of the twentieth century. At the beginning, it was focused on the configuration of language (i.e., the structural foundational rules which govern the sharing of meaning through verbal and textual communication). Particularly, De Saussure (1974) employed structuralist-linguistic methods to explain how languages are composed of various signs, and how the structural foundations of all signs consist of both signifiers (e.g., words) and the signified (i.e., concepts to which the words refer). In the second half of '900, structuralist practices moved beyond the borders of linguistics to be applied more broadly within the social sciences. Subsequent development of this theoretical approach start to compare mainly thanks to the contribution of Piaget (1970) and Althusser (2006) . In this period, structuralist practices were applied to human activity in order to uncover the underlying framework that govern phenomena like intelligence, social interaction, and human culture. Specifically, Levi-Strauss's masterpiece that allows to introduce the metaphor of bricolage was The Savage Mind, a work written in 1966. In this project, author employed the bricolage metaphor to highlight structures that govern human meaning-making. More specifically, however, he used the metaphor in the context of his challenge to the, then-dominant, thinking within anthropology which bifurcated mythical and scientific rationality.

rigor and complexity: the interpretive bricoleur,[13] the methodological bricoleur,[14] the theoretical bricoleur,[15] the political bricoleur,[16] and the narrative bricoleur[17] (*ivi*, p.4; Weinstein). Drawing on Becker (1998: 2), Denzin and Lincoln (1999: 4) explain that: "the qualitative researcher as bricoleur, or maker of quilts, uses the aesthetic and material tools of his or her craft, developing whatever strategies, methods, and empirical materials are at hand". Particularly "the combination of multiple methodological practices, empirical materials, perspectives, and observers in a single study is best understood, then, as a strategy that adds rigor, breadth complexity, richness, and depth to any inquiry" (Flick 2002: 229; Flick 2007: 102–104). For this reason, as the authors highlight "qualitative researcher who uses montage is like [...] a jazz improviser" (1999: 5). According to this idea, stitching and putting slices of reality together enables researcher to create a strict connection within psychological and emotional unity to an interpretive experience (Denzin and Lincoln 1999).

Qualitative methodology addressed the plurality and complex political dimension of knowledge work. This overview provides a thick description of phenomenal growth in this research methodological field in the last 20 years[18] (Atkinson et al. 2001), in order to give the epistemological framework on which following data have

---

[13] Adopting an interpretative bricolage approach enables researcher to understand the dialectical and hermeneutic nature of interdisciplinary inquiry, knowing that the boundaries between image and representation is the resultant of a reflexive collage or montage. Therefore, research is an interactive process shaped by one's personal history, biography, gender, social class, race, and ethnicity and those of the people in the setting. Particularly, reflexivity adds depth and plurality to the inquiry process and as Finlay (2002) argues, could be considered as a thoughtful, conscious self-awareness.

[14] Denzin and Lincoln's methodological bricoleur is a researcher who combining multiple research tools is adept at performing a large number of diverse tasks ranging from interviewing to intensive self-reflection and introspection. Therefore the product of his own solution (bricolage) denotes an emergent construction.

[15] Theoretical approach to bricolage allows bricoleurs to understand the different theoretical contexts in which an object can be interpreted—providing a multi-perspectival, post-structuralist perspective, showing the plurality of complexities that influence a phenomenon. In other words, for Denzin and Lincoln (2003) the theoretical bricoleur reads widely and is knowledgeable about the many interpretive paradigms (feminism, Marxism, cultural studies, constructivism, queer theory) that can be brought to any particular problem.

[16] According to political bricoleur there is no value-free science, for this reason he knows that each research implies political impacts, The notion of the political bricoleur influenced Kincheloe' s articulation of the critical bricoleur. As author this last one "stress the dialectical and hermeneutic nature of interdisciplinary inquiry, knowing that the boundaries between traditional disciplines no longer hold.

[17] For Denzin and Lincoln, narrative bricoleurs recognize that inquiry is a representation (i.e., a narrative), influenced by paradigms employed (e.g., positivism, post-positivism, constructivism). Thus research texts can only represent specific interpretations of a phenomenon. This means that narrative bricoleurs draw their techniques from multiple perspectives, voices, and sources.

[18] During the last years, scientific research has seen increasingly publication of qualitative articles in mainstream psychology journals. Specifically, the surge in popularity of qualitative approach in psychology can be traced to dissatisfaction with cognitive–experimental psychology in the 1960s and 1970s. Even more this methodological wave represents a novelty in the criminological research methods.

been elaborated. In 2008 Harper has listed the main research methods based on qualitative approach in clinical psychology field to explore a multiple range of topics. Qualitative methods which were widely represented include the Discourse Analysis (DA), the Conversational Analysis (CA), the Narrative Analysis (NA), the Grounded Theory (GT),[19] the Ethnography, Q-Methodology and Interpretative Phenomenological Analysis (IPA) (see also Del Corno and Rizzi 2010; Tweed and Charmaz 2012; Glaser and Strauss 1967; Glaser 1978, 1992, 1998; Larkin 2001; Langdridge 2007; Smith 1999, 2004, 2007).

Interpretative Phenomenological Analysis

Interpretative Phenomenological Analysis is a qualitative approach committed to the examination of how people make sense of their mayor life (Smith et al. 2009: 9).

The psychological interest in how people make sense of their experiences is the central issue of this form of elaborating data. It provides an established, phenomenologically focused approach to the interpretation of participants accounts. The mayor aspects of this kind of qualitative analysis include primarily an element of "giving voice" and "making sense." The first key point is connected to the possibility to capture and reflecting upon the principal claims and concerns of the research participants, while the second one is centered on the opportunity to offer an interpretation of material, which is grounded in the accounts, but may use psychological concepts to extend beyond them (e.g., see Larkin et al. 2006). These two key elements take considerable time and efforts. To ensure a right balance within these two key components is required to draw upon the context of supervision and peer support, which can facilitate the development and discussion of these elements. For this reason IPA researchers should be open-minded, flexible, patient, empathic, and willing to enter into, and respond to the participant's inner world (Smith et al. 2009, p. 61).

For researcher, being able to keep eye contact at the same time is taking notes is often crucial in the opening moments of the interview because, if captured accurately, what is revealed when the interview does begin to open up can be utilized to structure the rest of interview. In fact, starting from spoken words is very important to cultivate a heightened level of reflexivity in the research process.

For IPA the key conceptual touchstones are idiography and hermeneutic phenomenology. The idiographic level of analysis implies a focus on the particular rather than general. The issue is the quality; in other words, meaning-making is conceptualized at the level of the person-in-context.

At the same time, the second aspect that characterized IPA feels the effect of Husserl's transcendental phenomenology and Heidegger's existential theoretical and philosophical approach.

[19] If Grounded Theory builds a theory based on data experience, rather than on pre-established hypotheses, conversely, Interpretative Phenomenological Analysis identifies the possible connections within contents of inquired issues and behavior reasons of participants involved.

The study of "Being" (i.e., of existence and experience) is closely connects with IPA hermeneutic phenomenology. Especially, if for Husserl transcendental phenomenology overlaps with the essential core structures of a given experience, for Heidegger, persons (i.e., Dasein, "there-being") are inextricably involved in the world and in relationships with others. In fact, as Merleau-Ponty said, persons are always embodied too. According to hermeneutic phenomenology, existence is a situated enterprise and shapes our perception of the world. Thus IPA proceeds on peculiar epistemological assumptions. According to this perspective, employing an idiographic approach is fundamental in order to facilitate a detailed focus on the *particular,* and at the same time allows to the researcher to understand participants' human experience trough linguistic, relational, cultural and physical world lived.

In the same way as the Narrative interview Method, IPA encourages individuals to convey the complexity of their experience and preserve as much of the uniqueness of what was disclosed in the course of the data analysis. Is very important to encourage people to tell their own stories and then to ask questions that invited participants to elaborate further about own particular experiences (Smith et al. 2009). In this sense, doing qualitative research means capitalized the subjective inner world reactions in a complex way. It deals with an ongoing dialogue and a process of meaning construction that leaves from the dialectic relationship between inner world experience and outer-world phenomenon. IPA captures the richness of human experience and in this case is centered on the nuanced material to make sense of how particular individual feels about mafia crimes. The following paragraphs focus on what are symbolic and emotional acceptations that a Sicilian entrepreneur extorted by Cosa Nostra and one of the few justice collaborators belonged to 'Ndrangheta feel about own personal conditions.

For this reason, research question suit IPA does not test hypotheses, although is useful to have a few more refined or theoretically informed questions, treated as "secondary," because they can only be answered at the discussion stage.[20]

Data collection typically is in the form of a semi-structured, one-to-one interview (Smith et al. 2009). Other form of data can sometimes be used for IPA include written accounts (Smith 1999) and focus groups (Palmer et al. 2010). Moreover, an important role is played by the verbatim transcript of a first-person account, which has been generated by a research participant, usually in the response to an invitation by a researcher. For this reason, IPA studies require small sample sizes. This is because quality of data permits insightful analyses to be developed. Generally, number of participant will vary according to the aims, level and context of the research, and the time and resources of the researcher (Smith et al. 2009). According to Smith et al. (2009), IPA also lends itself to single case study analysis—although this may be more suited to more experience researchers. In this case, it can be helpful to interview participants twice, or to use diaries or other additional tools to facilitate

[20] For example, we might have a primary research question which is very open (such as "How do people make sense of their treatment decisions?"). More pointed questions (such as "How do accounts of the decision-making process relate to the model described in theory Y?") can be secondary.

understanding between the researcher and the participant. Expanding the design, to include interviews with related respondents can also be helpful (Smith et al. 2009).

To interpret qualitative data through IPA is fundamental to develop an organized, detailed, plausible and transparent account of the meaning of the data. To do this, first, is important to identify *patterns of meaning* in the data. This is the way in which sense-making process of what happens after extortion offense and after withdraw from a mafia organization it is analyzed. From the survey of emerging themes it was possible to highlight the mayor meaning-structures revealed through this qualitative analysis procedure. The identification of the emergent patterns (i.e., themes) within this experiential material, emphasizing both convergence and divergence, commonality and nuance (e.g., see Eatough and Smith 2008).

In particular, these patterns in IPA drawn from detailed, line-by-line commentary on the data, called "codes" (e.g., see Larkin et al. 2006). Meaning-structure could be represented trough visual and graphical output, as a hierarchical mode, i.e., family tree or by using a circular diagrammatic representation in order to present to the readers a global and synthetic analysis' overview.

It would also necessary to produce a narrative account of this structure for the analysis section of your report. Prevailing patterns have to put in evidence to underline the most important matters track down by participants and to understand what these things mean to them (e.g., see Larkin et al. 2006; Smith 2004; Smith et al. 2009: 85). Analytic work with IPA is *iterative*, *inductive*, *cycling* and *recycling* process.[21] Searching for connections within emergent themes makes possible the super-ordinate themes' development. A step that allows to find specific semantic and conceptual domains.

In particular, abstraction it could be considered the basic form of identifying patterns between emergent themes and developing a sense of what can be called a 'super-ordinate' theme. According to Smith et al. (2009: 103) this process involves putting like with like and developing a new name for the cluster. Clarifying core

[21] Analytic process in IPA provides for different steps. According to Smith the analysis has to begin at the level of individual case, with close, line-by-line. In this phase is very important coding experiential claims, concerns and understanding of each participant. It is also very important to detect the emergent patterns (i.e., themes) within this experiential material emphasizing both convergence and divergence, commonality and nuance. Joining up the researchers represents a necessary moment in the creation of an interpersonal dialogue to focus on what it might mean for participants to have these concerns in this context. Doing this operation means to develop more interpretative accounts and frame or gestalt which illustrate the relationship between themes. In this phase it would be possible to organize collected material in format that allows for coded data to be traced right through the analysis—from initial code on the transcript, through initial clustering and thematic development, into the final structure of themes. Supervision and collaboration would be very useful to ensure coherence and plausibility of the interpretation and would be also a very effective way to explore reflexivity. At this point of the analysis, development of a narrative, evidenced by detailed commentary on data extract, it could be supported through visual guide (simple heuristic, diagram, or table). Finally, according to Smith reflection on one's own perception, conceptions and process should occur throughout the process and is usually captured in a systematic fashion by keeping a reflexive journal.

content thanks to developing line-by-line coding and transcript excerpt tends to involve some parallel processes.

Whereas cases examined are two different single case designs, validation strategies employed consist of member-checking.[22]

Undoubtedly this methodology has already made an important contribution to knowledge in the mafias criminal organization field. IPA has had a great impact on the reflection about the realization of a systemic and multi-perspectival intervention addressed to mafias' victims. This analysis has inspired the conjunction of interrelated perspective by offering powerful new insights on mafias' world knowledge. Therefore to have had the possibility to deepen these cases study analysis by using this qualitative research methodology it could be considerate an important way to think carefully about situations emerging after mafias' offenses and to reflect on the degrees of vulnerability that are connected to these phenomena and their psychosocial, relational, economic and environmental terrible consequences.

Extortion Offense and Psychopathology. The Analysis of a Mafia Victim Experience

What is the relationship between extortion action and psychopathological consequences? Psychological literature on mafia victims experience, often moves towards crosscutting domains which characterized in a peculiar way the criminal organizations encounter.

The current contribution aims to deepen the understanding of the Mafia Psychism, as well as the devastating psychological and social impacts on its victims through the qualitative analysis of a single case.

The data collection started from the distribution of a purpose-built, semi-structured interview. In the present case, the action/research model shows a general

[22] However, in design with multiple participants is preferable to use sample validation (people eligible to participate, but who did not), peer validation (fellow researchers) or audit. According to Smith between general quality indicators that one might look for there are: the possibility to collect appropriate data by starting from an adequate selection of informants to interview; the importance to maintain the idiographic focus (i.e., the right balance between the particular experience of a singular participant and what is shared within a sample); the capacity to achieve an adequate schedule for a semi-structured interview; the ability to focus on "how things are understood," rather than on "what happened"; the importance to combine phenomenological details and interpretative work in order to develop a psychologically relevant account of the participant's' "engagement-in-the-world." At the same way quality indicators have to overlap with an appropriate use of triangulation (via methods, perspectives, data, analysis, fieldwork) or audit and/or credibility-checking (via respondent, supervisors, peers, parallel sample) in order to achieve trustworthiness. Moreover, according to this perspective, it is also relevant to promote an appropriate use of extracts and commentary to achieve transparency; to adopt appropriate level of contextual detail, to pay attention to analytic and reflexive components of the process employed to obtain meaning patterns and in closing to have an appropriate level of awareness of pitch and engagement with theory (in making sense of the analysis).

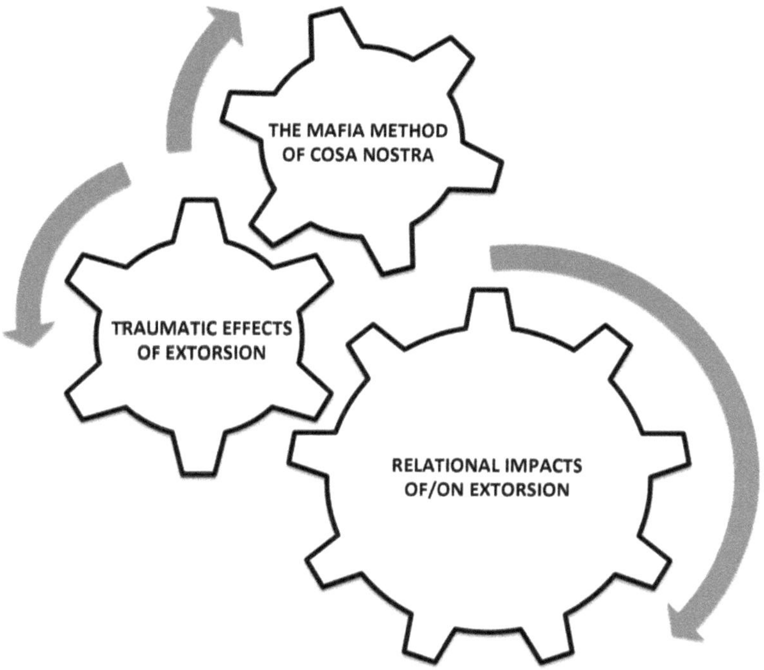

Fig. 7.1 Visual overview of the three semantic and conceptual domains achieved in analysis of experiences of a Sicilian businessman involved in research

framework of the key concepts required to understand the extortion crime characterization, starting from the complex and articulated signification map of the experience lived by the participant,[23] obtained through the interpretative-phenomenological analysis (Smith, 1995; Smith and Dunworth 2003; Smith, 2004; Smith et al. 2009) of the transcription. In the present case, sense-making process of what happens after extortion offense was built starting from the survey of emerging themes. In order to find specific semantic and conceptual fields, patterns identified have been connected in super-ordinate themes. In particular, three are the main macro-areas[24] in which it was possible to bunch up clusters obtained through the analysis:

- Mafia Methods employed by Criminal Organization
- Traumatic Effects of extortion action
- Need-help. Relational impact on/of the extortion crime (see Fig. 7.1).

[23] Participant involved in this research is a Sicilian entrepreneur extorted by Cosa Nostra. Mafia encounter will be documented, starting from participant's eyes above the tragic first-hand experiences.

[24] Figure 7.1 shows the three main semantic and conceptual domains achieved through participant's IPA analysis (1).

Mafia Methods Employed by Criminal Organizations

There is a parallelism drawn by organizational construction which defines criminal organizations and mafia methods employed by the same. In the organizational culture (Weick 1973, 1995) which characterized Cosa Nostra, in fact, offender is able to produce intimidating effects thanks to the capacity to impose its symbolic dictatorship over mind and territories (Zegrebelsky 2010). The dialectical pattern of the criminal behavior (Fattah 1976), typically associated with extortion action has a key role in the social construction of the victimization (Scarcella Prandstraller 2012), as it could be influenced not only the level of responsiveness externalized by the victim after the exposition to criminal event, but also his community reactions (see Fig. 7.2).

What Are the Extortion's Consequences?

The first conceptual level is associated to "mafia methods" employed by Cosa Nostra criminal organization. This issue highlights the distinctive characterization of this kind of offense. Extortion crime produces a process of repeated and multiple victimization.[25] In the experience of the participant, the "domino effect" generated by extortion crime acts primarily on a subconscious and phantasmatic level and at the same time it produces a deep transmutation of the mental representations[26] about life, death, future and self-schemas previously owned by participant. This situation contributed also to the appearance of an high level of feeling of insecurity,[27] and of perceived vulnerability. Threating by Cosa Nostra, in participant's experience means to feel a deep sense of identity disintegration. The seriousness of the dangerous event lived, leads participant also towards an increasing of personological consistency subjectively perceived. One of the another superordinate themes that appears in this conceptual and semantic area showed the disastrous effect of extortion action on the drastic modification of the previous idea of future. In particular, seems that participant's experience is sprinkled with a new concept of temporality. In the case under analysis, it emerges the emptying of the present

[25] Multi-victimization process activated by extortion action exposes one person to different crimes in the same period of time, while repeated victimization provokes the same offense towards the same person several times.

[26] The mental representation is the mental imagery of things that are not currently seen or catched by the sense organs. In our mind we often have images of objects, events and settings that could influence our inner world experience, our idea or feelings on interpersonal relationship, the way to perceive its own life condition and more over to give sense to own self-experience.

[27] The feeling of insecurity includes two factors. In particular, *personal fear* is the anxiety sensation that can you feel when you think to be affected by a crime which depends, in particular, in the perception of the probability that such an eventuality becomes a concrete reality. While *social concern* is, instead, the uneasiness deriving from the crime affecting a country in its various forms. Inter alia, reactions included in the insecurity feeling do not necessarily manifest themselves at the same time.

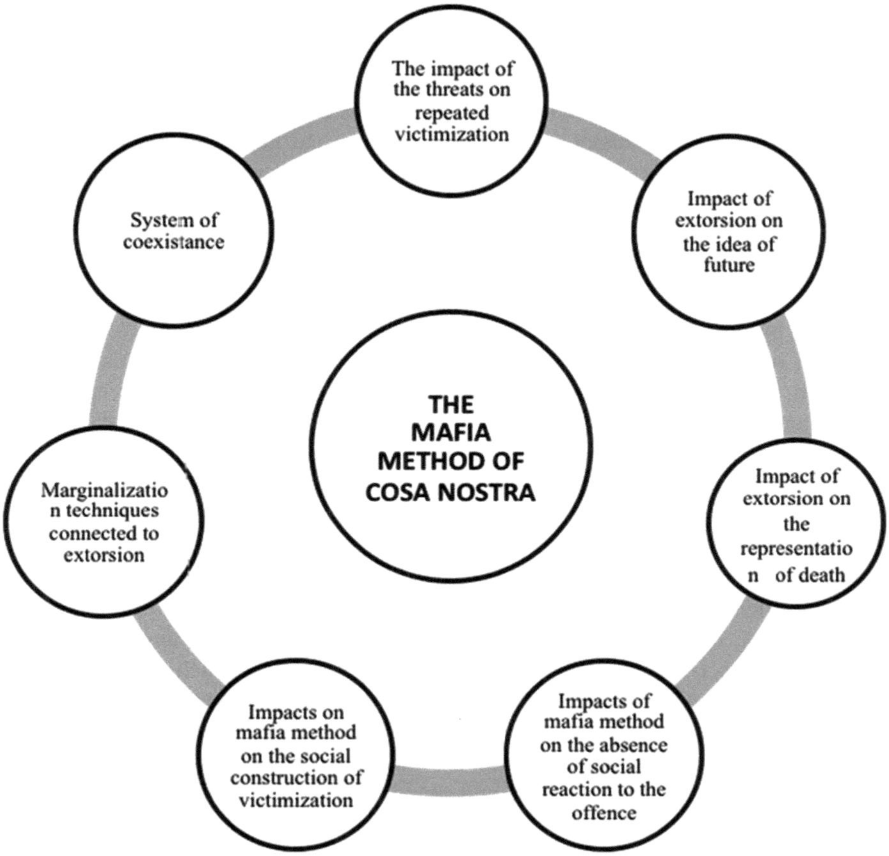

Fig. 7.2 Visual overview of the first semantic and conceptual level detected trough Interpretative and Phenomenological Analysis. The Graphic summarizes the main super-ordinate themes associated to this macro-area that are briefly discussed in the paragraph below

temporality (surviving), zeroing of the temporality which reflects on the future (obfuscation even of the desire of having children, and therefore interruption of the generative planning) (Cigoli and Scabini 2000). Another consequence of non-payment of the blackmail money is that the idea of death becomes more pervasive. The recurring thought of death provokes feelings of powerlessness and horror, becoming a *memento mori*. It overlaps with feeling of being imprisoned in a static-movement. The participant involved in research perceives often himself and his everyday reality as a sentenced to death. The thought about death, in participant's experience declines also in a real possibility to be physically annihilated. Particularly, this experience sharpens mainly when he listening again wiretapping material. Concerning the existential collapse experienced by the participant, it seems to be directly connected to the ability of marginalization techniques employed by the mafia organization of influencing not only the recognition of their own victim status, but also the social community representation of the same condition. The techniques act in order to turn victim in a "thing," to transmute it in an "object." *The other is annihilated; the other is nothing* (Calandra and Giorgi 2015, p. 88).

It happens that the social response is selective and based on specific circumstances (Henry and Lanier 1998).[28] Therefore, mafias' criminal offenses overlap with *invisible crimes*, in this perspective, organized crime has a key role in *social construction of victimization process* (Scarcella Prandstraller 2012). After the initial trend to the "normalization" of the crime happened to avoid the tragical aspects connected to event lived, extorted entrepreneurs usually choose to bow to the "law of silence," by remaining imprisoned in an oblivion curtain, that precludes any possibility of social proximity and communication. At first, participant involved in this research, was obliged to maintain a "low profile," by remaining for 2 years abandoned and unknown by his community. Specifically, the impossibility of his community to recognize his status after his exposure to extortion requests, in the case under analysis has provoked a significant in the capability of the participant to perceive himself as a victim in need of help. Thus, mafia methods have influenced participant's *moral career* of *self-ridefinition*[29] together with the evolution of victimization process (Viano 1983). The experience told by the participant underlines how the libelous loop diffused by the organization provokes a condition of social emargination, exasperating isolation feelings perceived. He became a victim of derision, suspect and aversion from his own community.[30] Such community has shown an incapability to react to what happened. The passiveness of people has delayed the awareness of his own status of victim. At the beginning silence has a particular meaning for the participant. It is perceived as the only escape route, but actually it just worsens his isolation and abandon status experienced. There's a great gap between the individual perception of his own condition and the social perception of it. At the same time it emerges the impossibility of living with tyranny and oppression behavior performed by the criminal schemings which, through a fascination strategy, are able to transform civil rights into extraordinary concessions. The

[28] *Invisible crimes* according to Henry and Lanier include all harmful acts perpetrated by organizations, corporation, professionals, government officials, powerful people, or organized crime. This definition is taken from a scheme called "*crime prism*" which is used to describe crime and victimization phenomena through variables as crime visibility, social agreement on crime, extent of victimization, and selectivity of social response to crime (*ivi*).

[29] Participant's experience could be marked by a radical ridefinition of his own identity and social relationships especially in case of serious crime. In these circumstance the person is forced to "reassess his/her personal choices and priority." Moreover, this condition after crime exposure denotes the beginning of a secondary victimization process.

[30] "*Libel diffused by mafia methods has created scorched earth around me.*" These the words with which participant evokes during the interview, the marginalization strategies employed by Cosa Nostra in order to make him untrusted and invisible (11.835: this interview fragment is positioned in page 11, line 835 of the original transcript). And so on "*if before I was a pusher, after denouncing I have become a cheater, a fool, who had made it all up*" (14.1056: this interview fragment is positioned in page 14, line 1056 of the original transcript). Both these slice of interview are collocated in the super-ordinate theme "Marginalization techniques connected to extortion."

participant shows also feelings of disgust and hostility towards corrupted people. But some driving values such as honesty, conscientiousness, courage and irreproachability together with the possibility to develop concrete social choices, are perceived as the only means to fight mafias.

Traumatic Effects of the Extortion

Extortion action is configured as a traumatic event for the person who suffers. This is because the stressor potential connected to this crime violates social basic principles and symbolic provisions of coexistence basis, determining a greater riskiness on victimization process and its trend. In fact, literature on traumatic disorders suggests that an injury is more likely to become a source of pathological suffering when the stressor is the result of a severe trauma caused intentionally by a man against his counterpart. It means that traumas intentionally provoked by a person could have a primary destructive effect on the sense of self-esteem and on attachment relationship (De Zulueta 2009). Usually, the shame and the guilt experienced, deprive the victim of the buffering and protective effects connected to social networks and lead to be exposed to an additional condition of risk. In addition to fear and mistrust feelings towards your own kind, it is possible to detect the appearance of dissociative symptoms and the related subjective powerlessness lived, the experience of extreme fear, the perception of a threat for life and of a potential physical violence (March 1993), until arrived to the development of a complex post-traumatic stress disorder (Liotti and Farina 2011) (see Fig. 7.3).

Psychosomatic and Psychopathological Reactions to the Extortion

In the experience of the participant it is possible to find signs of psycho-existential and affective-somatic repercussions, which emerge through psychosomatic and psycho-pathological reactions that could be attributable to post-traumatization symptoms. The patterns revealed are connected to:

- *Affective deregulation, shown in the increase of arousal reaction*
- In the experience of the participant anxiety is pervasive and nonspecific and could be explained as a deep sense of persecution and arises primarily from the awareness of being an *instrument in someone else's game*. Anxiety itself it could be associated with a condition of hyper vigilance which increases the sense of acted suspiciousness. This frame depends on the anguish of death and it is due to threats received. The gravity of this condition coerces the participant to produce an extreme cognitive effort in order to protect himself. The fear experienced is so terrible that it creates sleep disorders. For the participant the only way to fall asleep is sleeping with a *gun* under his pillow.
- *Use of a defense system that acts on post-traumatic stress management.*

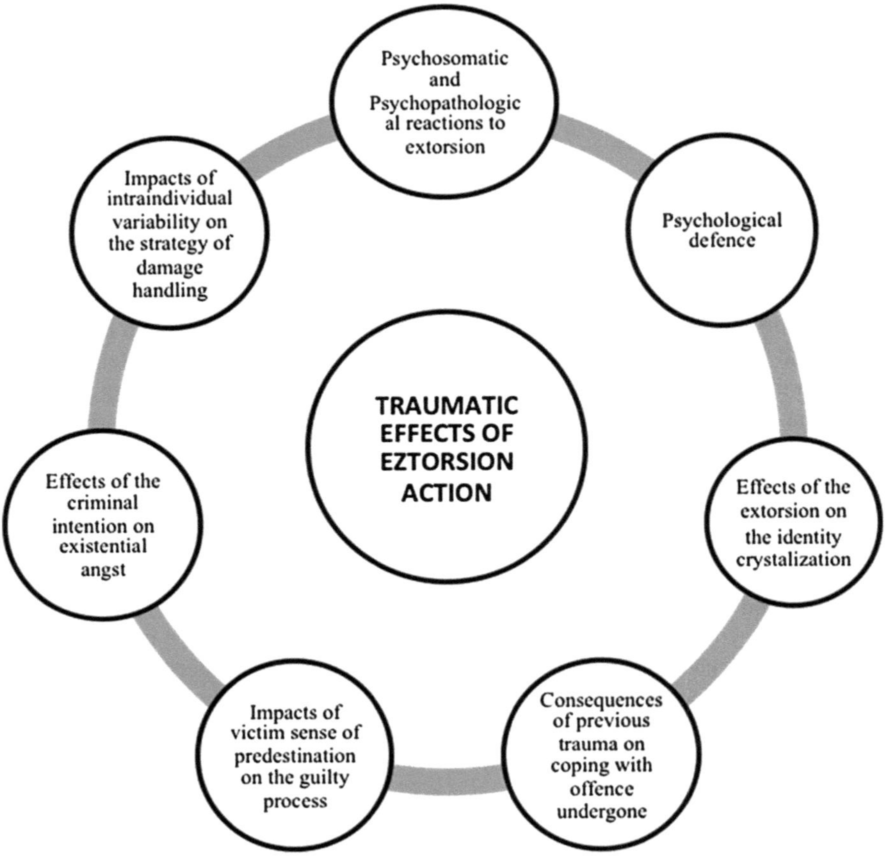

Fig. 7.3 Visual overview of the second semantic and conceptual level detected trough Interpretative and Phenomenological Analysis. The Graphic summarizes the main super-ordinate themes associated to this macro-area that are briefly discussed in the paragraph below

- In the case under analysis, most of the experiences lived by the participant are due to the massive use of dissociative psychological mechanism which expresses mainly in terms of depersonalisation.[31] There is a gap between the feeling of being an observer and the one of being a participant. In the same way, derealization monopolizes the self-experience and of the world around him becoming an overwhelming aspect of the participant's life. It emerges the necessity to control the dramatic nature of the experienced lived, so the participant often draws upon

[31] To refer to the tragedy condition lived after exposure to extortion action, during the interview, participant says it is "as if I were an angel of myself." Through this words is possible detect dissociative reaction due to offense received. This part of interview has collocated in superordinate theme connected to "Psychosomatic and Psychopathological reactions to extortion" (15.1110: this interview fragment is positioned in page 15, line 1110 of the original transcript).

the tendency of rationalizing what happened. Affective isolation and the propensity to freezing reactions appear more than once in what the participant told. Moreover, it is not rare the presence of hypermnesia during the narration of the story; it was also observed flashbacks of the event and the fear that the event could happen again.

- *Decrease of general reactivity and emotive detachment*
- At first, the emotive and relational detachment is influenced by guilt and anger feelings, which are due to the awareness of the level of gravity of the offense suffered.

Specifically, anger is the main reason why the participant decides to denounce to fight against the mafia crime organization. Reassurance and social support represent the only real solutions able to reduce the sense of guilt and powerlessness lived and to guide the anger felt. "Insanity" is the major pattern to cope the difficulties imposed by the events. In this case, *insanity* is the synonym of the tendency to reject the reality, and it could be considered the only way to survive.[32] This is because it is able to create a state of static movement and identitary crystallization and paralysis at the same time. On the one hand, insanity is the sign of a strong character, but on the other hand it represents a point of escape, in which there have been conducted the destructive and negation tendencies. The foolish behavior is the only way to refuse the sorrow experienced and in the same way it could be considered a mental refugee with a strong protective effect. The only way to survive to such an experience is to act like ostriches, that is to have his head in the sand.

The event lived for the participant represents the repetition of old traumas. Also his father, even if innocent, had been involved in legal proceedings connected with mafia issues, so he feels obliged to denounce his persecutors. This choice is characterized by contrasting feelings. He has not chosen to denounce but he thinks it is a duty, a form of predestination, from which he cannot escape.

Some aspects of his personological profile have affected his way of reacting, characterizing at the same time the protective factors in front of the stressor events.

The personality functioning schema is marked by the presence of neurotic tendencies. In this case, conscientiousness, obstinacy and tendency to control represent the most important aspects of the organization of the participant's life experience. In the specific case indicated, the obstinacy, which in the participant's experience is equal to recklessness and perseverance, overlaps with the coping strategy usually used in front of submission sensation, helplessness experience and weaknesses perceived as insurmountable difficulties.

Cognitive, affective and relational predisposition, together with values and self-efficacy beliefs, have played a central role in the crossing of risk condition, by becoming an undisputed and exclusive part of the resource to deal with painful events lived after exposition to extortion crime.

---

[32] In one of the pieces of the transcript included into the superordinate theme "effects of the extortion on the identity crystallization," participant talks about the meaning of his *madness*, by saying "*Each normal person would be enough the 1 % of what I have to live every single day to became insane, but thanks to my insanity I do not became aware of what I live*" (7.470: this interview fragment is positioned in page 7, line 470 of the original transcript).

Without his insanity, his perseverance, his tenacity, the participant has not been able to react to the tragedy lived; no possibility of rebellion to mafia dominion or acknowledgement of his condition it would be possible. Undoubtedly, his drive to act is the purest motivation that every day leads him to face with tight fists his struggle against mafia criminal organization. In particular, social support perception like social community proximity, in the experience of the participant, represent an essential aspect for the mafias' defeat.

Need-Help: Relational Impacts on/of the Extortion Crime

The last one thematic area detected from data analysis allows to focused on the consequences of the formal and informal response of victimization (Bandini et al. 1991, 2003). The victimization processes are the product of social constructions where the actors who have suffered a crime define their condition, give a meaning to it and assimilate it in the context of a structural conditioning, as a response to labeling and social reaction process (Scarcella Prandstraller 2012). Therefore, there is a circular connection between extortion action, and social and relational network which belongs to the person who has suffered crime. In particular social effects provoked by extortion action and primary harms associated to this offense concern relational impacts *on* the extortion crime, while the relational relapses *of* extortion actions' detection are focused on the secondary harms[33] on victimization "career." Therefore, the articulated character which defined extortion action it need to be addressed through differentiated and integrated intervention acts capable of operating simultaneously on the containment of the risk associated with the primary and secondary harmfulness of the crime and on their effects on the victimization process (see Fig. 7.4).

Relational Impacts on Making Sense to Extortion Crime and on the Victimization Process

The super-ordinate themes that are includes in this last conceptual domain highlight the effects intrinsic in the secondary harmfulness, which together with those connected to the primary harmfulness determine an amplification and summation effects of the traumatization status generated by extortion offense. Specifically, after being exposed to crime above-mentioned, participant has felt the police officers behavior as discordant to his previous expectation. He has perceived what happened during interrogatory as detrimental of his own dignity and self-esteem.[34]

[33] Primary harms is the direct health, material, economic, emotional or psychological consequences of the crime on the victims, while secondary harms are the consequences deriving from formal/informal response to victimization.

[34] "*For seven hours, police officers who have collected my statements during the interrogation, treated me as if I were Bin Laden.*" These are participant's memories after denouncing extortion action. This fragment underlines the importance of cops' reaction during interrogation in reducing

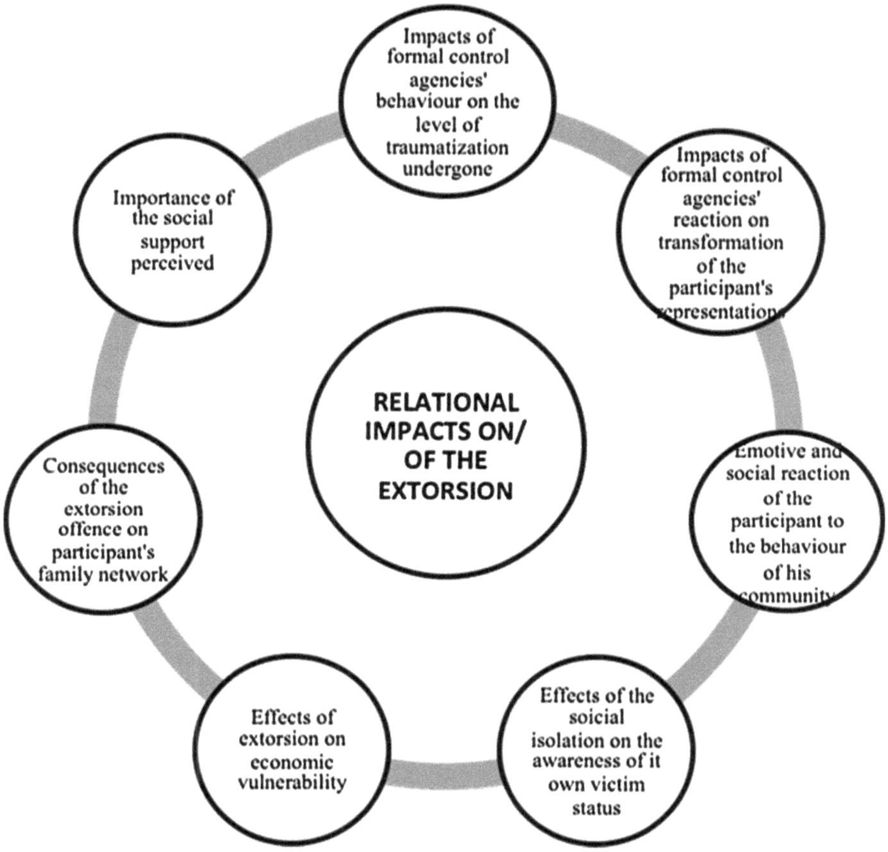

Fig. 7.4 Visual overview of the third semantic and conceptual level detected trough Interpretative and Phenomenological Analysis. The Graphic summarizes the main super-ordinate themes associated to this macro-area that are briefly discussed in the paragraph below

On one side, the sense of injustice for other episodes lived becomes intolerable, even for the connection with past events. Because of his mistrust in bureaucracy, the participant has postponed his help request, ignoring in this way the identification of his own victim status.

According to him *bureaucracy which could kills sometimes more than mafia.* For him, this aspect affects the amplification of the sense of social isolation experienced. Next to this negative idea, participant believe also in the importance of the support that every day he has received from the policemen who patrolling his house, his job, his family and who protect his safety, when he has suffered other threats from Cosa Nostra. In the story of the participant, there is another element that has

of the risk connected to secondary victimization process and is collocated in super-ordinate theme "Impacts of formal control agencies' behaviour on the level of traumatization undergone" (10.721: this interview fragment is positioned in page 10, line 721 of the original transcript).

worsened the isolation condition lived mainly in the first moment of his tragic experience, it consist in his social community inability to react[35] to his victims status. At the beginning, participant has considered by his own community as a "victimless crime." It means that he has socially constructed as "*non-victimizing*." In this case the failed labeling as person who has undergone to mafia offenses, it led him initially in a state of deep isolation and of extremely anguishing feelings.

People think he deserves what happened, they perceived situation occurred as a question of "setting of scores" and participant as a "*pusher*" and a "*cheater*." In this specific case, initially he had felt a "leper," perceived the worries of the people to stand by him and feels guilty for having denounced. After deciding to send an "appeal not to die" to his own town, community starts to became more close to him and to the terrible tragedy that had involved him and his family. His brave act has had various consequences. Specifically, the choice of denouncing overlaps with the loss of his relationships, with the crash of his family bounds and with significant economic losses, too. In particular, the aptitude to negation in familiar context has a *protective value* because it allows to reject the *death angst* and the sense of tragedy of the experiences lived. Without taking into consideration that the fact that his loved ones are get involved in this situation increases his sense of guilt and his worry for their integrity. Economic damages provoked by mafia organized crime have obliged him to deal with the failure of his own business.[36]

However, despite the fact that this kind of consequence has represented an extremely anguishing experience, his obstinacy has emerged. Even though what he has experienced has determined the activation of a "*moral career*" of *self-ridefinition*, the participant has underlined the importance of values like family and social support to cope the difficulties imposed extortion offense.

The Collaborator of Justice. Between Criminal Identity and Psychopathology

Who is the collaborator of justice? Why does his choice to leave the criminal organization could determine the appearance of psychopathological consequences and the breakdown of his own identity?

---

[35] The participant's memories after the fire at his dealership are connected to the perception of passiveness of his own community. "I remember a lot of people who watching without help me. They stand still, with folded arms as if what happened it was a show, a movie or a fiction." Through this word is simply to understand the deep sense of social loneliness, who participant has felt for refusing to pay extortionextortion request. This piece of transcript is included in the super-ordinate theme "Emotive and social reaction of the participant to the behaviour of his community" (11.789: this interview fragment is positioned in page 11, line 789 of the original transcript).

[36] Mafia offense has provoked not only the formal and informal networks crush, but also economic consequences and the progressive destruction of participant's professional finish line. During the interview, with sorrow he remember "*After treats I have to oblige to lay off staff*" [...] "*For two years, I see to collapse sales volume*" (14.1043: this interview fragment is positioned in page 14, line 1043 of the original transcript). Specifically, this issue it could be found in super-ordinate theme: "effects of extortion on economic vulnerability."

According to the Council of Europe (recommendation rec, 2005/9, of the Committee of Ministers to member states on the protection of witnesses and collaborators of justice), a collaborator of justice is a person "who faces criminal charges, or has been convicted of taking part in a criminal association or other criminal organization of any kind, or in offenses of organized crime, but who agrees to cooperate with criminal justice authorities, particularly by giving testimony about a criminal association or organization, or about any offense connected with organized crime or other serious crimes." In Italy, the latest report achieved by the Public Security Department of Home Office, related to the people who request the inclusion in a protection program until 30 June 2014 highlights a significant increase of requests. The protection program holders actually are 1244, of which 1158 are collaborators of justice. Specifically, the distribution of the collaborator of justice seems to be characterized by a significant heterogeneity. The collected data show that the criminal organization with the greatest number of people who decide to cooperate with justice is the Camorra with 521 people, followed by the Cosa Nostra with 139, the 'Ndrangheta with 139 and the SCU with 113, while remaining people belongs to the other minor criminal organizations. It means that the choice to collaborate with justice depends more on the specific structural and functional characteristics that define each mafia organization. Specifically, the single case analyzed is mainly focused on the phenomenological and interpretative analysis of the experience of a collaborator of justice who comes from 'Ndrangheta. Therefore, through this contribution it is possible to examine one of the most powerful and fearsome criminal organization of mafia, starting from the sight of a man who before was an affiliate to this mafia organization and who after has preferred to collaborate with justice. Especially in the present case study, the main semantic and conceptual areas that are found could be connected to the three following clusters:

1. The "Brand" 'Ndrangheta
2. The 'Ndrangheta inside
3. The Traumatic effects of justice collaboration (see Fig. 7.5)

The 'Ndrangheta Brand (see Fig. 7.6)

Who is an affiliated to 'Ndrangheta criminal organization? Why is it possible to talk about a 'Ndrangheta "brand"? Based on the collaborator of justice words, being affiliated to the organization mainly means to be designated to cover a well-defined role inside the organization. The structural foundations of the criminal organization correspond with the affiliate's biological family. As the participant highlights, "if you are born 'Ndranghetista (i.e.: a person affiliated to the 'Ndrangheta), you already are an honorable young man ("*giovane d'onore*"), which means, already affiliated to 'Ndrangheta (3.162)[37]" and "the family is really important (3.184)." This way belonging to the family ensures cohesion and organizational stability. It is

[37] (3.162: this interview fragment is positioned in page 3, line 161 of the original transcript). It is possible to use the same reading procedure in all of the other fragments mentioned in the chapter.

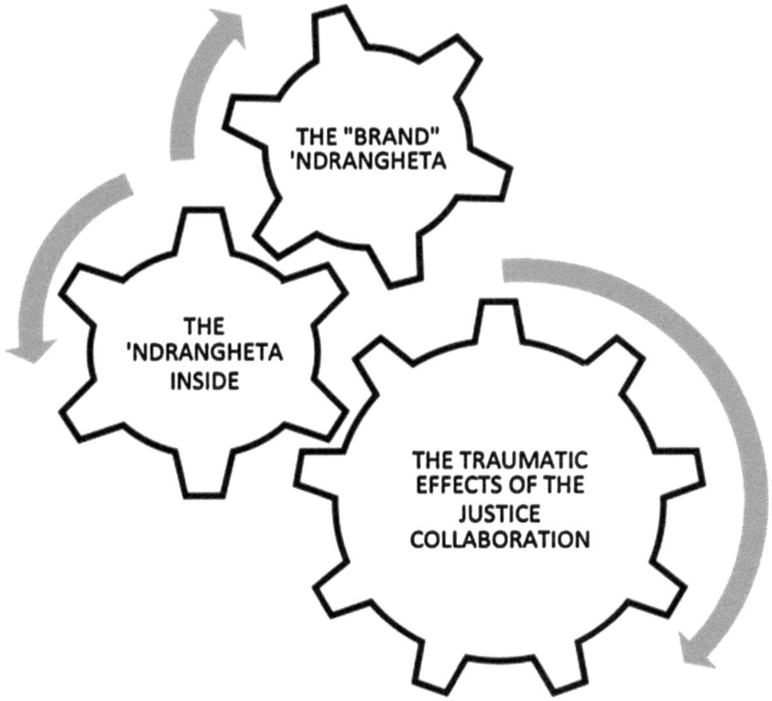

Fig. 7.5 Visual overview of the three semantic and conceptual domains achieved in analysis of experiences of the justice collaborator involved in the research

relevant that nothing can be thought outside of the family bond. The participant stresses also that "separation is worse than death if you are a 'ndranghetista (12.849)" and that "if you are born in a family and you think you can lose it on the existential plan, then you really don't exist (3.157)." For the former affiliated the 'Ndrangheta "is the family (15.1096), but it is at the same time a cannibal world (22.1517)."

However, the family has a strong fascination power on its components affiliates, since it employs a strong organizational culture that aims at idealizing the exclusiveness of its membership and to create a gap between what is 'Ndrangheta and everything that is not. As it emerges from the participant's interview, "the 'Ndrangheta classifies human species (3.152)" and "for them, there only are '*ndranghetisti*, then "*contrasts*" ("contrasti"), "*honored contrasts*" ("contrasti onorati") and the infamous people ("infami") (3.153)." 'Ndrangheta's organizational culture and the propensity to idealization, which is widely used in symbolical sense, are primarily aimed at legitimize power relationships and, then, organizational stability. The rules' value is of paramount importance. Rules, which constitute the organization's symbolic foundation, are fundamental for maintaining the power relationships and preserving the organizational structure.

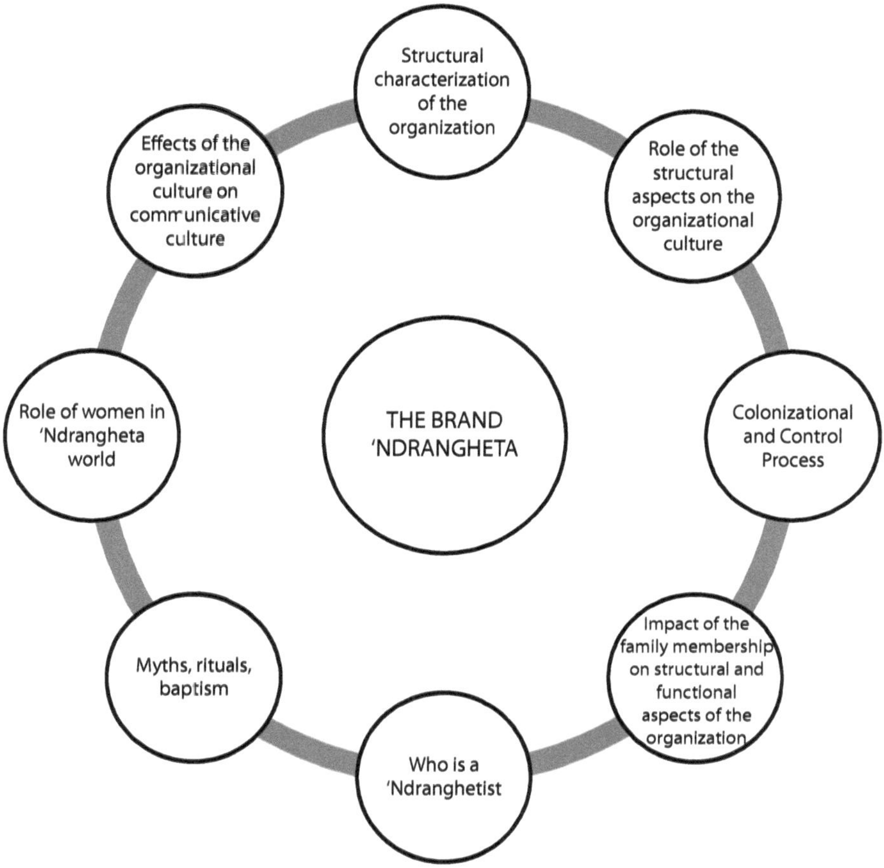

Fig. 7.6 Visual overview of the first semantic and conceptual level detected trough Interpretative and Phenomenological Analysis. The Graphic summarizes the main super-ordinate themes associated to this macro-area that are briefly discussed in the paragraph below

Respect for rules does never allow to act in autonomy, because "the mom is the mom." The undisputed centralization and control vertex stays in Calabria, the land where it all began, the land that is the mother of the organization.

While myth aims at preserving the original structural equilibria of the criminal clique, rules aim at legitimating the exercise of power and any other form of violence. There are rules about how to live, how to die, how to betray (Saviano 2011).

The sacred nature of some principles and the possibility to modify them in relation to specific environmental circumstances allows the organization's survival and, at the same time, it makes its structural layout more fluid. It is not a case that this peculiar organizational structure is the only one with the ability of duplicating itself like a fractal in very different areas of Calabria and to extend its dominion at a global scale (Forgione 2008).

As the participant recalls, 'Ndrangheta is "the only criminal organization that can be found in all of the five continents (32.2490)." Nevertheless, "Calabria is the Mom, the cradle, the vertex where the organization was born (20.2217)" and, once again, "the mom is always the mom (31.2222) [...] there, it is like Jerusalem for Christians (35.2727)." The geographical *core* of the organization is not susceptible of any chance of change, since for all of the affiliates it corresponds with the symbolic origin of the power. This is confirmed by the participant's words, "who attempted to subvert this order has been killed (31.2224)." Everything for 'Ndrangheta affiliates is instrumental to power; even the link with one's own land is secondary if compared to the chance of colonizing (Dalla Chiesa and Panzarasa 2012) and expanding his hegemony.

The mixture between new and old, myth and ordinary, favors the organization's embeddedness capability with respect to the civil society and the surrounding social fabric.

In the participant's opinion, this way the organization "needs popular consensus like any other institution (20.2217)." 'Ndrangheta's criminal world, in fact, is "a legend (33.2389) [...] a chivalric code" (33.2390) with an initiation ritual, the baptism, that is executed in the same exact way at all latitudes since the mythical organization's foundation that derives from the history of three legendary Spanish knights: Osso, Mastrosso and Carcagnosso (Gratteri and Nicaso 2009). The affiliation ritual contributes to make the bond with the organization sacred and inviolable, in such a way that during the investiture the participant felt some emotion stem from the awareness of the covered role, the weight of his assignment and his feeling like a "soldier."[38] Therefore, as the participant's highlights, little by little, "the participant perceives the organization as if it were a living being [...] a protective entity (15.1103)," in which the rigid categorization of roles is coded by the baptism. The participant's words describe everything that happens during the affiliation ritual: "I then become "*Camorrista di sangue*[39]" and then you must bite your finger and choose the rival, who then becomes your blood mate, it means he must protect you and you must protect him forever (20.1454)."

The "*punciuta*[40]," that is followed by the choice of the "compare di sangue" ("blood mate"), seals the link between adepts and between them and the organization. The belonging to the organization becomes a holy fact and then intangible and immutable. Since then, the adept "acquires the citizenship right, which means the full exercise of his rights and duties." Based on the experience of the former 'Ndranghetista, each behavioral code was only the product of a communicational culture centered on becoming familiar with the violence. Values such as obedience, silence, disregard for the feminine, mythicization of manhood, negation of subjectivity, homophobia, slowly incorporated by the participant, little by little start to be

[38] The participant tells that during the baptism, he "felt a certain kind of emotion." He felt, actually, the emerging difference of the new role he just was assigned too, "between ruler and affiliated" (16.1183).

[39] A role acquired by the 'Ndrangheta affiliated.

[40] The act of biting your finger with a needle.

"the basis of all of his own world's existence." The feminine conveys the "pedagogy of the revenge" and is central but submerged at the same time (Principato and Dino 1997). Women are allowed to temporarily handle power and they carry out a vicarious role with respect to their fathers, brothers or husbands. It is, then, a kind of pseudo-emancipation (Ingrascì 2007).

Therefore, the feminine is accurately exploited by the organization too. The marriage bond, for instance, is an instrument to preserve organizational equilibria, it is mostly constituted by "arranged unions," and it is the result of imposed cultural codes that serve the myth of the marital loyalty. Command and power require self-control, readiness, indifference, that have to be acquired sacrificing Eros and any other chance of encounter and exchange. These are the basis for one of the organization's "commandments" (Gratteri et al. 2008) that says: "*cummanari è megghiu 'i futtiri*" ("commanding is better than having sex").

The 'Ndrangheta Inside (see Fig. 7.7)

Another central nucleus around which the former affiliate's collaboration experience revolves, is the relationship and the bond with his own natural family, and specifically with his own mother and father. Both the educational models received and their heterogeneity has been crucial to the choice of the participant to leave the organization. The former 'Ndranghetista, subject of this research, allowed to deepen the understanding of the organization from the inside. By analyzing his experience, it was possible to find characterizing and distinguishing elements of the affiliation to a criminal organization that reveals itself as dogmatic and totalitarian. Specifically, among the super-ordinate themes, it emerges the one connected to the controversial relationship with the father. The majority of the emergent themes found during the data analysis stressed the sense of "predestination" that the affiliated perceived like a sentence. In this case, the relationship with the father is like a jail, like an inescapable constraint obligation.

It is not a case that the "dowry" ("dote," the role covered inside the organization) received through the blood relationship, in the participant's experience, is felt to be a form of predestination,[41] a way of being, thinking, and living, and that begins even before being conceived. Then it continues through the infancy, without ever stopping for the rest of one's own existence. A 'Ndranghetista is trained to believe himself to be a "superior being"[42]; 'Ndrangheta and its affiliates are the most important thing; this way each 'Ndranghetista learns to feel as a part of a "perfect race[43]."

The received training is completely absorbing and strict, and its most relevant traits are the de-humanization of the other, and the normalization of violence.

[41] I think I have been "thought" in such a way that my life, my destiny, was already traced (5.320).

[42] As the participant says, referring to his own experience: "There a code that makes you different and you are raised with it… This way you are the superior being" (12.872).

[43] From the interview: "'Ndrangheta and its affiliates come first, as if it were the perfect race" (8.542).

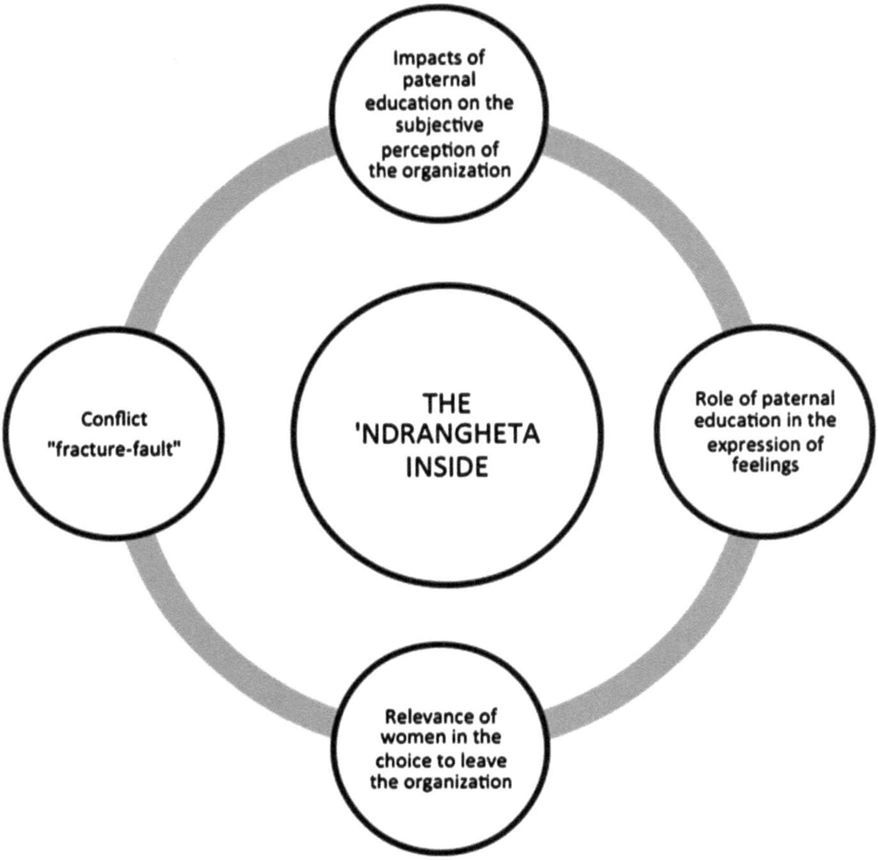

Fig. 7.7 Visual overview of the second semantic and conceptual level detected trough Interpretative and Phenomenological Analysis. The Graphic summarizes the main super-ordinate themes associated to this macro-area that are briefly discussed in the paragraph below

The same traits will be a stable presence in the affiliate's behavior. As the participant recalls: "sometimes I compare my training with the German shepherd one (12.887) [...] such a training usually begins close to the new year's eve (12.902), first by shooting at the shutters, then to bottles and finally by murdering someone." Then, as the participant recalls: "when you start shooting to people, at the beginning you think it is the same thing (13.925). Only when you see them falling down and bleeding, you start to understand that it's a completely different situation (13.927–13.928)." He continues: "the first training you receive is the psychological one [...] and maybe that is the hardest one" (9.605), and "it's all a matter of preparation, it's the air you breathe everyday (11.776) [...] your relatives continue to prepare you, to make you understand that blood need to be taken (11.779) [...] that vengeance is a need (11.793). 'Ndrangheta is a war context (8.573), then, where emotions are weaknesses and they are not admitted." By recalling the memory of his first homicide, the participant affirms: "I have seen the blood squirt, blood mixed with brain parts (15.1132) and I even felt my heartbeat accelerating" (15.1072). Moreover, he says: "Even having another person's brain on my shoes (16.1158), I don't think I have felt any emotion (22.1533), because I was psychologically prepared, I had been trained this way (15.1073)."

It is surprising, then, the way the training the affiliate receives is able to determine a clear splitting between the state of augmented physiological activation, perceived after executing a criminal action, and the recognition of the emotion and the associated mental states. It is highly probable that the observation of such a phenomenon depends on the fact that, after the training, as the participant suggests, "you become an automata (14.1045) [...] I felt completely like a robot, right after my first homicide" (15.1188).[44]

Another goal of the training is the idealization of the inviolability of the affiliation link with the organization. The organization exists above all, even above the life of one's own natural family.

As the participants describes, after taking the road of the collaboration with justice, "the father recounted it, then the "family"[45] gathered and they took various decisions" (20.1489) and, "from my father I had two ambushes in twelve hours" (20.1467). 'Ndrangheta punishes, it does not tolerate any possibility of separation, and nevertheless what disturbs the most the participant after his choice "it is not such a big deal to hear the bullets, but the betrayal [...] (20.1428), your father decided to murder you, and that's it (20.1432)."

Anxiety, hatred, and rancor are the direct effects of the deep conflicts with the father. However, the participant's history would have had a different finale if it had remained delimited to the sole paternal lineage. In organizations like the 'Ndrangheta, in fact, there is no way of escape. Nevertheless, in this sequence of events, what allowed the participant to break his bond with the organization was the role of the feminine carried out by his mother,[46] in explicit contrast with the one normally acted out by women in mafia context. Even representing an exception,[47] the participant's maternal lineage is not linked to the codes of any criminal system and for this reason it certainly represented a concrete chance of escaping from 'Ndrangheta, offering them already in his childhood an alternative cognitive and educational model.

[44] The emotion stays confined to a somatic level, so that a murder, for instance, produces the acceleration of one's own heartbeat, but it does not have a sufficient entity to prevent the execution of one's own assignment. The tendency to the emotional detachment end desensitization are, then, a strategy to rationalize and contain the normalization of violence.

[45] In this case, the term "family" refers to the criminal organization.

[46] In the participant's experience, the role of the women, in the conjugal and maternal sense, represents a protection factor and acts as an *intergenerational buffer*. In essence, the maternal education first and then the presence of his wife, softened the unfortunate effects of the 'Ndrangheta conditioning.

[47] My father managed to get married for love (10.754). As the participant recalls, both his father and his grandfather, even belonging to one of the most strict criminal organizations, managed to marry the woman they wanted for love.

The meeting of two diametrically opposed generational lines has created a strong moral conflict inside the participant, bringing him to such a strong sentiment of laceration, to make him consider a radical choice that gradually allowed him to separate himself from the organization.

The maternal education, as the participant recounts, provided him the "building blocks" (9.636) that allowed him to detach himself from the mafia identity received by his father.

Other than his mother, even his partner supported him in the choice of collaborating, "a situation that cannot be absolutely faced without having the right person by your side" (10.683).

In addition to the "feminine" experienced by the participant, also the concern for his own children represented a strong motivation in favor of the decision to change his own destiny. This way, little by little he felt the duty to protect their children from a world that, for many years, had looked like the only possible world, and that, as he recalls, "infects you, takes you" (33.2392).

The Traumatic Effects of Collaboration (see Fig. 7.8)

Next to the all of the previously discussed aspects, the collaborator with justice choice implies dealing with a double trauma.

On one hand, his own world and existence crumble away, and it entails the loss of its familiar and organizational identity. On the other hand, he faces the impossibility of an actual reintegration in the civil society. Hence, the last semantic-conceptual areas that emerges from the interpretational-phenomenological analysis of the participant's experience, is mainly related to the psychopathological, psychosomatic and relational impact following the collaboration choice, that highlights the logistic difficulties he will have to face.

The first *superordinate* themes found during the analysis and belonging to this conceptual domain, is connected to the detection of a significant number of *emerging themes* that revolves around the representation of the "detachment" from the organization as death, disintegration and loss of the self.

After undertaking the choice, the participant recalls that his greatest fear was "the nightmare of disappearing" (12.854) and, again, "my world had disappeared; everything had disappeared (23.1653) [...] the world was collapsing on me (23.1653) [...] nothing existed anymore (23.1656)." The participant has reaffirmed the rarefaction of his own presence and identity, during the interview, several times: "existentially you are nothing" (23.1656).

The collaborator with justice words are very clear: "the decision of collaborating has been to me an enormous trauma (21.1504); I was dead at a psycho-emotional level, existentially (21.1506) [...] because everything had disappeared (21.1557)."

The annihilation sense experienced by the participant after beginning the collaboration is so strong that, in his words: "I didn't see myself in the mirror anymore

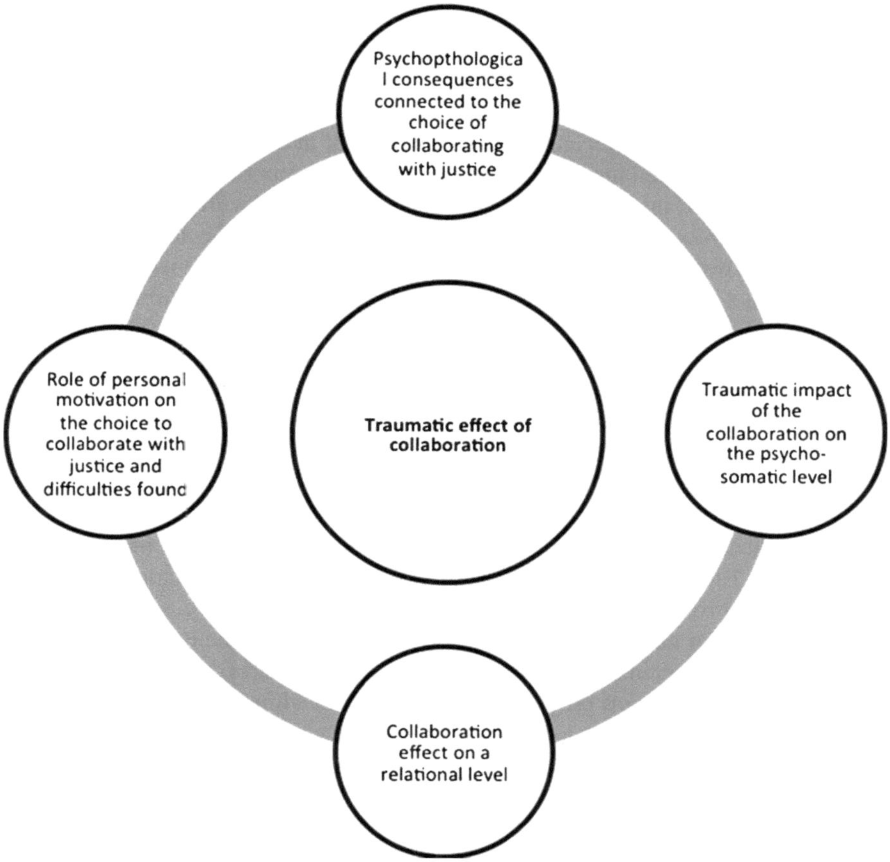

Fig. 7.8 Visual overview of the third semantic and conceptual level detected trough Interpretative and Phenomenological Analysis. The Graphic summarizes the main super-ordinate themes associated to this macro-area that are briefly discussed in the paragraph below

[…] I got sick of depression and this accompanied me until March 2010, it has been terrible" (23.1680).

The seriousness of the depressive psychopathological drift and its psychotic trait, in the collaborator's experience, has been so high that it has led to suicidal intents and to concrete attempts.

The depressive emptiness is to some extent still referred to the relationship with the father. The participant affirms: "he had already killed me before the shooting" (20.1457). Undoubtedly, the relevance of this theme amplified the perceived sense of collapse, as he has repeatedly stated, "you don't think, every minute you want to die" (23.1657). And again: "every hour I wanted to die (22.1625) […] I tried to suicide (25.1793), but I did not succeed (25.1795) […] I thought it was the better solution for my children, my family and maybe for myself too (25.1796)."

The accurate interpretational-phenomenological analysis of the transcript highlighted how the experimented psychopathological drift, in the participant's experience, results also in the appearance of psychosomatic elements, by taking the form of sleep disturbances, tremors, sense of paralysis, sleep apnea and panic attacks. Leaving the organization means, then, to find oneself in a "middle earth," paralyzed and suspended between inside and outside. During his report, he affirms, in fact, to have suffered from "insomnia" (25.1813), and "sleep apnea" with tremors (27.1927), but to have been caught by motor deficits to be probably attributed to conversion symptoms: "I was awake and I could not move" (27.1934). The separation from the organization, as long as leaving the familiar bonds, represented a stressful and conflictual factor that has not to be underestimated.

In his experience, also the lack of institutional measures amplify the pain caused by his sentiments. This issue has emerged clearly during the interpretational-phenomenological analysis of the transcript, in terms of logistic criticalities connected to the collaboration path indeed.

The participant experiences a deep sense of abandonment by the institutional system appointed to the protect former affiliates who choose to come out of the mafia organization. In the participant's opinion, also collaborators of justice "are victims" (26.1990), since they cannot have any chance of reintegration in the civil society, neither to be forgiven nor supported by their relatives.

When a former affiliate does not receive protection from the institutions, like in this case, he is forgotten or he lives with other former affiliates of the same organization during the protection program; this aspect makes him fear for his safety and amplifies the psycho-physical stress and trauma already caused by the collaboration itself.

The sense of emptiness cannot be alleviated by only administering psychopharmacological drugs, but in the participant's experience, it converts also into the research of closeness to the institutions. In his opinion, therefore, institutions should employ multidisciplinary teams to re-educate and provide psychological support to people who operated this choice, to avoid further amplification of their isolation sense.[48]

As the collaborator affirms "we walked embraced (23.1714), we had to be supported both on the psychological and the social plan (23.1714)." The only help he received was by his woman: "no one but my wife helped me. She was able to support me until a certain point, then she needed to be too (23.1708)."

The hope that animates the collaboration choice is fostered by the strength and the high motivation that his wife and his children gave him, and that allowed him to repudiate the heritage he received. He decided to fight for his children to avoid that they followed his steps. He recalls: "today we are here so that my children can have freedom of choice (10.721)," "I would not have tolerated to know that my son came back home after having killed someone (36.2615), now I hope to give a contribution (1.26), to be useful [...] hoping that 'Ndrangheta can be defeated (1.27) [...] and

[48] During the interview, the participant affirms: "they should find sociologists, educators, social workers and psychologists... why do these things do not exist? (37.2661).

avoid that others will experience what I experienced (19.360) [...] this way, while they grow up I relive a taste of childhood" (35.2623).

To this extent, dissociate themselves from the organization, for the participant, means having the chance to give a sense to the deprivation of his infancy and to contribute to actively fight the criminal power; that same power that gave him live, but also death.

An Example of Intervention Perspective in Mafia's Victim Handling

In the light of the above, the aim of the current contribution is to focus not only on the difficulties that the mafia victims have to face, but also on the intervention tools that could be useful to fight against the harmful that is connected to this type of crimes. Although the conditions for granting protection measures vary for witnesses and for collaborator with justice, and since both witnesses and collaborators tend to play a similar role in trial proceedings, in Italy the existing legislation framework on protection of witnesses and collaborators with justice is ruled by the same Decree Law. Specifically, it deals with the legal provision and the established practice connected to the Decree Law No. 8 of 15 January 1991, which was converted into a Law (No. 82) on 15 March 1991 and subsequently amended by Law No. 45 of 13 February 2001, "New provisions on kidnapping and on witness protection and protection and punishment of criminals collaborating with justice." Protecting people either who have already cut off their links with a criminal organization or give evidence of relevance to a preliminary investigation or trial proceedings, is not a simple task. Nevertheless with the current system is possible to guarantee both collaborators and witnesses protection and assistance, almost the existing system is a *low intensive model*, focused more on a strategies of economic countervailing. These strategies are not completely available for this people and often are inadequate to counteract the main psychic costs produced by mafias. Since these costs and consequences are usually related with the development of an heterogeneous system of variables it could be important reflecting on the possibility to create a model of intervention that could be able to overlap on each specific aspects of the issue in order to prevent for example the risk of the crash of its own social network, of the way to exchange with the external world, the lonesome and isolation, the feeling of failure, paranoia, depression and fear experimented, the mental-crush and the post-traumatic diseases that could emerge. Therefore, It is also important to reduce the mistrust in Institutions. Specifically, in the first case analyzed the complicated characterization which marks the consequences of the extortion action can be dealt with by using a model of intervention composed by multiple levels, capable of acting simultaneously both on the restraint of the primary harmfulness and on the interruption of the other effects of traumatic summation, connected to secondary harmfulness. The first step is to act on formal and informal social network at different levels starting from the valuing of community and human capital (citizens' awareness, community association and voluntary work and development of a system of multi-agencies services). The second one is connected to get to the possibility to develop plans of collaborative-assessment addressed towards the victim, and his family promoting the employment of an individual, group and family settings. Last but not least, is the possibility to promote training intervention addressed to the operators of the law enforcement agency. The same kind of intervention could be pointed towards the situation lived by the collaborators of justice involved in the research, by shaping for example the model on the specific critical issues that are associated to this condition. An example of concrete actions connected to the possibility to improve the networking tools to achieve multidisciplinary actions of prevention for mafia victims is provided by the research on the voluntary associations born in Sicily in '90 after mafia attack against the two judges involved in the "maxi trial" against Cosa Nostra. Thanks to one of these associations named "Addio Pizzo," entrepreneurs start to react to mafia threats and to rebel against the criminal organization (Coppola et al. 2011). The first aid provided by this association to the entrepreneurs who refused to pay protection money, was simply the divulging of an information support on how removing the glue from the padlocks of the portcullises of their shops and to denounce anonymously. It could seem a trivial solution, but gradually the number of the entrepreneurs who is being denouncing this offense is significantly increased, also thanks to the birth of other associations against all types of mafia as "Libera" for example. However, usually, when the claim is done, especially after the request to entry in a protection program as a witness, is probable that who denounce is obliged to lose his own right to work, to life and to security. For this reason the biggest challenges, before listening the sufferance of the victim, has to primarily guarantee to these people the real possibilities to maintain his own occupation, in order to preserve their sense of dignity, self-confidence and decrease the feelings of learned helplessness. Beside the voluntary associations, the new form of the "cooperation culture against mafia's traumatization methods it would be the proximity policing. The Situation and social prevention together with the creation of partnership network make possible the creation of mutual trust and knowledge between police and citizens. The diffusion of healthy ties of belonging it could be useful to implement the action of governance and to make the community able to develop a collective well-being in a circular way. Another possibility to do networking is operating on the people sensitization, in fact, only this way is possible to choose one viewing direction. Another way to act directly on mafia victims is take in consideration the possibility of elaboration of the traumatic experience lived, not only for themselves, but also for their families. The assessing activities have to be integrated in a more wide intervention model. For this reason, working with the mafia victims means assuring also the well-being of who are designed in the concrete handling of people involved in protection programs. Therefore acting on the training level could be assuring not only the possibility to prevent the risk of work related stress in police officers, but also the possibility to reduce the further form of victimization of which the victims may suffer due to the detachment attitudes that could be used by officer who daily have to communicate with victims, especially, if these are collaborators of justice. The adoption of this articulated perspective guarantees to work synergistically on the mainly points of weakness perceived by people directly or indirectly expose to mafia offenses and on the vulnerability elements that characterized the guardianship system currently in force in Italy, in order to improve the handling strategy employed through the adoption of better practice in the accompaniment and in the defense of those who benefit from these protective measures.

References

Althusser, L. (2006). Ideology and ideological state apparatuses. In A. Sharma & A. Gupta (Eds.), *The anthropology of the state: A reader* (pp. 86–111). Malden, MA: Blackwell.

Arlacchi, P. (1983). *La mafia imprenditrice*. Bologna: il Mulino.

Atkinson, P. A., Coffey, A. J., & Delamont, S. (2001). A debate about our canon. *Qualitative Research, 1*(1), 5–21.

Bandini, T., Gatti, U., Gualco, B., Malfatti, D., Marugo, M. I., & Verde, A. (2003). *Criminologia. Tomo I*. Milano: Giuffrè.

Bandini, T., Gatti, U., Marugo, M. I., & Verde, A. (1991). *Criminologia. Il contributo della ricerca della conoscenza del crimine e della relazione sociale*. Milano: Giuffrè.

Becker, H. S. (1986). *Doing things together*. Evanston, IL: North-western University Press.

Becker, H. S. (1998). *Tricks of the trade*. Chicago: University of Chicago Press.

Berry, K. S. (2004a). Structures of bricolage and complexity. In J. L. Kincheloe & K. S. Berry (Eds.), *Rigour and complexity in educational research: Conceptualizing the bricolage* (pp. 103–127). Maidenhead: Open University Press.

Berry, K. S. (2004b). Feedback looping for increasing complexity. In J. L. Kincheloe & K. S. Berry (Eds.), *Rigour and complexity in educational research: Conceptualizing the bricolage* (pp. 128–146). Maidenhead: Open University Press.

Berry, K. S. (2006). Research as bricolage: Embracing relationality, multiplicity and complexity. In K. Tobin & J. L. Kincheloe (Eds.), *Doing educational research: A handbook* (pp. 87–116). Rotterdam, The Netherlands: Sense Publishers.

Berry, K. S. (2011). Embracing radical research: A commentary on 'To the next level: Continuing the conceptualization of the bricolage'. In J. L. Kincheloe, K. Hayes, S. Steinberg, & K. Tobin (Eds.), *Key works in critical pedagogy* (pp. 279–284). Rotterdam, The Netherlands: Sense Publishers.

Calandra, F., & Giorgi, A. (2015). *Io non pago. La straordinaria storia di Gianluca Maria Calì*. Milano: IPOC.

Ciconte, E. (1992). *'Ndrangheta dall'Unità a oggi*. Roma-Bari: Laterza.

Ciconte, E. (2010). *'Ndrangheta padana*. Bari: Rubettino Editore.

Cigoli, V., & Scabini, E. (2000). *Il famigliare. Legami, simboli e transizioni*. Milano: Raffaello Cortina.

Coppola, E., & Formica, I. (2014), La 'Ndrangheta e la strada. Gruppo esperienziale con gli agenti dell'unità mobile di Reggio Calabria, Narrare i Gruppi (9), (pp. 101–112).

Coppola, E., Giordano, C., Giorgi, A., Lo Verso, G., & Siringo, F. (2011). *Trame di sviluppo. Il volontariato e la ricerca psicologica per il cambiamento nei territori difficili*. Milano: Franco Angeli.

Coppola, E., Giunta, S., & Lo Verso, G. (2010). La 'ndrangheta tra la realtà detentiva e l'idealità organizzativa: una ricerca psicologico-clinica. *Rivista di psicologia clinica*, n.1.

Dalla Chiesa, N., & Panzarasa, M. (2012). *Buccinasco. La 'Ndrangheta al Nord*. Torino: Giulio Einaudi Editore.

De Saussure, F. (1974). *Course in general linguistics*. London: Peter Owen.

De Zulueta, F. (2009). *Dal dolore alla violenza. Le origini traumatiche dell'aggressività*. Milano: Raffaello Cortina.
Del Corno, F., & Rizzi, P. (2010). *Teoria, pratica, vincoli metodologici*. Milano: Raffaello Cortina. La ricerca qualitativa in psicologia clinica.
Denzin, N. K., & Lincoln, Y. S. (Eds.). (1999). *The SAGE handbook of qualitative research* (3rd ed.). Thousand Oaks, CA: Sage Publications.
Denzin, N. K., & Lincoln, Y. S. (Eds.). (2003). *Collecting and interpreting qualitative materials* (2nd ed.). Thousand Oaks, CA: Sage.
Denzin, N. K., & Lincoln, Y. S. (2008a). *The landscape of qualitative research* (3rd ed.). Thousand Oaks, CA: Sage.
Denzin, N. K., & Lincoln, Y. S. (2008b). The discipline and practice of qualitative research. In N. K. Denzin & Y. S. Lincoln (Eds.), *The landscape of qualitative research* (3rd ed., pp. 1–47). Thousand Oaks, CA: Sage.
Devers, K. J. (1999). How will we know "good" qualitative research when we see it? Beginning the dialogue in health services research. *Health Services Research, 34*(5), 1153–1188.
Dino, A. (2012). Women and transnational organized crime: the ambiguous case of Italian Mafias. In F. Allum & S. Gilmour (Eds.), *Routledge handbook of transnational organized crime*. London: Routledge.
Direzione Nazionale Antimafia. (2010). Relazione annuale sulle attività svolte dal Procuratore nazionale antimafia e dalla Direzione nazionale antimafia nonché sulle dinamiche e strategie della criminalità organizzata di tipo mafioso nel periodo 1° luglio 2009-30 giugno 2010.
Eatough, V., & Smith, J. A. (2008). Interpretative phenomenological analysis. In C. Willig & W. Stainton Rogers (Eds.), *Handbook of qualitative psychology* (pp. 179–194). London: Sage.
Elliot, R., Fisher, C. T., & Rennie, D. L. (1999). Evolving guidelines for publication of qualitative research studies in psychology and related fields. *British Journal of Clinical Psychology, 38*, 215–229.
Elliot, L. J., Slade, A., & Bergner, S. (2010). *Da mente a mente. Infant Research, neuroscienze e psicoanalisi*. Milano: Raffaello Cortina.
Faj, I. (1973). *Ethnic succession in organized crime: summary report*. Washington: GPO.
Fattah, E. A. (1976). The use of the victim as an agent of self-legitimation: Towards dynamic explanation of criminal behaviour. In E. Viano (Ed.), *Victims and societies*. Washington: Visage.
Finlay, L. (2002). "Outing" the researcher: The provenance, process, and practice of reflexivity. *Qualitative Health Research, 12*(4), 531–545.
Flick, U. (2002). *An introduction to qualitative research* (2nd ed.). London: Sage.
Flick, U. (2007). *Designing qualitative research*. London: Sage.
Forgione, F. (2008). *'Ndrangheta. Boss, luoghi e affari della mafia più potente al mondo. La relazione della Commissione Parlamentare Antimafia*. Milano: Dalai Editore.
Foulkes, S. H. (1975). *Group analytic psychotherapy: Research and practice*. London: Gordon and Breach.
Gabbard, G. O. (2007). *Psichiatra Psicodinamica*. Milano: Raffaello Cortina.
Gadamer, H. G. (1960). *Verità e Metodo*. Milano: Bompiani.
Gambetta, D. (2009). *Codes of the underworld: How criminals communicate*. New Jersey: Princeton University Press.
Giannini, A., & Cirillo, F. (2012). *Itinerari di vittimologia*. Milano: Giuffrè Editore.
Giannone, F., & Ferraro, A. M. (2014). Le vittime del racket. Imprenditori e commercianti alle prese con Cosa Nostra, 'Ndrangheta e Camorra. *Narrare i Gruppi, 9*, 113–128.
Giorgi, A. (2007). Oltre il pensare mafioso: sviluppo umano e beni relazionali. *Rivista di psicologia clinica, 3*, 263–283.
Giorgi, A., D'Angelo, C., & Calandra, F. (2014). Lo sviluppo economico e della persona in contesti mafiosi: il ruolo dei beni relazionali. *Narrare i Gruppi, 9*, 129–142.
Giorgi, A., & Lo Verso, G. (2011). Gruppoanalisi Soggettuale e beni relazionali. In G. Lo Verso & M. Di Blasi (Eds.), *Gruppoanalisi Soggettuale* (pp. 235–257). Milano: Raffaello Cortina.
Glaser, B. G. (1978). *Theoretical sensitivity*. Mill Valley, CA: Sociology Press.

Glaser, B. G. (1992). *Basics of grounded theory analysis*. Mill Valley, CA: Sociology Press.
Glaser, B. G. (1998). *Doing grounded theory: Issues and discussions*. Mill Valley, CA: Sociology Press.
Glaser, B., & Strauss, A. (1967). *The discovery of grounded theory*. Chicago: Aldine.
Gozzoli, C., Giorgi, A., & D'Angelo, C. (2014). 'Ndrangheta in Lombardy: Culture and organizational structure. *World Futures, 70*, 401–425. Taylor and Francis.
Gratteri, N., Nicaso, A., & Borrelli, M. (2008). *Il Grande Inganno. I Falsi Valori della 'Ndrangheta*. Cosenza: Pellegrini.
Gratteri, N., & Nicaso, A. (2009). *Fratelli di sangue. Storie, boss e affari della 'ndrangheta, la mafia più potente al mondo*. Milano: Mondadori.
Gupta, A., & Ferguson, J. (1997). Discipline and practice: "The field" as site, method, and location in anthropology. In A. Gupta & J. Ferguson (Eds.), *Anthropological locations: Boundaries and grounds of a field science* (pp. 1–46). Berkeley: University of California Press.
Harper, D. (2008). Clinical psychology. In C. Willig & W. Steinton-Rogers (Eds.), *The Sage handbook of qualitative research in psychology* (pp. 430–434). London: Sage.
Henry, S., & Lanier, M. M. (1998). *Essential criminology*. London: Westview.
Ingrascì, O. (2007). *Donne d'onore. Storie di Mafia al femminile*. Milano: Bruno Mondadori.
Keller, C. M., & Keller, J. D. (1996). *Cognition and tool use: The blacksmith at work*. New York: Cambridge University Press.
Kellner, D. (1999). Theorizing McDonaldization: A multiperspectivist approach. In B. Smart (Ed.), *Resisting McDonaldization* (pp. 186–206). London: Sage.
Kincheloe, J. L. (2001). Describing the bricolage: Conceptualizing a new rigor in qualitative research. *Qualitative Inquiry, 7*(6), 679–692.
Kincheloe, J. L. (2004a). Introduction: The power of the bricolage: Expanding research methods. In J. L. Kincheloe & K. S. Berry (Eds.), *Rigour and complexity in educational research: Conceptualizing the bricolage* (pp. 1–22). Maidenhead: Open University Press.
Kincheloe, J. L. (2004b). Redefining rigour and complexity in research. In J. L. Kincheloe & K. S. Berry (Eds.), *Rigour and complexity in educational research: Conceptualizing the bricolage* (pp. 23–49). Maidenhead: Open University Press.
Kincheloe, J. L. (2004c). Questions of disciplinarity/interdisciplinarity in a changing world. In J. L. Kincheloe & K. S. Berry (Eds.), *Rigour and complexity in educational research: Conceptualizing the bricolage* (pp. 50–81). Maidenhead: Open University Press.
Kincheloe, J. L. (2004d). Redefining and interpreting the object of study. In J. L. Kincheloe & K. S. Berry (Eds.), *Rigour and complexity in educational research: Conceptualizing the bricolage* (pp. 82–102). Maidenhead: Open University Press.
Kincheloe, J. L. (2005). On to the next level: Continuing the conceptualization of the bricolage. *Qualitative Inquiry, 11*(3), 323–350.
KLPD. (2011). *The 'Ndrangheta in the Netherlands: The nature, criminal activities and modi operandi on Dutch territory*. Amsterdam: National Crime Squad National—Police Agency of the Netherlands.
Langridge, D. (2004). *Research method and data analysis in psychology*. Harlow: Pearson.
Langdridge, D. (2007). *Phenomenological psychology: Theory, research and method*. Harlow: Pearson.
Larkin, M. (2001). Understandings and experiences: A post-constructionist cultural psychology of addiction and recovery in the 12-step tradition. Doctoral Dissertation, Nottingham Trent University, Nottingham, UK.
Larkin, M., Watts, S., & Clifton, E. (2006). Giving voice and making sense in Interpretative Phenomenological Analysis. *Qualitative Research in Psychology, 3*, 102–120.
Lévi-Strauss, C. (1966). *The savage mind*. Chicago, IL: University of Chicago Press.
Lincoln, Y. S. (1999, June 3–6). Courage, vulnerability, and truth. Paper presented to the Re-claiming Voice II Conference, University of California-Irvine, Irvine, CA.
Lincoln, Y. S. (2001). Varieties of validity: Quality in qualitative research. In J. S. Smart (Ed.), *Higher education: Handbook of theory and research* (Vol. 16, pp. 25–72). New York: Agathon Press.

Liotti, G., & Farina, B. (2011). *Sviluppi traumatici. Eziopatogenesi, clinica e terapia della dimensione dissociativa*. Milano: Raffaello Cortina.

Lo Verso, G. (1998). *La mafia dentro. Psicologia e psicopatologia di un fondamentalismo*. Milano: Franco Angeli.

Lo Verso, G., & Lo Coco, G. (2003). *La psiche mafiosa. Storie di casi clinici e collaboratori di giustizia*. Milano: Franco Angeli.

Lo Verso, G. (2005). L'io fondamentalista e la psiche mafiosa, in Narrare il gruppo. *Prospettive cliniche e sociali, 3*, 87–93. Roma: Armando.

Lo Verso, G. (2013). *La mafia in psicoterapia*. Milano: Franco Angeli.

Lo Verso, G., & Di Blasi, M. (2011). *Gruppoanalisi soggettuale*. Milano: Raffaello Cortina.

March, J. S. (1993). What constitutes a stressor? The criterion A issue. In J. R. T. Davidson & E. B. Foa (Eds.), *Post-traumatic stress disorder: DSM-IV and Beyond*. Washington: American Psychiatric Press.

Marecek, J. (2003). Dancing through minefields: Toward a qualitative stance in psychology. In P. M. Camic, J. E. Rhodes, & L. Yardley (Eds.), *Qualitative research in psychology: Expanding perspectives in methodology and design* (pp. 49–69). Washington, DC: American Psychological Association.

Miles, M. B., & Huberman, A. M. (1994). *Qualitative data analysis. An expanded source book*. Thousand Oaks, CA: Sage.

Nelson, C., Treichler, P., & Grossberg, L. (1992). Cultural studies: An introduction. In L. Grossberg, C. Nelson, & P. Treichler (Eds.), *Cultural studies* (pp. 1–16). New York: Routledge.

Norman, K. D., & Lincoln, Y. S. (2008). *The sage handbook of qualitative research*. London: Sage.

OFAC. (2012). *Narcotics: what you need to know about U.S. sanctions against drug traffickers*.

Palmer, M., Larkin, M., De Visser, R., & Fadden, G. (2010). Developing an interpretative phenomenological approach to focus group data. *Qualitative Research in Psychology, 7*, 99–121.

Paoli, L. (2003). *Mafia brotherhoods: Organized crime, Italian style*. Oxford: Oxford University Press.

Paoli, L. (2007). Mafia and organised crime in Italy: The unacknowledged successes of law enforcement. *West Eur Polit, 30*, 854.

Piaget, J. (1970). *Structuralism*. New York: Basic Books.

Principato, T., & Dino, A. (1997). *Mafia Donna: Le vestali del sacro e dell'onore*. Palermo: Flaccovio Editore.

Rogers, M. (2012). Contextualizing theories and practices of Bricolage research. *The Qualitative Report, 17*(T&L Art.7), 1–17.

Saviano, R. (2011). *Vieni via con me*. Milano: Feltrinelli.

Scarcella Prandstraller, S. (2012). La vittimizzazione come costruzione sociale. In A. Giannini & F. Cirillo (Eds.), *Itinerari di Vittimologia*. Milano: Giuffrè Editore.

Smith, J. A. (1995). Semi-structured interviewing and qualitative analysis. In J. A. Smith, R. Harre, & L. Van Langenhove (Eds.), *Rethinking methods in psychology* (pp. 9–27). London: Sage.

Smith, J. A. (1999). Towards a relational self: Social engagement during pregnancy and psychological preparation for motherhood. *British Journal of Social Psychology, 38*, 409–426.

Smith, J. A., & Dunworth, F. (2003). Qualitative methodology. In K. Conolly & J. Valsiners (Eds.), *Handbook of developmental psychology* (pp. 603–622). London: Sage.

Smith, J. A. (2004). Reflecting on the development of interpretative phenomenological analysis and its contribution to qualitative research in psychology. *Qualitative Research in Psychology, 1*, 39–54.

Smith, J. A. (2007). Hermeneutics, human sciences and health: Linking theory and practice. *International Journal of Qualitative Studies on Health and Well-being, 2*, 3–11.

Smith, J. A., Flowers, P., & Larkin, M. (2009). *Interpretative phenomenological analysis: Theory, research, practice*. London: Sage.

Tweed, A., & Charmaz, K. (2012). Grounded theory methods for mental Health Practitioner. In A. R. Harper & D. Thompson (Eds.), *Grounded theory methods for mental health practitioners* (pp. 131–146). West Sussex: John Wiley & Sons, Ltd.

U.S. Department of State. (2011). *International narcotics control strategy report: Vol. I. Drug and chemical control*. Washington: U.S. Department of State.
Van Maanen, J. (1988). *Tales of the field*. Chicago: University of Chicago Press.
Viano, E. (1983). *Victimology. Enciclopedia of crime and Justice* (Vol. 4). London: Free Press.
Viano, E. C., et al. (2003). *Transnational organized crime: Myth, power and profit*. Durham, NC: Carolina Academic Press.
Vygotsky, L. S. (1978). *Mind in society*. Cambridge, MA: Harvard University Press.
Walker, R. (1985). *Applied qualitative research*. Gower: Ashgate.
Weick, K. (1973). *La Psicologia dei processi organizzativi*. Milano: Isedi.
Weick, K. (1995). *Senso e significato dell'organizzazione*. Milano: Raffaello Cortina.
Willig, C. (2001). *Introducing qualitative research in psychology: Adventures in theory and method*. Buckingham: Open University Press.
Zegrebelsky, G. (2010). *Sulla lingua del tempo presente*. Torino: Einaudi.

Chapter 8
Social Network Analysis and Organised Crime Investigation: Adequacy to Networks, Organised Cybercrime, Portuguese Framework

Joana Neto

Introduction

The social network is the principal concept being used to study organisational structure for noncriminal and criminal social relationships (Morselli 2009) and refers to the set of actors and links between them (Wasserman and Faust 1994). In regard to this, organised crime groups should be perceived and studied as networks (Block 1999; Wasserman and Faust 1994) as they are constituted by several individuals in collaboration with each other and occupying different roles (Xu and Chen 2005). The use of the Social Network Analysis (SNA) concepts and methods for describing, modelling and analysing criminal networks have had considerable developments in the academic community, the criminal investigation services and intelligence since the events of September 11, 2001. Focusing on its tributes, this paper has three specific goals. Firstly, to describe what the SNA is, why and how it fits in the study of organised criminal networks. Secondly, examine the importance of the SNA in cybercrime research. And thirdly, provide a critical analysis of the use of this form in Portugal. In general, this paper examines these sets of issues through its application in the criminal investigation services mainly, as well as in the academic, procedural and political level.

The criminal investigation and the law enforcement agencies can improve their struggle and prevention activities of organised crime by identifying and targeting actors of complex networks. According to Clark (2007), the lack of network analysis in a more objective sense is one of the main reasons why law enforcement and intelligence can fail. That is why a variety of tools is regularly used, both in the process of tactical and strategic analysis (McDowell 1998), and the standard procedure for investigating collaborations amongst criminals is the SNA (Hulst 2008).

J. Neto (✉)
University of Porto, Porto, Portugal
e-mail: joanasmneto@gmail.com

E.C. Viano (ed.), *Cybercrime, Organized Crime, and Societal Responses*,
DOI 10.1007/978-3-319-44501-4_8

A study by Mainas (2012) in order to test the usefulness of the SNA into the analysis of criminal organisations found it is an effective approach to knowledge of complex criminal structures.

Specifically regarding cybercrime, it is believed that we're before a rapid expansion in the illegal industry. McGuire's (2012) review found that up to 80 % of cybercrime could be the result of some form of organised activity. However, because of the novelty of the phenomenon, there is still a considerable lack of research on how these virtual networks are structured in cyberspace and how they work (Tropina 2012). Although there is little use of the SNA in this matter, it can be a powerful way to identify these networks, know how they are constituted, and analyse their relationship patterns.

In Portugal, there is limited formal information published on the SNA. Their capabilities are still little known. In terms of police and criminal investigation this technique is already widespread in analyst services; although few practical concerns. Nevertheless, in the political and academic context, contrary to what happens in other countries, this method is not widespreadly employed in the comprehension of criminal networks.

This being said, the first part of this paper addresses the adequacy of organised crime's analysis as a social network, and clarifies what the SNA is. It will be then identified the capabilities and innovations that the method brought to the study of the criminal phenomenon and its difficulties as well as limitations. A second part will discuss the use of the SNA in organised cybercrime and discerning about the existence of organised criminal networks within the cyberspace. The third and final part of this paper will cover the current overview of the Portuguese framework providing some constructive critics along the way.

Part I—The Social Network Analysis in Organised Crime

Organised Crime and Social Networks

Nowadays, the social network is the principal concept being used to study organisational structure for noncriminal and criminal social relationships (Morselli 2009). At a more basic level, societies are organised around relationships and these constitute the networks (McIlwain 1999)—the new social morphology of our society (Castells 1997). They are relational structures of groups or a larger social system that consist of the pattern of relationships amongst the various actors. The concept refers hence to the set of actors and links between them (Wasserman and Faust 1994). These are open structures able to expand limitless, integrating new nodes as long as they share the same communication codes (Castells 1997); are adaptive and change with the passage of time (Bertalanffy 1975). These are also the characteristics of organised criminal structures that should be studied as networks (Block 1999; Wasserman and Faust 1994) as they are composed of many individuals in collaboration and occupying different roles (Xu and Chen 2005). Moreover, criminal conduct is predominantly related to social behaviour (Warr 2002), and criminal organisations may be illegal but their management principles are common to any other network: human and social capital (Hulst 2008).[1]

"Whether in a marginalized subset of society, a problematic neighbourhood, a deviant subculture, a criminogenic geographical space, or in the criminal marketplace, networks are in place and it is within such organisational system that criminal opportunities are generated and collaboration to seize such opportunities is organised and executed" (Morselli 2009, p. 3). Nonetheless, criminal networks are not simply social networks operating in a criminal environment. The covert settings that surround them demand specific interactions and relational features within and beyond the network (Morselli 2009). That said, law enforcement agencies can improve their fight and prevention activities of organised crime by identifying and targeting the participants and relationships of such complex networks. And, it is in this field that the SNA constitute a fundamental instrument (McAndrew 2000; Morselli 2005; Schwartz and Rouselle 2008; Xu and Chen 2005).

The Social Network Analysis

A better grasp of relational structures is vital to understand complex phenomena (Freeman 2006). Originated in ethnography and sociometry (Klerks 2001) the SNA refers not only to the perspective that social relationships provide crucial knowledge about human behaviour—an approach—but also to a set of analytical tools that allow the study of these social relations—an operational method (McGloin and Kirk 2010).

As an approach, it defends that individuals are interdependent and these interdependencies have an impact on their behaviour. The SNA is derived from a scrutiny of the social structure empirically, based on the observed relationships between the actors, instead of predetermined classifications. Explaining human behaviour or social process only through properties and categorical standards is not enough. The individual manifests itself in a socially relevant way especially in its relationship with others. Mapping these relationships, network examination helps to uncover the emergent and informal communication patterns surrounding organisations (Haythornthwaite 1996; Wasserman and Faust 1994; McGloin and Kirk 2010; Klerks 2001). It presupposes a structural analysis based on two central goals: (1)

[1] On the one hand, the human capital frame people with the right skills and competencies to optimise overall performance. So the core or the model of the criminal operations includes a strategic design (e.g. the organisational structure) and an operational design (e.g. roles and processes) which intends integrate people, information and technology to optimise their efficiency and effectiveness. On the other hand, another key issue to create organisational success is to generate competitive advantage through social connections that facilitate the achievement of objectives that would not be possible in its absence. The advantages that result from social networks are known as social capital, which is to say that actors and entities with better access to valuable social resources are more successful in their performance (Bourdieu 1986; Coleman 1990).

the identification of certain patterns of social interaction, and (2) understanding the influence of these patterns on the behaviour of social entities (Wasserman and Faust 1994).

As a method, it reflects in practice the goals of the theoretical approach as it is a means of visual mapping and measure of relationships between nodes after the data is entered into a matrix (Wasserman and Faust 1994; McGloin and Kirk 2010). The software[2] allows the exploitation of data that is done by displaying the nodes and links in various layouts and assigning colours, size and other advanced properties, after its examination through mathematical and statistical tools. Indeed, in addition to network graphics views and sociograms, the SNA is an arithmetic technique that examines and quantifies relational patterns of nodes and connections based on mathematical calculations—the analysis parameters[3] (Knoke and Yang 2008, cited in Mainas 2012).

According to the SNA, the social network is, thus, a structure composed of either actors or entities that are represented by nodes being connected by relationships that are social ties, represented by lines, where a variety of resources are changed (Randjeloviü and Popoviü 2011). First, the actors can be individuals, groups, organisations and populations and their characteristics are examined as attributes. This includes, for example, demographic or behavioural characteristics, socio-economic status and competencies (Bruinsma and Bernasco 2004; Haythornthwaite 1996; Hulst 2008; Wasserman and Faust 1994; Wellman 1992). Second, social ties are the connections between nodes that indicate some form of activity or relationship amongst them in which a variety of resources is exchanged. There can be more specific types of interdependency, such as values, ideas, financial interests, common interests, amongst others (Haythornthwaite 1996; Randjeloviü and Popoviü 2011; Hulst 2008; Wasserman and Faust 1994). Third, actors continually exchange a variety of products and materials and intangible services with others who are critical to achieving goals. These resources may vary from money to information (instrumental resources) on social support (significant resources) dependently, for example, of their socio-economic position, their experience, their knowledge or their specific capabilities and connections with others (Haythornthwaite 1996; Hulst 2008; McIlwain 1999; Wasserman and Faust 1994).

[2] For example *i2 Analyst's Notebook*, *SocNetV*, *NodeXL*, *Sentinel HL*.

[3] There are five main parameters for analysis that can be measured at the individual level—ego-cantered network—or at the group level—whole network (Haythornthwaite 1996; Wasserman and Faust 1994): the structural positioning—allows the assessing of the structural position of actors in relation to other actors in the network; the range—indicates the extent of the network, i.e. calculates the number of nodes that an actor can have within a specified distance; cohesion—scans the cluster nodes according to the intensity of common relations, measuring the degree to which all members of a network interact with other members; structural equivalence—studies the cluster nodes according to the similarity of the relationship; and brokerage—indicating the bridge of inter- or intra-network connections.

Capabilities and Innovations in the Criminal Networks Analysis

SNA has a major set of capabilities that will be identified as well as the most notorious innovations that this method brought to the criminological knowledge and investigative practice will follow. Specifically, its advantages could be divided into three different levels: (1) criminal investigation and intelligence level, (2) procedural level, and (3) political level.

Concerning the criminal investigation and intelligence level there are several benefits from the tool. Due to the capacity to quantify the network parameters in addition to graphics, the interpretations of the network characteristics are less sensitive to subjectivity and limit the risk of loss of important signals (Hulst 2008). Moreover, the tool introduced dynamics to the static understanding of social structures than traditional organisational diagrams convey (Klerks 2001). The instrument not only draws attention to the established contacts, but also to the relationships that do not seem to exist and are probably hidden. Recruitment processes become clearer by analysing the previous connections and makes it possible to track the transfer of criminal knowledge and innovations (Klerks 2001). The device also allows the identification of aliases, identical roles and substitutes. That is, it identifies the names of the participants in a database that appear as aliases based on the similarity in the standardisation of social ties (e.g. equivalency roles) or to identify subgroups of actors who use identical roles (substitutes). This makes finding potential successors for key players that are removed or eliminated (e.g. by imprisonment or death) (Hulst 2008).

Moreover, the *Intelligence-led Policing* emerges as a policing model to reduce crime proactively based on the use of criminal information (Ratcliffe 2008). It permits the monitoring, evaluation and prediction of potential threats associated with individuals or networks. Additionally, based on the information of (suspected) networks and criminal activities, specific targets can be identified as the probable cause of disturbances by criminal activities ongoing or planned. In consequence, this technique provides investigators with tactical options for destabilisation networks (or booster) (Koschade 2006; Hulst 2008). Thus, the examination and evaluation of the information verified become the mainstay for defining the strategic planning of criminal investigation (Rostami and Mondani 2015).

In the procedural level, the SNA is to be able to provide support for procedural decision as evidence. Hearing that, it can become a powerful instrument to support the application of criminal law, accounting for actors in their role and for their involvement (Hulst 2008). This could be handy within the same judicial case by analysing a certain network—intra-process—, and helping cross networks relationships amongst several cases—inter-process.

In the political level, the outcomes of the SNA allow to develop important political strategies that inform and guide decisions on crime and security public policies (Rostami and Mondani 2015). The scrutiny of the SNA information enables to create strategic measures to fight and prevent organised crime. This would be a result of empirical knowledge acquired by this method in the various intelligence services, criminal investigation and academic research that would inform policymakers of the patterns and dynamics of crime that should be targeted by measures.

Difficulties and Limitations in Criminological Analysis

Despite all the capabilities and the methodological innovation, the SNA technique is not immune to certain limitations and disadvantages. That is why the SNA is a valuable device when reconciled with other research methods and ways of conceptualising (Boissevain 1979). However, it has been argued that the neglect of the SNA in criminology and specific methodological problems has hampered the ability to neutralise organised crime (Bruinsma and Bernasco 2004; McIlwain 1999). Below are listed some of the most frequent difficulties when applying the SNA.

Firstly, the method faces human, financial and time constraints. Collecting, encoding and data analysing are labour-intensive. Simultaneously, the amount of time to deliver results is often very short which conflicts with the need to work accurately (McDowell 1998). It requires qualified and experienced researchers and analysts in the use of this device, which also assumes an economic investment (Hulst 2008).

Secondly, data sources could configure some barriers. Researchers have to rely on methods that could result in incomplete data (e.g. wiretapping, notes, e-mail, files, informants, witnesses) as long as they are not necessarily representative of the entire network or are subject to a limited period of time (Hulst 2008). Consequently, there may be an array of nodes and relationships to which researchers will not have access to (Sparrow 1991a). Moreover, the data is usually evaluated in terms of reliability and validity of the information source (McDowell 1998). There is, however, no a convenient method or routine available in the SNA that considers the different degrees of valid and reliable data (Hulst 2008).

Thirdly, some premises need to be done prior to encoding. It is needed to define the network boundaries could be a hard task. The problem defining the limits is that the extension of networks is uncertain (Wellman 1992; Sparrow 1991a, b) which affects the scope and structure of a social network (and, therefore, investigation results). So, there must have been a previous task which allows for elements defining to be considered. But most of the time decisions will be based on theoretical considerations or practices and comply with the research needs issue (Scott 2000). In addition, before any research, which needs to be consistent and clear, information about the social connections should be coded (e.g. which actors are considered friend or foe, what events are considered important or key issues) (Hulst 2008).

Fourthly, a network is changing over time. The SNA is based on a special composition of actors and links at a given point in time. However, its composition and activities are contingent. Changes in network activity (e.g. increases of specific flows of trade, rapid emergence of new players and ties, changing directions cash flows) can be a key element indicating various stages of an event or a planned operation (Krebs 2002; Sparrow 1991a, b) but makes the traceability and study of these structures more difficult.

Fifthly, the interpretation of outputs could become a problem. As the number of actors can be considerably the sociograms quickly become difficult to read (Haythornthwaite 1996). In addition, the perception of relational patterns is strongly affected by the provision of graphics (McGrath et al. 1997, 2003).[4]

Part II—The Social Network Analysis in Cybercrime Investigation

Since the late twentieth century, we have lived in a period of transformation of material culture by the mechanisms of a new technological paradigm organised around information technology (Europol 2011; KPMG 2011; McCusker 2006). According to Castells (1997), we're expanding a culture of the real virtuality in the sense that there is no marked difference between the real and the virtual, and the influence on one another is binomial. This new communication system allows the inclusion and breadth of all cultural realities, including the criminal one. Indeed, as said the historical trend, dominant functions and processes in the information age are increasingly organised around networks. And the increasing dependence of society on information technology raises concerns about the vulnerabilities in cyberspace and the dark side of these networks (KPMG 2011; McCusker 2006; Tropina 2012). One of these vulnerabilities is the phenomenon of cybercrime[5] which is an internet-criminal business model based on logical services that drive innovation and provides access to a wide range of instruments that facilitate crime (Europol 2014) and enhance the financial or another material benefit (Moneyval 2012).

Is SNA a relevant method to adapt to the analysis of cybercrime? To answer this question is, however, necessary to clarify another one: Is cybercrime also a kind of organised crime? These are the questions that will be answered further on.

The Organised Crime and Cybercriminal Networks

When internet and computer networks link people as well as machines, they become social networks (Wellman 1997). The cyberspace reflects the trend towards an interconnected world and enhances the turn towards networks and away from groups (Wellman and Hampton 1999). More recently, emerged the question whether the

[4] Some research has shown, for example, that people tend to believe that the actors in the centre or at the top of a chart are the most important, and the actors who are in close proximity to each other belong to the same group (McGrath et al. 1997, 2003).

[5] There is no consensus on the definition of cybercrime. However, two levels of cybercrime could be highlighted. In a narrow sense, the strict computer crime refers to any illegal behaviour directed by means of electronic operations that targets the security of computer systems and the data processed by them. In a broad sense, the computer-related crime denoted any illegal behaviour committed by means of, or in relation to, a computer system or network, including such crimes as illegal possession, offering or distribution information by means of a computer system or network (United Nations 2000, p. 5).

internet was hosting a kind of organised criminal networks. To better answer this we first need to clarify what organised cybercriminal networks are.

Despite sharing the "organised" label with conventional organised crime in its nomination, it does not mean it also shares the same definition. Quite the contrary: one kind and another are different in their essence and, consequently, in their conceptualization. Indeed, current definitions of organised crime do not reflect the digital underground activity (Europol 2014), seeing that they are different from traditional organised criminal networks (Europol 2011, 2014; Lusthaus 2013; Tropina 2012).

Generally, although they may be coherent and project-based, they could lack the structure and hierarchy of a traditional organised crime entity. Relationships between cybercriminals are often transient or transactional (Europol 2014). They are mainly temporary networks of people who collaborate even though they may live in different countries, making cybercrime activities inherently fluid and flexible. Moreover, they do not need their own technical expertise and access to commit cyber offences, because they can buy it (Australian Crime Commission 2013).

Many cybercriminal entities are indeed small, loosely structured and without a clear agenda (Lusthaus 2013), but some computer (related) crime offenders can be highly networked and cooperate with each other to commit offences (Hutchings 2014). Complex illicit operations, cybercrime infrastructure, the level of specialisation as well as the division of roles show the characteristics that define structured organised criminals who work together to obtain financial or other material benefits (Moneyval 2012). With regard to the structure, a hierarchy with designated roles and responsibilities often exists, mainly in forums and marketplaces. This allows for these infrastructures to effectively police themselves, controlling population levels, and rooting out unwanted or troublesome members (Europol 2014). The hierarchy, although quite similar, varies with the analysis target and study.[6] The world of cybercrime has evolved to the point where, like conventional crime, there is a division of labour and various cybercriminals have specialist skill sets, not all involving elite computing abilities (Lusthaus 2013).[7] Networks are resilient and they may be composed of many features. Actors in networks do not have to be geographically concentrated, formally organised, or united by a common value system. There is a possibility of the organisational confines associated with the hierarchy and the flexibility maintained within more decentralised configurations. The network is a self-

[6] For example according to Lusthaus (2013) forums generally have an administrator(s), moderators and then members. Yip (2011) noted that a typical western online carding forum is constituted by administrators, moderators, reviewers, reviewers vendors and then members. Europol (2014) found that online payment fraud is composed of the ring leader, the trustee and then by a panoply of actors, namely technical experts, skimming cells, online trader, runner coordinator and runners, mule herder and mules, and good reseller. Aiken, Moran and Berry (2011, cited in Europol 2014) state that the child exploitation online could be tiered by experts, closed traders, open traders and then simple viewers.

[7] For example some can recruit others to do the technical work for them. Others can buy and exploit code created by expert coders. Some simply specialise in the risky business of 'cashing out' profits made online into tangible physical assets (Lusthaus 2013).

organising structure that is essentially driven by the emergent behaviour of its parts. Such parts may include a variety of actors, subgroups, clusters and even hierarchies that are absorbed in the network structure. Moreover, considering that a network is built on flexibility and lacks formal organisation does not mean that the network cannot be centralised around certain poles of action (Morselli 2009). Thus, virtual communities should be perceived and studied as social networks (Wellman 2001; Wellman and Gulia 1999).

In relation to the virtual infrastructure, organised cybercrime structures could act in the regular web: online social networking sites such as social networks, blogs, online gaming and online dating have opened a route for the personal information theft (Australian Crime Commission 2013). But this constitutes just the tip of the iceberg once a more comprehensive host is the portion of the internet not indexed by search engines—the Deep Web. More specifically it is the Dark Web as peer-to-peer networks within the Deep Web operating using anonymity technologies that are hosting the majority of networks through underground forums and criminal marketplaces.[8] These underground forums[9] provide a location for the trade of goods and services and are a hub for networking, creating an organised set of criminal relationships. Forums dedicated to drugs, hacking, carding and child abuse material[10] can all be encountered on the Darknet. The criminal marketplaces offer a place to acquire illicit commodities or services. There are marketplaces devoted to drug trade, selling stolen goods, weapons, compromised credit card details, forged documents, fake identification documents, and the trafficking of human beings, amongst many others (Europol 2014). Another area of the Dark Web is the "bulletproof hosting".[11] In this type of hosting the provider secures a place for cybercriminals to operate illegal activities, safe from being shut down by authorities. As a result, such bulletproof hosting is very attractive to cybercriminals and is well known for providing services to pornography sites and spammers amongst others (Lusthaus 2013).

Concerning criminal offences, there is a vast organised cyber threat landscape: crime-as-a-service, malware, child sexual exploitation online, payment fraud, criminal finances online, crimes relating to social engineering, data breaches and network intrusions and vulnerabilities of critical infrastructure (Europol 2014).

Summing up, not every criminal structure operating in cyberspace is a network or organised, but many of them can indeed configure organised cybercriminal

[8] However, we need to mention these marketplaces are also frequented and utilised by sole offenders. As well as those who may actively participate in discussions but not participate in illegal activities themselves. Furthermore, organised criminal networks may not necessarily operate in online marketplaces (Hutchings 2014).

[9] For example *CardersMarket, DarkMarket, Ghostmarket.*

[10] Notwithstanding child sex offenders and producers make increasing use of the Darknet and other similar platforms to exchange child abuse material, some offenders affiliate themselves with each other in order to share physical access to children, therefore facilitating the production of new material, as well as its customisation (Europol 2014).

[11] For example the *Russian Business Network* (Lusthaus 2013).

networks, even in different templates when compared to the conventional ones. Morselli (2009) argued that the scope, forms and contents of criminal organisation systems vary across an extended continuum, from the less organisational forms to a vast criminal organisation. What is lacking in the understanding of criminal organisational systems is a concept that offers enough flexibility to incorporate that wide variety. And it is reflected in cybercrime research as well. Having said this, the answer to the proposed question is definitively yes. To examine this issue, focusing on the structure, organisational culture, offences and environment I would consider an organised cybercriminal network[12] a *flexible* complex system of multiples unities (actors or entities) connected within a structured organisation (with rules, resources, information flows, coordinate roles), driven by specific purposes. His elements collaborate through the use of networked computers or Internet technology to the facilitation or commission of serious computer or computer-related illegal offence(s). And, if committed, would likely result in a direct or indirect benefit (material or not) by the network or any networks unity. Randomly formed structures to commit one single illegal act do not fit in this definition.

With this said, three types of organised criminal networks have been identified as operating in cyberspace (Choo and Grabosky 2013; Choo and Smith 2008; Australian Crime Commission 2013): (1) as a new way, (2) as a new form, and (3) the ideologically and politically motivated. On the one hand, we're facing the growth of organised cybercriminal networks as a new way, which refers to the traditional organised criminal networks that use information and communications technology to enhance their regular criminal activities (Australian Crime Commission 2013; Europol 2014).[13] They are hybrid organised cybercriminal networks. In addition to carrying out online offences themselves, traditional organised criminal networks may employ professional hackers for their own specialised skills[14] (Hutchings 2014). On the other hand, we can find organised cybercriminal networks as a new form, which refers to networks that operate solely in the online environment (Hutchings 2014; Australian Crime Commission 2013) and whose members are highly technically proficient (Hutchings 2014). That is why members are likely to know each other in the online environment only, meeting and planning with each other through the internet. These are usually less structured, smaller, more likely to operate across borders, and are less hierarchical than conventional networks (Hutchings 2014). They are likely to band together only for a limited time so as to carry out their specialised tasks. They are purely organised cybercriminal networks. Finally, we can also find networks ideologically and politically motivated

[12] The aim is not to dissect on the definition of organised cybercriminal networks. This task deserves a better and extends reflection that I cannot provide here concerning the space constraints. However, the brief work I developed on the definition helps understanding this phenomenon in the paper's goals.

[13] For example the *Asian triads* and *Japanese Yakuza*, whose criminal activities adopted computer software piracy and credit card forgery and fraud (Organisation for Economic Co-operation and Development 2008).

[14] Or engage money mules in laundering funds (Hutchings 2014).

like terrorist organisations and those relating to *hactivism* (Choo and Smith 2008). They can be organised cybercriminals who have a great deal of technical expertise to offer to terrorist networks[15] in terms of communications, intelligence, propaganda and psychological warfare, recruitment, and training. Or yet, many criminals operate cyberspace functionalities to harass or threaten political adversaries. These actions could be made by patriotic hackers or even by the government itself despite official sources deny participation (Choo and Grabosky 2013).

Reflection on the Usefulness of Social Network Analysis

The internet is particularly attractive to criminals and organised criminal networks. Internet technology increasingly facilitates a wide range of serious and organised crime activity as communication, research, logistics, marketing, recruitment, distribution and monetisation instruments. This is due to the anonymity provided by the anonymisation techniques, the geographical dispersion, the access to countless victims and resources, the fast, low-risk and easy accessibility, and the ineffective legal instruments in place or with insufficient capacity to fight (Australian Crime Commission 2013; Europol 2011, 2014; Lipson 2002; Raab and Milward 2003). That is why it is anticipated that the organisational and technological capabilities of cybercriminals, especially in the absence of a global counter-strategy, will increase in future (KPMG 2011; Lipson 2002; Rush et al. 2009).

The need for a different approach to fighting and prevent cybercrime confronts the responsible entities with new challenges (Europol 2014). However, as there is no clear grasp on the phenomenon of organised criminal networks in cyberspace to solve this problem in development it becomes an uphill battle and difficult to correctly implement these purposes (Sarvari et al. 2014). There is, above all, a lack of research in the examination of new forms of online organised criminal structures (Tropina 2012). The unclear understanding of the phenomenon—although already powerful is still in an early stage of its development—comes from a lack of data to identify and understand which is the level of their organisation and its relationship patterns to then create strategies. With regard to the lack of reliable data on cybercriminal networks, it is very dangerous to make sweeping classifications about how several cyber networks might constitute organised crime (Lusthaus 2013).

Nevertheless, and as a result, the drawing up process of specific legal strategies to combat organised e-crime is still not mature enough. The exploitation of the weaknesses of immature legal developments in some countries will take these networks to look for countries with few resources for detecting and combating this type of crime, so can get their profits easily (Europol 2011; Tropina 2012).

To understand the organised cybercrime, researchers and analysts should focus on finding the pattern of relationships and understand how and why they occur. And, as by definition, organised crime offenders are offending with others, they thus

[15] For example *Imam Samudra* and *Tamil Tigers*.

require a communication platform. Analysing these communication channels provide a rich source of data about offenders and their activities (Hutchings 2014). The application of the SNA methods on this matter could clarify the current activities and potential future risks, identify actors, their position in the network and pattern of relationships, as well as also assessing the consequences (Yip 2011). The SNA could, in particular, help to realise some issues that have been raised within the scientific community, law enforcement agencies and political entrepreneurs about the crime perpetrated by organised networks on the internet: Who are the actors?[16] What are the infrastructures?[17] How to trace cybercriminal networks?[18] Who are the targets?[19] Which are the motivations?[20] What kind of crimes?[21] The answers to these questions would clarify some of the most fundamental queries about this emerging problem and thus create and tailor more effective and efficient preventions and countermeasures that would be better suited to their real outlines.

Above all, the application of the SNA can help clarify the ultimate question: Are we effectively facing an organised cybercrime? Is it a tendency for a new form or a new way? Whilst it is obvious that the conventional organised criminal networks can significantly benefit from the use of information and communication technologies (Shelley 2003), it is not yet clear to what extent cybercrime can be attributed to traditional organised criminal networks or to cybercriminal networks (Tropina 2012). Taken together all the information gathered by the SNA it will then allow to finally describe, explain and interpret this growing phenomenon that still proportionate so much discussion.

But there is always the reverse side of the coin regarding the use of this instrument in the study of networks in organised e-crime and some barriers. I highlight three of them. First, the anonymity (Australian Crime Commission 2013; Europol

[16] Many researchers have questioned whether the leaders of the Dark Web can be identified using their interaction with other members (e.g. L'Huillier et al. (2010). Moreover, it is assumed that a single individual or group of actors may represent separate or concurrent users which make its complex and interwoven structure (Tropina 2012). The SNA could clarify if the relations between cybercriminals are transient or simply transactional, and if criminals rarely know each other offline. There is also a recent theory which maintains that cybercriminals, although they may hypothetically operate in loose networks, while in group its members are located in geographical proximity, even when attacks go beyond national borders. It could, then, help to know if, as in other types of organised crime, small local networks, kinship groups and relational are significant actors (Kshetri 2013, cited in Broadhurst et al. 2014).

[17] Knowing where organised cybercriminal networks can operate is very important to their combat. The device can be used to analyse underground forums, criminal marketplaces, online social networks, and bulletproof hosts, amongst others. Thus, their constitution and dynamics will be better understood.

[18] Analysing private messaging, public posts, emails, text mining, web servers, amongst others, through the use of the SNA, will allow identifying and targeting criminal networks, its actors, links and patterns of relationships.

[19] The method could clarify if states, organisations or individuals are the objective victims.

[20] The device will clarify if we're tackling profit-driven or non-Profit-driven networks.

[21] The tool will then describe the typology of crimes committed, from crime-as-a-service, malware, child sexual exploitation online, payment fraud, criminal finances online, crimes relating to social engineering, data breaches and network intrusions, to vulnerabilities of critical infrastructure.

2011, 2014; Lipson 2002; Raab and Milward 2003) could be translated into difficulties accessing actors, links and sources. Second, the countless internet network users, transnational nature of the Internet and its decentralised architecture (Tropina 2012) are reflected in an "over-complexity" of cyber networks and, consequently make the definition of network limits difficult and their traceability too. Third, there is a notorious under-reporting and under-prosecution of these kinds of crimes (Hutchings 2014) which can cause a partial usefulness of reports and prosecutions as data.

This method, as said before, is not enough by itself. It is a complementary instrument. But its capabilities and innovation and its adequacy to organised networks in cyberspace have, without a doubt, proved to be a good wager.

Part III—The Social Networks Analysis in Portugal

Owing to technical and methodological developments in Portugal, SNA was introduced in the late 90s as a complementary tool for the processing and analysis of criminal and judicial information. Since then, this procedure has marked its place in the analysis of organised criminal networks. Nevertheless, this short lead way has also been conditioned by some problems and limitations that need greater attention.

Criminal Investigation Scope

The SNA has revealed itself as a fundamental tool in the Portuguese police system[22] when analysing police information in the Police Forces and Security Services (FSS) in general, and criminal information in the Organs of Criminal Police (OCP) in specific. Focusing now on criminal information, network analysis can be a consequence of the procedures and investigations of the OCP at judicial processing level, particularly during the investigation stage[23] or inquiry stage.[24]

[22] The Portuguese police model is centralised and pluralist being composed by two public security forces—*Policia de Segurança Publica* (PSP) and the *Guarda Nacional Républicana* (GNR) and two specialised security forces—the *Policia Judiciária* (PJ) and *the Serviço de Estrangeiros e Fronteiras* (SEF) (Oliveira 2006). These forces jointly with the Service of Information Security constitute the FSS (Diário da República 2008b). The criminal analysis information, in the strict sense, is restricted to the generic competencies of the first three organisations namely, the PSP, the GNR and the SEF being thus de-nominated as the OPC (Diário da República 2008a).

[23] The investigation stage entails a number of diligences that have as priority the investigation of the existence of a crime, determining of the agents as well as their responsibilities, discover and collect evidence required by law on decision of the accused (*Código de Processo Penal* 2015, art. 262, no. 1).

[24] The inquiry stage aims the judicial evidence regarding the decision of reducing the accusation or closing the investigation so as to either take or not take the case further to court of law (*Código de Processo Penal* 2015, art. 286, no. 1).

This activity analysis varies according to the organisation of each police force, territorial criteria and speciality (Oliveira 2006).

The practical application of the SNA in criminal investigation and police intelligence in the Portuguese police system is executed by a network of intelligence analysts. Regarding the analyst figures in Portugal there are four main points to emphasise. Firstly, and in general terms, the number of analysts is below average and lacking when comparing to needs. Secondly, it is more than common to verify the inadequacy of the analysts' work regarding the specific requirements. In third place, its rentability is not performed in the same way along the various FSS (Pereira 2013). In fourth place and finally, these professionals are equipped with specific training in information analysis, e.g. the "Analysis Course of Criminal Information" in PSP police force (Fernandes 2013, cited in Pereira 2013) however, as far as it was ascertained, there is no specific training on the software being used, i.e. there is no external training organisation or specific course dedicated to the use of this method of analysis and information processing. So being, knowledge is mainly transmitted by practice and companionship in each unit. Regarding the software, *i2 Analyst's Notebook* is the programme transversely used in the OPC. Yet, the available version is obsolete—due to the high licencing costs for the institutions (Ferraz 2015)—which determines the efficiency and effectiveness of intended goals. In addition it worths mentioning that to safe-guarding the confidentiality criteria of the available information, for ethical reasons, at the end of its legal life, all the information gained from the software must be destroyed.

Regarding the data sources for the software, analysts using the SNA can consult the following key sources: the Information Systems (IS),[25] open sources,[26] human sources.[27] Information that can be of confirmed or speculative nature (Luizio 2009, cited in Pereira 2013).

Restricting ourselves to the IS whilst systems interact with *the i2 Analyst's Notebook* there are two major issues to be analysed. The first refers to the storage and processing of the data. It is already known that the SNA requires previous work, in the sense that this tool must be accurate and have reliable data sources. Regarding the quality of information entered, on the one hand, we find that "a wide range of fields aren't in many cases completed. And even admitting that there might not be initial information available, when it is collected during the investigation, the registration is not completed" (Gomes 2013, cited in Pereira 2013, p. 33). On the other

[25] On the national level Portugal has various systems of information that are segregated to different entities. The introduction of the Integrated Criminal Information System (Diário da República 2008a) permitted action against the diversity and the lack of interoperability existent. On an International level, it is quite frequent to exchange data and information through the agencies of Interpol, Europol and SIS-Schengen Organisms (Diário da República 2009).

[26] As open sources we have as a basis information which is freely available without any sort of restriction be it through newspapers, publications, books, reports or radio and TV broadcasts, amongst others (Shulsky and Schmitt 1993).

[27] As human sources we consider all the bases of information collected by individuals who have resorted to the observation of direct behaviour, events or objects (Fernandes 2014, cited in Ferraz 2015).

hand, there is a difficulty to cross information (e.g. names, phone numbers, addresses, vehicles) scattered in various fields, eliminating the possibility to establish a connection with other elements/processes. The problem exists in every system, and is exponentially more notorious in the sharing amidst the IS. So being, it is essential that there be higher levels of quality control of information inserted as well as training provided (in all the IS) (Gomes 2013, cited in Pereira 2013).

The second problem relates to the sharing of data. On the one hand, in intra-institutional terms, professionals have a technical channel[28] based on a logic of efficiency and optimization of services for an easy access to all resource types. On the other hand, in inter-institutional terms, despite the duty of cooperation (Diário da República 2008a, art. 10), there is a lack of a true sharing of information culture and intelligence between the OPC (Pereira 2013; Torrado 2012). Each OPC has its own system with its own characteristics, in most non-interoperable cases, depending on the circulation of requests for research and information (Pereira 2013). Although attenuated in 2008 with the Criminal Investigation Organization Act—which provides the duty of cooperation through an integrated system of criminal information (Diário da República 2008a, art. 11)—, and with the Internal Security Act—that declares the coordination and cooperation of the FSS through the provision of information (Diário da República 2008b, art. 6)—this problem still seems to persist.

One should, however, acknowledge that being aware of the strategic importance of Information and Communication Technologies for its operational performance, Portugal have been making enormous efforts in the last few years to modernise and update this area. Guidelines have also been established to promote the use of technologies on a transversal and intensive way, through an integrated and focused approach to resource rationalisation (Polícia de Segurança Pública 2013). In fact, "to meet the challenges security is at present and in the future facing, FFSS is and will be required to provide constant upgradeability of methodologies of action and innovation of the technological component, associated with a cooperation (police and judiciary), the adequate and continuous training of researchers/analysts, the availability of resources and sharing (of "disinterested") information, for those eligible, in order to face a criminal phenomenon of increasing complexity" (Pereira 2013, p. 35).

Regarding the issue of cybercrime, the competence of their research is re-served to the Judiciary Police.[29] Information processing from organised networks in cyberspace

---

[28] A technical channel has the intention of being a intermediary means parallel to the hierarchical chain being informal so as to guarantee a direct communication between the technical information entities (Ferraz 2015). This channel, which has its foundations on the efficiency and effectiveness of its services, aims to hasten and facilitate communication through a less formal contact and so quicker with superior entities or even essential services during a specific activity as well as in determined situations where the typical formalisms are not, exceptionally of course, justifiable. We are targeting, for example, the enlightenment of doubts/queries, contact authorization, amongst others.

[29] It is of the utmost interest to undergo a more detailed analysis concerning the use of this tool in Police Entities nonetheless, and due to the absence of information sources, this was made impossible.

in Portugal using this method remains to be seen. However, it is of utmost importance to the Portuguese legislator that the security of cyberspace, mainly the organised cybercrime, be considered a national priority (Diário da República 2015).

Judicial Scope

From the judicial point of view, the methodology is seen as a new design of presentation for criminal evidence in several areas of crime (Cabral 2015). On the one hand, the information compiled using the SNA can be an asset in a particular case—intra-procedural utility. On the other, the SNA will assist in crossing information with other processes that may correlate actors or criminal activities—interprocedural utility.

Yet there was initially some resistance from the judges and prosecutors, probably because they were not aware of the tool's use. However, as the SNA advantages were producing results the acceptance of this technical evolution by various professionals became unquestionable. But here we find a gap: despite being extremely useful in legal terms, sometimes judges and prosecutors do not possess the adequate knowledge to analyse the more practically outputs of the SNA. In fact, for these professionals the SNA is merely a more advanced visual tool and a facilitator to understand a network of relational patterns. Not all realise the importance and significance of each software tool and thus the importance of the parameter establishment. It would thus be recommendable to offer training on the issue to these professionals.

Academic and Scientific Scope

With reference to academic training, there are some postgraduate courses in which, amongst other issues, the concepts and methods of the SNA are taught and applied. However, their approach is not at all the core of the training according to what we can ascertain. Moreover, although being focused amongst others on OPC professionals and magistrates, the *i2 Analyst's Notebook* is not used for the practical part being replaced by others software. Which, in short, results in there being no external formal training on the software used at OPC.

Also on the scientific level—and as a result—this tool has not yet gained much ground, unlike some more criminological developed countries as is the case of Canada and the US, where there are numerous academic studies based on solid empirical data provided by the various police agencies.

A real commitment to developing academic and scientific work in this area in Portugal (particularly in courses related to the area of crime) could enhance the empirical knowledge gained through the SNA which, as a consequence, would be a real asset in helping the understanding of the phenomenon of criminal networks.

Conclusion

Theorists and analysts in the area of crime can gain important knowledge focusing on social networks, as shown by the growing literature in criminology (McGloin and Kirk 2010). Throughout this paper we analysed the usefulness of this methodology in the criminal investigation manly, as at an academic, procedural/judicial and political level, fccusing three aspects: (1) the SNA in the study of organised criminal networks; (2) the SNA in the study of organised cybercrime; and (3) the SNA in Portugal.

The SNA was described as well as its importance in criminology as an analytical method for organised criminal networks. It was found that the scrutiny of the actors, exchanged links and resources more than just identify and describe, helps to know the criminal networks. It is, therefore, a promising and useful device. With regard to intelligence issues and criminal investigation the SNA sets an important support instrument at a strategic, tactical and operational level which allows services and forces to obtain knowledge that will support the assessment, planning and decision making in the fight and prevention of organised crime. At the procedural/judicial level, the use of the SNA allows clear views and direct decisions on the judicial process once it provides a clear picture of the complex structure of the network on trial—intra-procedural—or other parallel—inter-procedural. At the political level, it could lead to major criminal policies.

However, the SNA although constitutes an innovation in science it also presents some difficulties and limitations especially on the methodological and logistical level. Examples are human, financial and time constraints, difficulties in access to data and its sources, difficulties in defining the limits of the network, the need for prior encodings and strategies for certain obstacles, reliability data problems, contingencies in the network structure in space and time and a certain discretion in interpreting outputs. For these reasons the SNA is an approach that should be complementary to other network analysis techniques.

In a second part, attention was focused on the use of the method of cybercrime research. Here this paper tried to clarify two fundamental questions: Is cybercrime also a form of organised crime? Will the SNA be a relevant methodology to adapt to the analysis of cybercrime? It was found that, despite the controversy surrounding the definition of the problem, we are effectively moving towards organised cybercrime whether it be a new form or a new way. So, as in other types of organised crime, the SNA can also make an important contribution to the development of knowledge on this issue. Above all, fighting and prevention measures could be complementary based on the SNA findings.

Finally, the situation of Portugal concerning the use of the SNA was described and analysed, especially by the criminal investigation services. Here was referred the practical situation concerning the use of this method, addressing resources and operational dynamics through a descriptive analysis and discussion. The principal problem encountered was mainly the lack of literature sources. Yet it was found that in Portugal there are some human and technical limitations that need further attention at the criminal investigation level. Regarding the academic field there is not even a routine study of criminal networks. Many are therefore the critics and work to develop.

Nonetheless the importance that the SNA was shown in these three parts this paper also found some transversal problems that confirm what Carrington (2011) shared. First, the difficulties accessing data enhances the need to develop and study means to firm validity and reliability in sources. Second, the majority of network studies only focus on the composition or characteristics of the actors, forgetting the structure of network relationships. Third, most of the analyses are impressionistic, depending on visual examination of sociograms, rather than being computational. And, even in this case, tend to limit themselves to the simplest network concepts and indices. This is especially notorious not only in crime analysis but mainly at a procedural level. Fourth, in the criminological field, the SNA is in its infancy as not many criminologists appreciate the usefulness of the SNA in modelling concepts and propositions or use network analysis software. Fifth, and last, few professionals are trained in network methods, that is why it is desirable to provide training initiatives.

More specifically, concerning the normative field and organised cybercrime it is extremely important and well a known issue to draw national and international norms on cybercrime. We're facing a metamorphosis in social relationships, in crime environments and techniques and, consequently, in crime assessment and investigation. This is a cycle: news ways of connection are arising, which provides new infrastructures and instruments for criminal phenomena and, consequently, demands better strategic and tactical activities. It is a new paradigm. Bearing in mind the cyclical influence, how can we fight and prevent the organised cybercriminal phenomena? There is no consensus on organised crime and on the cybercrime definition, there is no consensual legal framework, there is a lacking in the study of these networks, and law enforcement agencies are still tackling data constraints. Developing a socio-normative framework means knowing what to handle. But, as observed, we do not exactly know what the problem is. Is important to know if we are confronting groups or networks, computer or computer-related crimes, a new way or a new form of organised cybercrime. Some studies have been performed, but a guideline on it is still missing. Law enforcement agencies, police-makers and decision-makers need to adapt their fight and prevent goals and strategies regarding this new technological paradigm. There is a need to integrate the empirical and theoretical knowledge in stable and extend conceptual structures and create communication dispositives amongst scientific investigation, criminal policies and crime investigation. The SNA could be a way to assess and identify the patterns of relationships, a stepping-stone to create a consensual knowledge on the problem. Knowing what to fight reveals how to fight it. In sum, a developed socio-normative framework will appear when the norm object becomes clear.

There is still much work to be done to establish a sophisticated tool for criminal analysis. More research, practical applications and development activities are needed to identify patterns and other regularities in organised criminal networks (Hulst 2008) whether it be conventional or in the cyberspace.

References

Australian Crime Commission. (2013). *Cyber and technology enabled crime*. Commonwealth of Australia.

Bertalanffy, L. (1975). *Perspectives on general systems theory (Scientific-philosophical studies)*. New York: George Braziller.

Block, A. (1999). *East side, west side: Organized crime in New York, 1930–1950*. New Brunswick: Transaction Publishers.

Boissevain, J. (1979). Network analysis: A reappraisal. *Current Anthropology, 20*(2), 392–394.

Bourdieu, P. (1986). The forms of social capital. In J. Richardson (Ed.), *The handbook of theory: Research for the sociology of education* (pp. 241–258). New York: Greenwood Press.

Broadhurst, R., Grabosky, P., Alazab, M., & Chon, S. (2014). Organizations and cyber crime: An analysis of the nature of groups engaged in cyber crime. *International Journal of Cyber Criminology, 8*(1), 1–20.

Bruinsma, G., & Bernasco, W. (2004). Criminal groups and transnational markets: A more detailed examination on the basis of social network theory. *Crime, Law and Social Change, 41*(1), 79–94.

Cabral, J. (2015). Ética e Corrupção. *Julgar*, 24.

Carrington, P. (2011). Crime and social network analysis. In J. Scott & P. Carrington (Eds.), *Sage handbook of social network analysis* (pp. 236–255). London: Sage Publications.

Castells, M. (1997). *La Era de la Información: Economía, Sociedad y Cultura* (Vol. 1, La Sociedad Red). Madrid: Alianza Editorial.

Choo, K., & Grabosky, P. (2013). Cyber crime. In L. Paoli (Ed.), *The oxford handbook of organised crime* (Vol. Oxford Handbooks, pp. 482–499). New York: Oxford University Press.

Choo, K., & Smith, G. (2008). Criminal exploitation of online systems by organised crime groups. *Asian Journal of Criminology, 3*(1), 37–59. doi:10.1007/s11417-007-9035-y.

Clark, R. (2007). *Intelligence analysis: A target-centric approach* (2nd ed.). Washington, DC: CQ Press.

Código de Processo Penal. (2015). Portugal: Almedina.

Coleman, J. (1990). *Foundations of social theory*. Cambridge: Harvard University Press.

Diário da República. (2008a). Law 49/2008 27 of August 2008 approves the Organisation of Criminal Investigation Act. *Diário da República, 1st Serie, No. 165* (pp. 6038–6042). Portugal: Assembleia da República.

Diário da República. (2008b). Act 53/2008 of 29 August approves the Internal Security Act. *Diário da República, 1st Serie, No. 167* (pp. 6135-6141). Portugal: Assembleia da República.

Diário da República. (2009). Act 73/2009 12 of August 2009 establishes the conditions and procedures that shall apply to ensure interoperability between information systems of criminal police bodies. *Diário da República, 1st Serie, No. 155* (pp. 5217–5220). Portugal: Assembleia da República.

Diário da República. (2015). Resolution of the Ministers Council No. 36/2015. *Diário da República, 1st Serie, No. 113*. Portugal.

Europol. (2011). Threat assessment (abridged): Internet Facilitated Organised Crime (iOCTA). *Europol Public Information* (pp. 1–11). Europol.

Europol. (2014). The Internet Organised Crime Threat Assessment (iOCTA) 2014. (pp. 1–92). Europol.

Ferraz, R. (2015). *Facebook e o Planeamento de Grandes Eventos: Um Contributo Operacional na Área das Informações*. Lisbon: Instituto Superior de Ciênciasa Políciais e Segurança Interna.

Freeman, L. (2006). *The development of social network analysis: A study in the sociology of science*. Vancouver: Empirical Press.

Haythornthwaite, C. (1996). Social network analysis: An approach and set of techniques for the study of information exchange. *Library and Information Science Research, 18*(4), 323–342. doi:10.1016/S0740-8188(96)90003-1.

Hulst, R. V. D. (2008). Introduction to social network analysis as an investigative instrument. *Trends in Organized Crime, 12*(2), 101–121. doi:10.1007/s12117-008-9057-6.
Hutchings, A. (2014). Crime from the keyboard: Organised cybercrime, co-offending, initiation and knowledge transmission. *Crime, Law and Social Change, 62*(1), 1–20.
Klerks, P. (2001). The network paradigm applied to criminal organisations: Theoretical nitpicking or a relevant doctrine for investigators? Recent developments in the Netherlands. *Connections, 24*(3), 53–65.
Koschade, S. (2006). A social network analysis of Jemaah Islamiyah: The applications to counter-terrorism and intelligence. *Studies in Conflict & Terror, 29*(6), 559–575.
KPMG. (2011). Cyber crime—A growing challenge for governments. *Issues Monitor, 8*, 1–24.
Krebs, V. (2002). Mapping networks of terrorist cells. *Connections, 24*(3), 43–52.
L'Huillier, G., Alvarez, H., Ríos, S., & Aguilera, F. (2010). *Topic-based social network analysis for virtual communities of interests in the dark web.* Paper presented at the Workshop on Intelligence and Security Informatics, Washington, July.
Lipson, H. (2002). Tracking and tracing cyber-attacks: Technical challenges and global policy issues (pp. 1–85). Pittsburgh: Software Engineering Institute of the Carnegie Mellon University.
Lusthaus, J. (2013). How organised is organised cybercrime? *Global Crime, 14*(1), 52–60.
Mainas, E. (2012). The analysis of criminal and terrorist organisations as social network structures: A quasi-experimental study. *International Journal of Police Science & Management, 14*(3), 264–282.
McAndrew, D. (2000). The structural analysis of criminal networks. In D. Canter & A. Laurence (Eds.), *The social psychology of crime: Groups, teams and networks* (Vol. 3, Offender Profiling Series, pp. 51–94). Aldershot: Ashgate.
McCusker, R. (2006). Transnational organised cyber crime: Distinguishing threat from reality. *Crime, Law and Social Change, 46*(4), 257–273.
McDowell, D. (1998). *Strategic intelligence: A handbook for practitioners, managers and users.* Cooma: Istana Enterprises Pty Ltd.
McGloin, J., & Kirk, D. (2010). An overview of social network analysis. *Journal of Criminal Justice Education, 21*(2), 169–181.
McGrath, C., Blythe, J., & Krackhardt, D. (1997). The effect of spatial arrangement on judgments and errors in interpreting graphs. *Social Networks, 19*(3), 223–242.
McGrath, C., Krackhardt, D., & Blythe, J. (2003). Visualizing complexity in networks: Seeing both the forest and the trees. *Connections, 25*(1), 37–47.
McGuire, M. (2012). *Organised crime in the digital age.* London: John Grieve Centre for Policing and Security.
McIlwain, J. (1999). Organized crime: A social network approach. *Crime, Law and Social Change, 32*(4), 301–323.
Moneyval. (2012). Criminal money flows on the Internet: Methods, trends and multi-stakeholder counteraction (pp. 1–93). Council of Europe.
Morselli, C. (2005). *Contacts, opportunities, and criminal enterprise.* Toronto: University of Toronto Press.
Morselli, C. (2009). *Inside criminal networks (Studies of organized crime).* New York: Springer.
Oliveira, J. (2006). *As Políticas de Segurança e os Modelos de Policiamento: A Emergência do Policiamento de Proximidade.* Coimbra: Almedina.
Organisation for Economic Co-operation and Development. (2008). *The economic impact of counterfeiting and piracy* (p. 397). Paris: Organisation for economic co-operation and development.
Pereira, C. (2013). *Análise Criminal e Sistemas de Informação.* Pedrouços: Instituto de Estudos Superiores Militares.
Polícia de Segurança Pública. (2013). Visão Global de Operacionalização da Estratégia para as TIC na PSP, 2013–2016. In D. N. d. PSP (Ed.) (p. 8). Lisboa.
Raab, J., & Milward, H. (2003). Dark networks as problems. *Journal of Public Administration Research and Theory, 13*(4), 413–439.
Randjeloviü, D., & Popoviü, B. (2011). *Visual analytics instruments and theirs application in social networks analysis.* Paper presented at the 19th Telecommunications forum (TELFOR), Belgrade, November.

Ratcliffe, J. (2008). *Intelligence led policing*. Cullompton: Willan Publishing.
Rostami, A., & Mondani, H. (2015). The complexity of crime network data: A case study of its consequences for crime control and the study of networks. *PLoS One, 10*(3), 1–20. doi:10.1371/journal.pone.0119309.
Rush, H., Smith, C., Kraemer-Mbula, E., & Tang, P. (2009). Research report: Crime online. Cybercrime and illegal innovation (pp. 80–87). CENTRIM, University of Brighton.
Sarvari, H., Abozinadah, E., Mbaziira, A., & McCoy, D. (2014). *Constructing and analyzing criminal networks*. Paper presented at the IEEE Security and Privacy Workshops, San Jose, May.
Schwartz, D., & Rouselle, T. (2008). Using social network analysis to target criminal networks. *Trends in Organized Crime, 12*(2), 188–207.
Scott, J. (2000). *Social network analysis: A handbook* (2nd ed.). London: SAGE Publications.
Shelley, L. (2003). Organized crime, terrorism and cybercrime. In A. Bryden & P. Fluri (Eds.), *Security sector reform: Institutions, society and good governance* (pp. 303–312). BadenBaden: Nomos Verlagsgesellschaft.
Shulsky, A., & Schmitt, G. (1993). *Silent warfare: Understanding the world of intelligence* (2nd ed.). New York: Brassey's.
Sparrow, M. (1991a). Network vulnerabilities and strategic intelligence in law enforcement. *Journal of Intelligence and Counterintelligence, 5*(3), 255–274.
Sparrow, M. (1991b). The application of network analysis to criminal intelligence: An assessment of the prospects. *Social Networks, 13*(3), 251–274.
Torrado, H. (2012). *A Partilha de Informação Criminal e a Cooperação*. Lisboa: Academia Militar.
Tropina, T. (2012). *The evolving structure of online criminality how cybercrime is getting organised*. Paper presented at the Eucrim.
United Nations. (2000). *Crimes related to computer networks: Background paper for the workshop on crimes related to the computer network*. Paper presented at the Tenth UN Congress on the Prevention of Crime and the Treatment of Offenders, Vienna, April.
Warr, M. (2002). *Companions in crime: The social aspects of criminal conduct*. Cambridge: Cambridge University Press.
Wasserman, S., & Faust, K. (1994). *Social network analysis. Methods and applications*. Cambridge: Cambridge University Press.
Wellman, B. (1992). Which types of ties and networks give what kinds of social support? *Advances in Group Processes, 9*, 207–235.
Wellman, B. (1997). An electronic group is virtually a social network. In S. Kiesler (Ed.), *Culture of the internet* (pp. 179–205). Mahwah: Lawrence Erlbaum.
Wellman, B. (2001). Physical place and cyberplace: The rise of personalized networking. *International Journal of Urban and Regional Research, 25*(2), 227–252.
Wellman, B., & Gulia, M. (1999). Net-surfers don't ride alone: Virtual communities as communities. In B. Wellman (Ed.), *Networks in the global village: Life in contemporary communities* (pp. 331–366). Boulder: Westview Press.
Wellman, B., & Hampton, K. (1999). Living networked in a wired world. *Contemporary Sociology, 28*(6), 1–12.
Xu, J., & Chen, H. (2005). Criminal network analysis and visualization. *Communications of the ACM, 48*(6), 101–107.
Yip, M. (2011). An investigation into Chinese cybercrime and the applicability of social network analysis. In *ACM WebSci'11, Koblenz, June 2011* (pp. 1–4).

Chapter 9
Drug Trafficking Trends and Its Responses: A Case Study of Vietnam

Hai Thanh Luong

Introduction

Vietnam's economic performance has been remarkable since the first decade of the twenty-first century. Vietnam has managed to sustain an average Gross Domestic Production (GDP) growth rate of 7.25 %; by 2010 the average income per capita reached US$1,200—up from less than US$ 400 in 2000 UNODC (2012c). In just over two decades Vietnam went from being a poor, underdeveloped economy to reaching middle-income country status and improving the living conditions of millions of people. Moreover, generally, Vietnam has met most of the Millennium Development Goals (Socialist Republic of Vietnam 2010, p. 11; UNDP 2013, pp. 5–7). As the country enters the current decade, it has the ambition of becoming a modern industrialized nation, with an overall goal of increasing GDP per capita by 70 % by 2015, up to US$2,100 per person (NAV, 2011). In the pursuit of this objective, the Government of Vietnam (GoV) intends to reform and modernize governance, overcome disparities and gender inequalities, fight corruption and crime, including all of drug-related activities. Through signed bilateral drug control cooperation agreements with many countries in the Asian region, the Government has strengthened prevention and suppression responses to counter drug trafficking activities, both domestic and international. Although law enforcement agencies (LEAs) have implemented strict measures to detect, investigate, and prosecute syndicates who illegally traffic drugs on land, sea, and air routes, these efforts have not yet been sufficient in financial and technical terms to address the emerging challenges and the increasingly sophisticated modus operandi of drugs traffickers. Basing on the secondary data from official statistics of LEAs, this chapter draws briefly the drug trafficking situation in Vietnam of two popular types, namely heroin

H.T. Luong (✉)
School of Global, Urban, and Social Science, RMIT University, Melbourne, Australia
e-mail: haithanh.luong@rmit.edu.au

E.C. Viano (ed.), *Cybercrime, Organized Crime, and Societal Responses*,
DOI 10.1007/978-3-319-44501-4_9

and amphetamine type stimulants (ATS) at the first section. The second part analyzes main characteristics of drug trafficking networks through locating and mapping on its operations. In the third part, the chapter briefly presents the National Strategy of Vietnam to combat and control drugs through 2020 with orientations toward 2030.

Two Popular Illegal Drugs Trafficking in Vietnam

An assessment of the United Nations of Drugs and Crime (UNODC 2013d, pp. 57, 69) on transnational organized crime in East Asian and the Pacific evaluated that Vietnam, at the moment, has been increasingly becoming as one of the transited and destination point, particularly with heroin and ATS. In terms of domestic drug users' demands, both of these types of drugs have become the more prevalent choice than the rest of narcotics since nearly one past decade (Devaney et al. 2006; UNODC 2010; UNODC Vietnam 2013). The Annual Report of the Ministry of Public Security of Vietnam (MPS 2010) states that drug addicts have become a widespread phenomenon not only in urban areas but also in the countryside, affecting all strata of Vietnamese society. Statistics on seizures and drug-related arrests confirm that throughout the 1990s, Vietnam has been continuing to face illegal drugs concerns, particularly for heroin (DEA 2003, p. 1; UNODC Vietnam 2013), and ATS (UNODC and SODC 2012, pp. 2, 4). As a consequence of this expanding transnational flow, the number of drug-related cases in Vietnam increased considerably over the last decades with respect to both the number of seizures made and of people involved in trafficking.

In fact, during 5 years before and after the *Doi Moi*, the period 1981 and 1990, when drug-related crimes was not regulated in the Criminal Code of Vietnam (CCV), the whole of country had only 1698 cases of drug-related crime. However, only one decade afterward, from 1991 to 2000, drug law enforcement agencies investigated and prosecuted 43,211 cases, a 27-fold rise (Vinh 2002). Particularly, after the 1999 the Criminal Code was approved with one separate chapter entitled "drug-related crimes," 112,642 cases of drug-related offenses were detected during 10 years, 1997–2006 (Vinh 2002). Figure 9.1 shows that the rapid increase, both of cases and offenders connected to drug trafficking in Vietnam in from 2008 to 2014. It can been seen clearly that around the midpoint of the decade, the total drug cases of this timeline were much higher than the total case of 10 years before, 126,078 cases between 2008 and 2014 compare to 112,642 cases in the period of 1997–2006. One noticeable point from this figure is that although the total case from 2008 to 2014 was considerably stable with an average of about 18,011 cases per years, the number of offenders involved has increased considerably, one and half times after 7 years, that is 30,000 offenses recently compared to 20,000 before.

More specifically, at the end of 2013, there were over 180,000 drug addicts (to be estimated), an increase by 5.4 % with 9,396 cases compared with 2012 with heroin and synthetic drugs at the highest percentages in the total types of drugs with 75 %

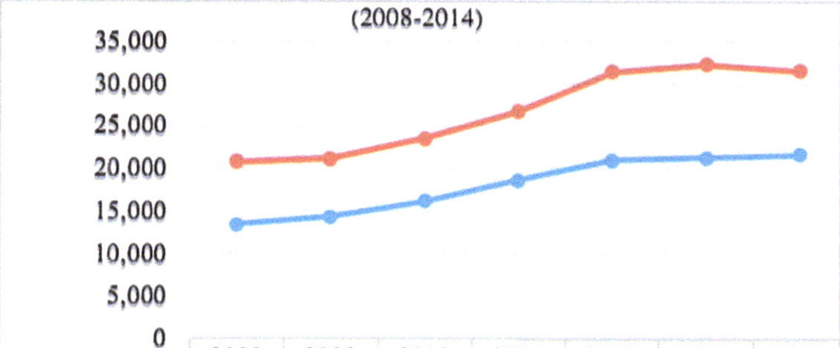

	2008	2009	2010	2011	2012	2013	2014
Cases	13,371	14,237	16,123	18,623	20,917	21,188	21,619
Offenders	20,781	21,086	23,497	26,687	31,419	32,332	31,551

Cases Offenders

Fig. 9.1 Drug-related cases and arrests in Vietnam (2008–2014). *Source*: Adapted from the Annual Reports of Vietnam at the ASEAN Inter-Parliamentary Assembly Fact Finding Committee (AIFOCOM), between 2007 and 2014

and 10 %, respectively (AIPA 2014b). The number of male drug users accounted for 96 % in comparison with 4 % of female (MPS 2015). The heroin users now account for the largest proportion of drug abusers with 84.7 %, followed by synthetic drugs with 6.5 %, opiates with 6.4 %, cannabis with 1.6 %, pharmaceutical drugs with 0.3 % and finally other drugs with 0.5 %, respectively (UNODC Vietnam 2013). The Vietnam's authorities also recognized that "the real figure of the drug addicts might have been higher than that documented" (AIPA 2014b, p. 4). Although gathering reliable statistics is fraught with difficulties, as is any attempt at a thorough analysis of these data, the official report of the UNODC (2015a) affirmed that in Vietnam, heroin and the ATS are two of the most popular illegal drugs.

Heroin

The Annual Report of Drugs of UNODC shows that Afghanistan maintained its position as the number one producer and cultivator of opium globally (2011, p. 30), meanwhile, Myanmar reached second place in opium production (Paoli et al. 2009, p. 111; UNODC 2011, p. 59). According to McCoy (2003, p. 285), most heroin production of the Golden Triangle extends from the Shan hills of North-eastern Burma through to Northern Thailand and to the Hmong highlands of Laos. As a result, some of these proportions were trafficked into Vietnam from Laos via either international gateways or unofficial roads (INCSR 2013, p. 225). One survey of Kramer et al. (2009, p. 47) observed that heroin at both the Southeast Asia and Golden Triangle, frequently, is sold in various forms and amounts, for instance, "a compressed block of heroin on the China-Burma border weighs 350 g and measures

6 × 4 × 3½ in. (15 × 10 × 9 cm)." It can be concluded clearly the heroin producing area of the Golden Triangle is central to the Southeast Asian drug trade. As a part of supply and demand scale, it continued to impact directly or indirectly this regional market and Vietnam has also not escaped this trend (Chin 2009, p. 8; INCSR 2013, p. 18; UNODC 2012d, p. 1).

Historically, in Vietnam, the opium has been cultivated and used by groups of ethnic minority people in the mountainous regions with the purpose of maintain their habits and cure addition since the feudal societies (Cam 1999a, b; Uc 2000; Yem 2003). Meanwhile, in respect of heroin, during the American War years of the 1960s and early 1970s, it made a significant appearance in the south of Vietnam (DEA 1992; Michaud 2000a, b). Smoking and injecting heroin mainly occurred amongst the United States and South Vietnamese soldiers and smaller numbers of the general community (Michaud 2000b; Shear 1993). Heroin did not come to widespread attention again until the middle years of 1990s with the large quantities from the Golden Triangle countries and Southern China initially entered into Vietnam through a corridor in the north of the country, and from here was transported south or exported to international destinations (Griffiths 2006; Hoa 2008; Rapin 2003). As a tropical storm with a severe damage, currently, heroin enters at a multitude of points along the 3,800-km land border with all of 63 provinces in Vietnam, including five municipalities such as Hanoi, Haiphong, Danang, Cantho, and Ho Chi Minh City (UNODC 2010; Van and Scannapieco 2008). In recent times, with the increased availability of heroin and its falling street price, the Vietnam have been faced with the rapidly increasing numbers of young people using heroin (MPS 2014; UNODC Vietnam 2013). After all, apart from the sudden emergence of the variety of the amphetamines, heroin is still the most concerned issue in the illegal drug's market in Vietnam (AIPA 2012b, 2013; Byrne 1999; UNODC 2005, 2015a; UNODC and SODC 2012).

Amphetamine Type Stimulants (ATS)

The ATS covers two groups of synthetic substances: amphetamine-group substances including amphetamine, methamphetamine (methyl-amphetamine), and methcathinone; and ecstasy-group substances such as MDMA (ecstasy) and its analogues (UNODC 2011, p. 127). Different from opium and coca plants, the ATS's production is adaptable and the places to produce it are easily changeable. Thus, the ATS laboratories are frequently located in close proximity to illicit markets for ATS's demand (UNODC 2011, p. 146). Regarding the manufacture process, the ATS are likely to come in many forms such as powder, paste, liquid, tablets, or crystals (WHO 2013). To date, the UNODC warned of a rapid expansion in the global ATS market since 2009, with the total quantity of seized ATS almost doubling to reach over 144 tons in 2011 and 2012, the highest level since they began systematic monitoring. It remained at a comparatively high level in 2013 (UNODC 2015b, p. xvi).

Regionally, Blickman (2009, p. 52) also raised the alarm that the ATS boom in Southeast Asia is "an example of what can be described as 'displacement': a campaign against one drug (opium and heroin) can lead to the rise of an equally or more dangerous substitute (methamphetamine)." More complexly, one of the current concerns is the appearance of "new psychoactive substances" (NPS) if one compares the today's list with the United Nations Conventions of 1961 and 1971, such as synthetic cannabinoids, synthetic cathinones, ketamine, phenethylamines, piperazines, plant-based substances, and others (UNODC 2013e, pp. 59–60; UNODC 2015b, pp. xvi–xvii).

Nonofficial report of drug enforcement authorities assert that these NPS and ATS can be manufactured at Vietnam. Instead, notwithstanding, almost all the amphetamine-group substances and ecstasy-group substances are smuggled into Vietnam from Cambodia, China, Lao PDR, Myanmar, and Thailand (UNODC 2012b, p. 117). One national research and survey scale in Vietnam of the UNODC noted that there are many different types of the ATS available and circulating in Vietnam. They come in a variety of forms including tablet, crystal, and powder (UNODC and SODC 2012, p. 12). In fact, although no clandestine methamphetamine manufacture has been reported in the country, the ATS market continues to expand and diversify with a 65 % increase in the country's methamphetamine pill seizures in 2011. Especially the number of youth users has increased (INCSR 2013, p. 318).

In addition, the trafficking and use of various ATS, including methamphetamine and the bulk of NPS sold on the streets, more particularly with "ecstasy," has swiftly become a second top drug consumed in Vietnam after heroin's markets, for three main reasons (UNODC 2013e, p. 52). Firstly, Vietnam was also growingly vulnerable to the threat of precursor chemical's types due to Vietnam's geographical position in the neighborhood of the world's major hubs of synthetic drug manufacture in the Golden Triangle and China (INCSR 2014; UNODC 2014b). In addition, secondly, the high valuations and considerable benefits of illegal drug trafficking are economic stimulant factors to motivate traffickers for trading (Battersby 2014; Kramer et al. 2014). As a result, it has led to the increase in the number and amount of ATS trafficking (INCB 2005; INCSR 2009; UNODC and SODC 2012; UNODC Vietnam 2013). Thirdly, regarding to the element of, since 2003, the use of both of methamphetamine pills and ecstasy has enlarged gradually in metropolitan areas and has also expanded in rural markets, a more complicated situation (UNODC and SODC 2012).

Vietnam is concerned that the ATS trafficking has increased and that it is likely to become a major drug consumption's country in the Southeast Asian region the soon (INCSR 2010, p. 658). In fact, the quantity of ATS abusers has risen remarkably since 2008 and it has overtaken opium as the second most widely used drug in Vietnam since 2010 (UNODC and SODC 2012; UNODC Vietnam 2013). Therefore, alongside with heroin, the ATS have been challenging to Vietnam's LEAs to control drugs and combat their threats.

Transnational Drug Trafficking Routes Between Vietnam and Its Neighbors

The UNODC has established a liaison office in Hanoi as one of the official representatives of the Regional Office for Southeast Asia and the Pacific since 1994. Vietnam has not yet published data in terms of drug-related crimes following up the Annual Reports Questionnaire.[1] This paradox has been widely acknowledged by both Vietnamese LEAs and international organizations working in Vietnam. Particularly with foreign press agencies, their information collection and sharing procedures are often inadequate and need to be restructured (UNODC 2009). In addition, the effectiveness of these agencies is being obstructed by their current processes which are neither effective nor inadequate, particularly the dearth of a structured system to improve the speedy flow of data between agencies with all levels (UNODC 2005, 2009). As a result, it led to limitations in collecting and examining the reality and situation of illegal drugs, more particularly to barrier visualization and formation of its network in Vietnam. Also, the lack of academic research and journal articles to gauge drug trafficking and its operation in Vietnam's context is regrettable. Logically, it also hampered the comprehensive understanding of the overall illegal narcotics situation and its specific drug trafficking activities in Vietnam, involving both transnational and domestic market. Therefore, based on the official report of Vietnam's authorities at the annual meeting of the ASEAN Inter-Parliamentary Assembly (AIPA) fact-finding committee to combat the drug menace (AIFOCOM), between 2008 and 2014, this chapter strives to present and analyze the main routes of drug trafficking and their characteristics within cross border between Vietnam and its neighbors.

Located closely to the Golden Triangle, as one of the largest opium-producing over the world, Vietnam has expanded considerably as a transit route for illegal drug trade's networks to and through in recent times. According to LEAs of Vietnam, at the current time, illegal narcotics trafficking activities, seemingly, have spread across the whole of the country, including rural and urban domain, from metropolitan to mountainous areas, not distinguishing between economic or poor conditions (AIPA 2012a; SODC 2013b). A critical analysis by the UNODC notes that:

> With efficient opium poppy eradication efforts, it is estimated that as much as 95 % of illicit drugs being transported inside Viet Nam, for either transit or domestic consumption, have been smuggled in *from neighboring countries*. Cross-border and domestic drug trafficking relay on increasingly organized and sophisticated methods. The traffickers take advantage

[1] At the reconvened 53rd session of the Commission on Narcotic Drugs, in December 2010, Member States adopted a revised Annual Report Questionnaire (ARQ) to enable the monitoring of and the biennial reporting to the Commission on the implementation by Member States of the Political Declaration and Plan of Action on International Cooperation towards an Integrated and Balanced Strategy t to Counter the World Drug Problem, as well as for the reporting to the Commission mandated by the three international drug control conventions. The first reports resulting from the revised ARQs have been considered by the Commission on Narcotic Drugs at its 56th session in 2013.

> of the long and porous land borderline and the coastline. Heroin, opium and amphetamine-type stimulants (ATS) are smuggled into Viet Nam across the north-western, central-northern and southern borders. Heroin and cannabis are trafficked from Viet Nam into China. Inside the country, drug hot spots are mainly located in the cities (pp. 6–7).

It shows that under the direct impact of regional drug trafficking, Vietnam has still faced complex situations with the crossings of its borderland with neighbors, particularly focusing on three borderland routes, namely central northern coast, north-east, and south-west (AIPA 2008, 2009, 2010b, 2011, 2012b, 2013, 2014b, 2015)

At the Central Northern Coast borderline: Vietnam and Laos

In terms of the boundary between Vietnam and Laos, it covers about 2,340 km of length and stretches across Vietnam's 10 provinces (National Border Committee 2010c, 2011). These include Dienbien, Sonla, Thanhhoa, Nghean, Hatinh, Quangbinh, Quangtri, Thuathienhue, Quangnam, and Kontum. All of these territories of Vietnam are adjacent to ten southern provinces of Laos, namely Phongsaly, Luangprabang, Houaphan, Bolykhamsay, Khammoune, Savannakhet, Salavan, Xiengkhouang, Sepon, and Attapeu. Most borderland areas between Vietnam and Laos require going over the top of or through mountains and tropical forests with the lowest place above the sea being about 300 m and the highest around 2,700 m (National Border Committee 2010c). Between the two countries, there are a lot of high mountains difficult to walk (National Border Committee 2011). Residents living along the border are mostly people of ethnic minorities who live in villages scattered far apart and across borders (Giang 2012; Michaud 2009). Transport and travel between the two sides in the border areas are very difficult; there is almost no motorized traffic, except for a few international and national border-gate areas with densely populated living, either some roads from the war's period or new forest roads open seasonally and are outdated for mobilization (Hoang 2007; Lintner 2008).

Crossing mountainous commutes, villages and provinces between Vietnam and Lao PDR have still continued to maintain a sizable acreage of poppies, covered by a long-history of opium cultivation by local minorities (Griffiths 2006; Michaud 2000a; UNODC 2013c). Cultivating poppy by ethnic minority groups such as Hmong, Thai, and Laotian Hmong from both sides continues today (Michaud 2000b; Rapin 2003). For example, on the Laos side, although the Laotian government has strived to reduce the cultivated area and declared its success in significantly decreasing opium poppy cultivation in 2006 (UNODC 2006, p. 37),[2] the potential production of dry opium for 2013 could yield 23 tons from 3,900 hectares under cultivation (UNODC 2013c, pp. 21, 26). Additionally, traffickers use Laos

[2] On 14 February 2006, Laos declared to the world that it was virtually opium free. Opium poppy cultivation has declined to just 1,800 hectares in 2005, down from 26,870 hectares in 1998, a 93 % decline. Moreover, domestic opium consumption has been reduced by over 68 % over the same period.

routes as a drug trafficking transit between the Southeast Asian countries and third nations through borderlines of Laos and its neighbors, including Vietnam (INCSR 2011, p. 357). In particular, at deeply internal border areas, they take advantage of forest trails, streams, and rivers to deliver illegal drugs from Laos to Vietnam (UNODC 2005). To avoid monitors of LEAs during stockpiling and transporting, drug traffickers have used a variety of sophisticated tricks and cunning mode of operation. Right at the borderline, a number of transnational drug trafficking groups closely incorporated with the local drug traffickers store a significant amount of drugs that is then trafficked into Vietnam whenever suitable (Cong an Nghe An 2013). Moreover, the criminal who have a lot of previous convictions are ready to use weapons and firearms against investigations and operations of LEAs (MPS 2012b; SODC 2012, 2013b). All of these features challenge LEAs' effectiveness to prevent and combat drug trafficking.

One Annual Report of the Supreme People's Procuracy of Vietnam (SPP), between May 2011 and April 2013, show that all LEAs investigated and prosecuted over 5,700 cases and arrested more than 7,300 drug-related offenders across the Vietnam's borders with Laos. This accounted for approximately 17 % of total national drug cases (Hieu 2013). Drug trafficking syndicates traffic drugs from the Golden Triangle into Vietnam, more particularly at cross border between Vietnam and Laos (AIPA 2013; INCSR 2014). Accordingly, there are two main borderlines as the hot-spots of the drug trafficking networks. Firstly, the north-west route with particular provinces along the No.6 Highway and Laos border, involving Dienbien, Laichau, Sonla, and Hoabinh, have been used to transported ATS from "blurred points" between Laos and Vietnam borderland to domestic Vietnam markets (SODC 2012). They have frequently combined both ATS tablets and heroin to transport them at the same time, from Laos via the small trails and inter-district roads to the No.6 Highway and onto other provinces for consumption (UNODC and SODC 2012, p. 16). Secondly, the are the Central Northern Coast routes crossing five provinces, namely Thanhhoa, Nghean, Hatinh, Quangbinh, and Quangtri characterized by the vast mountainous terrain from two sides. Traffickers can use both official ways via the International Border Gates such as the Nameo (Thanhhoa province), Namcan (Nghean province), Cautreo (Hatinh province), Chalo (Quangbinh province), and Laobao (Quangtri province) and unofficial ways via narrower paths.

Along this route, many containers of heroin have been illegally trafficked into Vietnam by various armed criminal groups (AIPA 2010a, p. 1; AIPA 2014b, p. 2), especially ethnic minorities groups who are living at the "blurred points" between Vietnam's borderlands and the Laos areas (Rapin 2003, pp. 80–81; Thanhniennews 2013; Tuoitrenews 2013). Many Hmong and Thai local ethnic groups of Vietnam colluded with Laotian criminals to establish networks for illegal trafficking and transporting heroin across the Laos border areas, mainly on the opposite side of Hatinh and Nghean province, into Vietnam or to a third country (AIPA 2012b; MPS 2012a). Moreover, the Laotian drug traffickers collude with their complicit networks, involving relatives, family and friends in Vietnam to facilitate drug transportation into Vietnam's borderland before spreading out to other domestic markets (MPS 2013, 2014). Yet, at both these above routes, one noticeable point has been established: the East-West Economic Corridor (EWEC) with official connection between Northeast Thailand, Central Lao PDR, and North Central Vietnam, the so-called Asian Highway (ADB 2010). It not only facilitates trade's opportunities between the Greater Mekong sub-region (GMS). It is also likely to create potential threats and risks for national security and social order with shared countries, such as Vietnam and Lao PDR (Giang 2012, p. 78). Accordingly, apart from the expected economies that can be achieved in the future when ASEAN becomes a community in 2020, there are some international border-gate and economic corridors that can be targeted by nontraditional crime threats, especially with transnational drug trafficking (AIPA 2014b; MPS 2014).

At the Northern borderline: Vietnam and China

A second route is the Northern line between Vietnam and China border that covers around 1,463 km to flow over seven provinces of Vietnam, including Quangninh, Langson, Laocai, Hagiang, Caobang, Dienbien, and Laichau close to and shared with Yannan and Guangxi of China considered as one of hot-spot domain at the Northern borderlines in drug trafficking activities (UNODC and SODC 2012, p. 16). On this frontier, four international, three national and fourteen provincial border gates have been built surrounded from the northeast of Vietnam (National Border Committee 2010b). Yet there are a myriad of unofficial paths followed by local people, who have relatives on the other side of the border and frequently meet each other (Shira and Associates 2011; Turner 2010). In addition, there exists vast track running and small roads (*duong mon* va *tieu ngach*) alongside commutes, villages, and districts of both sides (Michaud 2009; Thuy 2009). As a result, this leads to more flexible movements and comfortable environments for local authorities and minority groups for cultural exchanges, social cooperation, and shared resources (He 2012; Xiaosong and Womack 2000). To some extent, however, it can create natural conditions to commit a crime, such as smuggling of counterfeits and illegal narcotics (Chin and Zhang 2007; Salter 2004; Zhang and Chin 2015). According to Vietnam's anti-narcotics authorities, the situation of heroin and ATS illicit trafficking across the Vietnam borders with China's Northern provinces is more complicated than whenever since the last two decades (Chalk 2000; DEA 1992; Rapin 2003; UNODC 2013b). Furthermore, with mountainous terrains and tropical climate, the operations of drug traffickers have challenged and created considerable difficulties and barriers for two national LEAs (AIPA 2009; MPS 2010; UNODC 2007).

There are two discrepant drug trafficking routes able to operate at the same time (AIPA 2010b, 2011). As China is a major source of clandestinely manufactured ATS thus, the first tendency is to transport psychotropic substances, including diazepam, seduxen, and other types of synthetic drugs from China into Vietnam (INCB 2005, para 468). In the other direction, meanwhile, the tendency is to deliver heroin and opium from Vietnam to China after collecting it from the Golden Triangle region, particularly cross border Laos and Vietnam (AIPA 2012b; SODC 2012). At the current situation, seemingly, at almost all national border gates, open-economic zones, trading areas on the Vietnam–China borderline drug trafficking flourishes, especially when the China route becomes more portable and convenient to link the two countries' roads and create greater individual freedom of travel in China (MPS 2014, 2015). According to both Vietnamese and Chinese police offices, among some national border gates such as Mongcai, Tanthanh, Huunghi, and Laocai, they often investigate drug trafficking cases with great amount of drugs (Hammett et al. 2005; INCSR 2010; MPS 2012b). For example, during the period 2012–2013, LEAs of Vietnam cooperated with China's authorities to prevent and combat 4,402 case with 5,623 offenders, seized 229.9 kg of heroin, 81.5 kg of opium, 11.4 kg and 211,312 tablets of the ATS, and 7 kg dried cannabis (MPS 2014). It can be seen obviously that the battle of fighting drug trafficking across two border's countries also will continue and need more cooperated from two sides.

At the Southwestern Borderline: Vietnam and Cambodia

With respect to Vietnam and the Kingdom of Cambodia, they share their borderland with around 1,137 km, to start on a triangulated location between Vietnam, Lao PDR and Cambodia and to end at the sea's point between Kiengiang province, Vietnam and Kampot province, Cambodia (National Border Committee 2010a). It flows by 10 provinces in Vietnam, namely Kontum, Gialai, Daklak, Daknong, Binhphuoc, Tayninh, Longan, Dongthap, Angiang, and Kiengiang, shared with nine provinces in Cambodia, including Ratanakiri, Mondulkiri, Kartie, Kampong Cham, Preyveng, Svayrieng, Kandal, Takeeo, Kampot. Apart from advantageous conditions of natural, geographical, and cultural exchanges between both sides, the weakness in control, the lack of intensive cooperation to prevent, and the limitations of capabilities of LEAs from the two sides create potential threats for national security and social order in these areas, including drug trafficking concerns (AIPA 2013; MPS 2013; SODC 2013b).

The official publications of both the two national authorities state that on the Southwestern border with Cambodia, cannabis and ATS are considered as the major type of drugs trafficked into Vietnam (AIPA 2013, 2014a, b). Firstly, with respect to cannabis, according to the International Narcotic Control Board, Cambodia has become a major source of illicit cannabis for regional and global markets (INCB 2005, para 438). Geographically, there are four areas, namely Angiang, Dongthap, Tayninh, and Kiengiang of Vietnam that have been identified as consumer markets for Cambodian cannabis smuggling and trafficking due to they shared borderland with Cambodian provinces (SODC 2013b). Secondly, in respect to the synthetic drugs, Cambodia is also considered a transit country from the Golden Triangle region to transport into Vietnam where ice form of methamphetamine is one of the popular ATS types (INCSR 2005, p. 306). Some amounts of the trafficked illicit drugs are used to satisfy the demands of drug abusers at the social evil pots and casinos around the Mocbai and Takeo International Border Gates; and the rest spreads out to the Ho Chi Minh City's market and some provinces of the South-West part of Vietnam (MPS 2014; UNODC and SODC 2012). Along with that on this route, furthermore, the fact has showed that precursors trafficking have been increasing for the recent years, particularly through air routes (SODC 2013a). Predominately, traffickers have selected the Tan Son Nhat International Airport as destination's transit to deliver illegal drugs into and out of Vietnam (AIPA 2013; MPS 2014).

Vietnam's Responses to Prevent and Combat Drug Trafficking

Following up the Communist Party's formulation, even after the Soviet Union collapsed, Vietnam is one of the limited countries to still catch up with political development, compared with others in ASEAN region (Thayer 2010 pp. 427–428). However, sharing experiences with ASEAN's member on drug issues, Vietnam has also recognized that to control drug and combat transnational drug trafficking is one of the highest priorities in the Initiative National Program of the Vietnamese Government since 1993. One should be aware of the importance of drug prevention and control, over the past years, of the Communist Party (CPV) and the Government of Vietnam (GoV). They have adopted and promulgated guidelines to enhance the effectiveness of drug prevention and control. The National Strategy for Drug Prevention, Combat, and Control in Vietnam through 2020 and orientated towards 2030 (hereafter call "*the National Strategy*") is considered as the most specific documents of Vietnam to concretize viewpoints, targets, and solutions in this battle (Prime Minister 2011).

Viewpoints

Both the recent Constitution of Vietnam after *Doi Moi* (the 1992 Constitution) and the serial documents of CPV have affirmed the process of prevention, combat, and are controlled under the direct leadership of Party Committees.[3] Similar to the Communist Party of China's drug control policy, drug prevention, combat and control must be integrated with the implementation of the relevant programs and strategies derived from the Communist Party (Zhang and Chin 2015). Accordingly, the Vietnam's authorities consider that investment for drug prevention, combat and control is an investment for sustainable development of the country and thus, it requires patience, determination and close and synchronous coordination of agencies and

[3] During the period of 1992–2006, there are two strategy documents in terms of the central role of the CPV to drug's issues, including the Instruction 06-CT/TW dated November 30, 1996 of the Politburo on consolidating the leadership over drug prevention, combat and control Directive 21-CT/TW dated March 26, 2008 of the Politburo on consolidating the leadership over drug prevention, combat and control in new circumstances

mass organizations (SODC 2013b). In addition, the CPV, GoV, and SoV secure resources mobilization for drug prevention, combat, and control in accordance with its capacity and socioeconomic conditions in each stage of development, while calling for contributions and aid from the international community (UNODC 2012c; Vuong et al. 2012). The *National Strategy* emphasizes that their strategies and policies have to not only concretize to improve the recognition of community about the importance of drug prevention, combat and control, but also foster socialization by encouraging sectors, mass organizations, economic sectors, nongovernmental organizations, and citizens to involve themselves (Political Bureau of CPV, 2008; Prime Minister 2011). Besides that, as one of the positive members in the Southeast Asian region and around the world, Vietnam also wants to enhance international cooperation and implementation of international commitments to drug prevention, combat and control as their responsibilities (Prime Minister 2011; SODC 2012).

Targets

Under the CPV, GoV, and SoV viewpoints, drug prevention, combat, and control are one of the key tasks that are both urgent and regular. Yet this battle is needed to focus on both general and particular targets. With respect to general target, Vietnam's authorities have looked forward for improving the responsibility of individuals, families and the whole society in the war on drugs (AIPA 2014b, 2015). The *National Strategy* stated that gradually stop and push back drugs vice and minimize the consequences caused by drugs that are considered as one of the long-termed expectations of Vietnam to create a healthy society for national development (Prime Minister 2011). To do this, the *National Strategy* also identifies that putting a brake on the increase of the number of new drug addicts, reducing the rate of people using illegally drugs in communities, particularly among high-risk groups, and offering detoxification in an effective and sustainable manner are general aims (Prime Minister 2011).

In respect of specific targets, to achieve these above general targets, there are two main milestones. First, in terms of establishing drug-free zones at local community, the Vietnam's authorities at all levels, including headquarter, provincial, districts and communes, strive for keep 70 % of communes, wards and residential areas and 90 % of State agencies, organizations, army units, businesses, and schools free from drugs menace (Prime Minister 2011). Second, regarding to amphetamine-type stimulants (ATS) concerns, the State will not only tightly manage legal trading activities of precursor substances, addictive substances, and psychotropic substances, but also prevent illegal production of synthetic drugs in Vietnam (UNODC and SODC 2012). Third, in relation to drug addicts' concerns, the National Strategy expects to reduce at least 30–40 % of drug addicts' number in Vietnam (MPS 2014; Prime Minister 2011). Furthermore, 100 % of the addicts are detected and managed; 90 % of them are treated, detoxified and provided with vocational training; 100 % of the addicts in detention, education and rehabilitation centers are detoxified; pull the rate of drug readdiction down to 10–15 % compared with the current figure (MPS 2014; Prime Minister 2011).

Conclusion

In the time to come, the drug menace in Vietnam will still be complicated due to the regional and international drug situation. Drug trafficking could regularly change approaches, tricks, operational boundaries, and team up with international drug rings across the Vietnam's borderland with its shared neighbors. They can also collaborate with corrupt criminals, money laundering rings, and weapon traders in order to trade and produce synthetic drugs inside the country. The number of people dependent on synthetic drugs, new addictive medicines, and other new types of drugs tend to increase, especially among young people and students in urban areas. The possibility of people regrowing opium poppy is still latent in many localities. Hence, if synchronous and long-term solutions were not adopted, the drugs scourge would be out of control, resulting in serious and unpredicted consequences for society. By promulgating the National Strategy with its specific targets, programs, and solutions, Vietnam is looking forward to expecting an efficient and sustainable manner to prevent and eradicate the menace in society. Further, it will not only help the Vietnam's construction and development but also contribute to build "free zone drugs" in the Southeast Asian region when it becomes one Community in 2020.

Acknowledgments The author would like to express his respect and gratitude to his PhD primary supervisor, Associate Professor. Paul Battersby Deputy Dean, School for Global, Urban, and Social Science, RMIT University, Melbourne, Victoria, Australia for his helpful comments.

References

ADB. (2010). *Strategy and action plan for the Greater Mekong Subregion East–West Economic Corridor*. Mandaluyong City, Philippines: Asian Development Bank (ADB).

AIPA. (2008). Drug situation in Vietnam in 2007. In the ASEAN Inter-Parliamentary Assembly Fact Finding Committee (AIFOCOM) (Ed.), *Country report of Vietnam*. Singapore: AIPA.

AIPA. (2009). Drug situation in Vietnam in 2008. In the ASEAN Inter-Parliamentary Assembly Fact Finding Committee (AIFOCOM) (Ed.), *Country report of Vietnam*. Chiang Rai, Thailand: AIPA.

AIPA. (2010a). *Country report of Vietnam: drug situation in Vietnam in 2010 viewed 10 August 2013* (p. 5). Ho Chi Minh City, Vietnam: Asean Inter Parliamentary Assembly (AIPA).

AIPA. (2010b). Drug situation in Vietnam in 2009. In the ASEAN Inter-Parliamentary Assembly Fact Finding Committee (AIFOCOM) (Ed.), *Country report of Vietnam*. Ho Chi Minh City, Vietnam: AIPA.

AIPA. (2011). Drug situation in Vietnam in 2010. In the ASEAN Inter-Parliamentary Assembly Fact Finding Committee (AIFOCOM) (Ed.), *Country report of Vietnam*. Phnom Penh, Cambodia: AIPA.

AIPA. (2012a). *Country progress report of Vietnam. The 9th Meeting of the ASEAN Inter-Parliamentary Assembly (AIPA) Fact Finding Committee (AIFOCOM)*. D.I.Y. Yogyakarta, Indonesia: The ASEAN Inter-Parliamentary Assembly (AIPA).

AIPA. (2012b). Drug situation in Vietnam in 2011. In The ASEAN Inter-Parliamentary Assembly Fact-Finding Committee (AIFOCOM) (Ed.), *Country report of Vietnam*. Yogyakarta, Indonesia: AIPA.

AIPA. (2013). Prevention and combat against drug and drug-related crimes between 2010 and 2012—Process and outcomes. In The ASEAN Inter-Parliamentary Assembly Fact-Finding Committee (AIFOCOM) (Ed.), *Country report of Vietnam*. Indonesia: ASEAN Inter-Parliamentary Assembly.
AIPA. (2014a). *Cambodia's country report at The 11th Meeting of the AIPA Fact Finding Committee to Combat the Drug Menace (11th AIFOCOM)*. Vientiane, Lao PDR: ASEAN Inter Parliamentary Assembly (AIPA).
AIPA. (2014b). *Country progress report of Vietnam at the 11th Meeting of the AIPA Fact-Finding Committee (AIFOCOM)*. Vientiane, Lao PDR: ASEAN Inter Parliamentary Assembly (AIPA).
AIPA. (2015). *Country report summary of Vietnam at the 12th Meeting of the AIPA Fact Finding Committee (AIFOCOM)*. Kuala Lumpur, Malaysia: AIPA Fact Finding Committee (AIFOCOM).
Battersby, P. (2014). Global crime and global security. In M. B. Steger, P. Battersby, & J. M. Siracusa (Eds.), *The SAGE handbook of globalization* (Vol. 2, pp. 697–719). London: Sage Publications Ltd.
Blickman, T. (2009). The ATS boom in Southeast Asia. In T. Kramer, M. Jelsma, & T. Blickman (Eds.), *Withdrawal symptoms in the Golden Triangle—a drug market in disarray* (pp. 52–69). Amsterdam, Netherlands: Transnational Institute.
Byrne, J. (1999). *Drug culture in Vietnam: An investigation Melbourne*. Australia: Department of Human Services Victoria.
Cam, L. (1999a). Luat Hinh Su Viet Nam Truoc The Ky XV. *Tap Chi Dan Chu va Phap Luat, 5* [trans: Cam, Le 1999, Criminal code of Vietnam in prior XVth century. *Journal on Democracy and Law*, vol. 1995].
Cam, L. (1999b). Luat Hinh Su Viet Nam Tu The Ky XV den cuoi the ky XVIII. *Tap Chi Dan Chu va Phap Luat, 8* [trans: Cam, Le 1999, Criminal code of Vietnam: From XVth century to the ends of XVIIIth century, *Journal on Democracy and Law*, Vol. 1998].
Chalk, P. (2000). Southeast Asia and the Golden Triangle's heroin trade: Threat and response. *Studies in Conflict and Terrorism, 23*(2), 89–106.
Chin, K.-L. (2009). *The Golden Triangle: Inside southeast Asia's drug trade*. Ithaca: Cornell University Press.
Chin, K.-l., & Zhang, S. X. (2007). The Chinese connection: Cross-border drug trafficking between Myanmar and China. *Final report to The United States Department of Justice Office of Justice Programs National Institute of Justice*.
Cong an Nghe An. (2013). Annual Meeting on Bilateral Cooperation on Preventing and Combating Drugs Across Borders between Vietnam and Laos, XIIIth. Nghean, Vietnam (*Vietnamese*—Internal Publication) Steering Organization on Prevention and Combat Drugs Eight Provinces of Vietnam and Laos.
DEA. (1992). Opium poppy cultivation and heroin processing in Southeast Asia. In U.S. Department of Justice (Ed.). Washington, DC: National Institute of Justice.
DEA. (2003). Vietnam: Country brief—Status in international drug trafficking. In Drug Enforcement Administration (Ed.), *Drug intelligence brief* (p. 6). USA: Drug Enforcement Administration (DEA).
Devaney, M. L., Reid, G., & Baldwin, S. (2006). Situation analysis of illicit drug issues and responses in the Asia-Pacific region. In Australian National Council on Drugs (Ed.). Canberra, Australia: Australian National Council on Drugs.
Giang, B. N. (2012). Potential economic corridors between Vietnam and Lao PDR: Roles played by Vietnam. In I. Masami (Ed.), *Emerging economic corridors in the Mekong region*. Bangkok, Thailand: Bangkok Research Center.
Griffiths, P. (2006). A shot in the arm: Transboundary flows and opiate transition in Vietnam. In P. Thomas (Ed.), *Illicit drugs and development: Critical issues for Asia and the Pacific* (pp. 59–64). Canberra, Australia: Development Studies Network.
Hammett, T. M., Bartlett, N. A., Chen, Y., Ngu, D., Cuong, D. D., Phuong, N. M., et al. (2005). Law enforcement influences on HIV prevention for injection drug users: Observations from a

cross-border project in China and Vietnam. *International Journal of Drug Policy, 16*(4), 235–245.

He, Z. (2012). Migration and the sex industry in the Hekou-Lao Cai Border Region between Yunnan and Vietnam. In T. E. Blair (Ed.), *Living on the edges: Cross-border mobility and sexual exploitation in the greater southeast Asia sub-region* (pp. 1–43). Thailand: Southeast Asian Consortium on Gender, Sexuality and Health.

Hieu, L. (2013). *Drug trafficking across the Vietnam and Laos borders*. Retrieved 28 June 2013 (*Vietnamese*).

Hoa, P. T. N. (2008). *Legislative implementation by Vietnam of its obligations under the United Nations Drug Control Conventions*. Ph.D., University of Wollongong, Wollongong, New South Wales, Australia.

Hoang, V. L. T. (2007). Vietnam's quest for influence and its implications for the management of border disputes with Laos and Cambodia. *Journal of Current Southeast Asian Affairs, 26*(2), 6–38.

INCB. (2005). *Report of the International Narcotics Control Board for 2005*. Vienna, Austria: Vienna International Center.

INCSR. (2005). *International Narcotic Control Strategy Report 2005 Southeast Asia* (Vol. I (Drug and Chemical Control), pp. 295–364). Washington, DC: United States Department of State, Bureau for International Narcotics and Law Enforcement Affairs.

INCSR. (2009). *International Narcotic Control Strategy Report 2009* (Vol. I (Drug and Chemical Control), p. 638). Washington, DC: United States Department of State, Bureau for International Narcotics and Law Enforcement Affairs.

INCSR. (2010). *International Narcotic Control Strategy Report 2010* (Vol. I (Drug and Chemical Control), p. 674). Washington, DC: United States Department of State, Bureau for International Narcotics and Law Enforcement Affairs.

INCSR. (2011). *International Narcotics Control Strategy Report 2011* (Vol. 1 (Drug and Chemical Control)). Washington, DC: United States Department of State, Bureau for International Narcotics and Law Enforcement Affairs.

INCSR. (2013). *International Narcotics Control Strategy Report 2013: Volume I. Drug and Chemical Control* (Vol. 1 (Drug and Chemical Control)). Washington, DC: United States Department of State, Bureau for International Narcotics and Law Enforcement Affairs.

INCSR. (2014). *International Narcotics Control Strategy Report 2014*. Washington, DC: United States Department of State, Bureau for International Narcotics and Law Enforcement Affairs.

Kramer, T., Jelsma, M., & Blickman, T. (2009). *Withdrawal symptoms in the Golden Triangle: A drugs market in disarray*. Amsterdam, Netherlands: Transnational Institute.

Kramer, T., Jensema, E., Jelsma, M., & Blickman, T. (2014). *Bouncing back—Relapse in the Golden Triangle*. Amsterdam, Netherlands: Transnational Institute (TNI).

Lintner, B. (2008). Laos: At the crossroads. *Southeast Asian Affairs, 2008*(2008), 171–183.

McCoy, A. W. (2003). *The politics of heroin: CIA complicity in the global drug trade—Afghanistan, Southeast Asia, Central America, Colombia*. Chicago: Lawrence Hill Books.

Michaud, J. (2000a). A historical panorama of the Montagnards in Northern Vietnam under French Rule. In J. Michaud (Ed.), *Turbulent times and enduring peoples: Mountain minorities in the Southeast Asia* (pp. 51–79). Surrey: Curzon Press.

Michaud, J. (2000b). The Montagnards and the state in Northern Vietnam from 1802 to 1975: A historical overview. *Ethnohistory, 47*(2), 333–368.

Michaud, J. (2009). Handling mountain minorities in China, Vietnam and Laos: From history to current concerns. *Asian Ethnicity, 10*(1), 25–49. doi:10.1080/14631360802628442.

MPS. (2010). Vietnam drug report 2010. Hanoi, Vietnam *(classified and unpublished document):* Department of Police Force Prevention and Suppress Anti Narcotic, Ministry of Public Security of Vietnam.

MPS. (2012a). *Status and result on preventing and combating drug trafficking of Vietnam*. Paper presented at the International Drug Enforcement Conference East Fair Regional Working Group Meeting (IDEC EFRWGM), Danang, Vietnam.

MPS. (2012b). Vietnam drug report 2012. Hanoi, Vietnam *(classified and unpublished document)*: Department of Police Force Prevention and Suppress Anti Narcotic, Ministry of Public Security of Vietnam.
MPS. (2013). Annual report for drug situation in Vietnam. Hanoi, Vietnam (*Vietnamese language*): Department of Police Force Prevention and Suppress Anti Narcotic, Ministry of Public Security of Vietnam.
MPS. (2014). Annual report for drug situation in Vietnam Hanoi, Vietnam *(Vietnamese language)*: Department of Police Force Prevention and Suppress Anti Narcotic, Ministry of Public Security of Vietnam.
MPS. (2015). Annual report for drug situation in Vietnam. Hanoi, Vietnam *(Vietnamese language)*: Department of Police Force Prevention and Suppress Anti Narcotic, Ministry of Public Security of Vietnam.
National Border Committee. (2010a). *Borderland between Vietnam and Cambodia Hanoi.* Vietnam: Ministry of Foreign Affairs.
National Border Committee. (2010b). *Borderland between Vietnam and China*. Hanoi, Vietnam: Ministry of Foreign Affairs.
National Border Committee. (2010c). *Borderland between Vietnam and Laos*. Hanoi, Vietnam: Ministry of Foreign Affairs.
National Border Committee. (2011). Overview on borderland between Vietnam and Laos. *Vietnam's sovereign boundaries*. Retrieved 22 March, 2014, from http://123.30.50.199/sites/vi/tongquanchungveduongbien-gid-19430525-nd-f8444a7e.aspx.
Paoli, L., Victoria, G. A., & Reuter, P. (2009). *The world heroin market: Can supply be cut?* London: Oxford University Press.
Prime Minister. (2011). Decision No 1001/QD-TTg issued 26 July 2011 of Prime Minster on Approving the National Strategy on Drug Prevention and Control in Vietnam till 2020 and Orientations Toward 2030 (2011).
Political Bureau of CPV. (2008). Directive No21-CT/TW issued on 26 March 2008 of the Party's National Congress on Continuing to Enhance Management and Leadership in Prevention, Suppression and Control Drug in New Situation.
Rapin, A.-J. (2003). *Ethnic minorities, drug use and harm in the highlands of northern Vietnam: A contextual analysis of the situation in six communes from Son La, Lai Chau, and Lao Cai*. Hanoi, Vietnam: Thegioi Publishing.
NAV. (2011). *Resolution on the Five-Year Socio-Economic Development Plan 2011–2014*. Hanoi, Vietnam: National Assembly of Vietnam (NAV).
Salter, M. B. (2004). Passports, mobility, and security: How smart can the border be? *International Studies Perspectives, 5*(1), 71–91. doi:10.1111/j.1528-3577.2004.00158.x.
Shear, W. G. (1993). The drug war: Applying the lessons of Vietnam: DTIC Document.
Shira, D., & Associates. (2011). *China's neighbors: Who is influencing China and who China is influencing in the new emerging Asia*. Asia Briefing (Ed.), China Briefing: The Practical Application of China Business.
Socialist Republic of Vietnam. (2010). *Vietnam: 2/3 of the way achieving the millennium development goals and towards 2015*. Hanoi, Vietnam: New Technology Printing Joint Stock Company.
SODC. (2012). *Vietnam country report*. Paper presented at the Seventeenth Asia-Pacific Operation Drug Enforcement Conference (ADEC), Tokyo, Japan.
SODC. (2013a). Situation and the results of drug prevention in Vietnam. In Ministry of Public Security of Vietnam (Ed.), *The SMART Vietnam National Workshop*. Danang, Vietnam: Standing Office on Drugs and Crime (SODC).
SODC. (2013b). *Vientnam National Report*. Paper presented at The Twenty-third Anti-Drug Liaison Officials' Meeting for International Cooperation (ADLOMICO), Busan, Republic of Korea.
Thanhniennews. (2013). 3 Lao Drug Smugglers Arrested in Central Vietnam. Retrieved 2 April, 2013, from http://talkvietnam.com/2013/04/3-lao-drug-smugglers-arrested-in-central-vietnam/.
Thayer, C. A. (2010). Political legitimacy in Vietnam: Challenge and response. *Politics & Policy, 38*(3), 423–444.

Thuy, T. D. (2009). *The implementation of Vietnam-China land border treaty: Bilateral and regional implications* (Vol. 173). Singapore: S. Rajaratnam School of International Studies (RSIS).
Tiem, T. L. (2010). *Enhancing international co-operation on crime prevention and suppression challenges facing global security in the 21st Century*. Hanoi, Vietnam: Interpol.
Tuoitrenews. (2013). Laos-Vietnam drug trafficking ring busted. Retrieved 5 March, 2013, from http://tuoitrenews.vn/society/9261/laosvietnam-drug-trafficking-ring-busted.
Turner, S. (2010). Borderlands and border narratives: A longitudinal study of challenges and opportunities for local traders shaped by the Sino-Vietnamese border. *Journal of Global History, 5*(02), 265–287.
Uc, D. T. (2000). *Luat Hinh Su Viet Nam, Quyen I-Nhung Van de Chung* (Vol. 1). Hanoi, Vietnam: Nha xuat ban khoa hoc xa hoi [trans: Uc, D. T. (2000), *Handbook on criminal code of Vietnam*, Vol. 1 (General Provisions), Hanoi, Vietnam, Social Science Publishing].
UNDP. (2013). *Consolidated report on Vietnam's post-2015 consultation process*. Hanoi, Vietnam: UNDP in Vietnam.
UNODC. (2005). *Vietnam country report*. Hanoi, Vietnam
UNODC. (2006). *Opium poppy cultivation in the Golden Triangle: Lao PDR, Myanmar, Thailand*. Bangkok, Thailand: United Nations on Drugs and Crime.
UNODC. (2007). *Strategic programme framework Vietnam 2005–2007*. Hanoi, Vietnam: UNODC.
UNODC. (2009). AD/VIE/H65—Strengthening Drug Law Enforcement Agency Information Collection and Sharing Procedures. In UNODC VIet Nam Country Office (Ed.), *Projects*. Hanoi, Vietnam: United Nations on Drugs and Crime.
UNODC. (2010). Statistics on drug trafficking trends in East, South-East and South Asia, Oceania and worldwide.
UNODC. (2011). *World drug report 2011*. Vienna, Austria: UNODC.
UNODC, & SODC. (2012). Amphetamine type stimulants in Vietnam: A review of the availability, use and implications for health and security in Vietnam. "*Support for developing effective ATS prevention strategies and measures for East Asia: A Pilot in Viet Nam*" *VNM/J93*. Hanoi, Vietnam: UNODC Vietnam Country Office & Standing Office on Drugs and Crime of Vietnam.
UNODC. (2012b). *AD/VIE/H65—Strengthening drug law enforcement agency information collection and sharing procedures*. Hanoi, Vietnam: UNODC Regional Programme for East Asia and the Pacific.
UNODC. (2012c). *Patterns and trends of amphetamine-type stimulants and other drugs: Asia and the Pacific 2012*. Bangkok, Thailand: UNODC.
UNODC. (2012d). *Vietnam country programme 2012–2017*. Hanoi, Vietnam: UNODC, Vietnam Office.
UNODC. (2012e). *World drug report 2012*. Vienna, Austria: UNODC.
UNODC. (2013a). *Needs assessment for establishing a national referral mechanism in Vietnam*. Hanoi, Vietnam: Regional Centre for East Asia and the Pacific.
UNODC. (2013b). Patterns and trends of amphetamine-type stimulants and other drugs: Challenges for Asia and the Pacific. In Global SMART Programme (Ed.), *A report from the Global SMART Programme*. Bangkok, Thailand: United Nations on Drugs and Crime.
UNODC. (2013c). Southeast Asia Opium Survey 2013. In Regional Officer for Southeast Asia and the Pacific (Ed.), *UNODC's Illicit Crop Monitoring Programming (ICMP)*. Bangkok, Thailand: United Nations on Drugs and Crime.
UNODC. (2013d). *Transnational organized crime in East Asia and the Pacific: A threat assessment*. Vienna, Austria.
UNODC. (2013e). *World drug report 2013*. Vienna, Austria: UNODC.
UNODC. (2014a). *Border control training to fight transnational organized crime in Vietnam*. Quangtri, Vietnam: UNODC Regional Programme for East Asia and the Pacific.
UNODC. (2014b). *World drug report 2014*. Vienna, Austria: United Nations on Drugs and Crime.
UNODC. (2015a). *Expanding synthetic drugs market inhibiting development in east and southeast Asia and Oceania*. Bangkok, Thailand: UNODC Regional Centre for the Southeast Asia and the Pacific.

UNODC. (2015b). *World drug report 2015*. Vienna, Austria: United Nations on Drugs and Crime.
UNODC Vietnam. (2013). ATS second-most popular illicit drug in Vietnam, Heroin Still No. 1. Retrieved 8 July, from United Nations Publication.
Van, T. N., & Scannapieco, M. (2008). Drug abuse in Vietnam: A critical review of the literature and implications for future research. *Addiction, 103*(4), 535–543.
Vinh, Q. V. (2002). *Hoan Thien He Thong Phap Luat co Lien Quan den Cong Tac Phong, Chong Toi Pham ve Ma Tuy*. Paper presented at the Hoi Thao ve Thuc Tien Dau Tranh Phong Chong Ma Tuy va Van De Hoan Thien Phap Luat Trong Phong, Chong Ma Tuy, Hanoi, Vietnam [trans: Vinh, Quang Vu 2002, 'Improving the Legal Framework on Prevention and Suppression Drug-Related Crimes', paper presented to the Conference on Practices on Preventing and Combating Drug-Related Crimes and Some Issues to Improve Vietnam's Legal Framework on Drug Control, Hanoi, Vietnam].
Vuong, T., Ali, R., Baldwina, S., & Millsa, S. (2012). Drug policy in Vietnam: A decade of change? *International Journal of Policy Analysis, 23*, 319–326.
Vuving, A. (2010). *Vietnamese perspectives on transnational security challenges*. Paper presented at the Issues for engagement: Asian Perspectives on transnational security challenges, Hawaii.
WHO. (2013). Amphetamine-type stimulants. *Management of Substance Abuse*. Retrieved 21 September, 2013.
Xiaosong, G., & Womack, B. (2000). Border cooperation between China and Vietnam in the 1990s. *Asian Survey, 40*(6), 1042–1058.
Yem, X. N. (2003). *Mai dam, Ma tuy, Co bac, Toi pham thoi hien dai*. Hanoi, Vietnam: Nha xuat ban Cong an nhan dan [trans: Yem, Xuan Nguyen 2003 *Prostitution, Narcotics, and Gambling: Crimes at the Present Time* the People's Public Security Housing, Hanoi, Vietnam].
Zhang, S., & Chin, K.-l. (2015). *The Chinese heroin trade: cross-border drug trafficking in Southeast Asia and beyond*. New York: New York University Press.

Chapter 10
Post Trafficking Victims in Mexico and Their Reintegration Process: An Analysis of the Government's Response

Arun Kumar Acharya

Introduction

Trafficking in persons became the subject of renewed international concern towards the end of the twentieth and the start of the twenty-first centuries (Wijers 2015; U.S. Department of State 2015). In a globalized world with increasing polarities of wealth both within and between countries, with an increased demand for cheap labor in developed countries, with increased possibilities for travel and telecommunications broadcasting, and images of western wealth around the world, those living in relative and absolute poverty tend to migrate in search of a better life (ILO 2005). This gives origin to a number of different situations. Since many migrants are often undocumented or "illegal," they may depend on smugglers to be taken into their country of destination. Others may actually not want to migrate, within or outside their own country, but are forced to do so for various reasons, almost all illegal and criminal, like being sold by his or her parents into servitude to pay the family's debts or improve their livelihood, or are tricked into accepting onerous labor contracts that enslave them to organized crimes organizations whose only goal is to mercilessly exploit them, often with the connivance of corrupt officials. While trafficking of women for sexual work has received a lot of attention, people are trafficked for all sorts of work, most often per se legal (like working in orchards, farms, restaurants, mines, etc.) and can be national or international, Basically, trafficking is a modern form of slavery.

This global crime generates billions of dollars in profits for the traffickers. The International Labor Organization (ILO) estimates that around 20.9 million people are victims of forced labor globally. This estimate also includes victims of human trafficking for labor and sexual exploitation; however it is not known how many of these victims were trafficked (UNODC 2014). On the contrary, the 2015 Trafficking

A.K. Acharya (✉)
Universidad Autónoma de Nuevo León, Nuevo León, Mexico
e-mail: arun.kumara@uanl.mx

E.C. Viano (ed.), *Cybercrime, Organized Crime, and Societal Responses*,
DOI 10.1007/978-3-319-44501-4_10

in Persons Report given by U.S. Department of State indicates that as many as 27 million men, women, and children are trafficking victims at any given time (U.S. Department of State 2015). The 2014 Global Report on Trafficking in Personas indicates that women and girls comprise around 75 percent of victims of trafficked persons, among which 58 percent are used for sexual exploitation and 36 percent are exploited for forced labor (UNODC 2014).

Accordingly, when national governments came together in Palermo in December of 2000 to address the issue of human trafficking, they adopted a comprehensive definition of the term. The United Nations Protocol to Prevent, Suppress, and Punish Trafficking in Persons (the Palermo Protocol) defines human trafficking in Article 3 as:

> "The recruitment, transportation, transfer, harboring or receipt of persons, by means of the threat or use of force or other forms of coercion, of abduction, of fraud, of deception, of the abuse of power or of a position of vulnerability or of the giving or receiving of payments or benefits to achieve the consent of a person having control over another person, for the purpose of exploitation." Exploitation shall include, at a minimum, the exploitation of the prostitution of others or other forms of sexual exploitation, forced labor or services, slavery or practices similar to slavery, servitude or the removal of organs.

Research on trafficking of women states that young girls and women mainly trafficked for the purpose of sexual exploitation and forced prostitution are often suffering from extreme physical, sexual, and psychological exploitation, which leads to a high risk of unwanted pregnancy and sexually transmitted diseases (Saxena et al. 2007; Zimmerman et al. 2008). Raphael and Deborah (2004) for example, indicated that: trafficked women suffer extremely elevated physical and sexual violence. In the case of Mexico, trafficking of women and girls is difficult to ascertain, as there is little empirical data available. To date, there is no exact official statistics on trafficking of women, but once Teresa Ulloa, President of Regional Coalition Against Trafficking of Women and Children in Latin America and the Caribbean (CATWLAC in Spanish) said that every day 400 women enter into prostitution (this figure includes trafficked and non-trafficked women) in Mexico City, out of which 80 percent are there against their will (González 2003). Goldenberg et al. (2012) studied 624 female sex workers in Tijuana and Ciudad Juarez, Mexico and found that: 42 percent were entered into sex work as minors and they experienced a higher prevalence of sexual violence and substance abuse, which relates to health impacts.

The physical, psychological, and behavioral violence and exploitation spoiled the victim's life (Crawford and Kaufman 2008; Kempadoo and Doezema 1998), and often it is extremely difficult for many women to survive on their own. As a result, they not only suffered prom poverty, but also a life lifetime social exclusion (Kara 2009). Thus, the Palermo Protocol emphasizes two important elements in relation to human trafficking. First it states an effective prevention of trafficking through prosecution of traffickers, and secondly, protection of human rights and victim assistance to ensure their rehabilitation and reintegration into society. The protocol also refers that integration is a process of recovery and economic inclusion of an individual after a trafficking experience and it is the Government's responsibility to provide a safe environment, economic opportunities, medical assistance as well as social and emotional support.

However, most of the literature on trafficked persons indicates that many post trafficking victims suffered wide ranges of psychological, physical, socioeconomical, and cultural obstacles, which limited their process of reintegration. Lack of proper assistance as well as a support network makes victims vulnerable and potentially complicates the reintegration factor in the social, cultural, and personal spheres. Thus, in this chapter an attempt has been made to analyze the effort endured by Mexico's government to address the reintegration of post trafficking victims in the country. For this study, we have utilized the information available from the government. Some information was also obtained from the National Institute for Access to Information and Data Protection (*INAI* in Spanish).

Trafficking of Women and Children for the Purpose of Sexual Exploitation in Mexico

The 2015 Trafficking in Persons Report provided by the U.S. Department of State indicates that Mexico is a source, transit and destination country for women, children and men subjected to sex trafficking and forced labor. According to this report, Mexican women, children as well as men are exploited in forced labor in agriculture, domestic service, food processing factories, construction, the informal economy, begging, and vending in both the USA and Mexico. The most vulnerable groups to human trafficking in Mexico include women, children, indigenous people, individuals with mental or physical disabilities, migrants, and LGBT Mexicans (U.S. Department of State 2015).

Human trafficking for the purpose of prostitution in Mexico has become a public concern in the last few years, especially with respect to the prostitution of children (Esteinou 2011). Mexico ranks second in the world in terms of prostitution of underage persons (Monroy 2010). Available evidence suggests that children are commonly trafficked from poor areas of the country and are often exploited by American tourists (COHA 2009; Ruiz Torres, M.A, 2003). Prostitution has been practiced in the country since the pre-Hispanic period, and is still commonplace throughout the country (Franco 1973; Ríos de la Torre 1991). According to Azaola (1998) the rapid increase in the number of children for commercial sexual exploitation is due to the following factors: (1) The deterioration of living conditions of poor families, (2) the promotion of child prostitution by close family members, (3) the use of sexual activities as a means of survival by street children who escape from an abusive home, (4) the recruitment of children as sex workers by organized crime network and, (5) the illegal transfer of children as sex workers from developing countries to developed countries.

In the last few years, some significant effort has been made to understand the trafficking in persons issue in the country. It also evidenced that both domestic and international trafficking of persons, especially of women and children has increased (U.S. Department of State 2015; Montalvo 2014[1]; CNDH 2013[2]), however, trafficking-related corruption among public officials, especially local law

[1] http://www.animalpolitico.com/2014/11/victimas-de-trata-en-mexico-se-duplican-en-el-ultimo-ano-la-mayoria-son-mujeres-y-ninas/

[2] http://www.senado.gob.mx/comisiones/trata_personas/docs/Diagnostico_Trata.pdf

enforcement, judicial, and immigration officials remains a significant concern in Mexico. Some officials extort bribes and sexual services from adults and children in prostitution; extort irregular migrants, including trafficking victims; falsify victims' documents; threaten victims with prosecution if they will not file official complaints against their traffickers; accept bribes from traffickers; facilitate movement of victims across borders; operate or patronize brothels where victims are exploited; or fail to respond to trafficking crimes, including in commercial sex locations (U.S. Department of State 2015). Given that the Mexican Government does not fully comply with the minimum standards to eliminate trafficking, the country is currently at a Tier 2 level.

With respect to Trafficking in Persons Reports from 2001 to 2015, in the last 15 years Mexico has faced some key challenges. For example, the 2001 Trafficking in Persons Report ranked Mexico as source and transit country. According to the US State Department, Mexican women, children and men were trafficked into the USA, Canada, and Japan for the purpose of sexual exploitation and forced labor, and Mexico is a transit country for persons from various countries, especially Central America and China. There are an increasing number of persons from Brazil and Eastern Europe transiting through Mexico, some of whom are trafficked Salvadorans and Guatemalans, especially children, trafficked into Mexico for prostitution, particularly at the Southern border (U.S. Department of State 2001). The report classified Mexico as a Tier 2 country, given that the government does not yet fully meet the minimum standards and there are no specific laws in place to prohibit the trafficking of persons, and this continued until 2003. However, since the 2002 Trafficking in Persons Report, the U.S. Department of State extensively recognized Mexico as a source, transit, and destination country of women and children trafficked for the purpose of sexual exploitation.

According to official information, after implementing the 2012 Anti-Trafficking Law in the country, there are 253 trafficking cases under investigation by the Federal Government, and at least 196 trafficking cases are under investigation by States entities in 2014, as compared to 139 federal investigations and 458 State investigations reported in 2013 (ONC 2014). Mexican authorities reported sentencing three traffickers at the federal level and at least 108 at the State level in 2014; this represented an increase in reported sentences from 2013 when authorities did not issue any federal trafficking convictions and only 73 at the State level, including 38 in the federal district (U.S. Department of State 2015).

The Government of Mexico continued to increase its law enforcement efforts and in June 2012 Congress approved the new anti-trafficking law, which was also reformed in 2014. Although there is a lack of coordination, officials' complicity, and some officials' limited understanding of human trafficking, it has been observed that to this date most States have specific anti-trafficking legislation in line with national trafficking laws and only in some States the law criminalizes all forms of trafficking. These inconsistencies among States laws complicate inter-state investigations and prosecutions.

Some studies demonstrate how child prostitution has increased all over the world (UNODC 2014; Shelley 2010), however, during the last few years, Mexico has undergone deep changes regarding trafficking of women (Azaola and Estes 2003). Firstly, it is an important country of origin, destination and transit for international trafficking, and secondly, it is one of the most important countries with regards to domestic trafficking. Our previous research indicates that every year approximately 10,000 people are being trafficked within Mexico, particularly to the following six cities: Cancun, Acapulco, Mexico City, Tijuana, Ciudad Juarez and Monterrey, and approximately 5000 are trafficked into the USA (Acharya and Bryson 2014). This study also found that in Mexico seven out of ten trafficked women are being trafficked within the country and three out of ten are taken abroad (Acharya 2010). In addition, every day an estimated 400 women enter into prostitution (this figure includes trafficked and non-trafficked women) in Mexico City, out of which 80 percent do so against their will (González 2003).

In 2014, the National Citizen Observatory conducted a 4-year analysis (January 2010 through July 2013) of human trafficking in Mexico including 31 States, the Federal District, and the federal government. The present study found persistently high levels of impunity for the crime, demonstrating how incomplete and contradictory official information contributes to bury the true scope of the problem. Over the time period, 16 states reported a total of 846 victims, while the rest failed to provide information. Jalisco had the highest number of victims, with 283, representing about a third of the total. This was followed by Baja California, with 136, and Puebla, with 122. The national Attorney General's Office (PGR) registered 347 victims during this time period, and the Ministerial Federal Police (PFM) registered 121 (ONC 2014). Likewise, information regarding sex, age and nationality was provided for only a portion of the total victims reported by these States. Of these, around 87 percent were women and approximately the same percent were victims of sex trafficking, and nearly 90 percent of victims were single, Mexican citizens and were under 18 years old (ONC 2014). The important issue here is that regarding the process of reintegration of trafficking victims in the country is not clear, which we will try to explore in the following section.

International Legislations and Recommendations on Human Trafficking for Mexico

International laws are a powerful conduit for combating human trafficking, and the Government of Mexico has signed and ratified most of the significant conventions implemented by the United Nations, ILO as well as the Organization of American States. The important instrument of international law signed and ratified by Mexico on human trafficking is the United Nations Convention against Transnational Organized Crime and its two related protocols: The United Nations Protocol to Prevent, Suppress, and Punish Trafficking in Persons, Especially Women and Children, and the United Nations Protocol against the Smuggling of Migrants by Land, Sea, and Air, which entered into effect in 2003–2004. As a means of

Table 10.1 International and regional conventions ratified by the Mexican Government

International conventions	Status of the Mexican Government
1. United Nations Protocol to Prevent, Suppress, and Punish Human Trafficking especially Women and Children	Signed and ratified
2. United Nations Protocol against the Smuggling of Migrants by Land, Sea, and Air	Signed and ratified
3. American Convention on Human Rights	Signed and ratified
4. United Nations Convention against Transnational Organized Crime	Signed and ratified
5. Inter-American Convention on the Prevention, Punishment, and Eradication of Violence against Women	Signed and ratified
6. ILO Convention 29 on Forced Labor	Signed and ratified
7. ILO Convention 105, Abolition of Forced Labor	Signed and ratified
8. Convention on the Rights of the Child on the Sale of Children, Child Prostitution and Child Pornography	Signed and ratified

Source: self elaboration

enforcing these instruments, Mexico has ratified other international conventions as well as regional conventions (see Table 10.1).

The Government of Mexico submits regular progress reports regarding their level of compliance with the treaty and receives regular inputs from international committees as well as from nongovernmental organizations. However, in spite of ratifying these treaties, the 2015 Human Trafficking Report ranked Mexico as a Tier 2 country, meaning that the government does not fully comply with minimum standards of the Trafficking Victims Protection Act, but it is making significant efforts to comply with those standards. This report recommends that Mexico's government increase funding to provide specialized victim services and shelters in partnership with civil society, and refer victims of all forms of trafficking to services and provide them with adequate protection; strengthen efforts to investigate and prosecute trafficking offenses, and convict and punish traffickers, especially for forced labor crimes; increase efforts to hold public officials complicit in trafficking accountable through prosecutions and convictions (U.S. Department of State 2015).

Similarly, it is necessary to enhance the formal procedures to identify victims among vulnerable populations, such as people in prostitution and undocumented migrants, and to refer them to appropriate care; modify anti-trafficking laws at the federal and state levels to reflect the international anti-trafficking law; increase the ability of regional and state coalitions and specialized units to more effectively respond to trafficking cases through increased funding and trained staff; verify through increased training and monitoring that victims are not coerced into testifying against traffickers or treated as traffickers; strengthen data collection efforts; provide effective protection for witnesses and victims testifying against traffickers; increase training on victim identification and treatment for government employees; and improve coordination mechanisms between federal, state, and local authorities (U.S. Department of State 2015).

Protection

According to the 2015 Trafficking Report, the Government of Mexico continued to provide limited specialized services for trafficking victims. Some government institutions had informal victim referral procedures, but most government officials lacked clear guidelines for identifying and referring victims to care services. It is also seen that, immigration agents continued to ask detained migrants if they were trafficking victims and lacked in-depth screening mechanisms. The anti-trafficking experts and people in prostitution reported officials often did not always differentiate between sex trafficking victims and women in prostitution due in part to the overly broad anti-trafficking law making victim identification statistics unreliable. Although the government did report identifying trafficking victims, it did not report how many were exploited in forced labor or sex trafficking. It is also unclear how many of the identified victims received particular services such as shelter and victim services, in most parts of the country these services remain inadequate in light of the significant number of trafficking victims identified by NGOs and officials.

In the year 2014, the Special Prosecutor's Office for Violence Against Women and Trafficking in Persons (FEVIMTRA) received ten million pesos ($680,000) to address the rights of assistance to female victims of extreme violence, including human trafficking. Similarly, many NGOs also received foreign donations or private funding, which provided the majority of specialized assistance, however, to date it is observed that the coordination between the government and the private sector on victim services is weak (U.S. Department of State 2015).

In Mexico City, FEVIMTRA operated a high-security shelter for female victims of sex trafficking and other forms of extreme violence who were participating in the legal process against their exploiters. The shelter housed an unspecified number of trafficking victims for up to 3 months; victims were not allowed to leave the shelter alone, reportedly due to safety concerns. Similarly, many nongovernmental (private) agencies at federal and state level also provide shelters for victims with emergency services, such as medical attention, food, and temporary lodging (see Table 10.2).

Prevention

According to the 2015 Human Trafficking Report, the federal and state authorities engaged in a range of anti-trafficking prevention efforts, though overall prevention efforts were inadequate given the magnitude of the problem. The interagency anti-trafficking commission met twice a year to coordinate federal government efforts and released the anti trafficking report. The government has released a national action plan for 2014–2018, which contains the strategies for prevention, protection and prosecution, to promote and coordinate cooperation among local public institutions, inspect and watch programs, actions and programs, design prevention and educational campaigns, promote local development programs aimed to prevent

Table 10.2 Center of attention and shelters for victims of trafficking in persons

	Public	Private	Total	Total w/shelter
Aguascalientes	8	0	8	0
Baja California	1	0	1	0
Baja California Sur	8	0	8	0
Chiapas	7	0	7	3
Chihuahua	5	0	5	1
Coahuila	12	1	13	0
Colima	2	0	2	1
Distrito Federal	42	22	64	18
Durango	19	0	19	1
Guanajuato	39	0	39	1
Guerrero	11	0	11	0
Hidalgo	23	0	23	1
Jalisco	7	1	8	1
México State	10	1	11	3
Michoacán	3	0	3	0
Morelos	1	0	0	0
Nayarit	9	0	9	0
Nuevo León	4	0	4	0
Oaxaca	4	1	5	2
Puebla	4	1	5	5
Querétaro	4	1	5	2
Quintana Roo	1	0	1	1
San Luis Potosí	6	0	6	1
Sinaloa	18	0	18	8
Sonora	1	0	1	0
Tabasco	26	1	27	5
Tamaulipas	2	0	2	0
Tlaxcala	18	2	20	3
Veracruz	20	0	20	2
Yucatán	1	0	1	0
Total	*316*	*31*	*346*	*59*

Source: Government of Mexico

trafficking, gather statistic data regarding Trafficking in Persons crimes, ensure adequate repatriation for foreign victims, promote agreements with NGOs for a better compliance of the National Program, educate the public on denouncing aggressors, and foster public awareness on Internet and social media risks. The federal and state governments engaged in a variety of awareness-raising activities distributing educational materials, including in indigenous languages and sign language, and publicizing phone numbers to report trafficking crimes anonymously. In the 2014 Government Report, nearly 9000 public officials were trained on the human trafficking material (see Table 10.3).

The National Human Rights Commission (CNDH) conducted extensive anti-trafficking training and awareness sessions for a range of audiences. The Federal District government provided funding to set up an anti-trafficking hotline in the capital. Officials continued efforts to prevent child sex tourism through training sessions, partnering with the tourism chamber of commerce, and distributing awareness

Table 10.3 Government agencies trained on human trafficking material

Government agencies	Number of public officials
National Institute of Penal Sciences (INACIPE)	1702
National Institute of Women	88
National Institute of Migration	898
Office of the Attorney General	938
Secretariat of Transportation and Communication	170
Secretariat of Social Development	372
Secretariat of Education	3822
Secretariat of Health	259
Secretariat of Tourism	168
Secretariat of Foreign Affairs	38
Secretariat of Labor	50
National System for Integral Family Development	449

Source: Government of Mexico

materials to reduce the demand for sexual exploitation of children in tourism destinations. While the government investigated some child sex tourism cases, it did not report how many child sex tourists it prosecuted or convicted, if any, and some NGOs alleged that some corrupt local officials allowed child sex tourism to occur. Authorities reported no efforts to reduce the demand for forced labor. The government provided anti-trafficking training or guidance for its diplomatic personnel.

Process of Reintegration of Post Trafficking Victims in Mexico

Victims of human trafficking face major problems being reintegrated into their home communities when they are freed from the situation into which they were trafficked. Social stigma and personal emotional scars must be overcome during the process of reintegration. Many victimized women may have been treated by law authorities as criminals, either for prostitution or illegal migration, and, therefore face additional problems of employment or other forms of reintegration. Assisting victims to resettle and start a new life is a daunting challenge for concerned governmental agencies and NGOs. In addition to psychological and social considerations, the victim faces the practical financial consideration of providing for life's essentials. Thus, it is important that government agencies and NGOs in Mexico work together to establish programs that provide practical assistance and help returning victims reintegrate and become productive members of their communities. In this section, I have analyzed the efforts and Government's response for the integration process of trafficking victims in the country.

In 2012, the Government of Mexico introduced and approved a new anti-trafficking law, taking down the 2007 juridical instrument. This General Law to prevent, punish, and eradicate crimes on human trafficking and to protect and assist victims of these crimes, defined trafficking as an organized crime activity, and therefore its prosecution is a task exclusive of Federal agencies, leaving the protection of victims in hands of local governments. Both local and federal governments are responsible for preventive actions. The law also prohibits all forms of human trafficking, prescribing penalties of 5–60 years imprisonment depending on the form of trafficking; these penalties are sufficiently stringent and equal to those prescribed for other serious crimes, such as rape (Cámara de Diputados del H. Congreso de la Unión 2012). However, 2 years later in 2014, Congress reformed the Anti-Trafficking Law, though this reform law remained the same as the 2012 Anti-Trafficking Law, very few changes have been made. For example, the most notable issue in this new legislation was the elimination of the term revictimization, replacing it with "avoiding the criminalization of the victims due to activities related with their trafficking situation." Additional changes in the law relate to language assistance for victims and local governments regaining their faculties to prosecute the crime of trafficking, which is possible only when it does not involve organized crime (Cámara de Diputados del H. Congreso de la Unión 2014).

In the process of reintegration, the main objective of the government is to provide a safe, dignified and enduring entry of the victim into society and a normal life. Reintegration assistance for victims of trafficking can include a wide range of services from assistance for housing, medical care and psychological, social and legal counseling, enrollment in school and professional training. In Section 6, Article 2 of the anti-trafficking law it states that it is necessary to establish an integral, adequate, efficient and effective mechanism to repair the damage already suffered by the victims. Similarly, Article 3, Section 1 states that, the Government must provide the maximum protection to all trafficked victims as well as protect their privacy, identity, liberty, security, and human rights. It is also the responsibility of the government to implement measures to ensure the total physical, psychological, and social healing of victims of human trafficking.

In Article 4, Section XIV and Article 64, Section V, the Federal trafficking law defines that government agencies should provide protection and support to victims from the moment of their rescue until they are fully reintegrated into society. However, on Article 68 the law stresses the need to protect them during the trial against the offender. On Article 88, section II the trafficking law requires the federal government to design and manage the anti-trafficking policy. That policy should cover the prevention and prosecution of the crime, and the protection, assistance and social reinsertion of the victims.

For the smooth reintegration of victims, the Federal trafficking law also requires many Secretariats to take care of those victims who need different types of assistance at the shelters. For example, Article 89, Section VII assigns the Secretariat of Health (SALUD) the physical and psychological attention for the victim in the appropriate shelters; section VIII demands the Secretariat of Labor and Social Welfare to promote agreements with the private sector aimed to provide labor guidance and job opportunities to the victims; section XI appoints the National System for Integral Family Development (DIF) the care of minors; in sections XIII the National Institute of Migration (INM) is responsible of guaranteeing the permanence of foreign victims and provide voluntary repatriation; according to section

XIV the National Institute of Women is the one in charge of assisting women victims of trafficking. Similarly, Article 90 assigns the federal government the design and management of victims' assistance and protection models that should provide at minimum legal counsel, physical and psychological attention and schooling, labor training and job opportunities.

Typology of the Center for Reintegration

The reintegration process for trafficking victims is a moral and legal responsibility of the Government of Mexico, and it is the duty of the State to provide protection to trafficked victims according to the laws. After analyzing and assessing the situation, victims are channeled into different types of shelters. In Mexico there are two types of shelters:

1. *Albergue*. These are basically a kind of shelter, which provides care for people who are in vulnerable situations during a short period of time.
2. *Refugio*. These are shelters that provide long-term support.

There are currently 59 short and long-term shelters in Mexico, which provide counseling, family reintegration, medical facilities, family support grants, legal assistance, education, vocational training and safety, among other services. The reintegration of victims of trafficking is accomplished in three phases. *Phase 1* is the initial support where shelters provide accommodations with clothing, food, medical assistance, psychological services, vocational training, physical security, translation facilities, and family reunification (at the request of the victim). Female lawyers who represent, advise, litigate, and manage administrative procedures provide legal assistance. Similarly, the psychological treatment is also provided by female staff and should be offered in a safe, private, comfortable, and cozy space. Psychological care is aimed to prevent the women from committing suicide and to manage depression, helping to stop the violence cycle and empowering women to achieve their autonomy. Medical care, although comprehensive, will be focused on the reproductive and sexual health of the victim. Social work covers a variety of tasks, coordinating and following up on victims care. The anti-trafficking law recognizes that each type of violence should be treated accordingly, and it is therefore up to social workers to assess and determine whether a victim has completed their process or not, and if they are able to reintegrate into society.

Phase 2 is a mid-term support, where victims of trafficking are empowered to establish their own small business, and the last phase (*Phase 3*) is a long-term support, where victims are ready to lead an independent life. However, shelters have an obligation to follow-up in order to ensure the smooth reintegration of victims. It is the responsibility of shelters to check if victims of trafficking continue to be with their families when they go back to their families and whether they received the appropriate support. In case the victim is living on her own, it is necessary to observe how well she is progressing in her business as well as adapting to society. Some time shelters also evaluate victims' security process, in case they complain about any type of anomaly on their security, it is the responsibility of the government and the shelter to provide adequate safety.

The reintegration process of trafficking victims is very complex and long lasting as it involves violence and exploitation, which have direct consequences on their physical, psychological, and social health. However, it is has been observed that there are three factors responsible for the smooth reintegration of these victims. The first one is the State institutions that provide support in terms of counseling, employment, training courses, health care, and various forms of protection. The way in which State institutions address human trafficking has direct effects on their process of reintegration. The second factor is the community's attitude, which is a prerequisite for the reintegration. The community must be tolerant, inclusive and must have positive attitudes towards the victims. They should not judge victims for their past at any point in time. The last and third factor is the role of civil society and organizations; these play an important role in providing information and services for victims of trafficking.

Conclusion

Trafficking in persons has an impact on the individuals; it victimizes them in all areas of their lives. At every stage of the trafficking process victims suffer physical, sexual, and psychological abuse and violence, deprivation and torture, the forced use of substances, manipulation, economic exploitation, and abusive working and living conditions. Unlike most other violent crimes, trafficking usually involves prolonged and repeated trauma. Thus, when women victims of trafficking are rescued they need special attention for their reintegration. Social, economical, cultural, religious, and political stability are some of the important factors usually considered to be most influential within the reintegration process for victims of trafficking.

In 2014, the Special Prosecutor's Office for Violence Against Women and Trafficking in Persons (FEVIMTRA) in Mexico received ten million pesos ($680,000) to provide assistance to female victims of extreme violence, including human trafficking, which is not adequate to address the trafficking problem in the country. This poor funding situation is often an obstacle for the program of reintegration process of victims.

On the other hand, the sociocultural environment into which a victim of trafficking is reintegrated plays a major role in their economy and health, but also psychological situations. Reintegration to a great extent depends on the way family relations, as well as relations in the larger social environment, are able to support and cope with victims of trafficking. This is again partly dependent on individual characteristics and behavior of the trafficking victim. For the reintegration process, it is also often required a certain readaptation from the person being reintegrated. Where issues of social acceptance and individual readaptation are not properly addressed, stigmatization can become a dominant force of condemnation affecting a victim of trafficking in such negative ways that some feel pushed back into their former situation.

These different issues regarding reintegration need to be approached from different perspectives, which although different, may complement each other. As an individual, reintegration is influenced by their feelings of shame and low self-esteem, dissatisfaction with life, and unfulfilled responsibilities regarding economic contributions for the family. From the point of view of the family, considerations regarding family relations, family honor, but also expectations regarding economic contributions play an important role in the reintegration process. In the social, cultural, and religious environments, the incorrect behavior and contagion can lead to gossip and social stigmatization with regard to victims of trafficking.

Although during the last 15 years Mexico has worked hard to fight against trafficking, to date the response from the government is not very effective in terms of prosecution, protection, and prevention of human trafficking in the country. There is an urgent need to increase funding, train staff, provide effective protection for witnesses and victims, increase training on victim identification and treatment for law enforcement officers, immigration officials, labor inspectors, prosecutors, judges, social workers, and other government employees; ensuring that anti-trafficking legislation at the federal and state levels reflect international anti-trafficking laws; and improve coordination mechanisms between federal, state, and local authorities.

References

Acharya, A. (2010). Feminization of migration and trafficking of women in Mexico. *Review of Research and Social Intervention, 30*, 19–38.

Acharya, A. K., & Bryson, C. J. (2014). Trafficking of women and vulnerability to HIV/STI infection in urban Mexico. *Genus*, 70(2–3). doi: 10.4402/genus-603.

Azaola, E. (1998). *Prostitución infantil. Salud, IV Informe sobre los derechos y la situación de la infancia en México* (pp. 297–315). México: Colectivo Mexicano de Apoyo a la Niñez.

Azaola, E., & Estes, R. J. (Eds.). (2003). *La Infancia como Mercancía Sexual: Mexico, Canada, Estados Unidos* (1st ed.). Mexico: Siglo XXI.

Cámara de Diputados del H. Congreso de la Unión (2012). Ley General Para Prevenir, Sancionar y Erradicar los Delitos en Materia de Trata de Personas y Para la Protección y Asistencia a las Víctimas de estos Delitos. Nueva Ley DOF 14-06-2012, Government of Mexico. Retrieved June 16, 2015, from http://www.inmujeres.gob.mx/inmujeres/images/stories/normateca/legislacion2014/lgpsedmtp.pdf

Cámara de Diputados del H. Congreso de la Unión (2014). Ley General Para Prevenir, Sancionar y Erradicar los Delitos en Materia de Trata de Personas y Para la Protección y Asistencia a las Víctimas de estos Delitos. Última Reforma DOF 19-03-2014, Government of Mexico. Retrieved June 16, 2015, from http://www.diputados.gob.mx/LeyesBiblio/pdf/LGPSEDMTP.pdf

COHA (Council on Hemispheric Affairs) (2009). Modern Day Slavery in Mexico and the United States. December 21, 1250 Connecticut Ave, N.W., Suite 1C Washington, D.C. Retrieved June 16, 2015, from http://www.coha.org/modern-day-slavery-in-mexico-and-the-united-states/

Comisión Nacional de los Derechos Humanos (CNDH). (2013). *Diagnóstico sobre la Situación de la Trata de Personas en México, Primera edición: diciembre, ISBN: 978-607-729-047-6, Comisión Nacional de los Derechos Humanos, Periférico Sur 3469, México, D.F.* Retrieved June 16, 2015, from http://www.senado.gob.mx/comisiones/trata_personas/docs/Diagnostico_Trata.pdf.

Crawford, M., & Kaufman, M. R. (2008). Sex trafficking in Nepal: Survivor characteristics long term outcomes. *Violence Against Women, 14*(8).

Esteinou, R. (2011). Selling bodies and sexual exploitation: Prostitution in Mexico. In D. Rochelle et al. (Eds.), *Global perspectives on prostitution and sex trafficking: Europe, Latin America, North America and Global*. Lanham, MD: Lexington Books.

Franco, R. (1973). *La prostitución*. Diana: México.

Goldenberg, S. M., Rangel, G., Vera, A., Patterson, T. L., Abramovitz, D., Silverman, J. G., Raj, A., & Strathdee, S. A. (2012). Exploring the impact of underage sex work among female sex workers in two Mexico-US border cities. *AIDS Behaviours, 16*(4), 969–98.

González, R. (2003). *Violencia contra las mujeres deja un millón de víctimas anuales en México*. Mexico: CIMAC. Retrieved April 14, 2015, from http://www.cimacnoticias.com.mx/node/30338.

International Labour Organization (ILO) (2005). *A global alliance against forced labor*. International Labour Conference, 93rd Session, International Labor Office, Geneva.

Kara, S. (2009). *Sex trafficking: Inside the business of Modern Slavery*. New York: Columbia University Press.

Kempadoo, K., & Doezema, J. (Eds.). (1998). *Global sex workers: Rights, resistance and redefinition*. New York: Routledge.

Montalvo, T. L. (2014, November 26). *Víctimas de trata en México se duplican en el último año: la mayoría son mujeres y niñas, Animal Político*. Retrieved June 16, 2015, from http://www.animalpolitico.com/2014/11/victimas-de-trata-en-mexico-se-duplican-en-el-ultimo-ano-la-mayoria-sonmujeres-y-ninas/.

Monroy, P. (2010). *México: pasividad ante explotación sexual infantil*. Septiembre, México DF: Contralínea. Retrieved October 7, 2015, from http://contralinea.info/archivo-revista/index.php/2010/09/05/mexico-pasividad-ante-explotacion-sexual-infantil/.

ONC (Observatorio nacional ciudadano de seguridad, justicia y legalidad). (2014). *Estadística sobre la eficiencia en el combate a la trata de personas en México: un ejercicio de acceso a la información 2010–2013*. México: Observatorio nacional ciudadano de seguridad, justicia y legalidad.

Raphael, J., & Shapiro, D. L. (2004). Violence in indoor and outdoor prostitution venues. *Violence Against Women, 10*(2), 126–139.

Ríos De La Torre, G. (1991). La prostitución femenina en la ciudad de México durante el Porfirismo. Master thesis. México, UNAM.

Ruíz Torres, M. A. (2003). La Explotación sexual de Niños en Dos Ciudades Turísticas: Cancún y Acapulco. In E. Azaola, & J. R. Estes (Eds.), *La Infancia como Mercancía Sexual: Mexico, Canada, Estados Unidos*. Mexico: Siglo XXI.

Saxena, P. M., Patel, V. S., Maj, M., Maselko, J., Phillips, M. R., & Rahman, A. (2007). No health without mental health. *Lancet, 370*(9590), 859–877.

Shelley, L. (2010). *Human trafficking: A global perspective*. Cambridge: Cambridge University Press.

United States Department of State. (2001). *The trafficking in persons report-2001*. Washington DC: U.S. Department of State. Retrieved April 3, 2015, from http://www.state.gov/g/tip/rls/tiprpt/2001/.

United States Department of State. (2015). *The trafficking in persons report-2015*. Washington DC: U.S. Department of State. Retrieved April 3, 2015, from http://www.state.gov/g/tip/rls/tiprpt/2015/.

UNODC. (2014). *Global report on trafficking in persons 2014. Global report on trafficking in persons unit, research and trend analysis branch division for policy analysis and public affairs*. Vienna: United Nations Office on Drugs and Crime.

Wijers, M. (2015). Purity, victimhood and agency: Fifteen years of the UN trafficking protocol. *Anti-Trafficking Review, 4*, 56–79.

Zimmerman, C., Hossain, M., Yun, K., Gajdadziev, V., Guzun, N., Tchomarova, M., Ciarrocchi, R. A., Johansson, A., Kefurtova, A., Scodanibbio, S., Motus, M. N., Roche, B., Morison, L., & Watts, C. (2008). The health of trafficked women: A survey of women entering post-trafficking services in Europe. *American Journal of Public Health, 98*(1), 55–59.

Chapter 11
Measures in the Background of Piracy in Entertainment and Software Industry in India

Sanjeev P. Sahni, Garima Jain, and Indranath Gupta

Introduction

This chapter revolves round the idea that movie and software piracy is rampant in India. Reports concerning India suggest increasing rates of piracy with direct consequences leading up to economic loss. These reports, however, are limited to private assessments of piracy in a country. There are limited resources at a governmental level to suggest the level of piracy. Therefore, piracy as it stands in the movie and the software industry in India must be understood through the lens of private initiatives. Without going into the obvious questions surrounding the issue of methods followed in these reports to the questions as to consistency in relation to the findings, this chapter engages with the recent measures that have been considered in the movie and software industry. Although these methods have been believed to be useful in curbing piracy, their utility can be further questioned in the absence of adequate data about digital piracy. There is no reliable data to suggest and gauge increase or decrease the level of piracy in movie and software industry. The chapter concludes on a note that there is not enough evidence to connect piracy to the measures and the measures to the possible rates of piracy. It is necessary to engage in ascertaining the real dangers and the possible remedial measures to deter possible pirates.

Background

The piracy in India has been a contentious issue for a considerable period of time. This issue has been pointed in number of reports including the special 301 report published by the United States Trade Representatives. While acknowledging the

S.P. Sahni (✉) • G. Jain • I. Gupta
Jindal Institute of Behavioural Sciences, O.P. Jindal Global University, Haryana, India
e-mail: drspsahni@jgu.edu.in

E.C. Viano (ed.), *Cybercrime, Organized Crime, and Societal Responses*,
DOI 10.1007/978-3-319-44501-4_11

positive developments in maintaining a strong IP regime in India, the report has been critical about the prevailing IP enforcement issues in the country (Froman 2015).

Internet piracy has now taken center stage as far as enforcement is concerned. The study conducted by Envisional and Motion Pictures Association (MPA) (2009) suggested that the condition of online piracy in the Indian film industry is significant. The MPA study shows that Indians constitute the fourth largest illegitimate movies downloaders in the world. According to the study, the two main internet piracy methods used in India are the file-sharing "bit torrent" network, and web-based "cyber-lockers." As per the estimates made under this study, 8.2 % of the visitors to the top 10 cyber-lockers in the world are Indian users.

Often India has been criticized for its failure to curb digital piracy. Reports publishing the Indian scenario and response to piracy have shown that the rates of piracy have gone up with rapid development of technology. While the reports featuring piracy in India have cited the economic predicaments of those who are involved in the production of digital media, such reports have been published by primarily by two or three organizations (Liang and Sundaram 2011). The reports published by these organizations are not limited to the Indian subcontinent but spread across other continents. In the background of all these reports, this chapter reflects on the measures followed by the movie and software industry in the background of piracy reported in India.

Measures in the Background of Movie Piracy

"The Effects of Counterfeiting and Piracy on India's Entertainment Industry," a study released by the US Business Council (USIBC) with Ernst and Young (2008), showed that 800,000 direct jobs are lost every year due to piracy in India. It has been argued that the movie piracy rate is worst in India, although the report has quoted negligible effect on internet piracy. In 2014, for the first time, India was included in the International Piracy Watch List by the USA, a list of four countries where piracy is rampant (Srivas 2014). Nehru Place and Gaffar Market in New Delhi; Chenoy Trade Center and Hong Kong Bazaar in Hyderabad; Lamington Road and Manish Market in Mumbai are known for notorious piracy markets in India (The New India Express 2014). In 2010, PricewaterhouseCoopers reported that piracy cost the film industry nearly 1.8 million jobs and $6.2 billion to the Indian economy (The Times of India 2010). Similarly, in 2009 Motion Picture Distributors Association listed India in the top 10 countries where online piracy is the highest.

According to a report on Counterfeiting and Piracy in Indian entertainment industry by Ernst and Young (2008), the India movie industry, commonly known as Bollywood produces more than 1000 films every year on an average as compared to 500 films by Hollywood. It is further reported that Bollywood overtook Hollywood in terms of worldwide audience of 3 billion as compared to 2.6 billion for Hollywood. But surprisingly, Bollywood made only half the revenue to Hollywood (Chakravorty 2014). Report by US India Business Council and Ernst and Young (2008) stated counterfeiting and piracy as the chief causes behind shrinking revenues. It has been further reported that as an English speaking country India has the highest level of film piracy after the USA, Great Britain, and Canada (Borpujari 2009). This gives us the impression that in India, piracy is a very significant issue in film industry. Every year, the industry loses a massive portion of its potential profits to digital piracy (Lorenzen and Taube 2008). However, an important observation that needs to be made is that the domestic theatrical revenue is consistently growing every year in spite of an increase in the number of Internet users and consequent increase in digital piracy of movies (Scaria 2013).

Multiple Releases of Print Across the Country

Indian film industry is expected to grow from $1.8 billion in 2011 to $2.8 billion in 2016, i.e., Compound Annual Growth Rate of 9.9 % for the next 5 years (Prabhakar 2013). Confederation of Indian Industry, PricewaterhouseCoopers (2012) reported that at these rates, "the Indian box office is among[st] the fastest growing markets in the world next only to China in a market greater than $276 million." According to a report by Deloitt, 60 % of the Bollywood movie box office collection is made during their first week of release (DNA India 2016). "It is expected," moreover, "that in the next few years, the Indian (box office) market will surpass the UK market (as well as that of Australia) and will be the fifth largest market in the world by 2016" (DNA India 2016). Looking at the recent trend, box office revenues have quadrupled since 2000. Since 2008, the movies surpassing box office collection of $ 1 billion and above have increased steadily (Table 11.1) (DNA India 2016).

There is a progressive increase in the number of movies making the $ 1 billion dollar mark (Mitter 2016). The aforementioned table prime facie raises an important issue in connection with the growing piracy concerns in India. In the context of the widely accepted economic argument that piracy reduces incentive, the Indian film industry is flourishing even at times when piracy has been claimed to be rampant.

Table 11.1 The Revenue of Indian Box Office (2008–2015)

Year	No. of movies	Highest ($M)
2008	1	17.88
2009	1	31.75
2010	2	21.78
2011	5	23.34
2012	9	31.17
2013	8	44.58
2014	9	53.4
2015	4	46.28

Piracy is not perhaps a straightforward economic argument but it is an outcome of one of the possible steps taken by stakeholders (Mitter 2016).

Delayed release of films across small towns in India is the leading cause of piracy in movie industry (Mane 2013). Before digitization, movie releases were confined to Tier 1 and Tier 2 cities (Dubey 2012). The film industry sought to combat piracy through technological and innovative distributions. The CEO of UFO Films, Rajesh Mishra explains, "Films are promoted heavily in India through every possible medium, reaching every possible person, down to the smallest village. But filmmakers in past ended up releasing in only a few centers. So you created a hunger but didn't give the food to everyone" (Hammer 2014). By the time the legitimate prints of the movies reach the screens in the small towns, the pirates filled the vacuum by supplying CDs/DVDs at cheaper rates (Dubey 2012).

In an attempt to cut piracy in 2006, Telugu Film industry began mass screening of movies in Andhra Pradesh, which saw an increase in revenues (Kumanath 2006). Owing to digitization, the distribution cost have reduced considerably by two-thirds (Mane 2013). Cost of printing and physical transportation of the films from one place to another has been completely eliminated. As a result, it has become possible to release a film all over India at given time and day. This opportunity has increased the screening of movies, thereby, contributing towards reducing piracy and increasing revenues (Mane 2013). For instance, it was possible to release 800 prints of *Kahani*, a small budget film, and it accumulated a gross revenue of INR 69 crore. Had it been pre-digitization era, the movie would not have been released more than 200 prints (Mane 2013). It has been estimated by FICCI-KPMG entertainment (2011) that domestic theatrical industry is expected to grow at a Compound Annual Growth Rate of 10.8 % to cross $ 2230 Million in 2017.

Early Television Premier of Movies

In order to tackle piracy, Indian film producers have been releasing movies for television viewers (Table 11.2).

The aforementioned table represents some of the popular films and their television premiers (Filloux 2012). According to Ernst and Young Report (2012), the revenues from the theater segment constitute 60 % of the total revenue for the producers. Further, producers have started pre-selling the satellite and home-video rights to alternative media (e.g., offering apps and websites where movies are avail-

Table 11.2 Early Premier of Bollywood Movies on Television

Movie	Release date	TV Premiere
Agneepath	Nov 2011	June 2012
Ek Tha Tiger	Aug 2012	Nov 2012
Rowdy Rathore	May 2012	Nov 2012
Son of Sardaar	Nov 2012	Jan 2013

able on rent) (CII, Pricewatercoopers 2012). With the advent of 3G services on mobile phones, producers are introducing mobile gaming and online platforms to reduce the movie's dependence on theatrical performance (DNA India 2016).

Shortening release windows, expanding the number of screens, and increasing the number of media do not take pirated prints off the market (Hammer 2014). Nevertheless, by increasing the availability of legitimate copies, producers are de-risking their business model by making pirated copies less attractive for the consumers (Hammer 2014).

Direct to Home/Satellite Innovation Broadcast

Historically, home video market in India has been highly fragmented. Prior to 2007, no single company had been able to capture significant market share as none had the distribution capability or a large content base in multiple languages. Further, there was rampant piracy eating into the market share of brands. As a response, T-Series, Ultra, Time, and Venus attempted to set up an association called "Video Federation of India" in 2001. The association estimated that video industry market including video cassettes and video CDs was estimated at $ 7.84 Million in 2001. Including the pirated market, the size was 10 times more and was estimated at $ 78.425 Million (Subramanian 2001). In 2002, IMI estimated a loss of INR 200 crore owing to music piracy, while in 2008, USIBC-E&Y US (2008) Chamber's Global Intellectual Property Centre reported a loss of $4 billion.

The "legal" players used to price home VCD/DVDs at a premium and stressed upon the quality difference compared to pirated videos. Though this approach created a profitable channel, home viewing formed a much smaller share of film industry revenue than it did in markets like the USA.

In 2006, a Chennai based manufacturer of Optical Media, Moser Baer reconfigured the issue of piracy in terms of affordability and immediate access (Business Today 2010). They began offering CDs and VCDs at a substantial low rates from $ 0.44 to $ 0.53. Through this strategy they claimed to have reduced piracy by 20–30 % (The Hindu Business Line 2009).

According to a report by Global advisory firm Deloitte, Bollywood is now resorting to use Electronic Sell Through (EST) mechanism to check piracy. Through EST, consumers can buy digital copies of films for unlimited viewing on demand via mobile, Internet and cable in exchange of a transactional fee (DNA India 2016). In 2014, the Film and Television Producers Guild of India (FTPGI) in association with Motion Picture Distribution Association, India launched a new website www.findanymovie.in with the aim of giving access to movies and television shows of high definition quality legally.

In 2016, arguably India's black market of piracy got its biggest competitor in the form of Netflix (Poorvaja and Kandavel 2016). It has revolutionized the entertainment industry in western country through its video streaming service. In a study (2014), Waterloo, Ont., tech company estimated that Netflix alone accounts for 35 %

of all downloading traffic during peak hours in North America (Harris 2015). Whereas, BitTorrent (an illegal file sharing tool for pirated content), accounted for 2.8 % of the same traffic as compared to 7.6 % in 2011 (Harris 2015). However, the role of Netflix in Indian market to curb piracy remains speculative. Netflix offers a minimum subscription of Rs. 500 per month for unlimited access to all content in standard definition resolution, which appears steep when compared with home grown competitors. Eros Now's subscription starts at Rs. 49 per month, while Hotstar is available for free (Srivastava 2016). Second challenge for Netflix in Indian market is slow internet speed and slow data caps. For instance, in order to stream movies and TV shows in HD quality, Netflix recommends that its users need a minimum of 0.5 Mbps per second for broadband connection and an Internet speed of 5 Mbps (Srivastava 2016). Despite of existing challenges, the fact remains that Netflix has over 75 million subscribers over 190 countries and believes in delivering personalized, advertising free, high quality at a time convenient to the viewer (Srivastava 2016). Netflix's business model is simple. They offer a month's free trial and once users experience the exclusive, original, and gripping content in HD, users will be willing to pay the subscription price for a good quality. It will be interesting to see the trend of piracy with upcoming of Netflix in years to come (Srivastava 2016).

Awareness Through Education Campaigns

According to a recent report by Ernst and Young (2008), there is a substantial "lack of consumer awareness about the implications of copyright infringement" within India.

Wikimedia Foundation (2013) conducted a series of interviews in Pune to study how people view copyright violation. Every interviewee admitted that copyright as an issue is not as important in India as in the USA or Europe. Respondents further revealed that copyright was never taught in Indian schools. (Wikipedia)

> "People (in India) have absolutely no idea about copyright ... There's just no cultural awareness of copyright. It only happens when you go to master's or grad level. Then you understand a little more about copyright. It's the same for software. If you want Word, you just download a bootleg copy."
>
> "(Response to question: Was copyright/plagiarism ever mentioned in any of your classes in India?) "Never. Not a word."
>
> "I don't think any of my professors ever used the term copyright or plagiarism."

The study clearly raises the issue of lack of sensitization about copyright and piracy at schools. To rectify this problem of awareness, Telugu film industry launched an iMovieCopp app in 2013 (Rao 2014). The users were educated about anti-piracy laws, copyright infringement, and content protection through various interactive activities (Rao 2014).

Although these campaigns are relatively recent, it appears that they have had some success. Not only have reports emerged of consumers refusing to purchase or download illegal copies (Kaushik 2014), it also appears that the educational campaigns may have even mobilized consumers to take direct action against camcorders.

The 12th 5 Year Plan set out an "anti-piracy initiative" to deal with "audio-visual" piracy (Laghate 2012). A majority of their work deals with creating awareness about piracy. They propose to implement these measures by "training judicial and administrative officials ... about the Copyright Act," "including anti-piracy awareness materials in the school curriculums," "conducting debates/essay competitions in schools and colleges about anti-piracy" among other initiatives Laghate 2012).

Federation of Indian Chambers of Commerce and Industry (Hereinafter referred to as FICCI) in collaboration with the Ministry of Human Resource Development launched an "Anti-Piracy Coordination Cell" (Kumar 2008). A substantial amount of their work involved spreading awareness about the ill-effects and illegal nature of piracy to the common public. This included mandating theaters to display FICCI's "anti-piracy" posters before every screening and conducting debates at schools and colleges among other plans (FICCI 2014). Creating these posters and in addition producing films on anti-piracy issues was also one of their initiatives.

The FICCI Committee against Smuggling and Counterfeiting Activities Destroying the Economy (CASCADE) teamed up with the Odisha Judicial State Academy (2015) in order to curb piracy and similar activities. They stated an urgent need for state officials to be made aware of how activities like piracy take place and what effects they have, since legal enforcements were not able to create the "desired deterrence" and there was a "delay in inflicting the penalties." Events of this nature seem to be of growing importance since the one mentioned above was attended by "70 trainee judges and a number of sitting high court judges."

Culture of Indian Cinema

Indian government recognized 16 major languages, but in reality there are over 700 languages with their own dialects (Lalmalsawma 2013). It is surprising to know how Indian cinema is catering to the needs of such diversified audiences (Kaur and Sinha 2005). According to India Today report from 2000 states that no film in India did well in 1999 both in urban as well as in rural India (Srinivas 2002). Nevertheless, Indian audience remained resilient and it has been estimated that around 10–15 million movie tickets were sold every day in India during 1990s (Rajadhyaksha 2003). It has been suggested that there is something unique about Indian film culture which ensures its resilience despite widespread piracy (Srinivas 1998). Unlike western countries, where audiences are silent and disciplined in their viewing style, movie experiences in India involve families, friends, and coworkers (Srinivas 1998). The emotional experience of watching movies in Indian theater is different from the contemporary Western audience of Hollywood films. Indians prefer to go to theaters in groups and indulge in group conversations about movie stars or about on screen events (Srinivas 1998).

Thus, it may be the case that the continued resilience of the Indian film industry has nothing to do with filmmakers' specific efforts, but is due to the unique place of the movie theater within Indian society and the inability of pirated films to replicate the theatrical experience (Dubey 2012). However, it must be stated that the data above is dated (from 2003) and in the absence of recent data, the authors are not making any claims as to the present day situation in India.

In the midst of the claim that there are rampant cases of piracy in the Indian entertainment industry, "box-office" figures for some of the films have been excellent. In a report released by Ernst and Young (2008), it is revealed that the producers have been able to recover $ 15.58 million in the first week. Furthermore, the aforementioned alternative measures is a true reflection of the effective use of technology and other innovative ways to maximize returns of investments made in films. Without the available options it would have been difficult to recover the money invested at the current pace. On the contrary, one may argue that producers were forced to innovate to minimize the negative effects of piracy; however, there is the need to conduct further research to authenticate such claims. Even if we link these efforts to curb digital piracy, there is not enough evidence to suggest that piracy rates have gone down since these efforts have been adopted. Instead, the ever increasing rates of piracy at stated in multiple reports do suggest that these efforts have not been adequate.

The Complexities of Software Piracy: Availability of Data and Measures to Curb

Software piracy, while recognized as a major concern and threat to the nation's economic and creative landscape, still lacks proper infrastructure to ensure that it remains at a minimum. Various reasons have been cited for the same, ranging from cultural dissonance towards IP, where we as a culture do not recognize or respect individual creations enough to value them monetarily to plain economic reasons of affordability in a huge developing market where first time users would tend to resort to piracy (Global Annual Piracy Study, BSA 2006). However, all of this being said, there still lacks statistical data from India which shows us at what rate software piracy in India occurs (Froman 2015). There seems to be only one consistent source for the same, namely the Annual BSA-IDC Global Software Piracy Studies.

Reporting of Software Piracy in India and Role of Business Software Alliance (BSA)

The BSA is a "nonprofit trade association created to advance the goals of the software industry and its hardware partners" (BSA 2015). A majority of the organizations work involves curbing piracy and infringement of their member organizations intellectual property. Their goals, among others, involve "opening markets to barrier free trade," "data security," and "software innovation and choice" (Froman 2015). The initiatives trickle down to detecting piracy committed by end users. They routinely track activity on auction sites which gives them firsthand data about pirated software and the distribution of the same (Froman 2015).

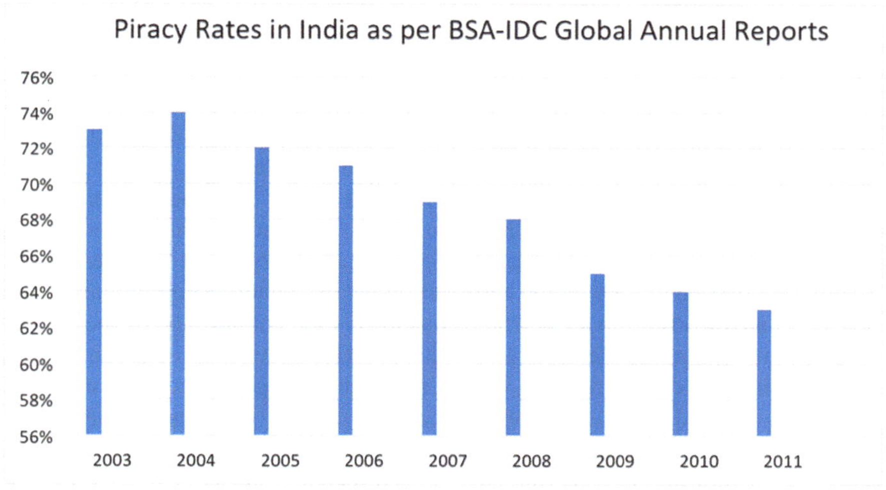

Fig. 11.1 Piracy Rates in India as per BSA- IDC Global Annual Reports

One of BSA's most noticeable works involves their Annual Global BSA-IDC Software Piracy reports. Started in 2004, these reports have served as one of the only statistical sources available which provide piracy statistics on a global scale (Global Annual Piracy Study, BSA 2006). BSA collects data for these reports from their member companies, which are published along with the International Data Corporation (BSA 2015).

In addition to conducting audits and raids to put a stop to software piracy (Fox News 2007), they encourage people to report instances of software piracy that they might have come across at workplaces and sometimes promise hefty rewards (Fig. 11.1).

BSA and India

In the 2004 study India was one of the top 20 pirating countries, featuring at the last place with a piracy rate of 73 %. According to Fourth Annual BSA and IDC Global Software Piracy report (2007), the situation since then seems to have improved. BSA has cited substantial number of reasons explaining the decline, ranging from conducting "search and seizures" (Anton Piller orders[1] in the State of Karnataka (6th Annual BSA/IDC Piracy Study 2008) to "government and industry education

[1] http://www.businessdictionary.com/definition/Anton-Piller-order.html (Anton Piller orders are issued for the sake of evidence not being destroyed. Defendants have to allow Plaintiff's to enter their premises and also to conduct searches. These orders are prevalent in cases of copyright infringement.)

and enforcement efforts, software vendor activation controls, and an increase in PC market share by multinational vendors (5th Annual BSA/IDC Piracy Study 2007)." The 2007 report also mentions that "the slower market growth in the developed world since 2000 has heightened awareness about the importance of lowering piracy in emerging economies." Regardless of the decline, the piracy rates still remain fairly high since around 60 % of software used is unlicensed.

Emerging economies have consistently higher piracy rates because there is a constant influx of new users who resort to piracy. More access to internet in these countries increases the level of piracy, however, this argument is based on the assumption that new users would resort to piracy by default. The rationale is that new users are mostly from areas where consumers may not have the finances available to purchase legitimate software. Culture is also thought to be a contributing factor to piracy in certain regions, where "intellectual property is viewed more as a common good and not the creator's property." Further, "weak institutional infrastructure" makes it difficult to educate people about piracy. The threat of piracy has therefore "driven investments that have helped increase anti-piracy education and enforcement and, through partnerships and joint ventures, helped drive local industry revenues (5th Annual BSA/IDC Piracy Study 2007)"

The stronghold that BSA has in India can be witnessed in the 227th Parliamentary Standing Committee Report (2010). The report discusses the Copyright Bill of 2010, which went on to become the latest Act. While commenting on several aspects of the bill, opinions of BSA and other organizations like Yahoo India, Google India and Indian Performing Right Society Limited were considered by the Committee.

For instance, BSA's input was considered, while deciding upon the scope of an "infringing copy." The bill attempted to introduce a proviso, which stated that any work from outside India, if brought into the country with the permission of the author would not be considered as an infringement. BSA stated that such a proviso would render it difficult or even impossible for law enforcement agencies to "apprehend illegal copies." Further, it would cause "imbalance of trade and counterfeiting activities across borders."

While there may be questions as to the methods adopted in all these BSA reports, there is considerable amount of monopoly of BSA in case of software piracy reports. Although in a limited way the comparison reports of the movie and software industry show that there is a reduction in the rate of software piracy, credible empirical evidence and further research must be conducted to establish the ground realities.

Measures Adopted to Curb Piracy: Industry and Government Initiatives

In an effort to curb the rampant software piracy, one evolving measures adopted by software industry is the use of cloud based technology (Etherington 2013). Adobe for instance, with its 2013 version of Photoshop, made sure that some of the features and services were only available on the cloud, for which a subscription was necessary (Etherington 2013). The company has also made sure that the process of subscribing and using the cloud is less cumbersome than manually installing the software, therefore deterring possible pirates (Etherington 2013).

Microsoft recently gave away Windows 10 for free to existing Windows 8 users as an attempt to curb piracy (Tassi 2015). As a part of this unusual move, they ensured that all existing users with "qualified devices" running on either pirated or genuine software could upgrade to Windows 10 for free (Tassi 2015). This move has been seen as a way for Microsoft to give users of pirated software a "clean slate" (Tassi 2015). If they could successfully turn existing pirates into actual customers, the same people would perhaps be likely to buy their other products (Tassi 2015). What is common in all the recent initiatives is an effort to centralize the resources available to the customers, whether it be through cloud based technology or through using websites to generate license keys.

According to a survey conducted by BSA, 43 % of computer users in India admitted to acquiring pirated software (Gupta 2013). To curb the menace, BSA in 2013 started working in collaboration with Department of Information Technology, Government of India, large enterprises and SMEs in India to raise the awareness about software in India.

It is argued that escalating cost of software is a major concern for the price sensitive customers in India (Jena 2007). However, Brian Campbell, Director, Original Software Initiative, Microsoft India commented on the high cost of software and said, "People pirate software because buying it is too expensive is oversimplifying the issue. People are willing to pay for content they value, if it is priced reasonably and if they see adequate benefits in purchasing original content versus pirated. If customers see value, they will be willing to pay the price and this is what we are focused on. One must remember that low cost software is not the only response to piracy as even low priced software can be pirated (Jena 2007)." To better understand status of software piracy in India, Microsoft conducted a survey in 2010 with 2000 respondents in India. It was found that 75 % of the customers in India believe that genuine software is more secure and stable. 86 % of respondents said that they were ready to pay for genuine software; while 79 % felt that there is need to create awareness about illegal software (The Economic Times 2010). As a response to their understanding of Indian market, Microsoft adopted three pronged approach which focused on education, engineering and enforcement (Jena 2007).

Microsoft India is working with policy makers, government and judiciary to educate consumers about consequences of piracy. They are establishing IPR courts in different parts of the country; e.g.: Karnataka and West Bengal and providing IPR scholarships to the National Law College. They are spreading awareness among customers, business and SMEs about IPR laws and the fact that pirated software are more vulnerable to virus attacks than genuine software (Suryanarayana 2007).

Secondly, they are making use of engineering and technology to deal with the piracy menace where if the user is not using genuine Windows software, then they will operate in "Reduced Functionality Mode," where the user cannot download anything other than security updates (OneIndia 2006).

Their third lever is Enforcement. Microsoft India have partnered with FICCI and NASSCOM for channelizing enforcement of laws (Suryanarayana 2007). They have acknowledged that users in India are gradually recognizing the risk of using counterfeit software. In 2010, Microsoft reported that 6000 Indian customers reported incidents of pirated or illegal software to them (The Economic Times 2010).

Similarly, Adobe has also established case support system which comprises of experienced legal experts who help build and prosecute piracy cases (Gupta 2013). Besides, BSA is also running several Software Asset Management (SAM) seminars since 2008 for SMEs in India (Jena 2008).

In June 2014, BSA conducted a poll in partnership with International Data Corporation (IDC) in 34 markets including 22,000 consumers and business PC users and more than 2,000 IT managers. It was found that there was a mere 4 percentage point decline in 2013 as compared to 2011 regarding the rate at which counterfeited and illegal PC software were installed in India. Less than half of the IT managers were confident that their company's software is properly licensed. Furthermore, only 33 % of the companies' studies have written policies in place on intellectual property right (Businesswire 2014).

Conclusion

Government and industries are introducing sensitization programs at the community level to spread awareness about the cost borne by the producers (low profitability), government (low revenues), and society (unemployment) due to piracy. Similarly, producers and industry are constructing innovative business model to deal with the issue of piracy (e.g., improving distribution channels by the film producers/cloud based technology).

While there has been a concentrated effort to increase revenue generation at least in the movie industry, there is little evidence to link these measures with the issue of prevailing piracy in the same industry. These efforts may be useful to curb piracy to an extent but their origin can be traced back to technological developments. In comparison, the efforts emanating from the software industry are connected to the reported loss in the reports. While the efforts in both the industries are worth reflecting, there is a need to explore the rates of piracy and the measured efforts. We have already observed legislative changes based on industry reports. In the background of the overwhelming piracy rates, developments in relation to piracy rates must be carefully scrutinized before bringing about any further changes in future. Therefore, there is a need to promote a platform for various stakeholders (government, industry, producers, legislators, policy makers, and researchers) to devise an effective model to deal with the situation more efficiently.

References

Borpujari, U. (2009). India major online film piracy hub. Deccan Herald. Retrieved from http://www.deccanherald.com/content/41541/india-major-online-film-piracy.html

Business Software Alliance, Global Annual Piracy Study. (2006). *Fourth Annual BSA and IDC Global Software Piracy Study*. Retrieved from http://globalstudy.bsa.org/2007/studies/2007_global_piracy_study.pdf

Business Software Alliance, Global Annual Piracy Study. (2008). *Sixth Annual BSA and IDC Global Software Piracy Study*. Retrieved from globalstudy.bsa.org/2008/studies/globalpiracy2008.pdf

Business Software Alliance. (2015). About BSA and Members. Accessed March 8, 2016 from http://ww2.bsa.org/country/BSA%20and%20Members.aspx

Chakravorty, V. (2014, January 25). Our films, their films: A comparison between Bollywood and Hollywood. *India Today*. Retrieved from http://indiatoday.intoday.in/story/our-films-their-films-a-comparison-between-bollywood-and-hollywood/1/339715.html

Confederation of Indian Industry, PricewaterhouseCoopers. (2012). India Entertainment and Media Outlook 2012. Retrieved from http://cii.in/WebCMS/Upload/em%20version%202_low%20res.PDF

Dubey, B. (2012). Digitization renders film reels redundant. *The Times of India*. Retrieved from http://timesofindia.indiatimes.com/entertainment/hindi/bollywood/news/Digitization-renders-film-reels-redundant/articleshow/11669556.cms

Envisional and Motion Pictures Association, India: Internet Piracy Landscape Audit. (2009). *India: Internet Piracy Landscape Audit*. Retrieved from aact.co.in/downloads/reports/Sep2009-IndiaInternetPiracyLandscapeAudit.pdf.

Ernst and Young. LA – India Film Council, Film Industry in India: New Horizons. (2012). *Film industry in India: New horizons*. Retrieved from http://indiainbusiness.nic.in/newdesign/upload/news/New_Horizons_Final.pdf.

Etherington, D. (2013, June 21). Adobe Photoshop CC Proves That The Cloud Isn't A Cure-All Refuge From Software Piracy. *Techcrunch*. Retrieved from techcrunch.com/2013/06/21/adobe-photoshop-cc-proves-that-the-cloud-isnt-a-cure-all-refuge-from-software-piracy/

Federation of Indian Chamber of Commerce and Industries with Intellectual Property Office. (April, 2014). *World Intellectual Property Day*. Retrieved from http://ipindia.nic.in/iponew/world_IP_Day_22August2014.pdf

FICCI-KPMG India Media and Entertainment Industry Report. (2011). Hitting the High Notes. Retreived from http://www.kpmg.com/IN/en/IssuesAndInsights/ArticlesPublications/Documents/FICCI-KPMG-Report-2011.pdf

Filloux, F. (2012, November 26). Different release times of films and TV shows boost global piracy. The Guardian. Retrieved from http://www.theguardian.com/technology/2012/nov/26/films-tvs-global-piracy

Froman, M. B. G. (2015). United States Trade Representative. 2015 Special 301 Report. Retrieved from https://ustr.gov/sites/default/files/2015-Special-301-Report-FINAL.pdf

Gupta, Y. (2013, March 12). Software Piracy: Will Joint Effort By Vendors And Industry Associations End The Menace?. *ChannelWorld*. Retrieved from http://www.channelworld.in/features/will-joint-effort-vendors-and-industry-associations-end-menace

Harris, S. (2015, May 7). Netflix helps reform hard-core movie pirates, but at a cost. *CBC News*. Retrieved from http://www.cbc.ca/news/business/netflix-helps-reform-hard-core-movie-pirates-but-at-a-cost-1.3063800

Here's How Bollywood Aims to Fight Piracy. (2016, Feb 7). DNA India. Retrieved from http://www.dnaindia.com/money/report-here-s-how-bollywood-aims-to-fight-piracy-2174996

Hammer, B. (2014). Smooth sailing: Why the Indian film industry remains extremely successful in the face of massive piracy. *Harvard Journal of Sports & Entertainment Law, 5*, 147.

Jena, C. (2007, September 24). Miles to go before curbing Software Piracy. Firstpost. Retrieved from http://m.firstpost.com/business/biztech/views/features/miles-to-go-before-curbing--software-piracy-1861963.html

Jena, C. (2008, June 17). Software Asset Management Enhances Business Productivity. *Firstpost.* Retrieved from http://www.firstpost.com/business/biztech/views/features/software-asset-management-enhances-business-productivity-1864633.html.

Kaur, R., & Sinha, A. J. (2005). *Bollyworld: Popular Indian cinema through a transnational lens.* New Delhi: SAGE Publications Private Limited.

Kaushik, P. (2014). Camcorder video piracy in India and who it affects the most. *The BusinessInsider*. Retrieved from http://www.businessinsider.in/Camcorder-Video-Piracy-In-India-And-Who-It-Affects-The-Most/articleshow/45601157.cms

Kurmanath, K.V. (2006, September. 29). Finding new ways to curb piracy. *The Hindu Business Line*. Retrieved from http://www.thehindubusinessline.com/todays-paper/tp-economy/finding-new-ways-to-curb-piracy/article1747515.ece

Kumar, V. R. (2008). Software body working on anti-piracy task force. *The Hindu Business Line*. Retrivedd from http://www.thehindubusinessline.com/todays-paper/tp-info-tech/software-body-working-on-antipiracy-task-force/article1632064.ece

Laghate, G. (2012). I&B Ministry approves anti-piracy initiative in the XII plan. *The Business Standard*. Retrieved from http://www.business-standard.com/article/economy-policy/i-b-ministry-approves-anti-piracy-initiative-in-the-xii-plan-112112803003_1.html

Liang, L., & Sundaram, R. (2011). India. Karaganis, J. (Ed.). *Media piracy in emerging economies*. Lulu. com.

Lorenzen, M., & Täube, F. A. (2008). Breakout from Bollywood? The roles of social networks and regulation in the evolution of Indian film industry. *Journal of International Management, 14*(3), 286–299.

Mane, T. (2013). Lights, Camera, Digital. *Outlook Business*. Retrieved from http://www.outlookbusiness.com/the-big-story/lead-story/lights-camera-digital-309

Microsoft Launches Genuine Software Initiative in India. (2006, May 31). *OneIndia*. Retrieved from http://www.oneindia.com/2006/05/31/microsoft-launches-genuine-software-initiative--in-india-1149073478.html.

Mitter, S. (2016). Journey of the 100-Crore Bollywood Film. *ForbesIndia*. Retrieved from http://forbesindia.com/blog/business-strategy/journey-of-the-100-crore-bollywood-film/

Moser Baer Claims Decrease in Film Piracy. (2009). *The Hindu BusinessLine*. Retrieved from http://www.thehindubusinessline.com/todays-paper/tp-marketing/moser-baer-claims-reduced-film-piracy/article1040072.ece

Most Indians Ready to Pay more for Genuine Software: Microsoft (2010, November 18). *The Economic Times.* Retrieved from http://articles.economictimes.indiatimes.com/2010-11-18/news/27606556_1_counterfeit-software-piracy-illegal-software

Nehru Place, Gaffar Market Notorious Markets for Piracy: US. (2014, February 13). *The Indian Express*. Retrieved from http://indianexpress.com/article/india/india-others/nehru-place-gaffar-market-notorious-markets-for-piracy-us/

Lalmalsawma, D. (2013, September 7). India speaks 780 languages, 220 lost in last 50 years – survey. *Reuters*. Retrieved from http://blogs.reuters.com/india/2013/09/07/india-speaks-780-languages-220-lost-in-last-50-years-survey/.

Odisha State Judicial Academy. (2015). Judiciary Sensitization Programme on Smuggling, Counterfeiting and Piracy. Retrieved from http://ficci.in/events/22409/ISP/Judiciary-report-11-4.pdf

Piracy Cost Bollywood $959m: Report. (2010, March 20). The Times of India. Retrieved from http://timesofindia.indiatimes.com/india/Piracy-cost-Bollywood-959m-Report/articleshow/5703165.cms

Prabhakar, B. (2013, February 3). Bollywood no longer talks of piracy; but ignoring dangers of online can be costly. *The Economic Times*. Retrieved from http://articles.economictimes.indiatimes.com/2013-02-03/news/36704530_1_piracy-box-office-alliance-against-copyright-theft

Poorvaja, S. & Kandavel, A. (2016). Mixed Reactions to arrival of Netflix. *The Hindu*. Retrieved from http://www.thehindu.com/news/cities/chennai/mixed-reaction-to-arrival-of-netflix/article8080584.ece
Rajadhyaksha, A. (2003). The 'Bollywoodization' of the Indian cinema: cultural nationalism in a global arena. *Inter-Asia Cultural Studies, 4*(1), 25–39.
Rao, C. S. (2014, October 11). Film industry's iMovieCop app to fight anti-piracy may get a mascot. *The Times of India*. Retrieved from http://timesofindia.indiatimes.com/city/hyderabad/Film-industrys-iMovieCop-app-to-fight-anti-piracy-may-get-a-mascot/articleshow/44784763.cms
Scaria, A. G. (2013). Online piracy of Indian movies: Is the film industry firing at the wrong target? *Michigan State International Law Review, 21*(3), 647–663.
Srinivas, L. (1998). Active viewing: An ethnography of the Indian film audience. *Visual Anthropology, 11*, 323–353.
Srinivas, L. (2002). The active audience: Spectatorship, social relations and the experience of cinema in India. *Media Culture & Society, 24*(2), 155–173.
Srivas, A. (2014). U.S. government panel puts India on piracy watch list. *The Hindu*. Retrieved from http://www.thehindu.com/business/Industry/us-government-panel-puts-india-on-piracy-watch-list/article6148666.ece
Srivastava, R. (2016, February 2). Can Netflix win over India and other stories. *Livemint*. Retrieved from http://www.livemint.com/Companies/sxYn2mTT2BeCStYsyulTiK/Can-Netflix-win-over-India-and-other-stories.html
Software 'Police' Accused of Targeting Small Businesses. (2007, November 28). *Fox News*. Retrievedfromwww.foxnews.com/story/2007/11/28/software-police-accused-targeting-small--businesses.html
Subramaniam, N. (2001, October 21). Video cos form united front against piracy. *The Hindu Business Line*. Retrieved from http://www.thehindubusinessline.com/2001/10/21/stories/14218703.htm
Suryanarayana, P. S. (2007, August 22). "Ignorance of software piracy can no longer be excused". *The Hindu*. Retrieved from http://www.thehindu.com/todays-paper/tp-opinion/ignorance-of-software-piracy-can-no-longer-be-excused/article1896444.ece
Tassi, P. (2015, March 19). Why Microsoft is Giving Away Windows 10 to Pirates. *Forbes*. Retrieved from www.forbes.com/sites/insertcoin/2015/03/19/why-microsoft-is-giving-away-windows-10-to-pirates/
U.S.–India Business Council, Bollywood–Hollywood Initiative. Ernst and Young, (2008).*The Effects of Counterfeiting and Piracy on India's Entertainment Industry.* Retrieved from http://infojustice.org/wp-content/uploads/2011/02/Ernst-Young-PIracy-report-India-2009.pdf
Wikipedia: India Education Program/Analysis/WMF Interviews. Available at https://en.wikipedia.org/wiki/Wikipedia:India_Education_Program/Analysis/WMF_interviews

Chapter 12
Crime and Antisocial Behaviors in Male Adolescents: An Exploratory Study in the City of Ribeirão Preto, São Paulo Brazil

André Vilela Komatsu and Marina Rezende Bazon

Introduction

Adolescence is a stage of life that concentrates risk behaviors, including those that constitute violation of any law (Farrington et al. 2006; Vermeersch et al. 2013). Thus, criminal behaviors, to some extent, are part of a statistically normative process, related to age and to the typical tasks associated with the development of identity and self-regulation and in a context to gain personal autonomy, according to studies carried out in different social settings (Le Blanc 2003; Mun et al. 2008). For a number of adolescents, however, this type of behavior becomes more frequent and diverse and sometimes results in serious and violent actions (Hoge 2009). In this case, the behavior does not seem to be related solely to typical developmental tasks, but to difficulties and to important psychosocial lags, revealing a significant level of criminal engagement (Carrington et al. 2005; Le Blanc 2010).

Several taxonomic clusters based on different variables were proposed to provide parameters to guide the socio-judicial monitoring of juvenile offenders, and consequently, to obtain additional data on the phenomenon, considering its intrinsic heterogeneity. Previous cross sectional studies, which were based on clinical samples, dealt with information related to a single dimension analysis. Dembo et al. (1987) for example, used the nature of the offense committed by the adolescent as a categorization criterion (crime against person or property). In turn, Quay (1987) used some personal characteristics related to youth personality traits, such as immaturity, anxiety and socialization. Sorensen and Johnson (1996) combined the scores from both the Minnesota Multiphasic Personality Inventory (MMPI) and the Jesness Personality Inventory (JPI) and were able to indentify five groups of juvenile offenders based on their psychological profile. Similarly, Stefurak et al. (2004), who used

A.V. Komatsu • M.R. Bazon (✉)
University of São Paulo, Ribeirao Preto, São Paulo, Brazil
e-mail: mbazon@ffclrp.usp.br

E.C. Viano (ed.), *Cybercrime, Organized Crime, and Societal Responses*,
DOI 10.1007/978-3-319-44501-4_12

the Millon Adolescent Clinical Inventory Introduction (MACI), identified four groups of juvenile offenders. In 2010, Mowder identified four groups of juvenile offenders using the resilience level as a criterion measured by The Resiliency Scales for Children and Adolescents.

At the same time, some studies implemented with a behavioral development perspective in the lifecourse, began to advocate the importance of categorizing the adolescents by taking into account the levels of criminal engagement and by considering the variations of the manifestation of criminal behavior over time. Loeber (1990) argued that there are different developmental pathways to distinguish groups of juvenile offenders and the categorization of these youngsters and the investigation of their peculiarities may assist researchers to detect risk factors and unique processes related to each pathway. In this context, the independent variables should be those that describe the construct of criminal engagement: precocity, diversity, and frequency of criminal behaviors in adolescence (Le Blanc 2010; Piquero and Moffitt 2008).

According to Piquero and Moffitt (2008), the association between the age of the first offense and the continuation of a certain behavior that progresses into delinquency are well documented in studies on the topic. The sooner an individual commits an offense, the higher the probability of committing new crimes and even more violent offenses later. Furthermore, research data in different contexts show that an antisocial behavior at early age is also positively related to greater frequency and different types of crimes committed by adolescents (Le Blanc 2010; Moffitt 2003).

In this way, Moffitt's Theory of delinquency (1993) proposed two distinctive pathways of juvenile delinquency: (1) life-course persistent, for offenders who engage in criminal activity in childhood and continue criminality in adulthood; and (2) adolescence-limited, when the antisocial behavior only exists during the teenage years. The author described that the combination of a poor social environment and neuropsychological deficits leads an individual down a pathway for persistent criminal behavior. For those individuals who engage in deviant behaviors only during adolescence, the cause is justified by their exposure to models (generally in pairs) that present antisocial behaviors and their search for social support. Moffitt (1993) estimated the predominance of two types of trajectories using data based on *rates* of *antisocial behaviors* provided by parents, teachers and the adolescents. According to the author, chronic offending is relatively rare, as only 5 % of adolescents persist in antisocial behavior into adulthood. The average of offenses in this group was *more than* one *standard deviation* above the norm of more than 1000 adolescents participating in the study.

With the similar perspective, Le Blanc (2003, 2010) suggested three meta-trajectories that describe differences in the level of criminal engagement in adolescence: common, transitory, and persistent (or distinctive). For *common delinquency*, the offenders are occasionally involved in a criminal activity motivated by the search for pleasure and excitement, set in a life context of respect for the laws and social rules. This would be presented by the majority of young people and tend to cease spontaneously. *Transitory delinquency* differs from C*ommon delinquency* to the extent that its early manifestation, the number and diversity of the offenses make it more serious, with causes that go beyond merely situational aspects. It is essentially the result of adolescence crisis and the transgressive acts may represent more than a recreational activity with pleasant benefits; it is also a rebellious act against social rules and may become a personal identification, mainly when affiliated with deviant peers (Le Blanc and Morizot 2000). Adolescents with a criminal behavior pattern which characterizes *Transitory delinquency* would be more susceptible to being arrested or getting involved in legal matters. According to the author, *Persistent delinquency* is manifested by a minority of adolescents. However, they would present what the literature refers to as "criminal engagement," which is characterized by early antisocial acts, frequent and diverse offenses, becoming increasingly serious and may also include the use of violence against anyone (Carrington et al. 2005; Le Blanc 2010).

This proposition is the result of the studies carried out by Le Blanc and Fréchette (1989) and with the participation of 1684 Canadian non-offenders and 470 adolescents with legal problems, ages between 7 and 25 years. Some self-report questionnaires were applied in 2-year intervals to allow the authors to follow the process of activation, aggravation, and desistance. The authors have also determined that some offenses were common to most adolescents, such as theft of less valuable objects, while other offenses, such as aggravated assault, were committed by adolescents engaged in more serious criminal acts.

In Brazil, no studies on this topic were carried out so far, although the *juvenile crime* rate has soared. The state of São Paulo, alone, has more adolescents arrested due to criminal activities than all countries in South America (Fundação CASA 2011). According to sources, the rates of criminal acts by adolescents may be increasing. A survey (Uribe 2013) has shown that the rate of arrested adolescents, aged between 12 and 18, increased 14.3 % in 2012 compared to the past year, and were responsible for 18 % of the total number of arrests in the country in the same year.

With regards to the severity of crimes committed by adolescents, according to the annual publication of the Fórum Brasileiro de Segurança Pública (2014), only 12 % of violent crimes, such as homicide, robbery or rape, may be attributed to them. However, these offenses are widely publicized by the media, which can explain the Brazilian population claims to control these criminal activities. A research institute revealed that 87 % of the Brazilian population was in favor of reducing the age of criminal responsibility from 18 to 16 years (Datafolha 2015). It was believed that the adolescents had great responsibility for the increasing rates of criminality and this reduction would provide better conditions to correct such delinquent behavior.

The current legal framework for the protection of children's and teenagers' rights in Brazil includes references to juvenile justice and was subject to further specific legislation in 1990, when the Statute of the Child and Adolescent came into force. The juvenile justice law establishes that 18-year-old individuals should not be criminally responsible. It provides specific social legal frame for the investigation, trial and penalties of individuals responsible for offenses, with ages between 12 and 17, according to the Beijing rules adopted by the UN in 1985. The current law imposes to the judicial-decision making a requirement towards an evaluation that should consider not only the needs of society, but also the circumstances and the needs of a minor. It should be an evaluation that goes beyond a simple analysis of the criminal act, which has brought the individual to juvenile justice, in a way that the sanction, much more than a punishment, would be a socio-educational action to recognize that these adolescents are still at an early stage of human development, and therefore, require special attention and assistance, aiming at their physical, mental and social development, and a legal protection to bring them peace, freedom, dignity, and security.

In the context of the Brazilian juvenile justice, one of the challenges is to recognize the needs of the adolescents seized by police for committing offenses, and to identify among them those whose behavior is characterized as *common delinquency* and those whose behavior refers to *persistent delinquency*. Such a distinction can have positive effects on public policies in the area, contribute to make the system more dynamic and also offer relevant data for public debates about juvenile delinquency and ways of prevention and crime control. The distinction by profiles and typology would favor the adolescents to the extent that they would have their need for legal and psychosocial intervention fulfilled beyond the offense by which they are caught by police and brought to justice. It would also benefit the professionals who make decisions about the guidance to be given to young people and to those who are responsible for the socio-educational follow-up interventions. Therefore, these professionals would have more elements to plan and manage the treatment programs. Furthermore, from an institutional point of view, such a distinction would certainly reduce the intervention costs (considering the number of places in the new *socio-educational* system for *adolescents* in conflict with the law) and better quality of services offered (Maruschi and Bazon 2014).

Therefore, this study aimed to evaluate a sample of students and of juvenile offenders and to identify groups based on the levels of criminal engagement (considering the criteria of first early offense, the number and diversity of the self-reported offenses). After determining the groups, the other objective was to categorize the adolescents in terms of age, economic class, and education, use of psychoactive substances and types of offenses.

Methods

Participants

This study took place in Ribeirão Preto a medium-size city in the State of São Paulo – Brazil with approximately 600,000 inhabitants. The population with ages between 10 and 19 years represents approximately 15 %, with 7.5 % male (Atlas Brasil 2014).

A total of 193 male adolescents participated in this study, 133 were students, recruited from three public schools in the city (mean age of 14.9 years; SD = 1.4), and 60 juvenile offenders recruited from probation programs (mean age of 15.8 years; SD = 1). The criterion used to compose the samples was intentional; however, they were set up for convenience considering that the institutions had to authorize the participation of the adolescents in the study, i.e., in schools and in probation programs. Data were collected only from those participants who were willing to take part in the study and whose parents/responsible provided their free and informed consent according to resolution 466/96 of the Brazilian Health National Council (BRASIL 2012).

Instruments and Measures

The following variables were used in this study:

Divergent and criminal behaviors: Information on divergent and criminal behaviors were obtained using an instrument similar to that applied in 2006 in 30 countries based on the *Second International Self-Report Delinquency Study* (ISRD-2, Breen et al. 2010), which is used to obtain self-report delinquency data. This instrument comprises questions with focus on socio-demographic background information. There are also questions about some illegal behaviors, which are misdemeanors, according to the Brazilian Law, specifically on substance abuse (marijuana, focused on the present study) and alcohol. Fourteen questions refer to criminal behaviors that are considered crimes (damage, personal injury, fight, assault, personal injury with the use of instrument, abuse against animals, possession of stolen property, shoplifting, stealing and robbing from someone, items stolen from car, bike theft, vehicle theft, illegal gun possession, and drug trafficking). The offenses covered by the questionnaire were described in behavioral not in legal terms. For example, to investigate a crime of shoplifting, the question asked was: "Have you ever got something and didn't pay for it in a store (shops, supermarket, etc)?"

For each behavior, the respondents were asked if they had "ever" done something (regardless of whether or not they were caught by the police); this information, which referred to a group of respondents, provided the number of individuals who have committed a crime once in their lives (measuring the prevalence). Upon the affirmative response of the respondents, they had to answer the following questions: "Have you committed a similar offense in the "last 12 months" and "How often have you committed a similar offense." The information obtained from the groups of respondents made it possible to determine the prevalence of adolescents by category of behavior and frequency of each act and for each teenager during that past year.

Procedures

Data collection in schools was carried out in small groups with 10 adolescents each in a classroom. The participants read and responded the questionnaire individually. Doubts were solved by the researchers upon request. Data were obtained from each juvenile offender in a reserved room of the institution. The individual application of the questionnaire in this group created the ideal conditions for data collection, with a structured interview format, since the vast majority of adolescents in conflict with the law in Brazil are behind in their school levels. This situation reflects their poor reading and/or interpretation skills.

The data obtained were stored in spreadsheets and submitted to statistical analysis. First, a cluster analysis was carried out to place the individuals in subgroups based on similar traits. The clusters were categorized following some predetermined selection criteria that in our study was the level of criminal engagement. The parameters used to measure the levels of criminal engagement were those mentioned previously: age of first offense (the lower the age, the greater the engagement); the diversity of crimes throughout life (the greater the number of different types of offenses, the greater the criminal engagement); and the total number of offenses in the past year (the greater the total frequency of offenses, the greater the engagement).

This clustering was performed using the *Ward method***.** The results *were used* as *input* for *K-mean* clustering algorithms to adjust a non-hierarchical relocation in groups, establishing internal homogeneity (in groups) and external heterogeneity (between groups). The use of this procedure brought high performance in the relocation of individuals, which offered great results, because the two combined methods allowed hierarchical and non-hierarchical procedures to be used as complements, with a view to obtaining more effective results. After clustering, a description of the data was done to summarize the sample information and to organize them by means of descriptive measures. Chi-square tests were conducted to determine the differences between the clusters in relation to their frequency in the categorical variables of socioeconomic class, level of education and use of alcohol and marijuana (or Fisher's Exact test, when the cell counts were less than 5). Finally, an analysis of variance (ANOVA) was performed to compare the groups with respect to mean age when the first offense was committed, diversity of offenses, and frequency of total offenses associated with the level of engagement. Subsequently, the Tukey post hoc test was used to show the difference between the groups. For all the analyses, the significance level was set at 0.05.

Results

After the statistical analysis was performed to cluster the participants, five groups were formed. Table 12.1 shows an overview of the five groups in relation to the three variables with regard to the level of criminal engagement based on the early onset (age of first offense), diversity (number of different types of offenses committed in life), and number of offenses (total frequency of crimes committed in the past 12 months).

The results shown in Table 12.1 revealed an ascending order (group 1 to group 5) for the intensity of criminal engagement. Group 5 comprised adolescents whose

Table 12.1 Means and standard deviations for age of first offense (early onset), the number of types of offenses committed in life (diversity), and the total number of crimes committed over the past year (volume)

	Age of first offense		Diversity of offenses		Number of offenses	
Group	M	SD	M	SD	M	SD
1 (n=31)	0	0	0	0	0	0
2 (n=52)	12.5	1.3	1.4	0.7	0.3	0.5
3 (n=37)	11.0	1.6	2.1	0.9	1.7	2.0
4 (n=37)	10.1	1.7	4.2	1.9	5.0	3.8
5 (n=36)	9.1	1.6	9.3	2.7	22.8	14.3

Table 12.2 Analysis of variance (ANOVA) and Tukey post hoc test for the analysis of the differences between the means of the groups in relation to the precocity, frequency, and diversity of offenses

	Groups										
	1	2		3		4		5		F	p
Age	0	12.5	c	11	b	10.08	ab	9.08	a	130.64	0.001[a]
Diversity	0	1.44	b	2.05	b	4.24	c	9.33	d	205.99	0.001[a]
Frequency	0	0.25	a	1.73	ab	5	b	22.78	c	81.55	0.001[a]

[a]Means with the equal letters in the same line do not show significant differences between them, where: a<b<c<d

criminal conduct was manifested earlier, and was the most diverse and the most frequent in the last 12 months. It should be noted that the first group was composed of all those adolescents whose responses indicated no criminal activities, therefore, all their values shown in the table are zero.

Table 12.2 shows the result of the analysis conducted to determine the differences between the groups for the variables referring to criminal engagement. Significant differences between the groups were found in almost all comparisons, which are consistent with the methods used in the cluster analysis, Ward and K-Means, considering those variables taken as criteria for the formation of groups.

The groups are described in Table 12.3 in terms of current mean age, sample origin, education and socioeconomic class according to *Brazil* Economic Classification *Criterion—ABEP* (2012).

Considering the importance given to commonsense, science, and to the association between juvenile delinquency and the use of psychoactive substances, a specific analysis concerning this behavior was carried out based on the groups formed. Thus, Table 12.3 shows the percentage of adolescents per group that reported the use of alcohol and marijuana. It also reveals the number of teenagers who reported the use of both substances and the number of those that use drugs frequently (at least once a week), as well as their respective percentages in relation to the group itself. It can be observed that in group 5, 33 individuals (92 % of the group) reported having consumed alcoholic beverages and 6 (17 %) consume them at least once a week. With regard to marijuana, 34 individuals from this group (94 %) revealed that they have used the substance and 22 (61 %) use it once a week (Table 12.4).

Table 12.3 Characterization of groups according to age, sample origin, education, and socioeconomic class

	Group 1 ($n=31$)		Group 2 ($n=52$)		Group 3 ($n=37$)		Group 4 ($n=37$)		Group 5 ($n=36$)		X^2	p
Current mean age (years)	14.7		15		14.7		15.7		15.8			
Juvenile offender	*n*	%	*n*	%	*n*	%	*n*	%	*n*	%	46.31	0.5
Yes	0	0	12	23	8	22	14	38	26	72		
No	31	100	40	77	29	78	23	62	10	28		
Education	*n*	%	*n*	%	*n*	%	*n*	%	*n*	%	41.21	0.05
Up to 5th year	0	0	0	0	0	0	0	0	2	6		
6 th year	0	0	1	2	0	0	0	0	0	0		
7 th year	4	13	4	8	5	14	3	8	8	22		
8 th year	3	10	12	23	9	24	9	24	8	22		
9 th year	13	42	11	21	8	22	8	22	10	28		
1st year High School	4	13	8	15	7	19	4	11	7	19		
2nd year High School	5	16	11	21	2	5	9	24	1	3		
3rd year High School	2	6	5	10	6	16	4	11	0	0		
Socio-economic class	*n*	%	*n*	%	*n*	%	*n*	%	*n*	%	23.76	0.48
A1	0	0	0	0	0	0	0	0	0	0		
A2	2	6	2	4	3	8	5	14	0	0		
B1	3	10	8	15	2	6	8	22	6	17		
B2	8	26	13	25	12	33	10	27	10	28		
C1	14	45	22	42	13	36	10	27	17	47		
C2	4	13	7	13	5	14	3	8	3	8		
D	0	0	0	0	1	3	0	0	0	0		
E	0	0	0	0	0	0	1	3	0	0		

Table 12.4 Percentages of adolescents per group who have already consumed alcohol and used marijuana and those who use the substances at least once a week

	Have already consumed alcoholic beverages		Consume alcoholic beverages at least once a week		Have already smoked marijuana		Smoke marijuana at least once a week	
Group	*n*	%	*n*	%	*n*	%	*n*	%
1	10	32	0	0	0	0	0	0
2	32	62	3	6	10	19	1	2
3	27	73	1	3	8	22	4	11
4	35	95	4	11	15	41	0	0
5	33	92	6	17	34	94	22	61
	$X^2=38.8$; Phi=0.45; $p=0.001$*		$X^2=10.5$; Phi=0.22; $p=0.03$*		$X^2=80.7$; Phi=0.65; $p=0.001$*		$X^2=84.0$; Phi=0.66; $p=0.001$*	

Table 12.5 Number of crimes that each group committed in the last 12 months

Group	Number of crimes committed	% of the total crimes reported
1	0	0 %
2	13	1.2 %
3	64	5.9 %
4	185	17.1 %
5	820	75.8 %
Total	1,082	100 %

Table 12.6 Number of adolescents who committed each one of the crimes and the percentage in relation to their group

Investigated crimes	Group 1 (*n*=31)		Group 2 (*n*=52)		Group 3 (*n*=37)		Group 4 (*n*=37)		Group 5 (*n*=36)	
	n	%	*n*	%	*n*	%	*n*	%	*n*	%
Damage	0	0	12	23	15	41	25	68	34	94
Personal injury/hurt someone	0	0	7	14	13	35	32	87	31	86
Group fight	0	0	10	19	8	22	17	46	28	78
Personal injury with any instrument	0	0	0	0	0	0	3	8	21	58
Abuse against animals	0	0	4	8	1	3	2	5	12	33
Receiving stolen goods	0	0	0	0	3	8	17	46	35	97
Bicycle theft	0	0	0	0	0	0	3	8	18	50
Shoplifting	0	0	22	42	24	65	29	78	31	86
Items stolen from car	0	0	0	0	1	3	0	0	19	53
Vehicle or motocycle theft	0	0	1	2	1	3	2	5	17	47
Rob someone	0	0	5	10	2	5	11	30	24	67
Steal someone	0	0	1	2	2	5	7	19	20	56
Illegal gun possession	0	0	5	10	1	3	15	41	35	97
Drug trafficking	0	0	13	25	6	16	8	22	25	69

Table 12.5 summarizes the results of the contribution of each group in relation to the total number of crimes committed last year, revealed in the sample as a whole. It should be highlighted that group 5 was responsible for most of the crimes reported (total of 75 %), while group 4 was responsible for 17 % of the total. Together, these groups were responsible for 93 % of the total number of crimes committed last year, according to information given by the adolescents.

Table 12.6 presents the number of adolescents from each group, who reported having committed each of the 14 crimes investigated in the study. Furthermore, it shows the percentage that represents the number of adolescents within their group. It is worth mentioning that in group 5, 35 individuals (97 % of this group) reported having already carried a gun, while in group 4, 15 individuals (41 % of this group) did the same.

Discussion

The data presented in the present study, such as those observed in studies conducted in other sociocultural settings (Le Blanc and Fréchette 1989; Farrington et al. 2006) showed that the engagement of adolescents in criminal activities is quite common, considering that approximately 84 % of the respondents reported being involved in crimes.

However, this involvement ranges from "lack of criminal activity" (Group 1) to "quite early, diverse and extensive criminal activity" (Group 5), which demonstrates a heterogeneous level of engagement among the adolescents studied, whether they were recruited from the general population or from a judicial program.

It should be highlighted that all groups were composed of school students and juvenile offenders, except group 1, although in group 4, and mostly in group 5, the number of juvenile offenders was higher. Group 1 represented 16 % of the total sample and according to Table 12.5, the individuals reported that they have never been involved in criminal activities. It is possible that some of them would eventually get involved in criminal activities by the end of adolescence. This can be explained by the average age of the adolescents (14.7 years), which refers to a period of transition from the first half of adolescence to the second, when the risk of young people to engage in some risky behavior increases (Le Blanc 2010). It is also possible that others will continue without getting involved in criminal acts until adulthood, and therefore, be part of a group similar to those described in the literature that generally represents a minority (Le Blanc 2003). In Canada, it was found that only 5 % of youth reported that they have never been involved in criminal activities, and for this reason they were called "abstinent" (Le Blanc 2003, 2010).

Following are the groups formed by individuals that have revealed a certain level of involvement in illegal activities. Groups 2, 3, 4, and 5 presented an ascending order of values for the variables analyzed, which were all used to measure the level of criminal engagement. These findings confirmed that the levels of engagement range from lower to higher or more intense, based on precocity (the age of onset), diversity (variety of offenses committed), and total volume of irregularities (higher frequency of crimes committed in the past year). Moreover, groups 2 and 3 were less engaged and intense compared to groups 4 and 5. Group 2, specifically, clusters individuals whose first offense was committed later ($M = 12.5$ years), the variety of offenses experienced was the lowest ($M = 1.4$), and the number of offenses over the past year was also the lowest ($M = 0.3$). These objective parameters confirmed that the adolescents in this group were involved in illegal activities in their early teens and experienced one to two different offenses. In addition, in the past year, many of them were not involved in any criminal act, which indicated a non-persistent behavioral pattern. This group comprised 77 % students and 23 % juvenile offenders, representing 27 % of the total sample.

Group 3 represented 19 % of the total sample. Although significantly different from group 2 with regard to the criminal engagement variables, these two groups (2 and 3) are similar in their composition. The group 3 comprised 78 % students and 22 % juvenile offenders. Their criminal engagement can be considered minor, although it was higher compared to group 2. Based on the objective parameters, it can be said that the adolescents in this group got involved in criminal activities in the transition from childhood to adolescence (average age 11 years), which was considered too early. Anyway, the adolescents in this group would have experienced only two types of different offenses ($M = 2.1$), and in the past year, one or two offenses only ($M = 1.7$).

It seems that the adolescents from both groups (2 and 3), which represented 46 % of the total sample, exhibited what Le Blanc (2003, 2010) denominates *common delinquency*, which refers to an occasional type of offense during adolescence. According to Le Blanc and Fréchette (1989), *common delinquency* comprises a small number of offenses, which are not diversified. It is associated with hedonist motivation, e.g., the youth are involved in situations to seek leisure, pleasure, and excitement, and not in acts that involve planning or the use of instruments.

Richards et al. (1979) mentioned by Le Blanc (2003), argue that *common delinquency* is a kind of game for the teenagers; a recreational activity that occupies part of their free time, especially when they get together with peers and without adult supervision. This activity is a typical developmental task of young age, that relate to norms and autonomy (Le Blanc 2003, 2010).

For the adolescents clustered in groups 2 and 3 in our study, "shoplifting" was the prevalent offense (Table 12.6); in these groups, 42 % and 65 %, respectively, of young people were engaged in this type of crime. However, it was evenly distributed across all groups, which seems to indicate that this is a common crime in adolescence. The percentage of teenagers who have shoplifted at some point in life ranged from 20 % to 29 % between groups. This type of crime confirms some of the information aforementioned, as it occurred when these adolescents were involved in leisure activities, with no adult supervision and the stolen items were under surveillance.

In group 2, the second most prevalent type of crime was drug trafficking, which was reported by 25 % of the participants. This rate was only lower than that found in group 5. From a legal point of view, this offense is considered quite serious. In 2011, in the state of São Paulo, Brazil, among the total number of juvenile offenders deprived of freedom, 42 % of them were arrested for drug trafficking (*Fórum Brasileiro de Segurança Pública* 2013, pp. 88–90). The fact is that, although the criminal engagement of these adolescents was insignificant, this act was considered legally serious. This apparent contradiction deserves some reflection. On one hand, if the legal criterion to the severity of the offense that brought the offender to justice is considered, the insignificance of the criminal engagement by this group is questionable. On the other hand, if one considers that the concept of criminal engagement is more complex because it necessarily implies a set of variables, what is questionable is the Brazilian juvenile justice system, in which different teenagers are probably treated similarly, considering that only the offensive act has bought them to face a judge, which denies both the Beijing Rules (ONU 1985) and the Brazilian Law (Brazil 1990).

In this scenario and according to specialized literature, the most fragile variable to support the analyses that would allow a better understanding of the adolescents and their behavior is the type of crime they have committed, especially when acted alone (Herrenkohl et al. 2000). Currently, there is relative consensus among researchers regarding the concept of criminal engagement and the relevance in considering, concomitantly, different variables for the analysis of the levels of criminal engagement.

It should be observed that the most robust variables were those used in the present study, which allowed the sample clustering (Le Blanc 2010). For those variables, the adolescents clustered in group 2 did not exhibit high levels of criminal engagement, although some of them have been involved in a legally serious act. Such behavior may be explained by the social conditions in which some adolescents live. In some Brazilian urban areas, the *illicit drug abuse and trafficking rates are* very high. This condition not only promotes a drug subculture but also gives those young residents, with different levels of criminal engagement, the opportunity to engage in drug trafficking.

For group 3, the offenses that include "damage" (41 %), "personal injury" (35 %), and "fight" (22 %) are those that involve more adolescents. The nature of the "damage" suggests that this kind of crime occurs during group activities, such as leisure and entertainment, in which the adolescents are not under adult supervision and are easily targeted by offenders. These factors would be most likely determinants of the so-called *common delinquency*. For interpersonal forms of violence that include "personal injury" and "fight," the question that arises is whether these forms represent a more significant criminal engagement issue. However, according to the reflections made previously for "drug trafficking" in group 2, it is likely that the behaviors that imply these crimes are quite widespread in the communities where many of these young people live, which also include recreational and entertainment activities. Therefore, it seems that the fact that these adolescents were engaged in "personal injury" and "fight" alone could sustain the argument that the adolescents in group 3 exhibited any delinquent behavior other than the one described in *common delinquency.*

Group 4, which represented 19 % of the total sample and comprised 62 % of students and 38 % of juvenile offenders, included a cluster of adolescents with greater offensive activity, compared to the groups previously discussed. For this group, an average of five crimes was committed in the past 12 months. Furthermore, they have been engaged in four different types of crimes and committed the first offense with 10 years of age.

The individuals in group 4 seem to represent what Le Blanc (2010) classified as *Transitory delinquency* and Moffitt (1993) described as *adolescence-limited delinquency*. The latter differs from *common delinquency* to the extent that the offensive acts, in view of their early onset, diversity and amount; the engagement is more significant and its determinants are more than merely situational aspects. According to Le Blanc (2010), *Transitory delinquency* appears essentially during adolescence crisis and the offending act represents more than a casual recreational and pleasurable activity; the antisocial behavior of this typology is also a rebellious attitude towards social norms and may become a reference for personal identification, especially if these youngsters maintain relationships with their peers who share similar or more severe problems (Le Blanc and Morizot 2000). Therefore, young people with criminal behaviors that characterize *Transitory delinquency* would be more susceptible to be apprehended by the police or referred to the juvenile justice.

With regard to group 4, the variety of offenses revealed, the most prevalent incidents were objectively more severe than those practiced in groups 2 and 3. There was a predominance of offenses in this group that may imply some degree of violence that often involves a victim. Among the total number of adolescents clustered in group 4, 87 % have reported being involved in activities that resulted in "personal injury." It should be observed that a considerable percentage of adolescents reported having access of weapons and 41 % admitted "carrying a gun." In groups 2 and 3, this behavior was revealed by only 10 % and 3 % of adolescents, respectively.

Group 5 represented 19 % of the total sample, comprising 28 % of students and 72 % of juvenile offenders. The adolescents clustered in this group more clearly presented the most significant level of criminal engagement, which have started very early age (9 years old). It was also diversified and in great number. They were involved in an average of nine different types of crimes and committed an average of 23 offenses in the previous year, which was four times greater than the number observed in group 4.

With respect to the incidence of "bicycle theft," "car or bike theft," and "items stolen from car theft" combined with "personal injury using an instrument," comprised a list of crimes committed mostly by the adolescents in group 5. More than 80 % of the total number of offenses was reported in this group. The majority of individuals (above 50 %) mentioned having committed all the crimes investigated, except "abuse against animals" (33 %) and "car or bike theft" (47 %). In terms of prevalence, the rate of teenagers per offense in this group was always higher than that observed in the other groups, with the exception of "personal injury," which was observed in group 5 (86 %) was equivalent to that in group 4 (87 %).

Moreover, there was a high prevalence of adolescents who revealed having committed crimes with some degree of violence against a person in the group 5: 86 % had engaged in "personal injury," 78 % in "fight," 58 % in "personal injury with the use of instrument," and 56 % in "theft" (with the use of violence to rob anything from anyone). Furthermore, 97 % reported "firearm possession." Considering that this behavioral profile is strongly associated with violent crimes against a person, combined with the most significant level of criminal engagement, which characterizes this persistent behavior of the adolescents' repertoire, it could be suggested that the mechanisms and processes that maintained this criminal conduct in this group were also responsible for its severity. Based on the longitudinal investigations, Le Blanc and Fréchette (1989) reported that the severity of the criminal behavior is associated with greater precocity, intense diversification, and high frequency of the crimes committed.

It should be noted the concept of severity implies not only the participation in offenses that involve a victim, but also in a large number of crimes against property, as these offensive acts involve stealing of valuable items (Hoge 2009). The data we found corroborate this proposition. In group 5, we evidenced a high prevalence of adolescents who have committed "shoplifting" (86 %), a typical activity showed by the groups with less significant criminal engagement. However, 53 % of individuals of this group also reported having "stolen some item from a car," 50 % committed "bicycle theft" and 47 % "car or motorcycle theft." It is noteworthy these three types of crime were mostly reported by the adolescent clustering into group 5.

Following the same line of thinking with regard to the concept of severity, there should be some reflection on the high prevalence of adolescents in this group that reported having "received stolen goods" (97 %) and "trafficked drugs" (69 %). It is likely that such activities are, somehow, very common in the communities where these adolescents reside, similar to those in group 2. This situation offers greater opportunity for their participation in these serious offenses, but it does not explain the level of criminal engagement. However, the behavior of these adolescents engaged in frequent "reception of stolen goods" and "drug trafficking" seems to indicate a closer relationship of those teens with criminal networks, considering that these illegal acts imply interpersonal contact with other criminals.

Thus, the criminal behavior pattern observed in this group seems to refer to what is described in the literature as *persistent/chronic delinquency* (Moffitt 2003; Farrington et al. 2006; Le Blanc 2010). The *persistent delinquency*, based on different empirical studies, in other sociocultural settings, is characterized by early onset, (8–10 years of age), diversity, severity, and frequency. The motivation for the criminal activities in this case, according to literature, is instrumental or utilitarian in nature, concerns the expectations of consequences, indicating that it fulfills the needs and is almost always planned and involves the use of instruments to commit the offensive acts. When victims are involved, the offender may use physical force and/or intimidation (Le Blanc 2003). The determinant factors for this behavioral pattern go beyond those related to the typical tasks of young age, and in most cases, refer to significant difficulties and important psychosocial lag (Carrington et al. 2005; Le Blanc 2010). For Le Blanc (2003), the psychosocial functioning that underlies the persistent delinquency is based on the interactions between the individual and the environment along the years, from childhood to late adolescence (as well as at the beginning of adulthood). Over the years, they become more resistant to changes; therefore, it is wise to say that interventions aimed at preventing the development of this behavior model should also be early and intensive (extended over a reasonable time).

It is noteworthy that the adolescents in group 5 were responsible for 75 % of the total crimes revealed by the sample, which explains the idea of behavior stability during this period and reinforces the behavior defined as *chronic delinquency*. This data was consistent with those observed in other investigations, in other sociocultural contexts and showed that the subgroup of adolescents with higher level of criminal engagement was usually responsible for most crimes whose authorship could be attributed to adolescents (Le Blanc and Fréchette 1989; Le Blanc 2003/2010; Carrington et al. 2005; MacRae et al. 2008). In England, for example, Farrington et al (2006) found that only 7 % of arrests were of adolescents responsible for more than half of the *criminal offenses* recorded on the *Criminal Register.*

At this point it should also be emphasized that, with the exception of group 1, all other groups, in which some criminal activities was identified at some level, with less or more criminal engagement, were formed by adolescents with and without a history of juvenile criminal records. This finding shows that, on one hand, there are adolescents with significant level of criminal engagement until then had no contact with justice; on the other hand, a considerable number of adolescents whose behavior is not representative of a significant criminal engagement are in the Juvenile Justice System, submitted to a judicial measure. Therefore, the evidence shows that juvenile offenders very different in terms of criminal engagement are submitted to the same judicial measure. It indicates a lack of *refinement* in the *evaluation* of the offenders when *decisions have to* be made by a judge. These findings are in agreement with some authors that criticize the massification treatment towards juvenile offenders by the Brazilian juvenile justice, which is often based on the analysis of the crime for which they were detained by police (Maruschi and Bazon 2014). According to these authors, more important than to consider the severity of the offense committed by the adolescent, for the court to make a decision, it is necessary to evaluate the level of criminal engagement, aiming to adjust the legal and psychosocial responses to fulfill the needs of adolescents.

The adolescents without significant criminal engagement, eventually arrested as a result of any offensive or casual act, may be submitted to treatments that negatively affect their development. This occurs because of labeling and/or a possible intensification of interactions between these and other teenagers with higher level of criminal engagement and in settings where the judicial measures are being applied. Meanwhile, adolescents with significant offensive criminal engagement can undergo treatments that do not fulfill their needs because they were arrested for a mild offense. This fact contributes to deny them the type of psychosocial treatment they need and are entitled to, leading to the aggravation of the problems bound to the development of their criminal engagement. Besides the observations made about the necessary adjustment of the evaluations that involve the needs and difficulties of every adolescent that enters the justice system, it should be emphasized that the mistakes made in these situations contribute to the loss of financial investments and human resources made by the state and society.

Furthermore, it is necessary to highlight the other variables analyzed in this study, especially the similarities and differences presented by the adolescents in all five groups. These groups had a similar socioeconomic background and most individuals in two groups were from the same social classes (B2 and C1), according to the ABEP (2012). Their families were living with a monthly income ranging from R$ 1.333,00 to R$ 750, 00 (approximately US$ 350, 00 to US$ 198, 00, respectively).

These findings are of paramount importance as they reinforce the idea that the *socioeconomic* variables act *indirectly* and are mediated by more determining factors or by factors that have more direct influence on the shaping of social conduct in adolescence. In other words, the results indicate that the adolescents who live under the same socioeconomic conditions may present significant differences in terms of socialization, mainly due to their exposition to psychosocial risk factors. This observation requires a better reflection on public policies for the prevention of juvenile delinquency, especially those aimed at the underprivileged strata of the population.

These programs and services should focus on those psychosocial risk factors and reach beyond the actions aimed at improving the socioeconomic conditions of their underprivileged families, by granting social benefits and/or professional qualification with the purpose of providing conditions to those youngsters and their families to find a job.

For the level of education, no any significant differences were observed between the groups, indicating that all participants were equally represented in all school years. However, the adolescents in groups 1, 2, and 3 were on average, a year younger than those in groups 4 and 5. This suggests that the adolescents in these last two groups exhibited age-grade gap. For Le Blanc (2003), adolescent misbehavior is amplified by weak school bond and poor school performance; in turn, adolescent crime increases, leading to higher levels of adolescent delinquency, especially when associated with other risk variables.

For the association between criminal engagement and consumption of substances, the most relevant information was that most adolescents in all groups reported having consumed alcohol, except those in group 1, in which approximately 32 % revealed this behavior. This data seems to indicate the important correlation that exists between the occurrence of different antisocial behaviors in adolescence (Mun et al. 2008). With regard to one adolescent in particular, more than information on whether he had or not displayed an antisocial behavior, it is important to comprehend his behavioral pattern. It is emphasized that it is only in groups 4 and 5 that the frequent alcohol consumption is referred to by more than 10 % of adolescents. For the use of marijuana, the adolescents in group 1 reported not having used this substance. In relation to other groups, there was a gradual increase in the percentage of teenagers who had used this substance: in group 2, 19 %; in group 3, 22 %; in group 4, 41 %; and in group 5, 94 %, respectively. In the latter group, in addition to the prevalence of those who reported having used this substance, the percentage of those that have used marijuana at least once a week was also high (61 %).

In the scientific literature, there are reports on the significant co-occurrence between the behaviors of psychoactive substance use and criminal behavior, and at least three different models on the positive association between them. The first model determines that the criminal behavior is prior to the use of substances (Choquet et al. 1991). The second suggests the opposite, i.e., that the substance use predates the criminal behavior (Fagan 1993). Finally, Hirshi and Gottfredson (1994) proposed that the relationship between these variables is hypothetical, whereas the fact that the use of drugs during adolescence is considered illegal, and therefore, considered a subtype criminal act. Thus, both substance use and other offenses seemed to be caused by the same set of risk factors. Further longitudinal and prospective studies are necessary to better understand the connection between these problems.

In summary, the results of this study showed that the vast majority of youth has manifested antisocial behaviors and a significant proportion also committed offenses in the course of adolescence. However, the manifestation of these behaviors, especially the violation of laws, did not occur homogeneously among teenagers.

Based on the measurement of criminal engagement of individuals, it was possible to identify five different groups of adolescents whose criminal activities ranged from absent to early onset, from very diverse to frequent. Further investigations should be under way to identify the personal and social differences of the participants in each group.

The study has some limitations. First, we used an instrument that was suitable to collect information to meet the objectives this study, however, it was a self-report method, which was not adapted to our population, and consequently, *brings into question* the *validity* of the constructs *measured*. Although most of the results obtained were consistent with those found in the literature, which suggests a strong external validity, some effort should be made to validate the questionnaire used for our population. Second, the size of the sample used was not so large than is desirable. This restricted the possibility of generalization of the results presented here for this population, especially because the study only included representatives of certain social segments, in contrast to the great cultural diversity that often characterizes the same Brazilian city. Finally, we sought to follow all statistical parameters established for similar studies, involving multivariate analysis. According to what was suggested by Hair Jr. and colleagues (2006), a minimum number of participants was used to reach the figure of five times the number of variables analyzed, and for comparison between groups, each one of them had at least 20 participants. Therefore, we can say that our statistical analyses were robust enough and consequently, supported the results obtained and the considerations that can be made about them.

References

ABEP - Associação Brasileira de Empresas de Pesquisa. (2012). Critério de classificação econômica Brasil. Retrieved March 15, 2015, from http://www.abep.org/new/criterioBrasil.aspx

Atlas Brasil. (2014). Atlas do Desenvolvimento Humano no Brasil 2013. Perfil do Município de Ribeirão Preto – SP. Retrieved November 12, 2015, from http://atlasbrasil.org.br/2013/pt/perfil_m/ribeirao-preto_sp

BRASIL. (1990). *Estatuto da Criança e do Adolescente: Lei 8.069/90, de 13 de Julho de 1990*. Brasília: Senado Federal.

BRASIL. (2012). *Resolução n° 466, de 12 de dezembro de 2012*. Brasília. Retrieved September 1, 2016, from http://conselho.saude.gov.br/resolucoes/2012/Reso466.pdf.

Breen, J., Manning, U., O'Donnell, I., O'Mahony, D., & Seymour, M. (2010). Ireland. In J. Junger-Tas, I. Marshall, D. Enzmann, M. Killias, M. Steketee, & B. Gruszczynska (Eds.), *Juvenile delinquency in Europe and beyond: Results from the second international self-reported delinquency study* (pp. 111–124). New York, NY: Springer.

Carrington, P., Matarazzo, A., & de Souza, P. (2005). *Court careers of a Canadian birth cohort* (Crime and justice research paper series, Vol. 6). Ottawa: Canadian Centre for Justice Statistics.

Choquet, M., Menke, H., & Manfredi, R. (1991). Interpersonal aggressive behaviour and alcohol consumption among young urban adolescents in France. *Alcohol Alcohol, 26*(4), 381–390.

Datafolha. (2015). 87% dos brasileiros são a favor da redução da maioridade penal. Retrieved June 20, 2015, from http://datafolha.folha.uol.com.br/opiniaopublica/2015/04/1620652-87-dos-brasileiros-sao-a-favor-da-reducao-da-maioridade-penal.shtml

Dembo, R., LaVoie, L., Schmeidler, J., & Washburn, M. (1987). The nature and correlates of psychological/emotional functioning among a sample of detained youths. *Criminal Justice and Behavior, 14*, 311–334.
Fagan, J. (1993). Interactions among drugs, alcohol, and violence. *Health Affairs, 12*(4), 65–79.
Farrington, D. P., Coid, J. W., Harnett, L., Jolliffe, D., Soteriou, N., Turner, R., & West, D. J. (2006). *Criminal careers up to age 50 and life success up to age 48: New findings from the cambridge study in delinquent development* (Home Office Research Study, Vol. 299). London: Home Office.
Fórum Brasileiro de Segurança Pública. (2013). Anuário do Fórum Brasileiro de Segurança Pública. São Paulo: Fórum Brasileiro de Segurança Pública, Ano 7. Retrieved November 12, 2015, from http://www2.forumseguranca.org.br/novo/produtos/anuario-brasileiro-de-seguranca-publica/7a-edicao
Fórum Brasileiro de Segurança Pública. (2014). Anuário de Segurança Pública. São Paulo: Fórum Brasileiro de Segurança Pública, Ano 8. Retrieved November 12, 2015, from http://www.forumseguranca.org.br/produtos/anuario-brasileiro-de-seguranca-publica/8o-anuario-brasileiro-de-seguranca-publica
Fundação CASA. (2011). CASA é destaque em seminário no Chile. November 12, 2015, from http://www.fundacaocasa.sp.gov.br/View.aspx?title=-casa-e-destaque-em-seminario-no-chile&d=594
Hair Jr., J. F., Anderson, R. E., Tatham, R. L., & Black, W. C. (2006). Análise multivariada de dados. Tradução de A.S. Sant'anna e A. Cloves Neto. 5a Ed. Porto Alegre: Bookman, 593 p.
Herrenkohl, T. L., Maguin, E., Hill, K. G., Hawkins, J. D., Abbott, R. D., & Catalano, R. F. (2000). Developmental risk factors for youth violence. *Journal of Adolescent Health, 6*, 176–186.
Hirshi, T., & Gottfredson, M. (1994). *The generality of deviance*. New Brunswick, NJ: Transaction.
Hoge, R. D. (2009). Serious and Violent Juvenile Offenders: Assessment and Treatment. 139th International Training Course: Visitin experts' papers.
Le Blanc, M. (2003). Trajetórias de delinquência comum, transitória e persistente: uma estratégia de prevenção diferencial. In I. Alberto (Ed.), *Comportamento Antissocial: Escola e Família* (pp. 31–80). Coimbra: Centro de Psicopedagogia da Universidade de Coimbra.
Le Blanc, M. (2010). Un paradigme développemental pour la criminologie: Développement et autorégulation de laconduite déviante. *Criminologie, 43*(2), 401–428.
Le Blanc, M., & Fréchette, M. (1989). *Male criminal activity, from childhood through youth: Multilevel and developmental perspectives*. New York, NY: Springer.
Le Blanc, M., & Morizot, J. (2000). Trajectoires délinquantes commune, transitoire et persistante: une stratégie de prévention différentielle. In F. Vitaro & C. Gagnon (Eds.), *La prévention des problèmes d'adaptation chez les enfants et les adolescents* (Vol. 2, pp. 291–334). Québec: Les Presses de l'Université du Québec.
Loeber, R. (1990). Development and risk factors of juvenile antisocial behavior and delinquency. *Clinical Psychology Review, 10*, 1–41.
MacRae, L., Bertrand, L. D., Paetsch, J. J., & Hornick, J. P. (2008). *A profile of youth offender in Caligary: an interim report*. Calgary, Alta: Canadian Research Institute for Law and the Family.
Maruschi, M. C., & Bazon, M. R. (2014). Justiça Juvenil: a aplicação e a execução das medidas socioeducativas pelos parâmetros do modelo "risco-necessidade-responsividade". In A. Jakobsson (Ed.), *Prêmio INNOVARE: 10 anos—A justiça do século XXI* (1st ed., Vol. 01, pp. 42–72). Rio de Janeiro: Instituto INNOVARE.
Moffitt, T. (1993). Adolescence-limited and life-course-persistent antisocial behavior: A developmental taxonomy. *Psychological Review, 100*(4), 674–701.
Moffitt, T. E. (2003). Life-course-persistent and adolescence-limited antisocial behavior: A 10-year research review and a research agenda. In B. B. Lahey, T. E. Moffitt, & A. Caspi (Eds.), *Causes of conduct disorder and juvenile delinquency* (pp. 49–75). New York, NY: Guilford Press.
Mowder, M. H. (2010). Resiliency scales for children and adolescents: Profiles of juvenile offenders. *Journal of Psychoeducational Assessment, 28*(4), 326–337.

Mun, E. Y., Windle, M., & Schainker, L. M. (2008). A model-based cluster analysis approach to adolescent problem behaviors and young adult out comes. *Development and Psychopathology, 20*, 291–318.

Organização das Nações Unidas. (1985). Resolução 40/33, de 29 de novembro de 1985. Regras mínimas das Nações Unidas para administração da justiça da infância e da juventude – Regras de Beijing. http://www.gddc.pt/direitos-humanos/textos-internacionais-dh/tidhuniversais/dhaj-NOVO-regrasBeijing.html

Piquero, A. R., & Moffitt, T. E. (2008). Explaining the facts of crime: How the developmental taxonomy replies to Farrington's invitation. In D. P. Farrington (Ed.), *Integrated developmental and life-course theories of offending* (pp. 51–72). New Brunswick, NJ: Transaction.

Richards, P., Berk, R. A., & Forster, B. (1979). *Crime as play–delinquency in a middle class suburb*. Cambridge, MA: Ballinger.

Quay, H. (1987). Patterns of delinquent behavior. In H. Quay (Ed.), *Handbook of juvenile delinquency* (pp. 118–138). New York, NY: John Wiley and Sons.

Sorensen, E., & Johnson, E. (1996). Subtypes of incarcerated delinquents constructed via cluster analysis. *Journal of Child Psychology and Psychiatry, 37*(3), 293–303.

Stefurak, T., Calhoun, G. B., & Glaser, B. A. (2004). Personality typologies of male juvenile offenders using a cluster analysis of the millon adolescent clinical inventory introduction. *International Journal of Offender Therapy and Comparative Criminology, 48*(1), 96–110.

Uribe, G. (2013). Cresce participação de crianças e adolescentes em crimes. Retrieved November 12, 2015, from http://oglobo.globo.com/brasil/cresce-participacao-de-criancas-adolescentes-em-crimes-8234349

Vermeersch, H., T'Sjoen, G., Kaufman, J. M., & Van Houtte, M. (2013). Social science theories on adolescent risk-taking: The relevance of behavioral inhibition and activation. *Youth Society, 45*(1), 27–53.

Chapter 13
Mareros and *Pandilleros* in Honduras: The Reintegration of Youth Gang Members

Ellen Van Damme

Introduction

Honduras and its neighboring countries El Salvador and Guatemala are highly affected by the violence of gangs and drug traffickers. With 90.4 murders per 100,000 citizens, Honduras has the highest homicide rate of the world. Gang related homicides have even increased the past years and Honduras currently accounts for most gang related murders (30 per 100,000 citizens). In Honduras' neighboring country, El Salvador, the two rivaling gangs *Mara Salvatrucha 13* and *Barrio 18* agreed upon a truce, which caused an immediate decrease of homicides and other gang related violence. However, this truce only lasted for 1 year, as homicide rates increased again (Gurney 2014). A similar truce was attempted in Honduras, but it did not result in a lower homicide rate (UNODC 2013). Not with standing the former, according to Salvadoran citizens, the alleged truce has barely, if at all, reduced the delinquency rate in El Salvador (IUDOP 2012).

This chapter is based on my Master's Thesis in Criminology, written in 2013–2014, and revised to fit this content. My research is made possible with the help of many people, which I would like to thank. First of all I want to thank my promoter, Prof. Dr. Stephan Parmentier and co-promoter, Dr. Barbara Van Wijnendaele, for their guidance and enthusiasm. I would also like to express my gratitude towards the University Arbitration Committee on Risk Destinations, which approved my research application. Furthermore, I would like to thank all respondents I interviewed in Honduras, Nicaragua, Costa Rica, El Salvador and Guatemala. I am very grateful for their cooperation and friendliness. A special thanks to IUDPAS in Tegucigalpa, Honduras. The University institute facilitated me during most of my interviews in Honduras. I want to thank Dir. Migdonia Ayestas for welcoming me at IUDPAS and Ronny Barahona for facilitating the contacts with key figure respondents in Honduras. Finally, I would like to thank the family Macedo Hernandez who hosted me during my time in Tegucigalpa. I am very grateful for their hospitality and care.

E. Van Damme (✉)
Catholic University of Leuven, Leuven Institute of Criminology, Leuven, Belgium
e-mail: Ellen.VanDamme@law.kuleuven.be

E.C. Viano (ed.), *Cybercrime, Organized Crime, and Societal Responses*,
DOI 10.1007/978-3-319-44501-4_13

However, in a country where 20 % of the youngsters are not studying and are likely to get involved in a gang (Floresi et al. 2004), few financial efforts have been made to protect these vulnerable youngsters. Nearly 200 million dollar (4137.1 million Honduran Lempira) or 4.6 % of the central administration expenses of Honduras, goes to security (i.e., the police forces), whereas only 308 thousand dollar (6.4 million Lempira) or less than 0.01 % of the central administration expenses is spent on the national program of prevention, rehabilitation, and social reintegration (Secretaría de Finanzas 2013).

Many studies have already been done on the origin, creation, and activities of youth gangs as such, but not as many on the reintegration processes of youth gang members (Wood and Alleyne 2010). Therefore, the goal of this research is to focus mainly on the reintegration of youth gang members, by investigating which intervention methods are effective in helping gang members to reintegrate into society. In order to understand these processes of reintegration, attention will also go to the context of gang membership, i.e., reasons for youngsters to join a gang.

The main research question is: "How can the reintegration of young gang members into society best be facilitated?" In order to respond this research question, the following sub-questions are investigated:

1. For what reasons can young gang members leave the gang?
2. Which intervention methods can facilitate young gang members in their process of leaving the gang and reintegrate in society?

Qualitative methods are used to gather research data. In accordance with the guidelines of KU Leuven and for the safety of the researcher, as well as of gang members and local informants, gang members or ex-gang members as such are not interviewed. Rather, data are gathered by interviewing Honduran social workers who work with (ex-) gang members in a reintegration program or academics who have studied the reintegration processes of youth gang members. The goal of this investigation is to find out which programs, focusing on the reintegration of (ex-) gang members, are available in Honduras, which intervention methods are used and which of these methods are effective when taking into account the specific setting of the intervention.

In this chapter we first give an overview of existing research on gangs in Honduras, related to the aspect of reintegration. Secondly, we discuss our data results concerning gang involvement, leaving the gang, and the reintegration into society. We conclude by giving some recommendations for further research.

Mareros and *Pandilleros*: Gangs in Honduras

Maras and *pandillas* are present in all Central American countries, but most of all in El Salvador, Guatemala and Honduras. Despite their presence in several countries, there is no official definition of gangs which criminologists have agreed upon

(Katz 2004).[1] With the concepts *maras* and *pandillas* we refer to juvenile gangs in Central America. Though there is some disagreement regarding the meaning and difference between the terms *mara* and *pandilla*. According to Aplícano Cubero (2012), the concepts of *mara* and *pandilla* are merely synonyms and thus refer to the same phenomenon.[2] But according to Cruz (2010) and Rodgers, Muggah and Stevenson (2009), there certainly is a difference between *maras* and *pandillas*.[3] In this chapter we refer to *maras* and *pandillas* as synonyms for juvenile gangs.

Furthermore, there is also some disagreement regarding the origins of Central American *maras* and *pandillas*. Some say they migrated from the USA (see for example Aplícano Cubero 2012; Reisman 2006); others say they have always been present in Central America (see for example PNPRRS 2011). However, according to Cruz (2010) *maras* exist due to local conditions (i.e., marginalization and law enforcement strategies) as well as transnational processes (i.e., migration flows and the spreading of Southern California gang identities).

There is not only a discussion on the decent and definition of *maras* and *pandillas*, also the number of gang members is highly being discussed. Depending on statistics of governmental or nongovernmental organizations, the range of gang members in Honduras lies between 4728 (National Program for Prevention Rehabilitation and Social Reintegration/PNPRRS 2011) and 12,000 to 35,000 (UNODC 2012; Rubio 2002; USAID 2012). One major difference is that the PNPRRS (2011) does not include *simpatizantes* (youngsters who sympathize with a gang, but are not (yet) initiated into the gang) in their statistics. Also, there are slightly more gang members belonging to the *Mara Salvatrucha*, compared to the *Barrio 18* (PNPRRS 2011; UNODC 2012). Although statistics do not make a distinction between male and female gang members, research indicates that men as well as women are active within a gang (Proyecto Victoria 2013). According to the PNPRRS (2011) most gang members are male (80 %) and only a smaller part of the

[1] However, according to Eurogang "*a street gang (or troublesome youth group corresponding to a street gang elsewhere) is any durable, street-oriented youth group whose involvement in illegal activity is part of its group identity*" (Weerman et al. 2009, p. 20).

[2] Aplícano Cubero (2012) states that the word *mara* is derived from "*marabunta*," an African ant that attacks in group. The concept *pandilla* would refer to a group of people who have a close relation and share the same philosophy. As friends, they take action in group, which contains for example going out to party, but also committing crimes and even murder.

[3] Rodgers, Muggah and Stevenson (2009, p. 6) state that *maras* "*are a phenomenon with transnational roots*" and can be found in Honduras, El Salvador and Guatemala. This is closely related to Cruz's definition of *maras*. In his opinion *maras* are "*a vast network of groups of people associated with the identity franchises of two street gangs that had their origins in the city of Los Angeles in the USA, but whose development no longer depends upon the American dynamics: the Mara Salvatrucha Thirteen (MS-13) and the Eighteenth Street Gang (also known as Barrio 18).*" *MS13* emerged from a division of *Barrio 18* (Cruz 2010, p. 382 and 384). *Pandillas*, on the other hand, "*are more localized, home-grown gangs that are the direct inheritors of the youth gangs that have been a historic feature of Central American societies. Pandillas were initially present throughout the region in the post-conflict period but are now only significantly visible in Nicaragua – and to a lesser extent in Costa Rica (where they are often called 'chapulines')*" (Rodgers et al. 2009, p. 6).

gang consists of females (20 %). The role of female gang members differs in some aspects from that of male gang members. Female members are often violated via sexual abuse within the gang, but they are also violators towards others. For example, female gang members are often given the task to collect the "war tax" or *impuesto de Guerra* (IUDOP 2010).[4]

Most youngsters enter a gang before the age of 15 (PNPRRS 2011), and have an average age of 13–16 years old (Merino 2004). According to the Honduran law for the prevention, rehabilitation and social reintegration of gang members, almost all gang members in Honduras are in between 12 and 25 years old.[5]

The reasons for youngsters to join a gang, often at a very young age, are similar for boys as for girls, although girls often seek refuge, within a gang, from external sexual violence (Interpeace 2013). Youngsters connect with a gang, when they have the feeling they need to be protected from violence in their neighborhood; when they have weak family ties, experience domestic violence, and live in poverty; but also when they are being excluded from good formal education and the legal job market (Santacruz Giralt et al. 2001). Youngsters who cannot relate on a sense of belonging to school or for example a sports club, find this same feeling of solidarity and belonging in a gang (Aplícano Cubero 2012). Despite the aggressive attitude towards external people, within the gang there is much solidarity in sharing food and shelter. As stated by Merino (2004, p. 128–129), "*Uno para todos y todos para uno*." Nevertheless, according to Cruz (2010), the reasons to join a gang and the gang activities have changed over the years. In the 1980s and 1990s, youngsters who were in search for their identity, found a sense of belonging in a gang. At the beginning of the twenty-first century, *mareros* could find solidarity, respect and support in a gang, but more important to note is the increase of instrumental violence with a more economic purpose. In 2005, *MS13* and *B18* became actual criminal organizations, whose main purpose was to preserve control on the criminal economy. In 2006, the gangs had completely developed their extortion practices.

By combining information from different instances (Aplícano Cubero 2012; PNPRRS 2011; Proyecto Victoria 2013), we can create a better understanding of the structure and hierarchy of the gang. The *maras* and *pandillas* are organized according to the following hierarchy: every neighborhood (*barrio*) has its own clique (*clica*),[6] which is led by chiefs and sub chiefs (*jefe* and *sub jefes*). Additionally, there are the members of the gang (*hommies* or *homeboys*),[7] who are responsible

[4] According to Wells (2013), "*criminal organizations reportedly 'tax' businesses according to how much profit they make. A small shop or market stall must pay around $7.50 a week, larger ones $10, and shop owners $15*."

[5] *Ley para la Prevención, Rehabilitación y Reinserción social de personas integrantes de maras o pandillas.* Retrieved from http://www.pnp.gob.hn/Archivos%20Para%20Descarga/LEY%20del%20PNPRRS.pdf.

[6] *Barrios* are slums or "*socially disadvantaged neighborhoods*," where most of the *maras* flourish (Cruz 2010, p. 394).

[7] *Hommie* comes from the English Word 'homeboy'. It is used when referring to male gang members (Interpeace 2013).

for the implementation of the commands of the chiefs; as well as a coordinator (*coordinador*), who is in charge of the facilitation of the relations between the other members and responsible for the supervision on the fulfillment of the rules inside the group. Before a youngster is accepted in a gang, he needs to go through different stages before reaching the (top level in the) gang hierarchy. Five levels of participation can be distinguished: the sympathizer (*el Simpathizante*), the aspirant (*el Aspirante*), the rookie (*el Novato*), the permanent gang member (*el Pandillero Permanente*), and the leader (*el Líder* or *Cabecilla*). *Simpatizantes* are youngsters, aged 10–16 years old, who live in the neighborhood where a certain gang is active. They admire these gang members for their power and way of living. *Simpatizantes* do not form part of the gang. Still on a low level, but closer to the gang, is the function of *el Aspirante. El Aspirante* is part of the gang, but does not participate in the local or national meetings. *Aspirantes* are mainly being used as *bandera*, which means that they have to guard the borders of their neighborhood and report to the gang who enters and leaves "the gang's territory." Their commitment to the group (and possibility to go to the next level) will be evaluated over a period of 1–3 years. When the *Aspirante* goes through the initiation process (*el bautizo*),[8] he becomes *el Novato*. This means he forms part of the gang and there is no way back, but he still needs to earn the confidence of the group. The main activity of *el Novato* is collecting the *impuesto de guerra. El Novato* has 1 year to adapt himself to the lifestyle and rules of his new family. As a *Novato* you can still have contact with your family, but once you are a *Pandillero Permanente*, you have to cut all family ties, because you are living with a new family now. *Pandilleros Permanentes* have to do more important (and also more dangerous) tasks. They are also willing to die for their fellow gang members. Finally, the *Líder* or *Cabecilla* is the one who is at the top of the gang. A gang member can get to this level by committing cruelties and being feared and respected by the other members.

Nevertheless, according to Merino (2004), the gang as such is not bad, but they often commit violent crimes. Fortunately, not every youngster who is part of a gang commits these crimes, which can be an important aspect regarding their rehabilitation process. As such, the mutual fights between the different gangs are often to protect their territory. This implies that gang violence is limited to the area where the gang operates, i.e., the area which the gang arrogates. According to Cruz (2010), violence that extends beyond the boundaries of the barrio would be futile, because the violence is mainly used to protect the borders of the barrio.

The so-called "war taxes" (*impuestos de guerra*) or "protection taxes" are raised from small businesses, transportation units and even from people, in order to be able to fund the *mara* expenses (Cruz 2010). Interpeace (2013) states that mainly female gang members are used to collect these taxes, as they look more innocent than male *pandilleros* and thus raise less suspicion among bystanders.

[8] The initiation process contains being beaten up for 13 (*MS13*) or 18 (*M18*) seconds. Women who want to enter the gang can chose between a 13 or 18 s of beating (*la paliza*) or 13 or 18 s having sex with several gang members (Interpeace 2013; IUDOP 2010).

Honduras has a history of so-called gang legislations and prevention and intervention measures. Since the 1990s, with the rise of *maras* in Central America, Honduras has been governed by different political parties who alternately implemented repressive and preventive measures regarding gangs. Carlos Roberto Flores Facussé (President from 1998 until 2002), from the Liberal Party, was aware of the fact that repressive measures are not effective in tackling the violence and crime generated by *maras* and *pandillas*. According to Flores, the problem needed to be handled by focusing on the underlying causes; this is the reason why he implemented the Law for the prevention, rehabilitation and social reintegration of members from *maras* and *pandillas* (*Ley para la prevención, rehabilitación y reinserción social de personas integrantes de maras o pandillas*).[9] This law also provided the country with the legal foundation of the National Program for Prevention Rehabilitation and Social Reintegration (*Programa Nacional de Prevención, Rehabilitación y Reinserción Social*/PNPRRS), which aims to prevent, rehabilitate and reintegrate members from *maras* and *pandillas*.[10] On the other hand, Ricardo Rodolfo Maduro Joest (President from 2002 until 2006), from the National Party, did not believe in supportive measures and implemented a harsher strategy towards the *maras* and *pandillas* in his country, which was known as a "Zero Tolerance" (*Cero Tolerancia*) policy. In 2003 he changed the article 332 of the Criminal Code of Honduras,[11] making it possible for the police to arrest and detain people who they suspected to form part of a gang (Carranza 2006). The reformation of article 332 of the Criminal Code was soon referred to as the law *Mano Dura* ("Hard Hand") or Anti-gang law (*Ley Antimaras*). According to Aplícano Cubero (2012) and Samayoa (2011), the implementation of the *Mano Dura* law was the start of a severe "war against crime." They argue that instead of reducing the crime rates, Maduro fostered processes of stigmatization by focusing on youngsters from marginalized and poor neighborhoods, who were suspected to form part of a gang due to their looks and language. Manuel ("Mel") Zelaya (President from 2006 until 2009), from the liberal party, just like his liberal party predecessor chose to implement a less repressive, but more balanced approach in dealing with the problem of youth gangs (Reisman 2006). The last two presidents, Porfirio ("Pepe") Lobo Sosa (2010–2014) and Juan Orlando Hernández (2014–...), both from the National Party, tried to implement some supportive measures, like the "Honduras for life" ("*Honduras por la vida*") and the "Everyone for a Better Life Plan" ("*Plan de Todos para una Vida Mejor*"), in order to create jobs, but also to give youngsters a better prospect for the future, and at the same time reduce delinquency in the country (*El Heraldo* 2012; *Gobierno de la República de Honduras* 2014).

[9] *Ley Octubre 31 2001 para la prevención, rehabilitación y reinserción social de personas integrantes de maras o pandillas, Exposición de Motivos*, p. 2, http://pdba.georgetown.edu/Security/citizensecurity/honduras/leyes/8.pdf.

[10] Art. 2, *Ley Octubre 31 2001 para la prevención, rehabilitación y reinserción social de personas integrantes de maras o pandillas*.

[11] Art. 332, *Código Penal de Honduras*, http://www.oas.org/dil/esp/Codigo_Penal_Honduras.pdf.

Despite these good intentions, Durán Chavarría (2012) states there is a general lack of preventive measures in dealing with juvenile delinquency and he emphasizes the importance of preventive projects to prevent children and youngsters from committing a crime and enrolling into the juvenile justice system.

The Reintegration of Youth Gang Members

Although many general theories on gang formation and reasons to join a gang are available, not as many discuss the reintegration or rehabilitation process of gang members. Criminological theories on gangs can help us understand why a youngster gets involved with a gang. Subsequently, we can better comprehend the reintegration processes of these youngsters, along with its difficulties. Nevertheless, according to Wood and Alleyne (2010, p. 100) "*our knowledge on gangs is still limited and rather muddy*." In what follows, we discuss the results from our interviews in relation to key criminological theories on gangs. To start with, we first discuss Thrasher's findings of his pioneering research on 1313 gangs in Chicago, as he made some specific recommendations on reintegration of gang members.

Thrasher (1963) does not focus on eliminating the gang and pushing them to the borders of our society. Rather, he argues that the gang must be given a place in their community. According to his findings, two institutions need to take care of this: those who advocate for the interests of the youngsters in the gang, and those who represent the law.

Firstly, with regard of the legal powers in our society, Thrasher (1963) considers that there is no sympathy for the situation of young gang members. Policemen have the feeling they need to suppress the gang and address them in a harsh way, without providing any suitable leisure alternatives.

Secondly, Thrasher (1963) argues that most treatment programs were not successful, because they isolated the boy from his gang and did not take the group factor into account. The delinquent's group plays an important role in the individual's life when he is constructing his own identity. Thrasher argues that, when developing a program for the treatment of gang members, attention must go to all groups in society to which the boy is affiliated. In other words, attention must be given to "*not merely the gang alone, but the family, the neighborhood, the school, the church, the occupational group, and so on*" (Thrasher 1963, p. 345). It is of importance to adapt the program to the person concerned, i.e., the role the youngster had in his gang needs to be replaced by another meaningful role within society.

Thirdly, according to Thrasher (1963) there are only two ways for a gang member to be reintegrated into society: complete removal from the gang and the associated social structure, or reformation of the gang. Regarding the first option, Thrasher (1963, p. 350) concludes that "*sending a gang boy away to an institution turns out to be little more than one method of evading the real problem – that of adjusting him in his actual social world*." He states that the second option shows more potential, for example by turning a gang into a Boy Scouts, because there is a "*need to develop a program into which the activities of the gang and its members can be incorporated and through which they can be given significance in a larger plan of life*" (Thrasher 1963, p. 359).

In the following sections we discuss our results regarding the reasons why youngsters in Honduras join a gang, the reasons to leave their gang, and the process of reintegration into society.

Gang Involvement

Before discussing the reasons for youngsters to join a gang, we need to clarify the presence of gang members within society. It is not an "us" versus "them" story, as gangs are present in all big (and even small) cities in Honduras. With more or less 35,000 gang members in the country (USAID 2012), 80 % of them living in the two biggest cities (Tegucigalpa and San Pedro Sula), it is not unlikely to come in contact with gang members. This implies that regardless of the following factors, which might have an influence on whether or not a boy or girl will become a gang member, children are confronted with the presence of gangs from a very young age onwards, and they basically grow up in communities where one gang or another is present. The latter implies that, as stated by Sutherland (1947), when youngsters find themselves in a place where criminal behavior forms part of the social structure of that neighborhood, they are more likely to become involved with the present delinquent groups.

According to our data the lack of socio-economic opportunities in Honduras, a person's instable family and environmental situation, the willingness to belong, and the persuading factor of gangs, can all contribute to the fact that a youngster joins a gang.

> *Imagine a child, an adolescent, without the possibility of going to school or they [his parents] did not register him into school; in his household there is possibly no father or the present father is violent or a violent stepfather; the economic situation is very limited; there is access to drugs; his community is dark 24 hours a day; he does not have, let's say, services which middle class boys have. That is, all those limitations lead him towards the side of these groups* (D. Urbina, personal communication, August 22, 2013).[12]

First of all, more than half of the children in Honduras grow up in poverty, often without a father, and in an environment that lacks proper healthcare, education, recreational space, and employment opportunities. Several researchers (Aplícano Cubero 2012; Merino 2004; Reisman 2006; Santacruz Giralt et al. 2001; Thornberry 1998) confirm that this is an ideal situation for the practices of gangs. During one of

---

[12] "*Imagínate un niño, un adolecente, que no tiene posibilidades de ir a la escuela o no le matriculan en la escuela; que posiblemente es su hogar no exista un papa o el papa que existe es un violento o un padrastro violento; el nivel económico es muy limitado; existe acceso a drogas; las 24 horas del día su comunidad es obscura; no tiene, digamos, servicios que tienen los muchachos de clase media. O sea, todas estas limitaciones lo guían hacia la parte de estos grupos*" (D. Urbina, personal communication, August 22, 2013).

our interviews, O. Lopez and M. Obando stated that not going to school forms a risk for gang involvement. Knowing that, according to M. Flores, 816,000 youngsters in Honduras are not going to school or working, and the fact that there are "only" 35,000 gang members, one might wonder what happened to the other children and what made the difference for them not to form part of a gang. Or, in the words of Matza (1964), how come that some youngsters drift more towards criminal and other more towards norm conformist behavior?

Secondly, many children in Honduras are raised by a single mother (up to 70 % according to C. Díaz) or grow up with the experience of domestic violence. The latter can have an influence on a child's vision towards problem solving. Though not all gang members come from poor families, they most likely seek for emotional support within a gang, when this is lacking in their own family (cf. Thrasher 1963).

> *Next, it became attractive especially for the youngsters who have suffered from domestic violence, who have lived in the streets, who have become orphans. So they encounter, within gangs, a surrogate home; where they are fed, where they are dressed, where they are accepted, they have their norms of the violent situation; but it is something the family or society cannot give them* (Pastor, personal communication, August 23, 2013).[13]

This also reminds us of Hirschi's (1969) and Reckless' (1967) control theory. When a youngster does not feel a strong attachment to his family or school or is not influenced by this outer containment, he is more likely to get involved with nonconformist activities. However, we cannot state this is due to a child's behavior; rather it is the responsibility of the family and the school to keep a youngster occupied and involved, and subsequently away from the streets (cf. Thrasher 1963).

Thirdly, youngsters encounter, in a gang, a place where they can belong and develop their identity. As a gang member you can exercise power, be respected and protected against external violence. Also the PNPRRS (2011) and Reisman (2006) stated that youngsters are attracted to gangs, because they can provide them with economic goods and give them a place in the group to develop their social identity (cf. Shaw and McKay 1969; Thrasher 1927).

> ***Interviewer**: And what do they find within a gang?*
>
> ***Interviewee**: The feeling of belonging, which they do not have at their homes; unconditional support, despite of what they do; and also the economical aspect. And all the prestige, reputation within the communities where they live* (Community police officer, personal communication, August 30, 2013).[14]

---

[13] "*Luego, fue como atractivo especialmente para jóvenes que han sufrido violencia familiar, que han vivido en la calle, que han quedado huérfanos. Entonces ellos encuentran, al interior de las pandillas, como un hogar sustitutivo; donde se alimentan, donde se visten, donde ellos son aceptado, tengan sus normas de la situación violenta; pero es algo lo que la familia o la sociedad no les puede dar*" (Pastor, personal communication, August 23, 2013).

[14] "***Entrevistador**: ¿Y que encuentran entonces en la pandilla?*

***Entrevistado**: El sentido de pertenencia, que no tienen dentro de sus hogares; apoyo incondicional, a pesar de lo que hagan; y también el aspecto económico. Y tanto de prestigio, reputación dentro de las comunidades en las cuales ellos habitan*" (Community police officer, personal communication, August 30, 2013).

Though we might ask ourselves, as stated by I. Pereyra, why it is that some youngsters, in the course of developing their identity, try to find their place within society by joining a gang? Should there be more alternative youth movements in Honduras, like boy scouts? These, according to Thrasher (1963) sometimes have the same structure or hierarchy as a gang, but with a positive attitude towards the community and society.

Fourthly, youngsters, who are not interested in joining a gang in the first place, can, according to some of our respondents, also be persuaded by their local ruling gang to perform a certain task, and by doing so get even more involved with the gang. Though we need to mention that when youngsters (who basically grew up with gang members living in their neighborhood) are asked to perform a certain task (e.g., sell some marihuana to earn a bit of money), they do not immediately link this act with forming part of a gang; as to form part of a gang, they need to go through an initiation rite first. To some extent we could link this to Cohen's (1955) subculture theory on status frustration; as Cohen states that youngsters who want to achieve a certain social status (i.e., having economic goods), but do not have the legal means to achieve it, will be tempted to use illegal means in order to get what they want. On the other hand, we were not able to confirm Cohen (1955) and Whyte's (1937) distinction between a corner boy, a college boy and a delinquent subculture—more research should be done regarding this aspect.

Leaving the Gang

Though there are youngsters who want to leave their gang, it is not always easy to do so. We first discuss the (personal) reasons to leave the gang, followed by the different ways to do so and the related difficulties.

Our respondents gave several reasons why youngsters want to leave their gang. Firstly, they want to leave as a consequence of the process of maturing. Secondly, they want to leave for the fear of being assassinated by a rivaling gang, the police, someone from the community, or by one of their fellow gang members. Thirdly, the gang member might be willing to leave his gang for family reasons and/or when he encounters external opportunities.

First of all, as our respondents mentioned, at a certain age youngsters mature and realize that what they are doing is not right. Moreover, they have had enough of all the violence. This process of maturing is what Moffitt (1993) identified as adolescent limited antisocial behavior.[15] More research should be done to find out at what age youngsters start to mature; thus at what age youngsters will be more willing to leave their gang.

[15] Moffitt (1993) developed an age-crime curve, whereby she demonstrates that most delinquency is committed at the age of 17 and the amount of crime committed decreases severely by the age of 20 and even more by the age of 25.

Secondly, gang members want to leave the gang when they are aware of how life in a gang really is in practice, i.e., committing crimes, such as robbery, murder, drug consumption, or suffering from internal (by their own gang) and external (by other gangs or the police) violence (cf. Cruz 2010; Merino 2004). After committing all these crimes, gang members realize they have built up a network of enemies and subsequently start to fear for their lives.

> *So, motivation: no longer doing this, because they end up having four enemies: enemy number one: the opposite group, the opposite gang; enemy number two: the police, that in a fight, a ... until he converts into an enemy, a member of the group with the police and they kill one another, so they are perceived as an enemy; three: people in society who have felt aggrieved or offended by this group. Many people, who suffered a death of a relative, are seeking for this group, this member, in order to kill him likewise; and the fourth enemy comes to be his own friend or partner of the group. When he wants to leave, this leads to the death; this is what they call in their jargon 'giving green light'* (M. Flores, personal communication, August 29, 2013).[16]

Thirdly, as stated by our respondents and confirmed by the literature (cf. Rodríguez Bolaños and Sanabria 2007; Aplícano Cubero 2012), youngsters are willing to leave their gang when they are offered a job or educational opportunity (cf. Hirschi 1969; Matza 1964). Our respondents also mentioned that when a gang member gets a child, he or she starts to think differently and often does not want their child to grow up as a future gang member. Although finding a job, going back to school or starting a family seems to be quite obvious reasons to leave a gang, it is not always that simple. First of all, there is a great lack of employment opportunities within the country and even if a gang member finds a job, he will most likely be refused because of his history (cf. Aplícano Cubero 2012; UNDP n.d.). Some other difficulties are discussed in the next part.

According to some of our respondents, there are only a few options to leaving the gang: converting to religion, starting a family or dying (cf. Matza 1964; Merino 2004). Even when a gang member wants to leave his gang to dedicate himself to the word of God, he always needs the permission of the gang. Other ways of leaving the gang is by seeking refuge in an institution (e.g., Casa Alianza or Proyecto Victoria) or even by fleeing the country. Though these options cannot be seen in the light of reintegration, as in the first case (for example Proyecto Victoria) ex-gang members often stay inside the rehabilitation center for a long time without going back to their community (for safety reasons), and in the second case ex-gang members literally move to another city or another country in order to avoid reprisals.

---

[16] *"Entonces, motivación: ya no seguir haciendo esto, porque llega tener cuatro enemigos: enemigo número uno: el grupo contrario, la mara contraria; enemigo número dos: la policía, que en una refriega, una ... hasta que se convierte enemigo, el miembro de un grupo con la policía y se mata uno otro, entonces se toma como un enemigo; tres: personas de la sociedad que se han sentido agraviadas o ofendidas por esto grupo. Muchas personas, que sufrieron una muerte de un familiar, andan buscando ese grupo, ese miembro, para darle muerte igualmente también; y el cuarto enemigo viene ser su mismo amigo o compañero del grupo. Cuando el ya se quiere salir, este le termina dando muerte; es lo que llaman en el jargón de ellos 'darle luz verde'"* (M. Flores, personal communication, August 29, 2013).

While some youngsters, depending on their situation (cf. supra), are willing to leave their gang, they are also aware of the dangers of doing so; one of them being, as we just mentioned, the risk of reprisals by the gang (cf. Rodríguez Bolaños and Sanabria 2007; PNPRRS 2011). Although not every gang member has equal chances to leave his gang; for a Sympathizer, Aspirant or Newbie it is easier to leave than for a Permanent Member or Leader (cf. Proyecto Victoria 2013). With this in mind, it might make sense to focus reintegration programs on the specific needs of each category or to choose to only focus on the reintegration of Sympathizers, Aspirants and Newbies. Another difficulty that a gang member is most likely to face when leaving his gang is the issue of stigmatization by society (cf. Aplícano Cubero 2012; Samayoa 2011). This stigmatization is even more severe when the person has tattoos. Whether or not the removal of tattoos can prevent an ex-gang member from further stigmatization; it is up to society to become more aware of giving second chances to ex-gang members.

> *It is extremely difficult for a person to leave a gang, here in Honduras. In the sense that we are a society that stigmatizes people. It is to say, here, the simple fact that you see a tattooed person, here they already associate the person with being a drug addict, they associate him with being a person that can be involved in criminal activities* (Community police officer, personal communication, August 30, 2013).[17]

Until now we have only discussed reasons and methods to leave the gang. However, some of our respondents (e.g., E. Bardales, I. Pereyra, and the Pastor) mentioned that leaving the gang is not always a good option (cf. Rodríguez Bolaños and Sanabria 2007; Thrasher 1963); they would rather opt for preservation (i.e., giving a place within the community), though reformation, of the gang.

> *It is that removing them from the context of the gang, in my way, viewing the things in my experience, cannot be an objective. You have to see that they already constructed a set of values and within their set of values do not think one of their values is to kill the people that are my enemies, no. It is defending my neighborhood and loving it. It is a concept of love of belonging; of respect, like I said* (I. Pereyra, personal communication, August 27, 2013).[18]

---

[17] "*Es sumamente difícil para que una persona abandone una pandilla aquí en Honduras. En el sentido de que somos una sociedad que estigmatiza a las personas. O sea aquí, el simple hecho que usted vea a una persona tatuada, aquí ya lo asocien que es una persona adicta a las drogas, le asocien a que es una persona que puede estar involucrado en actividades criminales*" (Community police officer, personal communication, August 30, 2013).

[18] "*Es que sacarlos del contexto de la pandilla, a mi modo, ver las cosas en mi experiencia, no puede ser un objetivo. Usted tiene que ver que ellos ya tienen construido un conjunto de valor y dentro de su conjunto de valores no crea usted que uno de sus valores es matar a todas las personas que son mis enemigos, no. Es defender mi barrio y amarlo. Es un concepto de amor de la pertenencia; de respeto como le decía*" (I. Pereyra, personal communication, August 27, 2013).

Reintegration into Society

When leaving the gang, our respondents stated that the process of rehabilitation and reintegration of young gang members into society should contain different aspects, and implement these aspects simultaneously in a holistic approach (cf. Dowden and Andrews 1999; Howell 1998; Thrasher 1963).

First of all, as most of our respondents stated, the reintegration process should take place in the local community of the youngster, including his family, educational training and religion (cf. Andrews and Bonta 2010; Merino 2004; Shaw and McKay 1969; Thrasher 1963). The relationship with the community, as well as with one's family should be strengthened, in order to ensure the local reintegration process (cf. Howell 1998; Shaw and McKay 1969). Also the educational aspect of going to school and having access to extracurricular activities (e.g., the "Open School" system), should keep youngsters occupied and away from the street (cf. Hirschi 1969; Lipsey 1995; Lipsey and Wilson 1998; Thrasher 1963). One example of an additional school-based method to keep children of the street is the "Open School" ("*Escuelas Abiertas*") system.

> *The teachers are now obliged to go [to school] the Saturday mornings. Said the minister of education the other day, and he is right, if Saturday in the morning of the day the teachers do not give classes or they do not want to do anything with the children, the mere fact they are at school already separates them half a day from the street. So with the Scout Association of Honduras, the National Prevention Program is making an effort to train teachers. And those weekends the school remains open, but not only for the children, also for the parents, to do some activities* (M. Obando, personal communication, August 28, 2013).[19]

While Proyecto Victoria isolates the youngster from his community, and does not have contact with the youngster's school, Casa Alianza emphasizes the importance of rehabilitating the youngster in his own environment. One might wonder whether it would be useful to reintegrate an ex-gang member in the same environment where he grew up, as it would include the same aspects which moved him towards the gang in the first place. In this regard we might ask ourselves if we can speak of a culture of violence in (certain parts of) Honduras,[20] and if it would thus

---

[19] "*Los maestros están obligado ahora ir los sábados por la mañana. Dice el otro día el ministro de educación, y tiene mucha razón, si el sábado en la jornada de la mañana los maestros no le dan clases o no quieren hacer nada con los niños, el solo hecho que estén en la escuela ya los separa media jornada de la calle. Entonces con lo Asociación de Scout de Honduras, el Programa Nacional de Prevención está haciendo un esfuerzo de formación de los maestros. Y estos fines de semana la escuela permanece abierta pero no solamente para los niños, también para los padres, para hacer algunas actividades*" (M. Obando, personal comunication, August 28, 2013).

[20] We can find some factors referring to a culture of violence, as described by Waldmann (2007) on the case of Colombia, which are similar to the case of Honduras; e.g.: high homicide rates, a culture of machismo and revenge, a lack of state monopoly of violence, ineffectiveness of the rule of law, dominance of drug cartels, etc.

make sense at all to reincorporate a rehabilitated ex-gang member in such an environment. According to the community police officer (personal communication, August 30, 2013) it can be necessary to:

> *"Also relocate them to other places where the environment is not that hostile. Because it is of no use to grab a gang member, remove him, take him for a treatment and put him back in the same place. He will return to [do] the same thing."*[21]

Secondly, psychological aspects should also be included in the reintegration process. Our respondents agreed upon the fact that psychological treatment should be given individually as well as within a group or family context. Though the literature confirms the effects of psychological treatment, they are rather critical regarding the different psychological intervention methods (cf. Lipsey 1995; Lipsey and Wilson 1998; Shaw and McKay 1969). In line with Merton's (1938) strain theory and Reckless' (1967) containment theory, we would recommend psychological treatment to focus on the person's self-control. The effectiveness of the different kinds of psychological interventions should be investigated in future studies on the rehabilitation and reintegration of gang members.

Thirdly, besides psychological, also medical aspects should be included in the reintegration process. Our respondents highlighted the importance of medical treatment, from providing general healthcare to specific attention for drug addicts and the removal of tattoos. General medical attention can be an important asset for youngsters who have limited access to health care within their community; though the effectiveness of the removal of tattoos was still open for discussion (cf. Merino 2004), since according to A. Rodriguez (personal communication, August 26, 2013).

> *It leaves behind scars and that was a mark. So, we created a conclusion in our study: the society is the one who has the tattoo. The social tattoo is there, it is on the other side; because they do not allow the reintegration process of youngsters.*[22]

Fourthly, there is some disagreement among academic researchers whether vocational training aspects should be included in the reintegration process or not (cf. Dowden and Andrews 1999; Lipsey 1995; Lipsey and Wilson 1998). According to our respondents it should. C. Díaz (personal communication, August 28, 2013) outlined an example, of what she witnessed in El Salvador, of how a group of religious people supported gang members in their process of reintegration:

> *They grabbed all the gang members that were willing to leave and created a macro workshop. They have carpentry, they have welding, they have – so, they create microenterprises right there. For example, the ministry of education of El Salvador tells them "we need*

[21] "*reubicarlos también en otros lugares donde el ambiente no sea hostil pues. Porque de nada nos sirve agarrar un miembro de la mara, sacarlo, llevarlo dar un tratamiento y volver meterlo en el mismo lugar. Vuelve de lo mismo*" (Community police officer, personal communication, August 30, 2013).

[22] "*Quedan cicatrizas y esa era una marca. Entonces, en nuestro estudio creamos una conclusión: el tatuaje lo tiene la sociedad. El tatuaje social está allí, está en el otro lado. Porque no permiten el proceso de reinserción de los jóvenes*" (A. Rodriguez, personal communication, August 26, 2013).

2000 school desks; you [can] make them". So they make 2000 school desks, they buy the materials and they distribute the profits among all the partners. So over there it is working a lot.[23]

A future study, regarding this aspect, should investigate which vocational skills are most useful for ex-gang members who want to reintegrate into society. From this study we remember that vocational skills, which focus on employment, micro enterprises and commercial or administrative business skills, can facilitate the reinsertion process on the labor market.

Following the discussion of our results in relation to well-known criminological theories and other literature; we would like to conclude by singling out one theoretical approach which in our opinion is most related to the phenomenon of youth gang members and their reintegration into society, namely, the approach of labeling theories. We consider this approach to be related to the specific situation of *maras* and *pandillas* in Honduras for the following reasons. First of all, when Ricardo Maduro implemented the so-called Anti-gang law, he created a platform whereby it was possible for police officers to arrest and detain youngsters who were (often allegedly) being suspected to form part of a gang (cf. Carranza 2006). According to our respondents and confirmed by the literature (Aplícano Cubero 2012; Samayoa 2011), due to this Anti-gang law many youngsters were being stigmatized by their looks, economic situation and area where they lived; to state it with the words of Becker (1963), those youngsters were labeled as outsiders. Secondly, as Lemert (1951) argued in his theory on primary and secondary deviation, or before him Tannenbaum (1938) with his theory on dramatization of the evil, the disapproving reactions of the government, the media and subsequently the community on primary deviant behavior, fostered further secondary deviant behavior, as the youngster has the feeling he is already pushed into a certain category. The latter is particularly important regarding this research, as our respondents repeatedly mentioned that the Honduran society is very stigmatizing towards youngsters with a history of gang membership, especially towards those with tattoos; subsequently they are not eager in giving second chances. In order to avoid these processes of stigmatization, outsiders should be relabeled as insiders, and they should be given a space within society.

"*We need to integrate the boys. Because I am not in favor of policies – like this policy, which they are discussing in North America – the policy of affirmative action. Because they are segregationists. Gang members, regardless their condition, should be integrated into society. Whatever their condition is. Not creating segregated communities just for them, no*" (E. Bardales, personal communication, August 22, 2013).[24]

---

[23] "*Ellos agarraron a todos los mareros que querían salir y crear un macro taller. Tienen carpintería, tienen soldadura, tienen – entonces, ellos allí mismo crean microempresas. Por ejemplo, el ministerio de educación de El Salvador les dice "necesitamos 2000 pupitres, háganlos ustedes". Entonces ellos hacen 2000 pupitres, compran los materiales y las ganancias se distribuyen entre todos los socios. Entonces allí está funcionando mucho eso*" (C. Díaz, personal communication, August 28, 2013).

[24] "*Hay que integrar, hay que integrar a los muchachos. Porque yo no estoy a favor de las políticas – como se dice esta política, que en lo Norte-Americana hablan – de la política de la acción afirmativa. Porque son segregacionistas. Los miembros de pandillas independientemente su condición deben ser integrados a la sociedad. Independientemente su condición. No crear comunidades segregadas, solo para ellos, no*" (E. Bardales, personal communication, August 22, 2013).

Conclusion and Recommendations for Further Research

The purpose of this research was to find an answer to the question: "How can the reintegration of young gang members into society best be facilitated?" In order to respond to this research question, two sub-questions have been investigated:

1. For which reasons can young gang members leave the gang?
2. Which intervention methods can facilitate young gang members in their process of leaving the gang and reintegrate in society?

We used 14 qualitative semi-open interviews with stakeholders, living in Honduras, to research this subject.

Regarding our first sub-question, we can state that there are several reasons for gang members to leave their gang. Those reasons are: the fear of being assassinated by a rivaling gang or to die within the gang; the family of the gang member who wants him to leave the gang; and encountering a better alternative of living (e.g., formal education or a legal job). These are some push and pull factors for gang members to leave their gang, but actually doing so is not that obvious. According to most of our respondents, a gang member can only leave his gang if he converts to religion (and goes to church on a daily basis) or when he dies. The options to leave the gang are scarce and there is always the risk of reprisals by the gang. When a gang member leaves his gang, for one of the reasons mentioned above, he is followed up by his gang for 1–2 years. If he trespasses one of the conditions for leaving the gang (e.g., if he stops going to church or commits a crime), the gang gives him "green light" (*luz verde*), which means they kill him for the mistake he made.

Regarding our second sub-question, we can state that the process of reintegration of young gang members into society can best be facilitated when it contains different intervention aspects, which are simultaneously implemented in a holistic approach. This research highlights the importance of making a distinction between the different levels of gang membership; rehabilitation and reintegration interventions should focus on the Sympathizers, Aspirants, and Newbie's. The reintegration process should take place in the local community of the youngster, if possible. Otherwise, the youngster should be relocated to another community. During the process, the youngster's family and school or educational formation should be incorporated. The reintegration process should also contain psychological aspects, focusing on one's self-esteem and the youngster must be provided with the required medical treatment. Ex-gang members, who tattooed themselves, should also get the opportunity to remove their tattoos, as (mostly visible) tattoos have a stigmatizing effect regarding one's chances on the job market. Finally, our respondents also stated vocational training aspects should be included in the youngster's reintegration process, though the literature is more critical towards this aspect.

Concerning further investigation, we could make the following suggestions. First of all, while focusing on gang members in general, we did not distinguish between male and female members. We briefly highlighted the different roles of men and women within a gang, but it could be of interest to elaborate more on this issue. Secondly, the focus of this dissertation was on the reintegration of *maras* and *pandillas* in Honduras. No distinction was made between the different gangs. This could be another recommendation for further research, i.e., to investigate the difference between the *Mara Salvatrucha* and the *Barrio 18*. By investigating the differences, and also the similarities, between those two gangs, we could have a better view on the potentiality of a truce, which was initiated by Bishop Rómulu Emiliani. Subsequently, we could elaborate more on the differences and similarities of the *MS13* and *B18* in Honduras and the rest of Central America and even in the USA, where those gangs are active. Finally, while we focused on extramural reintegration methods, it could be of interest to investigate which rehabilitation and reintegration methods within an intramural setting, i.e., within jail or other closed centers, are most effective.

References

Andrews, D. A., & Bonta, J. (2010). *The psychology of criminal conduct* (5th ed.). New Providence, New Jersey: LexisNexis Group.

Aplícano Cubero, A. (2012). Relato de vida de una expandillera de Honduras. In M. Ávalos Quispal (Ed.), *Historias y relatos de vida de pandilleros y ex pandilleros de Guatemala, El Salvador y Honduras: Inicio de diálogo desde su realidad y percepciones* (pp. 287–321). Guatemala: Insituto de Estudios Comparados en Ciencias Penales de Guatemala.

Becker, H. (1963). *Outsiders: Studies in the sociology of deviance*. New York: Free Press.

Carranza, M. (2006). Del asistencialismo a la incidencia y el cabildeo: las diversas respuestas de la sociedad civil organizada al fenómeno de las pandillas en Honduras. In J. M. Cruz (Ed.), *Maras y pandillas en Centroamérica: las respuestas de la sociedad civil organizada (Volumen IV)* (pp. 235–328). San Salvador: UCA.

Cohen, A. K. (1955). *Delinquent boys: The culture of the gang*. Glenceo: The Free Press.

Cruz, J. M. (2010). Central American maras: From youth street gangs to transnational protection rackets. *Global Crime, 11*(4), 379–398.

Dowden, C., & Andrews, D. A. (1999). What works in young offender treatment: A meta-analysis. *Forum on Corrections Research, 11*, 21–24.

Durán Chavarría, D. (2012). *Prevención de la violencia juvenil y fortalecimiento del sistema de justicia penal juvenil*. San José: ILANUD.

El Heraldo (2012). *Lanzan programa Honduras por la vida*. Retrieved June 30, 2014, from http://www.elheraldo.hn/csp/mediapool/sites/ElHeraldo/Pais/story.csp?cid=573167&sid=299&fid=214

Floresi, H., Mejía, J., Mejía, J. A., SJ, I. M., & Serrano, O. (2004). Políticas juveniles y rehabilitación de mareros en Honduras. In ERIC, DIRINPRO, NITLAPÁN, IDIES, & IUDOP (Eds.), *Maras y pandillas en Centroamérica: vol. III. Políticas juveniles y rehabilitación* (pp. 187–292). Managua, El Salvador: UCA Publicaciones.

Gobierno de la República de Honduras (2014). *Juan Orlando Hernández—presidente de la república de Honduras: plan de todos para una vida mejor*. Retrieved June 30, 2014, from http://www.presidencia.gob.hn/

Gurney, K. (2014, March 8). Homicidios en El Salvador alcanzan niveles previos a la tregua. *InSightCrime*. Retrieved August 28, 2014, from http://es.insightcrime.org/noticias-del-dia/homicidios-el-salvador-alcanzan-niveles-previos-tregua

Hirschi, T. (1969). *Causes of delinquency*. California: University of California Press.

Howell, J. C. (1998). Promising programs for youth gang violence prevention and intervention. In R. Loeber, & D. P. Farrington (Eds.), *Serious & violent juvenile offenders* (pp. 284–312). London: Sage.

Interpeace. (2013). *Violentas y violentadas: relaciones de género en las maras Salvatrucha y Barrio 18 del triángulo norte de Centroamérica*. Guatemala: Interpeace Regional Office for Latin America.
IUDOP. (2010). *"Seconds in the air": Women gang-members and their prisons*. San Salvador: UCA.
IUDOP. (2012). *Encuesta de evaluación del año 2012*. San Salvador: Universidad Centroamericana José Simeón Cañas.
Katz, J., & Jackson-Jacobs, C. (2004). The criminologists' gang. In C. Summer (Ed.), *Blackwell companion to criminology* (pp. 91–124). London: Blackwell.
Lemert, E. M. (1951). *Social pathology*. New York: McGraw-Hill.
Lipsey, M. W. (1995). What do we learn from 400 research studies on the effectiveness of treatment with juvenile delinquents? In J. McGuire (Ed.), *What works: Reducing reoffending* (pp. 63–78). Chichester, UK: John Wiley & Sons.
Lipsey, M. W., & Wilson, D. B. (1998). Effective intervention for serious juvenile offenders: A synthesis of research. In R. Loeber, & D. P. Farrington (Eds.), *Serious & Violent Juvenile Offenders* (pp. 313–345). London: Sage.
Matza, D. (1964). *Delinquency and drift*. New York: Wiley.
Merino, J. M. (2004). Políticas juveniles y rehabilitación de mareros en Guatemala. In ERIC, DIRINPRO, NITLAPÁN, IDIES, & IUDOP (Eds.), *Maras y pandillas en Centroamérica: vol. III. Políticas juveniles y rehabilitación* (pp. 89–186). Managua, Nicaragua: UCA Publicaciones.
Merton, R. K. (1938). Social structure and anomie. *American Sociological Review, 3*, 672–682.
Moffitt, T. E. (1993). Adolescence-limited and life-course-persistent antisocial behavior: A developmental taxonomy. *Psychological Review, 100*(4), 674–701.
Programa Nacional de Prevención, Rehabilitación y Reinserción Social, (2011). *Situación de maras y pandillas en Honduras*. Tegucigalpa, Honduras: Programa Nacional de Prevención, Rehabilitación y Reinserción Social.
Proyecto Victoria. (2013). *Maras y Pandillas: sinónimo de violencia, dolor y muerte*. Tegucigalpa: Proyecto Victoria.
Reckless, W. C. (1967). *The crime problem*. New York: Meredith Publishing Company.
Reisman, L. (2006). Breaking the vicious cycle: Responding to Central American youth gang violence. *SAIS Review, 26*(2), 147–152.
Rodgers, D., Muggah, R., & Stevenson, C. (2009). *Gangs of Central America: Causes, costs, and interventions*. Geneva: Small Arms Survey, Graduate Institute of International and Development Studies.
Rodríguez Bolaños, J. A., & Sanabria, L. (2007). *Maras y pandillas, comunidad y policía en Centroamérica*. San José: DEMOSCOPÍA S.A.
Rubio, M. (2002). *La violencia en honduras y la región del valle de Sula*. Washington, DC: Departamento Regional de Operaciones II.
Samayoa, C. V. (2011). *Ejecuciones extrajudiciales de jóvenes estigmatizados en Centroamérica: estudio de situación de Guatemala, El Salvador y Honduras, 2009*. San Salvador: Programa de Seguridad Juvenil.
Santacruz Giralt, M. L., Concha-Eastman, A., & Unidos, H. (2001). *Barrio adentro: la solidaridad violenta de las pandillas*. San Salvador: Instituto Universitario de Opinión Pública.
Secretaría de Finanzas. (2013). *Presupuesto ciudadano. Ejercicio Fiscal 2013*. Honduras: Secretaria de Finanzas.
Shaw, C. R., & McKay, H. D. (1969). *Juvenile delinquency and urban areas: A study of rates of delinquency in relation to differential characteristics of local communities in American cities*. Chicago: The University of Chicago Press.
Sutherland, E. H. (1947). Differential association. In J. E. Jacoby (Ed.), *Classics of criminology* (pp. 225–227). Illinois: Waveland Press.
Tannenbaum, F. (1938). *Crime and the community*. Boston: Ginn.
Thornberry, T. P. (1998). Membership in youth gangs and involvement in serious and violent offending. In R. Loeber, & D. P. Farrington (Eds.), *Serious & violent juvenile offenders* (pp. 147–166). London: Sage.

Thrasher, F. M. (1927). *The gang: A study of 1,313 gangs in Chicago*. Chicago: The University of Chicago Press.

Thrasher, F. M. (1963). *The gang: A study of 1,313 gangs in Chicago*. Chicago: The University of Chicago Press.

UNAH-IUDPAS. (2013). *Observatorio de la violencia: boletín enero-diciembre 2012 (Edición No. 28, Enero 2013)*. Tegucigalpa: Instituto Universitario de Democracia, Paz y Seguridad.

UNDP (n.d.). *Honduras en breve*. (n.d.). Retrieved November 4, 2013, from UNDP Honduras website: http://www.hn.undp.org/content/honduras/es/home/countryinfo/

UNODC. (2012). *Transnational organized crime in Central America and the Caribbean: A threat assessment*. Vienna: United Nations Office on Drugs and Crime.

UNODC. (2013). *Global study on homicide 2013*. Vienna: United Nations Office on Drugs and Crime.

USAID. (2012). *Snapshot: Deconstructing gang structures & operations*. Washington, DC: U.S. Agency for International Development.

Waldmann, P. (2007). Is there a culture of violence in Colombia? *Terrorism and Political Violence, 19*(4), 593–609.

Weerman, F. M., Maxson, C. L., Esbensen, F., Aldridge, J., Medina, J., & van Gemert, F. (2009). *Eurogang program manual background, development, and use of the eurogang instruments in multi-site, multi-method comparative research*. Retrieved March 31, 2014, from http://www.umsl.edu/ccj/eurogang/EurogangManual.pdf

Wells, M. (2013). *Teen gang fighting Honduras Maras for extortion profits*. InSight Crime. Retrieved July 28, 2014, from http://www.insightcrime.org/news-briefs/teenage-gang-fighting-honduras-maras-extortion

Whyte, W. F. (1937). *Street corner society*. Chicago: University of Chicago Press.

Wood, J., & Alleyne, E. (2010). Street gang theory and research: Where are we now and where do we go from here? *Aggression and Violent Behavior, 15*, 100–111.

Part III
Society's Responses to Crime

Chapter 14
The Surveillance Society: A Criminological Perspective

Rick Sarre

Introduction

Almost four decades ago I was backpacking with friends through Europe, and took the opportunity to visit Checkpoint Charlie, the cross-over point through the Berlin Wall that divided East and West Berlin. After conceding that there was no alternative but to put up with the rigmarole at the crossing (which involved handing over passports and converting the required amount of West German deutschmarks to East German deutschmarks), my friends and I dutifully stepped quietly into East Berlin. Walking through empty streets toward the virtually deserted Brandenburg Gate, we observed dozens of pairs of eyes watching us from "pillbox" observatories. We remarked to each other that the difference between the "free" West and these authoritarian regimes was the level of surveillance of their citizenry.

Fast forward to 2015, and modern, democratic Berlin is now home to tens of thousands of Closed Circuit Television (CCTV) cameras, millions of mobile (or "cell") phones (usually equipped with cameras), and a significant (and growing) number of publicly and privately owned portable "drones," referred to more appropriately as Remotely Piloted Aircraft, or "RPAs" (Fung 2013). The actual numbers of CCTVs, portable telephones, and RPAs are completely unknown, principally because most are in private hands. No one recorded our visit to East Berlin in 1979. But there could be dozens of hours of CCTV footage of the visit that my wife and I made there in 2015. Our mobile phone records will, upon retrieval, tell the reviewer exactly where we were, who we called, and for how long (Michael and Clarke 2012; Atlantic 2012; Tassone et al 2013). Our credit card purchases will tell a story about where we walked, and what our shopping preferences were (Norris and Wilson

R. Sarre (✉)
School of Law, University of South Australia, Adelaide, Australia
e-mail: rick.sarre@unisa.edu.au

E.C. Viano (ed.), *Cybercrime, Organized Crime, and Societal Responses*,
DOI 10.1007/978-3-319-44501-4_14

2005, p. 409). While we did not see any RPAs, they could have been deployed without our knowing and could have been delivering our Internet Service Provider's wireless signal connection (Hern 2015).

In the modern digital age, data, especially personal data, have become not only ubiquitous, but profoundly political (Bennett et al. 2014). In the modern big city police, intelligence agencies, corporations, employers, media, and property owners, many by using their privately contracted security personnel and service providers, are all now capable of observing, filming, and monitoring the activities of others very easily and very cheaply. What we see today is a surveillance society that one would never have dreamed of in decades past (Lyon et al. 2012). It is not a new story at all. These trends had been predicted for many years (Neyland 2006) and are now coming true (Helgesson 2011; Smith and Brooks 2013; Sarre 2014).

Let us begin with a definition of surveillance. A very useful one is found in a recent report by a Canadian team that studied the growth of the phenomenon for 7 years. Surveillance, they said, is

> any systematic focus on personal information in order to influence, manage, entitle, or control those persons whose information is collected. (Bennett et al. 2014, p. vii)

Indeed, such a systematic focus on citizens is now readily available by the tools of the modern digital world. These tools are regularly available to police and policing and military agencies but are increasingly becoming available to (and affordable for) individuals and private organizations (Sarre et al. 2014). This is a phenomenon that will continue to manifest itself rapidly as our technological sophistication continues.

> From time immemorial, detailed records have been accumulated on the health, morality, cognitive development, motivations, sexualities, incomes, work activities and whereabouts of certain populations … [what *has* changed is the] significant intensification and diversification of technologically facilitated surveillance mechanisms …. (Smith 2012, p. 1)

Given that surveillance is on the increase, should it be a matter of concern? The Universal Declaration on Human Rights provides us with a first step toward making our way through the ethical maze. In 1948, its proponents agreed as follows:

> No one shall be subjected to arbitrary interference with his privacy, family, home or correspondence, nor to attacks upon his honour and reputation. Everyone has the right to the protection of the law against such interference or attacks. (Article 12)

How does this admonition, written a half a century ago (before television, wireless phones, and the internet were invented), play out in a world that leaves very little of public (if not private) space untouched by some form of visual surveillance? Some believe that society is living under a unique modern day privacy threat. Others, however, have few worries about living in a "watched" society, arguing that surveillance allows citizens to enjoy the benefits of instantaneous communication on a scale only dreamed about by our forebears. They consider that any interference with privacy is simply an annoying by-product of a very useful and highly convenient trend.

Consider also the modern phenomenon of social media which facilitates, with the permission of the user, the sophisticated surveillance of those who participate in this form of communication. Take, for example, the massive reach of Facebook today. Its technological capacities are mind-boggling.

> Facebook announced in June [2011] that it was implementing face-recognition technology that scans all the photos in its database and automatically suggests identifying tags that match images of a user's friends with their names. (Rosen 2011)

Users of Facebook, LinkedIn, or similar sites provide details about themselves and, by recommendation, their friends and associates (Arnold 2012, p. 58). Not only does Facebook build a profile of users, but by using the *like* button to indicate one's interest in pictures, comments, or advertisements, one allows a far more detailed picture of him or herself as a consumer to be built. Information about our preferences, affiliations, and purchasing patterns may be extrapolated to populate a personal profile. Today this information is a highly commercialized and thus valuable commodity. One can extrapolate from the numbers of subscribers who continue to use Facebook that they do not seem to care too much about their potential for commodification.

What do we make of all of this? Are the tools of modern surveillance blessings or curses? To answer these questions, we first need to examine briefly some cultural issues.

On the One Hand, the Culture of Control

There has been, and continues to be, a massive expansion of overt and covert surveillance internationally, through an ever-expanding technological revolution that has left no part of the globe untouched. There are those, like Elliot Cohen, who view this trend as a manifestation of a new "culture of control" that presents an ever-present and insidious danger:

> As we begin to accept increasingly greater and greater restrictions on our civil liberties, the technology to further abridge these liberties continues to expand and leads the way to even greater abridgements. (Cohen 2010)

Surveillance, Cohen and other advocates say, serves the interests of data-hungry social and commercial institutions. These institutions then apply formulae and protocols in order to classify and sort information, label and categorize abnormalities and identify particular patterns (Marks 2012). Citizens are the pawns in the process of enriching those who have the power to observe, monitor, and assemble data on them.

While there are arguments that the tools of surveillance allow us to feel safer, Marcella and Stucki are not so sure. By using a series of rhetorical questions posed as follows, they point to the dangers of any such views:

> Does giving up my right to privacy ensure my improved safety and security? How can I prove this? Can I see improved safety? How do I know I am secure? I can quantify and tangibly identify when I am asked to provide personal data, or when my privacy may be challenged either directly or indirectly. Scarier, however, is my total lack of knowledge of the times my personal confidential and private data is accessed, reviewed, analysed, cross-referenced and mixed, without my knowledge and/or consent. (Marcella and Stucki 2003, p. 12)

Hence there are fears associated with the technology and the political powers held by its users. In the case of the public sector, this involves the emboldening of police and other agencies to spy upon the legitimate activities of those whom the authorities deem "undesirable."

The American Civil Liberties Union (ACLU) expresses well the dangers their members see in governmental surveillance generally. They issue this challenge for legislators:

> Rules must be put in place to ensure that we can enjoy the benefits of this new technology without bringing us closer to a "surveillance society" in which our every move is monitored, tracked, recorded, and scrutinised by the government. (ACLU 2007)

We should, says the ACLU, be very cautious of these trends. How can we be sure, their members ask, that the controllers of the tools of surveillance are not privileging some sectors of society vis-à-vis others? Should we not be suspicious of the political persuasions of those who would suggest, install, and monitor the means of surveillance? (O'Malley 2008)

In the case of the private sector, power is manifested by the availability of data for sale pertaining to the spending and other patterns of behavior of millions of customers. The culture of control thus extends to the collection of information data. Increasingly, nations are accessing metadata (communications between people by mobile telephonic means) for international intelligence analysis (Smith 2006; Prunckun 2010) and requiring national and private telecommunications companies to store it for lengthy periods of time. In Australia, for example, laws were enacted in 2015 requiring metadata to be stored for 2 years, even in the face of growing evidence that open-source anonymizing network services can be employed without requiring the user to reveal any information about themselves at all (Flick 2013).

According to the culture-of-control theorists, there are the additional dangers of public and private institutions failing to vouchsafe data security. The poor track record of certain companies in this regard is a matter of public concern. In May 2011, for example, Sony's PlayStation data network was breached by hackers and the private data files (including the banking details) of almost 70 million people were stolen (BBC 2011).

The dangers appear to have become even more sinister in recent years:

> And now we have the risk of hacking computer-based, networked drug dispensers, and changing the doses which they are told to administer, or hacking motorcar computers so as to disable the brakes or the power-assisted steering. And there is "ransomware", which is malware which encrypts your documents or other computerised records so that you cannot get access to them, and then you are asked to pay the encrypter a substantial sum to disencrypt. (Neuberger 2015, § 49)

On the Other Hand, the Culture of Connection

On the other hand, the above trends are of little consequence to millions of the world's citizens who do not feel compromised by the modern trend of pervasive monitoring. They say that the extra surveillance is simply a desirable by-product of the demands of consumers for security in the aftermath of the attacks on the World Trade Center and the Pentagon on September 11, 2001, if not other terrorist attacks before and since, including, for example, the horrors of the shopping mall attack in September 2013 in Nairobi, the storming of the parliament in October 2014 in Ottawa, and the multipronged shootings and bombings of citizens in November 2015 in Paris.

Millions of people around the world, on a daily basis, add material to their social media sites, walk through shopping centers where there are clearly CCTV cameras, and use retailers' loyalty cards which are electronically linked to their private banking details. Indeed, the growth of these linkages shows a seemingly insatiable desire of citizens to embrace them. For example, the Apple Corporation revealed in 2012, when it launched its new iOS 6 operating system, that 100 million devices were updated within the first 3 days of its release (Apple 2012).

There is a strong argument that modern citizens indulge in a privacy-benefit trade-off, and calculate that their lives can be enhanced by having access to all of the modern social media platforms such as Instagram, Facebook, Viber, and Facetime without worrying too much about the consequences for their personal privacy. They point to the phone "apps" that provide instantaneous data that can provide very useful tourist advice, taxi services, maps, and safety and protection information when one is lost, or has been a victim of crime.

These apologists point to the high profile manhunts solved by the use of mass CCTV surveillance. In April 2013 two young men planted bombs near the end of the Boston marathon route. Their faces, captured on CCTV, were on the front page of most American newspapers within 48 h of the bombing.

The most recent high profile example in Australia was a case in Melbourne in 2012 when a young journalist named Jill Meagher was attacked and killed by a man who approached her in a commercial street late at night. CCTV footage (from a private shopfront) showing the victim walking from a bar along the street toward her home at 1:40 am on the Saturday morning and being met by a man known to police was crucial to solving the case. Prior to then, investigating police were uncertain about any of the circumstances of her death and had no suspects at all (Le Grand and Gosper 2012).

It is not just violent crime that has been solved by electronic means. Banks can cast their surveillance "eye" over millions of credit card and other transactions, and look for anomalies, for example, transactions that have been made in a number of places simultaneously that could not have been physically possible (Woodward 2013). In this way they can forestall much electronic crime including cybercrime.

Into the surveillance "mix" has come a new player entirely: the drone or Remotely Piloted Aircraft (RPA) which is becoming common in urban skies. A sophisticated RPA is now available to the public for less than US$10,000. It can be hired (with an operator) for as little as US$1500 per hour. A far less sophisticated RPA is available for sale for less than US$1000. They are very common today. One of the main manufacturers, DJI, has forecast that it will sell US$1 billion worth of products in 2015 (Marsden 2015).

RPAs can be very useful. They can be deployed, for example, for crime prevention, agricultural and mining surveying, aerial photography, traffic control, bushfire spotting, beach patrolling, sports webcam broadcasting, and for search and rescue (Maiolo 2012; Bracken-Roche et al. 2014). They may have a use in diplomatic circles also. The President of the Organisation for Security and Cooperation in Europe (OSCE) said, in September 2014, that they plan to use RPAs to monitor the Russia–Ukraine border in their mission to broker deals between Ukraine's warring sides (Sarre 2015). RPA ubiquity has, for the most part, been greeted favorably.

There are a number of questions that arise not only from RPAs but from the modern surveillance phenomenon more generally: are our societies better off (e.g., in terms of crime reduction or safety or knowledge) by the deployment of tools of surveillance? If so, are these benefits worth the financial costs, the opportunity costs, and the loss of privacy occasioned thereby? Is there something more sinister that we need to be concerned about? It is to that question we now turn.

Are We Better Off in a World of Mass Surveillance?

To maintain one's dignity, one must be able to control access to oneself, and to be protected against unwanted scrutiny and judgment in private or in public. In a world of mass surveillance, that protection is becoming more difficult to guarantee.

> Grounded in this rationale is the entitlement to anonymity, which should ensure that encounters with others in public remain at arm's length and that a person is subjected to only fleeting and impersonal appraisal. Like all privacy-related claims, anonymity is of particular value in fending off the controlling powers of the state. (Larsen 2011, p. 185)

Our anonymity is now at grave risk, says Larsen. Once the power of control is in place, it is very difficult to take it back.

> [O]nce the process of surveillance and collection of information is set in motion, and with new methods of electronic processing, facilitating the sorting and identification of people, it only needs the political will to assert the control that the accumulated knowledge allows. (Larsen 2011, p. 186)

As the former parliamentarian Craig Emerson wrote in November 2013,

> with every new closed circuit television camera installed, every retina reader in public and private places, every deployment of face-recognition technology, a decision is being made in favour of [public protection] over privacy. (Emerson 2013)

All of this paints a somewhat frightening scenario, but there is another side to the coin. The millions of little phones and cameras that are now within everyone's reach have provided us with a great tool against tyranny. Who can forget the exposure of the appalling practices of the Los Angeles Police Department by the public filming of the Rodney King beating in 1991? (Kearon 2013, p. 418) Who does not believe that public officials are now being held to greater standards of accountability knowing that handheld cameras on telephones are never too far away? (Goldsmith 2015) Mobile telephone cameras owned by private individuals will continue to be regularly utilized to expose criminal behavior. Moreover, security technology will continue to enjoy the great confidence of the commercial sector given its indispensable capacity to protect assets from theft and damage (Welsh and Farrington 2004; Norris and Wilson 2005; Draper et al. 2012; Prenzler and Sarre 2012).

The deployment of RPAs likewise provides the potential for enormous public benefit. True, the breach of privacy possibilities is obvious. How many of us would want our neighbors deploying an RPA over our backyard while we were sunbaking or attending to the family barbecue? How many of us would like to see journalists from the local newspaper or television station trying to get closer for a photograph of a family during a moment of private grieving? On the other hand, as listed before, if deployed appropriately, RPAs can be vital to citizen safety and welfare, and in the detection of criminal activity (Australian Government 2014; Sarre 2015).

It is possible that current and future generations will be less concerned with their individual privacy, driven by ever-increasing desire for connectivity at a relatively minimal cost, and even with a clear understanding of what it is that they are exposing. There is a strong sense that people indulge in a privacy-benefit trade-off, and calculate that their lives can be enhanced from having databases, say, that allow any embassy or hospital anywhere in the world to access their travel and medical records, or to have a global credit rating available electronically that can be relied upon to allow purchases to proceed in any country without difficulty (Sarre and Prenzler 2009).

By the same token, it is also possible the public *does* want there to be limits upon the ability of public and private institutions to delve into their private lives. A recent report on community attitudes by the Office of the Australian Information Commissioner (OAIC 2013) found that Australians of all ages *do* care about improper information sharing. They *do* worry about the collecting and processing of data by government agencies and private businesses (Arnold 2013). They *do* worry about how long it will be stored, and how it will be used. They *do* worry about how they may not be able to stop it being misused.

Many individuals will thus continue to develop a heightened expectation of privacy, given the possibility that any one of us might be under observation by a tool of surveillance (publicly or privately operated) at any time.

> It is at times tempting to accept the pithy observation made by one of the founders of Sun-Microsystems, who said that the effect of the internet is that "You have zero privacy. Get over it." But that is not the way to go. The state has a duty to protect its citizens against the excesses of the state itself as well as the invasions of rights by others. People care about their privacy, even if they often do little to protect it. And with its substantial potential for criminality—hacking, cyber-fraud, illegal pornography, grooming and bullying—as well as for defamation and other civil wrongs, electronic communication systems have to be subject to a degree of regulation and control. (Neuberger 2015, § 62)

The types and levels of control are matters for all of us to consider seriously. These are not questions that can be dismissed lightly.

It has often been said that anyone who has nothing to hide should not worry about high levels of surveillance and monitoring. That is not a strong argument. What makes a person of little interest to governments and corporations today can change overnight for the most spurious of reasons (Woodward 2013). The old adage that the price of freedom is eternal vigilance has never been more apt.

Conclusion

Will the expectation of privacy reduce over time, especially as technologies become more widespread and accepted? It is difficult to say. Some people will remain unconcerned about incursions into their individual privacy, driven by an ever-increasing desire for global connectivity at a relatively minimal cost, and even with a clear understanding of the data footprint that they are leaving behind. Others will continue to harbor concerns that they will never be able to escape the public and private eyes that will continue to follow them whether they like it or not, even if the purposes for doing so are not dishonorable.

Government policy-makers, legislators, and the courts alike are thus challenged to find the required balance between appropriate levels of surveillance and the rights of individuals to be free from the prying eyes of others. At the very least, these institutions must hold those organizations that wield surveillance power to high levels of public accountability. Citizens themselves must make their preferences known. Will their opinions change over time? How will legislators respond? We await the future with some trepidation but also with great interest.

References

ACLU (2007). Surveillance Society Clock, 4 September 2007. Retrieved November 11, 2012, from http://www.aclu.org/technology-and-liberty/surveillance-society-clock-more.

Apple (2012). iPhone 5 first weekend sales top five million. Retrieved November 11, 2012, from http://link.amtac.net/tjvn4.

Arnold, B. (2012, October 20). Face off, agenda. *The Weekend West*.

Arnold, B. (2013, October 10). The Australian public cares about privacy: do politicians? *The Conversation*.

Atlantic (2012, April 7). *Total surveillance society: mobile phones increasingly used by local police for tracking*. The Extinction Protocol. Retrieved November14, 2012, from http://www.theextinctionprotocol.wordpress.com/.

Australian Government (2014). *House of representatives standing committee on social policy and legal affairs. Eyes in the sky: inquiry into drones and the regulation of air safety and privacy.* Retrieved from http://www.aph.gov.au/Parliamentary_Business/Committees/House/Social_Policy_and_Legal_Affairs/Drones/Report

BBC (2011). Sony investigating another hack. Retrieved from http://www.bbc.co.uk/news/business-13636704

Bennett, C., Haggerty, K., Lyon, D., & Steeves, V. (2014). *Transparent lives: surveillance in Canada*. Canada: Athabasca University Press.

Bracken-Roche, C., Lyon, D., Mansour, M., Molnar, A., Saulnier, A., & Thompson, S. (2014). *Surveillance drones: privacy implications of the spread of unmanned aerial vehicles (UAVs) in Canada*. A report to the office of privacy commissioner of Canada. Surveillance Studies Centre, Queen's University, April.

Cohen, E. D. (2010, October 24). Mass surveillance and state control: the total information awareness project, *Psychology Today*, www.psychologytoday.com.

Draper, R. A., Ritchie, J., & Prenzler, T. (2012). Making the most of security technology. In T. Prenzler (Ed.), *Policing and security in practice: challenges and achievements*. New York: Palgrave.

Emerson, C. (2013. November 2). No escape from electronic eyes, *The Australian*. p. 20.
Flick, C. (2013, October 9). Silk road bust unmasks our misconceptions on anonymity. *The Conversation*.
Fung, B. (2013, August 16). Why drone makers have declared war on the word 'drone'. *Washington Post*.
Goldsmith, A. (2015). Disgracebook policing: social media and the rise of police indiscretion. *Policing and Society, 25*(3), 249–267.
Helgesson, S. (2011). Public-private partners against crime. *Surveillance and Society, 8*(4), 472–484.
Hern, A. (2015, July 31). Facebook launches Aquila solar-powered drone for internet access. *The Guardian*. Retrieved from http://www.theguardian.com/technology/2015/jul/31/facebook-finishes-aquila-solar-powered-internet-drone-with-span-of-a-boeing-737
Kearon, T. (2013). Surveillance technologies and the crises of confidence in regulatory agencies. *Criminology and Criminal Justice, 13*(4), 415–430.
Larsen, B. (2011). *Setting the watch: privacy and the ethics of CCTV surveillance*. Oxford: Hart Publishing.
Le Grand, C., Gosper, S. (2012, September 28). Meagher's body found; man charged, *The Australian on line*. Retrieved from http://www.theaustralian.com.au/news/nation/meaghers-body-found-man-charged/story-e6frg6nf-1226483028702.
Lyon, D., Haggerty, K., & Ball, K. (Eds.). (2012). *Routledge handbook of surveillance studies*. London: Routledge.
Maiolo, A. (2012). Drones to the rescue. Retrieved from http://www.campusreview.com.au pp. 10–11.
Marcella, A. J., & Stucki, C. (2003). *Privacy handbook: Guidelines, exposures, policy implementation and international issues*. Hoboken: John Wiley and Sons.
Marks, P. (2012). *The surveillance & everyday life research group*. University of Sydney, Home page editorial. Retrieved November 11, 2012, from http://sydney.edu.au/arts/research/surveillance/.
Marsden, R. (2015, October 22). Geek mythology. *The Independent*, p. 35.
Michael, K. & Clarke, R. (2012). Location privacy under dire threat as "uberveillance" stalks the streets. *Precedent*, January-February, pp. 25–29.
Neuberger, D (2015). Is nothing secret? Confidentiality, privacy, freedom of information and whistleblowing in the internet age. *Singapore Academy of Law Annual Lecture 2015*, Singapore.
Neyland, D. (2006). *Privacy, surveillance and public trust*. Houndmills Hants: Palgrave-Macmillan.
Norris, G., & Wilson, P. (2005). Crime prevention and new technologies: The special case of CCTV. In D. Chappell & P. Wilson (Eds.), *Issues in Australian crime and criminal justice*. Chatswood, NSW: Butterworths.
O'Malley, P. (2008). Neo-liberalism and risk in criminology. In T. Anthony & C. Cunneen (Eds.), *The critical criminology companion* (pp. 55–67). Sydney: Hawkins Press.
OAIC (2013). Office of the Australian Information Commissioner. Retrieved from https://www.oaic.gov.au/media-and-speeches/speeches/setting-the-scene-privacy-law-in-australia.
Prenzler, T., & Sarre, R. (2012). Public-private crime prevention partnerships. In T. Prenzler (Ed.), *Policing and security in practice: Challenges and achievements* (pp. 149–167). Houndmills Hampshire: Palgrave Macmillan.
Prunckun, H. (2010). *Handbook of scientific methods of inquiry for intelligence analysis*. Plymouth UK: Scarecrow.
Rosen, J. (2011, September 12). *Protect our right to anonymity,* blog *on the subject of US v Jones*.
Sarre, R. (2014). The use of surveillance technologies by law enforcement agencies: what are the trends, opportunities and threats? In E. Pływaczewski (Ed.), *Current problems of the penal law and criminology* (pp. 755–767). Białystok, Poland: Temida Publishing House.
Sarre, R. (2015). Eyes in the sky. *Drone Magazine, 1*, pp. 48–51.
Sarre, R., Brooks, D., Smith, C., & Draper, R. (2014). Current and emerging technologies employed to abate crime and to promote security. In B. Arrigo & H. Bersot (Eds.), *The Routledge handbook of international crime and justice studies* (pp. 327–349). Abingdon, Oxford: Routledge.

Sarre, R., & Prenzler, T. (2009). *The law of private security in Australia* (2nd ed.). Pyrmont, NSW: Lawbook Co.

Smith, C. L. (2006). Trends in the development of security technology. In M. Gill (Ed.), *The handbook of security* (pp. 610–628). Houndmills Hants: Palgrave-Macmillan.

Smith, C. L., & Brooks, D. J. (2013). *Security science: Theory and practice of security*. Waltham, MA: Elsevier.

Smith, G. J. D. (2012). Constitutional statement and manifesto, the surveillance & everyday life research group. Retrieved November 11, 2012, from: http://sydney.edu.au/arts/research/surveillance/about/index.shtml viewed.

Tassone, C., Martini, B., Choo, K.-K. R., & Slay, J. (2013). *Mobile device forensics: a snapshot, Trends and issues in crime and criminal justice, No 460*. Canberra: Australian Institute of Criminology.

Welsh, B. C., & Farrington, D. P. (2004). Surveillance for crime prevention in public places: results and policy choices in Britain and America. *Crime and Public Policy, 3*(3), 497–526.

Woodward, A. (2013, September 20). Pick your battles when fighting financial spying. *The Conversation*.

Chapter 15
An Investigation into Criminal Regulatory Science—An Approach from the Perspective of "Law and Economics"

Toshiko Sawaguchi

Introduction

Criminology has always been assigned broad as well as narrow meaning. A traditional, German-language magazine called *Kriminologie* was published in Germany (the country that provided the origins of forensic medicine in Japan). It saw criminology as almost synonymous with criminal policy, thus interpreting it in a narrow way. Recently however, many elements of the social sciences have been incorporated in criminology research even in Germany.

The Japanese Association of Criminology was founded on 2nd July 1913, and at that moment it was already an interdisciplinary association. The Association's founding members included Kuniyoshi Katayama, Shuzo Re, Tongo Takebe, Takuzo Hanai and Kaoru Sugie, all of whom were Tokyo University professors who worked in the fields of medicine, psychology, law, and social science 1). From this point onwards, Japanese academics were already aiming to develop criminology as a "unified criminology". A World Congress by the International Society for Criminology held in Japan several years ago provided an opportunity for the links between various criminology-related associations, such as the Association of Sociological Criminology and the Association of Criminal Psychology, to be strengthened. Their network became more structured, developing to the extent that an office and a code of conduct were established (Kageyama 2013). This kind of

T. Sawaguchi (✉)
Department of Legal Medicine, Showa University School of Medicine,
National Institute of Public Health, Shinagawa, Japan
e-mail: sawaguchitoshiko@niph.go.jp

E.C. Viano (ed.), *Cybercrime, Organized Crime, and Societal Responses*,
DOI 10.1007/978-3-319-44501-4_15

consolidated criminology also includes areas (particularly within the Japanese Association of Criminology) that are heavily influenced by medicine and biology, such as forensic medicine and forensic psychiatry.

In the United States two partially unified theories, biosocial criminology and life-course criminology, have been proposed as twenty-first-century criminological theories. The aim in Japan is to completely unify these two theories (Kageyama 2013).

As this kind of criminology spread in this country in a unified way, it is not surprising that regulatory science sprung up as a policy science, a unique development to Japan (Saio and Kurihara 2010; Sawaguchi and Sawaguchi 2013a, b). The background to this is briefly explained later.

The concept of regulatory science has its origins in the United States. It is said to have been turned into a field of study that would deal with problems that science needed to, but could not, address by the American nuclear physicist Weinberg. It was then adopted by Moghissi of the US Environmental Protection Agency (EPA), who established the Institute for Regulatory Science at a time when policies needed to be evaluated despite scant or incomplete scientific information being available.

Of particular interest here is an approach that stipulates that the scientific agency (the emergence of scientific knowledge as required in policy planning) used in policy planning should be kept separate from policymaking processes, as suggested by Jasnoff, and an approach whereby the scientific knowledge that emerges in drawing up public policy is seen as useful to policy planning, as suggested by Salter.

In the midst of all this Japan's Mitsuru Uchiyama said that, although the administration continued to be based on science, the time had come to turn policymaking itself into a science, which he named regulatory science. Administration is where regulatory science finds application, while experiments and surveys are carried out as part of health science research, and so regulatory science involves the evaluative science of efficacy and safety. The research outcomes of evaluative science often turn up in guidelines and regulations, while regulatory science aligns the life sciences with evaluation of the administration and aims to generate societal value.

One could think of it as a science that optimises technological and societal development, in order to improve public health.

Regulatory science does not only include elements of law, but also of medicine and economics, making it integral to administrative development. However, modern criminology does not directly encompass the economic or social welfare viewpoints. At the same time, the evidence and frame of reference-based viewpoints that are required in the life sciences were lost when criminology was seen as a social science. To what extent is it possible to compensate for this loss by using intermediate approaches (that occupy an intermediate position between natural science, which includes the life sciences, and humanities, which includes social science) such as psychology and economics? As part of such an investigation we propose the concept of criminal regulatory science. For instance, we believe it is beneficial to consider how effective the field of "law and economics" would be within modern criminology when we look at it from this viewpoint.

The Contribution of "Law and Economics"

"Law and economics" is an academic discipline that has developed mainly in the United States and which analyses the social and economic effects of the law. One particular feature of this discipline is that it can be applied widely, to all fields of law including civil law, criminal law and public law. Through such application it is possible to understand the hidden functions of the law (Fukui 2008). Its methodological basis requires the rudiments of micro-economics. It is a field in which the same theory can be replicated and applied to different areas. The methodology is useful when dealing with legal disputes for its legal interpretation theory as norms in the courts, and as a basis for the legal claims of the parties concerned. At the same, it can also provide legislative authority as a law-making theory.

In other words, in a capitalist state "law and economics" is an academic area that can shed light on how to achieve a form of legal control that reflects economic factors, how standards can be applied to policies and strategies regarding taxes and budgets and the like, and how to provide a basis for the evaluation of policy by the public/citizens.

In this sense, when assuming the existence of a regulatory science within criminology, i.e. criminal regulatory science, we envisage "law and economics" as a pre-existing academic area that is able to provide a methodology that can be thought of as effective.

Legal Policy, Public Policy and "Law and Economics"

However, the academic area of "law and economics" also comes with its own, inherent problems. Law and economics are different academic areas, and so have differing schools of thought. In-between the two, there inevitably exist situations in which unsurmountable disagreements are created.

Nevertheless, there are many situations in which this methodology is useful. For instance, we consider it to be effective in public policy analysis. It is crucial to analysis of whether Japan's bureaucratic system is driven by political or a bureaucratic leadership, and to analysis of the efficiency and cost-effectiveness of the administration, as well as in producing the basis for fundamental measures for providing public services and outsourcing public services to the private sector (Tsuneki 2012).

As part of judicial policy (Fukui 2006), if we see the judiciary as a body that performs the task of giving firm definition to legal interpretation and enforcing what is contained therein, and which bears the responsibility of allocating rights to citizens, then it becomes clear that conventional legal interpretation theories are limited when it comes to such things as guaranteeing judicial evaluation standards and law enforcement, putting laws into practice and how precedents are set. In setting more concrete rules as part of legislative policies, it is possible to carry out a standard analysis within the "law and economics" framework.

Criminology and "Law and Economics"

In essence, "law and economics" has come to be seen as useful when it comes to crime. This came about as a result of the economic analysis of criminal law, in which the meaning of punishment is examined when it comes to crime prevention (Fukui 2008). For example, the following questions have been asked (Fukui 2008):

1. Why does criminal law exist, and who does it aim to benefit?
2. Within tort law, what are the different parts played by acts on compensation for damages and criminal law?
3. Is toughening measures against crime effective in reducing crime?
4. Why are less severe punishments applied to crimes committed by underage individuals than to impulsive acts, even if the end result of the crime is the same?
5. What examples can be given where the premise that criminal punishment prevents crime does not hold, such as when the perpetrator is mentally ill (non compos mentis)?
6. Is there a limit to the extent to which the social cost of criminal punishment can be controlled?

   In practical terms, if we see crime as a market, and treat the question of what kind of criminal punishment modifies the behaviour of the criminal in what way, and to what extent crimes as undesirable acts can be prevented, as directionality and causality in shifts in supply and demand curves, it is possible to examine the acts and psychology of criminals (Fukui 2008).
7. The possibilities of "law and economics" within criminal regulatory science.

   As shown earlier, "law and economics" can provide an effective methodology in relation to crime. In what way, then, can "law and economics" be useful in criminal regulatory science?

   As explained in the introduction, regulatory science is a science that optimises technological and societal development, in order to improve public health. The efficacy and necessity of this optimisation as a methodology can be predicted based on economic simulations carried out beforehand. The feasibility and objectiveness of such simulations are affected by the extent of cause-and-effect relationships predicted beforehand and, if this relationship is limited, the model must be seen as flawed. In either case, the "law and economics" approach aims to reduce the social cost of crime as much as possible, and in addressing, through economic analysis, the question of how the value of its future reproducibility can be ensured, data engineering methods that include big data processing need to be incorporated. We expect that an area such as "criminology and big data" will need to be set up in the future.

   Further, because flexibility is required in law-making (regulating) that stems from the administrative changes that accompany technological innovation, over-and-above making other laws it is essential to optimise the kind of simulations described earlier.

   Further still, it is possible to treat mistakes by the government seriously and pre-simulate strategies for dealing with situations in which the government is unable to improve market outcomes, and to carry out post-simulation of the reasons why improvements could not be achieved.

Finally, as per the intended theme, we think that criminal regulatory science has four particular features that have emerged in dealing with the issues seen in regulatory science and medical regulatory science.

8. Extending "law and economics" to criminal regulatory science in concrete terms. What follows are concrete examples of how "law and economics" can be extended to criminal regulatory science, including three measures and two problems.

   (a) Moving from family reintegration to social independence as the ultimate aim when dealing with child abuse cases.

       Increasing the maximum age for anti-child abuse laws from 18 to 20.

       Japan's falling birth rate and ageing population poses a pressing issue, and an increase in child abuse has been identified as a problem relating to children.

       So far, as the ultimate aim in treating victims and perpetrators (the parents) of child abuse, family reintegration has been held up as a policy aim. The Attachment Theory on the development of children provides the background to this. The theory hypothesises that, if a child does not experience close relationships collectively known as attachments with its immediate family members during the course of its development, this will greatly impact on what kind of human being that child grows into, manifesting itself biologically in the child's cognitive processes. It is thought that such a lack of attachments will eventually contribute to instances of criminal behaviour in adulthood.

       A concrete example of this are the so-called Ceausescu's children: Romanian orphans who grew up without loving carers and whose bodies and minds were severely damaged. These cases proved that the environment in which a child grows up can inflict serious developmental damage. However, recent neuroscientific research has shown that the ability to provide loving care is in no way limited to immediate family members (Raeburn 2009).

       In actual fact, even if family reintegration is cited as the ultimate aim in child abuse cases, there are many instances in which the family had already broken up when the abuse took place and there is no family unit to return to, or in which it was not possible to return the child, or in which abuse reoccurred even when the child had been returned to partly the original household, and so the success rate of family reintegration is extremely low. Generational chains of child abuse have been shown to exist and recently, in cases where the abuser has a history of having fallen victim to child abuse themselves, experiments featuring behavioural therapy such as role plays involving positive mother-and-child relationship have been carried out. However, even if such abusers react positively to an extent, there are still many cases of their child being taken back into care after having been returned to the home, and of the child being neglected. It is easy to infer that it is highly inefficient to spend money on policies such as family reintegration.

Given the above, might it not be more effective to switch the ultimate aim in treating child abuse from family reintegration to achieving social independence by the victim and the abuser?

In recent times, the welfare-based concept that children grow up in society rather than in the household has been proposed in Europe and the United States. Equally, as part of Japan's social care system, group homes and private facilities are being set up as "bridging systems" (intermediate facilities) that link the home and society to child consultation offices and children's institutions. These facilities provide support for children exiting child consultation offices and children's institutions, but they are too few in number, and those that do exist are severely underfunded. Moreover, it has already been demonstrated that in institutions managed by people who are not related to the children, how to manage close human relationships, and how emotional needs and emotional neglect affect children subconsciously, are extremely difficult matters.

It may be possible to introduce tax reduction measures for these social care facilities, or policies whereby donations to such facilities are exempt from taxation. We also believe it will become necessary to provide medical-economic estimates of how to encourage recruitment within this field, and compare the results with estimates for family reintegration measures. There are also many cases in which both the child abuse and the developmental damage inflicted are severe, and where it is not clear where priorities should lie. The number of children in Japan with minor developmental damage is increasing. It should be possible to estimate the economic effect of social care on the total number of children that have suffered mild developmental damage, if the calculation is limited to cases of child abuse.

Meanwhile, current anti-child abuse laws are aimed at children up to the age of 18. Victims of abuse can be taken in by children's institutions, after having been released from child consultation offices, until they are 18. When the victim is between 18 and 20 years old but cannot return to the home, we believe a system may be necessary whereby the child is temporarily given lodging and a mobile phone, has a mediator when they are job searching and receives support in achieving social independence.

In northern Europe a consistent system has been established that enables women to receive one-on-one care from a health care professional from the moment they conceive to when they are looking after their newborn, and that also addresses child care. Such a system may be useful in preventing child abuse.

In other countries, it has become clear that many incarcerated criminals were at one point victims of child abuse. We should provide an estimate of how much funding is needed to implement the earlier anti-child abuse measures, i.e. measures that prevent victims of child abuse from committing crimes and, further, to what extent the social cost of crime can be reduced.

Medical-economic estimates relating to child abuse have already been published in other countries. Due to the fact that it is difficult to obtain data from child consultation offices for unintended use, neither accurate trials (Wada 2013) nor the kind of estimates as per the viewpoints described earlier have been carried out in Japan.

The classical principle of "law and economics" states that, if a right is clearly defined and no cost is incurred in its application, no matter who this right is extended to, subsequent negotiations will produce optimum social and economic results. The judiciary and the administration control the distribution and discretion of rights, and fulfil the role of clarifying those rights and keeping the cost of their application to a minimum. When dealing with the earlier points in academic lectures, it becomes clear that not only victims and perpetrators of abuse but also the people who work in social care, as well as the wider public/citizens, have rights.

(b) Problems concerning regenerative medicine.

Medical regulatory science in Japan entails that all regulation relating to regenerative medicine is set under the guidance of academics and specialists. Three laws on regenerative medicine have already been enacted.

However, before these three laws took effect and while Japan as a country was failing to develop laws relating to regenerative medicine, a multinational venture company based in Korea began carrying out autologous stem cell transplantation in Japan's private clinics, leading to patient deaths. At the time, regulations that made special provisions for hospitals were already in force in Korea and the United States. Only in Japan did such regulations not exist, and this judicial failure to act resulted in these deaths (Sawaguchi and Sawaguchi 2013a, b)

In general, technological achievements precede the establishment of laws and law-based regulations, and the public/citizens are informed of these afterwards. It has been shown that there are many lags within Japan's welfare system, such as a drug lag and a device lag.

Conventionally, laws have always lagged behind technological innovation and changes in society, and are established retrospectively. When legal intervention takes place, questions are asked about when, how and under what conditions this should be done. Regulatory authorities should, at the very least, establish new laws or instigate a legal intervention after technological innovation has occurred but before societal changes take place. Documentation supplied by the Cabinet Legislation Bureau shows that, among developed countries, Japan's capability to deal with legislative processes can by no means be considered advanced, and the quality of lawmaker-initiated legislation is undeniably low. At the very least, we believe it is crucial to the stability of the times and the social situation that the formation of laws, i.e. when the law intervenes, precedes attempts at minimising legislative error in the event of failure to act and precedes awareness within the public opinion.

The establishment and implementation of the three laws on regenerative medicine was hurriedly debated after fatalities had occurred, meaning they will always be evaluated in light of this.

During the research and development of regenerative medicine and long before any legal intervention took place, medical and economic viewpoints were taken into consideration.

An example that comes to mind is the development of periodontal membrane cell sheets for the treatment of alveolar pyorrhoea. The fact that large numbers of people suffer from alveolar pyorrhoea, ensuring the existence of a market, provided the basis for development opportunities. In general, the state of the oral cavity reflects one's state of mind, and severe problems are common in psychiatric patients, victims and perpetrators of abuse, and incarcerated criminals. In such people, rigorously enforcing dental hygiene aimed at preventing alveolar pyorrhoea gives rise to difficult problems. Moreover, in patients that require tooth extraction due to old age, masticatory function is essential to maintaining an appetite, which is in turn fundamental to human life. Hence, this treatment was expected to be in demand among the elderly, and was also predicted to contribute to health improvements in the elderly population from the outset. In these situations, for example as part of medical insurance claims, the development/dispersion costs of periodontal ligament cell sheets, the economic effects of an increase in a healthy elderly population with good masticatory ability and the ex-post-facto cost of the emergence of the condition, costs relating to efforts to rigorously enforce dental hygiene from childhood so as to prevent alveolar pyorrhea and the cost of dealing with the psychoneurotic conditions that cause problems within the oral cavity, should also once more be compared and balanced against the costs incurred before occurrences of the condition.

In Japan, where national policy favours the advancement of regenerative medicine, the allocation of state research funding currently tends to focus on regenerative medicine at the expense of other research areas that come under the remit of the Health, Labour and Welfare Ministry. As this kind of policy spreads, the regenerative medicine being studied will expand to encompass not only those conditions that are considered rare and serious, but also those that affect a large part of the diseased population, such as diabetes. It will also move beyond the treatment of conditions that are already manifest to preventative treatment, such as prenatal treatment of illness and defects. We believe that this, or alternatively aiming to effectively apply the treatment to areas other than medicine, such as to the development of epithelial cell sheets through use of hair stem cells (Sawaguchi 1986), will greatly contribute to the possibility of affirming the medical-economic effects of regenerative medicine.

There have already been cases in which compensation for loss was sought from the state after the occurrence of legislative errors due to failure to act, and we suggest that it would be preferable to give consideration in various ways to allowing medical-economic validation to be routinely given to lag time-based arguments. There is also potential for criminal regulatory science to be applied in this way to regenerative medicine and cutting-edge medical treatments.

References

Fukui, H. (2006). *Judicial policy and law and economics*, iii–iv. Nippon Hyoronsha (Japanese).

Fukui, H. (2008). *Law and economics*, iii–viii (pp. 129–154). Nippon Hyoronsha (Japanese).

Kageyama, S. (2013). *100th Anniversary Conference of the Japanese Association of Criminology Abstracts* (pp. 7–9) (Japanese).

Raeburn, B. (February/March 2009). The father factor. *Scientific American Mind* (English).

Saio, T., & Kurihara, C. (2010). Regulatory science wars. *Clinical Evaluation, 38*(1), 177–187 (Japanese).

Sawaguchi, T. (1986). Localization of γ-GTP in epithelial transitional zones. *Okajimas Folia Anatomica Japonica, 63*(5), 293–309 (English).

Sawaguchi, T., & Sawaguchi, A. (2013a). Problem areas in Japan's medical treatment regulation and the potential of medical regulatory science. *Gakushuin Women's College Bulletin, 15*, 57–67 (Japanese).

Sawaguchi, T., & Sawaguchi, A. (2013b). Problem areas in Japan's medical treatment regulation and the potential of medical regulatory science. *Gakushuin Women's College, 15*, 69–85 (Japanese).

Tsuneki, A. (2012). *A public analysis using "law and economics"*, viii–xiii. Iwanami Shoten (Japanese).

Wada, I. (2013). The economics of child abuse. In T. Sugiyama (Ed.), *A new way of treating child abuse* (pp. 134–151). Gakken (Japanese).

Chapter 16
Restorative Justice in the Conditions of the Slovak Republic

Tomáš Strémy and Miroslava Vráblová

Origins, Aims and Theoretical Background of Restorative Justice in the Slovak Republic

Nowadays, traditional criminal policy is facing its limits and is unable to cope with the rising criminality. Current criminal justice based on repressive approaches is unable to face serious obstacles and problems, namely in inefficiency of punishment, poor protection of victims, and slow and overburdened criminal courts. New models of criminal judiciary based on principles of restorative justice have been unveiled while traditional systems of criminal justice are facing a serious crisis.

The conception of restorative justice is one of the most modern and progressive of current approaches to criminal law that deserves to be implemented into the Slovakian and, of course, other criminal judiciary systems. The foundations of restorative justice is a conviction that crime (criminal offence) itself does not mean only a breach of Criminal Code clauses, but it also means social conflict between individuals and an invisible breach of social and interpersonal relationships. Because of this, we think the conflict should be resolved at an elementary level of interpersonal relationships with the aim to restore damaged social relations and to compensate damages or other harms. Nevertheless, 100 % restoration of damaged social relationships is hardly ever possible. Thus, instead of repression we should focus on preventing criminality and protecting victims. The main goals of restorative justice are to decrease the number of those incarcerated, crime prevention, motivating offenders to make restitution, give up criminal activities and live in a socially responsible way. We should protect society against criminality with special attention to victim's rights.

This work was supported by the Slovak Research and Development Agency on the grounds of Contract No. APVV-0179-12.

T. Strémy (✉) • M. Vráblová
Comenius University. Trnava University, Bratislava, Trnava, The Slovak Republic
e-mail: tomas.stremy@flaw.uniba.sk

E.C. Viano (ed.), *Cybercrime, Organized Crime, and Societal Responses*,
DOI 10.1007/978-3-319-44501-4_16

Overview on Forms of Restorative Justice in the Criminal Justice System

The criminal judiciary in the Slovak Republic is based on the traditional continental criminal procedure. Substantive Criminal Law as well as Procedural Criminal Law are more or less rigid and there is not enough space for the independent actions of judges, attorneys-general, prosecutors and police to determine the best practices to cope with criminality and at the same time protect the interests of victims, offenders and the public as well. Modern features of restorative justice in the Slovak criminal judiciary are appearing and it could be the way out of the crisis of criminal judiciary in Slovakia.

Main reforms of Slovak criminal procedure were implemented in 2005 during the process of Re-Codification of Slovak Criminal Law. Some restorative measures and concepts came into effect on 01 January 2006, when Criminal Code No. 300/2005 Coll. and Code of Criminal Procedure No. 301/2005 Coll. came into effect, Act No. 215/2006 Coll. On Compensation to Injured Persons by violent criminal offences, as well as Probation and Mediation Officers Act No. 550/2003 Coll. which came into force few years before.[1]

First of all, criminal procedure had been amended via strengthening the position of victims and other injured persons (better chance to claim damages). There is another progressive move, an effort to make victims and other injured persons take part in the criminal proceedings in order to ensure quick and satisfactory claims of damages using so-called diversions. Finally, some modern informal processes had been implemented, e.g. Conditional Discharge, Reconciliation and Agreement of Guilt and Sentence (Arbitration and Mitigation in criminal proceedings).

Last but not least, substantive criminal law was amended through the implementation and application of alternative sentences. The most important of them is the Community Service Orders and the opportunity to impose Protective Supervision over juvenile offenders exercised by the Probation and Mediation Office in case of Conditional Suspension of Execution of Sentence of Imprisonment with Probation Supervision and Waiver of Sentence with Probation Supervision.

There is also a new institute of Mediation, a formal arbitration or mitigation proceeding outside the criminal procedure. It is an alternative to the criminal procedure, which creates an opportunity for imposing alternative sentences, using diversions in criminal procedure or substituting protective custody with less harmful protective measures. However, several concepts of restorative justice have never been implemented in the Slovak Republic, namely restorative group conferencing, police cautioning, community reparation boards and sentencing circles.

---

[1] Dianiška, G. (2011). A kolektív: Kriminológia. 2. vyd. Plzeň: Aleš Čeněk.

Reform History

The 1990s brought a broad discussion about possible implementation of restorative justice instruments such as Conditional Discharge and Conditional Discharge with enforcement by the Probation Supervision in Slovakia. Though it sounds strange, the first efforts to implement Conditional Discharge were in the 1980s during the totalitarian regime in the Czechoslovakian Socialist Republic (solving issues of criminal liability for minor criminal offences, misdemeanours, anti-social and moral derelict behaviour). There was also an issue of Criminal Conciliation outside the Criminal Trial Proceedings. The proposed conception of Criminal Conciliation Proceedings was mentioned as a diversion from the traditional course of criminal proceedings. The reforming effort was successful and some instruments of restorative justice have been finally implemented in the Slovak Republic.

First of all, the diversion in criminal proceedings, Conditional Discharge, was enacted by Amendment No. 247/1994 Coll. to the Criminal Procedure Code No. 141/1961 Coll. and came into force on 01 October 1994. Moreover, in Amendment No. 422/2002 Coll. to the Criminal Procedure Code No. 141/1961 Coll., which came into effect on 01 October 2002, the instrument of Criminal Conciliation Proceedings was implemented. Criminal conciliation ensures faster criminal proceedings as well as a strengthened position for victims and other damaged parties (to help them claim damages). In order to impose alternative sentences and non-custodial protective measures, the Probation and Mediation Service was created. The Probation and Mediation Officers Act No. 550/2003 Coll. was enacted and came into force on 01 January 2004. Last but not least, a new alternative sentence was implemented in Slovakia–Community Service Orders (Sentence of Community Work). Moreover, for juvenile offenders, there was an opportunity to create the Conditional Waiver of Sentence (or Conditional Restraint of Sentence).

Contextual Factors and Aims of the Reforms

According to the Submission Report sent to the Criminal Conciliation Implementation Act the criminal conciliation proceedings should enable agreement between the prosecution (the Slovak Republic, victim, other damaged parties) and the defence, outside of the regular formal criminal proceedings. Of course, regular statutory criminal proceedings cannot be diverted at all, but they could focus exclusively on matters of guilt and sentence. On the other hand, when a criminal conciliation agreement comes into effect, it influences regular criminal proceedings in various ways: First of all, to make conciliation proceedings successful, there should be an agreement of awarding damages to the victim. This will make criminal proceedings quicker, less expensive and far more efficient. Furthermore, if there is a valid and effective conciliation decision and an agreement of damages to be awarded, there is still space for Agreement of Guilt and Sentence at the criminal court.

Re-Codification of Criminal Law in 2005 created ideal circumstances for the implementation and application of concepts and approaches of restorative justice into the Slovak system of criminal justice.[2] The reform process had several main goals compatible with the concept of restorative justice, namely effort to decriminalize, de-penalize and help the overburdened courts. Moreover, trial proceedings had become less complicated and less time consuming as well as more efficient. Finally, the institute of Probation and Mediation Officers was created. They tried to solve as many criminal cases as they could outside the criminal proceedings and criminal judiciary.

Influence of International Standards

Criminal justice in Slovakia is being influenced by current European trends, such as extending the use of alternative sentences in substantive criminal law and diversions in procedural criminal law. Also international standards have played an important role in the process of Re-Codification of Slovak criminal law by introducing restorative measures.

Home Arrest in the Slovak Republic

Home arrest was introduced in the Slovak legal system by Act No. 300/2005 Coll., Criminal Code,[3] as amended (hereinafter as "Criminal Code"). It holds a crucial position within the system of alternative sentences, also due to the fact that the lawmaker has inserted it right behind the sentence of imprisonment within the enumeration of the types of sentences under S 32 of Criminal Code. The conditions for

[2] Dianiška, G. & Strémy, T. (2009). Introduction to criminology. Publishing Aleš Čeněk. Plzeň.

[3] *Section 53 Home Arrest*

(1) The court may impose home arrest for a period of up to 1 year on the offender of a minor offence.

(2) During the execution of home arrest, the convict shall be obliged, for the period of time determined by the court, to stay in his dwelling and premises adjacent thereto, lead a regular life and, if ordered by the court, submit himself to supervision by means of electronic monitoring devices.

(3) During the execution of home arrest, the convict may leave his dwelling only upon the previous consent given by a probation and mediation officer or an authority responsible for overseeing the convict via *technical devices, and only on the grounds of urgency and for the period no longer than necessary. This period of time shall be included in the calculation of the overall sentence.*

(4) If the convict does not comply with the conditions referred to under paragraph 2, the court shall convert home arrest into an unconditional imprisonment sentence in such a way that 2 days of unserved portion of home arrest shall be equivalent to 1 day of an unconditional imprisonment sentence, it shall also decide about how the sentence is to be executed.

imposing home arrest, its modifications, including other specifics of its content, are governed by the provision of S 53 of the Criminal Code. The execution of home arrest is governed by the provision of S 435 of Act No. 301/2005 Coll., Criminal Procedure Code, as amended, and of S 79a of Decree No. 543/2005 Coll., on Administration and office regulations for district courts, regional courts, the Special court and military courts, as amended.[4]

In the context of the Slovak Republic, the courts are missing the statutory option to impose the home arrest on a minor, because home arrest is not included in the enumeration of sentences under S 109 of Criminal Code which may be imposed on a minor.

Home arrest is a separate sentence and despite the fact that it presents a detriment to the personal freedom of the convict, the fact that during the execution of home arrest the convict remains in his natural environment with his social, family and economic bonds remaining intact, but with the concurrent monitoring of his behaviour, can be seen as a positive attribute. Home arrest should be imposed mainly in cases when the significantly lesser intensity of interference with personal freedom of the offender is required, given the nature and severity of the crime, the personality of the offender, his chance of re-socialization and taking into account his family background.[5] Introduction of home arrest was motivated by the requirement of the society to punish the offender and at the same time to eliminate the negative effects of unconditional imprisonment, which include the effect of so-called prison subculture that often leads up to the negative change in value orientation, whereas family and social bonds are severed or work habits are lost and the connection of the convict with the everyday reality is severed. This undoubtedly leads to a bad financial situation and the indirect increase of the risk of relapse. The financial intensity of imprisonment compared to home arrest is also an important attribute.

Punishment of Compulsory Labour in the Slovak Republic

Punishment of compulsory labour was introduced into our legal system by Act No. 300/2005 Coll. Criminal Code,[6] which is effective from 1 January 2006. Imposition and execution of this sentence are set forth in several legal regulations. Conditions

[4] Vráblová, M. (2013). *Slovak substantive criminal law*. Trnava: Publishing Trnava University.

[5] Ščerba, F.(2011). *Alternativní tresty a opatření v nové právní úpravě*. Leges. Praha.

[6] *Community Service Work*

Section 54

The court may impose on the offender, upon his consent, a community service work sentence for a period not less than 40 h and not exceeding 300 h, if it issues a ruling for a minor offence punishable by the term of imprisonment of not more than 5 years under this Act.

Section 55

(1) The convict shall be obliged to perform community service work within 1 year after the date on which the related court ruling becomes final. The court may, as appropriate, impose the restrictions and obligations referred to under Section 51 par. 3 and 4 on the offender, with the aim of encouraging him to lead regular life; as a rule, the court shall also order him to compensate, to

for its imposition are set forth in Act No. 300/2005 Coll. Criminal Code. Specifically, the provisions related to the conditions of its imposition are contained in S 54, S 55 and S 111. Execution of punishment of compulsory labour, its alternation as well as possibilities and conditions of waiving of the executions is regulated by a separate Act No. 528/2005 Coll. On Executions of punishment of compulsory labour. Provision of S 422 of Act No. 301/2005 Coll. Criminal Procedure Code which deals with executions of punishment of compulsory labour refers to the application of Act No. 528/2005 Coll. On Executions of punishment of compulsory labour.

Materials of the Council of Europe emphasize that the punishment of compulsory labour pro bono for the society has been one of the most progressive measures of the European criminal law over the last few years. The punishment of compulsory labour offers several possibilities for its use and the professionals put a lot of trust into it. The originality of this punishment is that the punishment actively contributes to the perpetrator's re-socialization, not only during the execution of the punishment. Furthermore, the relationships of perpetrator with his surroundings are not disturbed. The perpetrator is not exempted from social obligations or by his responsibilities. Thereby the perpetrator's re-integration to the society increases after the punishment. The detriment caused by this punishment is shown in the notable impact into the perpetrator's leisure time, as well as by not receiving any income for the work performed. In accordance with the principle of Decriminalization, it allows to impose this punishment mostly on those perpetrators for whom the imposition of another punishment would disproportionate to the severity of the crime.[7]

---

the best of his abilities, for the damage inflicted by the criminal offence. When calculating the period of participation in a community service work, it shall not be taken into account any period of time, during which the convict

a) could not perform community service work due to a temporary illness, or because he was not assigned any work during this period,

b) attended compulsory military service or other service instead of compulsory military service,

c) stayed abroad,

d) was remanded in custody, or was serving a term of imprisonment in connection with other offence.

(2) The court shall not impose community service work if the offender is on long term sick leave or has been disabled.

(3) The offender shall have an obligation to perform community service in person and during his free time without receiving remuneration.

(4) If the convict fails to lead regular life or perform, of his own causation, the service in the required scope, or if he does not respect the restrictions and does not fulfil the obligations imposed on him under the sentence, the court shall convert the community service work sentence or the remainder thereof into an unconditional imprisonment sentence execution in such a way that every 2-hour segment of unserved portion of community service work shall be equivalent to 1 day of an unconditional imprisonment sentence, it shall also decide about how the sentence is to be executed.

(5) The court may waive the execution of community service work, if the convict, during the serving of this punishment, has gone on long term sick leave or permanent disability without any fault on the part of him.

[7]Čentéš, J. (2014). Trest povinnej práce. In: Trest zákazu účasti na verejných podujatiach. In: Strémy, T. (ed.): *Restoratívna justícia a alternatívne tresty v teoretických súvislostiach*. Praha. Leges. pp. 340–351.

One of its characteristics is universality. The punishment of compulsory labour is not mentioned in the special part of the Criminal Code. Therefore, it may be imposed on all perpetrators, either as a separate punishment or along with another punishment (S 34 (6) and S 34 (7) of Criminal Code) for which an unconditional sentence of imprisonment may be imposed. It is obvious that all statutory requirements must be respected.

In all countries where this punishment is enacted, its main feature is that it lies in performing work as a benefit to society.

Financial Penalty in the Slovak Republic

Financial Penalties, unlike sentences of compulsory labour and punishment of house arrest, were introduced in Slovak law as a punishment which was already in the provisions of Act No. 140/1961 Coll. Criminal Code, as amended. The inclusion of a financial penalty to the fixed list of punishments did not affect the codification of criminal law, which regulated the conditions of new types of alternative punishments. Currently, the conditions of financial penalty, conversion to a term of imprisonment as well as other aspects of content are governed by S 56 to S 57 of Act No. 300/2005 Coll. Criminal Code, as amended (hereinafter the "Criminal Code"). The Procedure for the enforcement of financial penalties is governed by the provisions of S 429 to S 432 of Act No. 301/2005 Coll. Criminal Procedure Code, as amended and S 79b of Regulation 543/2005 Coll. On Administration and Office Rules for district courts, regional courts, the Special Court and military courts, as amended.

The Financial Penalty[8] is a specific type of punishment that is not an alternative sanction in relation to imprisonment, especially given that the court may impose

---

[8] *The Financial Penalty*

Section 56

(1) The court may impose a financial penalty of not less than 160 EUR and not more than 331 930 EUR the offender of an intentional criminal offence whereby he gained or tried to gain property benefit.

(2) In the absence of the conditions referred to in paragraph 1, the court may impose a pecuniary penalty for a minor offence if, in view of the character of the offence and the potential for rehabilitating the offender, it decides not to impose a custodial penalty.

(3) The court may, taking account of the amount of the financial penalty and the personal and property situation of the offender, allow the payment of the financial penalty in monthly instalments. At the same time, the court shall determine the amount of instalments, and the time limit for the payment of the financial penalty, which may not be longer than 1 year from the date on which the convicting judgment became final.

(4) The financial penalty that the sentenced person has already paid shall be credited towards the new financial penalty imposed in respect of the same offence, or the penalty imposed as a cumulative or concurrent sentence.

(5) The court shall not impose a pecuniary penalty if this would obstruct the payment of the compensation for damage caused by the criminal offence.

statutory conditions as an independent punishment but also attach them to another sentence, for example, to imprisonment. The Financial Penalty is an injury to the prisoner's property but its primary purpose is to affect the perpetrator's efforts to gain unfair advantage by means of keeping and using funds generated directly by crime or using them to commit other crimes. Provisions of S56 of the Criminal Code apply to those cases and the court will impose a financial Penalty rule, in addition to imprisonment.

A Financial Penalty as the sentence imposed separately is applicable to offenses of a less serious nature (misdemeanours). Its alternative nature is in relation to imprisonment and is governed by S 56 of the Criminal Code. The provision of Criminal Code creates a relatively wide space for its court application, taking into account the nature and seriousness of the offense, as well as the person and the circumstances of the perpetrator. The imposition of financial penalties however, has a major drawback because it does not only affect the perpetrator but also other people towards whom the perpetrator may have commitments, such as the actual victim or other creditors or his family.

Section 57

(1) When imposing the financial penalty the court should consider the personal and financial circumstances of perpetrator. The court doesn't impose a financial penalty if it is clear that the perpetrator will not be able to pay.

Effective until 31/8/2011:

[(1) In determining the amount of the financial penalty, the court shall also consider the personal and property situation of the offender. It shall not impose a pecuniary penalty if it is obvious that it cannot be collected.]

(2) The paid financial penalty shall constitute the revenue of the State.

Effective until 31/8/2011:

[(2) The confiscation amounts of financial penalty shall constitute the revenue of the State.]

(3) In addition to imposing a pecuniary penalty, the court shall deliver an alternative custodial penalty of up to 5 years to be executed, should the execution of the pecuniary penalty be deliberately prevented. The combination of such alternative penalty and the imposed custodial penalty may not exceed the statutory sentencing range.

(4) If the alternative penalty would exceed the range referred to in paragraph 3, or if a pecuniary penalty is imposed in combination with life imprisonment, the court shall impose no alternative penalty.

Section 114

(1) The court may impose a pecuniary penalty of not less than 30 eur and not more than 16,590 eur under conditions set out in this Act, if a young offender is gainfully employed, or the property owned by him enables such a penalty to be imposed.

(2) When imposing a pecuniary penalty on a young offender, the court shall deliver an alternative custodial penalty of up to 1 year to be executed, should the execution of the pecuniary penalty be deliberately prevented within the prescribed time-limit. The combination of such alternative penalty and the imposed custodial penalty may not exceed the statutory sentencing range reduced pursuant to S 117 par. 1.

(3) When a decision whereby a young offender has been imposed a pecuniary penalty becomes final and conclusive, the court, upon the statement of a young offender, may issue a ruling that its payment or unpaid remainder thereof be replaced in such a way that a young offender shall perform community service work within the probationary programme.

A Financial Penalty, pursuant to the provisions of the Criminal Code, can be imposed on a juvenile and the conditions for its application are governed by S 114–116 of Criminal Code.

Conclusion

This chapter focuses on the application of restorative justice in the Slovak Republic. The conception of restorative justice is just beginning to be implemented into the Slovak criminal justice system. Examples provided are the Probation and Mediation Office or other institute which works more theoretically than practically. At the end of the article, we mentioned alternative punishments like home arrest, compulsory labour or financial penalties which are used in the Slovak criminal judiciary system.

Acknowledgements This work was supported by the Slovak Research and Development Agency on the grounds of Contract No. APVV-0179-12.

References

Brunk, C. (2001). Restorative justice and the philosophical theories of criminal punishment. In: *The spiritual roots of restorative justice.*

Elizabeth, B., Kropf, N. P., & Leonard, P. B. (2011). *Social work and restorative justice.* Oxford: Oxford University press.

Burda, E. (2014). Trest zákazu účasti na verejných podujatiach. In T. Strémy (Ed.), *Restoratívna justícia a alternatívne tresty v teoretických súvislostiach.* Leges: Praha.

Čentéš, J. (2014). Trest povinnej práce. In T. Strémy (Ed.), *Restoratívna justícia a alternatívne tresty v teoretických súvislostiach.* Leges: Praha.

Dianiška, G. (2011). A kolektív: Kriminológia. 2. vyd. Plzeň: Aleš Čeněk.

Dianiška, G., & Strémy, T. (2009). *Introduction to criminology.* Plzeň: Publishing Aleš Čeněk.

Johnstone, G. (2013). *A restorative justice reader* (2nd ed.). Oxon: Routledge.

Kurilovská, L. & Lenhartová, K. (2013). EÚ ako otvorená cesta restoratívnej justície = EU as an open way of restorative justice. In: *Právny obzor.- roč.* 96, č. 3.

Kury, H., & Shea, E. (Eds.). (2011). *Punitivity – international developments* (Vol. 3). Bochum: Universitätsverlag Brockmeyer.

Liebman, M. (2012). *Restorative justice/how it works.* London: Jessica Kingsley Publishers.

Miers, D. & Willemsens, J. (2004). *Mapping restorative justice.*

Strémy, T. (2013). *Criminological aspects of property crime in The Slovak Republic.* Trnava: Publishing Trnava University in Trnava.

Clear, T. R. (2008). Community justice versus restorative justice: contrasts in family of value. In D. Sullivan & L. Tifft (Eds.), *Handbook of restorative justice.* Routledge: Routledge International Handbooks.

Vráblová, M. (2013). *Slovak substantive criminal law.* Trnava: Publishing Trnava University in Trnava.

Scheinost, M. (2003). Restoratívní justice. In: *Sborník příspevku a dokumentu.* Institut pro kriminologii a sociální prevenci. Praha

Ščerba, F. (2011). *Alternativní tresty a opatření v nové právní úpravě.* Praha: Leges.

Zehr, H. (2002). *The little book of restorative justice.* Intercourse, PA: Good Books.

Chapter 17
The Role of Institutional Legitimacy in Facilitating Judicial Reforms: Examples from Mexico

Jennifer Stave

Introduction

The cumulative death toll for the drug-related violence in Mexico continues to climb toward 100,000. Under President Felipe Calderón Hinojosa (2006–2012), policy makers implemented substantial reforms to their law enforcement institutions in order to strengthen the government's ability to impose a rule of law. They have created a federalized police force and mandated one of the largest overhauls of their judiciary in history, changing from an inquisitorial system based on Napoleonic-era laws to a mixed-adversarial system. This move to an adversarial system introduces oral trials into the courts and grants less discretion to public prosecutors' offices in prosecuting and to judges in sentencing. Legal scholars tout adversarial systems, such as that used in the USA, as more impartial because the court acts as a *neutral* moderator of the defense and prosecution; in inquisitorial systems, the court is more actively involved in investigating the facts.

To assess whether these judicial reforms have helped to reduce violence in the areas where they have been implemented, I conduct a quantitative analysis of Mexico's 2438 municipalities in all 32 of its states.[1] Each state is at a different stage of reform; all have a mandate to finish implementation by 2016. This variation allows for a timely analysis of the reform effort and identification of possible changes in implementation based on the experiences of the first states to apply the reform.

[1] This count includes the Federal District.

J. Stave (✉)
Justice Reform Initiative, Washington, DC, USA
e-mail: stave@justicereforminitiative.org

E.C. Viano (ed.), *Cybercrime, Organized Crime, and Societal Responses*,
DOI 10.1007/978-3-319-44501-4_17

I offer evidence, based on the first reformers' outcomes, that the judicial changes alone will not reduce violence in Mexico; institutional trust is an intervening factor that determines whether the reforms will have the intended effect. Specifically, the 2008 reforms have reduced violence only in states where residents have some semblance of trust in the institutions. My analysis suggests that distrust of rule-of-law institutions obstructs the reform effort by discouraging public participation, such as reporting crimes or offering witness testimony. Consequently, many crimes are not reported, criminals are not brought to justice, and the judiciary loses its deterrence effect. Indeed, from 2002 to 2009, the percentage of citizens who said they did not report a crime they witnessed increased from an already high 73 % to an even higher 78 % of the population (Instituto Ciudadano de Estudios Sobre la Inseguridad 2002, 2009). The main reason given was that the respondent thought that it would be a waste of time.

Instead of focusing on institutional trust and public participation, the reforms mandated widespread and indiscriminate structural changes, which theoretically were expected to strengthen performance, decrease corruption, and increase coordination. It was hoped the police and courts would investigate and prosecute more criminals, thus leading Mexico out of its downward spiral of crime. However, there is a flaw in this logic; my research indicates that structural changes will not achieve the desired result of violence reduction unless there is a *preexisting* trust in institutions. This trust is path-dependent and restricted by statewide histories of pockets of authoritarianism. Yet in some states, trust in institutions has been increasing for the past 30 years, just as statewide processes of democratization and economic prosperity have taken hold. This evolution in state-society relations helps to convince people that the state's institutions are in fact capable of transitioning to a new protocol (e.g., the adversarial reform in the judiciary). In contrast, where relations have not improved, people find it hard to believe that an illegitimate institution can master new protocols when it did not use the old ones ethically or efficiently. In summary, when trust in the institution exists, the reforms bolster public participation in the rule of law and help deter crime.

Theoretical Contribution

In the beginning of the twenty first century, scholars have taken a greater interest in how trust in political institutions affects governance. Their analyses illustrate that trust in institutions can have substantial benefits for deterring criminal behavior.

The main theory of crime control used to justify Mexico's institutional reforms is the deterrence effect: Increasing the likelihood of sanctions decreases criminal behavior. A legal sanction (e.g., a prison sentence, a fine, probation) has been historically touted as the most salient deterrent to crime (Tittle 1969), and indeed, this was an explicit rationale for Mexico's judicial reform (Cuevas 2011). The mechanism is straightforward: Legal sanctions deter people from criminal behavior because the higher probability of punishment is considered a disincentive to criminal action. The theory has a basis in academic literature and long-standing bodies of work in criminology, yet over nearly a century of writing, criminologists still debate the merits of the deterrence effect in explaining the judiciary's impact on crime. Notable critics include Nagin (1998) and MacCoun (1993), who find that the deterrence effect exists but its impact is negligible. Other scholars, such as Paternoster (1987), find that it has no effect.

In the course of exploring violence and justice in Mexico, I introduce an alternative view of the judiciary. Rather than looking at its ability to deter crime vis-à-vis sanctions, I adapt the approach from political psychologist Tom Tyler (2006) that shows that courts and police can often prevent crime more effectively by bolstering their status as legitimate and fair institutions, which in turn motivates people's self-regulation and participation in the system.

The impact of institutional trust on crime, unlike the deterrence effect, is not contingent upon an outcome (e.g., an arrest/legal sanction). Rather, trust affects security through the process by which outcomes are determined (e.g., a fair trial, accepted arrest protocols). In other words, people self-regulate their behavior in accordance with law because of a respect for and acceptance of the institution's operating protocols (McCluskey 2003; Tyler 2006).

Studies have found that in Chicago and New York, even with an absence of authorities, people's tendency to engage in illegal behavior was more influenced by their respect for procedural justice than by a fear of sanction (Tyler 2006, p. 89). When asked whether people will obey the law, even if it goes against what they think is right, Tyler explains, "Americans are generally found to express a strong sense of obligation to defer to law and to legal authorities" (2006, p. 88). Several judges in Mexico State have observed that this same reverence does not exist for the legal structures in Mexico. According to one judge, "In countries such as the United States or England, where oral trials have been used for some time, the adversarial model is effective because there is credibility and respect for the police force and prosecutors in those countries" (Méndez and Aranda 2007). In countries such as Mexico, in contrast, there are subnational pockets of lingering authoritarianism, and a concomitant dearth of institutional legitimacy, that hinder the government's ability to implement new institutional protocols efficiently.

According to Cleary and Stokes (2009), lack of trust in institutions is often a result of poor historical performance. Histories of corruption, mistreatment, and even torture plague the rule-of-law institutions in Mexico. These practices feed mistrust of the police and courts and fuel nonparticipation in the rule of law. A cursory glance at the petitions before the Inter-American Human Rights Commission reveals prolific abuses. For example, the Center for Justice and International Law (CEJIL) and the Human Rights Center of the Montaña filed a petition to the Human Rights Commission in 1998 for the government's "alleged kidnapping and torture perpetrated against Luis Gonzaga Lara, Magencio Abad Zeferino Dominguez and Miguel Antonio Zeferino Aquino, as well as alleged acts of intimidation against Gloria Eufracia Gonzaga Campos, Hermilia Gonzaga Campos, Pedro Gonzaga Lara, Costantina Uriozo Hernández, Antolito Gonzaga Urioso and María Isabel Aquino Reyes" (Inter-American Commission on Human Rights 2009, p. 130). There are many similar cases, such as the petition of Asdrúbal Araujo Castillo for the alleged "deprivation of liberty, torture, and threats by government agents" and for "violations of due process and the right to judicial guarantees" after his detention in 1999 for suspected robbery (Inter-American Commission on Human Rights 2012, p.). In 2001 and 2002, the National Institute of Migration in the Federal District detained a citizen of the Dominican Republic who was traveling through Mexico to the USA. The man, Luis Castillo Sepúlveda, alleges that in custody he "was the victim of consistent torture in physical, verbal, and psychological aggression by uniformed immigration and police officials, which had seriously injured him" (Inter-American Commission on Human Rights 2009, p. 1).

These situations contribute to the lack of trust in and resistance to the rule-of-law institutions. Histories of subnational authoritarianism in local political structures also inhibit the building of trust. While the tide of democratization was moving across Mexico in the 1980s and 1990s, some political elites in various states sought to reinforce local authoritarian structures to ensure their continued prosperity in the region. As a result, these institutions did not receive the benefits derived from increased civic activity, such as greater accountability and public participation. Instead, the institutions—including the judiciary—continue to serve the elite interests while remaining unaccountable to the populations. In Oaxaca, for instance, the PRI was able to keep the governing institutions consolidated under its authority and has since ensured that Oaxaca's institutional development remains stunted (Correa-Cabrera 2013). As described by democracy scholar Correa-Caberera:

> The Oaxacan government's failure to solidify separation of powers inhibited local democratic progress. Oaxacan governors' control over the state legislature gave them control over the state judiciary that did not challenge their use of funds, assaults on municipal autonomy, or their use of unfair electoral practices ... Oaxacan political institutions are still quite ineffective in general. Even now, authoritarianism, arbitrariness, and corruption characterize Oaxaca's government. The local justice system is highly dysfunctional. (2013, pp. 57–58)

This historical and continued dysfunction of the judiciary has proven to be a barrier for the reform initiative. Years after the implementation of the new justice system, people remain skeptical of what they see as a wolf in sheep's clothing. They resist participating in the new system, which some fear may help criminals escape sanction, especially if they have certain political ties or social connections. In the most extreme circumstances of resistance and fear, the people take justice into their own hands. The lynching of Jordi Alberto Gómez Ortega in 2010 is a prime example of this. At three in the morning on February 18, Gómez Ortega, 16 years old, and Guillermo de Espinosa Rodríguez, 25 years old, got into a taxi driven by Ángel Manuel Jiménez Vázquez and asked to go to the Costera highway. While in transit, the two men assaulted the driver and demanded that he give them all his money (Alegria and Moreno 2010). After the attack, a group of taxi drivers tracked down Gómez Ortega and beat and burned him. The drivers explained that they acted "because of the fear that the authorities of the Deputy Attorney General would release him [Gómez Ortega] *under the complacency of oral trials* [emphasis added]" (Blas 2010). They further referred to two previous instances when suspected criminals were brought before the courts and were inevitably found not guilty and set free (Blas 2010).

The lynching of Gómez Ortega was a direct refutation of the systems of oral trials and justice provision that allow presumed criminals to escape punishment. As observed in 2010 by Víctor Leonel Juan Martínez, a local journalist, "The lynchings are a product of immense police failures, irregularities, corruption, lack of professionalization and obstructive laws that characterize the inoperability of the institutions. For this, the population does not have trust in the institutions and prefers to take justice into their own hands." Even with the new institutional structures in place, lack of trust prevented the judicial process from providing a deterrence effect, with or without reform.

Other states in Mexico, however, have a different history in the late twentieth century. Baja California, for instance, achieved many municipal victories in the 1980s and then, exceptionally, it transformed these victories into greater political gains. In 1989, the state elected (and was permitted to have) the first opposition governor, Ernesto Ruffo from the PAN party. Coupled with decentralization in the 1990s, this gubernatorial win granted Baja California an unprecedented level of state and institutional autonomy to democratize its local structures (Shirk 1999). The same neoliberal policies that hurt many states' civil society and formal institutional development (e.g., Oaxaca, Michoacán) have manifested differently in Baja California; there, the rise of the maquiladora system after NAFTA in the 1990s and a burgeoning middle class with business ties to the USA have worked to create local institutions that are no longer beholden to the clientelistic network of the dying hegemony (Cleary and Stokes 2009, p. 37).

In addition, the same policies that decimated the agricultural industry in the central and southern states created wealthy industrial centers—complete with a middle class—in the northern region. Throughout the 1980s and 1990s, Baja California's civil society witnessed a rise in pluralism and public participation. A number of innovations built solid connections between society and governmental (non-party-based) institutions:

> [Tijuana] sought to reconstruct its relationship with citizens by creating three new channels for communication, dialogue, and influence: elected neighborhood committees that would replace the traditional clientelistic leaders; a participatory planning structure that employed the legal figure of [the Municipal Planning Council]; and a joint business-government roundtable for long-term planning on economic issues. (Selee 2011, p. 116)

These types of participatory structures involved the community in the democratization process. In Baja California, the creation of robust societal engagement has helped the judiciary (and other institutions) to maintain and increase trust throughout the past 30 years. Newspapers have hailed the oral trials and the reform as a success (see, for example, Cordero 2011). Since this first effort, Baja California has continued to expand the capabilities of the judiciary. It has written over 120,346 expert reports, completed 10,583 DNA analyses, taken 10,647 fingerprints, and processed 3,050 ballistics (Manjarrez 2012). This is in stark contrast to Oaxaca, which has seen a steady decline of oral trials since they were first introduced in 2007.

Regaining institutional trust is necessary to expand the capabilities of states such as Oaxaca. Bo Rothstein in *Social Traps and the Problem of Trust* illustrates that once societies lose trust in institutions, it becomes increasingly difficult to regain that trust. In his analysis, Rothstein offers a solution: "The deliberate action of the state and its leaders is crucial. Social trust comes from above and is destroyed from above. Simply put, they must be able to send trustworthy signals that they will guarantee and respect the impartiality of the relevant public institutions" (2005, p. 199.). This is similar to the conclusions of Cleary and Stokes (2009), who note that trust in institutions is based on a belief that the institution is impartial.

The reforms in Mexico were meant to increase the belief of such impartiality. However, this narrow view presupposes that people view the partiality of the institutional structure as the problem. Historically, the structure of the institution is not the violator; after all, torture and physical abuse have always been illegal and not permitted as a part of judicial functioning. Impartiality is demonstrated to society by a lack of malfeasance, not by structural arrangements. Citizens are able to trust institutions when they believe there is a modest amount of horizontal or vertical accountability in place that will restrain the institutions from committing abuses (Cleary and Stokes 2009).

In this analysis, I follow the scholastic lead of institutional trust scholars such as Cleary and Stokes (2009), Rothstein (2005), and Tyler (2006). The analysis provides evidence that structural changes to the judiciary will not significantly affect Mexico's rate of crime until the rule-of-law institutions deal with the crisis of societal trust—or lack thereof—in them.

Modeling the Role of Trust in the Institution in Crime Reduction

In this section, I test whether the judicial reforms or trust in the judiciary have reduced drug-related homicides in Mexico. I also explore the interaction between the reform and trust by testing whether the reform reduces violence *more* when there is trust in the judiciary, compared to areas without trust. First, I describe each variable included in the model and discuss how it is operationalized.

Drug-Related Homicide

Drug-related homicide is operationalized as the number of drug-related homicides in each municipality from 2007 to 2009. These data are counts and have a Poisson distribution (see Fig. 17.1). However, Poisson models often fail to account for over- or under-dispersion in the dependent variable, and as a consequence, produce inefficient estimates. The negative binomial model accounts for this incorrect dispersion. A Vuong test concluded that a negative binomial model was superior to a Poisson in

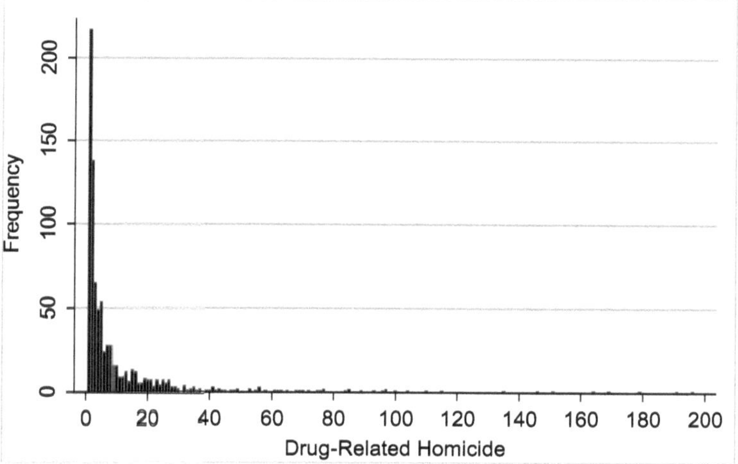

Fig. 17.1 Count of drug-related homicides per municipality, 2010

this case. A zero-inflated negative binominal (ZINB) accounts for the excess zeros in the dependent variable that may be due to an alternative process.[2]

Many municipalities have no drug-related homicides. This can mean one of two things: (1) There are no drug-related crimes because the rule-of-law institutions are working to keep illicit activity out of the municipality, or (2) there is never any illicit activity for the rule-of-law institutions to address. The zero-inflated model controls for the excess of zeros and alternative processes at work by separating the regression into positive counts and "sometimes zero" values in one group and "always zero" values in another group. ZINB estimates a count model for the former and a binary logit predicting the "always zero" group. Table 17.2 shows the output of a series of zero-inflated negative binomial regressions. Note that the "always zero" group—those municipalities where there is no crime to keep at bay—is separated out and run independently.

The ZINB model does not regress time-series data appropriately as it has trouble with time-series correlation of the dependent variable. Therefore, the model incorporates fixed effects for each year, which essentially renders the ZINB model a cross-sectional analysis with more data points than a one-year cross-section.

The dependent variable is the number of drug-related homicides per municipality. The counts range from zero to 2738 deaths, the highest of which was in the city of Ciudad Juárez in 2010. These municipal-level data are from the Office of the President in Mexico (Presidencia de la Republica n.d.). The independent variables lag one year behind. As such, I can test whether the independent variables each year had an impact on the following year's number of homicides.

[2] I compared the results of a zero-inflated negative binomial model and negative binomial. The zero-inflated model was superior in regard to the Bayesian information criterion (BIC) and Vuong test.

Figure 17.1 shows the distribution of the dependent variable, excluding zeros, for 2010; the distribution for other years is similar. Approximately half of all municipalities did not have one death from 2007 to 2010, and approximately half had fewer than 100 deaths per year during the same time period. Fewer than 25 municipalities account for most of the violence, reporting death tolls of hundreds or even thousands.

I have also run this model with a dependent variable that includes all homicides, not just those that are drug-related, and found no substantial difference. The reason, I believe, is clear: Most contemporary homicides in Mexico are drug-related. The "all homicides" variable is composed of very few non-drug-related murders. Furthermore, the reforms were intended to specifically address the rising drug-related violence, and therefore the model is best focused on crime in Mexico.

Judicial Reform

To measure the impact that the judicial reforms had on violence, I include a variable, judicial reforms, which is given the value of 1 if the oral trial, adversarial system is in effect (as defined in the law and by the government) and a 0 otherwise. In 2007, no states were operating a mixed-adversarial system. From 2007 to 2010, seven states had municipalities that implemented the reform: Baja California, Chihuahua, Mexico State, Morelos, Oaxaca, Nuevo Leon, and Zacatecas. For the year that the reform went into effect, and every year after, the variable is a 1. Note that there is within-state variation. For instance, Mexicali in Baja California implemented the reform in 2009, but Ensenada in Baja California had not as of 2010. The data account for this municipal difference. I use the Consejo de Coordinación para la Implementación del Sistema de Justicia Penal (CCISJP) designation of implementation status. This council, responsible for overseeing the national reform effort, designated four stages of implementation. For the purposes of the empirical model, only states that achieved "fully operational" status are coded as reformed.

To be sure, other classifications of judicial implementation exist. Other governmental agencies define the features of implementation differently, thus changing the list of states that have "implemented" the reform. For example, Matthew Ingram conducted a study of the criminal procedure reform in Mexico. He created an index based on state implementation in relation to Chihuahua (the most reformed state by his measure). Ingram determined the Code of Criminal Procedure's geographic spread within the state was the most important aspect by which to judge implementation. He found that Baja California, Zacatecas, Mexico State, Nuevo Leon, Yucatan, and Morelos had most fully implemented the reform (scoring over 80 out of 100 on the index). This varies from CCISJP's classifications just slightly. Ingram's index (based off of SETEC data and 80 % correlated to SETEC's own index of reform implementation [Ingram 2013, p. 10]) does not include Oaxaca and Durango in the highest tier of implementation, while CCISJP does. Ingram's index ranks Durango in the tier below this group (scoring 72 out of 100) and Oaxaca two tiers below this (scoring 57 out of 100). Oaxaca's faltering on this index is due to the large areas of the state still lacking the judicial reform. Because I use CCISJP's index *at the municipal level*, I account for part of Ingram's system of classification by also including the geographic spread of the reform as part of the operationalization.

Regardless of variations in the definition of implementation, it is clear that the judicial reform process was not motivated by geography or any other obvious trend. It is important to establish that the reforms in Mexico were implemented randomly. If the reforms were not implemented randomly, then the reform variable could in fact measure some other underlying quality. For instance, if the reformed states happen to have reformed because they have quality X, then we couldn't be certain whether the reform or quality X helps to deter violence. There is substantial evidence that the municipalities that have reformed are not correlated in any other regard. States from the south, central, and north have implemented the reforms. Education and income are also not factors: Both poor, less-educated Oaxaca and wealthy, industrialized Baja California are included among the reformed states. Contrary to what some people assume, the reforms were also not implemented based on who received US funding for them. Oaxaca and Chihuahua began the reform process a couple of years before the federal mandate in 2008 and had been working with the U.S. Agency for International Development (USAID). However, other states that do not receive programs and training from USAID were also among the first reformers, such as Zacatecas (Villalobos 2012).

One might also assume that violence and the impunity rate spurred the reform process. States that implemented the reforms first did not decide to do so because of higher- or lower-than-average impunity rating. Theoretically, both scenarios seem possible. Policy makers in a state with an exceptionally high impunity rating could decide that they need to do something about the lack of justice, so they push through reforms to the judicial system. On the other hand, policy makers in a state with an exceptionally low impunity rating could decide to capitalize on the well-functioning system by making even more improvements to the judiciary. A quick glance at overall impunity statistics show that in 2007, those states that had reformed their judiciary had an average of 83 % of crimes go unpunished because they were not brought before the court (ICESI—Estadísticas Sobre Inseguridad Pública n.d.). Those states without a reformed judiciary also had an average of 83 % of crimes go unpunished (ICESI—Estadísticas Sobre Inseguridad Pública n.d.). The fact that impunity is the same for both reformed and unreformed groups suggests that this was not a driving factor to the reforms.

Violence levels are also not a factor: They are similar for reformed and unreformed states during the first implementation. This suggests that states that were more violent than average did not implement the reforms at a faster rate in order to quell the violence. It also indicates that states that were less violent than average did not implement the reforms at a faster rate in order to capitalize on a time of peace.

Trust in the Judiciary

To measure institutional trust, I use data from LAPOP (Vanderbilt University n.d.). The survey asks respondents how much confidence they have in each of their political institutions. The measure for trust in the judiciary is the average ranking within the state. The scale is from 1, the lowest amount of trust, to 10. The state averages for a given year range from a ranking of 1–6. The measure for trust in the police is the ranking that people in the state gave when asked how much confidence they had in the police, on a scale of 1–10. The state averages for a given year range from 1 to 5.

Interactions Between Reform and Trust

I predict that the reforms will have a greater impact on reducing crime when the institutions are trusted. That is to say, the reforms to the rule-of-law institutions will work to reduce violence only when those institutions are trusted by society, regardless of their institutional structure. When they are not trusted, there will not be the same reduction in violence. To account for this, I create an interactive variable measuring the interaction between judicial reform and trust in the judiciary.

Control Variables

I include another reform-based variable, police reforms, in the model. Since police are an integral part of the justice system, it is important to control for their status as an effective institution. This variable is given the value of 0 through 7 for each "good" score on the seven requirements determined by the Executive Secretariat of the National System of Public Security in its FASP evaluation (Secretariado Ejecutivo del Sistema Nacional de Seguridad Publica n.d.). This is a statewide variable. Data at the municipal level are not available.

I use three other control variables in the model that are widely suspected to affect the count of homicides: female-led households, percentage of people who work in the informal economy, and income.[3] The first control variable, female-led households, is expected to have a positive correlation with homicide. "Broken" homes—single-parent households—are hypothesized to lead to criminal behavior among children, a theory that has penetrated academia and public discourse for over a century (Gilling 1933; Gordon 1937; Jackson 1957; Monahan 1957; Peterson and Becker 1965; Wilkinson 1974). In 2010, Iain Duncan Smith, the work and pensions secretary in the UK, proclaimed that children from "broken" homes are nine times

[3] I also included a measure of the number of police agents per municipality, but this variable was automatically dropped due to collinearity.

more likely to commit crimes than children from homes with two parents (Bloxham 2010). I include this variable with data from Mexico's census bureau on the percentage of homes per municipality that are led by a woman (Instituto Nacional de Estadística y Geografía n.d.). From 2007 to 2010, single mothers headed 17 % of all households in the average municipality. The values range from 0 to 43 %.

The second control is the percentage of people who work in the state's informal economy. This rate of employment is hypothesized to positively impact homicide because people who are not connected to government institutions—those who are more marginalized—are less likely to use them to report crimes and file complaints in the courts (Rothstein 2005; Strange 1996). Susan Strange's *Retreat of the State* (1996) creates a framework to show that a global world economy and neoliberal policies have given rise to nonstate authorities such as criminal elements, international organizations, and transnational corporations, to the detriment of the traditional source of authority, the state. Equally important is the work of Guillermo O'Donnell (1973), who coined the term "browning of the state" to describe areas of a polity where the state has retreated and private interests run amuck. These works show that in areas where privatization has decimated government structures, criminal elements will grow and exploit this abandonment. In an anthropological work on narcotics trafficking in Mexico, Victoria Malkin illustrates how people in the territories that were most affected by the neoliberal reforms of the 1990s were more likely to develop extensive narcotics trafficking organizations. The dearth of a state presence allowed narcotics traffickers to influence the growing strategies of farmers and link these local economies to the drug trade (Malkin 2001). In order to control for the increase in homicides due to this lack of state presence, I include a measure of the percentage of people in the municipality who work in the informal economy. In the average municipality in Mexico from 2007 to 2010, approximately 30 % of the people were in the informal economy. The data range from a low of 16 % to a high of 39 %. These municipal data are provided by Mexico's census bureau (Instituto Nacional de Estadística y Geografía n.d.).

Lastly, I also include income as a control variable. An increase in income is expected to decrease homicide rates. This is hypothesized because people will be less likely to risk illegal behavior if they have a means of producing income in a legitimate industry. I specifically looked at average taxed income per person within each municipality. From 2007 to 2010 in Mexico, the average taxable income in the municipalities was 198,798 pesos (approximately 15,531 US dollars). The data range from municipalities with, on average, no taxable income to municipalities that average 6,614,991 pesos (approximately 516,796 US dollars). These data are also provided by Mexico's census bureau (Instituto Nacional de Estadística y Geografía n.d.). The variable is at the municipal level.

Table 17.1 shows the results of six ZINB models that test whether the aforementioned variables impact the number of homicides in Mexico. Models 1 through 3 incorporate different combinations of the control variables, while Models 4 through 6 incorporate different combinations of the theoretical variables. Models 5 and 6 are the best fit. These models use all control variables and account for the judicial reform and police reform independently.

Table 17.1 Series of ZINB models estimating the impact of reform and trust on homicides

	Model 1	Model 2	Model 3	Model 4	Model 5	Model 6
Judicial reform	32.08***	34.26***	17.52***		4.37*	
	(13.43)	(15.02)	(7.62)		(2.34)	
Trust in the judiciary	0.76***	0.77***	0.15		−0.29***	
	(6.49)	(6.71)	(1.29)		(−4.23)	
Judicial reform X trust	−7.78***	−8.35***	−4.23***		−1.14*	
	(−13.46)	(−15.12)	(−7.46)		(−2.36)	
Police reform	−0.20	0.63	1.38***			1.10***
	(−0.39)	(1.34)	(3.73)			(4.03)
Trust in the police	−1.52***	−1.32***	−1.07***			−0.20**
	(−12.19)	(−10.96)	(−9.31)			(−2.72)
Police reform X trust	0.33	−0.01	−0.39**			−0.33***
	(1.89)	(−0.02)	(−2.99)			(−3.36)
Pct. broken homes		15.99***	14.62***	5.47***	5.60***	5.88***
		(18.11)	(16.67)	(8.01)	(8.13)	(8.64)
Pct. informal economy			−0.17***	−0.05***	−0.06***	−0.07***
			(−21.40)	(−9.70)	(−10.78)	(−12.11)
Average income				0.01***	0.01***	0.01***
				(17.47)	(17.23)	(17.31)
Year = 2008	1.38***	1.12***	0.86***	0.49***	0.50***	0.54***
	(13.38)	(11.11)	(9.31)	(6.44)	(6.64)	(6.75)
Year = 2009	−0.27	−0.04	0.51***	0.95***	0.86***	0.80***
	(−1.56)	(−0.27)	(3.29)	(12.77)	(10.32)	(6.35)
Inflate						
Pct. “broken” homes	−20.00***	−13.16	−13.13***	5.71**	5.46*	5.39*
	(−13.27)	(−0.98)	(−5.65)	(2.63)	(2.49)	(2.50)

(continued)

Table 17.1 (continued)

	Model 1	Model 2	Model 3	Model 4	Model 5	Model 6
Pct. informal economy			0.04	−0.04*	−0.05**	−0.05***
			(1.32)	(−2.53)	(−3.10)	(-3.30)
Average income				−0.01***	−0.01***	−0.01***
				(−4.87)	(−4.61)	(−4.69)
Aic	17,730.0	17,421.8	16,711.1	13,724.6	13,516.9	13,490.2
Bic	17,813.1	17,511.8	16,815.0	13,792.4	13,602.9	13,576.2

$p<.01$ *** $p<0.05$ ** $p<.10$ *

In Model 5 and Model 6, all variables are significant at the .10 level.

Table 17.2 ZINB model showing the impact of the judicial reform on the count of drug-related homicides in Mexico, 2007–2010

	IRR	Std error	*P* value
Trust in the judiciary X reform	.32	.15	.01
Judicial reform (1 = yes, 0 = otherwise)	79.21	147.83	.01
Trust of judiciary	.75	.05	< .01
Pct. of female-led households	271.15	186.85	< .01
Pct. in informal economy	.94	.01	< .01
Income	1.00	.01	< .01
2008 dummy	1.65	.12	< .01
2009 dummy	2.36	.19	< .01
Always zero predictors			
Pct. of female-led households	5.46	2.19	.01
Pct. in informal economy	−.05	.01	< .01
Income	−.01	.01	< .01
Number of police officers	−.07	.17	< .01

$N = 3{,}440$

The number of observations used in the model is limited by missing data, primarily for income. I ran the model without the income variable (increasing the number of observations to 7,517 in total, or 1,879 per year) and found similar results.

Nonzero observations = 1,799

Zero observations = 1,641

Table 17.2 presents the results of Model 5 using incident rate ratios for easier interpretation.

The interaction effects between reform and trust are significant and provide support for the theory that trust hinders the ability of the reforms to have a deterrence effect on violence. Three variables in the above model measure the interactive impact of judicial reform and trust on homicide: β_1 (trust in the judiciary X judicial reform), β_2 (judicial reform), and β_3 (trust in the judiciary). Because this is an interaction effect, these coefficients have slightly different interpretations than noninteractive coefficients.

The trust in the judiciary variable estimates the impact on municipal violence when a judiciary that is not reformed increases its trust by one point on the seven-point trust scale. This coefficient is significant and suggests that a one-point increase in trust (in nonreformed municipalities only) will decrease the expected number of homicides by a factor of .75 ($p < .01$).

The judicial reform variable estimates the impact on municipal violence when a judiciary that has no trust transitions from an unreformed system of justice to a reformed one. In the strictest sense, this situation is not possible, as even the most despised judiciaries have some trust, however fragile. The variable does, however, indicate that reformed municipalities with extremely low levels of trust will become more violent, by a factor of 79, if they attempt reform without trust. This suggests that areas where there is poor trust in institutions should not make an effort to reform. As mentioned previously, soon-to-be-reformed municipalities and unreformed municipalities had similar levels of violence before the restructuring. Thus, the difference in rates of violence is a consequence of the reform, not the other way around.

Why would the reform increase violence in communities where there is almost no trust? This is likely due to narcotics traffickers' presumption that they can "push back" with impunity due to society's distrust of government. Any reform in the judiciary or police threatens the livelihood of organized narcotics traffickers, so they may fight changes by intimidating the local community and sending threats to the government through violence. Unfortunately, this has been witnessed many times. In one of the most violent episodes, a narcotics trafficking organization known as La Familia killed over 16 police officers in the span of 3 days in retribution for the apprehension of one of their members, Arnoldo Rueda (Grillo 2011). Another sensational pushback features the detonation of a bomb in Tamaulipas, which killed two policemen, in retaliation for the arrest and prosecution of members of a narcotics trafficking group (STRATFOR 2012). However, when the judiciary or police have a high level of societal trust, narcotics traffickers may be more hesitant to violently resist reforms out of fear that the institution may be able to impose sanctions upon them for such acts.

The interaction effect shows that this difference in violence levels between reformed and unreformed municipalities diminishes when trust increases. When there are low levels of trust, reformed municipalities will have more instances of violence than nonreformed municipalities. But for each increase in trust, the *difference* in violence between reformed and unreformed municipalities will decrease by a factor of .32. In other words, when municipalities have average or high levels of trust in the institution, the reform will reduce violence.

In order to more specifically show what effect the reform would have on violence when there are high levels of trust in the institution, I ran a series of predicted

Table 17.3 Changes in predicted probabilities of homicide given levels of trust in the institution

Expected value of homicide	No reform	Reform
1	18.3	3.3
2	10.2	2.4
3	6.4	2.0
4	4.2	1.7
5	2.8	1.5
6	1.9	1.4
7	1.3	1.3
8	0.9	1.2
9	0.7	1.1

Presidencia de la Republica (n.d.)

probabilities.[4] These show the predicted probability of a certain outcome (e.g., homicide = 1) for different values of the independent variables. For high levels of trust (ranking = 7) and all other variables set at their mean, I computed the change in the predicted probability of increasing homicide for reformed and unreformed municipalities.

For highly trusted judiciaries, I found that when a municipality implements the judicial reform, the predicted probability of deaths decreases:

- For one death in the municipality, it decreases from 18 to 3 %.
- For two deaths, it decreases from 10 to 2 %.
- For three deaths, it decreases from 6 to 2 %.
- For four deaths, it decreases from 4 to 2 %.
- For five deaths, it decreases from 2 to 1 %.

The predicted probability of nine deaths is nearly identical in reformed and unreformed municipalities with high rates of trust (both are at 1 %). Table 17.3 lists these values.

This same decrease in predicted probability of violence is not seen when trust equals 3. *Only when trust is at high levels (over 6) does the model predict that a move from not reformed to reformed will decrease the chances of violence.* This helps to explain why many states do not think the reform has helped to impose any semblance of a rule of law. These states do not have high levels of trust in their institutions, which significantly impacts the reform's ability to reduce violence. Simply put, in areas where there is little or no trust, the reform will not reduce violence.

[4] These were derived using the pr value command developed by J. Scott Long (see Long and Freese 2006).

Discussion of Control Variables

With regard to control variables, the models confirm the suspected relationships between violence and income and violence and family structure. However, the informal economy control variable does not operate as expected. The percentage of the population that works in the informal economy has a negative impact on violence. This is a surprising result that runs in the opposing direction of the hypothesis. The model predicts that a municipality that has 100 % of its population working in the informal economy will reduce each count of homicide by a factor of 6, compared to a municipality that has 0 % of its population working in the informal economy. There are no municipalities with either 0 % or 100 % of the population in the informal economy, so this is an out-of-range estimate; however, the directionality of the coefficient still opposes extant theory.

A possible explanation for this finding is along the lines of bridging social capital: Communities without formal institutional structures supplement these with informal institutional structures as a means to keep control (Putnam 1993). In other words, a community that has its entire workforce in the informal sector has not fallen into anarchy; rather, it has replaced formal institutional arrangements with informal ones. Conventional theories predict that this is a recipe for more violence; however, it could also be the case that informal institutional arrangements have the potential to impose a rule of law. There are a number of examples of this sort of arrangement in Mexico. For example, in Ayutla de los Libres, Guerrero, a group of rural villagers decided to start community groups in 2012 with the sole purpose of imposing security (Thomet 2013). The small community was tired of violence, "fed up with the police," and "exasperated with their ineffective judicial system." They took up arms and started self-policing, arresting over 40 members of local gangs and narcotics-related groups. Similar groups have appeared in Chihuahua and Michoacán. These informal communities are marginalized from the state but are sometimes still able to maintain lower levels of violence.

The percentage of households that are headed by a single woman has a positive impact on violence. The count of homicides is predicted to increase by a factor of 271 when a municipality has 100 % of its households headed by single mothers, compared to municipalities with 0 %. This confirms what "broken-homes" theorists would expect to find.

Income is statistically significant ($p = < .01$) but substantially insignificant. It predicts no change for income growth even at such high multiples as a 100,000-peso increase.

The always-zero part of the ZINB model is a logistic regression that tests whether specific variables cause a municipality to go from nonviolent (zero deaths) to violent (one death). I do not expect that the theories I explore about rule-of-law institutions' ability to reduce violence apply here. Instead, I include some basic determinants to homicide: percentage of female-led households, percentage of population in the informal economy, and average taxable income. All of these variables are statistically significant and, with the exception of the percentage of the population that works in the informal economy, all operate in the hypothesized manner. A higher number of female-led households increases the likelihood of a municipality becoming violent (death = 1). When a municipality goes from zero female-led households to all female-led households, the probability that it becomes violent increases by a factor of 5. A municipality that increases average income by 100,000 pesos (slightly under 8000 US dollars) is less likely to become violent by a factor of 2. These operate as expected, except for informal economy work, which, once again, is an anomalous finding: A municipality that goes from no informal economy work to all informal economy work is 5 % less likely to become violent.

Conclusion

I offer here a critique of the conventional wisdom surrounding how rule-of-law institutions decrease crime, providing support for the claim that focusing reform efforts on institutional performance is not enough. The courts and police also need the people's trust. These insights should offer reformers in Mexico and other countries that are contemplating reforms a blueprint for moving forward.

There is little information about how to escape from a situation of stagnating trust, like that in Mexico. In his seminal work *Social Traps and the Problem of Trust*, Bo Rothstein explains that when institutions lose trust, it is incredibly difficult for them to regain it. This situation is what is known as a "social trap." Mexican states have different histories of attempts to crawl out of the social trap; the development of states, their institutions, and their leaders has varied dramatically across the country over the past four decades.

My work suggests that the development of institutional trust is a necessary precondition to institutional reform. Most policy makers assume that reform is the cure for mistrust. Yet, as history shows, shallow institutional reform begets only shallow institutional approval. And, as is evident today, shallow institutional approval hinders reform efforts.

Even so, much rhetoric continues to insinuate that trust will follow automatically after the reform is implemented. For example, Marco Antonio Higuera Lopez writes that the reform "derives a change in culture which requires a more active citizenry, who denounces and involves themselves in the process" (Nandayapa 2008). It is clear that this is not the case in many states' experiences with the reform (e.g., Mexico State, Oaxaca). People are more apt to involve themselves in the rule-of-law institutions when those institutions have trust—regardless of whether a reform has occurred. Trust *must* precede reform.

Along with Cleary and Stokes (2009), Rothstein (2005), and Tyler (2006), I illustrate that institutional trust is a key factor in determining development in governance. These findings have implications for reforms of political institutions. They suggest that underlying processes of democratization can be a bigger determinant in the success of an institution than the contours of institutional reforms. More specifically, these findings call for more inquiry into the relationship between historical processes of democratization and trust in the institution. Although researchers have long attempted to examine the role of trust in political institutions, the concept eludes measurement, and often understanding as well. This study provides a valid and reliable methodological foundation upon which to build future studies on trust in the judiciary in other countries or other political institutions in Mexico. My findings also have relevance for public policy, suggesting to policy makers that the benefits of a structural reform in the judiciary will remain obscured until trust in the institution is fostered.

References

Alegria, J. M. & Moreno, H. (2010, March 3). Taxistas asesinan a delincuente. *En Marcha: Realidad Municipal de Oaxaca*. Retrieved from http://www.revistaenmarcha.com.mx/reportaje/378-taxistas-asesinan-a-delincuente.html.

Blas, C. (2010, February 22). Salina Cruz, linchamiento y corrupción. *En Marcha: Realidad Municipal de Oaxaca*. Retrieved from http://www.revistaenmarcha.com.mx/columnas/cronicas-de-la-insula/371-salina-cruz-linchamiento-y-corrupcion.html.

Bloxham, A. (2010, November 4). Children from broken homes "nine times more likely to commit crimes." *The Telegraph*. Retrieved from http://www.telegraph.co.uk/news/politics/8109184/Children-from-broken-homes-nine-times-more-likely-to-commit-crimes.html.

Cleary, M & Stokes, S. (2009). *Democracy and the culture of skepticism*. Series on Trust. City: Russell Sage Foundation.

Cordero, M. (2011, February 4). Acreedor a primer juicio oral. *El Sol de Tijuana*. Retrieved from http://www.oem.com.mx/elsoldetijuana/notas/n1952631.htm.

Correa-Cabrera, G. (2013). *Democracy in "two Mexicos": Political institutions in Oaxaca and Nuevo Leon*. City: Palgrave Macmillan.

Cuevas, S. B. (2011). La implementación del nuevo sistema. *Nuevo Sistema de Justicia Penal: Revista Semestral Del Consejo de Coordinación Para La Implementación Del Sistema de Justicia Penal: Revista Semestral Del Consejo de Coordinacion Para La Implementacion Del Sistema de Justicia Penal, 3*, 14–30.

Gilling, J. (1933). *Social pathology*. New York: Appleton-Century.

Gordon, R. G. (1937). Delinquency in relation to the broken home. *National Institute of Health: Archives of Disease in Childhood, 68*(12), 111–117.

Grillo, I. (2011). *El Narco: Inside Mexico's criminal insurgency*. City: Bloomsbury Press.

ICESI—Estadísticas Sobre Inseguridad Pública. (n.d.). Retrieved from http://icesi.org.mx/estadisticas/estadisticas_encuestasNacionales.asp.

Ingram, M. (2013). *Criminal procedure reform in Mexico: Where things stand now*. City: Woodrow Wilson Center's Mexico Institute.

Instituto Ciudadano de Estudios Sobre la Inseguridad. (2002, May). Primera encuesta nacional sobre inseguridad public en las entidades federativas.

Instituto Ciudadano de Estudios Sobre la Inseguridad. (2009, October). Sexta encuesta nacional sobre inseguridad.

Instituto Nacional de Estadística y Geografía (INEGI). (n.d.). *Sistema Estatal y Municipal de Bases de Datos* (Mexico). Retrieved from http://www.inegi.org.mx.

Inter-American Commission on Human Rights. (2009, March 27). Report No. 52/09. Organization of American States.

Inter-American Commission on Human Rights. (2009, November 12). Report No. 130/09. Organization of American States.

Inter-American Commission on Human Rights. (2012, March 19). Report No. 61/21. Organization of American States.

Jackson, T. (1957). The differential impact of family disorganization. *American Sociological Review, 22*, 505–512.

Long, J. S., & Freese, J. (2006). *Regression models for categorical dependent variables using stata*. City: Stata Press.

MacCoun, R. J. (1993). Drugs and the law: A psychological analysis of drug prohibition. *Psychological Bulletin, 113*(3), 497–512.

Malkin, V. (2001). Narcotrafficking, migration, and modernity in rural Mexico. *Latin American Perspectives, 28*, 101.

Manjarrez, R. M. (2012). *Reformas constitucionales al sistema penal de Mexico y su implmenacion en el estado de Baja California*. Washington, DC: Procurador General de Justicia del Estado de Baja California, Woodrow Wilson Center.

Martínez, V. L. J. (2010, March 23). Linchamiento: La (in)justicia de los pobres. En Marcha: Realidad Municipal de Oaxaca. Retrieved from http://www.revistaenmarcha.com.mx/analisis/407-linchamiento-la-injusticia-de-los-pobres.html.

McCluskey, J. D. (2003). *Police requests for compliance: Coercive and procedurally just tactics*. City: LFB Scholarly Publishing.

Méndez, A. & Aranda, J. (2007, December 13). Magistrados rechazan juicios orales; Preferible capacitar personal, señalan. *La Jornada*. Retrieved from http://www.jornada.unam.mx/2007/12/13/index.php?section=politica&article=009n1pol.

Monahan, T. (1957). Family status and the delinquent child: A reappraisal and some new findings. *Social Forces, 35*, 250–258.

Nagin, D. (1998). Criminal deterrence research at the outset of the twenty-first century. *Crime and Justice, 23*, 1–42.

Nandayapa, C. V. N. (2008). Breves reflexiones sobre algunos de los retos en el diseño del nuevo proceso penal ordinario. Suprema Corte de Justicia de La Nación, pp. 72–78.

O'Donnell, G. (1973). *Modernization and bureaucratic authoritarianism*. City: Institute of International Studies.

Paternoster, R. (1987). The deterrent effect of the perceived certainty and severity of punishment: A review of the evidence and issues. *Justice Quarterly, 4*, 173–217.

Peterson, D., & Becker, W. (1965). Family interaction and delinquency. In H. C. Quay (Ed.), *Juvenile delinquency*. Princeton, NJ: D. Van Nostrand.

Presidencia de la Republica. (n.d.). *Homicidios*.

Putnam, R. (1993). *Making democracy work: Civic traditions in modern Italy*. Princeton, NJ: Princeton University Press.

Rothstein, B. (2005). *Social traps and the problem of trust* (Series of institutional design). Cambridge: Cambridge University Press.

Secretariado Ejecutivo del Sistema Nacional de Seguridad Publica. (n.d.). *Fondo de Aportaciones Para La Seguridad Pública (FASP)*. Retrieved from http://portal.secretariadoejecutivosnsp.gob.mx/?page=fasp.

Selee, A. (2011). *Decentralization, democratization, and informal power in Mexico*. University Park, PA: Pennsylvania State University Press.

Shirk, D. (1999, July). *New federalism in Mexico: Implications for Baja California and the cross-border region* (Briefing paper for Fronterizo Policy Luncheon).

Strange, S. (1996). *The retreat of the state*. Cambridge: Cambridge University Press.

Stratfor. (2012, July 3). *Mexico: Bombing retaliation for gang arrests—State attorney general*. STRATFOR Situation Reports.

Thomet, L. (2013, January 28). Vigilante justice is at work in Mexico. *Iol News*. Retrieved from www.iol.co.za/news/world/vigilante-justice-is-at-work-in-mexico-1.1459854#.USD3RWeQPNh.

Tittle, C. (1969). Crime rates and legal sanctions. *Social Problems, 16*, 417.

Tyler, T. (2006). *Why people obey the law*. Princeton, NJ: Princeton University Press.

Vanderbilt University. (n.d.). *Latin American Public Opinion Project (LAPOP)*. Retrieved from http://www.vanderbilt.edu/lapop.

Villalobos, A. G. (2012, October 15). *Interview*. Mexico, DF.

Wilkinson, K. (1974). The broken family and juvenile delinquency: Scientific explanation or ideology? *Social Problems, 21*(5), 726–739.

Chapter 18
Patterns and Modus Operandi of Crime and Disorderly Conduct on the Public Transport System in Abakaliki, Nigeria: A Descriptive Analysis

Smart Egwu Otu

Introduction

The Public Transport System (PTS)[1] in Abakaliki City is made up of minibuses (18+ seaters), coaches (42+ seaters) and taxicabs (8+ seaters). It provides the most important means of transportation for both rural and urban residents who commute to other locations for both their convenience and daily social, economic, political and health reasons. Residents and public transport users in Abakaliki do not see the PTS as a choice, and Gray et al. (2010) explained that individuals in extreme cases may become less mobile which they described as evidence of fear. Its proper management therefore is of paramount importance to provide safety for its many users and their property.

Ceccato et al. (2013) explained that security remains one of the many factors which influence the mobility of individuals, especially in an urban environment. They asserted that an increase in the rate of crime and public disorder on the PTS—whether static or non-static (that is non-moving or moving)—causes great fear on the part of its users within the city limits. Studies by Clarke (1997), LaVigne (1997), Church et al. (2000), and by Newton (2004) showed that forms of transport facilitate the occurrence of crime and public disorder in several ways, so that its safety for its many users and stakeholders can no longer be overemphasised.

Generally, the Public Transport System is a multifaceted system, and as such has characteristics which promote crime and public disorder. For instance, Newton (2004) in his studies of public transport system in UK observed that the design of its facilities, the internal design of the vehicles, and the environments (routes) which a vehicle crosses may influence the level and kinds of crime and public disorder

[1] The PTS is made up of two categories: one owned and/or managed by the government and/or its agencies, and the other owned and/or managed by private individuals or cooperative societies.

S.E. Otu (✉)
Federal University Ndufu Alike Ikwo, Ebonyi, Nigeria
e-mail: smart.otu@funai.edu.ng; smartotu@yahoo.com; smartotu@gmail.com

E.C. Viano (ed.), *Cybercrime, Organized Crime, and Societal Responses*,
DOI 10.1007/978-3-319-44501-4_18

experienced. Newton (2004), Weiser-Easteal and Wilson (1991) described the complex interaction of settings such as trains, trams and facilities (well-developed stopovers, stations and interchanges) as common characteristics of a well-developed PTS which help generate crime and public disorder. Weiser-Easteal and Wilson (1991) explained that a country and its mode of transport has a distinct set of problems due to its unique environment, and efforts to reduce those problems may well require a discrete set of solutions. According to Jochelson (1997), different types of crime occur in different places and vary over time.

The People's Daily (a daily newspaper in Nigeria) in its online publication when reflecting on the increase in crime and public disorder on the PTS, reported a tragic armed robbery incident which took place along a busy highway, during which many commuters either had their belongings stolen, or were maimed, raped or killed (see "The latest tragedy on Okene-Lokoja-Abuja Road" in http://www.peoplesdaily-online.com/opinion/editorial/18499-the-latest-tragedy-on-okene-lokoja-abuja-road). Daily reviews in Nigerian newspapers, tabloids and magazines show that crime and public disorder on the PTS in Nigeria are a common occurrence, and they include theft of commuters' luggage, robbery in bus stations and stopovers, drugging and hypnotising of passengers on moving buses/coaches/taxis, waylaying and robbing commuters on the highways, as well as various kinds of assault and insult on innocent commuters.

In a sarcastic, but well-founded treatise warning visitors to Africa entitled "So You're Planning a Trip to Africa", Bidstrup (1999, p. 3 and cited in Otu 2003, p. 56) a decade ago illuminated the seriousness of crime, and especially armed robbery on the public transport system in Nigeria. Bidstrup warned would-be visitors to Nigeria to be wary of armed bandits when travelling on Nigerian roads. As he put it *inter alia*:

> … Never travel at night. Armed robbery is always everywhere in Nigeria, but is much worse at night … Daytime travel isn't safe, but it is much safer than night time travel. Never carry all your money with you. If you get robbed, and they find your money (and yes, they will, no matter how clever you think you are), you'll end up penniless in a country that doesn't know the meaning of the words "credit cards", "wire transfers", "ATM", or "bank credit" … Cf. (Otu 2003, p. 56).

In Abakaliki, the capital of Ebonyi state, the PTS is not as multifaceted as its counterparts in more advanced cities in Nigeria such as Lagos, Port Harcourt and Abuja. It is far less multifaceted when compared with its counterparts in western countries such as the USA, the UK, Germany, France and Russia. In fact, the main and only PTS in Abakaliki is the automobile which includes buses, taxis and coaches. Sadly, the design of the facilities and the environments (routes) which public transport uses are poorly constructed, ran and supervised thereby providing a unique opportunity for all kinds of crime and public disorder to thrive. Available police records show that crime and public disorder on the PTS are not uncommon, including mainly theft, robbery, obtaining by pretence (OBT), unlawful possession, assault and insults (lumped together and reported); that is these offences are not discretely documented (see Police Crime Reports, State Police Command Headquarters, Abakaliki). The Table 18.1 below shows the distribution of reported cases of crime and public disorder (lumped together), arrests made, suspects charged in court, and the value of property stolen and recovered in the State between 2004 and 2012.

Table 18.1 Crime and disorder trends, arrests, suspects charged and value (in hundreds and thousand of US$) of the property recovered by the Nigerian Police in Abakaliki

	2004	2005	2006	2007	2008	2009	2010	2011	2012
Crime/disorder	Freq.	Freq.	Freq.	Freq.	Freq.	Freq.	Freq.	Freq.	Freq.
Cases reported	109	159	113	186	206	179	248	168	246
Arrests made	160	342	201	126	148	196	264	185	256
Suspects charged in courts	89	79	84	121	108	86	118	78	88
Value of property stolen	$22,439	$22,185	$60,840	$25,588	$31,145	$62,860	$38,865	$38,444	$42,850
Value of property recovered	$5240	$5340	$5964	$4875	$3479	$6285	$4850	$3556	$42,324

Source: Police Command Hqtrs. Abakaliki

A detailed study of the analysis provided by the Nigeria Police reveals that with the exception of OBT, all other crimes and public disorder on the PTS occurring each year in Abakaliki share a lambda (frequency) mean in the neighbourhood of 29.07 (see Police Crime Reports, State Police Command Headquarters, Abakaliki). It also reveals that in line with the eye of the law, crimes such as robbery, theft and assault are considered more serious and responded to as such by the Nigeria police than reported disorderly conducts. Certainly, when compared with other big cities in Nigeria such as Onitsha, Lagos, Port Harcourt, Kano and Aba, the reported cases pale into insignificance. However, their daily occurrence continues to cause serious concern for all the most important stakeholders in the public transport system in the city and state.

Abakaliki represents a perfect example of a fast growing and transitional city with increasing socio-political and economic activities. The environment within which public transport companies operate in Abakaliki is a very disorganised one. With no visible police officers, security staff or CCTV cameras at the stations, as well as very bad roads, the PTS in Abakaliki is certainly experiencing an increasing range of crime and public disorder in both the moving (non-stationary) and non-moving (stationary)[2] transport systems.

The lack of security when using the PTS in Abakaliki continues to erode the confidence of its many users. Therefore, for most Abakaliki residents who use public transport for their daily activities—both personal and property—security remains a major concern. However, it is not only commuters whose security is of concern, the safety of the staff who often are the first casualties of any crime and public disorder in this sector is also of primary concern (see also Crime Concern, UK. http://www.dft.gov.uk/rmd/project.asp?intProjectID=10488).

The Urban Environment in Abakaliki

While interest in crime and public disorder on public transport in more urbanised cities and countries such as Lagos, Port Harcourt and Abuja (in Nigeria), and the UK, Sweden, France and the US has grown considerably, this level of interest is yet to grow in less developed cities and countries such as Abakaliki and Nigeria. All these make the city a chequer board and good place to study crime and public disorder. Therefore, focusing on crime and public disorder on PTS in an emerging city such as Abakaliki adds to the growing body of literature on transportation challenges from the perspective of African sociology-criminology. This is more so as public transport systems and infrastructure in less developed cities and countries such as Abakaliki and Nigeria are largely underdeveloped and far less organised.

[2]Crime and disorder on stationary public transport refers to any criminal or outlaw behaviour which occurs on a bus, coach or taxi that is not in motion, i.e. in a state of inertia, while crime and public disorder on the non-stationary PTS refers to any criminal or outlaw behaviour occurring while the bus, coach or taxis is in transit (motion), or has just left its point of departure such as parks, stations etc. en route to its destination.

Abakaliki is a medium, urbanising capital city of Ebonyi State. The state was founded on October 1st 1996. The state has an estimated population of 2,176,947 according to the 2006 National Population Census. A quarter of this number is estimated to reside in Abakaliki, the capital city of the state. Although the residents of the city are mainly Ebonyians, the city is fast gaining a multicultural status as a result of increasing diverse ethnic people settling in the city pursuing various personal and group needs.

The city is a checkerboard of an emerging modern city with all the trappings of urban blight, social vices and crime (armed robbery, theft, vandalism), commercial sex work, cultism, youth unrest and disorder, including on the PTS. There are no trains or trams in Abakaliki. With more than three quarters of Nigerians projected to be using the PTS, and especially road transportation (see http://www.frsc.gov.ng/roadsafetyaudit.pdf), we project that over 90 % of the residents in the city use this means of transportation in Abakaliki city.

Transport companies operating in the city are mostly privately owned with a few owned, controlled and managed by government agencies. There is no remarkable difference between the two, except in the fares charged and strict adherence to carrying a normal number of commuters. The most popular names in the PTS in the city include Peace Mass, Romchi, Ifesinachi, Okeyson and Onitsha South.

Abakaliki has a poorly maintained road networks which constitute part of its governance challenges (see Ukoha and Chukwuma 2012). Parks stations have no streetlights which come on at night, giving a sense of eeriness to public transport users. In addition, typical parks/stations in Abakaliki are often overcrowded with waiting passengers, agberos (loaders), people accompanying passengers to the parks/stations, as well as people who come to take care of some kind of business or other. Most, if any at all, do not have provision for waiting rooms or even conveniences for their many users. With tricycles and motorcycles the main means of shuttles in the city, parks/stations are often flooded as operators come to drop off passengers. There is also a cacophony of blaring loudspeakers announcing to waiting passengers the arrival of buses/coaches from/to different destinations, thus making the atmosphere around parks/stations unbearable for their users. The park/station environment is important not only because it directly and indirectly affects visibility, but also because it can offer a sense of calm for its users (see also Jacobs 1961; Uittenbogaard and Ceccato 2014).

Objectives of the Study

The aims which make up the three key questions asked are: (1) Is crime and public disorder on both stationary and non-stationary (moving and non-moving) PTS discernible in Abakaliki even without due and diligent consideration for variations across time and space? (2) What are the patterns, dimensions and modus operandi which these crimes and public disorder consist of? (3) Which criminological model best explains these crimes and disorderly behaviour? This study brings Abakaliki city into focus in terms of challenges facing commuters using public transport systems on a daily basis in Nigerian cities. It highlights the various steps being taken by public transport operators and the government to check the menace of these crimes and public disorder and makes informed suggestions for further improving safety through crime prevention drawn from the principles of situational crime prevention, routine activity theory and rational choice theory.

Theory and Previous Studies

Crime and public disorder on both the stationary and non-stationary PTS depend on many conditions which occur at various levels of interaction within the environment (see Uittenbogaard and Ceccato 2014). These conditions are determined by the environmental characteristics of the stations, people's activities and daily habits, and the offenders' awareness and area of activity (see also Brantigham and Brantigham 1995). Working with this mind-set, the conceptual model of the present study relies on the principles of both *routine activity* and *rational choice theories* even though I acknowledge these two theories traditionally address more the issue of victimisation than offending behaviour. Both theories certainly cut across environmental criminology which has received wide criminological attention (Brantigham and Brantigham 1995; Cohen and Felson 1979; Smith and Clarke 2000).

As adopted in this study, the routine activity model from the perspective of offending behaviour describes how social change in Abakaliki city—as a new state capital in the post-military Nigerian era—had facilitated the convergence, in space and time, of likely offenders with the goal of committing crimes against suitable targets in the absence of capable and effective guardians. Cohen and Felson (1979) had argued: first, that the opportunity for crime may depend on a configuration of distinct (though not disaggregated) components of the criminal; second, a correlate of the first, that the lack of either of the first two components (criminal and target) or the presence of the third (capable guardians) would be sufficient in itself to prevent a potential criminal event from occurring. The rational choice model describes the capacity of potential offenders to evaluate their own risk factors before making a decision either to commit a crime or engage in public disorder or not. Among the factors identified include the location, environment, absence of capable guardianship (security agents), the presence of soft targets, potential opportunities to commit crimes; these factors are juxtaposed and synergised both in time and space (see Cohen and Felson 1979; Smith and Clarke 2000).

Writing from the perspective which explores the link between bus crime and its environs, Levine et al. (1986) used both survey and observational data to provide evidence which shows that incidents of bus crime are highest on bus routes which traverse high crime-rate areas. Pearlstein and Wachs (1982) support the view that most crimes on buses occurred on routes that pass through high crime-rate areas in general, and that all transit crimes were concentrated in these parts of the city where soft targets and the absence of capable guardian (security) exist. Ihlanfeldt (2003) with evidence from Atlanta, USA, showed that railway stations have a significant influence on the levels of crime in their neighbourhoods, and vice versa. This finding corroborates victims' accounts of robbery on moving coaches, which show that most robberies occur on routes that traverse high crime-rate neighbourhoods, towns, cities, and states in Nigeria. Weiser-Easteal and Wilson (1991) explained that each mode of the PTS has its own specific problems which come about because each one has its own distinct environment. In all these studies, it seems obvious that the basic assumption of routine activity and rational theories—commuters carrying large sum of money and valuables, lack of capable guardianship and good-to-go offenders who undertake minimum risks are discernible.

Ceccato et al. (2013) study of security in Stockholm's underground stations found a relatively large share of reported public disorder and crimes at the stations. Public disorder was mainly cases of drunken people on platforms, and the unjustified use of fire hoses or fire extinguishers. Crimes identified at the stations were fighting, vandalism, threats and other types of violence. The authors also found that property crimes were relatively common even though they were more often recorded by police than by the Stockholm Public Transport and Veolia databases. Importantly, these authors found that these crimes and public disorder were associated with specific features of the stations, the kind of neighbourhood where the stations are located, and the relative position of both the stations and the neighbourhood in the city—this reflecting the interrelation of space and time.

Loukaitou-Sideris (1999) examined the connection between criminal activity at bus stops and environmental factors based on empirical observations, mapping and surveys. By examining ten bus stops, the author found that bus stops with a high crime rate had a largely negative environment and a general lack of defensible space. This contrasted with bus stops with a low crime rate, which showed a lack of negative environmental factors and better surveillance opportunities. The author then identified some of these negative factors (within 300 ft of a bus stop) as including liquor stores, bars, adult bookstores, check cashing establishments, seedy motels, pawn shops, vacant lots and movie theatres. This finding corroborates Newton (2004), who examined criminal damage on bus shelters and found this damage was related in a systematic and predictable way to known attributes of a shelter's location. In a study of Green Line Light Rail Stations in Los Angeles, Loukaitou-Sideris et al. (2002) found a link between crime rates and stations with dark hiding places or with poor visibility in the surroundings which minimises the risk of apprehension. Liggett et al. (2001) extended the findings of Loukaitou-Sideris by investigating how environmental factors around a bus stop could be used as predictive rather than indicative measures to measure the amount of crime as a result of placing a bus stop in a particular location.

Block and Davis (1996) took a slightly different approach by opting to examine the spatial distribution of street crime in four districts in Chicago—to ascertain whether areas adjacent to busy transport stations are a focus for street crime or not. Their findings showed that in low crime-rate areas, street robbery was high and near (but not immediately outside) busy transit stations. In high crime-rate areas, robbery was prominent on the main streets near transit stations, with more robberies occurring at least on every block and mainly at night, thus reflecting the fact that area with high routine activities is a good crime and disorderly conduct attractor.

A survey carried out in 1996 and 2004 by "Crime Concern" for the Department of Transport UK on people's perceptions of personal security and concerns about crime on the PTS found that respondents generally expressed their fears with perceptions differing between variables such as sex, age, race, time and modes of transport. For instance, the survey found that the perception and fear of crime was higher among women after dark (at night) while waiting at train stations (especially underground stations). This was the case for younger and elderly women and minority groups. In statistical terms, the agency found that 10 % of their respondents reported experiencing deliberate shoving and hostile staring while using public transport. Five percent (5 %) of the male respondents reported being threatened with violence, and slightly less than 10 % of the women reported being a victim of sexual harassment, assault and men exposing themselves in front of them. Interestingly, the same agency found that when compared to workers in other occupations, public transport workers were more often associated with a higher risk of victimisation because the nature of their works requires them to maintain order, collect fares, handle money and work late at night—all which provide improved rewards for potential criminals.

The British Transport Police Statistics (BTPS) focused on crimes committed on the railways in the UK and identified that theft of passengers' property and other offences involving motor vehicles accounted for the highest number of offences recorded by the British police. Significantly, the BTPS attributed these offences to the convergence in space of both the offenders' and victims' awareness. In a similar manner, Crime Concern Reports (CCR) in England reported a wide range of disorderly conduct associated with homeless people, beggars, alcoholics and drug dealers loitering on public transport facilities.

The Bureau of Consular Affairs, a US Department of State, takes responsibility for providing information on the security situation to its citizens all over the world. In one release (see http://www.ngex.com/business/public/newsinfo.php?nid=22 posted on 29 August 2006), the Department showed that the level of insecurity associated with the use of the PTS in Nigeria was increasing. It warned *inter alia*: "travel by any means within Nigeria is risky …". The Department warned would-be-US visitors to Nigeria on the presence of touts and armed bandits at both Nigeria's Airport and on the nation's roads. The Consul reported a rise in smash-and-grab robberies in private cars and the PTS, particularly in Lagos. It illustrated the prevailing crime and public disorder on Nigerian roads thus:

> Road travel is dangerous. Robberies by armed gangs have been reported on rural roads, and within major cities. US citizens should avoid travelling by roads. Because of poor vehicle maintenance and driving conditions, public transportation throughout Nigeria can be dangerous and should be avoided. Taxis pose risks because of the possibility of fraudulent or criminal operations, old and unsafe vehicle, and poorly maintained roads … (2006, p. 2).

However, it is not only the nature of the external environment and its effects on public transport crime which has attracted the interest of PTS scholars. Mayhew et al. (1976) drew attention to the importance of the internal environment of buses as something that also needs to be examined. For instance, the authors examined the effects of supervision on damage to buses in Manchester in the UK and found damage was greater on buses without a conductor. They also found that the upper decks of buses were far more damaged than the lower decks, and buses with a rear staircase suffered far greater damage and vandalism than those without.

The Touts or "Agberos"

On the local scene, Okpara (1988) investigated the role of touts (popularly and colloquially known in Nigeria as *agberos*[3]) on passengers using the PTS. Okpara explains that *agberos* constitute a nuisance to the station's staff, passengers and all station users alike. Furthermore, *agberos* members often fight among themselves, bully and fight passengers, cause the loss of passengers' items, help in degrading the environment around stations, and even commit a lot more serious crimes as they weigh between the risk of apprehension by security agents and the rewards of satisfying their utilitarian and/or non-utilitarian criminal behaviours and/or misconducts.

In all these reviews, offenders showed they are purposive, goal oriented and would seek the most feasible opportunity and target within a convergence of space and time to commit crime and disorder on the PTS (see also Cornish and Clarke 1986). Offenders on the PTS in Abakaliki are therefore both "willing-to-do-crime" and are presented with suitable targets and the absence of responsible guardians. In making decisions and choices about what crime to commit and how to commit it, offenders are inclined to choose what would afford them the highest returns, minimise apprehension only constrained by time and the availability of information (see Felson and Clark 1998). Newton (2004) used this viewpoint to suggest that offenders who commit crime and engage in public disorder on the public transport sector would most likely exhibit some level of rationality while making these decisions and choices.

Research Methodology

The descriptive analysis of crime and disorder on the PTS in Abakaliki, Nigeria was based on responses from a cross-sectional survey conducted with park's/station's managers, a few representatives of identified victims and eye witnesses of PTS users, and reflective data. The empirical material with stakeholders examined in concrete terms four key objectives: (1) the epidemiology (trend) of crimes and public disorder on the PTS in Abakaliki, (2) the modus operandi (MO) of these crimes and disorderly behaviour (3) correlations with bus stations in Abakaliki and the

[3] The author conceptualised *agberos* as freelance workers who undertake the self-imposed duty of recruiting passengers for drivers, and bus/taxi owners for small commissions.

Table 18.2 Sampled transportation models and their correlates

PTS models	Correlates	Transport companies sampled
Popular/competitive	1. Heavy patronage by the public	Peace mass transit, Romchi
	2. Long and medium distance coverage	
	3. Owned and managed by private individuals	
	4. Many hawkers, preachers and freelance loaders.	
Luxurious/comforter	1. Luxurious and comfort services provided	Ifesinachi, G.U Okeke and Chisco transport companies
	2. Long distance coverage	
	3. Owned and managed by private individuals	
	4. Stations look more organised	
Hang-on transportation	1. Medium class comfort.	Abia line; Imo Transport Company (ITC) and Onitsha South
	2. Medium distance coverage.	
	3. Moderately popular and competitive in their operations	
	4. Owned and/or managed by the government	

routine activities of PTS users, which help calibrate the occurrence of these crimes and public disorder, and (4) the various strategies being adopted by public transport operators to deal with these challenges.

Design Procedure

The first step in the design and selection of interviewees was to conceptualise, categorise and model the PTS in Abakaliki into three broad categories, namely: "popular/competitive" (18+ seaters; buses), "luxurious[4]/comforter", (42+ seaters; coaches) and "hang-on transport" (16+ seaters minibuses). This was done by means of "distance coverage", "commuter patronage" and "carriage capacity". Next, we listed all the public transport companies operating in Abakaliki city and assigned them to the relevant model. The classifications and subsequent comparison of public transport companies provided us with a baseline upon which crime and disorder were examined and measured, and can even be statistically tested. The Table 18.2 below shows types of PTS identified with their corresponding identifiers.

[4] 'Luxurious' is a colloquial term commonly used by Nigerians to describe coaches which carry large numbers of passengers and their luggage over a long distance with a certain high level of comfort. Here passengers are provided with additional services such as video entertainment.

All transport companies operating in Abakaliki have the trappings and features of both external and internal operative structures which capture our specific routine activity and rational conceptual models. Some of these external and internal features are the absence of capable guardians (the obvious presence of security officers), the presence of “ready-to-go” otherwise described by Cohen and Felson (1979) as “motivated” offenders and unsuspecting targets (loiterers hanging around parks), poorly built and lit parks and stations, motor park touts (agberos), and overcrowding, all of which come together both in time and space to provide potential opportunities to commit crime and disorderly conduct in both moving and stationary PTS.

Guided by our rational and routine activity conceptual framework, we developed an interview guide with nine key areas of focus. These are the lambda (frequency), the patterns, the MO, the design of parks/stations, the facilities, company policy, operational hours, estimates of daily human traffic and security measures.

Sample Size

A total of seven public transport companies (both government and privately owned) were sampled and used for this study. There are over 16 public transport companies operating which were modelled in Abakaliki using our set of parameters. That is, all the 16 transport companies in Abakaliki were first aggregated and then disaggregated according to our correlations, and a simple random sampling technique was applied to select the seven transport companies for interview.

Interview Setting

In-depth oral interviews (IDIs) were conducted with park managers from all the selected transport companies (Ifesinachi, Onitsha South, Peace Mass Transit, Imo Transport Corporation, Abia Line, G.U. Okeke transport and Chisco). Park managers were our main primary source of information. Our reason for choosing them was because they remain in the front line of information flow in their various transport companies, and therefore are best positioned to provide information about crime and public disorder. Every occurrence in bus stations and off-station is first and foremost reported to a park manager, who then passes on the information to either the management.

All the interviews with our respondents were interspersed with sentence completion and/or word association so that the approach formed an important component of the interview process. This involved the interviewers saying half-completed statements or sentences and allowing the interviewee to respond or complete the sentences (see Otu 2003). This was done mostly on occasions when it was clear to us that the respondents did not comprehend the information we were looking for, or feared that negative information could have an adverse effect on the respondent’s business.

The data were collected systematically, but in a way that permitted engagement and flexibility with the respondents for finding out facts. In fact, much effort was made to encourage the respondents to give not only specific answers to the questions, but also insightful information that would be useful to furthering our understanding of crime and public disorder on the PTS in Abakaliki.

Given the tight schedules of the park managers, appointments for the interviews were made in advance with each park manager. The interviews took place in the park managers' offices, or any other place chosen by the park manager within the precincts of the park. Although the interviews were held in English, they were occasionally interlaced with Igbo (the local language spoken in our study area) both to boost the confidence of the park managers and to seek further clarification.

The interviews were started by the interviewers introducing themselves and an explanation of the objectives of the study. The respondents were told in clear terms that the aim of the study was not to discredit their companies for any acts of public disorder and crime which might have occurred, but to help provide better security for the passengers and staff alike. Each interviewee was asked to sign a consent form prior to participating in the research and was assured of their anonymity and confidentiality of the information given. The interviews took place after the morning rush hour, when park managers and staff are usually very busy.[5]

The interviews were conducted by the lead researcher and an assistant who was also taking notes. The interviews with each park manager lasted between one and two and a half hours. One observation made during the interviews was that most of the park managers were fairly engaging on the issues of crime and public disorder which affected their transport businesses in Abakaliki. At the end of each interview the notes taken were read out before respondents who authenticated them.

An important characteristic of all the park managers we interviewed was their long years of service in the public transport business. Most of our respondents had also served as park managers outside Abakaliki. All our respondents were male; they had undergone one kind of training or another organised by consultants for their respective companies. Thus by this long service and managerial experiences, we were optimistic and became convinced that all the respondents provided us with reliable information.

The interview guide included items (questions) which focused on the kinds of crime and public disorder so far experienced in the companies (moving and non-moving coaches and buses), the frequency (lambda) of crime and public disorder, and the *modus operandi* (MOs) of these crimes and public disorder. Other ancillary questions included the time (hours) these crimes and public disorder occurred, the most susceptible and victimised person(s), and what calibrated these crimes and public disorder.

We also asked the park managers whether or not they reported crime and public disorder to the police or handled it internally, the strategies they put in place to deal with the incidents of crime and public disorder, and finally, their views on using

[5] PT companies in most Nigerian cities tend to experience their peak hours both in the morning, at weekends and during public holidays.

police escorts on moving buses/coaches. There were some unlisted questions that cropped up during the process of the interviews, but which nevertheless were considered crucial to furthering our understanding of crime and public disorder on the PTS in Abakaliki.

Victim and Eye Witness Accounts

Our sources of information included true-life stories told by three victims and four eye witnesses on crime and public disorder which had occurred either at park stations or on non-stationary buses/coaches. These victims and eye witnesses were chosen purposively by means of a referral technique prior to the commencement of the field interviews of the park managers. The notes served as potential exploratory issues to be examined in the study.

Reflective Data

The reflective data was significant for the present study and included the recorded notes on personal thoughts, experiences, speculations, prejudices, feelings and ideas taken over time by the lead researcher on the subjects being discussed (for a similar approach, see also Bogdan and Biklen 1992, p. 121). Both the reflective and descriptive field data were constantly compared as the study progressed.

Research Validity and Reliability

Detailed information about crime and public disorder on the PTS that came from police sources helped us to update our interview guide and as such helped to come up with pertinent questions during the interviews. The interview guide was presented to a senior police officer in the Criminal Investigation Department (CID) and a colleague in the Department for the Purpose of validation. This triangulated approach allowed us to be aware of deviations and further helped validate the current study.

Data Analysis

The qualitative data generated were analysed using a qualitative analytic technique. This technique involves unitising and categorising the information (see also Glaser and Strauss 1967). Schatzman and Struass (1973) explained that the qualitative analytic technique enables analysis to begin early in the research process.

The data analysis started with the process of continually reviewing, coding and organising the data both chronologically and categorically, so that a kind of what Katz (2001) called an "analytic circle" thus emerged. This process led us to draw up a window description using some constructed themes showing the epidemiology, dimensions, *modus operandi*, as well as the contexts of crime and public disorder on both the stationary and non-stationary PTS operating to and from Abakaliki.

Constant comparisons and cross-checking of the field data with the reflective data from the police helped us to both identify and code these data into meaningful categories and common patterns. The sorting and coding of the data were done manually because of their relatively small amount, and also because of the relatively high level of similarity in the responses provided by our interviewed park managers.

Results

Stationary (Non-moving) PTS

Crime and public disorder in non-moving coaches, buses and taxis are common phenomena in the PTS in Abakaliki. All the park managers interviewed agreed they had experienced and continued to experience one form of crime and disorderly behaviour or another in their park stations. Notable ones identified are armed and violent robbery, theft, fighting, assault, verbal abuse (insults), drunkenness, indiscriminate smoking and defecating around the parks/stations. Crime and disorder on stationary PTS manifest in different ways and often overlap with the *modus operandi* of these crimes. They include the following:

Blitz Armed Robbery

This involves a gang of bandits storming a park and robbing the commuters and park staff as quickly as possible. According to our respondents, when this kind of robbery occurs, it is either one passenger or a group of passengers who are targeted. The park manager of the Chisco Transport Company explained that his transport company recently experienced a blitz robbery in its Abakaliki depot. As he put it:

> Some boys stormed the park one early morning while we were loading a Lagos-bound bus. They were well dressed and came in one big car. And we thought they were intending passengers. But before we knew it, they had robbed most of our passengers who were travelling that morning. They immediately drove off...

Stealing (Impostor Commuters)

According to the park managers, victims and eye witnesses we both interviewed and interacted with, as well as the police, reflective data and media sources of data, one of the most common kinds of crime and MO in most parks in Abakaliki is stealing from commuters' luggage while posing as a co-commuter. Stealing in non-moving transport often occurs when the passenger is either purchasing a ticket, their luggage is being loaded, or during the rush hour. The park managers of Peace Mass Transit, Onitsha South Mass Transit and two witnesses and victims from each company confirmed that theft occurred more in parks used most by commuters. Also associated with stealing is pick-pocketing in the parks. Ceccato and Haining (2004) strongly suggest that transport sites are often crowded but lack "capable guardians"— people who by their mere presence could possibly prevent some crimes from taking place.

Insults, Assaults, Bullying and Fighting

Our findings show that by far the most common disorderly behaviour in parks are verbal abuse (insults), assaults, fighting either between the co-passengers or between passengers and the park staff, and defecating around the parks. The park managers of the Chisco and Ifesinachi coaches are of the view that insults, assaults and fighting in the parks are mainly between passengers and park workers (loaders). Conflict often occurs either between passengers in dispute over seating inside the bus where there are no seat numbers, or between passengers and park staff (especially drivers and loaders) for either overcharging for luggage or unsatisfactory service delivery. The park managers interviewed explained that sometimes acts of disorderly behaviour on public transport are initiated by criminal groups who use them as diversionary tactics to rob targeted commuters. By causing a rowdy atmosphere, the "ready-to-go" offenders take the opportunity to execute their plan.

Non-stationary (Crime and Public Disorder on Moving PT)

The most dramatic, feared and discussed crimes and acts of public disorder on the PTS in Nigeria occur on moving buses, coaches and taxis. Newton (2004) explained that non-stationary crime events may have more than a single location—a starting point (the place the crime originated) and an end-point (when the crime finished). Whether at a single location or multiple locations, crime and public disorder on non-static transport companies operating to and from Abakaliki are numerous and varies from one form and *modus operandi* to another.

Stealing

As with crime on stationary transport, stealing is not uncommon on the non-stationary (moving) PTS operating to and from the environs of Abakaliki. Stealing takes various forms. From the interviews conducted, one of the most common kinds or modus operandi of stealing involves "ready-to-go" offenders posing as passengers and taking the rear seat near the luggage compartment. When the bus is in motion, the targeted luggage is expertly vandalised and stolen by the offender(s), who immediately get off (disembark from) the bus for one reason or another to avoid being caught. The park manager of Peace, Chisco and Onitsha South explained that most of the time, the victims are hypnotised with a sedative, thus making it easier for the perpetrators to easily executing their plan. The park manager of Peace Mass Transit explained that while there is strong dislike for the rear seats on the part of most commuters, ironically, they are usually the preferred place for these criminals.

Robbery

Armed robbery remains the most common, feared and talked about crime and act of disorder on non-stationary public transport in Nigeria (Otu 2003). Highways robbery on both the public and private transport system in Nigeria has caused much anguish for many road users and their families with many having met an untimely death at the hands of armed bandits (Agekameh et al. 2000; Otu 2003; victims and eye witness accounts [undated]).

The interviewees in this study explained that armed robbery on moving buses/coaches operating to and from Abakaliki is on the rise. Sometimes a robbery starts at the bus park and is carried out at a particular point on the bus/coach's route. Several *modus operandi* of armed robbery occur. A common MO involves the offenders posing as passengers to gain access to the bus/coach.

According to the park managers, non-stationary armed robbery usually involves a tip-off, and the targeted coach/bus is designated "high-value" (carrying passengers who are in possession of a large amount of money or valuables). The "target commuter" is often the crime attractor or generator, and other occupants who are attacked and robbed of their possessions are simply innocent victims. To successfully carry out the robbery, the perpetrators (motivated offenders) occupy seats in a manner that they can effectively maintain control over the commuters and driver. As the findings show, the seating arrangement inside the bus usually requires gang members to occupy the front, middle, back, window and aisle seats of the coach for effective control of the internal environment.

The arrival of cell phones has helped facilitate robbery on moving coaches/buses. The offenders are now able to pass vital information to gang members both inside and outside the coach/bus. Guns, cutlasses, clubs and other lethal weapons are often used in these robberies. Usually the weapons are concealed and smuggled into the bus or coach using all manners of tricks. The park manager of Peace Mass Transit and Ifesinachi explained that dangerous weapons have been found during routine screening, concealed in women's private parts, in fake body parts such as wigs, wall clock, with bandages, using children, in loaves of bread, small radio transistors (SRTs) or in shoes.

There is also another kind and *modus operandi* of robbery called the "blitz" (see Otu 2014). In a blitz, armed robbers either block the road with heavy logs to force the bus/coach to stop, or the bus is pursued, overtaken and forced to stop. Once stopped, there is spontaneous, noisy and fierce shooting followed by an attack on the commuters/victims inside the bus/coach, who are terrified. The park managers quoted victims and eyewitnesses who described scenarios consisting of indiscriminate shooting with guns, wild shouting and loud commands saying "Co-operate", "Give it up", "Don't fuck up" and "Don't move an inch", "Lie down everybody", etc. The aim of the indiscriminate shooting is to intimidate the victims and take charge of the crime scene (see Otu 2014).

Our findings show that the blitz robbery MO is common among public buses/coaches travelling long distances. This explained the use of police escorts on public transport, which are much despised by highway armed robbers. All the coaches and buses in this study have at one time and other fallen victim to blitz highway robbery. The park manager of Chisco bluntly put it this way:

> We have lost about six senior drivers to robbery on the highways, particularly on night journeys. These drivers were killed instantly as a result of indiscriminate shootings. So escorts and night journeys are bad and that is why we have banned them officially in our company. Any driver that wants to travel by night is at his own risk and is paid twice his allowance. We also give them a paper to sign indicating that they acted on their own freewill.

The park manager of Peace Mass Transit said:

> Our buses have been attacked more than once along the Abuja-Abakaliki road; they often shoot at them indiscriminately. It all happens in the late evening because we don't even operate at night.

With regards to buses/coaches going to and from Abakaliki, blitz robbery is not uncommon within the neighbourhood of Idodo—a small village which lies along the Abakaliki and Enugu route. Stories of incessant robbery attacks and a couple of rape incidences around this particular axis of the Enugu-Abakaliki highways abound (Victim-survivals and eye witness acoounts, undated).

Finally, our findings revealed special kinds and *modus operandi* of robbery which we describe as "one-chance" or "sharp-sharp" robbery on moving (non-stationary) public buses/coaches (Table 18.3). In "one-chance" (sharp-sharp) robbery, during the rush hour the "ready-to-go" offenders trick unsuspecting commuters into joining a bus or taxi, only to rob them at gun point along the way. One of the student victims we interviewed explained thus:

> … we were just waiting at the bus stop to catch a bus back to Ishieke (just four kilometres away from Abakaliki city centre) when a small taxi pulled up with two occupants (young men) already inside. We all rushed to get a space because we'd been waiting there for a while. Unknown to us, they were sharp-sharp boys. As soon as we passed mile four hospital (two kilometres from the city centre and two kilometres to Ishieke), we were ordered, at gunpoint, to give up everything in our possession. They slapped us and took everything we had. I lost my purse and cell phone and even thank God they didn't do (girls in the taxi) anything to us (rape) …

Findings

To sum up, the findings in this study point to the following:

First, our findings reveal the reality of crime and acts of disorderly behaviour on the PTS in Abakaliki, which are variegated. Our interview in general attested to this

Table 18.3 Common crimes and disorderly behaviour in both moving and non-moving transport companies operating to and from Abakaliki city

PTS model	Crimes	Disorderly behaviour
Stationary (non-moving) transport companies	1. Armed robbery	1. Fighting
	2. Violent robbery	2. Assault
	3. Stealing	3. Verbal abuse (insults)
	4. Theft	4. Drunkenness
		5. Bullying,
		6. Indiscriminate smoking
		7. Defecating
Non-stationary (moving) transport companies	1. Armed (blitz) robbery	1. Fighting
	2. Violent robbery	2. Assault
	3. "One chance" (sharp-sharp robbery)	3. Verbal abuse (insults)
	4. Pilfering (stealing)	4. Drunkenness
	5. Theft	5. Bullying
		6. Indiscriminate smoking

reality. The infamous park touts, popularly known as "agberos", remain one of the worst aspects of the PTS—causing incidents of crime and public disorder on public transport in Abakaliki. The phenomenon of agberos has become a nightmare for most public transport users in Nigeria (see Okpara 1988), becoming a converging point for bad boys and girls who exhibit different kinds of antisocial behaviour, cause disorder and engage in all kinds of crime on the PTS. The Chisco park manager was particularly eloquent about *agberos* when he retorted:

> Abolish the agberos. They are criminals who rob and also give information about passengers to other criminals.

Okpara (1988) described these agberos as freelance workers who contribute to the misery of public transport users in Nigeria.

Second, armed and violent robbery, theft, fighting, assault, verbal abuse (insults), drunkenness, indiscriminate smoking, bullying and defecating which are key findings on both moving and non-moving PTS are actions which are not only purposeful and calculative (rational model) but also reflect the routine activities around the parks and the routes which most public transports from Abakaliki commute. The convergence of a number of activities on daily basis both in the parks and along the various towns and cities where PTS transverse through such as the presence of touts along these routes, picking of passengers along the highways by drivers, travelling very early and late at nights, increase in the use of ATM before going to parks are some of the changes in structural patterns and experience of PTS users' daily activity in Abakaliki which configuration provided greater criminal opportunities. Pearlstein and Wachs (1982) provide evidence which shows that incidents of bus crime are highest on bus routes which traverse high crime-rate areas. Increased women's participation in the labour force and PTS use as well as an increase in number of vacations (holidays), trips outside Abakaliki, increased contact with strangers some who are possible offenders, are further components that converge in space and time and calibrate the commission of crime and disorder by motivated offender.

In addition, technological advances leading to use of mobile phones, Ipad and other mnemonics from the year 2000 in Nigeria with higher values and lower weights made them very attractive and easy to steal from crowded parks. Finally, the use of tricycles and motor cycles as a means of inner-city transportation system in Nigerian cities, generally increased crime both on stationary and non-stationary PTS in Abakaliki as both increased the visibility of passengers transporting themselves to the parks or back to their homes from parks. Both also facilitate the mobility of potential offenders who often operate with speed and relative ease of escape.

Still consistent with the principles of general traditional urban and environmental criminology, and our specific routine activity theory, situational crime prevention and crime prevention by design (see Newman 1972; Clarke and Felson (1993, we found that the social setting of Abakaliki acts as a driver for crime and public disorder on the PTS in Abakaliki. For instance, the specific environmental factors identified include a lack of adequate space in park, a lack of visible guardian (security) at parks, ubiquitous peddlers who loiter around the parks selling various items, presence of many touts as freelance workers scouting for commuters, poor lighting and the presence of liquor stores around parks. The configuration of these elements provide greater criminal opportunities, greater soft targets and greater absence of effective guardianships for increasing crime and disorderly behaviours occurring in both moving and non-moving PTs in Abakaliki.

In specific term for example, findings revealed that it is in the process of buying and selling in parks that dangerous weapons such as shotguns and knives for use in robbery on non-stationary coaches/buses are smuggled inside buses. The park manager of GUO Okeke Transport Company revealed that some confectionary which is commonly sold and purchased by commuters in the parks are sometimes spiked with certain sedatives which put the users at great risk of being hypnotised and robbed of their valuables.

Third, in line with our routine activity theory and in confirmation of our reflective data, the respondents criticised the neighbouring communities around where some crimes on non-stationary (moving) buses and coaches occur for harbouring the perpetrators. Motivated offenders along these routes often alert their colleagues from other locations on the time of passage of these PTs which they prey upon. Respondents also attribute some of these crimes to occasional police complacency and sometimes outright collusion with highway bandits, citing instances where highway robberies have occurred either within the area or on the spot where the police put up their road blocks. Marenin (1987) also emphasised this perception by most Nigerians (expressed in an anxious tone) when he explained that communities where robberies frequently takes place tend to harbour and shield criminals from arrest by the police.

Fourth, the use of police escorts in Nigeria has yielded the desired result. However, the findings show that it nonetheless has contributed more to endangering the lives of commuters on moving public transport during night journeys. All the park managers revealed that both the operators and other users of public transport businesses now frown on night journeys being continued because they lead to an increase in casualties among night journey passengers, police escorts and drivers alike. Apart from the greater opportunity which night journey presents for robbery and disorderly behaviours in both stationary and non-stationary PTS, motivated offenders know that the gain of robbing night travellers (majority who are on such trips for businesses) far outweigh the risk (almost negligible) of doing so in a clear manner reminiscent of rational choice theory.

Other significant findings which align with our routine activity and rational choice theories include (1) the arrival of cell phones has led to an upsurge in crime on both the stationary (static) and non-stationary (moving) PTS. From police reports and park manager accounts, buses and coaches going between Abakaliki and other locations have sometimes been robbed with the aid of these new communication gadgets. Therefore, making calls while a coach/bus is in motion is now well regulated, and most transport companies operating in Abakaliki have placed a ban on the use of mobile phones inside buses/coaches, especially long distance, (2) sometimes drivers, especially those operating coaches, collude with criminals when they carry high-value passengers, (3) some transporters have gone the extra mile to issue warnings to their passengers on the dangers of carrying large sums of money when travelling for business or other activities, (4) from time to time transport companies organise seminars for their park workers on security and public relations matters.

When the PTS in Abakaliki was reviewed both critically and analytically, we found that it involves all three elements of the routine activities of both the offenders and offendees: suitable targets (for example, staff, passengers, the presence of liquidity cash and valuable items), "ready-to-go" (potential) offenders (for example, unemployed youths, touts [agberos]), and the absence of capable guardians (for example, police officers as escorts, security staff, CCTV cameras). In addition, the PTS in Abakaliki is apparently unsystematic, and poorly organised and managed. The physical characteristics of the parks lack measures such as fencing, lighting, an open design and security hardware that would prevent crime and disorder; they also lack other state and local council support services (see also Harris (1971).

Public transport stations in Abakaiki are crowded with people who do not know one another, thus creating the right environment for crime and public disorder to occur with ease in these stations. Brantigham and Brantigham (1993, 1995) thesis showed that at a certain time in people's routine activities, the crowds and the characteristics they exhibit (for example, commuters using public transport during the morning and evening rush hour, or festive periods) create suitable conditions for certain kinds of crime (for example, attracting offenders who believe they have more opportunities either to pickpocket or steal valuables from holiday goers) so that both the parks and certain periods act as attractors of crime.

Fundamentally however, it is crucial to stress that offenders—whether robbers, thieves, assaulters, defaulters of conduct behaviours are not simply helpless agents of some inexorable external social forces acting under some psychopathic dispositions.

Instead they are rational and calculative ones who more often than not make a choice and decision which consists among other things a sequence of three important elements about (1) deciding to commit one crime or disorderly behaviour mainly for one gain or the other (2) deciding who and/or what target to direct the crime or disorderly behaviour to (3) deciding and planning when, what and where to do the crime and (4) how to escape (see also Conklin 1972; Cook 1990; Otu 2010). Once these key areas are addressed, the potential offender decides the tools to use to accomplish the crime and disorderly behaviour which constitute a crucial component of the routine activity theory.

Discussion

With an almost negligible interest in crime and disorderly behaviour on the PTS in Abakaliki, this study has drawn attention to the routine activities of residents in Abakaliki city over time and in space that are geared towards sustaining their daily social, economic, political and health interests and their convenience. It also explains crime and disorderly behaviour as an outcome of rationality over time and in space. First, the idea of time and space explains that during certain time and space windows, people converge or disperse through the transport system following certain constraints of movement, as discussed by Hagerstrand (1970). Ceccato and Uittenbogaard (2013) explained that for crime and disorderly behaviour to occur in a transport node, synchronicity between various elements in time and space must exist. That is, a "ready-to-go" offender who identifies a potential victim, based on his or her evaluation of the "right" time and "right" place.

Both models (that is routine activity and rational choice) are complimentary, and they suggest that people's patterns of activities (movement) are rhythmic—rush hours, weekdays and weekends, and winter and summer—and are what defines both temptations and opportunities to make a decision either to commit a crime and/or disorderly behaviour, or refrain from it on both the stationary (static) and non-stationary (moving) PTS operating to and from Abakaliki.

The temptations and opportunities here include the huge amounts of cash and valuables which ordinary public transport users in Abakaliki carry with them, and the lack of effective security at public transport parks/stations and on highways (routes). So for many offenders on public transport in Abakaliki, it appears that the muted risk is always worth it.

In addition, opportunities and temptations for crime and disorderly behaviour on the PTS in Abakaliki present themselves in a number of ways. These include (a) the presence of "ready-to-go" (motivated) offenders—many of whom are unemployed youths and touts (*agberos*) in and around the parks, (b) the absence of capable guardians—the absence of officials and private security personnel, (c) the unsystematic, poorly organised or managed, and lack of state and municipal support services such as good lighting in the parks serving the PTS in Abakaliki.

Conclusions and Policy Implication

Like other studies (see for example, Weiser-Easteal and Wilson 1991; Loukaitou-Sideris 1999; Liggett et al. 2001; Uittenbogaard and Ceccato 2014), this present study asserts that the social context (environment) within which the PTS operates in Abakaliki helps to explain the complex nature of crime and disorderly behaviour in this sector.

The findings in this study show that policy intervention that can limit the extent of the crimes and disorderly behaviour so far identified and restore confidence in public transport's users travelling to and from Abakaliki is imperative. In keeping with the spirit of policy-informed research, our policy implications are guided and informed by the respondents whose knowledge of the relationship between offending behaviour and the PTS on one hand, and between offending behaviour and park characteristics on the other within the context of routine activity and rational choice theories, are informative and educative.

In this light, our findings have a number of implications. First, the external and internal operative structures of the PTS in Abakaliki promote crime and public disorder within the system. There are motivated offenders who are "ready-to-go" (unemployed youths and *agberos*), suitable targets (those who habitually carry large sums of cash when travelling, poor roads and poorly organised parks), and the absence of guardians (the lack of an effective security system). Offenders are rational, purposive and calculative, and always find reasons to justify their criminal activities. They are aware that there will be no completely bad day since there will always be passengers willing to risk travelling with valuables, especially cash.

In addition, most parks are small, often overcrowded with little or no space for clear visibility. Security is a function of either the direct or indirect visibility of passengers; the possibilities of being and seeing others, that is to say natural surveillance (see Newman 1972). Ceccato et al. (2013) explained that poor visibility can also be translated into poor surveillance. With parks being often overcrowded, it becomes difficult to monitor and distinguish between genuine park users and those who are there to commit acts of crime and public disorder. Decongesting the parks by filtering out the unwanted elements there will go a long way not only to ensuring effective human surveillance, but also to preventing the possibility of causing a noisy distraction conducive for perpetuating one crime and or disorder or another.

Second, because most crimes and acts of public disorder start at the station, the need for a police/security presence is a strong step in the right direction. For most park managers, a police/security presence is a favoured measure. Leading criminologists (see for instance, Wilson 1975, 1983; Wilson and Kelling 1982; Brown et al. 1998) hold the view that a police presence can be a strong deterrent for crime and acts of public disorder. In the light of the above understanding, some park managers in Abakaliki make intermittent use of police or private guards to search and screen passengers after loading, particularly on the early-bird buses and coaches. For instance, in the Peace and Abia transport companies, uniformed policemen are sometimes visibly present and they conduct searches on buses about to depart. Passengers and hand luggage are thoroughly searched before departure. In the eyes of the park managers of these companies, the incidents of crime and disorderly behaviour have dropped significantly.

Third, the need to abolish *agberos* (touts) at the nation's parks remains a very strong approach to checking the spate of crime and disorderly behaviour on the PTS. *Agberos* (most of whom are freelance loaders) have been linked to missing passengers' luggage and valuables; they are also heavily implicated in leaking information to criminal gang members. They struggle to earn money since they receive their pay on a commission basis.

Finally, night journeys and the use of police escorts are beneficial for public transport users, although they have a serious downside. Besides an increase in road casualties, the use of police escorts is judged by park managers and commuters to make little difference to most highway robberies on moving coaches as the robbers always act like loose cannons by shooting indiscriminately and fiercely on moving coaches. Discontinuing both night journeys and the use of police escorts as some companies have adopted should be encouraged as national PTS policy. Drivers who want to make night journeys do so at their own risk and take the responsibility for their decisions.

Ultimately, the idea of Integrated Crime Prevention through Environmental Design (ICPTED), target hardening, cash-free policies and effective policing (not road blocking) of all the major highways in Nigeria remain important practical policies for addressing crime and disorderly behaviour on the PTS in Abakaliki. At the centre of this policy is the idea that situational factors such as poor spacing, lighting, policing, carrying large sums of money, a lack of effective personnel and camera surveillance and the presence of *agberos* all make crime and disorderly behaviour on the PTS something that is more likely to occur both at a particular time and space. However, pursuing this integrated policy approach would require an understanding of the routine activities, rationality and patterns of these crimes and disorderly behaviour. But it is important to do so with caution. The reason is because the specific PTS and the specific social context it operates in are key to enhancing this understanding and to the development of a specific context-based approach.

References

Agekameh, D., et al. (2000). Living under the guns. Nigerians are feeling more and more helpless as armed robbers and hired assassins hold the nation hostage. *Tell Magazine, 52*, 25–35.

Bidstrup, S. (1999). *Are you planning a trip to Africa? A page of advice to travellers to Africa.* Retrieved April 12, 2003, from http://www.saps.org/29/8.

Block, R., & Davis, S. (1996). The environs of a rapid transit station: A focus for street crime or just another risky place. In R. Clarke (Ed.), *Preventing mass transit crime. Crime prevention studies* (Vol. 6). Monsey, NY: Willow Tree Press.

Bogdan, R., & Biklen, S. K. (1992). *Qualitative research for education: An introduction to theory and methods*. Boston, MA: Allen and Bacon.

Brantigham, P., & Brantigham, P. (1993). Environment, routine and situation. Toward a pattern theory of crime. In R. Clarke & M. Felson (Eds.), *Routine activity and rational choice: Advances in criminological theory* (Vol. 5). New Jersey: Transactional Publishers.

Brantigham, P., & Brantigham, P. (1995). Criminality of place: Crime generations and crime attractors. *European Journal on Criminal Policy and Research, 3*(3), 5–26.
Brown, S., Esbensen, F., & Geis, G. (1998). *Criminology. Explaining crime and its context* (7th ed.). New Providence, NJ: Matthew Bender and Company.
Ceccato, V., & Haining, R. (2004). Crime in border regions: The Scandinavian case of Oresund, 1998–2001. *Annals of the Association of American Geographers, 22*(3), 807–826.
Ceccato, V., & Uittenbogaard, A. (2013). Space-crime dynamics of crime in transport nodes. *Annals of the American Geographers*. doi:10.1080/00045608.2013.846150.
Ceccato, V., Uittenbogaard, A., & Bamza, R. (2013). Security in Stockholm's underground stations: The importance of environmental attributes and context. *Security Journal, 1*(3), 33–59.
Church, A., Frost, M. & Sullivan , K. (2000). Transport and social exclusion in London. Transport Policy, 7 (3):195-205.
Clarke, R.V. & Felson, M. (1993). Routine activity and rational choice. In: Advances in Criminological Theory, Vol. 5. New Brunswick, New Jersey:Transaction Books.
Clarke, R. V. (1997). *Situational crime prvention–Successful case studies* (92nd ed.). New York: Harrow and Heston.
Cohen, L., & Felson, M. (1979). Social change and crime rate trends: A routine activity approach. *American Sociological Review, 44*, 588–608.
Conklin, J. (1972). *Robbery and the criminal justice system*. Philadelphia: J.B. Lippincott.
Cook, P. (1990). Robbery in the United States: An analysis of recent trends and patterns". In N. Weiner, M. Zahn, & R. Sagi (Eds.), *Violence: Patterns, causes, public policy*. New York: Harcourt Brace Jovanovich.
Cornish, D., & Clarke, R. (1986). *The reasoning criminal*. New York: Springer.
Crime Concern. (2004). Understanding the links between bus-related crime and other crime. *Analysis of crime and disorder audits strategies, Round 2–2002*. London, UK: Department of Transport.
Felson, M., & Clark, R. (1998). Opportunity makes the thief. *Crime detection and prevention, series* Paper 98. London, UK: Home Office.
Glaser, B., & Strauss, A. (1967). *Discovery of grounded theory*. Chicago, IL: Aldine. Retrieved February 10, 2014, from http://www.frsc.gov.ng/roadsafetyaudit.pdf. http://www.peoplesdaily-online.com/opinion/editorial/18499-the-latest-tragedy-on-okene-lokoja-abuja-road. *The latest tragedy on Okene-Lokoja-Abuja Road*.
Gray, E., Jackson, J., & Farrall, S. (2010). Feelings and functions in the fear of crime: Applying a new approach to victimization in security. *British Journal of Criminology, 51*(1), 75–94. doi:10.1093/bjc/azq066.
Hagerstrand, T. (1970). What about people in regional science? Paper of the Regional Science Association, 24: 7-21
Harris, O. (1971). A methodology for developing security design criteria for subway, Washington DC.Urban mass transit administration, Report no,:UMTA-URT-5(70)-71-4.
Ihlanfeldt, K. R. (2003). Rail transit and neighbourhood crime: The case of Atlanta, Georgia. *Southern Economic Journal, 70*(2), 273–294.
Jacobs, J. (1961). *The death and life of great American cities*. New York: Random House.
Jochelson, R. (1997). *Crime and place: Analysis of assaults and robberies in inner Sydney, general report series*. Sydney: NSW Bureau of Crime Statistics and Research.
Katz, C. M. (2001). The establishment of police gang unit. *Criminology, 39*(1), 37–74.
LaVigne, N. G. (1997). *Visibility and vigilance: Metro's situational approach to preventing subway crime*. National Institute of Justice-Research in Brief. U.S Department of Justice. Retrieved June 2015, from https://www.ncjrs.govt/txtfiles/1666372txt.
Levine, N., Wachs, M., & Shirazi, E. (1986). Crime at bus stops. A study of environmental factors. *Journal of Architectural and Planning Research, 3*(4), 339–361.
Liggett, R., Loukaitou, A., & Iseki, H. (2001). Bus-environment connection. Do characteristics of the built correlate with stop crime? *Transportation Research Record, 1760*, 20–27.
Loukaitou-Sideris, A. (1999). Hot spots of bus stop crime. The importance of environmental attributes. *Journal of the American Planning Association, 65*(4), 395–411.

Loukaitou-Sideris, A., Liggett, R., & Iseki, H. (2002). The geography of transit crime: Documentation and evaluation of crime incidence on and around Green Line Stations in Los Angeles. *Journal of Planning Education and Research, 22*(3), 135–151.
Marenin, O. (1987). The Anini saga: Armed robbery and the reproduction of ideology in Nigeria. *The Journal of Modern African Studies, 25*(2), 259–281.
Mayhew, P., Clarke, R., Sturman, A., & Hough, M. (1976). Crime as opportunity. In *Home office research studies number* (Vol. 34). London, UK: HMSO.
Newman, O. (1972). *Defensible space: Crime prevention through urban design*. New York: Macmillan.
Newton, A. D. (2004). Crime on public transport: 'Static and 'non-static' (moving) crime events. *Western Criminology Review, 5*(3), 25–42.
Okpara, E. E. (1988). The role of touts in passenger transport in Nigeria. *The Journal of Modern African Studies, 26*(2), 327–335.
Otu, S. E. (2003). *Armed robbery in the south-eastern states of contemporary Nigeria: A criminological analysis*. Being an unpublished doctoral thesis (D. Litt. Phil.), Department of Criminology, University of South Africa (Unisa), Pretoria.
Otu, S. E. (2010). Decision-making practices in armed robbery among armed robbers in Nigeria. *International Journal of Research in Arts and Social Sciences, 2*.
Otu, S. E. (2014). An analysis of the method of approach (MA) and modus operandi (MO) of armed robbery and armed robbers in contemporary Nigeria. *Security Journal*, 1–18. Retrieved from www.palgrave-journals.com/sj/.
Pearlstein, A., & Wachs, M. (1982). Crime in public transit systems: An environmental design perspective. *Transportation, 11*(3), 277–297.
Police Crime Reports. State Police Command Headquarters, Abakaliki.
Schatzman, L., & Struass, A. (1973). *Field research: Strategies for a natural sociology*. Englewood Cliffs, NJ: Prentice-Hall.
Smith, M., & Clarke, R. (2000). Crime and public transport. In M. Tonry & N. Morris (Eds.), *Crime and justice of the research* (Vol. 6, pp. 169–233). Chicago: University of Chicago Press.
Story of an armed robbery attack on a Enugu-Lagos bound luxurious bus (Undated).
Uittenbogaard, A., & Ceccato, V. (2014). Safety in Stockholm's underground station: An agenda for action. *European Journal on Criminal Policy and Research, 20*(1), 73–100. doi:10.1007/s10610-013-92128.
Ukoha, U., & Chukwuma, I. (Eds.). (2012). *Governance and insecurity in South East Nigeria*. Lagos: Malthouse Press and CLEEN Foundation.
Victim-survival and eye witness accounts of a robbery incident on Abakaliki-bound peace Mass Transit (Undated).
Weiser-Easteal, P., & Wilson, P. R. (1991). *Preventing crime on transport*. Australian Institute of Criminology.
Wilson, J. Q. (1975). *Thinking about crime*. New York: Random House.
Wilson, J. Q. (Ed.). (1983). *Crimes and public policy*. San Francisco, CA: ICS Press.
Wilson, J., & Kelling, G. (1982). Broken windows. *The Atlantic Monthly, 249*(3), 29–38.

Index

E.C. Viano (ed.), *Cybercrime, Organized Crime, and Societal Responses*,
DOI 10.1007/978-3-319-44501-4

MIX
Papier aus verantwortungsvollen Quellen
Paper from responsible sources
FSC® C105338

If you have any concerns about our products,
you can contact us on
ProductSafety@springernature.com

In case Publisher is established outside the EU,
the EU authorized representative is:
Springer Nature Customer Service Center GmbH
Europaplatz 3, 69115 Heidelberg, Germany

Printed by Libri Plureos GmbH
in Hamburg, Germany